THE RADIANT SAMENESS

Satpuruṣa Mahārājśrī Maṅgatrāmjī's

Samatāvilāsa

THE RADIANT SAMENESS

Satpuruṣa Mahārājśrī Maṅgatrāmjī's

Samatāvilāsa

Edited, Translated and Notes by

SOM RAJ GUPTA

MOTILAL BANARSIDASS PUBLISHERS
PRIVATE LIMITED • DELHI

First Edition: Delhi, 2010

ISBN: 978-81-208-3410-1

MOTILAL BANARSIDASS
41 U.A. Bungalow Road, Jawahar Nagar, Delhi 110 007
8 Mahalaxmi Chamber, 22 Bhulabhai Desai Road, Mumbai 400 026
203 Royapettah High Road, Mylapore, Chennai 600 004
236, 9th Main III Block, Jayanagar, Bangalore 560 011
Sanas Plaza, 1302 Baji Rao Road, Pune 411 002
8 Camac Street, Kolkata 700 017
Ashok Rajpath, Patna 800 004
Chowk, Varanasi 221 001

PRINTED IN INDIA

By Jainendra Prakash Jain at Shri Jainendra Press,
A-45 Naraina, Phase-I, New Delhi 110 028
and Published by Narendra Prakash Jain for
Motilal Banarsidass Publishers Private Limited,
Bungalow Road, Delhi 110 007

CONTENTS

Anubhava Four

Prounciation of Sanskrit, Hindi and Urdu words (a rough guide)

a may be pronounced as in *but*
ā as in *father*
i as in *bit*
ī as in *machine*
u as in *full*
ū as in *rule*
e as in *play*
ai as in *my*
ṛ as in *rich*
g as in *get*
c as *ch* in *church*
ś and *ṣ* as *sh* in *shut*
ṃ before *p* and *b* as *m*, elsewhere as *n*
Other consonants may be pronounced as in English

Preface

THE reader interested in understanding the philosophical implications of the sayings collected in this book should consult the Translator's biography of the Master, *To the Home that was Nowhere, An Encounter with the Life and Teachings of Śrī Maṅgatrām.* Some of these implications have also been explained in the End-Notes appended to each chapter.

I would, however, add here that this work shows us the path to find our fallen condition itself as redemptive. We are not merely to accept our pain and our mortal condition but to live these and become these. In becoming that pain lies our bliss, in living our mortality immortality. That alone is the highest bliss and the absolute, that alone is salvation the final, this our becoming one with our mortal and absolutely tragic lot. That is what the state of *samatā*, sameness, is. Only that man is a *mukta*, a liberated soul, who can look alike on *Māyā*[1] and Brahman, on reality and appearance, on bondage and liberation, on life and death, on misery and joy. Not that there is an actual state called the state of liberation, an actual bliss that is absolute and highest, for terms like 'absolute' and 'highest' turn out to be relative, and, therefore, misleading. Hypostatization of *samatā* would not work, for all hypostatization is rooted in our narcissistic passion.

Yet this work does not encourage us to look alike on these opposites constitutive of our mortal being as long as we remain mortals and fight a desperate fight against our inevitable and destined fate; a stern discipline we have to undergo before we can even think of *samatā*, not to speak of living it. For, not before dying unto himself can a man look alike on these dualities, the stuff our mortal life and being are made of. Mere theoretical deconstruction of these opposites will not do; he must live the uncertainty that he is as a [no-]being placed between these opposites, between the given condition and the transcendental urge in us, between the past and the present, between oneself and one's *other*, between life and death. He cannot but seek to escape from what he finds himself to be, cannot resist the transcendental thrust informing him, and cannot but engage in the fight between these two urges, namely, the urge to remain himself and the urge to transcend himself. He has to accept and live this his destiny, there is, there can be, no escape from this his role. And to accept and live this his unhappy condition, he has to have the humility to become a mere passive witness of these ever recurring deadly tensions and conflicts within him, to stand apart from these as if these latter were mere events happening *before* him and not in him. He has to, in other words, cease to be a doer, accepting all the uncertainty that goes with his being as a mortal, as a creature uncertainly placed between the two poles of birth and death. But not before dying before his actual death can he have the patience, the patience all passive, to live his mortality and be his mortality, undoing thereby both birth and death and what lies between the two, his so called life.

'Samatāvilāsa.' the title of this book, means 'Rejoicing in *Samatā*, in Sameness'. There is another *grantha*, holy book, called *Samatā-prakāśa*, 'Revelation of *Samatā*'. The *Samatāvilāsa* contains mostly Master's writings, some of them dictations. The *Samatā-prakāśa*, on the contrary, consists of revelations that descended upon him when the man in him had ceased to be to give place to the Word, to that alone. It was in *samādhi*[2] that he uttered those words, knowing not what he uttered and when he uttered. His scribe was Banārasīdās, or Bhagatjī, 'The Noble Devotee', as he was affectionately called by other disciples of the

Master. The reader must go to the Translator's biography of the Master to know how and in what manner and where the *bānī* (*vāṇī*), speech the revelatory, descended, replacing the man in the Master. The *Samtāvilāsa*, however, is, as already noted, a collection of his 'conscious'[3] writings or dictations; it is his hermeneutic of what he found and became, not an interpretation of an interpretation, as we the ignorant are fated to formulate, but an interpretation of the uninterpreted and the uninterpretable. We mortals find ourselves in the already interpreted world, but he beheld the uninterpreted to become, in the state of *samādhi*, that very uninterpreted. But when he came out of the *samādhi*, he explained that state and the means of attaining to it for the benefit of mankind in general. Rejoicing in the state of *samatā*, not becoming one with it, he spoke about it and the way to it. One can perceive the distance that is there between what is said and that about which it is said. The word does not coincide with the referent, does not become the latter's speech, does not become the word of the Word but is the word of a man about the No-man. The Master's diction and the peculiar syntax of his sentences that could, in our human writing, be a hindrance in the way of conceptual or poetic communication became in this work its strength, their very inadequacy speaking of the truth of the transcendental reality they fail to express. He constantly harps on the ineffability of the real, harps on very many occasions and in almost the same language. And yet this failure of his language to capture what he has to say, this living dramatisation of the encounter between the sheer penury of language and the infinite abundance of the Real, succeeds in conveying the truth of what he speaks about. The unwearied dwelling on the ineffable, the frequent inconsistency of views regarding that truth, the use of appositions regarding the same subject term not always in consonance with each other, the turns of phrases frequently at discord with the rules of grammar and syntax, and certain lexical items defying their commonly accepted connotations - all these go a long way in establishing the truth of the state of *samatā*. In the very struggle of language to perform the impossible feat, in its very failure to map up the real, in the very intensity of this encounter and the frequent confession of the sheer inadequacy of language for the task it is called upon to perform, one can experience the truth of what refuses to be expressed and explained, experience its sheer ineffability, of that truth. One becomes aware of it without conceptualising it and without enframing it, without, that is, phenomenlising it. Where command of language will fail, where precision will fail and learning and the power to conceptualise, lack of education almost to the point of illiteracy succeeds. The text does not so much ask us to believe, it generates that belief, enacts the act of grace, that sole giver of faith. That is the paradox about his style, paradox benign and gracious; in its weakness lies its strength, in its simplicity its depth.

A reader with a scholarly bent of mind, he who would grasp the matter expressed in a book as a whole, would articulate it to himself in clear and communicative terms, will find this work monotonous and inconsistent, if not riddled with contradictions, those his red rags. The book is, undoubtedly, repetitive, is, to be more accurate, repetition itself. We humans rejoice in the new and the fresh, not in the old and the stale. How could this title be given it then, the title, 'Rejoicing in *Samatā*'? The same, as we understand it, is ever and always repetitive and, for this reason, is uninteresting for us. Add to this the exasperation of the reader that would try to know what the book has to say in toto. He has to shed this his passion for grasping the meaning of the book in totality, he must read it haltingly and leisurely, lingering on each and every paragraph, on each and every sentence, or on a few paragraphs dwelling on a particular thought, shedding his anxiety to reach a conclusion and assessment regarding the theme of the book. One is not to *grasp* the meaning, one is to let the meaning express itself. The preferred way would be to hear it read out by someone else, not more than a page or two at a time, and let the words sink into oneself. This would lead the reader or the hearer to think about what those words have conveyed to him, think about it in existential terms, think about it not for mere theoretical understanding but in anguished, existential terms. For, it is in these terms, terms of anguish, that this book will speak, speak about our existential condition and the tragedy of it. Once this understanding sinks in one's mind, once one feels with every intensity the sheer magnitude of that tragedy, one would not be put off by the repetition in the book. For the book will constantly recall only what is perpetual in one's life and being, its unhappiness and its misery unmitigated. And since this misery, this tragedy of our life, is a sheer recurrence, occur as it does each and every moment of our life, since we are born each moment and die each moment, we will find the book only reflecting that our state of being or no-being. Recurrence will no longer then appear monotonous to us, it will be our life and being, for born are we already stale and decaying and are destined to be and to get what is already stale and decaying.

But how can this misery of being the same, the same misery and the same mortality, this tragic repetition, be our rejoicing? The realisation of the sheer magnitude of our pain, pain that the *Samatāvilāsa* is never tired of highlighting, would make us, if we have truly interiorised this its message, stand apart from our existential condition. This comes to be possible only when we distance ourselves from our eyes and ears, when we turn into seers of our sight and hearers of our hearing. When this comes to happen, we will find our concepts of things, concepts that enframe them in terms of relationships and contrasts, melting before us, blurring our sense of distinctions. No clear-cut distinctions will survive for us then, distinctions like those between one thing and another and between ourselves and the world and also between one word and another word. The world will turn into almost an undifferentiated presence then and language into a sound indivisible, a sound that will appear as our deepest interiority. Our text calls that sound *nāda*, or *śabda*, Word, or the *ātman*, the self. It is a sound ready to swallow all one's thoughts, all that one perceives and hears.

The text also says that this Word may also manifest itself as *śūnya*, as void, as nothingness as it were, as silence, silence that would appear as one's being, being on the point of swallowing into itself the man in us and his world the entire. It also says that the Word may also manifest as consciousness pure and thought-free, a bare awareness as if about to absorb the entire realm of the not-conscious into itself. This it calls the state of *parama-śānti*, peace the transcendent, peace the highest or, as I often translate, peace the absolute. This peace is experienced more often by those *yogins* who experience the self as the *nāda*, as the sound. Those whose lot it is to undergo agony of life itself, agony the existential, not the agony that goes with deprivation of this or that thing but deprivation of being itself will find their self as *śūnya*, as the void or nothingness, beyond the reach of both joy and pain. They are called upon to die into that nothingness, not to rejoice in it. The joy of the *yogin*, his rejoicing, will not be their lot, only pain will be, pain without a qualification. They have to live that pain and be that pain and when they do so, when they become their pain, the pain will cease but not to give place to joy. For, beyond the pale of pain and joy will their self appear to them, into which they have to die and will die.

Those among the seekers of the truth that find the self as bare consciousness will be made to find soon that consciousness is only a reflection of their true being, not that being itself. They will find themselves distant from every joy, every thought, every sound, their consciousness melting as it were into nothingness. The worshippers of *śūnya* or *kuṇḍalinī*[4] or Kālī, as the *yogins* would call it, are called upon to sacrifice themselves into it, to burn themselves into it; persons as bare consciousness will find all consciousness fading out on its own along with all that it is consciousness of. One may call their way the way of calm, that of the worshippers of sound as the way of joy and bliss and that of the sacrificers into *kuṇḍalinī* the way of *tapas,* of self-burning. One can see how all these ways converge ultimately to lead one to the state of being the text calls the state still, the state supreme and all peaceful:

> **To stay still in the Real:** When a being thus comes to stay still in the Real, there remains no darkness of delusion to darken him, no thought of the I, that is. His consciousness, his consciousness-with-its-other, melts into the Imperishable Word, that *ātman* of his, that Consciousness the bare, Consciousness without its *other,* to turn into that itself.[5] To *nirvāṇa*[6] it attains then, to the peace that it is. This comes to be possible, when the intellect, hailing the glory of the *Nāda,* of that Immortal Sound, contemplates that Sound the Uninterrupted each and every moment with utmost spontaneity, contemplates it in its varied forms and facets. There will be moments when it will find that Sound beyond the reach of any dualities, dualities with their negation written into them. And there will be moments when that Sound will appear beyond the sphere of any *guṇa* of *prakṛti,*[7] with nothing to stay with, nothing to strive for and nothing to transcend. A-dual that Sound will appear to it, in which no desire can stir up and no action can originate, where the very self, self the false, one has projected oneself into, self the *other,* comes to be extinct. This coming to rest of the process of birth and death will the *buddhi*[8] find in It, and also the all silent ***śunyā,*** that void and stillness absolute, in that Sound. And at the same time, this very Word the Silent will appear all-knowing to it and Light the self-same. Contemplating the *Nāda* this way, the *buddhi* will lose itself into that its own being, its own self, the conflicts of opposites, the dualities that

> the mind, the body and the organs are, no longer touching it. Transcending these all, it will stay, no thought stirring up in it, no fear to disturb it. All still it will stay in that state supreme and all peaceful, in that final coming to rest of the ever moving wheel of recurring births and deaths. With every effort should a man try to attain to that supreme state, with every right and genuine effort, and with every disposition genuinely oriented towards that end, and with firm and sustained contemplation. To attain to that state is his duty paramount, that is the goal he should ever strive for. (The Path of *Samatā*-knowledge, Section 2, Saying 5)

The text unmistakably points out the convergence of all the paths before they lead one to the ultimate goal. However, it dwells more often than not on the way of the *nāda* and the joy it gives but sternly warns about the pitfalls on the way. Thus it says:

> Only a rare man endowed with a rare power of discrimination tries to free himself from this self-identification with action, and only a rare man all dedicated to *sādhanā*, to striving for that goal, comes to attain to the state of not-doing, that blissful state ever the same. For, a man may resort to every sacrifice and every self-denial, may resort to every yogic meditation and give away his possessions all, spend himself in the service of others and otherwise do every physical penance and at every moment but no measures he adopts will lead to cessation of his *vāsanā*, to cessation of the darkness that it is. On the contrary, these high deeds of his will make his *buddhi* all the more proud to make it fall of its purpose true and lead it astray all the more into self-concern and self-indulence, with unending unrest for its portion.

All these measures were taken to bring *vāsanā* into its extinction, but, instead of that, the density of that darkness increased manifold. Surpassingly strange

indeed is this phenomenon! This living being cannot attain to the state of no-desire, that state blessed where one remains just oneself without a hankering for the *other*, cannot attain to that state if he is bereft of a clear sense of distinction between the real and the unreal and the grace of a true seer. No display can work here and no pretence.

Self-denial and learning, meditation and passive contemplation and such other measures are there to put an end to *vāsanā*. But if these means are adopted without true faith and belief in the real and without dedicating one's life to the goal of self-redemption, then of no avail will be that effort and that striving. For, instead of purifying the mind, these measures will increase one's vanity to fierce proportions to inflame one's *vāsanā* as never before.

Teachers of holy lore abound here in plenty and men given to charity and men of learning and knowledge, their number swelling ever. But hard it is to find, extremely hard indeed, a man whose *vāsanā* has come to be extinct. It is their sense of identity with those acts, of these men given to noble acts and to the sacrifice of their lives in great acts of piety, that does not let their *vāsanā* die down and let them find the bliss of no-desire. Their resort to noble deeds of varied kinds does not mean the end of desire for their fruit in terms of happiness, it persists unabated in their hearts to lead them to further births and deaths. [Anubhava Five, On Understanding *Vāsanā*, Sayings 41-44).

The way to salvation advocated by the text consists mainly of yogic meditation and its prerequisite in the form of moral discipline. The latter consists of primarily four principles, namely, that of simplicity, that of truthfulness, that of service unto others and that of *sat-saṅga*, association with truth, in common parlance, holy association. These four principles are regulative principles and must be, the text is never tired of repeating, adhered to if one is to succeed in the path of *yoga*. At the same time, it warns us, as we can see in the quotations above, that *yoga* and its prerequisites may create more obstacles in the way than ever before, that a man of high moral character practising *yoga* runs the risk of falling a victim to *vāsanā* as never before to bring about ruin for himself. The man on the Path has to be endowed with extraordinary power of discrimination between the real and the unreal to succeed in his endeavour.

This power of discrimination does not, however, come from mere thinking. One's thinking is always narcissistic, prompted as it is by one's desire to *be*. All concepts are the products of this passion to *be*, flow out from one's projection of oneself as the I. This thinking has to be reflection on the word of a seer. But even that is not enough to make that thinking living and lucid. One has to pass through the hard test of life, through all the pain and anguish of life, pain and anguish not merely personal but what may be called ontological, pain and anguish inscribed into existence itself. The joy accompanying the manifestation of the *Nāda* is a temptation that has to be resisted, but man being what he is, he cannot but celebrate it and, as a consequence of that celebration, lose it. For, the humility required for self-extinction is lost in self-celebration. The result is a return to anguish manifold of the anguish of the suffering man before he embarked upon the path of *yoga*.

The redeeming feature of this suffering, however, is its purgatorial character. The joy changes into misery, misery too deep for description, a life long misery leading eventually to extinction of self-love. The *Nāda* then reappears but not as sound but as silence, as void, as nothingness, demanding the demise of the person on the path. And he has to die into that silence because life holds absolutely no promise and consolation for him. Worship of the *Nāda* has to give place, in very many cases, to self-submission to one's unhappy lot and to the silence and void that the *kuṇḍalinī* is. Even realisation of oneself as consciousness still and passive has to die in most cases into the misery that one turns into in the presence of that nothingness, that *kuṇḍalinī*. This does not, however, mean that there cannot be pure souls who can pass on from the state of *Nāda* or that of pure consciousness into the state of *samatā*, that Patience the Absolute, where all becomes one, all becomes the same. But the majority of pilgrims cannot escape the purgatorial fires that must succeed their joy sublime and high.

The message of the book will, therefore, be lost on a self-righteous person, one who is vain of his piety and meditation. Moral preparation is an imperative prerequisite for embarking on the path of *yoga*, and humility is indispensable for success in that path, a humility that comes to a man not through his conscious effort but through the giant agony he undergoes after his fall from his yogic ecstasies. That fall is truly the grace abounding, and he who can drink that bitter cup will live the life immortal, not he who rejoices in his bliss. For, his bliss has to have misery as its defining *other*, has to be related to the latter in terms of contrast. Fall from that bliss is, therefore, inevitable.

Every methodology, every *sādhanā*, every understanding and knowledge will, ultimately, fail to be of much avail to a mortal being, except the spirit of self-surrender to his mortal lot. That is the beginning and that is the end of his pilgrimage. In between are many puzzles, many struggles, many hardships, many disciplines and many meditations. But not until these disciplines give place to acceptance, total and unquestioning, of one's mortal lot can they be of any use. As long as the demon exists in man he has to resort to virtuous and noble life. As long as the man lives strong in him, he has to give away his means of life in service of others. Through the sacrifice of these two, his insensitive cruelty and his acquisitiveness, he will turn into a god, god that lives for others, whose life consists in *their* life. But even that god has to die, for the passion to *be* waxes strong in him too and not before that passion dies can he find what he seeks, ever seeks. Therefore, the man of goodwill in him has to die, man the giver in him has to die and also the god in him, he who lives not just for others but *as* others. The last has to take the agony of existence itself upon himself, has to turn into that existence, into the death that all that is in its truth is. It is as god the mortal, god that is mortality itself that he will be redeemed, will find the same and stale as bliss itself, not man the greedy and demon the cruel. And even this seer of sameness too has to die, as our text will say:

> *On* **samadarśī**, *on the seer of the Same:* To be beyond the reach of happiness and sorrow, to be free from the desire for the fruit of one's actions, to remain ever established in the *ātman*, to remain still when the organs of sense and action are active. And to perceive the same *ātman* within and without and to perceive all that happens in the world as grounded in it, to rise above the sense of me and mine with regard to the body and to remain ever given up to the *ātman*. And to remain distant from all the dualities like those of friend and foe, profit and loss. These are the characteristics of a seer of the Same. In sum, to remain self-same in activity and inactivity, to remain firmly established in the *ātman*. The seer of sameness is also called *jīvana-mukta*, one who has become liberated in his life itself. A man of this attainment is a blessing for the world.
>
> *On* **samavṛtti**, *one who lives the Same and has become the Same:* There is no taking for him and no giving, his being only the bliss that is the *ātman*, so deeply absorbed is he in it. Transcends he the body even while alive, the formed and the gross having disappeared for him. Not a trace of doership remains in him, for all oblivious he remains of his doings and what they bring about. Only Brahman he knows, only Brahman he becomes. The great men who have attained to this state are unable to do any good to the world, for they can neither

speak nor hear. Ever immersed they remain in the bliss of their *ātman*, of their being.

This means how even he who rejoices in *samatā* has to transcend that state. And when one perceives not and thinks not, where is the question of finding the varied things he perceives as one and the same? Even the vision of sameness he will cease to have, even that bliss. What he will be we cannot know and cannot imagine, for there remains no one to speak about it. All our categories are left behind, all our concepts, even our dualities and ambiguities, even what we may call the unsayable or the undecidable. For, we have to *be* in order to speak about the unsayable, but when we are not where is the place to say that things are unsayable or undecidable? Even silence will lose its meaning, as being will and no-being will, or being-no being will. For, silence too can be thought, but not *that* [?] that survives when we are not. But blasphemes like these cannot, alas! be avoided by us prattlers.

Through describing the state of *samavṛtti*, of one who has become the *same*, the Master does not negate what he has said. For, one cannot become a *samavṛtti* without first becoming a *samadarśī* (*samadarśin*) the seer of the Same. But in a way he negates all that he has said, negates all his formulations, disowns them and recants them. Even his own realisation he disowns, declaring himself yet on the path to become a *samavṛtti*. This way he reenacts the way of seers, who formulate every truth but only to disown it, only to recant it. The seer of the truth has to cease to be the seer of the truth in order to be the truth and to undo the truth he sees and perceives. One who has attained to the Supreme still finds himself a pilgrim, but a pilgrim without toil. For, the end of the pilgrimage will come on its own, it cannot be reached or attained to. No more this pilgrim has to make progress, he has only to wait in a spirit of complete self-submission. Self-submission then is the ultimate for us mortals, not the truth, not the destination and the goal. We have to be content with our fate, we have only to prepare us for that contentment. The rest does not belong to us. We do not know to whom it belongs or does not belong, or whether there is any scope for speaking about 'the rest'.

However, a word about the *Samatā-prakāśa, Revelation of Samatā*. How the revelation descended upon the world has been, as I said above, described in the said biography. The point to note is that the person or the man in the Master was, in that state of being, replaced by the Word of Revelation. The Master spoke without the knowledge that he spoke. He was not and yet the Revelation was. There was only the Revelation and not the hermeneutic because the man was not there to do the act of hermeneutic. The revelation descended in verse and has to be heard recited, the recitation softening down one's passion for interpretation, culminating eventually in a disposition of passive opening out to the voice of the Word. But even the word of revelation was, Gurudeva said, not the essence, not, as he put it, butter but only butter-milk. The butter remained within him, only the butter-milk flowed out for the benefit of the world. A *saṃavṛtti,* however, transcends the Word too; there is, there can be, no flowing out of the Word from him, no outflow of revelation. A brief description of such a seer the reader will find described in the said biography, the description about a sage at Srīnagar, Kaśmīr. To appreciate the content of this book to a satisfactory extent, the reader must be familiar with the life of the Master.

However, the immediate curiosity of the reader may perhaps demand that a few words may be said about the person that the Master was. Mahārājajī, Revered Lord, as his disciples would address him, was born on November 24, 1903 at a village called Gaṅgoṭhiān in the district of Rawalpindi (now in Pakistan). At the age of three he found himself in a state of being in which, as he put it once, one could not perceive either the morning or the evening. All mystery and enigma was the Being that presented itself before the child, all darkness and all silence until he was thirteen, when, at the dead of a night, he found a light blazing all bright within and without him, with the *Nāda* resounding loud and clear to kill his thoughts, even his perception of things and of the room he was sleeping in. The vision of his past births flashed before him with the vividness of perception but all seemed 'insignificant' to him. In a short while he left his room and found himself moving towards a dense forest in the vicinity of the village, called the Forest of Pīr Khwājā, spending the night there in ecstasy all oblivious of himself and his surroundings. Next day, in the depths of that forest, three words of the *Mahāmantra*, quoted at the beginning and the end of the book here, were revealed to him, and on the following two days, the rest of its words. After the revelation of the *Mahāmantra*, he found rhythmic words of the *bānī* (*vānī*) - revelatory speech - well up in him in the solitude of jungles to flow out spontaneously, without an effort and a thought. But all those words flowed out only to fade away into air, for no one was there to write them down, no one until Bhagat Banārasīdās came to act the scribe.

It was in the year 1938 that the *tapas*[10] of his nights and days culminated eventually in *sahajasamādhi, samādhi* the constant and spontaneous, at Jalmādā (Kashmir), a mile or two above the bed of the Jhelam, the *tapas* there reducing his body to a skeleton as it were. There follow then fifteen years of constant wandering from village to village, from town to town, accompanied by discourses and silent *tapas* at night with a yearly gap of two or three months when the Master would do his *tapas* in dense and dangerous jungles. A story miraculous is the story of these fifteen years, of the man whose nights were spent in the open, who never slept after the age of 25, whose daily intake was only a bowl of tea, later, when his health was perilously ruined, replaced by one of milk. He died on February 4, 1954 at Amritsar. I can say on the basis of what I saw on the following day: Nothing became him and the earth and the sky so much as his death. What a revelation it was for me, what a disclosure! The vision stands all vivid before me, stands before me with the vividness of perception, not of memory. But this is not the place to recall it or describe it. Years before his *mahāsamādhi*, the great *samādhi*, the *bānī* (*vāṇī*) had stopped to flow out, his interest in the spiritual well being of the common people fading out fast and quick. Awake he seemed lost, his formulations in response to some questions becoming brief and aphoristic, sometimes giving way to utter silence. In awe the questioner would be then struck mute, forgetting his question and his desire to know and comprehend. Imperceptibly though fast the *Samavṛtti* seemed to be replacing the *Samadarśin*.

A doubt may well arise in the mind of a thinking being: If all is one and the same, Brahman and *Māyā*, reality and appearance, fall and redemption, bondage and liberation, why strive for liberation and seek redemption from our fallen condition? If there is nothing to choose between mortality and immortality, then why the agony and despair of *tapas*, of austerities, should be endured? The answer is: we, with all our cunning and cleverness, cannot ultimately escape from that agony and that despair of *tapas*. It is our portion to die and we have to accept that portion. All our life we, however, fight against that portion, our life is little else than struggle against death. Our misery, our sordid love and sinister hatred, our mean virtues and our deadly sins and, eventually, our tragedy absolute are the results of that our struggle. We cannot escape from that tragedy and the despair of it unless we come to accept that tragedy and that despair, do so with utmost meekness and a spirit of sincere resignation. We must, have to turn from helpless victims into willing martyrs. In that alone lies the freedom we seek, in that acceptance, total and without a qualification, of our mortal lot.

We cannot escape this stern duty laid down for us, this duty of acceptance of our lot, we cannot escape that role of the martyr; it is written into our nature, is inscribed in our being, that role the inevitable. As I said earlier, the philosophical aspects of the work have been explained in the Biography and, to some extent, in the Notes, but there is one point that must be mentioned here regarding the imperative of this acceptance. The *jīva,* the living being, this mortal being, finds himself, the text says, projected as a doer, into a being related and situated, related to others and situated in the world but ever obliged, as a doer, to disown and undo every situation and every relationship, to disown and undo, in other words, his own being. Not to be is the being of this being. His self-projection as the doer implies his self-projection into the body with the seemingly infinite world as its constitutive *other.* Three conditions are there to constitute this being, namely, condition the given, condition he finds himself situated in; condition the transcendent, condition that compels him to transcend his given condition, every possible condition; and since this call of the beyond never lets him *be,* he seeks to sabotage his sense of the inevitability of that call through projecting himself in other existential conditions and situations. These three urges, namely, the urge to remain himself, the urge to transcend himself and the urge to project himself into a world situation are called respectively, *tamas, sattva* and *rajas.* The call of the *sattva,* that call of the beyond is stern and forbidding and inviolate, no mortal can escape it. If he tries to do so through projecting himself in other conditions, his punishment will be no less than death itself. Man has to die as a being situated because he will not die into the transcendental thrust in him. Once he gives himself up to that thrust, he will disown every situation, every existential condition; he will become that urge to undo himself and undo that urge itself. His being is that urge, the urge that demands his death and he has to obey its call. So every mortal, every doer has to die before his actual death by self-submitting to that urge in him, by identifying with that urge. Only then will his misery end, only when he dies into it and with his death makes that urge too die with him. For, no transcendental urge can survive the death of the being related and situated. Hard is the task before him, exceedingly hard, but he cannot but undertake it, his desire demands it, his primordial and ultimate desire, his very being demands it. His lack will not be made up, his existential wounds will not be healed unless he turns a martyr, a meek sufferer of the tragedy that inflicts being itself, existence itself.

Many a conceptual speculator would ask this question: why this fall, this love of oneself, this projecting of oneself as this being or that being and the obligation to disown that being? In other words, why this self-projection as the doer? The question is not as silly as it might seem, for it speaks of, rather shows forth, the very condition in which every doer finds himself. For, the being placed uncertainly and inflicted with every anxiety cannot but hypostatise his *arche* and his *telos*, invest the two with a sort of 'objective reality'. He believes that if he strives hard and with all sincerity he may escape from his *arche* and attain to his *telos*, putting an end to all his existential agony. All civilisations have been pursuing this end, to some extent. 'Civilised' people seek to escape from the jungle and from the beast to live in civilisation to puruse the ideals the civilisation in question has formulated for them. But no civilisation has been successful in this its endeavour. The Greek Tragedy enacts this failure with a poignant force and conviction. For it, the beast and the infernal furies will ever pursue man and the gods will ever elude him. Precariously placed between the two he will enact his tragic role of failure, a *moira* he can never hope to avoid. The Christian vision, as immortalised by Dante, finds the dark forest of despair, the hell and the purgatory as heaven itself, but only after the pilgrim has lost himself in the darkness of unknowing, unknowing lying 'twenty centuries deep in him', past any recall. Even the vision of all as heaven does not let him know the truth he seeks, for that secret deep and mysterious does not tolerate the presence of man. So

Divine Comedy does not turn out to be either divine or a comedy, for the Divine spurns man sternly, demands his death, death final and irrevocable. Where is the end of his journey, where is the *telos* he strove for? But many a visionary who seek their salvation through self-sacrifice imagine the real as a cosmotheandric sacrifice, where man and his world die into god and heaven and god and heaven die into man and earth to keep the world going and alive as the act of sacrifice. They do not realise, these pious souls, that their god and their heaven are only projections of the pilgrim placed between beast and god and that when he ceases to be, god and heaven too will cease to be. So, the question, why god sacrificed himself into a mortal is a question that will cease to have any meaning when man has sacrificed himself into god, for the god will not survive man. We as doers, placed between the past and the future and between the state fallen and the state redemptive cannot but strive for the latter. That is our *bhāgya*, our portion, portion that we must and have to accept.

The three-fold condition of our life, condition that has made us doers, has ceased to attract the notice of modern world in its contemporary phase of late or decadent capitalism. Some recent thinkers have pointed out that all our talk about the threefold structure of our being is not very meaningful because neither can our *arche* be intelligibly formulated nor can be our *telos*, and as a consequence thereof, nor can be our so-called present existential condition. We talk about these terms, they say, in relation to one another when the terms themselves are in question. So all this talk about *arche* and *telos* is unintelligible or, as they would put it, undecidable. These thinkers perhaps did not imagine that their thought will be taken so lightly and so frivolously as the contemporary world has, in fact, taken it. What their thought implies, as one can see it, is that if the two poles of our being, our *arche* and *telos*, are undecidables, then our existential condition, condition placed between these two, too is an undecidable. But the contemporary world forgot about this formulation and decided, out of sheer perversity, that our life, that undecidable between the *arche* and the *telos*, alone matters and that there is no sense in deciding what is the degraded, what is the normal and what is the ideal. So man and his desire became the absolute legislators of truth, of morality, of aesthetics and all that humanity tried to cherish but could not always do so. The result is that there is a collapse of all that mankind has imagined, striven for and dreamed about; only desire matters now, only passion and self-love and self-gratification.

During the 'creative' phrase of this civilisation, scientific development became the guiding principle of life. Mankind diverted their attention from the *telos* and directed it towards the world. This is how they sabotaged the transcendental urge in man, the principle of *sattva* in him. Forgetting about their actual existential condition, the condition that disowns itself ever and always, they tried to place man firmly in the world context, trying to master its ways and laws as much as they could. The result of this their commitment to *rajas* was unprecedented knowledge of Nature and the power that knowledge gave to man. Soon their commitment to knowledge gave way to consumer culture, encouraged by and encouraging technology more than science proper. The Master envisaged all this condition and its disastrous implications with a prophetic insight, (Vide Supplement 1, *On World Peace*). A passage or two would call for our immediate attention:

> *Saying 6.* Immersion in the pleasures of the body it is that prompts the *buddhi* to investigate the external and gross elements, to find that investigation the only genuine investigation. This investigation of the gross elements leads to the discovery and invention of many a wonder, wonders that make it ever restless and blind to its own truth and being. These wonders, those results of investigation of the elements, lead to tragic and

disastrous results. To seek peace the true in them is a sure sign of stupidity. One should understand this truth about this commitment to the I-sense. Dedication to this false I-sense may end up in mastery over the sun, the moon, air, water and other forces of nature but it cannot put to rest the unrest that troubles every mortal being. For, every investigation of external elements, investigation that has the passion for the pleasures of the organs of sense and action for its cause, and the discoveries and inventions that this investigation leads to for the supposed happiness of mankind, are, as a matter of truth, the source of every unrest, unrest in the extreme, and every fear. That is the truth about this investigation, truth that every thinking being should understand. And this precisely is the effect that scientific investigation of these days is producing on everybody's mind. Instead of finding ways to sustain life, people are inventing ways to destroy it. One should be aware of what this external investigation leads to, this excessive commitment to the gross, material world. It can lead, this worship of matter, only to killing tensions, degraded ways, fraud and deception and self-destruction. Instead of investigation of matter, it is the life force within that should be investigated. For, only that investigation can lead one to the way to peace the supreme, that goal true of life, only that can make human life truly successful.

Saying 7. Dedication to matter, to, that is to say, the pleasures of the functions of sense-cognition and action cannot but have complete disaster for its result. When mankind in general totally give themselves up to a consumer culture, with no thought of its implications, their *vāsanā* swells to lead them to all kinds of evil and mischief. People in the grip of this kind of *vāsanā* ever think of finding ways to destroy others, inviting retribution on themselves. That is the result of their excessively evil and wicked ways.

Saying 8. Tainted by the I-sense, the *buddhi* finds itself completely identified with the body of the five elements to seek final satisfaction in the modifications of those elements, in their subjective counterparts, namely, sexuality, wrath, greed, stupidity and egoity. Its increasing immersion in these passions pollutes it further to lead to all kinds of troubles and miseries for it. Not a moment can it find to breathe freely and without fear. That in sum is the worldly mode of life and being. Worship of matter, dedication to it, inflames these passions to an excessive extent, leaving no scope for any possibility of self-restraint. Human beings then turn worse than beasts, inviting complete destruction upon themselves. For worship of matter leads to increase of desires, resulting in exploitation of others for one's own pleasures and well being, provoking consequences that cannot but create every unrest for beings, unrest in the extreme. This is the life style of demons, the very embodiment of complete self-destruction.

Investigation of matter or scientific investigation has these disastrous results for mankind because to sleep over the call of the beyond inevitably provokes the deadly nemesis. We mortals live at the mercy of that call of the beyond, we cannot sleep over it out of our arrogance of knowledge and power. But sleeping over that call, we moderns in our perversion have committed ourselves to progress. And progress is progress in a context, that is, in the world-context. To believe in progress is to sabotage the transcendental thrust in us, the thrust that is there to undo all contexts. It is to sleep over our native sense of our fall and loss, our original and ontological lack and deprivation. Our paradise is in the future, of us born in this arrogant age, and for this reason, is to be fashioned and forged and not to be regained. This *hubris*, this our commitment to *rajas*, commitment almost complete and unqualified, cannot but end up in complete ruin and devastation. We have to pay heed to the prophetic warning of the Master, if we would survive. Or is it already too late for the act of atonement for us?

These are some of the ideas that will occupy the reader when he goes through this book. The Notes dwell on some of them at some length and the biography in some details. The Notes demand concentrated attention and reading; a man of easy faith may find them too condensed and difficult but not a man disillusioned with his thought, his endeavour and with the assumptions and goals of modern civilisation and its decadent culture.

The Translator found it impossible recapture the style of the work translated here. For, only an illiterate seer of the truth can command that style. No writer can, no poet can, no thinker can, howsoever great or sublime. I would readily part with my little learning for the ability to write merely a page or two in his style, style extracted direct from the mine of his experience that was no experience - rough, unpolished but burning with the light of revelation. As for the revelation of *Samatā-prakāśa*, one has only to self-submit to it and not to reflect on it. The *Samatāvilāsa*, however, demands reflection and constant meditation.

The Master uses the normal Hindi versions of some of the Sanskrit terms. He uses, for example, the term *ātmā* and not the Sanskrit *ātman*, the term *Brahma* and not *Brahman*, *yogī* and not *yogin*, *samadarsī* and not *samadarśin*. In the translation, I have invariably used the terms *ātman* and *Brahman* because they are more familiar to the English knowing non-Hindi speaking reader versed in these matters. Occasionally, I have used some other terms too this way. This work would not like to remain confined to merely the North Indian reader.

The work in the original was written basically in Hindi language but in what is called the Persian script. But quite a few words of Persian and Arabic origin entered into it, especially those related to Islamic tradition and the Quran and also of the Judo-Christian tradition frequently in use in that tradition. The work repeatedly invokes the identity of the end of all religions and also similarity of many of the means adopted for attaining to that end. Hence the shape of its language, a mixture of words of high Sanskrit origin and also, to a much lesser extent, of high Persian and Arabic origin. The unlearned Master had the learning of scholars at his ready command but in the shape of unlearned learning. His accent, his pronunciation and his syntax would not let any learning spoil the simplicity of his language, his direct appeal and the force of conviction, conviction born out of experience, direct and immediate. I may add that the Master received education only up to the eighth class or standard and that too at a village school.

To conclude with:

A Note on the Text: The six ANUBHAVA[S] of the text constitute the *Samatāvilāsa* as originally compiled during the Master's life and approved by him. The two SUPPLEMENTS presented here as an appendix were compiled by his disciples after his (the Master's) *mahāsamādhi*. Some of the sections of the supplements consist of letters written to disciples and others in response to their queries, some of them of his blessings on certain occasions. A few of them the reader may find redundant. The Translator nevertheless translated them because of the request made to him to translate the entire book. The bulk of the supplements, however contains themes of paramount importance.

And an Acknowledgement: The Translator expresses his thanks to Mr Anil Bahmi, a devotee of the Master, for supplying him digitally improved versions of two photographs of the Master.

Translator

Notes

[1] *Māyā*, as will be explained in the Notes below, is often taken, in Śaṅkara, to mean names and forms that conceal the Real. You cannot determinate what these names and forms are; you cannot say whether they are different from the *ātman*, the self, or the Real or one with it. They remain *anivarcanīya*, unsayable and unthinkable. That is why they are called *Māyā*, derived from the root *mī*, to measure. Names and forms are what we measure phenomena with, determinate them, set limits to them. There is another term called *avidyā*, often translated as ignorance, but which actually means false knowledge, or what we may call propositional knowledge. *Avidyā*, that primal ignorance, superimposes names and forms on to the real to determinate it in terms of relationships and contrasts. It also superimposes the Real on to names and forms to falsely invest these latter with a semblance of reality. In the Samtāvilasa, however, *Māyā* and *avidyā* are not so sharply differentiated because of their interdependence. One cannot perceive names and forms, cannot even imagine them, without superimposing the Real on to them, and one cannot delimit and enframe the latter, without names and forms. Names and forms thus depend on the act of superimposition and the act of superimposition on names and forms. *Māyā* and *avidyā* thus constitute a duality and cannot, therefore, be separated from each other.

[2] Literally, putting together, joining with. The state of being where dualities that compose our mortal being cease to be, the state in which our constitutive *other* does not remain the other but becomes, to put the matter in the traditional terms, our own *ātman*, our own self.

[3] 'Conscious', conscious within quotes because for a seer of *samatā*; there is no difference between the state of *samādhi* and the waking state. A man who sees difference between the two is still a *sādhaka*, still a man on the path, and not a *siddha*, one who has attained to the goal.

[4] *Agni* (fire) derived from the root *ag*, to move tortuouslly, of the Vedas came to be called *kuṇḍalinī* by the *yogins*. Long practice of yoga rouses that Fire or *kuṇḍalinī* in the region of the navel. It rises from there to reach ultimately the crown of the head where it turns all black to pervade the entire body to swallow it into itself. *Kuṇḍalinī* rises like a serpent waving tortuously or like a flame of fire waving in the same way. The *yogins* also call it *jvālāmukhī*, the fire-mouthed,

that burns the individual no less than his world. The Vedic concept of fire fully reenacts itself in this symbolism of the *yogins*.

5. Notice how the text uses the terms, 'Word the Imperishable' '*ātman*', 'consciousness the bare', or 'consciousness without its other' as synonymous. We know that consciousness will cease to be consciousness when there is no *other* to constitute it. We also know that a word is a word in relationship and contrast with other words of a given language and that if it is a name it can have no meaning without its referent.

And we also know that language requires speakers and also the world context in which those speakers dwell and live. And we also know, further, that a word acquires different meanings in different contexts, contexts of life, contexts of syntax, contexts of time, thought and activities and those of different discourses or situations. . This way language is language in tension, in relationships that are contrasts and, for this reason, ever changing both in terms of meaning and form. So, how can a word become the Word, Word the Imperishable? That is the question which philosophers of language sleep over, with almost insensitive consistency. Though philosophers may take to crude humour to wish away the phrase, 'In the beginning was the Word,' yet the Word has haunted mankind since the beginning of language, at least since the advent of scriptures. We cannot avoid questioning the Word if we have not lost the sense of wonder and mystery with regard to language.

Our text would have this to say regarding the words that we speak and the Word dwelling in every word as its in-being, and, for that matter, dwelling in each and every being and the whole world as their in-being, as their very *ātman*, their self. The individual, the text says, finds himself projected as a doer with the indispensable *other* of his doing, *other* in the form of the body and the world, each the constitutive *other* of the other. And *others* as distinctions require concepts and concepts require language. As the doer is the projection of one's ontological self so the words or language are the projection of the Word. Similarly, consciousness, that *other* of its other, the doer and his world, is projection of Consciousness, Consciousness the self. So, the terms like the Word, the *ātman*, or the self and Consciousness without its other, are mere superimpositions on to the Real of the names of the phenomena of our experience, phenomena of our experience shorn of their constitutive others. Thus Word is word without its other, the *ātman* or the self is the self without its other and consciousness the bare is consciousness without its other. These names are used only to deny the notions these names indicate and suggest with regard to the Real because consciousness, the self or a word can have no being without their *others*. All that these terms indicate is that every thing is the Real when it ceases to be a duality and that this can happen only when one ceases to be a doer, ceases to be an I which needs must have its constitutive other. See also Note 4 p. 567.

6. *Nirvāṇa* means extinction of the self one finds oneself to be. With the extinction of that self, self the projected and posited, its *other* the world too gets extinct, and all the distinctions and the differences. In one word, *nirvāṇa* means the extinction of *Māyā-avidyā*. To interpret *nirvāṇa* in terms of complete negation is a misconception of the meaning of the term. To interpret it this way is to equate reality with interpreted reality. If the collapse of the interpreted world means nothingness in the literal sense of the term, then reality can only be propositional reality, which will be absurd in the eyes of a thinker like Nāgārjuna. Unfortunately, this sage-thinker has been interpreted as a nihilist by many of his admirers and opponents alike and in modern no less than in ancient times.

7. *Guṇas* and *prakṛti*. These oft-occurring terms the reader will find explained in the Notes below. But he should not be left guessing about their meaning while he is being introduced to a work. These concepts are very complex and should be clearly understood to avoid misunderstandings of many a forth-coming passage. *Prakṛti*, literally, *before* of creation, means names and forms in their unmanifest state, names and forms *before* they become manifest. The concept of *prakṛti* has been a stumbling block for many a scholarly interpreter of the Vedānta tradition. If Brahman is the single and sole reality, then *prakṛti* should be unreal, as it indeed has been referred to very many times. But the truth is that the concept of the Real as single and sole reality is itself a mere concept and cannot but have its constitutive other, which is *prakṛti*. The Real cannot be called one or many, or one-many or, for that matter, even real or unreal. All these terms and concepts are misleading. One has to be free of all concepts, those de-terminating functions, to be the Real one is.

Prakṛti has three *guṇas*, three strands, strands constituting this rope that holds every being in bondage. And these strands, these constitutive principles of *prakṛti* are: *sattva*, *rajas* and *tamas*. *Sattva* is the principle of transcendence, and *tamas* is the principle that makes one remain coincided with oneself, and the *rajas* is the struggle between these two principles. Every being lives as bound by these *guṇas*, these strands. He would remain himself and transcend himself and participate in the struggle between these opposing principles: the principle of inertia and the principle of transcendence. This struggle embodies the *rajas* principle. Structuralism is as old as man, as its modern propounders would readily admit, even loudly advocate.

[8] *Buddhi*, the faculty of knowing,. The word is often translated as intellect but it has implications that should not be lost sight of. When identified with the senses the *buddhi* turns into perception, when it identifies with thinking about the things of the world in terms desire and aversion, it turns into deliberation of what is called *manas*, that orientation towards the senses and their *others*, namely, the objects of the world. In the state of reflection it turns into determinating faculty, the faculty that places things in concepts, sets limits to them, classifies them in terms of relationships-contrasts. There is still another dimension to the *buddhi*, the dimension of its witness character, when it stays still as the passive witness of its determinating functions and of the deliberations of the *manas* and of perceptions of the senses. It turns then, to invoke the Upaniṣadic language, into the eye of the eye, the ear of the ear, the mind of the mind and the knower of knowing. In one word, it turns into a still and passive witness of all that a person is, all that he knows, perceives, acts and acts upon. That is the moment when it becomes ready to melt completely to become what we call or miscall the Real or the *ātman*.

[9] The concept of *vāsanā* will occupy us a great deal in the book, especially in Chapter 5, where its ontology is discussed in details. Here only the meaning of the term is being explained. Derived from the root *vas*, to dwell, *vāsanā* means the desires, passions, ideas and impressions inherited from one's past lives. These dwell in a being to determine his world-view, his inclinations and habits, even what he perceives.. They represent the burden of the past, the burden too heavy for this being, who is little else than an orientation towards the future. It is *vāsanā* that distorts one's urge for the beyond into all kinds of projections into the world, one's tragic *other*.

[10] *Tapas*, austerity or fervent ardour, means in the case of the Master, prolonged absorption in *samādhi*. During the time of *tapas*

he reduced his intake rather drastically. This way of his proved, ultimately, disastrous for his physical health.

Brahman is truth the absolute
and the ground of all that is.
Samatā *is the Power Infinite*

The Great Chant

aum brahma satyaṃ niraṅkār ajanmā advait purakhā sarab vyāpak kalyāṇ mūrat parmeśvarāya namastam.

Aum! Brahman is Being the Formless and Unborn,
Person the a-dual is He,
all-pervasive and all-benign!
To Him, the Lord Supreme,
is our salutation.

The Samatāvilāsa[1]

Anubhava[2] One

(i) Samatā-nidhāna, *The Treasure of* Samatā

Saying 1. The order of the world has the power of *samatā*, power ever the same, as its sustaining principle.

Saying 2. All the order, political and religious, is based on *samatā*, on sameness. The order not based on *samatā* leads to disaster and cannot last for long.

Saying 3. It was the realisation of *samatā-śakti*, the power that is ever the same, that liberated the great ones from the recurring cycle of birth and death and enabled them to show unto the world the path to peace the ever lasting.

Saying 4. Samatā alone is *dharma,* the way to redemption. When its light disappears from the world then those that have seen the truth and become the truth appear to light their ways, of the people lost and bewildered, to their redemption.

Saying 5. Samatā alone is the bliss that every being seeks in his in-being.

Saying 6. And *samatā* alone is life and being. Any thing or being that deserts it shall have its or his life desert it or him.

Saying 7. And self-rule too is *samatā*, for it alone can free one from the worldly mode of being, that bondage, and blesses one with the bliss supreme.

Saying 8. All that is, the world entire, is the manifestation of *samatā* itself. In delight of each other do beings and things exist.

Saying 9. All the scriptures of the world reveal the truth of *samatā*, of that alone. Any book that does not speak of it is not a revelation but a mere fabrication.

Saying 10. Samatā alone is the destination that renunciates given to poverty ever seek, attaining which they get cured of desire, that malady.

Saying 11. Samatā is the primordial light that shines as consciousness. To find this bliss is, therefore, a necessity for every being.

Saying 12. Human birth is considered the best only because man alone, among creatures, can attain to *samatā* as it truly is and can free himself from desire, desire that has made him its dwelling.

Saying 13. Bliss is *samatā*, eternal is *samatā*, the very cessation of the world, its extinction, is it. It is the light that irradiates the intellect, the intellect of each and every being. To seek it is the act divine, to pursue it is to pursue the human goal true.

Saying 14. To instruct a man in *samatā* is to instruct him into liberation. It sets at rest, this instruction about *samatā*, all the conflicts and tensions among faiths and of life.

Saying 15. He who teaches *samatā* is the teacher true, he alone. To futile controversies and endless debates leads every other instruction.

Saying 16. To dedicate one's life to the attainment of *samatā* is, in every truth, worship of the Lord. Worship not so directed is not worship the true but a mere pretence, a worship of desire and passion.

Saying 17. The ruler and the ruled will flourish and prosper alike when they come to know what the state of *samatā* means for their life and being. Bereft of this understanding, unjust will be their life and fraudulent their ways.

Saying 18. To think about *samatā* is to participate in the truth, to come into contact with it. That is the real *sat-saṅga* [literally, coming into contact with the truth], that is the holy congregation and that is the service true. It is participation in truth because it brings to extinction one's sense of identity with organs, both cognitive and motor, and the mind, and orients one's efforts towards attainment of that state of being they call the state of bliss. Congregations bereft of this participation in the truth are empty shows where ignorance alone breeds and flourishes.

Saying 19. Samatā is the very life of men established in truth. Deep and earnest reflection will reveal this truth.

Saying 20. Samatā is the cure for every affliction that a mortal being is subject to. Into the very being of love turns he that finds it.

Saying 21. To think of *samatā* with a mind still and free from thoughts is *yoga* in its truth.

Saying 22. Samatā is the eternal revelation, the wisdom primordial that ever remains what it has been. And he who finds it will find himself turned into that revelation, that wisdom itself.

Saying 23. To seek *samatā* is to be in bliss, bliss real and true. For he who finds it never finds himself mired in *karma*, in action, and what it leads to, the ever-recurring process of birth and death.

Section 24. One comes to find the beatitude that *samatā* is when one has lost all the taste for the pleasures of the sense- and motor organs.

Section 25. When a man comes to know all as the same, the sense of me and mine, that deviation from his true being, comes to cease, the sense of me and mine that is *Māyā* itself, the *Māyā* of the three strands.[3]

Saying 26. To know all as one and the same is to be free from the passion for the fruit of action; it is to turn into the state that is passivity itself, into the state free from every desire.

Saying 27. Knowledge of all as the same is a knowledge where time is not, action is not, desire is not, where nothing comes to be and nothing ceases to be. Free from all these stains is that knowledge, that bliss the eternal, knowledge that is full in itself, is infinity itself [with no *other* to constitute it].

Saying 28. All striving, all efforts will go waste if they are not dedicated to the knowledge that *samatā* is. From bondage to bondage moves the man who would not know the same and be the same.

Saying 29. Knowledge of *samatā*, the vision of all as one and the same, is what men of wisdom have ever realised since the beginning of the world. Blessed with that knowledge they roamed about in bliss in this transient and destructible world.

Saying 30. Only a man given to right action and right thought and of pure intake and faith can know all as one and the same, the false appearances of the world tempting him not, his desire and allegiance reserved only for the truth, for that alone.

Saying 31. One must live in the company of seers if one would have the vision of *samatā*.

Saying 32. Knowledge of *samatā* dawns on man when he discards the false sense of me and mine that the deviation called the body is.[4]

Saying 33. Freedom from desire will manifest in the man who knows the state of being the same. And so will freedom from pride. And so will disinterestedness, steadfastness and the desire to do good unto others. And, lastly, the effort to remain ever the same will wax strong in him. Of bliss the absolute are these traits the emanations, of that light the beams.

Saying 34. He who would know the way to *samatā* should do obeisance to one established in *samatā* and receive instruction from him. This is an imperative for that seeker. He should understand that *samatā* informs all religions, is their spirit and life. If he does not know the truth about *samatā*, he will find himself only lost in disputes and controversies.

Saying 35. With full faith and dedication should one stick to the way that leads to *samatā*. That alone is devotion and that alone is *yoga*, this dedication to *samatā-dharma*, to the path of *samatā*.

Saying 36. Only knowledge of *samatā* can bring about purification of *buddhi*, of the faculty that knows. And only that knowledge can free one from the fret and tension of action. Therefore it is incumbent on man that he reflect upon the way that can lead him to that state, the way supreme that his life can take to. And it is incumbent upon him that he strive for that state and get established in it.

Saying 37. **_Samatā_ means remaining self-same in every situation and condition, it means freedom from the desire to accept and reject. That, in every truth, is devotion to the Lord and that verily is _mukti_, liberation** from the process of living into death and dying into life, the process ever recurring and ever constant.

Saying 38. Only the principles that lead to the state of being ever the same can free this mortal being from thoughts of self-interest and make him merge into the Truth that he is. With that attained, that merger, no more will he whirl around in the world, that motion constant from birth to death and from death to birth.

Saying 39. Ever seek that beatitude, that blessed state ever the same. That alone will make whole the lack, the deprivation that pursued you life after life. Full will it make you and perfect here itself, in this very life.

Saying 40. That light, light ever the same, shines within each and every being. But oriented towards the mind as he is, he cannot find it.

Saying 41. One gets established in *samatā*, that Word the Imperishable, when one's mind and the organs of cognition and action give up their self-orientations and come to be one.

Saying 42. Spare you no effort and no pains to attain to the Real that is ever the same. For blessed will you be when that Knowledge shines in you.

Saying 43. That knowledge ever the same manifests itself when no sense of me and mine remains with regard to the body[-mind complex] and with regard to actions.

Saying 44. A being will find that knowledge ever the same when he gives himself up to contemplation pure and genuine, when, that is, he remembers the Lord as the Doer and the Undoer [and attributes no doing to himself, and no undoing].

Saying 45. The way to that knowledge lies in serving, without self-interest and without self-glorying, each and every being, finding him and the world entire as Lord the Manifest.

Saying 46. Bliss after bliss will find the man that follows the way to that Ever-the-Same. Discard will he all sins and taints, those adjuncts, and will come to be his own native being, being indivisible and entire.

Saying 47. He who knows that Truth, that Ever-the-Same, is a jewel among mankind, a hero is he, invincible and unconquerable.

Saying 48. Knower of all do they call him and the support of all, the man who knows that Truth, that Ever-the-Same.

Saying 49. Ever abides in bliss the man that perceives in him that Truth, perceives that Truth Ever the Same.

Saying 50. There is no thought like the thought of *samatā*, no knowledge like the knowledge of *samatā* and no contemplation like the contemplation of *samatā*. To contemplate within oneself that ever that Ever the Same, that Word the Brahman, is the striving without a parallel.

Saying 51. He who ever thinks of that real, that ever the same, will drive away the delusion of *Māyā* and will merge into Word the Truth. That is the abode ultimate, the abode unsayable and nameless. Blessed is he that finds it and blessed indeed is his glory.

Saying 52. That knowledge ever the same is not the knowledge that those dedicated to their sects can find, or those for whom their country is every thing, or those who would worship the whole cosmos and creation[5]. To dedicate oneself to one's sect is to dedicate oneself to one's selfhood, to worship one's country is to worship one's sense of mine, to identify oneself with the entire creation too is a bondage.

Saying 53. To worship knowledge ever the same means to perceive the one Lord in all, to have no ill will towards any being, to be good and pure in one's conduct and to be free of self-interest and selfishness. It means to depend and have faith only in the One Lord and worship Him and only Him. It means to give gifts in His Name alone, and in obedience to His command serve His world. Knowledge ever the same is not confined within the limits of a sect or a religion, it is the very base, the ground, of every religion. This knowledge alone can put an end to the disposition that finds one's being as that of a doer, to that disposition of selfhood, and leads one to peace the indivisible and absolute, to the Lord Himself.

Saying 54. The instructor that does not worship that knowledge, knowledge ever the same, does not worship that Lord the truth, consciousness and bliss and has no inkling of its glory, of that knowledge, is not an instructor but an impostor; to hatred, tensions and unrest alone give rise his teachings. [Ignoring him] one should seek the truth, truth only.

Saying 55. A man who worships the One Imperishable Lord and teaches the people to be good in their conduct and give themselves unto the worship of the Lord true and supreme is a teacher true, he only. And incarnation divine is he, and the one that has attained to the goal final and supreme. And a prophet is he and a Messenger. To the world brings peace his instruction and joy to those that follow his way.

Saying 56. Ever search *samatā*, that state ever the same. That is the Lord's commandment for you.

Saying 57. Samatā means oneness, equality, the state or disposition that remains ever the same. Investigation of *samatā* too is *samatā*. For, only its understanding, of the real as self-same, can dispel the sense of mine, that falling off, that *Māyā* that deludes one's mind and intellect.

Saying 58. Sameness indeed is the being of the Lord, the Power that rules the world. That ever the same being of the Lord abides ever the same though moving with the moving world. No thing can touch it, and no unrest. For abides it as bliss itself in all the three dimensions of time. Finding this state within him, the mortal being finds his bindings - his actions - cut asunder to attain to the peace that moves not.

Saying 59. From bondage to bondage leads one the *buddhi*, the determinating faculty, intent on its own interests. For, discontent never leaves a being inflicted with this kind of *buddhi*, whether he finds what he desires or does not find. Only when the vision of *samatā* dawns upon him will he be disposed to work without desire and acquire other traits [traits that will lead him to the state of *samatā*].

Saying 60. For, when he works without desire, he comes to be gifted with a desire-free and generous disposition and other high traits that will bring him peace that passes understanding. And the moment he comes to know the truth, know that Ever the Same, that very moment the passion for work will come to cease in him, the passion that is mere another name for coming and going, for that never ending motion from birth to death and from death to birth. And that is the moment when one finds the bliss immortal in this mortal life itself.

Saying 61. It is knowledge ever the same that gives birth to faith in the Lord, to realisation of Him as one's own being and to one's establishment in Him. As long as one does not perceive all as one and the same, one cannot be free from the blind desire that dwells in every being, the desire that even far flung empires can never quench. Only that knowledge can bring to an end the malady called *Māyā*, that primal ignorance and concealment. When faith and effort, true and earnest, make the mind, the intellect and the sense- and motor organs merge into each other, when they make them one, there sounds in man the Word Eternal, the Word Ever the Same, its thunder deepening with the deepening of the said merger. That is the moment of the cessation of all kinds of desire, desire (*vāsanā*) that has accompanied every being from birth to birth, and also the unrest that the three strands of *prakṛti*, that *before* of all creation, generate in every mortal being. And that is the moment when he comes to be established in Word the True.

Saying 62. As long as the sense of 'mine', that addiction to and obsession with self-interest, dwells in the mind, it, the mind, continues to be pursued by many a thought, many a doubt and many a desire. For the eradication of this sense of 'mine', this deviation from oneself that *Māyā* the fierce brings about, is this formulation about the state of *samatā*.

Saying 63. The Being of the all-pervasive Lord dwells ever the same and as ever itself in all beings. When a man comes to remember the Lord truly and is devoted to Him truly, there will manifest in him the thought of the one in the all, of Being in all beings. That is what *samatā* knowledge is, that thought of the one in the all.

Saying 64. Belief in Lord the Truth, remembrance of Him and contemplation of Him constitute the way to deliverance from desire for the result of one's actions, desire that pursues every embodied being each and every moment, giving rise to all kinds dualities like those of happiness and sorrow, profit and loss, heat and cold, acceptance and rejection - those deviations that set in motion the wheel of recurring births and recurring deaths.

Saying 65. With the increase in man's faith in the Lord decreases the desire for the fruit of actions and one comes to be still and passive, comes to be, that is to say, established in the Lord who is liberation itself.

Saying 66. Controversies and disputes flourish when one is asleep to the truth that one is. As long as one's mind is embroiled in them, the knowledge that is ever the same will not shine forth, knowledge that is bliss itself. So, let not hate and animosity ever seize you, not for even a moment, or dismay and dejection and pride and egoism. Freed from these taints, let you find the peace and love that the state of *samatā* is. That is the bliss eternal, this abiding in the state of *samatā*, the bliss that ever shines within each and every being but which he cannot think of because his follies would not let him do so.

Saying 67. Anger will cease to be when love springs up in man, love for every being and creature. And his pride and greed will cease to be when he gives himself up in service to them. And his desire and delusion when he remembers the Lord, thinking of Him and Him only as the truth [and nothing else]. When a mortal comes to have this disposition, when devotion to the Lord and service to His creatures come to occupy his mind, all blessed with knowledge of *samatā* will he be, leaving behind the fallen state that *Māyā* wrought for him. To state the highest will he have attained then, the state of peace the eternal and indivisible.

Saying 68. Let every being endeavour to find the happiness that he truly seeks [but never finds]. Let him know the path that would lead him to it. Let no sectarian thought occupy him, that other name of self-seeking. For, his afflictions deep are these, his self-seeking and his fanaticism. Let him seek, therefore, the knowledge of Ever the Same, seek it ever and always.

Saying 69. Every mortal being seeks freedom from his mortal condition, but given to the compulsion of identifying himself with this state or that, he comes to be tied to these [imagining himself to be those very states]. No possibility of freedom from those ties remains for him until he gives himself, truly and in earnest, to devotion to the Lord.

Saying 70. The primal bondage is the bondage of self-identification with action, with the thought, 'I am the doer'. That gives rise to the sense of self-identification with the body. That in turn leads to self-identification with one's family, clan or caste. This leads to the sense of one's identity as a being related to a sect and as sharing in its beliefs and faith. And that leads to desire for domination over other groups or sects, and from that desire is born the sense of identification with one's own country [as against the countries of others]. Infernal is this desire, this desire for being, for being an identity.

Saying 71. This passion generates the disposition of hatred and enmity, giving rise to hostility and aversion, disputes and controversies, the disposition that would not let the disposition of good will and harmony prevail. A man given to this passion lives only to inflict pain on others, give up as he does all the acts and all the duties ordained for him [by Being within him]. For in his pride, he will forget that there is such a Being as the Lord and that He has ordained some duties for him. With this happening, swift will move Nature, that Creation of Lord the Perfect, to undo and destroy him.

Saying 72. A man who does not see the presence of the One Lord in all that is denies, in truth, the very existence of God. And he who does not serve with regard unhappy people defies His order and command. When he becomes vain and arrogant of the phantoms he calls his riches and possessions, a prisoner he becomes of self-interest and self-regard, with no concern whatsoever for ethical norms. A victim of desire and maladies of a sinful life, he loses both, his world as much as his spirit. A creature of hell does he then turn into, the man that has come to this pass.

Saying 73. Only vision of the Lord, that Ever the Same, can release a being from this condition, the condition he finds himself fallen into. As he moves forward in his contemplation of [the Name of] the Lord, he finds these ties loosening their grip on him, letting him eventually to lose himself in Word the Eternal, Word the all-knowing and all powerful.

Saying 74. When he merges into the Word, he verily attains to the very Origin of the world and to peace that passes understanding, to state the highest he attains to then and to the goal ultimate of *yoga*. Released is he then, that mortal being, from the compulsive desire for action. For, finds he everywhere and in every condition the self-same Lord, that truth and bliss and omniscient, within him as much as without him.

Saying 75. This is the abode, this state of *samatā-jñāna*, this knowledge of the self-same, where a mortal being comes to find the final rest. There is no striving like this striving, striving for the self-same, for a being blessed with a human birth. Not to the lot of every being does fall this striving; so seek to find it with every effort. And with faith unflagging dedicate your life to the way of contemplation revealed unto you to find that life [the true] before you come to die. To think of truth the self-same indeed is to live with gain.

Saying 76. Let him who seeks to find the life true surrender all the results of his actions to the will of the Lord. Let him contemplate Him, that Truth, with exclusive devotion. If he does that his sense of me and mine, that darkness in which he finds himself lost, will be dispelled and the Word Indivisible, that Truth ever the same, will shine forth in him. With the Lord is he then united, his state the state that is bliss itself, bliss the highest.

Saying 77. To resort to sustained meditation of the [name of the] Lord, perceiving all that happens or does not happen as ordained by Him, by Him only, leads to the cessation of all the false appearances that delusion has set up and fashioned. With the cessation of those appearances, one comes to be established in Word the Imperishable, the Word whose being is it to ever remain self-same, the Word that is bliss the highest. This is all that is about devotion all exclusive. Let one be all discriminating and ever strive to this kind of devotion, for that is the way to liberation.

Saying 78. Word the Brahman, the Word that has no beginning and no end, dwells in all and transcends all and ever remains self-same in all the three dimensions of time. Invisible is that Lord, infinite and nameless. To remember [the Name of that Nameless] Lord and give oneself up to a passive contemplation of Him reveals unto man that Being whose being is to remain ever the same. So trust in full that Lord, trust Him ever and always, let your life and breath be tied *(viśvāsa)* unto Him.[6] And remember Him [meditate on the Name of that Nameless] as the Ordainer of all that comes to be and ceases to be. This disposition will lead you ultimately to the revelation of the self-same, revelation of all as the Lord, that son of Man the Primordial.

Saying 79. There remains no duality then for the being blessed with this vision. He gets absorbed in Lord the indestructible and ever the same. No further birth remains for him and no further death and no further action to give rise to perishable pleasure and pain to ensnare him in further action, the process that continues forever. Brahman the Absolute then he turns, that mortal.

Saying 80. Ever stick you to the path truthful. Give up desire, that delusion, that death, and perceive the Self-Same, Self-same the desire-free, that final death of births and deaths that will otherwise lie in store for you. That is the only gain this false and purposeless world can dispense to you.

Saying 81. Only the Word true, the Word that is Brahman, is [the state of] *samatā*, that Word the ever full and all pervasive, that inbeing of all in each. With intellect pure and mind concentrated, one can get an inkling of It in one's thought. So ever strive to know that indestructible reality.

Saying 82. Far on very high is the abode of the Self-Same; only those that strive, strive hard and without a let and pause can hope to attain to it.

Saying 83. From time will he be released and from death the action, will be released the man whose soul is illumined by the light of *samatā*. Lost remains he in *samādhi*, where all dualities become one and the same.

Saying 84. Every act of devotion, every worship and every striving have one single aim, namely, to find that Word Indivisible, that light of *samatā*, of the self-same.

Saying 85. It is imperative that man live in accord with the Moral Law. For, no light of the spirit will shine for him if he does not live so. Beyond his reach will remain the Same.

Saying 86. A being comes to believe in *samatā-dharma*, the way leading to the Same, only if he keeps his thoughts pure of every fault and blemish.

Saying 87. To attain to the Same is to attain to liberation and to the Real and to bring into extinction the ever recurring process of births and deaths [and that of the worlds, their constitutive *others*].

Saying 88. When the Word, Word that is *samatā* itself, sameness itself, thunders within man, all his thought processes come to merge into It. That verily is the *state* of bliss the supreme, that state of merger.

Saying 89. Destruction itself is this perishable body, only truth the self-same is the Indestructible, that dispenser of bliss. It is that real the self-same that they call the self, the light and Brahman.

Saying 90. But unless and until a man has been instructed by a teacher [that sees all as the same] and has given himself unto the service of others, there will be no possibility of his getting established in *samatā*.

Saying 91. Name, form, qualities and activity - these are the modifications wrought by *Māyā*. To liberate himself from their grip a man must give himself to the meditation of the Name, the Name that is the embodiment of *samatā*, of sameness. Let him resort to it with concentrated mind time and again.

Saying 92. Samatā alone is life. For a man to strive to attain to it is verily to strive in truth. Let him ever seek to find that abode stable and firm.

Saying 93. Let a man ever surrender his mind to the will of the Lord, for that will lead him to the bliss that *samatā* is.

Saying 94. As long as one does not realise that the world is destruction itself, one cannot possibly find truth the eternal, truth ever the same.

Saying 95. Mind and the sense- and motor organs are formidable temptations. One must adhere to the path of *samatā*, sameness, with a steadfast faith. That is the effort true and righteousness true.

Saying 96. Blessed is the man who thinks about *samatā*, that destroyer of all that binds man and renders him weak and helpless.

Saying 97. Samatā is true righteousness, *samatā* is true prayer, *samatā* is true knowledge; it alone is true striving and it alone is *prema,* love and devotion.

Saying 98. Liberate yourself from the sense of Me and Mine. The thought of *samatā* that the great ones have formulated is the way easiest towards that end.

Saying 99. Think with devotion about the Lord, that Full. Therein alone lies the use of life here. Control your thirst [desire]. For, therein lies the heroic mould.

Saying 100. The state of *samatā* is the state devoid of the sense of the I or the Me. Let no effort be spared to attain to that bliss, that your deliverance from the noise and tumult of the world.

Saying 101. Think of the truth, believe in the truth and remember the truth. Serve in truth, relate to the truth and strive for the truth. That is the way to take you to *samatā,* your home, that life of persons the true. To find that joy the true is an absolute imperative for every mortal. If he does not find it, he will fall time and again into the snare of *Māyā,* where only pain and torment will be his portion.

(ii) Treasure the Peerless

Saying 1. The Lord is the truth; in His refuge lies our bliss the supreme.

Saying 2. What is effort the great?

To tread the holy path that leads unto Him.

Saying 3. Who is one's friend in truth?

One's good deeds.

Saying 4. Who is the man of power in the world?

The man who does good unto others.

Saying 5. Who lives ever happy?

The man who wishes well of others.

Saying 6. Who lives ever satisfied?

The man that believes in God.

Saying 7. Which is the paramount power in the world?

Freedom from desire, and forgiveness.

Saying 8. What is life the pure?

The life given to thought of one's death.

Saying 9. Who is the perfect guru?

One who has been victorious over himself.

Saying 10. What is the right worship?

Worship with no self-interest.

Saying 11. What is true happiness?

To attain to the Lord.

Saying 12. Who is wise?

One without self-conceit.

Saying 13. Who has political and social wisdom?

One who cherishes unity.

Saying 14. Who is the man without a foe?

One who is ever intent on the good of others.

Saying 15. What is goodness?

To relieve others from their ills and misfortunes.

Saying 16. What is charity?

To serve the deserving person as much as one can.

Saying 17. What is hard to find in the world?

A perfect guru, spiritual preceptor.

Saying 18. What is true devotion?

To think pure and to have faith the firm.

Saying 19. What is *sat-saṅga,* holy congregation?

Where they reflect on the nature of truth.

Saying 20. Who is avatar, incarnation of God?

He who is devoid of every desire.

Saying 21. Who is a *devatā,* a god?

One who strives for the good of others.

Saying 22. What is the core, the quintessence of human life?

To seek the truth.

Saying 23. What is the place of pilgrimage?

Where they sing in praise of the Lord or where dwell those whom the Lord holds dear.

Saying 24. Which is the misfortune worse than death?

To pay no heed to one's heedlessness [to be insensitive to and oblivious of one's lapses and wrongs].

Saying 25. Who is dead while alive?

One who is selfish.

Saying 26. How can one attain to the Lord?

By following the teachings of one's guru, by doing good to others, serving them without a desire for a return or a reward.

Saying 27. How can one make one's faith firm and stable?

When one finds a true guru, one's faith will become firm and stable.

Saying 28. What is the power of the Lord?

The power that dispenses joy to the whole world.

Saying 29. What is *dharma*, the way one should adopt and follow?

That which leads to blessedness holy and true.

Saying 30. What is knowledge?

That which dispenses life the eternal, that is, light the eternal.

Saying 31. How does life come to be truly alive?

By sparing no effort to keep to path the righteous.

Saying 32. Which is the greatest sin?

To cause misery to others.

Saying 33. What is the greatest disgrace?

Not to think of one's own sins.

Saying 34. What is mind?

Reflection.

Saying 35. What is *buddhi*, that which knows?

That which determinates, sets limits to.

Saying 36. What is the I-sense?

To be the doer.

Saying 37. What is coming and going, the recurring process of birth and death?

To desire the fruit of one's deeds.

Saying 38. What is the source of desire?

The sense of lack.

Saying 39. What brings about release from desire?

Absorption in the Lord Supreme, that Person the Perfect.

Saying 40. Who is sick?

One who eats useless food.

Right endeavour, right thinking and right company sustain life. One should stick to them till the end of one's life.

Notes

[1] Literally, 'Rejoicing in *samatā*, sameness.' See the Preface for explanation of this title. 'Rejoicing' implies the other meaning of 'vilāsa', namely, manifestation.

[2] *Anubhava* means experience of a thing and also abiding in and as that thing.

[3] The three strands are *sattva, rajas* and *tamas*. The text will explain these constituents of *Māyā* in due course and at many places. We may however say roughly that the *sattva* is the principle of transcendence, the *tamas* is the principle that forces each and every being to remain coincided with himself or itself, the principle of *statis* we may call it. And the *rajas* is the struggle between these two forces of *sattva* and *tamas*, forcing one to project oneself into the world; its characteristic is activity, activity that would change the given situation into something else. It is these three strands that constitute *Māyā, Māyā* that conceals the Truth that *samatā* is.

[4] This means that the body is nothing but the sense of me and mine become objective.

[5] Or, it may mean identification with one's family, clan or caste. The latter meaning becomes possible if we read *kul* in 'kul zāt' as the Hindi or Sanskrit '*kula*', which means one's family line. 'Zāt" in Urdu can mean both Being or existence and caste. And 'kul' in that language means 'all' or 'the whole'. So if we read 'kul zāt' as pure Urdu, it will mean the whole of existence, or the Cosmos.

[6] *Viśvāsa*, often translated as faith or belief, is actually derived from the root *śvas*, to breathe. *Viśvāsa* implies utter dependence, it implies perceiving one's life and being rooted in what one believes in. The word thus has existential implications and not mere attitudinal, as the word *belief* has.

Anubhava Two

Samata-dhāma, The Abode of *Samatā*

(i) *Concealment of* Samatā-*bliss*

Saying 1. When the mortal being[1] finds himself caught up by the sense of *kartāpan*, by the ego of doing, when, that is to say, he comes to imagine himself a doer, desire for the fruit of his actions comes to seize him, pleasure and pain holding him in their inescapable grip. This hold of pleasure and pain over him breeds in him desires of all kinds, bringing in their wake the compulsion of planning many a new project, one after another. Fret and frustration come then to dwell in him, leaving him never. This unrest then conceals the Sameness, that blessed state — desire, wrath, infatuation and pride taking its place, with discontents and vexations the lots only of his life. [2]

Saying 2. This concealment, this ignorance, is *Māyā* itself, *Māyā*[3] with its three constituent strands. The moment this mortal being projects himself as a doer, he finds himself, as a result of his passion for doing and for the result that doing of his gives rise to, entrapped in the modes of *sattva, rajaṣ* and *tamas*.[4] Inflicted with this false notion about his self, notion of its being a doer, many a form he takes upon himself birth after birth. This is what is called transmigration - this taking upon oneself many a form as a result of imagining oneself as a doer.

Saying 3. This positing of his being as a doer is the primordial darkness that conceals the light that *samatā* is, making the mortal being a prisoner of the false appearances of the Me and Mine and of desires of countless kinds that this self-positing generates in him. To appease that desire, he indulges in all kinds of pleasures of the sense but to no purpose, the darkness he is lost in, the darkness of doership, never letting him know the peace that the state of *samatā* is.

Saying 4. All beings, alive or inert, wander lost in this darkness, in this projection of one's being as a doer, knowing neither peace nor rest. Every being seeks to slake his thirst [for the bliss of sameness] in accordance with the mode of being he finds himself identified with. But all vain proves that seeking of his, only anxiety and discontent, anxiety and discontent everlasting, becoming his portion, of this being deluded and self-intoxicated.

Saying 5. Positing his identity as that of an agent or a doer, the mortal being takes on himself the form he sets up as a result of that positing, and identifying himself with that form, he acts and desires as determined by that form. This is what the play of *Māyā* is, this state of darkness of ignorance, which he can neither escape from nor dispel. The duality he thus turns into taking a firm hold on him, he indulges in pleasures to find himself a being ever on the move, forgetting his own being, that blessed state of *samatā*.

Saying 6. Why and how the sense of doership arises cannot be explained, for no cause of it can be traced. As a ripple arises out of still waters, spontaneously and without a cause, so does this sense of *kartāpan*, of doership, this primordial form of *Māyā*, emerges from the Supreme Being.

Saying 7. Awareness of origin and end, birth and death is contingent upon confusing one's being with the being of a doer. All dualities, those false modifications of one's true being, fallings from it, are contingent upon that confusion. The truth, however, is that there is no such thing as the being of a doer, it has no base and no cause. That is why, they call it, this false sense of me and mine, a delusion, a bewilderment, a passing appearance which was neither in the beginning nor will be there at the end. In between the two, the beginning and the end, it appears ever on the move, its ambit vast and wide ranging.

Saying 8. Every embodied being, noble or ignoble, is a prisoner of this doer-sense. Whatever state of being he identifies with determines the way he acts and strives, but no action and effort can bear for him any fruit that can appease his thirst for being, thirst for being himself and abiding as himself.

Saying 9. From birth to death moves he, many things come his way and many desert him but not that that can appease his thirst, the repose that the blessed state of being ever the same is. Desiring and averting he lives, ever liking and ever hating one thing or the other, ever moving from one frustration to another. In lack and insecure does he live, whether a king or a beggar, whether learned or foolish.

Saying 10. It requires a deep and concentrated thinking to know this truth. In the absence of this thinking, man identifies himself with action, the result that action promises tempting him. Ensnared by that temptation, he finds actions both good and bad forced upon him to reap their fruits in the shape of happiness and sorrow.

Saying 11. From *kartāpan*, from the doer-sense, arises the faculty that de-terminates, sets limits *to*. From the faculty that de-terminates, sets limits *to*, arises mind, the faculty that thinks *of*. From this state of thinking *of* arises the desire for the five elements. From the desire for the five elements arises the tendency to act. This is how the embodied being comes to be constituted, how he/it is set up. The eight-fold *prakṛti*[5], the primordial nature, that *before* of creation, ensnares a mortal being because of his identifying his being with the being of the doer, the being that he is not. This identification with doing or activity leads to his identification with *prakṛti* and to forgetting of his own true and real being.

Saying 12. A prisoner of *prakṛti*, that being the formed, he attributes its *guṇas*[6], strands, to himself, superimposes these on to himself. *Prakṛti*, however, is ever changing, it is in its nature to change ever and always. And the being that confuses his own being with it, cannot but attribute its change to himself. Thus seizing and rejecting, ever compelled to choose between the constitutive poles of dualities[7], dualities devoid of being, fallings as they are from it, he forgets the peace that *samatā* is. This entire process of forgetting his very own native being is what is called the sate of *ajñāna*, of ignorance.

Saying 13. Every being that has come to live in this world finds this conflict between opposites ever perpetuate itself within him, he helplessly seeking bliss the true from it. This is the unhappy condition in which he finds himself, whatever his country and his religion, whatever his status, high or low. In the pleasures of *prakṛti* he seeks that bliss, such is the hold of ignorance on him. The pleasures of *prak*ṛti do not, however, last long nor does last long his capacity to enjoy them. Ever insecure he remains, his desires fulfilled or not fulfilled.

Saying 14. Identifying himself with the body [the eight-fold *prakṛti*], the being born here in this world finds himself given up to the pleasures of the body. The pleasures of the body do not, however, stay with him nor does the body stay. So all his efforts, all his strivings go in vain, born as they are out of his ignorance of the being that he really is. To be safe and secure never falls to his lot. That is the truth about him and his life.

Saying 15. Sense-experiences are happy-unhappy experiences. If on finding a thing a mortal being finds himself happy, his separation from it is sure to distress him. If a thing gives him pain, he is anxious to distance himself from it and seek his pleasure elsewhere. This way, neither the thing he loves and likes can undo his discontent nor can the thing he does not love or like. In no condition can he find the *samatā-śānti*, peace the transcendental that self-sameness is.

Saying 16. Whatever the body he finds himself embodied in determines the mode of his desire or thirst. The world that one perceives is nothing else but the reflection of the body, the spectacle projected by the waking, dream and sleep states of the organs, cognitive and motor. For, it is the kind of *kartāpan* that a being finds manifest in him that determines the kind of desire he finds himself prompted by. And it is the kind of desire that determines the kind of body he will have, that gross modification, that instrument of action. Thus it is only the play of his own *kartāpan* does a being perceive and experience.

Saying 17. The pleasures of five senses of cognition - that of sight, that of hearing, that of smelling, that of taste and that of touch - senses that emerge from the five elements, give rise in a living being to the passion for the manifest world.[8] For the satisfaction of this passion, he wanders about in that world searching all kinds of things. In the thing or the place he thus finds he would seek fulfillment of the desire that dwells in his mind and, in his infatuation, gets bonded to it, attached to it. But all this process proves futile, for fulfillment of desire eludes him in the end. Rather, the duality that his life is, he is forced to take upon himself the responsibilities of others[9] too. This is all that relationships and ties are. [10]

Saying 18. Many things he would gather and many relationships forge to appease his thirst[11], appease it through bodily pleasures. But the pleasures of the body cannot give him the peace he seeks. In the end, they come to cease, those pleasures, and so does the body, and hollow turn all his efforts, ending as they do in misery and woe.

Saying 19. All the modifications of the body, the twenty five states of *prakṛti*[12], cannot appease his thirst for peace[13]. All that one can get from the embodied state, all its joys and pleasures, are, in every truth, the cause of the misery that a being embodied has to undergo. But that being, blinded by the sense of Me and Mine, would seek his welfare in these only, in these very sources of his misery.

Saying 20. Let him understand that rich repasts are not going to appease his hunger, nor can flavours rich and many satisfy his passion for them. Rather they increase a being's desire for them, adding to his misery. This is equally true of other bodily pleasures, pleasures related to his organs, cognitive and motor; they too intensify his passion instead of appeasing it. Wandering long in the world and enjoying many a pleasure, the mortal being finds not a moment's respite from his desire and is condemned to die all miserable and in despair.

Saying 21. To fulfill that very desire, he finds himself a captive of *prakṛti* in a new form and shape. This way, he moves from birth to birth, one after another, a victim of the sense of Me and Mine and enjoys many a pleasure natural to the *prakṛti* he finds himself imprisoned in, the *samatā*-peace, that bliss supreme, ever eluding him.

Saying 22. Misery and unrest haunt him ever and everywhere, haunt this victim of the sense of Me and Mine, of that false projection of himself as the doer. Not until this sense, this dark ignorance, dies down in him will he be vouchsafed the rest he seeks, namely, the state of *samatā*. To get out of this misery, great souls showed unto the unhappy world many a path. If anyone follows any of those paths, his misery will be transformed into the blessedness of sameness, into that source and being of the whole world and his own.

Saying 23. A man has to reflect on this net spread out by the sense of Me and Mine if he would be blessed, a precondition, an imperative is it, this reflection on this snare of *Māyā*, for that purpose. When you have diagnosed the disease you look for its cure and him that knows the cure. Wise is the man who seeks to withdraw his mind from this dark and dense delusion spread out by *Māyā* and directs it all attentive to the beatitude he has ever sought in vain in that very delusion. And good is he, only he, and a man of knowledge and one given to holiness and devotion.[14]

Saying 24. Human birth is a promise of beatitude, for wide awake is a being blessed with it. If despite that opportunity, he remains a captive of Me and Mine and falls of his purpose, his fate will be like the fate of a drowning man who found a boat but would not board it.

Saying 25. One born as a man should, therefore, reflect with care on the primal *ajñāna*, that source primal of the unrest that he has come to be. And let him be ever diligent to dispel from him that delusion dense and dark. That is the duty, the highest duty, laid down for man.

Saying 26. If he remains identified with the embodied state, a wide net of actions he will spread out for himself, a captive will he remain of *vāsanā*, of desire sedimented deep in him, good and bad. To ponder over this flurry, this distraction that would make the world appear as real (*vikhep*, Sans. *vikśepa*) and to liberate himself from it is to live as a man true to his purpose.

Saying 27. All that is considered holy — *vidyā*[15], reflection, to seek and be in the presence of a holy seer, to render service to others, *yajña*[16], charity, *tapasyā*[17], and others — has only one purpose: to burn up one's sense of Me and Mine and to dissolve oneself into the Blessed Same. For that is the bliss mortals are really and truly in search of.

Saying 28. To reflect deeply on *Māyā* and to cut asunder that delusion is to live a life cultured and fruitful. Not to know the ties that bind them down and not to know how to untie them is the way of the foolish. For, every being that has come to be born in this world is born to find peace the transcendental, his final and ultimate choice (*niścaya* > *cī*, to choose). That is his search, his seeking the real [and original], right from his birth to his death. But knowing not where to find it and forging relationships false and ill, he loses his way to that goal of his, inviting misery in life and frustration in death. Let him, therefore, seek that peace the real every second and every hour of his life, for that is the way to fulfill all the desires and aspirations of his mind.

Saying 29. Consider with care the net that *karma*, that passion for doing, has spread out for you. Let it be understood that it is *karma* that binds and it is *karma* that liberates. It is *karma* that makes you stray and wander [in the mazes of the world] and it is *karma* that will lead you beyond it. Know well what the way of *karma* is, for reach shall you not your goal absolute, that rest the ontological, until you know that way.

Saying 30. Buddhi, the faculty that de-terminates, is *karma*, the mind that thinks is *karma*, the organs, cognitive and motor, too are *karmas*. The maze of *karma* is all these. The mortal being, a prisoner of the I-sense, of the ignorance that it is, finds himself ever bound to these forms of *karma* and what they forge and bring about. In his infatuation, he can neither find the Supreme, that blessed state of sameness, nor can he ever strive for that goal. Of folly is this way of orientation towards the mind [not towards one's true being]. No way opens out before this man of false vision, the way to his redemption, to his liberation from the recurring process of birth and death. Therefore, let every being blessed with the human birth give thought to this dark and bewildering labyrinth that *karma* has fashioned for him. And let him resort to the *karmas* that lead to his truth, to the truth that is the Lord of all. That is the way to fulfillment, to gain real and genuine, the way of those dedicated to the truth.

Saying 31. And that way is the way of giving up of *kartāpan*, of the sense of one's being as a doer, that is to say, of the I-sense.[18] It consists in discarding the desire for the fruit of actions, that duality false and imagined. And in giving up the idea that the body is real and in giving up the false sense that one *is* the body [and its precedents, the organs, the five elements, the mind, the intellect and *I* the agent]. And in perceiving the pleasures of the sense as unrest and discontent. And in probing into the cause, secret and hidden, cause that brings about birth and death and in deliberating about what constitutes good action and what bad action. And in reposing one's faith in the truth, in finding in that alone one's being and life. And in finding one's home true before this body comes to fall.

And to serve that end, a man needs must ponder over the lives of those who dedicated themselves to the truth, to that alone, and see to it that his life ever moves upwards, towards that truth. Let him also seek holy company, that of the seers of the truth, to purify his *buddhi*, the faculty that determinates, of its taints; and let him never fail to see to it that he does not deprive others of their portion in the affairs of give and take. Let him rather render service unto others with his thought, his body and his possessions - render it ever and always. And let him repose his faith and trust entire in Power the Supreme, that Light of Consciousness, that Creator of all that is and dedicate himself to finding that Truth the transcendent. This is the kind of *karma* that would lead a man to his goal, in that lies the beauty and glory of human birth.[19]

Saying 32. A being that does not resort to this path, would not care to orient himself towards these dispositions, and acts in ways in opposition to these is not a being that deserves any social relationship. For the disposition of self-serving going strong in him renders him unfit for any society whatsoever. Obsessed with himself and with self-celebration he lives, intoxicated with pride and arrogance. Jealousy and fraud, theft and lies, slander and backbiting are the stuff his life is made of. And sadism and unbridled sex and anger, his faith reposed in the dark ignorance, not in the *ātman*, his true being, but in fetishes and charms. Out of self-love, again, he worships many a god and his righteousness is merely self-righteousness. He resorts to good deeds for applause and praise, his goodness a mere veil to conceal the fraud that he is. For acquisitions he lives, acquisitions without a number, his being a mere body-being and his devotion to the Lord a mere pretence, his cunning his faith and his conceit all-despising. For, no one seems to him of any account. Dispositions and acts of this kind are dispositions and acts of evil, a veritable hell are they, the products of the shadows cast by *Māyā*. To give these up and resort to deeds that lead to the truth constitutes good life. That is what a gifted man lives for.[20]

Saying 33. Hard, exceedingly hard it is to come out from this whirl of *karmas*. That institutes the way the world moves, the way that permits no easy escape. To redeem himself from this whirl is the way of the man true, man dedicated to the truth that he really is, to the *sameness* blessed and still. Man must strive for that end, for if he does not strive for it he will not find it. Let him when alive think of his death, the end destined for him, and resort to the principles true that will lead him to the True. That is the way to Blessedness, this *sādhanā*, this striving for it.

Saying 34. A prisoner of doing is born every embodied being. The modes of good life and action that different religions preach are directed towards one purpose alone: to lead man out of his given condition to Sameness the ever still. To disputes and counter-disputes about those modes of life and action but not to adhere to them is nothing but barking oneself into hell.

Saying 35. Let every being redeem himself, let him reclaim the supreme blessedness that he is. That is the end his efforts should be directed to. Himself a prisoner of sins, he is not to show unto others the path of eternal peace. He will be only deceiving himself if he dares to do this and will provoke his doom. He can think of showing that path to others only if he has experienced the peace true within him, has seen that light and become that light and has burnt up all the passions that led his mind away from that light to wander and stray in the world. His life and speech, of the man of such eminence, will have the power to inspire the lost souls to reclaim their being and their truth.

Saying 36. To escape from the concealing darkness of *Māyā*, one should, first, think about what is truth and what is not truth, should discriminate between the two. That is the *sādhanā*, striving for the true goal, pure and unalloyed - this thinking about Being. For, that thinking dispels untruth that the false thought of 'I AM' is, that seed of all the woes and ills. That false identity, that of the doer, will not, however, die down easily and straightaway; one must take refuge in the embodiment of the truth that a seer is - must resort to that *truth* in order to know what the truth, the Real, in fact is, and, then, reflect with care on what he has been instructed about It.[21]

Saying 37. The Truth Supreme, that Lord the Supreme, the Truth that lights up this body and keeps it alive is what one is to think of and think about [and not the phantoms that *Māyā* has set up]. For, it is only when a man has come to know that truth for certain and his mind has come to find in it its being and anchor that he can hope to escape from the concealing darkness of *Māyā*, from that false delusion. Man will reclaim his being, the being he has lost, when he thus lives and breathes for that Lord the Truth, and knows for certain His glory as the source primal of all that is. And knows, further, that the latter, all that that has proceeded from Him, is merely a false appearance.[22]

Saying 38. A man must find the world of dualities as a fall from its truth and being, a fall that is sorrow and suffering itself. And realising this truth about his life, he must believe in the word of those that have become one with the truth and make that truth his sole refuge. That is the way to deliverance from *Māyā* and its darkness, the way to Blessedness ever the same.[23]

(ii) Emergence of Devotional Fervour for the Lord

Saying 39. When the worldly mode of being appears all sorrow and suffering and one's body as death and all the things of the world one desires and would have as of a moment's joy and when that fall from one's truth, that sense of Me and Mine, gives place to humility, that is the moment for the devotional fervour to well up within a man, devotional fervour for the Lord. The light of *samatā* itself is that devotion, the light that has no equal, for undoes it the doing-self, that darkness absolute. This, in every truth, is the state of the Blessed Sameness, this cessation of the doing-self. Attaining it, that blessedness, this mortal being gets free from duality, that fall and deviation, to find within himself Nārāyaṇa the Word, Nārāyaṇa the Son of the Primordial Man, to lose himself into That.[24]

Saying 40. Identification with doing is a recalcitrant condition, hard in the extreme to resist. With all his care and striving, the foolish mortal being cannot resist the temptation of turning all that happens into *his* doings to become subject to the dualities of pain and pleasure, joy and sorrow. To escape from this dread and mysterious play of *Māyā*, let him take refuge in devotion to the Lord, that dispenser of his true well being, for that alone, that refuge, can lead him to *prema*, that ecstasy of going beyond oneself, of exceeding oneself into infinity.

Saying 41. To love Him, Him the Father, to lose oneself in Him, with all the commitment one can think of is the only way open to mortals to that *still* ecstasy of self-transcendence or self-loss. Not until a mortal has found that truth the absolute can he reach the goal of his life, the goal final and ultimate.

Saying 42. Let man be tethered with all his being to that *parama-puruṣa*, that Man the transcendental, that centre of the whole moving world, that witness of the body. That is the imperative duty of every mortal being, to make that Person his sole refuge. He is the life and being of this ever moving world, the light that lights all that shines and He is the Being that ever is. The sorrows of the world do not touch Him nor do the joys of the world. To love Him, to flow into Him, is to be blessedness itself.

Saying 43. From Him proceeds all and in Him stays all and into Him merges all; time does not see His beginning, neither the time past, nor the time present, nor the time future. But dwells He in every being, dwells as ever the same, ever Itself. Blessed indeed is he, the being that thinks of Him.

Saying 44. By His own might is He All-Full and Himself the resort of Himself, the proof unequalled [of Himself]; a Light unto Himself is He and bliss itself is He. To repose all one's trust in Him alone is to know in truth.

Saying 45. No desire He has and no resentment to torment Him; into Him enters all but touches Him not. To remember[25] that Being is to remember the Joy and be the Joy.

Saying 46. He alone *is*, there is no Other for that Knowledge to be obsessed with. To think of that Knowledge is to be in bliss, bliss the supreme and transcendental.[26]

Saying 47. Like unto Him is there none. With Himself makes He one the being that approaches Him. For gracious unto the lowly is that Lord Supreme. Rare of the rare is the fortune to remember Him.

Saying 48. Saves He from all calamities, dwells He in all mortals, each and every, that Transcendental Bliss, that nearest among the near, that ever attained. To contemplate that Brahman the Supreme, that Lord the Transcendental is verily success the transcendental.

Saying 49. Knows He the deepest of the deeps within all but none is there to penetrate into the mystery that He is - that Knower of the all, that Full. To think and deliberate about Him is *sat-saṅga* in its truth, that holy congregation and service. [27]

Saying 50. To attain Him is to burn the passion for the world into extinction and find the satisfaction final and absolute. To contemplate Him, that benign and auspicious Son of Man, is the consummation, consummation veritable of life the human.

Saying 51. The worlds may end but not He, that all-powerful in Himself, that Being true of every being. To remember Him is to be blest, is to be redeemed.

Saying 52. The whole world is the Lord Himself, within every being He dwells and without him, dwells there dispensing being to every being, even unto a blade of grass. Apart from Him nothing could ever exist or will ever exist. All-full is He and all-perfect. To find Him is liberation and stillness ever the same. That is how that Lord of the all is to be remembered, that is how He is to be contemplated. For, that is His worship, His devotion true.

Saying 53. To know Him is to know all, to know Him is to lose all fears and all delusions. Knowing and attaining to Him, to that Fullness and Perfection, the *buddhi* merges into Him, Him its being full and perfect. He is Knowledge the highest, and to strive to know that Knowledge and be that Knowledge is to strive in truth and for the truth.

Saying 54. When the *buddhi*, the knowing faculty, becomes purified of its taints, it strives in earnest to be free from doing and its frailties, each and every, and lets not its vigil ever go asleep as to the temptations of sin. That is the moment when this being gets some foretaste of the peace he seeks.

Saying 55. When the *buddhi* comes to see, in truth and in fact, that the body is a mere process of decay and dying, and knows the *ātman* as the dispenser of being unto it, that is the moment when the man gifted with insight and virtue comes to yearn for the Lord, his passion for the world irrevocably spent. This disposition is truly the disposition that knows and sees the truth as against the untruth, the disposition that dispels the delusion [of *Māyā*] dark and blind, turning that being into an ecstatic excess, his soul a flowing abroad to bring to rest his strivings and his turmoils.

Saying 56. When the *buddhi*, the faculty that determinates, comes to be purified of its taints and blemishes, it finds the body ever moving towards death, finds it ever decaying and dying, and cannot but yearn for bliss the transcendental and absolute. A living being blessed with this vision and this yearning directs all his efforts to the attainment of that bliss, his desires appearing as but fetters, fetters he must break and undo. He takes refuge in the Blest, in the souls that have become the truth, and, in their company, purifies his thought to end up as a devotee of the Lord, surrendering his life to His will. This disposition eventually leads him to find with every clarity the *ātman*, the self, as the base and ground of his body and all the ills and sorrows that inflict his body-self as ordained by the will of that self, that Lord.[28]

Saying 57. When a mortal finds the *ātman*, the self, alone as his last resort and refuge, he finds no one hostile to him. In each and every being he perceives that very self, that Lord of all, and his soul flows out to them in love to serve them as he would serve his own self. This humility in service washes away all the crookedness of his mind and his mind, purified of the taint of pride and conceit, gives itself up to remembrance of the truth, his being, to cast off, eventually, every false belief and every fear. Only the Lord of the all then he perceives in the all, one and only. That, in every truth, is peace that is ever the same, peace that the state of *samatā* is.

Saying 58. But dauntingly formidable is the mind. It would assert its identity with the body once again. But with careful effort the *buddhi* retrieves it from this ignorance, from its identification with the body. At peace with itself then it abides to lose itself in joy into that peace the real, peace that abides ever the same.

Saying 59. A mortal finds himself doubly fettered, (1) by the self that is the not-self he identifies himself with, by self the doer, and (2) by the desire for the results of actions that he thus wrongly takes to be *his* actions. To break these fetters, there is only one genuine way open to him: that he surrender all the activities of the body-mind complex to the Lord [take them as ordained by Him] - surrender them each and every moment of his life and give his mind to the remembrance of the Lord.

Saying 60. This spirit of self-surrender will undo his self-projection as a doer, the joys and sorrows, those dualities of life, disturbing not his quiet equanimity. This disposition of quiet surrender is true renunciation, the very embodiment of the latter, renunciation that will culminate in one's immersion in Word the a-doing, Word the Brahman.

Saying 61. The primordial ignorance, that self-identification with doing, comes to cease when man thus devotes his mind to remembrance of the Name of the Lord, finding his body-mind complex ever decay and die and taking all his actions as ordained by the Lord. With the cessation of that primordial ignorance, a mortal will find the immortal within him, the immortal that is his very being, the immortal that ever abides as itself and self-same.

Saying 62. The bodily pleasures ever lead him astray, this mortal being. But this very mortal being comes to abide in the truth when his *buddhi*, his faculty of knowing, comes to be purified. And it comes to be purified when he sees, with every clarity and lucidity, his body decay and wither, decay and wither ever and always. And, as a result of this perception, he finds the Lord of all as his self, the support and ground of his being. *This is what is called the bliss supreme, this abiding in one's truth, the Lord.* Man comes to be delivered from the ever recurring cycle of births and deaths when his intellect thus comes to be absorbed in the self - in this very life, with his passion for the embodied state and its pleasures having worn out.

Saying 63. To live is to live as embodied. That is the real bondage, this compulsion of being embodied. It is this compulsive desire, desire to be embodied, that makes every living being move from birth to birth and from death to death. However, when he sees the body die from moment to moment and remembers and contemplates with devotion the Real that transcends the body and the world, that Witness of this ever decaying body, he will come to find Brahman the Supreme residing within him. To peace still and ever the same will he attain then, his pilgrimage from birth to birth having reached its end.

Saying 64. As long as the sense of identity with the body persists in man, he should persist with his reflection on the truth and sustained contemplation of it. He should not let his efforts slack in any way in this matter. Reflection on the truth means to perceive the body as decay and death itself. And sustained meditation means remembrance and contemplation of the *ātman*, the self, that dispenser of life unto the body - remember it and contemplate it with full and firm faith. For, unless one resorts to these two - remembrance and contemplation of the self - one's *buddhi* will never come to be steady and stable. To realise within oneself the omnipotent Lord and to remember Him with fervour is verily devotion the true and peace the true.

Saying 65. The body is ever associated with activity and the *ātman*, the self, has no activity to condition it. As long as this being wanders about in the world taking his body as a real entity, there can be no release for him from the grip of actions. It is only when the body appears as all unreal to him that he can contemplate the *ātman*, that passivity within, the contemplation leading him to merge in it, with no possibility of a return to the delusion of recurring process of birth and death. This cessation of activity and of the worldly mode of being is [what has been called] bliss the same, bliss that is sameness itself.[29]

Saying 66. One's sense of identity with the body is a hard nut to crack. Unless the mind gets pure, one cannot even become aware whether this sense of Me and Mine is a blessing or a curse. It is only when the *buddhi* becomes pure that it can perceive it, this sense of Me and Mine, for what it actually is, a mere whirl of false appearances. That, its perception, makes the *buddhi* lose all interest in it, in the sense of Me and Mine, makes it rise above it and direct its effort to the realisation of the Real, Real the absolute. A time comes when these efforts bear their fruit and the *buddhi* finds the bliss it sought, the bliss transcendent, eternal and timeless.

Saying 67. Purity of mind is a must for the realisation of this goal, making it imperative for the seeker of salvation that he resort to acts that lead him to the truth he seeks. He should adopt a mode of life given to simplicity, to service unto others, to association with the seers of the Real, to truthfulness and to remembrance of the truth that he is. To adopt in life principles like these is to undo one's false conceit and to believe steadfastly in the self, in the *ātman*. To know and believe that one is that *ātman* [and not what one knows and finds oneself to be] alone is devotion in its truth and knowledge in its truth And dispenser of redemption in its truth too is that knowledge and that belief. So, let that *ātman* be the concern of your thoughts and of your efforts. That is *yoga* itself, this thought and this endeavour.

Saying 68. The *ātman* pervades this perishable body but ever untouched does it remain by its deviations and perversions. In its pristine purity it abides there, this purity itself, this all perfection. Those who find this wonder, the great ones, cannot but lose themselves into it. Like unto butter in milk and like unto fire in wood, the *ātman* abides in this perishable body to give it life and being. But in the absence of right endeavour, none can find it.

Saying 69. The way to that Supreme Being, the way straight and best, lies [first] in purification of one's intellect through reflection deep on the truth and in disorienting one's mind from the tempting pleasures set up by *Māyā*, that false delusion. And in making the Lord, that Power Transcendental, one's sole resort and in giving one's mind, each and every moment, to His devotion. And knowing the Majesty that He is, in remembering Him with exclusive attention, keeping one's mind away from the temptations of the world. And, in addition, in rendering service to the people, His creatures. With this disposition attained, one becomes pure in mind and concentrated in thought and comes to experience and become one with Word the Imperishable abiding within one to attain the peace that passes human understanding.

Saying 70. Let one's food be pure, and one's dealings and one's association. For, it becomes relatively easy to do away with mind, that adjunct superimposed on to the self, when one is pure in one's conduct. Gifted with this purity, a man can readily strive for that Bliss the Transcendent and have the disposition oriented towards the Real to make of him a being blest and redeemed. This world is hard to transcend, this motion cruel from death to death. Those who did go beyond it, the great ones, had to struggle hard and exert hard. Only then could they find the Being they sought to lead here a life blessed, an example unto those that came after them.

Saying 71. When the *ātman*, the self, comes to manifest itself within the body, there remains no longer any fashioning, any determinating and any desire[30], and the *buddhi* attains to its being to lose itself into it. Blessed is the man who has attained to this joy [to this loss of himself].

Saying 72. To remember the *ātman*, the self, as it really is, to contemplate it and to love it, to lose oneself in love into it, is to attain to the highest goal. With a particular disposition should a seeker of the truth resort to this remembrance, this contemplation and this love. With his mind should he remember the *ātman*, with consciousness still and concentrated should he contemplate it. And knowing that it, the self, is the Real itself, he should be all devoted to it. This disposition puts an end to the whirl of births and deaths, that false appearance, and leads him to the highest goal of life, to the quiet stillness of sameness.

Saying 73. To be born is to be born a compulsive doer, to be conditioned by doing. That is the inexorable fate of every being, from which fate he does not know how to escape. Dualities of all kinds ensnare and overwhelm him, dualities like those of happiness and sorrow, of giving and receiving, of joy and pain, of friend and foe. Miserable they make him, these opposites that at once sustain and negate each other. Whatever the state of being he may identify himself with cannot answer his need. That is his malady, great and dense, malady innate and inborn. To get rid of it, he resorts to acts of great sacrifice, to *tapas*, to fervent ardour, and strivings hard of all kinds but to no avail, for the sense of identity with action does not come to die through these acts. The result is rebirth, high or low, in accordance with his deeds and not the state of passivity, of not-doing, that home eternal of Blessedness.

Saying 74. The straight and smooth way out of this obdurate condition, this appalling trap is to attribute every act and every event, every coming to be or ceasing to be to the will of the Lord. And to remember Him with full determination and faith and to perceive, each and every moment, all that happens or does not happen as ordained by Him. And to concentrate all the activities of the mind on the Truth within, contemplate it steadily and intently. When this contemplation becomes stable and sustained, the *buddhi* finds within itself the truth as it is in itself, finds it to flow in every love towards that truth and merge into it, become one with it. It is then alone that its identification with doing comes to cease and the wide net it wove comes to be cut asunder and one comes to find one's being, the passivity that is Brahman the Word. That, in truth, is the quiet of sameness, this coming to rest in Brahman the Word.

Saying 75. This mortal being lives all miserable and purposeless in the midst of [and conditioned by] the false appearances (*mithyā*) of names and forms set up before him. [Or, alternately: Setting up false appearances of names and forms for himself, this mortal being lives all miserable and purposeless].[31] To escape from this maze of ignorance, he should remember the Name True, a sustained remembrance of which is the way to the cessation of the false appearances set up by *Māyā* and to the supreme blessedness one ever seeks.[32] At long last the time will come when this meditation will culminate in the merger of that striver into the truth, the truth that is his very own being.

Saying 76. That indeed is the right effort, the effort that is directed towards the improvement of one's life. One blessed with human birth must, therefore, make the Primal Father his only resort and refuge and should ever think of escaping from the concealing darkness of *Māyā* and should refrain from giving himself up to the pleasures of the body. Like a mere animal is he who lives and behaves otherwise; sinks he further down in the scale of existence. No promise and hope is there for him to escape from the dense darkness of ignorance that envelops and encircles him. From birth to death he will ever move and from death to birth, that wheel set in motion by *Māyā* never coming to a stop for him.

Saying 77. Let man think everything as of the Lord, let him consider Him alone as his Master, let him surrender all his actions unto Him and His will, and let him contemplate Him with intent concentration. This is *sādhanā*, effort the redemptive, for it will undo his sense of Me and Mine and make him one with the Blessedness Supreme. All will then turn into the Lord for him, every thing and every being. That is his home blessed, of that pilgrim, home the real and ultimate and bliss the real and ultimate.

Saying 78. A being blessed with human birth should make it a point to open out to truth, that is the disposition he must adopt. If this disposition vis-a-vis Being does not flower in man, he is compulsorily drawn towards untruth, giving himself up entirely to sin to invite every misery upon himself. For, the fire of desire ever burns in him to scald him without a let and respite.

Saying 79. So let man believe in the *ātman*, his being true, let him repose the trust and care of his life and being in it and contemplate it with sustained intent and concentration, thinking of his body as ever given to decay and destruction. That is the way to be blest, this way of contemplation and self-surrender. Those who do not adopt this way and resort to meditations of varied kinds for the sake of some desire or purpose of their mind create only misery for themselves, misery great and big. For, meditation prompted by desire will not gain what beings are in search of, namely Bliss the eternal and transcendent.

Saying 80. A mortal ever remains unappeased, whether he finds the things he desires or does not find them. Only work without desire can lead him to the blessedness he seeks. So let him consider that all that is and all that he has is of the Lord and let him do every action for Him alone, remembering His Name with dedicated devotion. If he lives his life this way, all his evil desires will come to cease before long, giving place to the noble orientation towards the *ātman* to culminate in its realisation. This is the highest endeavour that man can undertake.

Saying 81. A man who has reposed his trust in the One Lord and knows Him to be the sole doer and undoer, and who sees this moving world to be His manifestation and adopts the righteous way without the ego of righteousness and surrenders all his deeds to His will alone— a man who lives this kind of life will find his sense of identity with the body fall off him, his self, his being in its very truth, reclaimed for him. Never will he return to the whirl of doing; to peace of *samatā* will he attain, to peace ever the same.

Saying 82. He who perceives the body as other than himself, who ever stays as himself, as the *ātman,* to stay apart from all actions and their fruits, he alone is the knower of Brahman, he alone finds the *samatā*-bliss to become that bliss. Becoming the self of all, he finds the peace that passes understanding.

Saying 83. Only that man is the yogī true who has heard Brahman the Word within him and focusses his mind all intent on that Word and in whom invoke no interest the nine doors and their functions and who stays still in the Place Void and Still. He it is that finds the bliss that transcends the world and the *before* of the world (*prakṛti*). No more shall he fall in the mazes of the world and in the *before* of it. [33]

Saying 84. He who has left the care about the results of all his actions to the will of the Lord and has made of Him his last and absolute resort, who finds the whole world His marvel and wonderment - a man disposed this way will find his actions fall off him, he himself turning into the Passivity that is the Word. Supremely blessed will be he, a pilgrim to the truth arrived at the truth.

Saying 85. A man who has merged his consciousness in the current of the *Nāda,* in the current of the Word, and has transcended the confines of the body to stay in the *brahmāṇḍa,* in the Cosmic Egg[34], with the Word his sole base and support - he is the man that will find his self as the self of all - all that is within him and without. He alone will know what *samatā* is, what that truth is. A rare among the rare is such a man, his life a wonder and his presence redemptive.

Saying 86. He alone is the knower, he alone is liberated, the man for whom the body has turned into a mere shadow and who stays a mere witness thereof, witness passive and innocent of himself. And whom action does not touch, nor does time the destroyer. And who has become the Word and is lost into It. No longer will *Māyā* have any hold on him, its wheel of births and deaths moving not for him. He alone abides self-same and at peace with himself. Adorable is he, worthy of every tribute is he.

Saying 87. He who knows how to restrain the outflow of breath and its inflow, and has surrendered all his acts to the Lord and has abiding faith in Word the truth, he alone is a *yogī* of the highest order, he alone is the knower of the way internal. He knows the peace that *samatā* is, knows that peace to become that peace.

Saying 88. He who ever makes his mind flow with the flow of breath, his consciousness given to remembrance of the Name of the truth, and who finds the Lord as the inbeing of all that is and ever remains alike and self-same in weal and woe - he alone is the seer of the truth, of truth the Word. He alone has gone beyond the reach of the passions and perversions constitutive of the body, he alone is the dweller in the truth, his inbeing.

Saying 89. As long as a man does not reflect on the truth, as long as his soul does not flow out to it and is not anguished for it and as long as he does not meditate it with a sustained intent, there can be no possibility of his restraining his formidable mind. And as long as his mind is not restrained, there can be no possibility of his finding the peace real and true. His sojourn in the world may extend to millions of years but the peace he seeks will not be his lot.

Saying 90. Firm and strong indeed is the hold of action on a mortal. Not for a moment can he find himself free from it. Therefore, let him, with every effort, orient his mind towards the truth, leaving all his actions to the will of the Lord. Let him take his body, his mind and his possessions as the gifts of the Lord [giving up all his claims upon them]. When he adopts this kind of contemplation, his mind will come to know and be the real as it is and come to be still, will get absorbed in *ātman* the action-less. This verily is the highest devotion [supremely genuine]. Blessed is the man who abides suffused with this spirit.

Saying 91. With his mind ever remembering the Lord, his life devoted with faith to the service of others, the man thus blessed perceives all that happens as decreed by the Lord, that Son of man [man the sacrificial offering given to the yogic fire burning within him]. Suffused with the supreme devotion to the Lord, he will soon be absorbed in Him, in that abode of truth.

Saying 92. Folly is a tangle dense and dark, that deviation from one's being and truth into what it is not [the body-mind complex]. This fall into the body, this sense of identification with it, does not end even when the latter is cut apart and asunder. This delusion drags its victim to births and deaths without a count. Only knowledge can lead a man to his home, and his disillusion with the world and its ways. That is how men of old regained their home, those souls true dedicated to the truth, that is how they came victorious over *Māyā* and its delusions. Of truly heroic mettle were they made, those victors of the war between good and evil. Blessed with the bliss that the state of *samatā* is, in the abode of eternity they came to rest and repose.

Saying 93. The I-sense lies deeply entrenched in the living being, hard to erase is this imagined *I.* Wisdom lies in discarding it, wisdom the supreme. But this ignorance, this falling from one's being, cannot easily be given up; one must resort to sustained meditation with faith and devotion to get rid of it and regain one's lost home, the sate that is ever the same. Blessed will be the man who follows this way.

Saying 94. Those benighted beings who would not repose the trust of their life and being in the Lord and would not care to have the disposition oriented towards the truth, they, the prisoners of their foolish and deluded thoughts, are condemned to be born from low and base wombs, with unabated woes and miseries for their portion.

Saying 95. So, let every man ever direct all his efforts towards attaining to the truth, his home and abode, if he would escape from the condition he finds himself in, from this false and ever moving wheel of life and death that his deluded sense [of his being a doer] has fashioned for him. Supremely fruitful indeed will turn his life then. The Lord is not far away from him; only his benighted intellect would not stay to perceive that subtle truth. When it strives to get rid of its tainted *vāsanās* and tainted deeds and does come to get rid of these, it finds within itself that Lord, that Bliss Supreme. Therefore, there is no *tapas*, no penance, like making one's *buddhi* wake up to that truth within. For, as long as the darkness of its ignorance does not get dispelled, its propensity for wickedness will continue unabated and so will the misery that wickedness breeds, the denser that darkness the deeper its wickedness and its misery. On the other hand, its wakening up to that inner truth orients it towards good and noble deeds, those promises sure of the supremely blessed state.[35]

Saying 96. The states of bondage and liberation exist for [or, depend on] the *buddhi* only, for the faculty that determinates and fixes. As long as the I-sense is there in the intellect, it will remain active and never come to stay. Therefore it is the bounden duty of man to purify his intellect of this its taint [of I-ness]. For this purpose, he must reflect on the truth and resort to a sustained contemplation of it. The gifted man who adopts this way will surely purify his intellect of its taint and will find his goal final and supreme.

Saying 97. The purification of the *buddhi* is matched by its giving up of desire. With its purification reaching its consummation, it comes to merge in Being the Bliss, an accomplishment unique and unmatched this on its part.

Saying 98. The passion to do lies deep in man to lead his *buddhi* astray. Not for a moment will it let the latter rest and repose. After many an effort and striving, those gifted with insight endeavour to wash it of the taint [of doership], living the way the Lord decrees them to live and surrendering their dilemmas and their tangled predicaments and the possible acts these give rise to, to His will. The supreme humility of their souls frees them from the *vāsanā* for doing, from the compulsive desire for action that has held them captive life after life. Verily to liberation will lead this way of theirs, this their endeavour and striving.

Saying 99. Let man ever adhere to the right path, let him equip himself with the saving traits. For he it is that has entangled himself in delusion, and it is he who has to free himself from it. Those who think that they are fated to live this, their condition, are dull of mind and foolish. For, every being has to work and strive, whether the right way or the wrong way [depending on the state of being he finds himself fallen into]. Those who sought the company of the seers of the truth and kept to the right path attained to the Good - to peace ever the same. But those ignorant fools who seek wicked company and stray away from the right path will find themselves lost in the dark ways of self-concern and self-interest. To die unappeased and unfulfilled will be their inevitable lot.

Saying 100. Finding himself lost in the ways of the world, let every being think of the truth and strive for the truth, so that he may find the bliss, the bliss beyond human understanding, with no further births set up for him. Knowing this way the Full, let him become the Full, his being and his reality. Rarely is born a man gifted with this disposition and given to this way of life, that pilgrim from the unreal to the real.

Saying 101. Desire is a deviation from one's being, a fall from it, a malady deep and strong it is. Only the right effort, effort directed towards the truth, can cure it. If a man, despite all his gifts and rich potentialities, does not strive for that end and lets himself sink in the pleasures of body, unhappy and unfulfilled he will leave the world, his thirst for being unquenched as ever. So as long as a man continues to breathe, let there be no let to his striving for his redemption. Redeemed he will be when he is free from desire and from the passion to set up and project objects to match that desire, and when, before his body sinks to rest, he comes to abide in the Real that he really is to find himself all blessed. His fear of death irrevocably gone, he will come to abide in the state that abides self-same forever to turn him into bliss itself. Adorable indeed is the man who has attained to this state and lives that state, his life purity itself, a blessing for the unhappy millions around him. Of this ever-changing world will be a support, that man the blessed.

Saying 102. As long as a man remains a prisoner of his sense- and motor organs and does not come to be free from the hold of desire, he will not find the peace he seeks, peace in its truth. Therefore, to give up the pleasures of the sense- and motor organs is indeed a weal and blessing. To remain attached to those pleasures and prattle wise and contemplative is to live a life noisy but of no purpose. This way of folly is not the way of the thoughtful that think wise and strive wise, keeping themselves away from the pleasures of the sense- and motor organs. For, only the self is their delight and their pleasure, of these souls of fervent devotion to the Real. These verily are the persons that find the truth to abide as the truth.

Saying 103. The persons deprived of thoughts of and about the truth, who would not care to assess their inner life in terms of those thoughts cannot hope to be free from tainted thinking [the thinking that mistakes the body-mind complex for their *ātman*]. Therefore, the man who would purify his thought should ask and ponder over questions like the following: What is this body and who is its maker?

From whence have we come and whereto shall we go? Born into this world, what is it that I should do? What is happiness in its truth and how can one find it? Pondering over these questions makes relatively easy one's journey to the truth. Those who do not care to ask these questions and assume without a question their existence as the truth itself as if their sojourn in the world was to last for ever will not but invite untold misery on them. For beings given to this kind of disposition the pleasures of the body are as it were the bliss absolute, their life immortal and their place in the world safe and secure. They mock at death as if it were of no account, their self-opinionated arrogance exceeding all limits. *Vāsanās*, passions of this kind dwelling deep in them, are passions tainted and sinful and bring to man nothing but disaster. Their bodies will, of course, come to cease one day, but not these tainted dispositions; they will pursue them to block their way to the transcendental peace [that object true of their inner, unconscious search]. In misery utter and absolute will they die, these self-complacent beings, and in misery will they be born again to die again.[36]

Saying 104. All the great men of the world, those who strove for the truth and became the truth, gave only one message to man the fallen that he know and find the Master of the whole world in this very life of his. All religions are there to set him on to the path to liberation through disciplines that can lead him towards that end. But foolish beings would not seek their salvation; they would waste their life in disputes and conflicts to die a death all miserable.[37]

Saying 105. A disease inflicts every being that has come to live in this world, not for a moment will it let him rest, this disease that inflicts him, the disease of desire. No power can appease that thirst of him, no fame and no glory. *Sat-puruṣa* is he, the Real Man is he, who has cured himself of this malady. He, verily, is a guide unto the whole world, his instruction alone the true instruction, a cure for the ravaging malady of desire, the malady ingrained in beings, each and every.

Saying 106. Let man think about this lack in him, think about it well, and seek, ever and always, to make himself whole, to be the being that he truly is and find the home that is truly his. When with the lack filled, his mind comes finally to rest, he will find the very abode of the world, its base and support. With his lack unfilled, he will ever wander and ever stray, no land will console him, no faith and no body - no state of being. For *hope* will ensnare him to make him wander again and stray again.

Saying 107. Let a gifted man seek his redemption through a *buddhi* directed towards Being, towards the truth. That clearly is the best of efforts. For, to direct one's *buddhi* towards sinful acts is to believe in what is untrue and nefarious and to fall into fraud and cunning. Suicidal is this way of life, fretful and restless without a let and a pause. They know, these sinful beings, that what they do is wicked, yet they allow themselves to fall into sins, dark and murky. There is no one to instruct them out of their wicked ways, nor do they care to listen to any instruction if available. Realisation comes to them too late and too late comes the sense of repentance and remorse. When the time has passed, what will their repentance do, and what will their realisation?

Saying 108. The blest ones, the prophets and seers, have only one message for mankind that the latter should work for their salvation. As they came to be blessed, so should others too by following in their footsteps. Let them not lose themselves, those men of the world, in the mazes of the world, forgetful of who they are in truth and reality. If a man knows and understands the teachings of the wise and yet in his pride does evil unto others, he is, verily, a predator of the faith he pretends to believe in. He knows not what faith is, what religion is, he knows only cunning and fraud. Such a man should be kept at a distance, to live with him is to live in pain.[38]

Saying 109. A man should, with every effort, develop a disposition that stills his mind, brings it to rest. Let man believe in the Real, let him have every faith in the Power Divine. Let him think of the truth, let him, in other words, understand that only the Lord is the truth, all else is a passing show, a mere delusion. Let him strive for that truth, for attaining to that Lord, every hour and every moment. Let him, for the purity of his *buddhi,* his intellect, participate in holy congregation to give his mind to reflections on the lives of the souls that attainted to their truth and being and to give his ear to the recitation therein of the words of revelation, revelation of the Real. Let him serve the creatures of the Lord, remove their miseries without desiring anything in return. Let him be truthful in word and deed and also simple in life, purifying thereby his desire. Let him eat what is pure and be honest and straight in his dealings, reducing his own needs and desires to fulfill those of others. And let him act nobly, remembering the end destined for him. Anyone who lives this way and with this disposition will find his *buddhi* purified of all its taints, making of him a being that lives all dependent on the Lord, his sole refuge and resort. The time is not far off when he will reside in the Truth and be that Truth. [39]

Saying 110. Religion, that Way Redemptive, is nothing else than living faithful to the instructions of the truth-becomes. That verily is the way to self-purification, the way paramount to that end. To follow in life the commandment of a *sadguru,* of a true teacher, alone is true *dharma,* the right way or conduct. Those of benighted *buddhi* who do not believe in the word of *sat-puruṣas,* of men the real, stumble at every step, their life a frustration and a misery. So let him who would be liberated adopt in his life what the teachers true teach and instruct. The mind tends to follow the direction it has been oriented to follow. Therefore, let it be directed towards the truth if one is to be blessed here as much as hereafter.

Saying 111. To know the Master of the body before the death of the body, to know Him as the source of the body's light and life, to know that Master as the Master of all that is, has been and will be, and, enriched with this knowledge, to contemplate Him with all faith and devotion is verily to be blessed, to be redeemed and to be liberated. When this being sheds his sense of identity with the body, when, that is, he sees all that is as of the Lord only, he comes to be established in his *ātman,* his real being, his passions all appeased. To believe in this truth is to live in faith[40], to live truly in it.

Saying 112. The *buddhi* comes to be pure and still through redemptive acts, *sat-karmas.* A mortal being lives deluded by three kinds of self-identification, namely, identification of his self with the body, with thoughts and with material possessions. It is this false sense of his being that makes him fall in the ever moving cycle of births and deaths, that delusion. Therefore, let him live all humility, taking all that he calls his as gifts from the Lord, that Father of the world. Therein lies his true well being, his redemption and liberation. He alone is gifted who does not link himself with his gifts, stays as only his self, away from them. Of the truth is he a manifestation, a man of this disposition, his life an articulation of it[41].

Saying 113. To live in humility is to live in peace, peace that passes human understanding. For, to be the self in truth is to die as self-the-body. Therefore, thinking every thing as His, let the seeker of the Real submit every thing to Him. This way, he will extinguish his desire for things false and unreal and will be suffused with remembrance of *Nārāyaṇa,* of the Son of Man the sacrificial victim, that self-same home of the ever self-same. That is the way man should ever seek to live. [42]

Saying 114. A man who has freed himself from the pleasures and the passions of the body is indeed man the blessed, the man that knows the Real as it is.[43] He has won the game that the world is. His self alone is his delight and pleasure, for remains he ever established in it, in the self, despite all the pleasures of the world at his call and command; for tempt him they cannot, those pleasures. Abides he ever, this man, in bliss, bliss without a desire - *vāsanā* - and without a thought.

Saying 115. The pleasures of the world are all stress and fever, to be the self is to be in peace, peace the transcendent. This is the truth, the very essence of truth. Therefore, let the being who has been blessed with human birth make the self, the *ātman,* alone his resort and support. Therein lies *the* achievement of life, its highest accomplishment and fruition. For unless, he makes that Real his resort and anchor, he cannot escape from the circle that *Māyā* has woven for him. So let it be the concern of every human being to consider with care the ideal the prophets and seers of old set for themselves and for mankind and seek his spiritual well being by aiming at that ideal, giving up all the false beliefs and practices. That verily is spiritual practice, its essence and pith. Those who do not think of their spiritual well being and resort to false beliefs and practices will find themselves completely overwhelmed by selfishness and the consuming misery it will wreak on them. Therefore, let man pay heed to his supreme interest instead of his self-interest, think of it and contemplate on it so that all his existential misery may come to be extinguished. Anyone who accepts this thought, makes it his *own,* will surely find it lead him to the blessedness he seeks.

Saying 116. Let man spare no effort to find Sameness, that home of his. For, when he comes to attain that state ever the same, there will be no falling back for him into the darkness of Me and Mine, that fall from his Being. His own being is that sameness, his very self and truth, forgetting which he wandered birth after birth all deluded and in woe.

Saying 117. To know and be the Real that the state of sameness is, is *yoga* itself, its highest form. Not until a mortal finds that state will the conflict of opposites, that deviation, come to cease for him, that deviation constituting his fallen life and being. Therefore, let him contemplate that state supreme of sameness with a sustained intent if he would be happy and blessed.[44]

Saying 118. To remember the Imperishable Word, that Brahman that ever abides self-same in time [Brahman the immanent but ever transcendent], is to be blessed indeed. Those who forsake that Real and remain lost in their bodies and their self-interests are beings oriented towards their minds [and not towards the *ātman*] and as such have nothing but sorrow and unrest as their portion.

Saying 119. The abode of *samatā* has ever been the goal of those whose life was dedicated to the truth, nothing but the truth. They were *sat-puruṣas*, persons (become one with) the real. Therefore, the primary means to attain to that end is to repose one's faith in the truth, in the Real, give one's very life to it and thereby free oneself from the bonds of *prakṛti,* that *before* of creation, that seed of names and forms. That is the way one can get established in Word the Real. Only the effort dedicated to the truth, to the Real, can liberate one from the bonds of *karma,* action. The moving wheel of this world is a bewildering appearance, beyond the ken of man. It is not there in reality, and yet it appears vast and limitless. Only an exceptionally gifted soul can penetrate into the truth hidden behind this appearance.

Saying 120. When a mortal forgets his true being, he projects a world around him; for, the world he perceives is nothing else but his own *kalpanā*, his own formation or *making,* projected vast and expansive. The greater the *kalpanā,* the greater the expansion of the world, the lesser the *kalpanā*, the smaller the world's worth and meaning. When he comes to know the real being that he is, the delusory appearance of the world too comes to its end. Only Existence he perceives then [not existents], only bare existence ever the same. [45]

Saying 121. When a man attains to this state, he no longer falls from his self into the body and its changes, changes in the form of dualities; remains he ever established in his real being. He, the great man, knows the truth of all, he it is that comes to be full, in his very own self comes to be full. Rare to find is such a person and rare to receive instruction from him.

Saying 122. The first step towards the state of *samatā* consists in resorting to good deeds. It is these actions that bring about the end of the excessive sense of Me and Mine, purifying thereby the *buddhi* of its taint [of orientation towards the body and the world]. With one's *buddhi* purified of this taint [of orientation towards the *other*], one comes to concentrate one's attention on the inflow and outflow of Name-breath. Sustained contemplation of Name-breath leads eventually to the realisation of the *ātman*, of the self. This is the way to rid oneself from the hold that the passion for doing has over every mortal being, the way happy and real open alike to those who live in the world and to those who have renounced it.[46]

Saying 123. A being that does not care for peace ever the same and, given to his narcissistic ways, wastes his life in endless disputes, is little else than a beast. His perversions will never cease to torment him. To no purpose is born a man of this kind.[47]

Saying 124. Every creature should, must, know the lack in him and the way he can undo that lack, make himself whole. He should understand that human birth is a rare gift. Let him, therefore, him that has been blessed with human birth, know the real ever the same, know that ever full, finding which is to find all that is there or could be there. Let him find it and be it before his body comes to fall.

Saying 125. The man who believes in the true Lord and has made Him his sole refuge, who acts solely for Him and as ordained by Him, no receiving affecting him and no giving, and who, his mind all still and inactive, ever remains absorbed within in the Word Indivisible - he alone knows the abode of *samatā*, he alone, that man the true. Let every being share in his holy love for that abode, every gifted soul, for that Master of the world, that Blessedness Absolute. Giving up all false beliefs, let him believe in the *ātman* alone, in that in-being of his, and strive to find it and be it. Let him attain to that state, that goal blessed, if he seeks his well being, let him reach it, holding firmly to the way to it, to that self same, to that gain the highest. Blessed is the man that finds it and blessed are those who hear his word.

Saying 126. To attain to that blessedness there is the straight way of believing in the *ātman* and of purifying the mind through participation in *sat-saṅga*, in holy congregation, and of being truthful and honest in one's dealings and interactions. And of perceiving in Person the Witness, in that Lord Supreme, one's well being and in giving oneself to His remembrance and to nothing else. This alone is devotion the pure, this way of life, this alone is the dispenser of peace that transcends all human reckoning.[48]

Saying 127. A good life is indispensable for freedom from the anguish of attachments and aversions. It is incumbent upon every being, one who seeks to escape from this dense and blind darkness, that he strive and live for the truth, for that only.[49]

Saying 128. To tell the *ātman* from the *anātman*, the self from the not-self, is the highest form of discrimination. That discrimination alone can enable a man to believe in the *ātman*, in the self, in the absence of which belief it is difficult to escape from the ill that the worldly mode of being is. To attain freedom from that ill and to be what one truly is, one must accept the word of the truth-become, of men *the real*, and live by it [and not by one's own beliefs and thoughts]. To be in the presence of those men the real is, however, not enough; it will do no real good to a man unless he gives himself up to what they reveal and instruct. So let him always purify his mind and thought [by paying heed to what those men say and living by their instruction].[50]

Saying 129. Only that thought can be of avail which is directed towards the self and only that action can be fruitful that is oriented towards the self and only that contemplation is meaningful that dwells on the self, for these alone can bring salvation to man. Let this be his conviction and his resolve: to direct his thought, actions and contemplation towards the self. For, no one can hope to extricate himself from the perverse passions of the body who does not make the *ātman* his sole support and refuge.[51]

Saying 130. Those who would not thus believe in and live for the self and entertain, out of their narcissistic concerns, many a false belief instead, will find neither their self-interest served nor their supreme interest. Idle they turn and slothful, victims of frustration without an end. Whether a being's self-concerns and self-interests are served or not served depends on his *prārabdha*, on those past acts and dispositions of his that brought about his present birth. Not until he has reaped the fruit of those acts and dispositions in terms of weal and woe can he escape from their grip, try as he may. Only his self-submission to the *ātman*, to the self, can bring about freedom from that their grip. Towards that purpose alone should his efforts be disposed, towards his self-submission to the Lord.[52]

Saying 131. A being bereft of earnest faith in the *ātman* loses the world no less than the Spirit, his goal the highest. For, to think of the truth and to work for it is indispensable for progress in either of the two spheres. Selfishness will not work, render impossible as it does one's access to the real purpose. Only dedication to the *ātman* can make one the sovereign of the entire world, not selfishness. Therefore, ever believe in this truth and reflect on it.[53]

Saying 132. It is the thought of the Real that makes one prosper and flourish as against the thought of the unreal that brings about one's decay and destruction. This is the way *Māyā* operates. The thought of the Real, its essence, means living with the Lord as one's sole refuge. Those who do not seek refuge in the Lord and depend on *sādhanās*, disciplines, of many a kind are mere impostors that will never find what they seek and aspire for.

Saying 133. To live with the *sat*, with the truth, as one's life and being is to live in truth. The being that has not made the Lord his refuge and anchor, lives ever restless, his mind never coming to dwell at anything. Therefore, let man take refuge in Him and His will; let all his efforts be directed towards that end. For, with his will given up to His will, he will find even his sojourn in the world as suffused with calm and peace, calm and peace the highest.

Saying 134. All knowledge and all wisdom have *ātman*, the self, as their base. So let man give his thought to that living force within him; let him know it and contemplate it, giving up all useless disputes and debates. Therein lie his faith and his *religio*, the path that unites him with his being. Through this way and this path alone did the noble-minded of old attain to their goal, to the peace supreme and transcendent.

Saying 135. When the knowing faculty - *buddhi* - identifies itself with the body, then thoughts of sin come to assail it, making its life a misery and anxiety. When it gives itself to the thought of the *ātman*, of the self, when it knows for certain that the self, that Lord, is its being and truth, it comes to be purified and finds the rest it sought. Therefore, let man ever dedicate himself to noble deeds and efforts, efforts that lead him towards the self that he in every truth is.

Saying 136. The true well being of a person lies in making the *ātman*, the self, that is beyond the reach of weal or woe, his sole refuge, be that person a householder or a renunciate. His Law, that of the Lord of the Universe, is the same for every being, the Law, namely, that dedication to the truth leads to *śānti*, to peace the transcendental, and the obstinacy of self-assertion, assertion in terms of this state of being or that, and the evil that goes with it, will lead to woe the absolute. This is the very essence of the truth of life.

Saying 137. Therefore, let every being dedicate his life to search for the truth. Let him not be embroiled in religious disputes and quarrels, which only lead the *buddhi* astray. For, self-assertion gives rise to attachment, to self-identification with what is not the self, and to anger. One should understand that religion consists in what the noble have taught mankind as the way to their salvation. Not to adopt that way and to reduce one's faith to mere fanatic disputes and quarrels is the way of the foolish, the way that will ever lead them away from the way to beatitude [the way they profess to believe in].

Saying 138. Anyone who has made it a point to attain to the highest abode, has resolved to do so, sure it is that he, that *sat-puruṣa*, that man the real, will attain to liberation through his effort right and true. The lives of persons the true teach man to strive for the eradication of his faults and frailties, not to lead others to light when he himself is lost in darkness. Let him be ever mindful in this regard.

Saying 139. A man of trust full in the Lord, his conduct right and his will well intentioned, well intentioned vis-a-vis others, adversity depressing him not and prosperity elating him not, for takes he all the happenings as the will of *Īśvara*, of the Lord - he alone, that man of gifts, knows the spirit of religion in its very truth.

Saying 140. Let every man investigate the Real to find peace the transcendental. *Dharma* or faith means only this that man, all heedful, should adopt the path to the truth. That is what the teachers of old did teach, namely, that man do the right and thereby be liberated from the cycle of births and deaths. So let the man in search of liberation know from a seer-teacher true the path of yogic meditation to liberation and cleanse his mind of all taints through that meditation, leaving all his cares to the care of the Lord. And let him follow a strict time schedule for his meditation and his worldly duties. He, that man of pure intellect, will surely reach the supreme goal, his progress towards it, of this pilgrim, smooth and straight. The man of a nature contrary to this, the man who flouts these principles and does not care to purify his thoughts and to be honest in his dealings, and would not repose his trust in the Lord - the man of this kind of disposition will only live in misery great and die in despair great. His sins will pursue him for many a life to make him reap the bitter fruit they will bear for him. Let him, therefore, think about his condition with every care to find the peace that endures ever the same.

Saying 141. Different is the *ātman* from the body, the *ātman* ever the same and the body ever coming to be and ever ceasing to be. But enveloped by ignorance, the living being identifies his self with the body and perceives the changes of the latter as changes in his self to turn a victim of desire and anger. Taking himself as the doer of actions and obsessed with their results, he wanders in delusion, that darkness, knowing no peace or rest.

Saying 142. All disciplines and all *dharmas*, righteous modes of life, are meant to dispel the illusion that one is the body and related to it. They constitute the right means through which this mortal being can wake up from that state of ignorance into realisation of the blessed self of his, that support actual and real of the world.

Saying 143. A man who does not resort to *sat-dharma*, to Way the true, for emancipation from this his fallen state and, instead, has recourse to meditation and austerities for the sake of mere self-celebration, vanity and self-interests, will find all his efforts gone awry. For, darken his soul further will these efforts of his, leading him to a misery greater than ever before.

Saying 144. The sense of mine with regard to the body is the stumbling block in the way to that which is knowledge itself. A darkness it is, this sense with regard to the body. Oblivious of his eternal being this being posits the body - that tense and strenuous mire of actions - as his own being, its pleasure and pain keeping him ever on the move. A man lost in this mire can never, not even for a moment, think of his witness-self.

Saying 145. Human birth is there to free the mortal being from the darkness of this ignorance and all the miseries that go with it, past and future, and find his home true, that blessed state ever the same. Since there is no limit set to this darkness, a man can redeem himself from it only if he resorts to *sahaja yukti* - the discipline that comes natural to man[54].

Saying 146. To lose all interest in the pleasures of the body is to take the first and straight step towards that goal. This disinterest comes to pass on its own when a man gives up his wicked actions and reflects on the truth, purifying his intellect thereby. With his freedom from sinful deeds accomplished, his actions turn noble - oriented towards the truth. With that happening, he comes to be convinced of the power of the Lord, reposing his faith in Him.

Saying 147. When his mind, of this pilgrim, comes to know that the power of his body is of no account in comparison with the sovereign power of the Lord, that the body itself has that Lord of the whole world as its support and base, then alone will dawn in him the realisation that the acts of the body are really and truly ordained by Him and Him alone. And that will be the moment when he will give himself to devotion of the Lord, will give himself to it the way the truth-become have taught him to do. With that devotion maturing, he will find his identity with the body melt away and the splendour of the self and its power burn bright in him.

Saying 148. When he comes to contemplate that power of the self, contemplate it in the right way, his mind ever intent upon the self all still - when this comes to pass, he will find his attachment with the body dying down, giving place to an anguished yearning for the Lord. That is the state of being of a true *jijñāsu*, a true seeker. All unreal to him will then appear the world and its things, all pleasures a pain and torture, his mind solely focussed on finding the true peace, the thought of it and contemplation of it ever occupying him.

Saying 149. With this effort continuing, he finds within himself the supreme and eternal reality, revealing his body as death itself and the *ātman* as eternity itself. Blessed with this vision, he sings ecstatic of the glory of the Lord, all humility he sings, thinking nothing of himself. For him all power is the power of Nārāyaṇa, the Lord born out of the self-sacrifice of man. This is devotion the highest and absolute, for it liberates that man the great from the pleasures of the body [those temptations that make one mistake it for one's being and self].

Saying 150. With his remembrance and contemplation of the Lord getting more focussed and intent, he finds the supreme bliss manifesting more and more in him, the bliss that he can be but cannot tell. Finding the whole world grounded in the Lord, he gives himself up to Him, all love and devotion, and to contemplation of Him to find his being different from the body. Eventually, he loses himself in that being, attaining *samādhi*[55], *sanādhi* the eternal and ever-lasting. He alone is man *the* wise who has attained to this state, the state of eternal *samādhi*; he alone has truly redeemed himself from the worldly mode of being to find the bliss eternal. No action remains to bind him and no time to undo him, him that has come to be absorbed in being the real and true, in that ever the same state. Truly blessed is he that has found this state blessed; blessed are his struggles and blessed are his strivings. This indeed is the way true to liberation true.

Let every man be a true seeker of this state, let him reflect on this highest truth, its essence, so that he may rise above his given condition. This in every truth is the commandment of the Lord and the teaching of the spiritual guides and preceptors. This thought about the abode of *samatā* will dispel all false beliefs and set those who pay heed to it on to the path true and to the truth. So reflect on it with mind pure and strive for your redemption. That is the blessing this body, this skin and flesh, can vouchsafe to you.

Let man think of the truth, let him discard the adjunct,
his mind,
And remember the Name blessed and pure,
Remember it with ardent love and deep.
Let him serve all that have come to be,
Serve them as a servant would his master,
Thinking ever, day and night,
His weal and woe as the will of Him.
His mind intent and turned within,
Let him dwell on Name the true,
And find the home secure and safe,
With the guru true his sole refuge.
Rare is, Mangat, the soul that knows and believes
That to find that home all still and unmoving
Is to be washed of every taint and sin.[56]

NOTES

[1] *Jīva*, literally, being that lives.

[2] Notice the paradox. It is the *jīva* that thinks of himself as a *kartā*, a doer or agent. But the *jīva* is nothing else than the doer. He who imagines and he that is imagined thus constitute a duality, one presupposing the other. This way, neither comes to be established as a real being to constitute his *other*. The paradoxical mode of description here highlights the unreality of both the *kartā* and the *karman*, of the agent and of his action and, for that matter, identification of the one with the other. See 6 & 7 below.

[3] *Vide* Note 6 and 13 below.

[4] *Vide* Note 2, Anubhava 1, and Note 5 below.

[5] *Prakṛti*, '*before* of creation'. In the *Sāṃkhya* philosophy *prakṛti* is postulated as the original or primordial stuff the visible world is evolved from. Here the process of the coming to be of the body-being is described in a different way. The primordial source of all that is lies in the Supreme State, the state of being ever the same. From that arises [seemingly] the sense of doership or the ego of agency. So what is called *prakṛti* or *pradhāna*, the Primal, in the *Sāṅkhya* is called here *kartāpan*, self-identification with the doer-sense. That (1) *kartāpan* and what follows from it, namely, (2) the faculty that determinates – the *buddhi* or intellect, (3 –7) the five elements — namely, earth, water, fire, air and *ākāśa*, space — and, lastly, (8) action or doing constitute *Prakṛti*.

[6] Namely, *sattva*, *rajas* and *tamas*. *Prakṛti* ever changes because it and every being in it are constituted by these strands of *prakṛti*, the rope that binds every being. *Tamas* forces a being to remain himself, to preserve and coincide with what he finds himself to be. *Sattva*, that principle of transcendence, would not let him be what he is, it ever calls him to rise above himself. To ever transcend oneself is, however, to disown every state of being, a frightening thought for a being that would ever *be*. So in order to subvert its call, call the imperative, the mortal being projects himself into the world and moves with it and turns a *kartā* there, a doer in it, the point of transition, as it were, for the past to move on into the future. This projection into the world, this contextualising of oneself, constitutes the strand called *rajas*.

7. *Dvandva*, duality. A duality has the *other* as its constituent. All the phenomena of the world are dualities, they are constituted by their others, by that which they are not. Negation is thus inscribed into the very being of every being. So when a *kartā* (Sanskrit *kartṛ*) chooses one state of being to the exclusion of its other, he by this very act, chooses that other too, the *other* that is the negation of that state. So all our choices and actions turn out to be self-negating, turn out to be tragedies absolute.

They are devoid of being, all the phenomena, are fallings from being because when one cannot be without its other, how can it constitute the other and the other constitute it? They are all appearances, false and untrue.

8. Notice the paradox that 16 and 17 have formulated, paradox that has led to all kinds of philosophical dilemmas. The senses perceive what these have originated from. From the subjective point of view, the world is a mere perception of it. From the objective point of view, the senses that perceive are merely modifications of the material world. The doctrine of *Samatā* would question both these positions. The world is a duality, sense-matter duality; one cannot choose one pole at the cost of the other. This means that neither of the two poles constituting this duality, the sense-matter duality, can be established as real, nor can the terms that name them be established as meaningful. The truth of this duality lies elsewhere. Life in the world is an unhappy life because it cannot answer our unconscious search for that truth, truth that has no *other* to constitute it.

9. Others that constitute him.

10. 16 and 17 fully highlight how the phenomenal world partakes of the nature of a duality. 16 states that the world is the constitutive *other* of the body and the organs, cognitive and motor. In the waking state, what we perceive is the *other* of the five senses – those of seeing, hearing, of smell, of taste and touch, and the other of the five organs of action. In this state mind and the senses function different from each other, often in conflict with each other, mind desiring one thing and the senses presenting world conditions hostile to that desire. The organs of action try to reconcile this conflict, if and when they function in accord with the world conditions. The world we perceive in dreams is the world the mind itself projects in terms of sense-content; it is the product of the mind with the senses sunk into it. That is why dreams are said to be wish-fulfilments, even the dreams painful and frightening. In sleep

one perceives neither thoughts nor objects of the sense but only a blank, the mind and senses having sunk into breath. For a while, the *buddhi* stays quiet and reposeful in this state, stays with itself and as itself, the world of the senses imposing no conditions on it and the mind no projects. Behind these phenomena revealed in the three states lie *vāsanā*-s, the traces left by one's past lives on the *jīva*, as their source, and behind *vāsanā* is *kartāpan*, the *jīva's* projection of himself as the doer.

At the same time, 17 describes the sense organs as emerging from the five elements— from earth, water, fire, air and *ākāśa*, space. The body fashioned by *vāsanā* and *kartāpan*, the body composed of the five elements, and the senses that perceive the world composed of those five elements emerging from the latter! So the phenomenal world is a duality, the so-called subjectivity sustaining the objective world and the objective world sustaining the subjectivity. This does not, however, mean that we are to stop here, for duality is only an appearance, not the truth of the world. For, at the root of man-world lies desire for being and behind desire lies *kartāpan*, identification with the passion for doing. Man the doer lies at the centre of the world, a link between its past and future, it is through that doer, that elusive, unidentifiable moment, that the world gets divided into past and present, those preconditions of action. In that moment, however, in that centre, you cannot say this is past and this is future and this is present, for all seem one and yet distinct. And so seem the doer and the so-called world, resisting division as much as unification.

11. That is, his thirst for being.

12. The twenty five constituents of *prakṛti*: The five gross elements; the five organs of sense; the five kinds of disposition, one associated with each of these organs; the five organs of action; the desire to act; the desire to experience the five elements, the mind, the intellect and lastly, *kartapan*, self-identification with the doing-ego. See 11 above.

13. Thirst for the true being that *samatā* is.

14. *Māyā* in the Vedāntic tradition is often equated with names and forms, and *avidyā*, false knowledge or propositional knowledge, with superimposition of these names and forms on to the self and the self on to them. Here, *ajñāna*, literally, not-knowledge, *andhakāra*, darkness, and *Māyā* are used synonymously. This should not

puzzle the reader. There can be no superimposition of names and forms on to the self if they are not already there to be superimposed. This means that *Māyā* is indispensable for *avidyā*, for the act of superimposition. Conversely, one cannot think of names and forms if the self is not superimposed on to them, for in the absence of being, of self, names and forms cannot be perceived and conceived. For, we do not perceive merely names and forms, we perceive them as names and forms as being *there*, as existents. So perception is a double perception, that of things and of their existence. Without *avidyā*, without superimposition, we cannot perceive names and forms and without *Māyā*, there can be no act of superimposition. So *Māyā* and *avidyā* too are dualities, originating as already dependent on each other and existing as such.

15. *Vidyā* is the threefold knowledge, namely, knowledge of earth, knowledge of the *antarikṣa*, midregion, and knowledge of *dyu*, the region of light. To know the earth is to extend with it to the horizons, and from the horizons to the zenith and beyond; it is to realise one's earthly being as cosmotheandic and beyond that being the cosmotheandric. It is to realise one's being as transcendence itself, as going beyond what one is and one can or could be. Knowledge of the midregion, *antarikṣa*, is the knowledge that the region of the air can provide, the knowledge of breath, knowledge in the form of a serene contemplation of its coming and going. And knowledge of *dyu*, of the region of light, is the knowledge of ecstasy, of ecstasy of self-loss, the consummation of self-sacrifice. This is how one comes to acquire knowledge of the three Vedas, that of the Ṛg Veda, that of the Yajur Veda and that of the Sāma Veda. Learning of the texts will not do. To attain to the *ātman*, however, implies extinction of all knowledge, cosmotheandric no less than what we call our human knowledge, sophisticated or the commonsensical.

16. *Yajña*, sacrifice. The concept of sacrifice underwent a great transformation in the Vedas, in the Brāhmaṇas and in the Upaniṣads and the Bhagavadgītā. For the Ṛg Veda, sacrifice is the centre of the world (Vide 1.164.34-35). The Śatapatha Brāhmaṇa (2.2.2. 8-20) emphasises that the true redemptive fire burns within man and that he should give an offering of himself to that fire. That, for it, is the way of gods as against that of the demons who resort to external ritualistic sacrifices. In the Upaniṣads and the Bbhagavadgītā, the concept of sacrifice is wholly internalised. Sacrifice there means sacrifice of every state of being into the

burning flame of the Real within.

[17] *Tapasyā*, self-burning. The word is ordinarily translated as austerity. But it actually implies burning of the false self one finds oneself projected into. To do *tapas* is to undo that self and through its undoing to undo one's sense of identity with it, with the false self. Austerities may burn gross desire, or appear to do so, but not until one's identity with the false self is burnt up will *tapasyā* reach its consummation. *Tapasyā* ultimately means burning of the sense of doership.

[18] The I-sense is the sense of a situated I, situated in the world. The I comes to know itself when it encounters a situation that poses a challenge to it, a threat to it. And the world being of the essence of change always poses a challenge to the I, to its security, necessitating its self-assertion in forms of action and struggle. The thinking or contemplative Cogito is only a derivative of this primitive I, I the doer.

[19] There are actions that augment one's sense of being a doer, and there are actions that negate that sense. One cannot simply rest with the thought that the I-sense is a false illusion and stand apart from it in a mere theoretical way. The *I* that acts is embedded in the body-self and the entire world, that other of the body-self. One has to distance oneself, in immediate and experiential terms, from the senses, from the mind and from the intellect and the shape the external world assumes in these varied states of distancing. The material world does not remain the external world when a man comes to distance himself from his eye, the eye itself becomes that world and the eye the world, the tiny eye the entire universe and the entire universe the tiny eye. And when a man finds himself distanced from his thought-process called the mind, his body and the world change into a succession of events, losing their solid appearance. And when he gets distanced from the intellect, then all distinctions tend to melt into a darkness of plenitude, each thing exceeding itself into unknown and immeasurable depth and magnitude, into what we humans call infinity.

All the actions mentioned at 31 are oriented towards this end, towards extinction of one's narcissism through rendering service to others, towards cultivating faith in the invisible, in that which the intellect cannot conceive, the mind think of and the senses perceive and the organs of action work upon. For that is the fulfillment of all desire, all strivings, all thought and all aspirations, *that* in which they come to be negated. This is the paradox one has to know and live for. It is clear that our narcissistic thinking cannot lead us there, cannot even conceive that state, and our desires cannot be directed towards it and so cannot be our actions. For, all these are oriented towards what we can enjoy and consume, can perceive and handle, can find to our liking or otherwise, and towards what we can firmly understand, put within the framework of our thinking. The way to *samatā* demands extinction, absolute cessation, of all these dispositions.

[20] Notice the criterion for judging whether one's acts are good or evil. Actions that negate the I-sense and the doer-sense are good, those that strengthen these are evil. It is not, as the modern world in general believes, my inclinations and desires that can decide what is good and what is not good for me, but the ontology of my existential condition. No man, or, for that matter, no being is autonomous, his place and relationships constitute him and, what is more, his own negation and the negation of his place and relationships. Man is born a mortal, a being that is ever dying, that is what his condition is, that is what he is. All his actions are directed towards the negation of this his reality, of his mortality. Therein lies the source of evil. Good life is acceptance of this mortal condition, and salvation is to live that condition, to live mortality. Not to remain *a mortal* that fights against mortality but to be *mortality* itself is the purpose of life, its sole purpose. That is goodness, that is the truth and that is abiding in the truth. The modern world, with its arrogance of power, has totally forgotten this truth and has left the decision of norms of conduct and life to the whims and passions of those who live for only one purpose: self-gratification.

[21] Mere thinking will not lead man to understanding of the truth that he is. He perceives what is not, thinks what cannot be thought, would determinate what cannot be determinated and desires what cannot be desired. What his senses reveal, his mind desires and his thought apprehends cannot be determined as 'this', for all that one perceives and conceives ever disowns itself, is, in truth, nothing but disownment itself. And yet in perceiving these disownments, one perceives them as existents, as suffused with existence or with being, being which they are not. The seer of the truth will point out to a seeker that being or existence, being or existence that he perceives but notices not, is aware of it without being aware of his awareness of it. Similarly, the seer will also point out to him how he believes himself to be a self but finds himself to

be nothing but a mere disowning, disowning of what he thinks himself to be. So all his knowledge is nothing but projecting of that which *is*, which is Being, on to that which is not, which is no being, is devoid of it. The seer stimulates, in the mind of a seeker of the truth, the thinking that is contemplative, thinking that participates in Being, to make him passively self-submit to It to be It and live It, and not the thinking that is the forte of thinkers, those who would capture that Being in concepts that are not, concepts that ever disown themselves as do the phenomena they refer to and seemingly determinate. The thinking that a seer gives rise to in him, reveals, is a revelation, as against the thinking of a thinker that merely classifies and conceals. So thinking here does not mean what is called rational or conceptual thinking, or, for that matter, thinking related to and directed to observation and verification and revision.

22. A paradox again! The world ever moves towards its truth and being, that is the end of its striving - of the entire world, of each and every being that has come to be born here. Yet that goal is also its beginning, its source. Proceeding from that source, it ever seeks it. That *arche* is its *telos*, that beginning its end. And the glory of that truth, that source of all that has come to be, lies in creating a world that is only an appearance, a false show, seeking an end which was ever there. Why, then, this tumult of birth, this struggle hard and harsh for life, this unrest of ambition, this pain of decay, this despair of death? Why lose the source for the sake of finding it? The source is great and glorious because it dies into creation, loses itself into it, becomes it, so that creation too may die back into that source, and in its dying partake of the greatness and glory of the source. If the Lord ever remained himself, there would have been no glory in him, no greatness. It is because he ever dies that he ever lives. And the creatures are not great and glorious because they *would* ever live. They are to know that life is mortality itself, and all their struggles are negation of the truth of their life. If they too freely die with their life, they too would turn into the Lord. In dying lies our Being and Truth, in dying ever and always, in living lies our death. The Lord is ever the same, is sameness itself because he is ever dying, does not even stay to know that he is dying. And that is what every being has to be. For in ever dying lies his immortality, in loss of himself lies his ecstasy, his immortal bliss. The world is the glory of the Lord because in turning into it the

Truth reclaims itself, reclaims itself as disowning of itself. For, in that lies its true being, in sacrifice of itself. And in that sacrifice can reclaim every being his truth.

23 As creation is the goal of the creator, the reclaiming of his being, so the creator is the goal of beings. They must find creation as of no avail and go back to the source, to their home and place of rest. In disowning their life and the worth of their life, they find the worth true. The creator and creation too are dualities. The creator owns up to his *other*, whereas man disowns his other. When man owns up to that other, he will find the creator-creature duality too change into the truth a-dual, truth ever the same. For, we should not forget that the Lord, Creator or God exists as the *telos* of the mortal being, his end and goal. It is the latter that finds that Ever-the-Same as his God, this being that has fallen from his self ever the same. Without the mortal being there can be no eternal God and without the latter there can be no mortal being, that seeker of the place of rest and repose. In the *Samatā*-vision, God and his creation are one.

24. Mortality is the being alike of man and of his God, being that is *the* curse for man but is the blessing for his God. It is the curse of man because he would disown it and fight against it. When a man finds his struggle all sorrow and pain and his desires and ambitions as of no account, he seeks a release from it into a state where all is repose and no strife. That becomes his aim, his sole goal, that state 'reposeful and tranquil'. He calls that state immortal and eternal and gives it the name of God. His God is an illusion because he, in his delusion, finds mortality itself a curse and not his struggle against it, and makes of his God the fulfillment of that passion, the embodiment of immortality that he would be. Yet it is this error that redeems him from his fallen condition. For, in devoting himself to his God, in reposing his faith in Him, and taking all his doings and what they bring about, suffering or happiness, as His doing, man becomes free from the idea of his being a doer and gives himself up to his mortal condition and endures with a meek patience all that that condition may inflict on him. The sense of one's being a doer is,however, too deep to be eradicated even by this self-submission to the will of the Lord. For even to be conscious is to be a doer, howsoever self-submitting and passive one's consciousness may be. Man can cease to be a doer only when he ceases to be. His God is eternal because He is *not* and a mortal is mortal because he *is*. Self-submission to the will of God is self -

submission to one's mortal condition and fate and self-submission to the mortal condition is not to know oneself. Unless and until consciousness becomes extinct, man cannot become the Being that he would be. Every state of being that one can conceive is ridden with duality, be it that of the mortal being or that of his God. But the paradox of salvation lies in accepting one's mortal state of being, in becoming that state of being. The being that becomes his mortality turns into the Still ever the Same, beyond the mortal and immortal states he goes, beyond both man and God. For God Himself would then become his Son, the Word that is Its own referent. On that Word we shall dwell at the appropriate time.

25. To remember that being as one's lost home. Meditation means remembrance, it is not oriented towards something unknown and yet to be known. Our ordinary knowledge is a discovery, but true knowledge is a recovery. To discover is to discover the Other, to recover is to recover the Self, that which is one's own and one's being. The Other is a threat, a misery; the Self is restoration and joy.

26. Knowledge as we know it, is always other-oriented; knowledge is knowledge-of. This knowledge can be had, can be acquired. But what about the knowledge that has no *other* to know? One simply cannot *have* it or *acquire* it. Knowledge without the other can have no knower, that agent of knowing that needs must have the other to know. Knowledge without the other is therefore knowledge without the knower too. It is a state of bliss because there is no other to contend with, the state that one ever seeks to find and be. One cannot contemplate that knowledge, turn it into an object, one can only remember it as lost. To contemplate that state where there is knowledge alone and no knower and no known is to contemplate the unthinkable. The ontology of knowledge will occupy us in the pages to come, where we shall try to elaborate the implications of knowledge without the knower and the known.

27 We may note how all that man can think about the ultimate truth is attributed to God. Transcendent is he and immanent, the goal ultimate of life and bliss absolute, the source of all and the being of all, and knowledge absolute and unthinkable. Devotion implies surrender of all one's concepts and one's sense of distinctions, all one's truths and aspirations to God. He is the ultimate truth beyond our ken and imagination, yet it is he who

should be known, should be adored and reached, he that is beyond our reach and adoration. Thinking about that unthinkable will purge us of all thinking, to aspire for him is to be free from all aspirations, to yearn for him is to be free from all yearning, to worship that truth is to undo the false sense of truth, the false sense that we have about our I or Me.

No one who is not disillusioned with every thought, every desire and every aspiration, and every 'reality' can have this kind of fervent devotion.

The analysis that I have given here is a temptation that a devotee would spurn and reject. And that precisely is what he should do. But pause! There is hope and a way also for those who cannot but think, think with pain and anguish. 49 considers these seekers too as devotees.

[28.] Notice the equation of the *paramātman*, the supreme self, with the *ātman*, the self within man. One becomes aware of the presence of that self within when the body turns into a process, losing its entity character. Now, this is not possible until man withdraws from desire and action. Desire makes the body appear as an entity, solid and stable, because it invests things it desires with the entity-character. The 'reality' of things sustains one's sense of the 'reality' of the body. Action too assumes the 'reality', the entity character, of the body, that instrument of action. When the *buddhi* gets purified of desire and the passion to act, it withdraws itself into a disposition of passive contemplation before which the body appears as a mere succession of sense-events instead of the solid thing it was. Being then deserts all that the intellect can perceive and conceive, its concepts no less than its thoughts and percepts. Only consciousness appears to be endowed with stability, consciousness that can see the rise and fall of the succeeding sense-moments that the body has now turned into. With its concentration deepening, even the moments cease to be perceived, the intellect itself dying with those moments, the moments that sustained its witness character. The death of the *buddhi* is its transformation into the *ātman*, into the self of all in each, into the knowledge that ever is. But to call it the self or knowledge too is to profane it, for they too smack of concepts. That is why it is called unknowable, the knower that knows all but is never known (vide 49). It is imperative, however, that man direct his thoughts to that self, for that is the way to free himself from knowing, that fetter last and final.

29. Notice how embodiment and activity go together. The body inevitably and inexorably moves towards death, is, in truth, a movement towards death, that is the end destined for it, that is its being and its truth. And man, like other beings, would *be*, would be a *be*-ing, would be an Is. To fulfil that end, he has to invest the body, that prop of his being, with *sat*, with *be*-ing, with the Is that he would be. And for that purpose, he would ever preserve it, preserve that unpreservable. This desire to preserve the body and have the feel of its being a *be*-ing, a presence, compels the being identified with it to be ever active, be that activity of his practical, theoretical or in terms of suffering or enjoyment. The disposition of activity assumes the body to be real and existent, this assumption of it making it apply the concepts of reality and unreality to what is desirable for it and not desirable for it. And it is the nature of the body that determines what is desirable and what is not desirable and what is truth and untruth. This way the body becomes the dispenser of the criteria of judgements: ontological, moral, aesthetic and others. The man who finds the body real, rather assumes this way that it is real, remains ever busy with getting and spending, with suffering and enjoyment, with ambitions and frustrations. Not for him even an inkling of the self within him, the self that dispenses him consciousness, consciousness of his desires and his thoughts, of his perceptions and his actions, and of the objects of the world around him. It is only when he distances himself from the body and the senses, when he turns a passive witness of not only these but also of his thoughts and the consciousness of thoughts that he comes to have an intimation of the existence of the *ātman* within him. And when this awareness of the self the absent becomes deep in him, the body manifests itself as what it is, a mere passing show and a shadow, and self the unknowable as reality itself. To say No to all that one is and one knows within him and without is contemplation of the self. Man cannot contemplate the self as he would an object. It is only his sense of being deserted by being that makes him bid goodbye to all that he desired and cherished and thought to be real and true and yearn in agony for the truth, the *ātman* that he in truth is. A time comes when his desire for being, being the true, becomes so strong that to live as a man becomes impossible for him, leading him ultimately to lose himself. This loss of his fallen self is his attainment to his real self; in thus sacrificing himself he saves himself.

[30] That is to say, no activity of the intellect and that of the mind. Before whom does the *ātman* manifest itself? The ātman manifests itself in the form of *Nāda,* or of *śūnya,* as a dark nothing or as consciousness or the *buddhi* as still and inactive. These manifest themselves as interior to one's breath, one's concepts, one's desires and passions and one's cognitive and motor organs. In this state, one stands apart from all these, all still and passive. A seeker of the truth cannot go beyond this passivity, that is the ultimate truth for him, for *him,* not the ultimate truth in itself. He has to give up all efforts and endeavours and stay as the Nāda, as the *śūnya,* as consciousness the still. It is only when he loses himself in all passivity into any of these that he is said to attain to the *'ātman'*. Attaining to the *ātman* then would mean not to be any of these states. Should we, can we, then, retain the term *ātman,* or Brahman or *śūnya* and, for that matter, any other terms? Can we say that there is or there is not such a thing as the *ātman* or the ultimate truth?

[31] Both the readings are admissible. We may recall how names and forms are superimposed on to the self and the self on to names and forms. Superimposition of each on to the other constitutes *māyā-avidyā* duality. We may also recall how a mortal being and the ego of agency constitute a duality. Here too the living being imagines names and forms as facts as it were, *imagines* them as given, as if they were ontologically prior to him. He, their creator, becomes their creature., their reality or unreality becoming his reality or unreality. Dualities are *mithyā,* false appearances, precisely because they are dualities, because they are *mithuyāḥ.* We may remember that *mithuyā* was the original form of *mithyā*. 'False appearance', however, can be a little problematic. For, dualities do not admit the predicates 'real' and 'unreal'. They are and they are not, one pole constituting them assumes and is assumed by the other pole. They reveal the real as Being or existence but as other than them. That is why they are equated with the veils of *Māyā,* with false appearances of the Real.

[32] Names are concept-names and forms are their sense-content. They originate, both names and forms, concepts and sense content, as dependent on each other, each inconceivable without the other. They are thus *dvandva-s,* opposites that sustain each other and negate each other. Names are thus the false appearances of the Word as forms are the false appearances of Being, each appearance affirming the other through negating it and negating it through

affirming it. But how can a mortal being, himself a *dvandva*, a duality, of name and form can remember the Name true, Name different from all the names he knows of?

Here the concept of *dīkṣā*, of consecration, becomes relevant. The *ātman* that ever remains itself, creating or not creating, doing or not doing – for this is what this passivity is - remains wholly unknown to man except in the form of the ontological lack that he finds within himself. The sage that has become one with the *ātman*, is *ātman* itself, reveals to a man in search of wholeness a name, which is the proper name of the self in him, the self that is his God too. A human being, a being that is not-being, a being whose being is not to be a being, is turned into the appearance of a being by what is called his proper name, proper name preceded by his common name. It is that name which makes of that a-identity a seeming identity, a being with a self as it were of his own. But this common-proper name ever remains adventitious to what he in fact is, a constant disowning of the identity character that his name would invest him with. So the common-proper name that would identify a given form in terms of class-individuality fails to be the name proper. It is a false appearance, this name, because what can *make* it a name, namely a form, ever eludes it. A name is a class-individuality duality, its constituent poles ever problematic. And equally problematic remains its referent, namely concept—sense-content duality. But the name a seer of truth initiates a man into is the name with no *other* as its referent, which itself is its referent. That name alone is the self for the initiate, his God and being and he has to breathe that name, live for it and as it. The name comes to be alive, comes to be the real name when man dies into it, instills his breath into it. It is man that dispenses life to the name, to turn it into the self, into God. God is not the imagination of man, He is the creation of man through his sacrifice of himself. How this remembrance of the name leads to the birth of God through the death of man we shall consider, as far as we can, when we come to the chapters on the yogic meditation.[*vide, Anubhava* 3, On Remembrance of Truth].

33. The nine doors are the two eyes, the two ears, the two nostrils, the mouth and the organs of generation and evacuation. A true *yogin* loses all interest in what the senses reveal and also in food and sex. A *yogin* mingles the Name of the Lord with his breath and sacrifices himself into that flow of the name-breath. His senses die into it along with the world they reveal, and so do his mind

and his thoughts. Eventually the motion of his breath will come to rest, the name getting transformed into the Word, the Word in which dwells all that is named or could be named. The Word he turns into is Word the Silent because there is no other to speak it or hear it. That is the ontological place of beings, the home still of the still.

The *yogin* is the primordial man, man the sacrificial victim who through his sacrifice fathers the Father, the *Nārāyaṇa*, the Son of Man. In other words, man turns into God when he sacrifices himself, God his *telos* absolute, at once the source and the end of the world. That Father of the world and man is the son of man not in the sense that they are the dualities that originate as dependent on each other. He is the son of man because it is the fallen man that creates him as his *telos*, as his source and end and it is the sacrificial man that brings him, that God, into being, becomes that God through sacrifice of himself in the yogic fire. Man finds his God desert him when he asserts himself, he turns into his God when he sacrifices himself, sacrifices himself to the Who? in him and in the world.

34. *'Brahmāṇḍa'*, the cosmic egg, refers here to the head where the consciousness of a *yogin* comes to stay after it has freed itself from the temptations of the nine gates. It is there that he dies into the name to become the Name, that home of all that is, the name that is its own referent, the Word silent and still.

35. There has been a fierce debate regarding the ethical norm among serious thinkers. They had many thoughts and insights to offer to mankind regarding this momentous question. To go into the history of ethical thought is not our concern here; suffice it to say that almost all the ethical norms formulated by thinkers of repute have been set aside by the convenient norm of *pragma* in our times. The disastrous implications of this trend we will take up later. Here the point focussed by the text at this point alone should receive our attention. The ethical norm is decided, the text says, by the extent of one's orientation towards finding the *ātman*, the true self within. Acts that help us undo our identification with the body, the senses, the mind and the intellect and lead us towards the *ātman* are good actions, those that lead us to the opposite direction are evil actions. Modern civilisation, in this phase of late capitalism, has chosen the latter way. Its attention is almost exclusively fixed on the safety and interests of the embodied being. It is our success or no success in manipulating Nature, that Other, that decides the meaningfulness or meaninglessness of our actions. This dangerous

doctrine has become the faith of our times, which cannot but prove, according to our text, disastrous for modern man and his civilisation.

[36] We may recall how modern civilisation has come to be a full embodiment of this disposition that the text here deplores. It will dwell at length on this its disposition with a grim warning of its tragic consequences.

[37] The saying implicitly refers to the communal tensions that raged in India in those days, leading, eventually, to the partition of the country into Bhārata , India, and Pakistan.

[38] Again, a comment on the communal hatred that had engulfed the people of India, especially those who lived in the Panjab, the scene of terrible and bloody riots at the time of the partition of the country.

[39] *Buddhi*, intellect, we may recall, is the faculty that determinates, sets limits to things, individuates them, puts them in categories and concepts. This is its fallen state, its taint and its disease. Its purification consists in its getting rid of this conceptualisation and in becoming all innocent and passive. All the virtues described above, all those dispositions are meant for this purpose, namely, to transform the *buddhi* into innocence complete and absolute. For that is its highest state, this state of passive innocence, that is the *ātman*, the self, that is *Īśvara*, the Lord, and that is Brahman, that consciousness that knows not that it is consciousness. Can we call it consciousness then?

It may also be noted that purification of the *buddhi* comes to be possible when one hears the words of revelation and reflects deeply on the lives of those who have become one with the Real. Unaided thinking, unaided by revelation, is thinking directed towards the world, it cannot direct itself to the truth. For concepts through which thinking is done are concepts in relation to sense-content, as sense-content is sense-content in relation to concepts, is informed by them. Concepts identify sense-content, individualise it, through classification, but a class is not an individual, it has no content of its own, it comes to be only in relation to an individual. And the individual too cannot be identified as an individual but only in terms of a class. Thus our thinking is thinking in terms that are always in question. Categorisation is our knowledge, not acquaintance. So every thinking, be it speculative, analytical or scientific, thinking that has the world of the senses as its point of reference, is ignorance itself and every discourse a distortion. To know the truth, the self, there is only one guide, namely, revelation, revelation that is *vidhi*, that is disruption. Thinking that is focussed on the words of revelation is the right kind of thinking precisely because revelation disrupts us into innocence. And the right conduct also is the conduct that obeys the commandment of revelation because that commandment also is *vidhi*, the commandment that disrupts the person in us, undoes him, to lead him find and be the *ātman* that he truly is. And the wrong conduct is the conduct that is oriented towards the *anātman*, to the not-self, to the world that *avidyā* has set up, that realm of the unidentifiable. It is in the lives of the great ones that we can find the embodiment of the right conduct. It is they that can provide us with ethical criteria, no usage can do it, no custom and no reflection, much less our pragmatic considerations.

40. *Śraddhā*, literally, abiding in truth.

41 *Sat-vādī*, one who speaks the truth and also one who believes in the truth, in reality as against its false appearances. The man truly truthful is not merely he who speaks what is the truth, reports what has really happened, but one who lives for his true being, strives to find it and abides in it. Therefore, those who rely on their reason and their perception and practice-experiments live as prisoners of falsehood, the truth of their being and that of the world ever escaping them. One must live as absolute aloneness to be the being that one is. To predicate a *state* of being of oneself is to negate being, for every *state* of being is a false appearance of being.

42 The yogic practice is called remembrance because it makes one remember one's real being, the being one has lost. It is the sense of one's ontological loss that makes one yearn for it. What is new, what is a discovery, augments one's ego, one's identification with this or that state of being, it cannot set aflame one's yearning for one's own being. So the sense of loss is true knowledge, not discovery of the new. The paradise we seek can only be the paradise we have lost. Needless to repeat, man comes to be born as God when he extinguishes himself in the yogic fire. It is man the sacrificial victim that is born as God. *Nārāyaṇa* is thus man himself, it is man the extinct that 'fathers' that being of his.

[43] Not as structured in terms of concepts and categories or as interpreted.

[44] We should make it a point to take terms like happiness, bliss and blessedness as mere figurative expressions. The state of *samatā* implies finding life as death and death as life, salvation as fall and fall as salvation, happiness as sorrow and sorrow as happiness, liberation as bondage and bondage as liberation, creation as no creation and no creation as creation. It is not to be equated with the mental state of equanimity. Nor should the word *śānti* be taken as peace of mind, it means cessation of all the states of being with which we identify ourselves. The faithful are often eager to anthropomorphise the real by taking such figurative statements as propositional statements.

[45] *Kalpanā* also means imagination or thought. To say that the world is the imagination of a mortal being is to make a misleading statement. It implies that the mortal being exists as himself, as independent of the world and that it is this self-existing being that imagines a world around him. The fact of the matter is that the mortal being and his world originate together as dependent on each other, one cannot be disassociated from the other, neither the mortal being nor the world. The mortal being is a *saṃsārin*, a being of the world. There is however one rider that we must look into. The mortal being finds the world as ontologically prior to him, all his actions and desires assume this priority of the world. This being derives the sense of his own reality from the world; his desires and actions are all directed towards it. To feel himself as a being, as a real being, he invests the world with reality. Therefore, the source of the world lies in his desire to *be*; it is that desire, the desire to *be*, that sets up the world to embody itself as a being, as an existent. That desire projects the world so that the individual may *be*. The world is not an independent reality nor is man nor is the duality man-world. It is the desire to *be* that embodies itself as the individual being and the world as its constitutive other, which the former in his life and thought invests with reality in order to invest himself with reality. It is ultimately his choice to remain immersed in the world or distance himself from the world and from the desire to *be* in order to be his real self.

So the responsibility lies on the individual whether the world is to be there or not to be there. In this sense he may be said to project the world as his constitutive other, he as the passion for being. We should be wary of equating this complex thought with neat subjectivism.

46. Good actions are those that set one on to the internal way and make one distance oneself from self-interests and self-concerns. When man comes to have this serene disposition, he finds himself a seer of the senses and of the mind, and even of the motion of his breath. When this contemplation of breath becomes deep and passive, the motion of breath turns gentle and eventually comes to be still. That is the moment when one turns into the *ātman*, the seer innocent of his seeing. The text will have much more to say about this mode of yogic meditation.

47. A grim reminder of the kind of life a man gifted with mere keenness of intelligence is destined to live. Beings of this kind would capture reality in their concepts, those embodiments of their narcissistic passions. They would determinate reality, set limits to it through concepts, to sustain their own limited self, self they can identify as this or that. Nor can these gifted souls know what is right and what is wrong, their love of their delimited self ever concealing the right way from them.

48. Human beings cannot think of their self without identifying it with some existential state or the other. The self in itself is just inconceivable for them. This passion for being something, some state of affairs, is *ajñana*, is ignorance, it is *avidyā*, false knowledge, it is *Māyā*, that other of *avidyā*, namely, the phenomena that the latter would determinate and identify. What we call knowledge is itself *avidyā*, for it can reveal reality only in terms of ambiguities like concept-image, only in terms that have their negation written into them. So, an unreal (concept) would be real through another unreal (sense-content) and the latter through the former. It is as if a blind man were to seek his sight through another blind man, to adapt the well known Upanṣadic analogy. To believe in the *ātman* means, then, to give up all states of being that *avidyā*, our propositional knowledge, has set up, to outlive them, to be innocent of them; it means, in common parlance, to be nothing, to die before one's death. That man alone is man of faith who can thus die unto himself, die even when alive. All the arguments that philosophers give in favour of the existence of the self will be of little avail to him, conceptually and existentially.

One can, for example, discard the view that the self is a mere succession of thoughts by invoking the fact of one's consciousness of that succession, consciousness that persists in the midst of that process, that change. But when one tries to think of the self in itself, one finds that one cannot simply do away with what that self, that enduring consciousness, is conscious of, namely, the succession of thoughts. The thought process and the self turn out to be a duality. Only that duality can one experience, neither mere the self nor mere thoughts. [Does not the term 'experience' then turn out to be as problematic as do the self and thought?]. In the same way, the body, that prop of the feeling of stability, of the feeling of being that the I has with regard to itself, too turns out, when genuinely attended to, to be a mere succession of sensations, its stability a mere illusion, the result of projecting of the self on to it, the mysterious self that seems to endure in the midst of change. The body, that support of thoughts, itself turns out to be grounded on the self, the self that one cannot find or conceive.

Yet this inconceivable self is the dispenser of being to man and to all he perceives and conceives. If the self was not there, there could be no man there and no world, no thoughts and their succession, no feelings and perceptions, no sensations and no concepts and no experience. It is as endowed with self that a being can desire and aspire, act and achieve. We cannot rest content with the dualities that we are and the duality that the world is because we live here to find our being, because we would be a self. And until we come to be a self we will remain unhappy creatures, subject to decay and death to fight against which consists what we call our life. But we would not be the being, the being in itself, we would be the being that we can feel and know and experience! And therein lies our unmitigated tragedy, in our passion to know and experience the being that we are. Our knowledge is thus our fall, fall into the worldly mode of being, that eternal desolation and frustration, where we cannot come to *be*, where we can only live as self-disowning and deprivation, where we live only to die, where our life is nothing but negation of itself.

Most people, including the majority of thinkers, would not know what they are in search of, they would continue to seek being in negation of being, in their possessions, in their bodies, in their passions and thoughts and in their knowledge and interpretations. They continue to live this barren tragedy because they would not *be*, simply *be*, but would be the being they can live and know. In other words, they would seek their being in the phenomena they *know*, the phenomena that their passion for this kind of being has set up. They would seek it in their thoughts and bodies and in the world, that *other* of their thoughts and bodies. Only a man who has realised the grim tragedy of this tragic error seeks to rectify it. He alone is the man to find his loss in acquisitions, his degradation in accomplishments, his ignorance in knowledge, and his death in life. He alone will seek the gain true, the redemption true, the knowledge true and the life true. And that gain he will find when he has given up all his gains here and his knowledge and his pleasures and, what is more, the false life he lives.

The way straight to true life and being thus lies not in the grim struggle for life where no life can be but in being faithful to the self, to the *ātman*, within, discarding the passion to place it and determinate it. When one ceases to seek to know it and place it, when one ceases to know and think, perceive and sense, desire and aspire, then alone does one come to be truly oneself. To be innocent of the self is to be the self; in innocence alone lies our being and our truth. The other way to this innocence lies in paying heed to what our perception reveals, namely, objects as existents. We perceive not only the objects of perception but also existence. The latter we do not care to notice because of our active concern for the former. We do not care for pure existence because we cannot perceive it without the objects of perception, without those existents. But if we would save ourselves from our tragedy, we have to be loyal to the existence part of the existence-object duality too. We must live that existence-existent duality and perceive that duality in every object, live it and be it. We must, that is, perceive without a self-interest to let the object concerned become suffused with existence, with Being, and, in consequence, become suffused with Being ourselves. No distinction will then remain for us, distinction like that between existence and the existent, between one existent and other existents.

Yet still another way to this innocence lies in accepting our mortal lot without a question and in ceasing to struggle against it. If we let ourselves flow to our destined end, live our mortality and not the life that is a futile struggle against it, then we will not stay to be the I to be and know thoughts and desires. And, further, we will not stay to be the percipients that we find ourselves to be. We will cease to be and with our ceasing to be our mortality too will cease to be. We will become innocent of death as much as of life, of dying as much as of living. Not to know that we are is our aim, that is our truth. And that truth can be attained to, as we said above, through distancing ourselves from our existential condition or through accepting and living the ambiguities that we are. The third way is the way of the genuine mortal that ignores the *ātman* and the *sattā*, the self and existence or being. It is the way of self-submission to *Māyā* and the deathly traps it has woven for us, of living the mortal condition and its grim tragedies, caring neither for truth nor for being. What is of significance is giving up our passion for selfhood in and through dualities. If we discard that passion and are loyal to either of the poles of the duality that we are, be it the self or the other of the self, be it Brahman or *Māyā*, we will become what we truly seek to be. And find it we will through another way too, the way of owning up to our ambiguity, living it without a question in a spirit of total surrender. Our truths will remain our errors, our goals our strayings, our joys our curse so long as we *are*. The moment we cease to be, our errors will turn into truth, our fall into our redemption, our curse into our joy, our illusions into being and truth and our mortality into immortality. The way is not the question, the goal is.

49. Good and evil present themselves before us as woven into each other. The errors of wisdom have often been the undoing of mankind. To choose some ideals as the absolute ones often end up in letting loose much that is evil and harmful. Thus the dilemmas of moral life stay persistent and unreconciled, mocking at our criteria of good and evil. The solution lies not in formulating norms and criteria but in undoing the source of those dilemmas and dualities, namely, our passion for false selfhood, selfhood placed and determinated or, as we may say, interpreted. We have to choose a course of action that makes us reconciled to our mortal lot, acknowledge it and own it up to. Often the choice will be difficult to make if we depend on our own judgement, biased as it always is towards the false selfhood we cherish. One must seek refuge in the word of those who have died into their being, the *sat-puruṣas*, men the real, if one has to escape from the evil inherent in our moral choice.

50. One may, *through careful thought*, salvage the *cogito* from its placement, from the situation it is equated with (in the way that Descartes did) but one cannot salvage the *ātman*, the self, from it,

the self that is not the cogito, cogito that constitutes one pole of the duality that is the being of every placed being. The cogito can be only the cogito-in-the-world, it cannot be the base, the support and being of the world that the *ātman*, that *sattā*, that bare existence, is. It is only the word of a seer of the truth that can make one believe in that self and give oneself up to it. And it is the life of a seer, that renunciation itself, that can make a man live by and as existence and not as existents or to own up to being the latter, to mortality and not to fight against it. To live by one's own thoughts is to live in darkness, to live by one's decisions is to live in sin, to fight for one's being, to place it secure, is to invite one's doom. In that false self, the self placed and interpreted, lie our tragedy, our frustration and our ignorance. Only *śraddhā* can save us, our placement in truth (*śrad*, truth, *dhā*, placement) and *śraddhā* means placing our trust in the word of the truth that the word of a true seer is.

51. Thought is by its very nature directed towards its objects, it is the *other* that occupies it. And action too is oriented towards the accomplishment of something that is not already there, towards making present what is not present. And contemplation too is intentional; it too dwells on an object with serene passivity. To direct these towards the self means to undo all these three: thinking, acting and contemplation, for they cannot make the self their object, cannot place it and identify it. Knowledge of the self thus means the end of all knowledge; to act for the self means to cease to act and to contemplate the self means to cease to be contemplative. It means to undo the idea of the self too, for the self also is a fabrication but a fabrication that negates all other fabrications. What the ultimate truth is, our thought cannot conceive, it would not admit even the self as its predicate.

52. There is a compulsiveness about our choices and actions, our modes of life and of our thought. When we find ourselves pursuing 'our' goals with utmost enthusiasm and energy, our compulsiveness is at its heights then. We act out of obsessions, irresistible and overweening. These compulsive obsessions are determined by our *prārabdha*, by those portions of our past lives and dispositions that are responsible for our present birth. The strength of our determination and the intensity of our interests and acts are not *our* strength and *our* intensity, they are the expressions of the past that we have already disowned and left behind but which, despite this, pursues us relentlessly, making what we take

to be our present, conscious being, being that would choose and determinate, as of little account. Our life is not our life, it is just thrust upon us and we thrown into it. We work and repose because we are *made* to do so, we laugh and weep because we have to; we create and feel free because we have to create and feel free. Our life is already determined; it merely unfolds itself before us.

But there is a freedom vouchsafed to us, freedom of identifying or not identifying our self with this unfolding. If we identify ourselves with it, we will live as miserable slaves; if we distance ourselves from it, we will find the true self and freedom, the self and freedom we seek ever and always. We will reclaim our lost being, our real being, if we do not appropriate that unfolding as *our* life. 'This is my life' is the assertion of a miserable slave.

53 Most people often draw a clear line of distinction between *svārtha* and *parmārtha*, between the worldly life and the life of spirit. They believe that prosperity and spirituality do not easily go together. That there is a great measure of truth in this view cannot be denied; it is a warning against the self-complacency of those who would have both the worlds. If we seek life, we cannot find the spirit in us. One has to die into the latter. This has been the belief and practice of those who seek the life true; they know and believe that he who seeketh life shalt lose it and he who loseth it for the spirit in him will find it. And this is the view of the present text too, the view it expresses repeatedly and emphatically. The life of the Master leaves no scope for doubt in this regard.

Yet we find the text teaching here that belief in the *ātman* is necessary for prosperity in life too, a belief that a pragmatist would find it hard to accept. But we have to understand that prosperity requires collective effort; it is as beings in relationship that we can succeed in harnessing the resources of nature for our benefit. And successful communal effort requires of us that we should be straight in dealing with one another, that we should be truthful and honest and fulfill our promises. It also requires of us that we have care and concern for others; only then can we win their trust and cooperation. And the greater our concern for others and their prosperity, the greater will be the prosperity of the society we live in. It is also of paramount importance that we live a life of simplicity, for the desire for pomp and show makes us insensitive to the needs and conditions of others, destroys our honesty and our truthfulness, makes us crooked and fraudulent, bereft of feeling and callous. When the successful among us spend their wealth not on their vain pleasures but in serving those that are deprived and unhappy, the civilisation they produce cannot but prosper in harmony and concord.

And our worldly well being also demands that we think seriously about what is real and what is unreal, what is good and what is evil, what is the goal of life and its meaning. For this purpose, the society we live in must hold regular *sat-saṅgas,* holy congregations, where people should raise these questions and try to find answers to them. These *sat-saṅgas* should not be professional like the universities. People should attend them for knowing the truth only, with no other aim. *Sat-saṅga* gives a pause to one's worldly pursuits, makes one think about their worth or no worth. It makes one step back from those pursuits to measure them and assess them in the context of the ultimate purpose of life. And, lastly, we must remember the self, daily remember it contemplatively so that we should ever be aware of the ontological lack in us, lack which no possession and no success can fill up.

It is absolutely necessary that we ask the ultimate questions and remember our *ātman,* remember that lost paradise. For, if we do not do so, we will neither remain honest for long, nor simple, nor sensitive to the pain of others, nor truthful. Honesty and consideration for others for pragmatic reasons cannot last for long, as one can see from the condition to which late capitalism has brought us. People in so-called advanced countries are becoming increasingly self-obsessed and self-concerned, their own 'life' the focus of their attention. And in the countries which are trying to emulate them, the situation is fast becoming much worse. I need not go into the corruption that has seized the body politics of these countries; it is rampant enough for every one to see. And the cause of this unrest is the callousness and insensitiveness of the successful and the greed of the less successful and criminality of the deprived. Since all of them, each one among them, are concerned only with the well being of what they deem to be their self, self the situated, no one can even think of discarding it. Thus if we cease to believe that there is a self behind and beyond our mind and body, the self real, we will be so deeply immersed in our passions and desires that we cannot but destroy each other for our individual gains. The text will dwell at length on this aspect of our life.

There is however, one situation that a man of true faith may/will encounter in his life. If a community has lost every awareness of the self, has become oblivious of it, and if almost all of its members have their concerns solely focussed on 'this life', then how should live a man who, in contrast to the society he lives in, is haunted by the memory of his lost home and self? Will he not be unhappy and miserable where no one is there to understand his agony, his pain and feel the value and meaningfulness of his apparent failures? Insults and humiliations, hardships and misery, poverty and want will pursue him without an end, pursue this misfit among the ambitious and the proud. Can we say in all honesty that his morrows will be taken care of and his needs and requirements? That is the question that a seeker of truth asks himself in the modern world, where he may not find an understnding person to know his agony and his despair. Will his *ātman*, his Lord, take care of his interests and safety, of his *yoga* and *keṣema*? Or, will he perish into the thin air like, as Arjuna in the Bhagavadgītā would say, a floating cloud?

To facilitate his appreciation of the matter in question, I would request the reader to recall an aspect of Kant's thought. Man finds himself, according to this thinker's vision, immersed in sense-content and tied by the laws and categories of Understanding. Determined through and through he lives by these two conditions of his being. Only the voice of the moral law, his sense of not what is but what ought to be, prompts him to do acts that are not determined by these two; free are those acts, genuinely originary and undetermined. But the sense of *ought* is not as free as it is imagined by our thinker, for what ought to be is already conditioned by what is. It is the given condition of being which serves as the point of departure for the urge for transcendence that the moral law embodies. Our moral acts are not determined as are our acts compulsively directed towards the world of sense and Understanding; but they are not entirely free from their hold, from the hold of sense and Understanding. The text here would add that the world of sense and Understanding that we find ourselves placed in is determined by a past world of sense and Understanding, it is not just inflicted upon man, something arbitrarily imposed upon him. When we think of the world and ourselves in terms of the categories of Understanding, we find it as objective and given, find it as a condition imposed upon us, a condition about which we can do little or nothing. The world we find ourselves placed in seems to us an objective world, world *there*, existing (as it were) independently of us. It has its past and will probably have a future too, all determined by the categories of Understanding acknowledged by Kant or other categories not recognised by him. But that world does not, truly speaking, exist independently of the percipient; it is world the perceived. The world is thus what we may call a man-world and the past of this world determining its present form too has to be a man-world. This precisely is implied by the theory of rebirth. The world that I perceive and experience is the world determined by what I perceived and experienced in the past. And *prārabdha* is nothing else than that part of that experience which has brought about this present man-world. To come back, however, to the question we raised regarding the predicament of the individual who finds himself helpless in a hostile culture. A happy and prosperous culture can sustain itself only if men and women enjoying it do not forget their sense of loss, do not forget that they are exiled from their home, home past their power to recall. But soon, too soon their prosperity overshadows that thought and that remembrance, bringing in the era of the decline and decadence of that culture. Clearly, thought and remembrance of the *ātman*, their lost home, is not enough and this is what the individual in question will find as the inescapable truth of life. In the hostile and cold atmosphere in which he finds himself, he will have to go beyond mere thought and remembrance of the self, he will have to step back from his senses and Understanding and even from his moral sense to turn into the witness of all these, witness passive and innocent of itself. If a thought arises out of that passive innocence, it will be a thought true in the real sense of the term; it will be a thought creative and fruitful, a thought that cannot but bring about what it is the thought of. It is this innocent thought that will take care of his interests and his safety, his *yoga* and *kṣema*. When it is said that the Lord takes care of the safety and interests of those who are lost in Him (*nitya-abhiyuktānām* - vide *Bhagavadgītā* 9.22), the reference is to this thought of passive innocence, a thought that cannot fail in its purpose.

Thus thought and awareness of our ontological loss sustains our collective life but it is stepping back from our conditioned state of being that will take care not only of our salvation but also of our safety and interests. It was necessary to dwell on this point at some length because we of these times have lost all sense of the sustaining principles of life and of the genuine creative springs within us.

[54] *Sahaja yukti* or *sahaja yoga* is the *yoga* of *prāṇa* and *apāna*, the outflow and the inflow of breath. One who resorts to it equalises the duration of the inflow and the outflow and contemplates it with serene attention. The text will dwell on the *sahaja yoga* in some details.

[55] See Anubhava 4, section 2, part 4 for explanation of the state of *samādhi*.

[56] Notice the paradox of thinking of the truth and distancing oneself from the mind, that *other*. Man cannot simply wish away the mind, the *other* he has ever mistaken for his self. Through mind itself can he discard that adjunct of his. Mind is by nature other-oriented. Let man not think of the other but think of the *ātman*, the *ātman* he cannot think of, and through thinking of the unthinkable undo his mind, that thinking of the other. Also notice how his love, deep and ardent, is to be reserved for the Name of the Lord, the only Name true and pure. The names we know of are not names the pure, constituted as they are by their others, the forms. But the Name true is name the pure because it has no other to constitute it. Man cannot contemplate the *ātman*, he can contemplate only its name. And the name of the *ātman* is the name that it itself gives to itself. The name that a man will give it will not be its name, but a name polluted and tainted, for it will be the name not of the self but of the *other*, of that which is not the self. There is a schism, a fissure, between a thing and the name we give it, but the name the self gives itself is not its other but is the self itself. So, to contemplate that Name pure is to contemplate the self itself.

How to know that name, how to find it, the name that is not the name among the names we know of, the names that constitute us but only to deconstitute us, for our death are they, those our constitutive *others*? That name is the name that only the one established in the self can reveal, the one who has become the self itself. For the name he reveals is the revelation of the self in the form of that name. If the name that the *sadguru*, the true teacher, has revealed to his disciple, the latter reveals to another man, it will cease to be the Name true, it will turn into a name among names, the names that are our death. It will be like the dead body of a living being, divested of every power to move and to act. That is the secret true of the name true, the name that is the named itself. In the name that the *sadguru* vouchsafes to a disciple dwells all that is and all that is beyond all that is. And until a man knows that name, vain is his knowledge and wisdom, knowledge and wisdom that can bring only death to him. No spring will come to delight him, only winter, dreary and eternal, will be his lot. So let him approach a teacher true, let the latter be his sole refuge and anchor, let him win his grace, win the Name from him, in order to be the name and the named.

Anubhava Three

Samatā-nīti, The *Samatā* Way

Instruction 1

The Way Perfect to Samatā-Vision

Saying 1. To make Brahman the Word Eternal and All-pervasive one's refuge and hope - the Word Eternal that ever was and, in addition to this, to remember that Word the Eternal and know and contemplate It with intent exclusive and still; and to discard the ignorance that the sense of me and mine is and to orient one's mind, each and every moment, towards the transcendental peace that the state of being ever the same is — this in sum constitutes the *samatā* way, *the* way to it.

Saying 2. ***Samatā-yoga*, making one the Word and consciousness of the Word**: **The first principle** that leads one to its accomplishment consists in dedicating one's life to righteousness, that is to say, to truthfulness, to simplicity, to service of others, to holy congregation and remembrance of one's being and truth, remembrance of it in the form of its Name the true.

The second principle, the second step, towards *samatā-yoga* consists in the *yoga* of remembrance, sustained meditation of the Name, in making the truth one's sole refuge and hope, in fervent devotion to the Lord and giving up the pleasures of the body and the senses.

The third principle consists in realisation of the Word [the Name that is the Named too] and contemplation (*yoga*) of It, giving up [the desire for] the fruit of one's actions, resorting, that is, to the way of *niṣkāma-karma*, action without a desire, discarding one's outward-orientation and establishing oneself in the Word.

Saying 3. For one in the know of *samatā*, thinking true and of the true consists in giving up all false beliefs and making *rāja-yoga*, meditation of the Name, alone his resort.

Saying 4. The principle ever binding and imperative in the path of *sahaja-yoga*, the *yoga* that leads one straight to the state ever the same, consists in remembrance of the Lord, in realising the Word and contemplating It, in holy association - association with the preceptor true - and in striving for the good of others.

Saying 5. To hold in every esteem prophets and founders of different religions, those paths to the truth, and to live the ideals of their noble lives and to orient one's life towards the *ātman*, to self the real [instead of to the *Other*, the world] - that is the *samatā-sat-saṅga*, association true and holy congregation, for those on the path of *samatā*.

Saying 6. All social customs should be observed with utmost simplicity. There should be no display of show on the occasions of marriage or much ado on those of death. For, display and exhibition are mere expressions of the narcissistic self. A man who gives in to these forms of self-display cannot believe in the Supreme Reality that the Lord is, cannot make Him his refuge and anchor, his vision of sameness becoming dim and perverted and his life a tale of misery in excess.

Saying 7. All the ceremonies connected with occasions of joy and sorrow must always be preceded by a tribute to the glory of the Lord. Worship of gods is of no use, for mortals are related only to the Lord; He alone is their protector and He their support. Only that Power Supreme should be relied upon and believed in and to Him only dedicated all acts and ceremonies. This is an imperative absolute for man.

Instruction 2

Reformation of Ethical Life, of Spiritual Life and of One's Country

Saying 1. Simplicity, truthfulness, service of others, holy association and remembrance of the truth, of the Name, are the imperative principles for re-forming ethical life.

Saying 2. Reflection on the lives of persons the real, of *sat-puruṣas*, devotion without a self-interest to the Lord, devotion without a narcisstic desire to the spiritual preceptor and devotion without that kind of desire to one's country are the principles for re-forming **life the spiritual**.

Saying 3. To believe (*khayāl*) alike, to think alike and harmony among religions constitute the principles for reforming one's **land and country**.

Saying 4. *Sat-saṅga* is there to establish the principles of good life and of those of the good polity. Establishment of *sat-saṅga* is therefore an imperative for every society.

Saying 5. Display and show should not have any place in one's life. One's life should be a genuine embodiment of the principles one believes in.

Saying 6. To make his country and religion wake up [to the real goal and purpose of human life], it is imperative for a man that he devote his body, mind and possessions to that end.

Saying 7. One should keep oneself away from places of exhibition and show and devote one's time to make one's *buddhi* pure of faults and taints.

Saying 8. One should ever undertake work that is solid and sound, and make every sacrifice to bring about communal concord and for diffusion of the principles of good life, life devoted to the Real. With care every should one reflect on the lives of those that brought about reformation in different religions. This is the way to put an end to fanaticism and vain disputes.

Saying 9. Let every man who would be peaceful here and hereafter reform his life. Let him be of service unto others, giving up his extravagant ways and make it a point to abstain from intoxicants. Let him ever follow, with all earnestness, the way that leads to *samatā*, that foundation very of Hinduism.

Instruction 3

On Faith and Not-faith

Saying 1. To believe in the truth as it is, to make it one's refuge and support and to contemplate it with a stable and sustained intent is to live in faith. To entertain other beliefs and practices is to live without faith.

Saying 2. To worship the planets, the ghosts and the spirits or the dead ancestors, and to worship the images unconscious of the ideals they embody makes of one a non-believer, a non-believer in *Īśvara*, that self of all in each. Worship of this kind breeds only false beliefs and fears.

Saying 3. A book that does not speak of the *ātman*, the self in its truth, the *ātman* that is Brahman the Word, but describes of things doubtful and uncertain can produce - a book of this kind - only beliefs false and deluded.

Saying 4. A book that does not discriminate between the *ātman* and *prakṛti*, between the self and the body[1], does not say how to place oneself on to the path to the *ătman*, and, in their place, describes many a magical charm and insignia is a book that will destroy one's faith in the Law and the Real as it truly is.

Saying 5. A book that describes the lives of enlightened persons and what they teach is a book that reveals the Law and inspires people to believe in their being the true and live for it.

Saying 6. To read a holy book but not to reflect upon and abide by what it teaches is to undo one's faith in one's *real* self and being.

Saying 7. To be a believer or a non-believer depends on one's *buddhi*, on the power that determinates, and not on loquacious formulations of thought. If the *buddhi*, ignorant of the power of the *ātman*, would repose its faith in the planets, ghosts, spirits and many a god and goddess, then it, the *buddhi*, so disposed, is *buddhi* the non-believer, its delusions ever persisting in it.[2]

Saying 8. To have faith means that one discriminate between the body and the *ātman*; it means striving for attaining the *ātman*, taking it as the very life and breath of one's being [*viśvāsa*, derived from *śvas*, to breathe]. This disposition delivers man from the perversions of the body to establish him in the *ātman*, in his being the true.

Saying 9. The thought that has the *ātman* as its content makes one a believer, the thought given to matter, to the worship of the inert, makes one a non-believer.[3]

Saying 10. The *ātman* alone is bliss, the *ātman* alone is Being and the *ātman* alone is the Lord of all that is. That alone pervades all brittle beings, that ever the same. To believe in that Power, that giver of life, is to believe in the Real. To believe in powers other than that Power is to be a non-believer, is to deny the Real.

Saying 11. The real preceptor is he that makes one believe in the *ātman*, makes one believe that it alone is the breath of one's life, and sets one on to the path of its realisation as one's being and truth. **Discrimination between the body and the *ātman* alone constitutes knowledge in its truth, knowledge that destroys all delusions and all false beliefs. Knowledge other than the knowledge that tells the body from the self is knowledge the delusion, knowledge that binds one to delusions [set up by *Māyā*].**[4]

Saying 12. Only that book and that *sat-saṅga,* holy congregation, can reveal *dharma,* the path redemptive, the book and the *sat-saṅga* that discourse about the *ātman,* about that alone, and so can the preacher dedicated to reflection on the *ātman* and contemplation of the *ātman,* only he and no one else. Mere impostors are they that propagate about magic and insignias, tombs and cremation grounds and about all kinds of gods and goddesses; destroyers are they of *dharma,* these self-servers.

Saying 13. A man who devotes himself to righteous deeds, taking the *ātman* as their witness, and **taking all that is and happens as the will of the Lord**, he alone is a believer, and not the man given to pride and intoxicated with arrogance. To self-serving ever given, the latter is a mere hypocrite and impostor resorting to charms of many a kind to serve his ends.

Saying 14. To know the *ātman* is to know in truth and to know the Real, and to deny the *ātman,* to deny that Being, is to be a *nāstika,* is to be a non-believer. The man on the path to the *ātman* is a believer in truth, one who deserts that path and relies on gods and goddesses for his salvation is a *nāstika* and an *ajñānī (ajñānin),* one who denies the real and is ignorant of it.

Saying 15. To live as the seers of the truth lived and to seek the ideals that they sought makes of a man an *āstika,* a believer. To merely worship their bodies [or their images], ignoring the ideals their life embodied, is to be a *nāstika,* a denier of the real. Delusions after delusions will *Māyā* weave for him, birth after birth.

Saying 16. To worship the *ātman,* self the ontological, to know the *ātman* and to contemplate the *ātman* is to be an *āstika* in truth, a believer in truth, a believer in the real. **To worship that which is not the *ātman,* to know it and contemplate it is to believe in the darkness of ignorance.** To lower forms of being will he sink, to lower births, the man who believes in that darkness.[5]

Instruction 4

Spiritual Uplift - Dharma *the True*

The five means to it: simplicity, truthfulness, service, holy congregation and remembrance of one's being.

Means the First - Sādagī, *Simplicity*

Saying 1. To find *śānti,* to find peace that passes every understanding, is born this living being - to live ever in search of it. But under the impact of *ajñāna,* of false knowledge, he experiences himself instead a slave of the functions of sensing and doing and, instead of finding the peace he seeks, he becomes a victim of calamities dire and disastrous. That is the fate of all beings, human, animal and others: restless and frustrated they live ever in search of fulfillment of their false desires, but only to find in the end nothing but remorse and agony for their portion. A mystery and wonder indeed is this sport of the Lord!

Saying 2. Even men of great sight and of insight find themselves helpless in this wonder, in this sport of the Lord. They do not know how and where to seek the peace they are ever in search of and where to find it. Whatever they cherish and hold dear turns into their anguish when it is taken away from them. Every being knows and perceives this unhappy state of affairs but cannot free himself from his error and self-oblivion, his unrest accompanying him even in and after his death.

Saying 3. Men of thought saw the great malady and pain of mortal life. And seeing that pain and that agony, they sought joy the real and true, making that seeking their life's purpose. When that purpose was fulfilled, when they came to be all- blessed with that joy the real, with that peace the eternal, they desired that the whole world too should be all blessed like them. For this purpose they taught it the way to that joy and peace. And that came to be called *dharma,* the Path and *īmān* or faith, that way those souls taught unto the world.

Saying 4. Many means have been formulated by gifted souls to attain to that Path, Path the Blessed. But the primary means to attain to that end consists of the five principles enumerated above. Easy and straight becomes his way to that goal, of one who adopts these primary principles. No effort will be of any avail to man if he does not adopt these regulative principles, these means sure to peace real and eternal.

Saying 5. There is no devotion like restraint of desire, and no prayer. And there is no folly like falling a victim to desire. That is the great malady that inflicts every being, the malady of desire that is never appeased whether one finds the thing one desires or loses it, making his life a misery and a misfortune. Desolate he lives from birth to death, life after life without an end.

Saying 6. Not until he fills up the lack in him, not until he finds himself content and fulfilled in full, there will be no release from actions for him, actions that bind him to the cycle of coming and going, of birth and death. What they call liberation or attaining to the Lord is only freedom from this bondage, from this compulsion to act [and reap the fruit of one's acts].

Saying 7. An unreal thing would he enjoy, this being that has come to live in the world, taking it as real, imagining it as such. That is his disease, *the* disease of his. But not for long can that thing last. And when it actually comes to cease, the very joy the thing in question gave him turns into his misery. And it is this very process that continues to constitute his life, day in and day out. But blind to this his predicament, he continues to entertain desires, new and very many, to perpetuate his misery, the peace he seeks ever eluding him.

Saying 8. Human life is meant to disentangle him from the mazes that *Māyā* has woven for each and every being. For, a being blessed with it, with human life, can purify his soul through many a way available to him and find his home true and real. If, despite this blessing, he does not care to free himself from this disease, the disease of desire, unwise is he, his life a mere life of a beast. His moment last will be a moment of despair, for greatly will he rue this folly of his.

Saying 9. He first projects the unreal as the real, this being fallen from his being; then he senses it, feels its presence, and, then, finds himself desiring it, feeling happy when he finds it and unhappy when he fails to find it or loses it after finding it. This is his bondage great to cause him fear great and without an end. That indeed is the despairing predicament of every being, of the whole world, this helplessness, with no promise and no hope of deliverance from it.

Saying 10. The man that has cured his soul of this malady, has delivered himself from this malady of his, is man the real, he alone. Brighter than the sun shines he, his life a life and light for the world.

Saying 11. Bliss the real and eternal, that need of all needs, that power one's own and not derived from the *other*, the power one's own that is the very life of the world - that light eternal shines in each and every body, that bliss and power intrinsic. Every atom is instinct with it, its being as an atom sustained by it. This power intrinsic is what is called the Power Divine, this life at the centre of every being, finding which he finds the rest he seeks, his malady deep mended and cured.

Saying 12. Dwells that power within all, but the individual cannot find it, led astray as he is by desire, desire that ever holds him under its sway. When, however, he comes to restrain his desires, he finds manifest that power within him, that bliss the true, all his chains and fetters left behind. Find shall he then what the wise call his home the transcendental and his goal the final. That indeed is the ultimate purpose of all, the consummation absolute of their life. Let every man seek that being true of him, that fullness itself, that bliss the eternal, that fruit immortal of his mortal life. In despair will he leave the world, if fails he to find that bliss within him.

Saying 13. Man is born to strive aright, to search for the truth that he in fact is. That is the mission of his life, that search and finding. Heedful should be he of his mortal lot, thoughtful of his fated end. To free himself from desire, that malady of his life, should be his effort and his endeavour.

Saying 14. No straight way is open to man to bring him freedom from desire forthwith. Let him, therefore, seek, as a first step, to free himself from unnecessary desires. A curse, indeed, are these for those that have come to be, these unnecessary desires. To put a check on them is to create the conditions promising of redemption, conditions conducive to acts and traits good and ennobling, acts and traits that gradually soften down the fierce fury of desire, eventually bringing it to extinction. The state of freedom from desire will he come to attain then, that life of *prema*, of love that flows out to all to become all.

Saying 15. To hold in check unnecessary desires, the means effective are these only: simplicity, truthfulness, service unto others, *sat-saṅga*— to be in the presence of a seer or to participate in holy congregation— and remembrance of the truth that one is. And, of course, recourse to other virtues of a similar kind. A man who incorporates these virtues in his life will come to have command over himself, that pith and essence of human life.

Saying 16. And the man that lives contrary to these principles will remain a prisoner of unnecessary desires, his life a disgrace and a shame.

Saying 17. The guides and preceptors of every religion had only one purpose, namely, that man, this mortal inmate of this passing world, should find the bliss real and absolute. But those that came after them, their followers, made dispute and wrangling their guiding principles to lead themselves to all kinds of conflicts and tensions. Few among them were there, those of mind and conduct pure, who came to understand the purpose real of their guides and prophets, and tried to follow in their foot steps and find peace the eternal and truth the eternal. Only a man of such a disposition knows the real purpose of life. Others with different purposes live in mere ignorance, with self-service alone their guiding principle. Every being should, therefore, make it a point to investigate the truth those guides and prophets revealed and follow their righteous ways. That alone will save him, not [mere glorification of] their greatness, of those guides and prophets.

Saying 18. The first noble principle that man should make it a point to adopt is the principle of simplicity - the principle that helps him shed many an unnecessary desire to make his mind pure, and direct his effort towards the realisation of bliss the true and genuine.

Saying 19. Simplicity means simplicity in dress, in food and in thought. Compelling is the grip of these three on every living being, a helpless captive he lives of these 'habits'. To free himself from these fetters, let him resort to simplicity [as his first step].[6]

Saying 20. Simplicity in dress makes one's soul flow out to other things and beings (*prema*)[7] and abide with them and as them; it means a disposition of humility and regard and respect towards others. One given to it can manage the affairs of life with even a small income and avoid the dark and evil ways inevitable for those of excessive needs and desires. Simplicity alone is life, self-indulgence is death itself. Simplicity makes a man truly thoughtful, makes him know where lies his good and where lies his ill. Simplicity is the life of gods, fashion that of demons. One should adopt simplicity in life, resisting every temptation. For in simplicity lies the secret of joy, of joy the true and real.

Saying 21. Simplicity in food keeps one healthy in body and pure in thought. It enables one to put a restraint on passions and desires of mind, passions and desires deeply sendimented in it (*vāsanās*). A man with improper intake like meat, wine and other intoxicants is a man doomed to remain deprived and destitute of the bliss he seeks, bliss the real and genuine.

Saying 22. One should not eat the food that adversely affects one's *buddhi*, one's power to determinate, and renders it incapable of discriminating between the real and the unreal. Those who think that food of this kind is beneficial for their physical health only delude themselves. They should know that the greatest strength of man lies in the strength of his *buddhi*, his intellect. If it, the *buddhi*, comes to be tainted by heedlessness, if it turns oblivious of what is and what one is to do, then no limb of one's body will work properly and to purpose.

Saying 23. The essence of all knowledge lies in purification of one's *buddhi*. That is the instruction of the noble elders, those blessed with wisdom, for creatures of the world. For, therein lies man's glory, in purification of his *buddhi*.

Saying 24. He who takes impure food can never find the truth. Meat, wine and other intoxicants make him proud and given to anger, acts of extreme cruelty coming natural to him.

Saying 25. Cleverness or cunning are not to be equated with wisdom, cunning that people addicted to this kind of food often have. Folly is their cunning, a disposition determined and directed by *manas*, by mind, that passion to sense and to act. Wisdom consists in knowing what is right and what is not right. It culminates in beatitude [as against cleverness, that undoing of man].

Saying 26. The kind of food one takes and the kind of clothes one wears leaves a great impact on the mind. It is necessary, therefore, that one take simple food and wear simple dress if one wishes to be blessed with joy the real.

Saying 27. Simplicity of thought means communication sincere and straightforward and free from every ill will. It means communication with others in terms simple and plain, unprejudiced and unbiased. It means speaking with thought and deliberation. This kind of speech composes one's mind and comforts the listener and is a balm for many a hurt and trouble.

Saying 28. Simplicity is the foundation of authentic life. Therefore, a man who would be free from his sins or would find peace the everlasting should resort to simplicity with firm and solid faith. That is the step he should first take to achieve those ends. For, the life of show and pomp is the very root of all sins; it ruins one's conduct and pollutes one's understanding, ruins and pollutes them absolutely, rendering him utterly incapable of bringing his mind under control.

Saying 29. Simplicity is the nucleus of joy the real and of love the real. Anyone who adopts it with his mind and heart will cross all sins to be blessed with joy the real and genuine, the very end of his life at his command. Simplicity is indeed the very foundation of *dharma*, of the way to the truth and the real.

Saying 30. Miserable indeed is the man obsessed with eating and drinking. He should understand that no food, howsoever dainty and savoury, is there to appease his innate hunger, that disease of his life, and no dress is there and no apparel to fulfil his heart's desire. Hungry and naked will he have to depart from here in the end. Let him, therefore, live simple in every way before that hour of departure arrives; let him live that way to be free of sins and to be suffused with *śānti*, with peace the true.

Saying 31. The fire of desire burns to consume every mortal. And like unto oblations of butter is gratification of the passions to sense and to act; to feed that desire all aflame is that gratification to scald him more and further. There is no remedy for this, his misery, except to reflect with all seriousness on what the revelation discloses and the sages say and utter (*vicāra*).[8]

Saying 32. With the intellect all still and stable should one do this kind of noble *vicāra*, this kind of thinking, to emancipate himself from the despair and unrest that his life is. That is the means proper to make his life pure of its taints and blemishes. In no way can a man devoid of this kind of *vicāra* find any rest and peace.

Means the Second* - Satya, *Truth and Truthfulness

Saying 33. Sat, the truth, means Being, the Real that ever is and ever stays still and stable. To seek that truth, too, is the truth and also to mould one's life in accord with it and oriented towards it. And also to think aright and act aright. Without investigation of the truth this way, no one can transcend desire, go beyond its reach.

Saying 34. And, further, to be truthful in one's speech is the truth, and to be honest in one's dealings and transactions. To say what one actually thinks and feels is the truth, and to give up one's sinful ways for its sake. The truth is the way, the truth is the means and the truth is *the* peace. To seek the truth is to pray, and to live for it is to worship and to be pure. In the mazes of the world remains lost the man who would not seek the truth and would not strive for the truth.

Saying 35. The world is the untruth and the One Lord is the truth. To believe in Him is to worship the truth. To go after the truth is to go beyond this ever dying world and the woes of the world. A predator of his sight and insight is the liar, a being of cunning and fraud. Never shall his soul find its rest and be at peace.

Saying 36. No fear is there for the man of truth and no isolation, his soul overflowing to each and to all. To seek the truth, to reflect upon the truth and to strive for the truth is the acme of life, its very highest reach. Never did despair leave the man that lived not for that end. To strive for the truth is to live for the Law, Law the original and primal.

Saying 37. Man should ever do his utmost to have faith in the truth. To live for the truth is the highest penance and the highest knowledge. But hard is the way to the truth, well beyond the reach of a man not pure of sin and thoughts of sin.

Saying 38. Upright turns the man that dedicates himself unto the truth, and content and generous and suffused with feelings of spontaneous empathy. In him manifests the disposition to stay ever alike in dualities [dualities like weal and woe]. All his deviations will these traits undo and all the failings that go with mortal life. For, to liberation itself will these lead, liberation from that eternal recurrence of births and deaths.

Saying 39. Fraud and pride, arrogance and jealousy, hatred, greed and infatuations come to posses and torture the man that would not have faith in the truth and would not live for it. An embodiment of ignorance will he live, a very pain and torment unto himself.[9]

Saying 40. True unto his own truth should live every being, ever on guard against his habits and inclinations. That should be his effort, whatever the cost. For, to be true to one's truth is beatitude itself, the very root of the entire ambit of *dharma*, of the righteous Law and Way.

Saying 41. Faithful ever unto his being is to remain this being, his self-interests are not to lead him astray. Resolve firm of this kind will wash away all his sins and all his blemishes. The truth is verily the essence of all knowledge; into angels shall you turn if you live for the truth and strive for it - ever and always.

Saying 42. No unnecessary desire will ever assail the man that lives for the truth. For, of his mind becomes he the master, and of his neglects and omissions a repentant. Unto peace shall he attain, that man of wisdom, peace the real and authentic.

Saying 43. The truth is life and the truth is glory, the truth is knowledge and the truth is contemplation, the very end of life is the truth, and its very final goal. Follow you the path that leads to the truth, follow it with earnestness absolute. For many are there in wait for you, many an evil to lead you adrift and astray.

Saying 44. To live for the truth is to live in truth and to live in bliss the real, with every doubt dispelled.

Saying 45. The truth is the teaching of teachers, the thought of holy books and the miracle of divine incarnations and messengers, their very perfection and attainment. To live for it is to live for *dharma,* is to live as the Law would have one live.

Saying 46. To search for *sat*, for truth the ever abiding, is to search in truth. And to think of *sat* is joy the true and bliss the true. And to speak the truth is to be victorious in truth. Unconquerable is acknowledged the man that believes in *sat* and lives for *sat*, that thinks of *sat* and strives for *sat* and, in his dealings, sticks to *sat*. At his service abides the entire world, at the service of him that believes in God and in the truth. To live [thus] alive, truly alive, is verily to live for the Truth.[10]

Saying 47. A man who does not believe in the truth, does not strive for it and does not think about it lives to no purpose and strives for no end. Ardent austerities and meditation, piety and charity and penance hard and stern have only one meaning or purpose, viz., that man get disposed towards *sat*, towards the truth that ever is, and seek to find it with every earnestness. For, the truth alone is bliss and the truth alone is liberation.

Saying 48. As he moves towards that truth, he will find the untruth, that misfortune and malady of his, getting dispelled at each step he takes. His doubts will disappear and so will his woes, a disposition still and stable will take their place. That will be the moment when he will succeed in bringing his mind under control, his efforts towards that end become effective. He indeed is man the venerable, man the perfect that man with his mind so stilled. Passed has he the test of life and departs he from here all blessed and in bliss.

Saying 49. Search for *sat* is not to depend on any particular religious way or faith. Nature is there within man to give him intimations of that truth. But the benighted being that he is, man takes no heed of these. Only the man that ever lives in fear of death can live for the truth, and not one that lives oblivious of it. Every religion is there to seek it, that *sat* is its goal and purpose. Therefore, one should ever seek to find it, giving up all debates and disputes.[11]

Saying 50. Let a man's mind be ever directed towards the truth, lest his disposition towards the untruth have the better of him. Only then will he live absorbed in the truth. Mind, that passion for the *other*, and the functions of sensing and doing are there to ever lead him to the untruth[12]. Only thoughts pure and faith pure, thoughts oriented towards the truth and faith in the truth, can undo their impact - that of mind and of the functions of sensing and doing. Only that orientation and that faith can make him live ever dedicated to it, to the truth. In the true heroic mould is made the man that lives in contemplation of *sat*, his natural bents restrained and subdued.

Saying 51. Anyone who devotes his life to doing good unto others, giving up his concern for his own interests is the man to attain to the real ideal of *sat*. His care and concern for others will bless him with the ability to concentrate exclusively on the truth.[13] Bliss the real and true will he find and bliss the real and true shall be he.

Saying 52. A man who knows the world as unstable and transient, knows it to be so with conviction and belief, and seeks, every moment, to shed his self-oblivion, he alone is the seeker of Being. Sooner or later, the day of his awakening will arrive to bless him with bliss the true and real.

Saying 53. A man who knows how misleading are the ways of the mind and does not let this awareness go dim in him and who lives in agony deep, all remorseful of his misdeeds - he is the man to find the truth, this seeker with intent noble and good.

Saying 54. Hard to tread is the way to Being, but the way to blessedness sure it is.

Only that should be sought in earnest and with effort, that which ends up in one's well being, but well being the true. You will have lived your life in its very essence and its spirit, if your mind has turned faithful to your being, has oriented itself to it. A man who has not attained to this end, to this faith and to this orientation, has lived to no purpose, a tale of mere conflicts and tensions has been his life and despaired of every hope will he die.[14]

Saying 55. Only the man who has oriented his mind towards the truth will know the right way, a faithful follower of his prophets and patriarchs will be he to find, one day, beatitude the full. Ever you live for your Being and truth, ever work for it and strive for it! Verily, to live for Being is to live for liberation. For, if you live for Being, no more will you die and no more will you be born.

Saying 56. The *sat* it is that sustains all the powers of the world And the *sat* it is that assigns their roles unto them, each unto its own. And under the command of the *sat* operate these powers, each faithful to the role assigned unto it. Like unto these powers should live a man too, ever faithful to the roles assigned for him, faithful to the principles the Truth has proclaimed for him. That is the way he can reclaim his being and his self, that is the way to his redemption and emancipation. The world has only woes to give you, and miseries great and in numbers great. Find then all that your mind really and truly seeks and strive for that end without a let or a go. And seek and attain what the prophets of old sought and attained.

Means the Third - **Sevā**, *Service*

Saying 57. A principle divine is the principle of service, the principle great and the means great to redeem this fallen being from his fallen condition. To Bliss the Supreme does it lead him to make him own up to and be that his very own Being. A disease great and serious is the *buddhi* focussed on self-interests and self-concerns. With infatuations it roasts a being and with desires without a count to tempt him on to sins great and appalling. Infernal indeed is this, his condition. From this darkness, blind and blinding, there is the benign spirit of service to lead him on to light. No more will he remain confined to himself, the man that in his wisdom has adopted this principle. For, unto the Real will it lead him, unto that beatitude blessed and supreme.

Saying 58. Three are the desires that hold, ever and always, this being under their sway: the desire to be embodied, the desire for possessions, and the desire to think of and deliberate about the objects set up before him and to enjoy [or avoid] those objects. Never would these let him be free and at rest, whatever be his status and influence and the extent of his pleasures. Ever infatuated he lives, oblivious of his truth and being, to end up in sin and ruin.

Saying 59. Service is the means, real and effective, to his freedom from these, his fetters three. Dedicated to it, he will dedicate himself to the Lord to find in His will the joy he truly seeks.

Saying 60. His desire for possessions will come to an end and so will the hope he reposes in them when he resorts to giving and to charity, his good will and service appeasing him and his desire. Devotion indeed is this spirit of service, renunciation supreme it is, and deliverance from every ill and calamity.

Saying 61. Service without a self-interest indeed is service the real and genuine. The service prompted by some self-interest will only thicken the darkness already thick, the darkness enveloping every being. A prisoner of infatuations it will make of him to swell his pride and inflate his ego. This base disposition can do no good to him, not until his service turns pure, pure of every self-interest.

Saying 62. Disinterested service is the very goal of life. Air is there to blow for others, water is there to flow for others, the earth is there to stay for others and the sun and the moon are there to shine for others. In doing these functions, they merely perform the roles assigned to them; no self-interest do they have to serve. In the same way, a man should also serve others, taking it as his duty and obligation. Then will he carry out, in truth and reality, the command of his Lord. Not long shall he have to wait for the Blessed Joy to own him up.[15]

Saying 63. Service rendered to others with his possessions, with his body and through his mind will release a man from all his aberrations and will lead him on to find the joy undying and eternal. Service indeed is the supreme righteousness, it indeed is the way to redemption. A man who would not serve others but only himself is man the evil; ever restless and anxious, a prisoner of greed is he, and of pride and arrogance and jealousy - these evil traits ever consuming him and making his life a hell. Not a moment of generosity does he find, that man the evil. Death itself is this, kind of dark disposition, every moment will this disposition tempt one into pleasures false and delusive, from one pleasure to an other. Service indeed is the sword to cut asunder this, his entanglement in those pleasures, an easy way to that end. Bliss the Real [that very being of his] will always elude the man who feels not for others and would not care to work for their good.

Saying 64. Each act of disinterested service a man renders unto others through his body, his mind and in terms of his possessions, will take him on towards that peace the eternal. The spirit of uprightness will dawn upon him, of contentment and forgiveness, and so will the power to know what is good and evil, what is real and unreal. The Real alone will become his refuge, his life and breath. His sins will melt away, sins one and all, his peace indivisible reclaimed. That is the way one is to worship, the way genuine and authentic.

Saying 65. The false appearances that delude the living being, those deviations and fallings from their truth and their being, will come to cease for the man that gives himself to disinterested service. With the Lord as his sole refuge and resort, he will come to be blessed with joy the everlasting. This verily is the way straight to blessedness, the way straight to liberation.

Saying 66. His sense of Me and Mine will not die out, that cause of his recurring births and deaths, if he does not resort to the way of service. Let man, therefore, have every good will for others and spend his resources on them. And let him do this service with every humility in his mind. This disposition of service with humility will undo his sense of Me and Mine, that death of him, giving rise to the vision of self-sameness, the vision that is liberation itself.[16] No desire will then rise to bind him, established will he be in his own being the eternal. And that is what is called *mokṣa* or liberation or Blessedness the Eternal, that state of his.

Saying 67. As long as the sense of Me and Mine persists in man, that miserable disposition of self-service, there will be no release for him from the desires that his mind ever generates in him. Nor can he know what *dharma* in its truth is, that regulative principle of life. A man in the grip of selfishness has no principles that could inspire trust and confidence in him. That cheat and fraud has only one principle - to exploit and use others for his own ends. This disposition of his is the disposition of *rākṣasas*, of beings evil and sub-human, a disposition that will ever burn him with desires that nothing can appease. A heavy load of calamity will he carry on to the lives to come.

Saying 68. If the mind is not directed towards service of others, it is bound to get oriented towards self-service. It is in the nature of mind to be ever active, to be ever disposed to act this way or that. If it is not directed towards observance of *dharma*, of the Law, sure it is that it will get immersed in evil. Let no one be oblivious of this fact.

Saying 69. Let your mind ever remain faithful to *dharma*, faithful to the Law so that you may be blessed with peace the true and be free from the misery that has ever scorched you life after life and death after death. To keep the mind under restraint and to orient it towards the Law is the prerogative vouchsafed to man to turn his death into an ecstasy and into release, release the final from every calamity, from the very possibility of it.

Saying 70. Let man spend his possessions in the service of the deserving, let him engage his body in the service of the unhappy, the miserable and the orphans and the people at large. And let him keep his mind in check to devote it to the worship of the Lord. That is the way of release for him, release from every sin and fall. Absorbed in the Lord will he remain, in that Blessed Joy of his.

Saying 71. The man that spends his possessions in evil ways, engages his body in evil acts and his mind in self-service should be taken as man the outcast, the sinner condemned to destroy his life. *Māyā* in its form most furious and fierce unfolds itself in his life. With every effort should a man keep himself away from these deviations, deviations natural to the mind, keep himself away from them so that he may emancipate himself from every torment.

Saying 72. To hoard and pile up possessions and wealth, to feel proud of one's figure and looks and to be of a mind all immersed in desires and passions is verily to weave a snare for oneself, a snare from which no being can find [an easy] release and escape. No amount of wealth can appease man's primal thirst, no honour and no pleasure, ever discontented he will remain, even a moment's rest eluding him. With service, that effective and unfailing weapon, should be undone *ajñāna*, the false knowledge that would equate the self with the *other* and the *other* with the self, *ajñāna* that ever keeps this living being unappeased and frustrated. Only then will he find the rest he seeks, the rest everlasting.

Saying 73. A man who has nothing but good will for others, who does not hesitate the least to place his body, his mind and possessions at the service of those in need is alone the renunciate true and the giver true. He alone knows what *dharma* is, the Law is and to where it leads. To serve others indeed is to discard one's sin. That is the ideal that man should cherish and strive for with every effort and at every cost. His sinful condition will he transcend, that condition fallen, if service becomes his way and his life.

Saying 74. A man dedicated to the service of others will find himself richly suffused with qualities noble and righteous. He will find himself blessed with the spirit of love for others, and with the disposition of empathy that will make him live one with and as others. Humility and the spirit of renunciation will his life embody, and dispassion, good will and contentment. In other words, *dharma* itself will come to be embodied in him, the very life that the *sat-puruṣas,* men become one with the truth, live. This world will be at his disposal, and so will be the world to come. Rarely is born a man to lead this kind of life, an example will it be for to others follow, an ideal to strive for.

Saying 75. Anyone who seeks liberation and the way true to it must make service the very way of his life. The very essence of joy, the very life of holy patriarchs is it, of holy prophets, this spirit of service unto others.

Saying 76. A mortal being cannot shed his ignorance unless and until he acquires the power to give up the false self his *ajñāna,* his false knowledge, has projected before him. For, a prisoner of that *ajñāna,* of that false knowledge, he takes the body, that false appearance and the very source and dwelling of all passions and desires, as his very being. This ignorance of his, this his taking his body as his very being, is the root cause of all his woes and fears, woes and fears that pursue him ever and always. To dispel this delusion, the spirit of service is the way straight and smooth. Let him place at the service of others the comforts and pleasures his body makes him crave for, and purify thereby his mind of all desires for those comforts and pleasures. This is the disposition that will lead him to his being the true and eternal, to the blessedness supreme that it is.

Saying 77. To save oneself from this all consuming fire of desire, a man must sacrifice his needs for the fulfillment of the needs of others. This is the right way to that end, to disinterestedness, this way of giving oneself up gradually to service. At long last, when his life becomes a life for others, when the good of others and their comfort become his deep concerns, he will come to be the quiet passivity, come to be that peace supreme that is his home itself. So let a mortal sacrifice his desires for the sake of others, sacrifice them at all times, and thereby attain to the state where no desire stirs up, where only bliss abides, that only.

Saying 78. Spiritual teachers, holy patriarchs, divine incarnations and messengers came to the world to lead a life dedicated to the good of others. Only a man that can control his needs and desires can hold his mind under control. And a man who can control his needs and desires has, out of necessity, to take care of the needs and desires of others. That verily is the Law Divine. When he thus lives for the sake of others, lives to serve others, his mind will merge into the Real Being that he truly is, the Being for which there is no falling, no deviation from Itself. Having attained to that blessed state, he will not fall back into the worldly state of being where one has to move from birth to death and from death to birth.

Saying 79. Great is the glory of service, of this way to the truth. Anyone who took recourse to this principle was purified of all his sins and attained to the blessed state eternal. Every being that breathes should therefore seek to have this redemptive quality if he wishes to be redeemed.

Saying 80. Let him not serve others with a personal motive in mind, for service of this kind will fail to bear for him the true fruit of service. One is to resort to service for the eradication of one's desires, not to serve those desires. But only the service rendered in the right spirit will be fruitful, not the service rendered with self-interest in mind, for no real purpose will it serve, the purpose of keeping under check one's wants and desires.

Saying 81. Any person that renders service to others to serve his own worldly interests will only strengthen the grip of his fetters, with every effort he will do so. For, this way of service can only tie him further to his false self, his sins persisting as ever. One should understand that the way of *sevā*, of service, is hard to understand. Only deep and serious reflection can find its truth. Service done in imitation of others is not the service to lead one to one's true goal.

Saying 82. To give relief, with a sense of duty, to the unhappy and distressed without any personal motive is to render service in its very truth. For the man dedicated to the true spirit of service there is no better use of his body, unreal as it is, than that it be of some use to others. He knows that the call for departure will be made for him some day or the other, so why not offer his unreal life unto the service of others? A man who believes this way and acts this way alone knows the meaning true of service and he alone, the man of this spirit, will find bliss the supreme in wait for him.

Saying 83. A man who renders service unto others, thinking that it will free him from his distressing circumstances, or resorts to it out of pride and vanity or for the sake of fulfilling some other desires will miss the meaning of service as the way to the truth. Nor can he practise this principle in the right spirit. The real service is the service that is rendered to others in all humility. In that spirit should a man serve others with his body, mind and possessions. Then alone will he attain to service in its truth, service that is peace itself, peace the highest. He it is who will know his God, he alone will be wise the perfect. Rare is the man who lives as dedicated to the true spirit of service. In this very life he will become peace itself to be a blessing for those who come near him. Blessed indeed is the man that cherishes and lives this ideal!

Means the Fourth - **Sat-saṅga,** *Association with the Truth*

Saying 84. Sat-saṅga, association with the truth, is the way *par excellence* to redemption, for even a dull witted person will attain to the state highest if he resorts to it. Therefore, one should resort to it with full determination and fervour. For, a ferry verily is *sat-saṅga* to take one to the other shore of freedom. In *sat-saṇga,* in that holy association, alone can a man know what is the truth and what is not the truth, and in that alone can one truly know the principles of good government. From *sat-saṅga* emanates the spirit of love and harmony and the knowledge of good and evil. *Sat-saṅga* is the dispenser of the highest peace, and of patience in the midst of weal and woe. There is no way like the way of *sat-saṅga* to liberation, so smooth and straight. *Sat-saṅga* makes one an all-conqueror, a blessing it is for rulers, for their subjects and for their country at large, a balm it is to every unrest and adversity, a source of concord and harmony. A panacea it is for every sin and evil, an indispensable means of purification, purification of *buddhi,* the power that determinates and sets limits to phenomena. As long as one's term of life lasts, one should participate in *sat-saṅga* to sanctify one's life. [17]

Saying 85. All that is great and all that is glorious have their source in *sat-saṅga*. Of faith it is the root and of righteousness and the sustainer of life the spiritual. A man or a place devoid of *sat-saṅga* cannot but come to ruin sooner than later.

Saying 86. A man's mind comes to be suffused by the truth through *sat-saṅga,* through association with the truth. What kind of being a man is and what kind of dispositions he has are fashioned by the kind of relationships he has with others. A mere not-knowing is a man at birth but as he comes into relationship with others, he comes to be aware of the world. It is his relationships that sustain his mental being, it is these that determine what traits he will have and what qualities. It is therefore necessary that he do his best to see to it that he associate with the truth, that he participate in *sat-saṅga*.[18]

Saying 87. Austerities sustained through millennia will not bear the fruit that a few hours' association with the truth can bear. For, it is at *sat-saṅga* that a man comes to learn, without much ado, thoughts about matters secret and hidden, it is here that a man of ignorance turns into a man of wisdom. *Sat-saṅga* is *the* place of pilgrim, the source of glory and the way to redemption. A man that does not care to forge a relationship with *sat*, with truth, through *sat-saṅga* is not a human being, but a being worse than an animal. Ill fares the land devoid of *sat-saṅga*, for oblivious of the way to their true well being live its people; they live together and come together only to hate one another and harm one another.[19]

Saying 88. One should, however, know what *sat-saṅga* in its truth is. Many holy congregations are held at all sorts of places and in all sorts of lands, but they, one finds, lead to discords and conflicts, not to concord and peace. The reason why this state of affairs prevails is that people convert even *sat-saṅga* into a means to serve their self-interests to hate and be jealous of each other all the more. Their *sat-saṅga* is not a holy congregation, it is *ku-saṅga*, an unholy gang, in which breed only wicked thoughts.

Saying 89. A true *sat-saṅga* is an assembly where its participants think together and in concord about what is good and what is evil, speak and hear about them, think about them all attentive and absorbed, and let the thought in question sink deep into their minds. Where *sat-saṅga* lacks this serious concern and content, it is will not be a *sat-saṅga* but a place for mere entertainment, a mere show and pretence. No use is that show, to participate in it is to taint one's understanding and make it blind and evil.

Saying 90. To think of all that happens in life, to think of the right way to live, to listen to and think of matters these in the right way is to participate aright in *sat-saṅga*. Music and melodies do not benefit as much as to pay attention to reflections on the right thought, pay it in an atmosphere of peace and harmony with one another. The real purpose of *sat-saṅga* is to make one understand aright whatever is said and reflected upon there. With this purpose accomplished, the mind then spontaneously does the rest [reflects further on what it has learnt and meditates upon it]. If one fails to understand the truth about the things discussed there, then no use is that hearing. As for sustained contemplation of the truth, it will simply be out of the question. Therefore only *sat-saṅga* held in the true spirit can be of purpose to one who would know and find the truth.

Saying 91. A *sat-saṅga* is a place to ponder over the lives of prophets and seers, all that they underwent and endured and experienced, to deliberate every point [of their teachings]. It is a place to know in full the way that takes one to the Lord and to discriminate between the real and the unreal. The so-called spiritual teachers that convert *sat-saṅga* into a mere means of their living and, for that purpose, narrate all kinds of events [real or imaginary] to their audience but would not act upon what they preach and narrate and are inclined to sectarian and divisive thoughts are the preachers out to destroy *sat-saṅga* as the way to the truth. A preacher of this sort does not really preach, a mere business transaction he makes of his instruction. One should know what is *sat-saṅga* and what is *ku-saṅga*, holy association and unholy association, before one decides to participate in an association. This knowledge and decision is necessary if one is to realise the purpose of one's life.

Saying 92. Sat-saṅga is where they think and reflect about that state in which no enmity is there, no distress, no doubt and no pride. Where this kind of thought is absent, there prevail only disputes and cavils. *Sat-saṅga* is the very basis of every religion, where one comes to know what is right and what is wrong, what is legitimate and what is not legitimate. But since it is not held as it should be held, *sat-saṅga* often breeds and augments instead the passions of enmity and jealousy leading to all kinds of troubles and tensions. A preacher who instructs his audience into the truth in a spirit of service and without any greed truly holds a genuine *sat-saṅga,* one that disseminates peace and harmony among them. Only right and comprehensive thought can lead one to the truth.

Saying 93. The first principle that constitutes the right kind of *sat-saṅga* is that of assembling, of sitting together. The second is to think about the ways whereby one can go ahead on the right way. The third consists in knowing what is true *dharma,* the true Law, and in acquainting oneself with the lives of all the holy patriarchs. The fourth, in knowing wherein lies the good, true and genuine, of one's life here, in the world. The fifth, in understanding the obstacles in the way of realising that good and in waking up to one's primordial duty. The sixth, in ridding oneself of blind faith and holding on to true faith. The seventh, to know the cause of one's fall and to redeem oneself from the misery that it is. Add to this the blessings without a count that it bestows on the participants. It is necessary, therefore, that a seeker of the truth holds on to *sat-saṅga* in his life, that fount of right thought, right belief and right endeavour, that basis and foundation of one's uplift. All love flows from it and all purity. With every determination should one resort to it.

Saying 94. Let those who are in search of their being sit together to reflect on the real as it truly is, to get rid of their evil ways and to follow in the footsteps of the founders of their respective faiths. Let them strive for the truth and think about the real duty of man. *Sat-saṅga* is there to equip them to undertake this task. Let them resort to it ever and always.

Saying 95. A man who has no love for *sat-saṅga* and the nation that has no thought of it will never progress towards their goal, notwithstanding their persistent efforts otherwise. *Sat-saṅga* is the lighthouse, the first one, to show them the way to their uplift. Let every one participate in it and benefit from it. In *sat-saṅga* dwells the life and prosperity of a nation and from it does spread the Law. A glory limitifess is *sat-saṅga,* let one participate in it to partake of that glory.

Means the Fifth - Sat-simaran, *Remembrance of the Truth*

Saying 96. Remembrance of the truth! It transforms a man into a god, a non-believer into a believer and one given to blind faith to one given to true faith. It delivers man from the shackle of recurring births and recurring deaths and from thoughts of enmity and meanness and gives him the patience to bear weal and woe. It sets at rest this restless mind and leads the *buddhi* on to its real home and abode. All worship is this, all devotion is this, all *yoga* is this, this remembrance of the truth. The essence is it of revelations, of the instruction of teachers and of the life of incarnations. It purifies man, delivers him from the snares of *karmas*, softens down his desire and blesses him with the bliss eternal. Remembrance of the truth is the foundation, the principle of principles, their very sustenance, of those other principles. To remember the truth is to live to true purpose, to make one's life prosper in truth and flourish in truth. The means ultimate it is to free the mind from its bonds. Every holy book reveals it, and every prophet and every seer. Having been born in this transient world let every being remember the truth to redeem himself from his fallen condition.[20]

Saying 97. Only remembrance of his truth, of his being true and real, can wash a man of his sins and make him find his Lord. So let him ever believe in this holy act of remembrance. Mind is remembrance itself, it becomes what it remembers. Remembering the things of the world, it has become subject to fear and pain. To undo this its remembrance, it should be made to remember the truth so that one may be freed from the grip of false appearances that weal and woe are and find the bliss everlasting.

Saying 98. Remembrance of one's being and truth leads to the cessation of the mind-process, brings its stirrings to their final rest and reveals the Lord [that it, that truth, is]. Let remembrance of that truth become the very regulative principle of one's life, that root of all endeavours for the truth, all strivings for it, this way straight to the Lord. Remembrance of the truth purifies the mind's *dhāraṇā*, its concentration. With the purification of *dhāraṇā*, one attains to *dhyāna*, the sate of passive contemplation, and with concentrated contemplation one attains to the Divine Bliss to become that Bliss, that mine of all the blisses. With *dhyāna* becoming firm and steadfast, one gets merged in the true being of the Lord. This is what is called *jīvana-mukta* [*jīvana-mukti*], liberation in life itself. All bliss flows out from remembrance of the truth. Therefore, one should approach a perfect teacher to know the method of this remembrance and live by it.[21]

Saying 99. To be non-active while being active, to be stable in the midst of instability is the gift that remembrance of the truth bestows on man. The highest bliss is it, this remembrance of the truth, the deliverer from the adjuncts that the mind conjures up to confuse the *ātman*, the self, with them, those adjuncts. There is no desire that it will not satisfy, no bliss that it will not bestow. To bathe in its waters is to bathe in all the holy waters. Knowledge is it, realisation is it, devotion is it, *yoga* is it, love is it and dispassion is it. The glory of the *gurus* it is and the right inherited of the disciple true it is, this destroyer of all sins, this way to the all-knowing Nārāyaṇa, that Son of Man.[22] It is the highest attainment, this remembrance of the truth, and the highest illumination. With stable mind should one contemplate the truth, to resort to it is to be perfect and to dispel the darkness that the sense of Me and Mine is. For, it leads this being that has identified himself with varied states of false being to know and be their witness [witness innocent of himself], know and be that his being the true.[23] Let the man who would find his true home make remembrance of the truth a regular practice of his life.

Saying 100. Only remembrance of the truth can make the mind one-pointed. Therefore, not for a moment should one forget it. It is remembrance of the truth that makes one realise the truth, become one with it (*anubhava*) and find what is life and what is death. The Lord Supreme, that Word, pervades each and every mortal to control and regulate his life. It is the meditation of His Name that reveals that Word.[24] With steadfast mind should, therefore, the Name be meditated.

Saying 101. Only remembrance of the truth can lead one to the inaccessible land, to the state invisible. It is the key fashioned by the Divine Law to the knowledge of the whole universe. To all the perversions of the mind it puts an end to, perversions that do not let it rest for even a moment. It illumines one's mind with the light of knowledge, knowledge of the real. Morning and evening, a seeker must spare some time for it. Purified will be he of every evil and every sin.

Saying 102. Men immersed in their worldly affairs may not find it easy to spare much time for this yogic meditation and the austere life of self-denial it demands. But they must make it a principle of their life to remember their Lord every morning and evening without an exception, for that observance, if regular, will certainly lead them to their goal. Formidable and dreadful is the mind. One should, therefore, gradually orient it towards remembrance of the Lord. It is imperative that man remember his Lord to dispel all his delusions and to find the Light illumine his mind.

Saying 103. Mental remembrance or meditation of the truth is superior to other forms of remembrances. For,, it is this silent remembrance that enables the man given to it to find all that he seeks. To repeat the Name with the tongue or to repeat it aloud is to make the Name ineffective. Internal meditation done with the mind concentrated within leaves a lasting effect on the mind and sets it at rest. To the *yoga* of remembrance shall attain the man who remembers the Lord with devotion, making Him his refuge and anchor.[25] But an impostor who makes a show of his meditation will ever remain immersed in sin.

Saying 104. Remembrance of the truth leads to union with the Lord; destroys it all sins, each and every. Every book of revelation hails it and pays tribute to it. Anyone who resorts to it in the right way and method will surely attain to the Lord - will slowly and gradually be transformed into Him, will be coloured in His colour. So give your mind to it with full determination, for the day will surely dawn when you will find the goal highest. Remembrance of Name the true encompasses every renunciation, every disinterest and dispassion and every yogic discipline. Destroy will it all folly and ill will to reveal the light of *samatā*. Its glory knows no end, only the man who finds it can know what it is, his tongue will fail to express it and his pen to write about it. A wonder of wonders, the very extremity of it, is what remembrance of the Name leads one to. But only one's effort can find that. Therefore, with every effort and every endeavour should one resort to the meditation of the Lord to attain to the state fearless, the state of the Word, that abode supreme and desire-free. The very essence of the world, the very essence of the knowledge of those who know, the very abode of bliss is the Lord. So, remember Him in your mind with devotion true and sincere to put an end to the sense of Me and Mine, the sense that has ensnared you into your worldly condition, and to reclaim the state of *samatā*, your being and your self.

Saying 105. These are the five means to lead man towards the attainment of his being and self the true. A seeker of the truth must adopt these redemptive means, make them the guiding principles of his life ever and always to find the state fearless. The aim of all knowledge and of all *yoga* in their very essence is to purify the mind of its sins and make it absorbed in its real being. This supreme state can be attained - and attained soon - if one adopts these five means, these five principles, the very ideals of the wise and gifted. Every man should and must adhere to these principles with sustained determination to dispel his deluded and sinful understanding - that darkness in which he is lost - and come to rest stable in the Real that his own *ātman*, his own self, is.

Saying 106. It is necessary that man make his life come truly alive, it is necessary that he seek the joy real, it is necessary that he strive to dispel the despair that his life is and that he seek to know and find the Real. Let his life be noble to disseminate nobility, let him find the state eternal and fearless before his breath ceases to move. This moving world lets no being remain himself and no thing remain itself. Let him free himself from its grip, by putting an end to his sins, adhering to these five means to redemption. That is the way to bliss and blessedness. Only the man blessed with good fortune seeks the real and strives for it to turn into the Real itself, that bliss the true.

Instruction 5

On Pilgrimage to Tīrthas, *to Places Holy and Blessed*

Saying 1. A *tīrtha* is a place sanctified with the birth of a man blest, or with his presence or with his death. It is also a place where a war for righteousness has been fought or where the principles of the Law have been formulated or where one has lived in *tapas*, in fervent ardour, for the sake of the Lord.

Saying 2. The purpose of going to places of pilgrimage is to think of these matters and happenings, to take a leaf out of the book of the lives of those holy souls of old.

Saying 3. To go to these places without this purpose in mind is to waste one's time and resources. To bathe in the 'holy' waters there is of no use if one does not reflect on the matters above.

Saying 4. The greatest *tīrtha* is the *ātman* itself, the *ātman* that abides in every mortal, for a dip in that holy water will heal all the burns and scars that life after life have given him.

Saying 5. No use is there to prefer places of pilgrimage for acts of piety. Any place where people give gifts [to those in need of them], do service to others and do other noble acts becomes a *tīrtha*, a place of pilgrimage.

Saying 6. At places of pilgrimage, people offer balls of flour to their dead ancestors and also perform ceremonies to ensure the latter's well being in the other world. This is a silly belief, for no one can save anyone else from the results of his deeds, the latter cannot but get rewards and punishment for what he has done. This verily is the Law of the *Māyā* of the Lord.[26]

Saying 7. Anything that cools down [the passions and desires of] the body and the mind is verily a *tīrtha*. *Satsaṅga* is a *tīrtha* because it cools them down and so are thoughts about the truth and the real, and so is service rendered in true spirit and so is remembrance of the truth. Instruction from a perfect teacher too is a *tīrtha* and so are the place of *tapas*[27] and the place where true knowledge[28] is given and learnt.

Saying 8. There is no particular need to pay a visit to the traditional places of pilgrimage. To act for the truth and live for the truth is to pay a visit to each and every *tīrtha*.

Saying 9. A pilgrimage to a holy place will not bear the fruit that association with the truth, faith in the truth and remembrance of the truth will bear.

Saying 10. The way pilgrimages have been extolled has led to the decline of *dharma*, of righteousness; it is a mere propaganda of the greedy and the grabbers.

Saying 11. A being cannot perform an act holy and render a help to others with a friendly disposition if he does not believe in the Lord and live for Him and His will. And in the absence of the purity of conduct, there can be no possibility of his unrest ceasing to pursue him. No pilgrimages will be of avail to him, howsoever regular and frequent.

Saying 12. A man who has come to live and breathe for the Lord has done the pilgrimage primal and final. For that alone will save him from his helpless condition, the condition of living into death and dying into life, this process continuing without an end.

Saying 13. If you have made your *buddhi* pure, if you have made it contemplate the Real [free of its enframing concepts], you will find every atom a *tīrtha*, a place holy and sacred.

Saying 14. The beauty of a place will not make a place holy nor will the flowing waters if that place and those waters are not sanctified by the Word of the Lord.

Saying 15. There is no place where hypocrisy and wickedness flourish as much as at places of pilgrimage. The Law daily meets its death there. Can a man in search of the peace of the *ātman* ever hope to find it there?

Saying 16. If your thoughts are noble and your will pure and good, then every place will turn into a place of holy pilgrimage for you. Ritualistic pilgrimages will buy only misery for you. Noble thoughts and good will alone should be your obligatory rites. When they become parts of your life, you will have performed every pilgrimage and taken every dip in holy waters.

Saying 17. Live for the Lord and breathe for Him, strive for Him and serve His creatures! Every holy place, every sacred river or water will come to pay their tribute to you. Your holy life will turn into a sanctuary, you yourself will turn into the Place Sacred, inviolable and eternal.

Saying 18. To serve your mother and your father, to be of service to the elders and the neighbours, to serve them with every good will and feeling is verily a great act of pilgrimage.[29]

Instruction 6

On the Principle of Giving

Saying 1. Giving is to be an act of obligation, not an act for a reward here or hereafter. To give with a hope of a reward is to give meanly and pettily.

Saying 2. To give not for public welfare but to appease one's gods and goddesses too is to give meanly and pettily.

Saying 3. To give for show too is to give meanly and pettily.

Saying 4. To give with a spirit of obligation and to give as much as one can and for the right purpose is to give in truth. The highest forms of giving consist in the following:

(i) to give for the spread of education;

(ii) to give for medical treatment;

(iii) to give for awakening one's country and one's social group to their obligations;

(iv) to give for the sustenance of saints and scholars of good conduct;

(v) to give for the upkeep of the poor and the orphans;

(vi) to give for the establishment of *sat-saṅga* and for bringing about harmony and concord in society at large;

(vii) to give for feeding and clothing the destitute;

(viii) to spend for the establishment of rest houses for travellers, for digging wells, tanks and reservoirs of water and on construction of roads and bridges.

These are the noble acts of charity that bring about great welfare [of the giver and the receiver alike].

Saying 5. Next to these high forms of giving come spending for the uplift of one's clan, for winning the favour of the rulers and the officials to serve one's self-interests, and for rewarding physicians and entertainers. To spend for winning the favour of the gods and on pilgrimages is giving of the inferior kind. The pith and gist of all this is that giving as an obligation, in measure big or small, is giving the noble and giving for self-interest is giving the mean.

Saying 6. No service rendered unto others with self-interest in mind can purify the *buddhi*, the intellect [of its enframing concepts], whatever be its magnitude. Only the service rendered as an [ontological] obligation can take one towards the *ātman*. Every being that has come to live in the world finds himself a slave of his possessions, of his body and his mind. To release him from this enslavement, the way of *tyāga*, of renunciation or sacrifice, has been formulated. That very renunciation is called *dāna*, giving. He who renounces or sacrifices with no self-interest in mind will break these fetters three - of possessions, of the body and the mind, and he who makes a sacrifice with some self-interest in mind will not escape from their grip; life after life he will remain their prisoner.

Saying 7. [Renunciation or sacrifice too is of three kinds}:

(i) *Renunciation of possessions:* To make this renunciation in the name of the Lord and for the sake of the public weal is a legitimate act of renunciation. To give without the ego of giving leads to liberation.

(ii) *Renunciation of the body:* Renunciation of the body means to spend its life and resources on devotion to the Lord and for the good of others. This kind of renunciation undoes the body-ego.

(iii) *Renunciation of the mind:* To surrender all that lies sedimented in the mind, all the thoughts, desires and passions inherited from past lives {*vāsanā* < *vas*, to dwell) to the will of the Lord and to perceive all that happens or does not happen as the expression of His will and to remember Him, meditate Him [His Name], with full intent is the renunciation of the mind, its highest penance. Renunciation of the mind leads to the state passive and a-doing, that bliss the highest, that Brahman the transcendent, that home real and true of this pilgrim.

Saying 8. In sum, a man who spends his body, his possessions and his mind for the sake of others, spends these without any motive to serve any of his self-interests, is the highest giver and the highest devotee. This disinterested disposition of his and the good he does to others with this disposition will lead him eventually to freedom from the wheel of birth and death that his ego of doing sets in motion, to turn him into passivity the still. All that lies sedimented in him in the form of desires and cravings, impressions and thoughts will then come to an end and he, this mortal, will turn into Brahman the Full. One should understand what giving in its truth is and where does it lead and, then, give oneself up to it, to this path of renunciation, missing no moment of opportunity for it. This is how one can redeem one's life. This verily is the settled conclusion of the *Samatā* Way.

Instruction 7

On Idol Worship

Saying 1. He who is a prisoner of *Māyā* is verily a worshipper of idols, lost as he is in the experience of names and forms, of the modes of *prakṛti*[30], and of motions and activities to enjoy these or suffer from these. At no time does he cease to invoke the perishable, to presence it and project it.

Saying 2. To worship is in the nature of the mind. If it is under the impact of names and forms, how can it worship the One?

Saying 3. As long as desires for sense pleasures keep a man under their sway, he remains a worshipper of idols. As long as he retains the sense of his identity with the body, he is in every truth a worshipper of these, of idols.

Saying 4. As long as he is immersed in work, its fruit, that *gross* deviation, deviation with a form, will hold him under its spell.[31]

Saying 5. The purpose [of the Law] is to take this being from his worship of the gross world of multiplicity to the One and Alone. But as long as he is under the spell of mental processes[32], there can be no worship of the One for him.

Saying 6. In the path of devotion to the Lord, worship of idols can be of use only to the extent one emulates the qualities of those the idols in question represent, and follows in their footsteps to realise what they in their life realised and worked for.

Saying 7. To worship idols without perceiving the ideal they symbolise is nothing short of a folly of the first order. This worldly being is already fallen into the inert *prakṛti* and lives for it. If he resorts to worship of the inert, sure it is he will have but sorrow and pain for his reward. From darkness to darkness alone will he move.

Saying 8. To fall into the snare of *Māyā* is to fall into the snare of the gross. To escape from this bondage, worship and devotion are resorted to. Those who escaped from the fetters of *prakṛti* have left behind them the example of their lives for others to emulate and follow, lives that would instruct every being to give up his worship of the gross, of matter, and attain to the *nirākāra*, to the formless.[33]

Saying 9. When you see the bodily form of a *sat-puruṣa*, a truth-become soul, it is necessary that you adopt the ideals he lived for. If you do not adopt those ideals and hope to attain to liberation merely by obeisance, by worship of his body and by drinking the wash of his feet, then it is ignorance, dark and dense, alone that you will worship. No rest and peace to you will be vouchsafed, only unrest and frustration will fall to your lot.

Saying 10. Remember that the bodies of the holy prophets, of the messengers of the Lord, of spiritual teachers and of incarnations are composed of the five elements as are the bodies of ordinary persons.

Saying 11. Only the power of knowledge that they had is to be worshipped, their establishment in the *ātman*, in the self, that light that illumined their life. Their freedom from desire is to be worshipped, their humility and their transcendence from the affairs of the world, and their stillness and their stability - the traits that are the affluence of the Grace Divine.

Saying 12. Those persons true triumphed over their *prakṛti*, their given state/s of being, and came to be established in their true being, their true self. From the state of the gross they moved to the state of the formless. That is what is to be emulated, this their movement from the formed to the formless. If instead of following in their footsteps, a person worships only their bodies, he will only show the extent and depth of his ignorance and folly. They, those persons true, died to their bodies even when they were alive. And it is those very bodies that their followers worship! Useless and of no avail is this their worship and devotion.

Saying 13. It is the *jñāna* of the persons true that should be adored, their knowledge that made them become what it revealed, not their physical forms. The worship of their physical forms will not liberate you if you do not adopt the ideals they embodied.

Saying 14. In different forms have appeared those persons true, their *prakṛti*, their respective identities, those seeming appearances, have had different names, different forms, different traits and different modes of action. But that which manifested within them as knowledge itself, as consciousness itself,[34] was one and the same.

Saying 15. Only that knowledge, that life itself and being itself, of the persons true, is to be worshipped [and not their *prakṛti*].

Saying 16. To follow their way to redemption, the way that led those great souls from the formed to the formless is to worship them in truth and reality. Blessed will you be if you adore them thus.

Saying 17. Let that life be an example unto you and let you lead the kind of life they led, those persons true. You will find Being itself manifest in your mind, dispelling the delusion that set up the gross before you and made of you a prisoner of it.

Saying 18. Whosoever be your spiritual patriarch, your prophet or your guide, whosoever commands your faith and allegiance, be you the knowledge that he was or is. That will be your worship of him, your worship true and authentic. For, as he went beyond the reach of *Māyā* to become Brahman the *Absolutus*, so will you too if you attain what he attained: the knowledge that liberates one from the fetters of name and form, attributes and action, those modifications of *prakṛti*, that *before* of creation, that Unmanifest.

Saying 19. Worship of the gross form of that your guide and preceptor, your faith in that form of his, will not give the peace you seek. Only your faith in his inner state, state that is knowledge itself, can make you find what you seek.

Saying 20. Every embodied being born into this transient world is born a prisoner of *Māyā*, be it of the tainted kind or of the pure kind. Only by attaining that which is the truth itself, that giver of life, the giver that has no sign to indicate it, no colour to present it and no shape to reveal it, only by attaining that truth the transcendental can one attain to the blessed state of liberation.

Saying 21. Sat-puruṣas, persons the true, only those men have been that attained to that blessed truth to become that truth. The ideal they embodied and the knowledge they had are there to bless others too, those that live as they lived and find the knowledge that they found. So worship what they sought and lived for, not the gross forms of *prakṛti* they appear to have assumed.

Saying 22. To worship an image can be fruitful if and only if one follows the ideal and the mode of life it represents. Those who would not strive for that ideal and would not live that life and, prompted by self-interests, would worship a mere image with elaborate rituals and rites will only strengthen the ties that bind them to *Māyā*, the door to blessedness closed on them.

Saying 23. It is only one's own effort that can bring about what one seeks. Therefore, he who would win the game of life that the transient world would play with him should make it a point to strive for his goal as men of wisdom, those persons the real, would direct him to strive. That is the way to win that game.

Saying 24. A man who would not follow the way of the persons true, would not make their life an example to emulate, and is content to worship their bodies will end up as an idler, a man fallen from the right path. His life to come will be a life in a hell dread and fearful.

Saying 25. Let a mortal put in every effort to become that knowledge, knowledge that the persons true came to be, knowledge in its very being and truth, that dispenser of peace the eternal and transcendental.

Saying 26. As long as a man is a slave of desire, in no way can he free himself from the tyranny of the gross over him - a worshipper of idols will he remain. The only way out of this dark falsehood is the way of *jñāna*, of knowledge true, the way, that is, of self-surrender to Word the Formless and steadfast contemplation of It. This has been the way of all teachers, of wise elders and of incarnations - this way of striving for knowledge true, striving that led them to the peace eternal. Therefore, a man should mould his life in accordance with the example they set for him to emulate in order to free himself from the clutches of *Māyā*. This will be his worship true. Everything else is a fraud and worship of darkness itself. With a pure mind should one meditate on this thought.

Instruction 8

On the Worship of Gods and the Planets

Saying 1. To worship means to worship any form of the Primordial, of that which was there before the beginning of the world.

Saying 2. A worship that leads to the birth of desire and to dreams of its fulfillment is a worship degraded and degrading.

Saying 3. A worship that leads to delusion, to fear and to greed is a worship degraded and degrading.

Saying 4. A worship that leads to conceit, fraud and cunning is a worship degraded and degrading.

Saying 5. A worship that leads to jealousies, disputes and the sense of Me and Mine is a worship degraded and degrading.

Saying 6. A worship that leads to grief, anger and pride too is a worship degraded and degrading.

Saying 7. A worship that leads to selfishness and infatuation too is a worship degraded and degrading.

Saying 8. A worship that augments the sense of duality, that delusion, is a worship degraded and degrading.

Saying 9. A worship that intensifies the passion for doing is a worship degraded and degrading.

Saying *10.* A worship that is confined to a particular place is a worship degraded and degrading.

Saying 11. A worship that sustains the illusion of this world and the other world is a worship degraded and degrading.

Saying 12. A worship that does not enable one to remain still and self-same in the midst of changes in the mind and the intellect and those brought about by action - that worship too is a worship degraded and degrading.

Saying 13. Worship of gods and goddesses and that of the planets cannot save one from these deviations and these fallings from one's true being, destroy as it cannot that deviation [behind these deviations] of desire. Worship is there to redeem this being the living from his fallen condition, from his state conditioned by *prakṛti.* A worship that cannot redeem him from that his condition and instead gives rise to all these kinds of failings and aberrations is not worship [of the Primordial] but of fall and darkness itself.

Saying 14. Worship of that which itself is helpless cannot bless the helpless mortal with the peace he is truly in search of.

Saying 15. Worship of that which comes to be and ceases to be cannot promise bliss the true.

Saying 16. Worship of that which is a slave of its disposition is not the worship to give you that bliss.

Saying 17. To worship many a god or a goddess and many a planet with a myriad of dispositions is to worship ignorance itself, an invocation is it to a further fall and deviation.

Saying 18. No power is there to undo the *prārabdha karma,* that portion of one's past lives, actions and dispositions that has borne its result in the shape of the present birth. No one is there to protect one from that result, happy or unhappy. One must endure it with the Lord as one's support. Of no comfort will be these modes of worship false.

Saying 19. It is one's *karmas,* what one does through the body, the mind and speech, that make one subject to recurring births and deaths. No god or goddess can save one from that condition, and no planet. To worship them is only to distress and delude oneself.

Saying 20. The planets move and exert their influence as regulated by the Law. No worship of them can change their courses and their influence. They cannot be made to give up their nature because their nature defines their being as it does the being of everything else. Fire is there to burn, water is there to flow, air is there to make things dry and the sun is there to give heat. Will any worship of them make them give up these their functions? To give up these their defining functions would mean their end. The same rule applies to everything else. That, one may know, is the Universal Law.

Saying 21. It is a being's past actions that determine what reward he is to get and what punishment to receive. No god can do anything in that matter nor can a goddess. Their worship will only bind a being all the more [to actions and their results] and augment his unrest and his delusion.

Saying 22. To emulate the deeds and traits of gods and goddesses is to worship them in the right sense of the term. One must know what power they had that made gods and goddesses of them and to what end was that power directed. This kind of worship sets one on to the right path.

Let one be as noble in one's acts as they were, let one be of service unto others as they were. That will be one's true worship of them. It is one's deeds that make one a god or a demon. Therefore, it is one's actions that one should seek to purify. For, that is the way of the gods and the goddesses.

Saying 23. To worship gods and goddesses with some desire in mind and not to adopt the way they act or the qualities they have is to worship in vain, is to worship for pain and misery.

Saying 24. Your actions alone can bring about what you desire, no god and no goddess can do that for you.

Saying 25. Actions are the cause of death and of birth, of woe and of weal. There is no power that can free you from these their results, no escape from them being possible. Teachers and holy men, incarnations and men of wisdom, prophets and divine messengers - all have to taste the bitter-sweet fruit of their past deeds. This is how the *Māyā* of the Lord plays its play.

Saying 26. Keeping these things in mind, let a mortal purify and reform his acts. That is the way out of his miseries.

Saying 27. Inevitable is the result of actions done with the mind, with the intellect, and with the sense- and motor organs. No one can deliver one from that result, no worship of gods and goddesses, worship performed with all one's mind and body.

Saying 28. To worship gods, goddesses and the planets is to lose one's faith in the Lord and in the way of right action. Of all sins lays the foundation this worship, if it is devoid of consideration of the life and qualities and functions of those powers.

Saying 29. To be free from desire and to care for others will ever remain beyond the reach of those that are dedicated to the worship of gods, goddesses and planets. Delusions and fears alone will be their portion. For mere greed would they waste away their priceless life.

Saying 30. Good deeds will make of you a god and wicked deeds a demon. So ever remain steadfast in your resolve to do the deeds that will lead you to your truth.

Saying 31. Worship performed with a self-interest in mind is worship against the spirit of the Law. From birth to birth it will lead you and from death to death.

Saying 32. There is no escape from this process of recurring births and deaths and the world they disclose, there is no escape from this worldly mode of life, so hard to escape from, than the knowledge that makes a mortal become one with the Lord, and the devotion dedicated unto Him.

Saying 33. That Lord the Omnipotent dwells within each and every mortal. He it is that makes the gods and the goddesses shine and also the planets. Who else is to be worshipped than Him, the Perfect? Of no avail will be worship of the perishable, for only delusions can it dispense unto you, the delusion of recurring births and deaths.

Saying 34. He alone is to be worshipped, that Lord the Witness within you. Only His worship will free you from the labyrinths of doing.

Saying 35. Whatever you have done cannot but bear its fruit and make you taste it. But devotion unto the Lord will undo your passion for that fruit. There will remain no dualities for you to contend with then, and no conflicts of the opposites. And that is what is called the state of joy the real, the state where no dualities obtain.

Saying 36. There is only one way to escape from the sooty confusion let loose by *Māyā*. And that is the way of devotion unto the Lord. And that is what one must adhere to.

Saying 37. Worship you must the Indivisible and Imperishable. For that alone will deliver you from desire, from that malady great of yours.

Saying 38. Contemplate the One Lord you must. In patience will you bear then the fruit of your deeds, past and present.

Saying 39. And must you contemplate the Lord if you'll be free of desire and of fear.

Saying 40. All that is glorious in the world, all that is of power in the world only worship of the Lord can give you, Lord the Omnipotent. So worship Him you must.

Saying 41. Not to worship Him but to worship the gods and the goddesses and the planets is an act of big folly, an act that denies Being and Reality.

Saying 42. There is no power like the mind. A god it turns when it comes to be established in the being of the Lord.

Saying 43. Verily, a god is he who acts for the truth and lives for the Lord.

Saying 44. The most proximate among the proximate is the Lord, that ever attained, that knower of each and every mortal. With purity itself as His being is that ever the same, that all-powerful in Himself, that light that illumines this perishable world. To worship the powers perishable, to worship the beings that themselves are victims of desire and not that Lord is to worship in vain. For darkness will you worship if you worship them, darkness alone and ignorance.

Saying 45. Worship the Lord whom gods have ever worshipped. It is imperative you adore Him and Him alone.

Saying 46. He is one and gods are many. And he who adores not the One but the many will not find his goal. Only doubts will he have - to gnaw him, and only woes to torment him.

Saying 47. Purify your thoughts and adore the Lord the way the gods adored Him. Their adoration of the Lord made the gods blest and wise. That was the worship true and that is the worship for you to adopt, that worship of that Primordial Father.

Saying 48. Ever adore Him, submit to His will, be your portion weal or woe. Rule over all the gods you will, if you devote yourself unto Him. Therefore, remember that Power the Supreme, that Son of Man, that Word. that All-pervasive. Think of Him, sing of Him, meditate Him and, all passive, contemplate Him. That is the true worship, that is the way to liberation.

Saying 49. Let the glory of the Lord suffuse your mind, only His glory and of nothing else. The glory of the gods is verily His glory, it is His glory that shines in them. He alone is to be adored, that Dispenser of every weal. With peace the eternal will be blessed this mortal being if he has faith in Him and if he worships Him.

Saying 50. That Power Supreme did they all worship, all the incarnations and the blessed ones, and the seers supreme and teachers, and men of wisdom and prophets and messengers. It is His glory that they revealed unto the world. But their self-professed followers concealed that glory and adoration of the Lord that the great ones had revealed unto the world. They urged the world, those false followers, to worship not the Lord but His worshippers themselves. Only to make their living certain and their pleasures secure was the purpose behind this their fraud.

Saying 51. That supreme *ātman*, that life and power, illumines all that is. Ignoring it, they of the world adored all kinds of gods and goddesses to turn self-centred and self-interested, jealous and fraudulent to generate only miseries for themselves.

Saying 52. Believe in the One Lord. Your *buddhi* should be directed towards that end, and rightly directed so. So should be your striving and so should be your thinking. Remember Him alone and contemplate Him alone. And see His light in the world entire. That is the way to worship Him, the way that blesses the worshipper with the joy blessed, the way that would make a god of him. So, let man ever believe in the Lord and serve His world. That is the duty supreme, the devotion supreme, the highest *yoga* and the highest attainment. All else is deception and fraud. With mind pure and unblemished should one consider this.

Saying 53. Selfish and self-killer is the man that makes offerings to gods and would not offer himself unto the Lord. No god will come to him to accept his offerings and shower favours on to him. This way of worship is the invention of the benighted souls, a mere means of their living is it. Only faith in the Lord and service of the people can pave the way to redemption, the way to godhood itself [and not this way].

Saying 54. The man who makes offerings of meat, wine and other things in the name of gods and the man who receives them are both impostors and frauds, destroyers are they of the way of *dharma* the true.

Saying 55. Worship of the Lord and service unto the world are the ways proper for man to attain to liberation. Those who sacrifice animals to the gods stray away from the Way and are born as sub-humans to receive punishment for their sins.

Saying 56. The state of *samatā* alone is the ideal that gods and goddesses live for. That is the state wonderful of the Lord - to be ever the self-same. One should therefore reflect on the lives of gods and goddesses and try to attain to that state, the state ever bright and blessed. That verily is the way true for you.

Instruction 9

On Ghosts, Wandering Spirits and the Fathers[35]

Saying 1. Every being born into the worldly mode of being has two constituents, namely, the conscious principle and the inert principle, that is to say, *prakṛti*, the power that causes manifestation. The conscious principle is purity itself, is eternal and ever the same, infinite it is and without a beginning and an end. That is the source of the world, that principle that ever subsists as itself in the midst of all the three dimensions of time.

Saying 2. Prakṛti, that power behind every manifestation, gives rise to varied elements [gross and subtle], elements that act and react with and against each other to undergo many a change and modification, and, in that process, ever come to be and ever cease to be. The changes they undergo, these elements, are termed birth and death and the world with its varied forms and appearances.

Saying 3. The conscious principle that appears to be in the grip of *prakṛti* is what is called *jīva*, the living being, one that experiences the elements, enjoys them or suffers from them. This *jīva* has no being of his own. Whatever bodily forms he assumes as a result of *vāsanā* - the ideas and the images, the thoughts and the passions, etc, inherited from his past lives and dwelling deep in him - that very form of *prakṛti* and its name he assumes to be his being and his name. This is what is called *ajñāna*, false knowledge, this identification with a form of *prakṛti*, assuming it to be one's own native being.

Saying 4. It is in the nature of *prakṛti* to be ever changing. A radical form of its change is called death. Coming to be and ceasing to be is what constitutes change of *prakṛti*. A mere deluded vision of the *jīva* is it, is *prakṛti*, a setting up by him.

Saying 5. When this living being discards one body, he creates, takes on himself, another body in accord with his *vāsanā*, the desire inhering in him. It is his *ajñāna*, his deluded understanding, that makes him identify himself with that other form, that other body. This way he assumes, that is to say, he manifests, varied forms of *prakṛti* under the compulsive force of his desire.

Saying 6. The name related to a particular body perishes with that body. The being that lives with the body has no name of his own. Therefore, the concepts about the forms of ghosts, spirits and fathers are all false and are mere delusions.

Saying 7. Whatever new form this being sets up and takes on, he identifies himself with that very form and the name of that form. His old name and form he no longer remembers and no longer identifies with.

Saying 8. Take the case of a dead man that assumes, under the impact of his tainted *vāsanā*, the form of an animal. In that state, it is that animal form of his that he knows to be his being, it is with that form alone that he finds himself identified and infatuated. His former human birth and nature, its name and form, he can have no experience of. Nor does he have any sense of his identification with it.

Saying 9. Therefore, there are no such things as ghosts, spirits and fathers, mere projections of the mind are they. Giving up one bodily form, the living being assumes another bodily form to assume the name of that very form. He himself has no permanent name of his. With his form changing, his name too changes. That is what is called the cycle of recurring births and deaths.

Saying 10. When he finds *Māyā* or *prakṛti* as merely a false appearance and comes to know his true being, being that is mere *bare* existence [and not an existent], there remains no longer any change for him, no death and no birth. Only his real being remains for him to merge into. As ice melts into water to become water, as an ornament melts to turn into gold, as a pot breaks to turn into earth, in the same way this being turns into his own true being, Being the eternal, when his ego-sense, that cause of birth, comes to cease. Then is he said to have attained to *mokṣa*, to liberation.[36]

Saying 11. Suppose for a moment that there is such a thing as a disembodied spirit. Even then, it will turn out to be a mere imagining, something the living being has set up to identify himself with. He will have to exhaust the deeds that brought about that state for him by going through the bitter and sweet results of those deeds. No ceremonial acts on the part of his descendents will free him from that condition. Anyone [a priest or someone else] who claims to free him from that condition is only a cheat and a fraud.[37] Every being has to answer for his deeds, there is no one to free him from that obligation.

Saying 12. The embodied state that a being finds himself endowed with consists of *buddhi,* the determinating power, *manas* or mind, that organ of desire and deliberation, *ahaṃkāra,* the I-sense, space, air, fire, water and earth. All these eight elements from *buddhi* to earth are set up by the *jīva* himself. These constitute *prakṛti,* these elements. Every being comes to be embodied through setting up these elements. As long as these eight elements do not come together, the being in question cannot come to be fully embodied.[38]

Saying 13. Ghosts, spirits and fathers have no being of theirs, they exist only in the imagination of those who believe in them. They do not have their being in *prakṛti,* that assemblage of the eight elements, an assemblage that becomes manifest only in a gross form. Apart from those elements, no being can ever exist. Therefore, there can be no such things as ghosts, spirits and spirits of the dead fathers, beings without the gross body. They are conjured up by the sense of fear, that product of one's sinful deeds. To sum up the matter: there are only four kinds of beings, those born of seeds, those born of eggs, those born out of moisture and those born out of water. To think of other beings is to think in ignorance.

Saying 14. Those of extremely wicked conduct are given these names. Beings of this kind are born in sub-human forms to continue with their wicked ways. They alone are evil spirits, men given to such wicked ways. As sub-human beings do they live, as the very images of those beings, identifying themselves with their dispositions, those of sub-human beings. They alone are called ghosts, evil spirits and the Manes. Not that there are in fact and truth such beings as ghosts, evil spirits and the Manes.

Saying 15. Let man ever believe in the Lord. Let him purify his actions. Let him give, give charities, in the name of the Lord alone, keeping himself away from thoughts of ghosts, spirits and the Manes. This mortal being is born in many a form in accordance with what he has done, but howsoever subtle those forms, they are *capable* of being visible. Of base and degraded states of being merely are these the names, the names given to these imagined phantoms, the so-called ghosts, spirits and the Manes; no objective reality do they have. Those who believe in and feel their existence, of these so-called disembodied spirits, and worship them will find themselves sink very low in the scale of existence. Therefore, man should give up such misconceptions and devote himself to noble deeds with the Lord as his support. Only this kind of disposition will lead him to the highest state, that blessed state of liberation from further births and deaths.

Saying 16. There is only one way to disentangle oneself from the net that *Māyā* has spread out to ensnare every being, namely, the way of devotion to the Lord and dedication to noble deeds. Those who worship ghosts, spirits or the Manes will never find themselves redeemed from their worldly mode of being.

Saying 17. Every being is rewarded or punished in accordance with what he has done. So, let him ever purify himself and his actions. He who himself wanders in darkness cannot possibly save the so-called spirits or the Manes from their unhappy condition. Let him take care of his own deeds, let him see to it that they remain pure and noble, and give himself up to remembrance of the Name and contemplation of the Lord. That is the way to his salvation.

Saying 18. Those who would not devote themselves to the Lord and would not give in His name and would not care to do righteous deeds and, instead, worship ghosts, spirits and the Manes are creatures lost in the darkness of their ignorance. They know not what *dharma* is, what the righteous way is. In delusion and superstition do they waste their life.

Saying 19. Let every being think of the goal of life and the way that leads to that goal. When he himself is in fetters, how can he hope to release others from theirs? The mere thought of it is absurd! So, let him reform himself every minute and every hour.

Saying 20. As long as this mortal being does not purify his conduct, his release from those fetters is out of the question. So, let him live as souls the real lived, those persons that had attained to their true being and self, and realise the goal of life and free himself from the bonds of *Māyā* to find that which is bliss the supreme itself.

Saying 21. No pilgrimage will be of any avail to him, no deity and no *mantra* until his acts and deeds do not get pure and clean. Purification of one's deeds is, in fact, salvation itself.[39] Those who would not purify themselves and hope to be saved by their children after their death merely live in illusion.[40]

Saying 22. He who strives will find. No one else will ever come to save him but his own pure ways and life. So let his life ever move towards righteousness if he would attain to his end.

Saying 23. A man who lets himself be deceived by such deluded beliefs will never find the peace his being and life ever seek. Discarding these false notions, let him rely on the Lord alone for that end, let Him be his sole support and anchor.

Saying 24. It is the ontological right of every mortal to attain to liberation from his worldly condition. But it is his own striving that can lead him to that end, he cannot rely on others [his children or others] for it. So let him strive for that end before death comes to overtake him [for, no ceremonial piety on the part of his children will help him in the other world].

Saying 25. Only he will be liberated who does not let himself entertain such false beliefs as those related to spirits and the Manes and lives with the One Lord as his only support. And with Him as his sole support, who gives himself up to noble deeds and avoids every thought of evil. And who remembers the Lord with every faith, thinking

Him alone as the maker and destroyer and viewing all that happens as ordained by Him and Him alone. And who serves others in all humility. Bliss the desire-free will such a being find, bliss the supreme. No more will *Māyā* weave its illusions to tempt him out of that blessed state, that goal final of mortal life. Let this be your belief and your conviction!

Instruction 10

To Religious Teachers

Saying 1. It is the bounden duty of a religious teacher to know the Way and follow the Way.

Saying 2. He is not competent to teach, has no right to teach unless and until his own mind becomes completely pure, pure of every *vāsanā*, every after-impression his past lives have left sedimented in him.

Saying 3. To teach for the purpose of awakening people to the Way, to teach them with the disposition of disinterested service and with empathy for their unhappy condition is to teach in the spirit right and true.

Saying 4. The teacher that teaches others to serve some purpose of his own, for his livelihood and for self-celebration or to mislead others [into acts of fanatic intolerance of other faiths] is a wicked teacher, a threat is he to his nation and to his faith.

Saying 5. A teacher who is not dedicated to a life of truthfulness, of simplicity and service to others and who does not believe in the truth [underlying and at the basis of all that he perceives and experiences], does not dedicate his life to that truth and does not remember it and contemplate it and who does not feel for others and feel with them is a teacher wicked and fraudulent, howsoever learned and erudite he may be.

Saying 6. A teacher who does not wear plain clothes, does not eat what is pure and does not speak plain and simple, who, in other words, is not humble and suffused with love and goodwill for others is a teacher out to destroy *dharma*, the Way.

Saying 7. A teacher who is vain of his learning and does not live simple and speak simple is also a degenerate teacher.

Saying 8. A teacher who takes intoxicants, is fond of shows [cinema, etc.], cards, chess and gambling and who eats meat is a teacher wicked and evil, a master of the four Vedas though he may be. His instructions will destroy the righteous ways and will spread only evil and sinfulness.

Saying 9. A teacher who has no feeling for orphans, for the helpless and the poor, who teaches for the sake of wealth and honour is also a teacher wicked and evil.

Saying 10. A teacher who does not teach in plain terms and is fond of talking about matters complicated and deep and is rude and arrogant in speech is also a teacher hypocritical and fraudulent.

Saying 11. A man given to pleasures of the mind is not the man to guide the world unto the right and the truth.

Saying 12. A teacher who is a mere book worm and has no *anubhava* of the truth, has not known the truth and become the truth, is not the man who can grasp the Way, much less make others have an inkling of it.

Saying 13. A teacher who narrates all kinds of ancient happenings and lore but has not adopted any of their precepts is a mere sham and swindler.

Saying 14. A teacher whose teaching gives rise to jealousies and disputes teaches only to undo *dharma*, to undo the Way.

Saying 15. A teacher who does not know Brahman and has not become one with It, whose faith is related to lower deities is a teacher petty and insignificant.

Saying 16. A teacher devoid of truthfulness, humility, desirelessness, disinterestedness and regard and concern for others is, despite all his learning, a fool indeed. His teaching cannot reveal the Way in its truth.

Saying 17. A religious teacher devoid of faith in the Lord, of good will towards others and generosity of spirit is a cheat and hoax. Unto darkness does he lead those who listen to his teaching.

Saying 18. Ruins he the Path, the teacher who identifies himself with the body, his clan and his caste and is proud of his learning.

Saying 19. A teacher who does not fear death and has no devotion for the Lord will never be delivered from his sins nor can he show unto others what is right and true.

Saying 20. A man who instructs others for their applause and not out of regard for them is verily a destroyer of faith.

Saying 21. A man who instructs others with his own interests to serve is verily a destroyer of *dharma*.

Saying 22. Realisation of the truth alone blesses a man with peace the absolute. A religious teacher whose heart has not been suffused with that peace cannot show unto others their truth and their good, whatever the extent of his learning.

Saying 23. A religious teacher who is a mere scholar and is devoid of devotion to the Lord and has all his desires unspent carries his learning as a beast would its burden.

Saying 24. A community which is replete with men of learning but has no one endowed with faith in *dharma*, in righteousness, is a community doomed to destruction, for learning without practice is learning for disaster. Let there be no doubt about this.

Saying 25. A religious teacher whose doubts have not come to be dispelled, nor have his deluded beliefs will not find the peace he seeks nor will he make others find it. Of no avail will be his learning to him or to others.

Saying 26. A religious teacher for whom religion is a mere pretence, a mere mask of an arrogant respectability that he must put on to serve a given occasion is a mere hoax and fraud.

Saying 27. A religious teacher who does not contemplate the One Lord with faith true and living, whose mind is ever tied to worldliness and has no good will for others and no active concern for their well being, is a man of sin, with all his study and learning.

Saying 28. A teacher devoid of regard and care for others, who believes in divisions and not in harmony, and is selfish and self-serving is a man unfit for any society.

Saying 29. A man who is arrogant and vain of his learning and who holds, in his mind, everyone else in contempt and is addicted to the pleasures of the organs of sense and action is not a man of learning but a dog who is there only to tear the world and consume it.

Saying 30. A religious teacher who is fond of preaching to women, is given to greed and is an easy turncoat is like unto a crow, ever cawing as it would. Nothing is sacred for him, neither *karma* nor *dharma*, neither a noble deed nor the Law.

Saying 31. A religious teacher who believes in one thing and preaches another is a cunning fraud, born only to bring ruin upon the world.

Saying 32. A religious teacher who is fond of singing and plays on musical instruments with much ado, now laughs and now dances is also a cheat and a hoax.

Saying 33. He whose mind has not risen above the temptations of the world, who does not fear sins and has no love for creatures in his mind - a man of such a disposition will never know what the Law is. In no way can he be a guide unto others on the way to the right and the true.

Saying 34. Learning is a must for a religious teacher and so is sustained meditation. And so is humility and so is freedom from desire. A teacher so equipped is indeed a blessing for the world.

Saying 35. A man of a mind pure of all its sins, his devotion and faith in the Lord firm and stable, his being ever given unto meditation of Him, with Him alone for his support and no thing of the world, is indeed a teacher true. He is the teacher to reveal to the world the way to its being and its truth. Duty bound he finds himself to serve all creatures, for perceives he them, those creatures, as the forms of the Lord, the forms that He Himself has assumed.

Saying 36. An asset for a community is indeed a religious teacher that teaches them how they are to make their life better, life social and spiritual, how to adopt it and live it.

Saying 37. The teacher who has known and realised the Real, who is patience itself and feels the pain of the unhappy and miserable and is straight and bereft of hypocrisy and pretence - a teacher of this kind is a teacher to proclaim the Law unto the world.

Saying 38. A teacher that embodies the true spirit of *tyāga*, renunciation, who has come to abide in the Bliss Divine and who wishes all the creatures well is truly the Law incarnate. That is the truth about him, the truth one should know.

Saying 39. With his sense- and motor functions well under his control and his mind completely at rest, with no desire welling up in it, a teacher true abides as patience itself whatever his portion, whether weal or woe. Verily, the Law itself is such a teacher, Law in the shape of a man.

Saying 40. A teacher who abides in the Same and strives for the Same and teaches the Same is verily the teacher to free people from their fetters of the Me and the Mine, fetters dreadful and appaling. He it is that speaks the truth and lives for the truth.

Saying 41. A teacher that abides passive in activity, abides so every hour and every minute, who, that is to say, abides as the *ātman* itself, and is suffused with love for creatures and has all his passions burnt out, is verily teacher the liberated. Of the entire world is he the teacher to reveal unto it the Way.

Saying 42. A man who has overpowered all the passions of the body, passions that ever deviate a being from his true being, and has attained to Brahman the Word and remains ever lost in devotion to the Lord is a man that knows the Real, the Real as It is. He alone is a teacher in truth, he that knows the truth.

Saying 43. He who finds Brahman as manifest in him and who has been liberated from that deviation called *Māyā*, is a teacher to grant liberation unto others, that goal final of life.

Saying 44. He who knows what it is that the whole world is destined to be, who knows how *Māyā* binds and releases, projects itself and withdraws itself, is a man to teach the world into blessedness.

Saying 45. A teacher that first knows the truth and then explains it is a teacher to make the ungifted gifted and the impoverished in spirit rich in spirit.

Saying 46. A man who has instructed his own mind into submission is truly a teacher to instruct the world into liberation.

Saying 47. A teacher who abides by his word and will not disown it for his life itself - he in truth is a teacher holy, a teacher dedicated to *dharma*.

Saying 48. A teacher that has offered his body, mind and possessions unto the Lord and is firm of resolve is a teacher true and genuine.

Saying 49. A teacher who is ever engaged in service of the unhappy, with no desire left in him for his own happiness, and is ever devoted to the Lord is, that teacher, verily the light itself of the Law.

Saying 50. A teacher ever given to righteousness, deeming himself a mere servant of the world, his mind replete with good will for each and every being, and his love alike for others and for his own, who is truthful in speech and well disposed in mind and is all devotion unto the Lord, and is full of humility and active compassion for every being - verily a teacher so gifted redeems the whole world, the very embodiment of the Law is he, the very incarnation of *dharma*.

NOTES

[1] It may be noted that the text equates *prakṛti*, that *before* of creation, with *śarīra*, the ever dying body. The meaning is that it is identification with the body that is the *before* of creation, the cause of its manifestation. With the rise of the body-sense rises the consciousness of the world. This should not be taken to mean that the text deviates from its earlier statement about *kartāpan*, the sense of one being a doer. Identification with the body and *kartāpan*, that root cause of the world, go together. To seek one's self in the body is to ever fight against its perishable nature, it is to turn into a doer. 'Śarīra', the word for the body, we may remember, means that which ever decays, that which ever dies *(śīryate)*.

[2] *Buddhi*, the power that determinates things, puts them in categories, comes to be a believer in the *ātman* when it ceases to conceptualise it, ceases to set limits to it, that is to say, ceases to make an object of it. If instead of the disposition of innocence it comes to entertain a disposition that would know and have beliefs, then it will deny the existence of the *ātman*, its real inbeing, and many a false and deluded belief will come to possess it. The primary delusion will be the delusion that mistakes the body for the self, superstitions and false beliefs will come later. Realism, the faith of modern times, realism that relies on the concepts of the *buddhi* for knowledge and power is no less false than the superstitious beliefs the text mentions. Rather, it is more pernicious than those beliefs. A superstitious man is at least aware of the limitations of his theoretico-practical powers, of which the man seized with the passion for endless knowledge and power has no inkling. Superstitions bring misery to man, the Faustian passion destroys him and his cilivilisations.

[3] Modern civilisation rejects worship of God and gods and other religious beliefs, sound or false, in favour of the worship of matter. That alone is the God supreme for modern man - matter along with its laws. This belief of his has made of him a *nāstika, a* disbeliever, this his disposition towards matter and its laws. The word *āstika*, derived from *asti*, 'there is or exists', means one who believes in being and existence, the word *nāstika* means one who denies reality, who is a nihilist absolute. A believer in matter as

the sole reality is a nihilist *par excellence*.

4. Knowledge that leads one to the *ātman* alone is knowledge in truth, knowledge of the *other* is ignorance itself and misery absolute.

5. A man who is aware of the not-self, aware of the world and the percipient of the world, and who finds these as real, the world and its percipient, is a denier of the real, and a man who is not aware of himself and the world, does not find himself placed in it and related/not related to other beings in it, is a true believer, is a man of true faith. To *be* is to deny one's being and not to be is to find it. Our superstitious beliefs murder the real, so does our worship of gods and goddesses and so do our knowledge and practice directed towards what we perceive, experience and think about. Our knowledge is our death and our actions suicidal, be our knowledge philosophical or scientific, be our practice mere foolish rituals or systematic experimentation.

6. For us, creatures of the world, food and clothes are our need and necessity. As for thinking, it is our compulsion, of us who are precariously placed between what we call past and future. But notice how the text reduces these our needs and compulsions into our *habits*. The need to eat is not our genuinely innate need, not of the *ātman* that we are, but of the body on to which we project it. The need of that *other*, we, in our ignorance, superimpose on to our self. This is the habit we have fashioned life after life, the habit of attributing the traits of the *other* to our self. Our natural needs are not natural needs but habits we ourselves have formed to make us helpless.

When we come to clothes, we do not confine ourselves to what we call our need, need that is only our habit, we extend this need to desire, desire to celebrate ourselves. Man is born a percipient of the world but he would not remain content with that condition, he would make himself the perceived and the noticed. Instead of taking notice of others around them, attend to their form and shape and their life, men and women would make others take notice of them, not of their life and being, but of how they appear. Obsession with dress makes a living being an inert object, it reduces his/her being to his /her looks, reducing the *others'* being too to a mere gaze and, eventually, to their looks – not their natural looks but looks that are made up and fashioned. Primal ignorance that makes one confuse one's being and self with the body and vice a versa murders the *ātman*, but fashion murders even that false self; it makes the perceiving being a perceived object, as if his/her life depended merely on the look of others.

Thinking becomes a compulsive necessity for us because when we identify ourselves with the body, we turn ourselves into mere contextualities, make ourselves problematic beings problematically situated in a problematic world, that network of relationships and contrasts, of cause and effect. We find ourselves as the present moment between the past of that world and its future, for that is what the present moment precisely is, namely, the uncertainty that we are, uncertainty between the past and the future, the past and the future that the uncertainty that we are renders too as uncertainties. This uncertainty that identified with the body in order to *be*, in order to be an identity and certainty, finds itself still in search of identity, forcing it to work and struggle for it. We who would be placed, thus ever find ourselves deplaced and desituated. As exiles we live, we who would be at home. Thinking becomes our necessity because we ourselves are problematic as our life is. The homeless and deprived cannot but think, think either to understand the nature and cause of their exile, or, in the majority of cases, fabricate homes where no home can be, make that their land where no land is. As men of greed seek ontological security in possessions, the gluttons in eating, the vain in show and pretence, men of thought would seek it in their thinking, forgetting the cause of their thinking – their ontological lack. There is a thinking done by the greedy, by the gluttonous by the pretentious and hypocritical and by what are called men of thought. Each of these kinds of thinking seeks reality in illusion, would slake its thirst in the mirage, to use the much used Indian phrase. Simplicity in thinking means thinking that does not impose what our passions seek on to what is real and make it answer to its own narcissistic needs, theoretical, practical or plainly hedonistic. Only an opening out is this kind of thinking, opening out straight and innocent, to what *is*, it is a thinking towards innocence and not towards what we call knowledge.

7. *Prema* or *preman* obviously cannot mean here the narcissistic love.

8. Independent thinking is, for the text, our bane, not our blessing, prompted as it is by our passion to be, to be this or that state of being. It is the primordial ignorance gone articulate, a covering and closure, not a revelation and disclosure. 'Vicāra' here means reflection on the word of revelation and of a seer, it does not mean thinking as the term is generally understood.

9. Belief in an eternal God has been frowned upon by many a gifted thinker of our times, who believe that to acknowledge one's truth of mortality and to live that truth is to be not only heroic but also to be true to fact and reality. The criticism is out of place, the result of a superficial understanding of the true nature of the religious belief. The truth is, our text says, that which ever *is* and the unreal is that which ever disowns itself. Our mortal condition disdains our attempt to project being on to the unreal, to superimpose our self on to it. We do not live as mortals, rather, to be more accurate, we do not live as mortality; we live only to fight against it in order to *be*. But no state that we know of can tolerate this our obsession, it ceases to be the moment we try to affirm our identity with it. To live as mortality, to live that disowning, is to undo our *ajñāna*, our primordial ignorance, ignorance that would superimpose our *ātman*, our self, on to that disowning.

To believe in and live for the transcendental and the eternal is a way to disown and undo that passion of us, the passion that would find being where being is not. It means not to seek our being in what we perceive, think of or imagine but elsewhere – in what is beyond our perception and conception. It means that we the knowers and perceivers cannot find that being, for all that we can find can only be a disowning of itself. But it will undo, that our belief in and our seeking of the eternal, our passion that would equate our being with a state of affairs. The Truth that we are does not admit the predicates of eternity or temporality or, for that matter, any other predicate. To accept the reality of eternity or our mortality – to accept and live as or for these untruths is only to undo our *ajñāna* that places us as uncertainties between these two polarities, it does not mean to affirm them as absolutely real.

10. How is truthfulness, speaking the truth in one's dealings with others, a means to attain to *sat*, to that which ever is? Man resorts to lying in order to protect himself from what he considers to be of harm to him; he has to, he would say, cheat and deceive others to be safe and secure. Sometimes he may lie just out of spite or malice or sheer perversity. The motive that lies behind these and other forms of lying is the same, namely, to serve his narcissistic interests in less sinister or more sinister ways. Man the truthful puts himself at the mercy of others, lets others do with him what they will. Instead of retaining his personal self, he lets others occupy that *place* of his, violate it. One who self-submits to his mortal lot undoes the Narcissus in him one way, one who self-submits to the eternal truth or God undoes him in another way. The way of man the truthful to undo the same Narcissus in him is the way of self-submission to others.

11. Genuine fear of death is possible in a man who realises in full what death implies for him. It means the negation of all that he considers the real, of the world no less than of him. A man who comes to realise, realise truly, what the mortal condition is in fact and truth, cannot find any meaning in life. For, all that they, the mortals including himself, perceive, think about, imagine or aspire for turn out, in his view and for him, to be mere false phantoms, their own selves not being excluded. The so-called bold men, men that die for a cause, conceal from themselves the truth of death. They would make the world a better place through their death, believing in the reality of their world and, by implication, their own reality and of the cause they live for. Heroism in this sense sleeps over the truth of mortality, it is an act of escape from our mortal condition, and is, for this reason, an act unheroic and self-deceptive. The man of true heroic mould accepts without an illusion the truth of death, that horror of every ontology. He it is that realises in full how our fight against mortality is vain and foolish, our power an impotence, our knowledge ignorance and our nobility a sham. He it is who seeks the eternal truth to undo his *ajñāna*, ignorance, that would seek the eternal in the transient. The seeker, of course, will die before he 'finds' the eternal and with his death will die 'the eternal' too.

12. Whatever man perceives, whatever he desires, whatever he thinks of and aspires for are all false and so are the senses that perceive, the mind that desires, thinks and aspires. The truth that he is ever in search of cannot be found in these false appearances.

13. On the Name that is, the name vouchsafed to him by a seer of the truth. Truth being eternal cannot be contemplated, only its name can be. See pp. 78-79

[14] He dies in utter despair. He despairs of hope itself, loses hope in hope itself, hope that makes life go on when every other prop has been snatched away.

[15] Do we have here a mere poetic fancy or a solid truth? That the cosmos is there to serve living beings is an assumption with man, with a man of the scientific disposition no less than with a man of the mythical temper. But we also know that the cosmos is there to also spite and destroy man. The mythical man sought to control it through chants and magic, the man of science seeks to do the same with his theories and experiments. But the *otherness* of the cosmos remains untouched, disdaining man's chants and knowledge. And the unknown *other* is always a threat, a source of fear for man, man the scientific no less than man the *mythical*. The Vedic mind sought to triumph over the Other through its vision of the world as a *maṇḍala*, a circle. The world as a *maṇḍala* has sacrifice for its centre, where the immortal gods sacrifice themselves for the mortals and the mortals sacrifice themselves to the immortals, thereby sustaining the world as the act of sacrifice. This is how the Vedas spiritualised the primitive concept of sacrifice. Earth, water, fire, air and space were gods in their vision with whom man the mortal could relate and they to him through participation in the act of sacrifice that the world was.

This vision was further spiritualised when the act of sacrifice that the world is came to be called the act of sacrifice on the part of the Lord. For, the world was not a mere cosmos where immortals sacrificed for mortals and mortals for immortals, it was a presence with absence inscribed into it. The transcendent was present in the world but as absence, as that which was no longer there. This act of sacrtifice on its part, the act of *presencing* itself as absence, sustained the world as informed by a purpose, by a *telos*. This going beyond itself is the very life of the world, this its thrust for the beyond and the absent. In its disowning of itself, in its dying, lies its life and being. This thrust for the beyond informs not only living beings but also what we call inert things, the latter too feel compelled to change and disown themselves. Every being and thing here is a thing-for ...?, and every being is a being-for... ?. Therein lies its being, in not remaining itself, in *absencing* itself. And man is to participate in this act of sacrifice, in this act of *absencing* oneself. The act of service that one renders to others is a preparation for this final act of absencing oneself.

[16] 'Vision of sameness' is a rendering of *samatābuddhi*, cognition of sameness. Liberation from birth and death comes to be possible when no consciousness-of remains. How can *samatābuddhi*, then, be equated with liberation? To seek an answer to this question one has to contemplate, in imagination, the vision of *samatā*. As long as the man in question thinks of himself as different from what he cognises, there can be no vision of *samatā* for him. Differences will persist and with differences the world of names and forms. It is only when all becomes the same for him, all that is there, has been, will be or could be, that [he] may be said to [have] the vision of *samatā*. And when all becomes the same, there remains no question of [his] perceiving anything. *Buddhi* as the determinating faculty sets limits

to things, differentiates them from their *others*. With all becoming the same, there can be no cognition of anything for it, no determinating. Vision of all as the same will thus mean negation of the entire phenomenal world, world that can be perceived only in terms of relationships and contrasts.

17. 'Sat-saṅga' is often translated as association with seers, more often as a religious congregation. 'Association with the truth' appears to be a better rendering because of its more comprehensive connotation. A seer of the truth is not a seer in the ordinary sense of the term, a seer of the truth is one who has become the truth itself. For, as long as we see something, know it and cognise it we enframe it in our concepts, superimpose these on to it, to make a divide between the reality and our knowledge of it. All discourses suffer from this disability, their knowledges are concealments and not revelations. We cannot know things, nor can we know ourselves, nor what is good for us and what is evil for us, cannot know them in reality, because our so-called knowledge or understanding stands between the truth and ourselves. All knowledge is thus ignorance of reality, all our ideals are our fallen states, our relationships are our alienations, our theories follies and our actions self-destructive.

There are many, with their visions blurred and their ears deaf, who would equate reality with our knowledge of it, or, as some would put it, with our interpretation of it. They perceive but would refuse to acknowledge that our interpretations are ever and always negations of themselves, everything that we know, including ourselves, rejects our knowledge of it the very moment we formulate that knowledge in what we term as intelligible terms. There is a lack, an absence, written into our knowledges and interpretations, a deep sense of loss and deprivation. Blind to it, we would seek other knowledges and interpretations without an end but we would not pause to notice that lack and deprivation, would not like to know why we and our world are a disinheritance, a fall and a loss and our life an exile. In falsehood we would forget our desolation, in our knowledge and the arrogance of that knowledge.

How can *sat-saṅga* , then, lead us to the truth when our discourses keep us away from it? *Sat-saṅgas* are often, and deservedly, dismissed as of no epistemological consequence, where people hear scriptures in silent attention but with no understanding and, of course, with no critical examination of what they hear. Our theories turn fruitful when they compel our critical attention, when we notice the element of inadequacy in them, for it is this our perception of their inadequacy that keeps the flame of knowledge burning, leading to new theoretical formulations and their practical tests or experiments. But at a *sat-saṅga* all that we hear is taken as truth, eternal and unquestionable, where the first word heard is the last and final word. So men of knowledge and science have no faith in *sat-saṅgas*, they may be holy but, surely, not enlightening. When all that we know and are is questionable, why not, then, the word of scripture? they would ask. How to hear a word there is to know the truth, when all the words we hear elsewhere are mere concealments of the truth?

This is a legitimate question, in view, especially, of the fanaticism of the participants of *sat-saṅgas,* fanaticism that has often turned into violent clashes, wars and suppressions in their extreme. Modern minded thinkers would keep religious faith, the product of *sat-saṅga,* away from social and political life and institutions, tolerating its presence, of this dangerous pastime, only as a private and personal affair of individuals. But the text here speaks of *sat-saṅga* in an absolutely opposite vein. *Sat-saṅga* brings us, it says, to the presence of the truth, it tells us wherein lies our good and the principles of ethical, social and political conduct. And it does not merely make us understand these matters but also make us live as oriented towards them. Can we of this age believe in what it claims for *sat-saṇga*?

A *saṅga,* congregation, becomes *sat,* true and holy, when a sage is present in it, a sage who is an *anubhavī,* one who knows the truth because he has become the truth, shedding all the equipments of knowledge, equipments that would enframe reality, put theoretico-practical limits to it. The man in him speaks the *anubhavī-vāk,* the word authentic, the word about what he has come to be. He speaks as the messenger of that truth, the truth he has become. In other words, when he returns from his abode and home into the world of man, the man in him revives struck with the wonder of what he has now become, and speaks, wonder-struck, of the glory of that truth. His speech resonates with an immediacy, has a force living and compelling, his thought a clear and lucid reflection of the truth, his mind its celebration, his body its embodiment, and his word its revelation. To perceive his body is to perceive the invisible, to hear him is to hear that cannot be heard, to think with his thought is to think of the unthinkable. A meeting space is he of man and the God of man, of the real and our knowledge of the real. We see our eternal night turning into the long wished for dawn in him, he himself is that transformation, that man and God at once. Only those who have met such a being know who he is, that disrupter of the death we call life and restorer of the death that is life. Claims made about *sat-saṅga* in the text appear as truths lucid, immediate and plain if one comes into contact with a seer true, for to perceive him is to perceive the truth itself.

When a sage is not present, his words should take his place. But his words that were once instinct with his presence or rather presence that was absence - for where was then the man in him? - and his silence cannot but present him now only inadequately. In truth, they partake more of the nature of memory than of presentation, for the absence of the speaker is felt too palpably to forget. There is however revelation to take his place, the *vāṇī,* the Word without a speaker, the Word that vouches itself to man. These two voices, the voice of the Word and the voice of the sage who has become one with the reality and yet still lives as a man to speak about it, has received our attention in the Introduction and need not be repeated here. The Word that speaks to man is the Word redemptive, it is truth itself, a manifestation of the latter. To give oneself up to it is the way to find it as what it is in itself, the truth and the revelation of the truth. We are to give our ear to it, we have to reflect deeply on it and we have to meditate it and contemplate it. This is how we will wake up to our truth and being, not through our discourses and their mazes, but through Word the revelation. If one gives oneself to it for long and with attention exclusive and concentrated, a time will come when the sound of its recitation will replace our thoughts and feelings. We will hear its chanting as if it were taking place within ourselves, we ourselves turning into a calm, a calm swelling to the extent of absorbing us into its depths. In that blissful death we will find or rather become the being that we truly are.

Modernity depends on science for its knowledge of the world and for man's power over the world; it relies on thought for finding the truth, and leaves to the individual the choice to decide the ethical questions, and on the collective will to decide about the forms of government. This is a false and ruinous view propagated by capitalism in its decadent phase. The *vāsanā*, desire for being, has set up the body and its other, the world, only to sustain itself; the world is the creation of that *vāsanā* for being no less than man is. Therefore, man's desire to know is as much an expression of that innate passion for being as he himself is and as his world is. His knowledge is a delusion and so is his world that he equates with reality; mere shadowy props are these two, the world and man's knowledge of it, to sustain the shadowy being that man is. And he, man, is there to keep alive the fury of *vāsanā*, that passion for being. Man would possess the world to sustain himself as the embodied self; he would seek ideals, ethical or moral or of other kinds, to idealise this embodied self of his; he will create his God to imagine himself as Man the perfect. So his life, his thought, his piety and his other cultural pursuits remain narcissistic to their core. His human self is fallen and fallen are the things he knows, works for, imagines or aspires for. A barren winter, cold and dreary, is his life, a vain endurance and a vain pursuit.

Revelation, augmented by the words of an authentic sage, his life and demeanour, or by the memory of his life and demeanour, will lead a man to the truth, reveal to him what the meaning of his life is, what is its purpose and its goal and what is the way to it. Through that alone can man learn these matters, not through his own narcissistic thinking. Thinking becomes serious and profound only when it is thinking on the *śruti* or *vāṇī*, not when it is pursued in obedience to the Narcissus in man. Questions about truth and untruth, reality and unreality, questions about what is good and not good, questions about social and political justice can be settled at *sat-saṅga* only, not through the arguments of philosophers or through the discoveries of science. These matters our text will take up and we will have occasions to dwell on them. Here we have to attend to another question, namely, why in a congregation and not in our solitary study can we enter into a passive communion with revelation.

Man as he finds himself in the world is not merely a being in the world, he is also a being in relation with and contrast to others. What he believes in as a social being is what others believe in, a good many among them. Only a few individuals are there who can question the assumptions and epistemes of the society they live in. Such beings find themselves alone in society, their situation in the world insecure and their relationships with others disrupted. They cannot but seek a new place, a new world, to dwell in and new relationships to sustain them. In short, they are in search of a new reality, for the old proves too meaningless to their disillusioned mind. It is these unhappy souls that would think, meditate and contemplate in their solitude. They cannot believe in any revelation as they cannot believe in the assumptions of their age or society. Such people are called geniuses, thinkers and men of knowledge.

But what are the concepts in which they would enframe reality? The concepts they may forge may have a new shape and mien but they as concepts cannot but be shared concepts, concepts that can be communicated if not in their own age but at least at some future time. So even when they are free from the stale beliefs and knowledge of their age, they are still prisoners of *ajñāna*, of knowledge that is ignorance. They would *place* the truth, set limits to it, enframe it, place it and set limits to it only to sustain their being situated and related. So their new knowledge and new findings are only *ajñāna* in a new garb and mask. They still remain beings tied to others and the world, their knowledge determined by the same old conditions.

The way to the real, therefore, lies in getting liberated from all knowledge, all enframing and all conceptualising, in, that is to say, becoming absolutely innocent and passive to let the real possess us and absorb us into itself. We that would be situated and related cannot easily divest ourselves of all concepts and frameworks, those preconditions and the bases of our being, being that would situate and relate itself. The way *immediately* open to us, us sunk in conceptions and misconceptions, is not, cannot be, the way of absolute innocence but the way of softening of these our conceptions and misconception. Since we cannot divest ourselves of all situational concepts, we are asked to situate us in a different context of relationships. We are asked to live in a sub-society that has a sage for its leader, a leader that is the very opposite of worldly leaders that embody our narcissistic ideals and aspirations, but a leader that embodies the very extinction of those narcissistic ends. What relates us to each other in that sub-society will not be our passion for self-hood, selfhood that we would sustain through our relationships, but our ability to shed that passion, ability that we the members of that sub-society would augment through our newly defined relationships, through getting our strength for that purpose from each other. Men and women in their ordinary situations are beings in relationships and contrasts with the world as the point of reference to determine those relationships and contrasts, for it is their respective places in the world that would determine what kind of relationships and contrasts constitutes their being. And our leader or leaders there are those who have succeeded in placing themselves more firmly than us in that world. Here, on the contrary, our guide is the man who has de-placed himself and de-related himself to make us too de-place and de-relate ourselves, for that is the point of our reference, that de-placement and de-relating, of our new existential condition. That is the paradox about this placement and relationship that it is there only to disrupt every placement and every relationship.

Sat-saṅga is then the place to de-place us, it is a relationship to de-relate us through our relationship with a sage. 'Sat-saṅga', association with the truth, thus means dissociation from relationships as our defining principles, or, as we often put it (wrongly, of course), as our informing principles. It implies the undoing of our passion for being situated and related through situating ourselves anew and relating ourselves anew. In our daily life we ever de-place ourselves and de-relate ourselves but only to place ourselves further and relate ourselves further. Here at the sat-*saṅga*, we place ourselves anew and relate ourselves anew but only to de-place us and de-relate us. How to transcend this new existential context, this *sat-saṅga*, is a matter that we will consider when we come to dwell on *sat-simaran*, remembrance of the truth.

18. Man without relationships is an inert being, not a living being. It is in relationship with others that he comes to be a being with a mind. Out of those relationships, there can be no mind. Relationships and awareness of the world rise together, only a being along with others can be a being in the world. *In* the world, not *of* the world, for a being *of* the world is a being *unaware of* the world. At *sat-saṅga*, man turns from a being *in* the world to a being towards the truth, a being oriented towards the transcendent, from a being in the world to a being having intimations of the beyond.

19. Man as a being fallen into the world and tied to relationships is being the evil, he is a being with others that is a being against others. His relationships make him conscious of the world as his place to seize as much of it as he can, depriving others of their opportunities for possessions, even of their possessions. Even in relationships he will become possessive. The sexual relationship, that relationship par excellence, the relationship on which other relationships are dependent, has an insurmountable and predominant element of sadism in it, a relationship pursued by furies out to destroy it. An inferno is the world that man is destined to wake into. Only full remembrance of his lost home can save him from the fury of seizing and possessing, can make him sit with others in peace and concord, not when he remembers only his false home, the world. And it is *sat-saṅga* alone that can make him aware of his lost paradise.

20. Simplicity, truthfulness, service rendered to others and *sat-saṅga* do not turn into a man's way of life until and unless he remembers his ontological loss, unless he realises, immediately and perceptibly, the deprivation that he is. Man confuses this his ontological lack with his needs, his wants and desires, and, prompted by these latter, he seeks to fulfill them through his knowledge and labour. It is his dissatisfaction with his given state of affairs that forces him to seek more and more by way of knowledge and possessions but there is no knowledge that is not ignorance and no fulfillment that is not frustration. It is when a man realises the ultimate failure of all his endeavours - cognitive, practical, ethical, hedonistic and aesthetic - that he comes to realise, with the

vividness of a perception, that these his efforts and their achievements are the result of forgetting of what he seeks and would find, his lost home, his being from which he has been banished into this unhappy world. It is this sense of his primordial loss that makes him see through the illusions that his desire and achievements weave for him, distracting him from his real pursuit of the real goal. It is before a man of this clear vision that the sense of truth and untruth dawns and that of good and evil and of well being and ill being, and it is to him that the power to make the right choice is vouchsafed. Those who do not remember their loss lose their way and their sense of goal, their life a waste and a misery, and, what is more, a depravity. No one who does not remember his lost home can be truthful, can be sincere, can be truly helpful and can be a man of insight. He lives only to ruin himself and ruin others, his life a folly and his acts mere sins. The self-complacent man should know this truth, he who has the presumption to believe that with his human power he can do good to others.

[21]. The sense of one's loss is one thing, to live by it, to have a sustained awareness of it, quite another. This sense of loss becomes a living truth for man when he, getting disillusioned with all that he is and all that he perceives, steps out of his senses, his mind and thoughts. This does not happen easily; he has to undergo all the agony of existence to become a passive witness of the human person in him - of his senses and what they perceive, of his desires and passions, of his sins and thoughts, good as well as bad, serious as well as frivolous. No thought can then attract him, no desire and no perception, all innocent he turns, as if on the point of melting into the silent and calm depths that reveal themselves within him in that disposition of his. He turns *antara-mukha*, oriented inwards instead of what he was, a being oriented outwards. Only the silent and calm depths within him, the depths he cannot know and measure, become his being then, his thoughts, his desires, his perceptions turning alien to him, turning something of a burden and pain which he must get rid of. Few are there to whom this grace is vouchsafed, the grace in the shape of a despairing agony and the patience to bear it. They are what they call the chosen souls, souls blessed by the anguish of life.

Others who cannot drink the bitter cup of blessedness have to strive hard for that impersonal state. They have to work hard for that state, make it the purpose of their life and endeavours. They have to become *sādhakas*, strivers for that *sādhya*, that objective. Instead of the grace in the form of a giant agony, they receive it, that grace, in the form of the Name. I was given a name by a priest who chanted the Vedic mantras to make that name a mark of my identity, the name that marked me out of the common name, Man, but it merely remained a label tagged on to me, it never became *my* name, the name that informed me. There was no concept signified by that name to encompass me. It is the irony of our life that we who would make ourselves identities can do so only through concepts, through class names. It is only in relationship and contrast to others that we come to be individuals, but individuals that are only uncertainties, uncertainties in search of our self or identity but never finding it. What we find here is only a name, a mere label; with that label we have to be satisfied, with that make believe, with that illusion. The Name that a seer of the truth bestows on us is, on the contrary, our name proper, name that is really and truly ours, that is our being and truth itself.

This Name is a *mantra*, a *mahāvākya*, a great utterance, that is made to flow with the flow of breath. Its first half is inhaled with *apāna*, the incoming breath, and the other half is exhaled with *prāṇa*, the outgoing breath. The Name equalises the flow of these two currents of breath, the *apāna*, incoming breath, moving down to the region of the navel to die down there to give rise to *prāṇa*, outgoing breath to mingle with the air of the atmosphere. This meditation of breath-name combine turns one into a witness of breath and of mind, distancing one from the senses and their perceptions. This distancing is what is termed in the passage here as purification of mind's *dhāraṇā*. *Dhāraṇā* means putting something on oneself - a dress, for example. And what it is that a mortal puts on himself? It is the body, the organs of sense and action, desires and thoughts and *buddhi*, the power that determinates, and, of course, breath. To purify one's *dhāraṇā*, then, means to give up these false *dhāraṇas* to turn into their *sākṣin*, their witness, silent and passive. This *dhāraṇā*, the *dhāraṇā* of being a witness, passive and still, of the false *dhāraṇas* opens up the depths within the person concerned, depths that absorb all its attention, of that witness self, making it exclusively concentrated on them. He comes to find a rest there, this long and exhausted pilgrim, in those depths, and, eventually, lets himself be swallowed by them to lose his false identity as the witness self too. In thus losing himself, he finds himself in truth and reality. That is his abode proper, his home real.

So, the Name is the true name, the name proper; it leads this lost soul to its real being, its self, makes it find itself and be itself. Other names remain adventitious to us, only the Name bestowed on us by a seer can give us the identity we seek. Mere word or words will not save us, only the gift of these from a seer will. This should be clearly understood. People do resort to meditation for relaxation, for relieving themselves from the stress of life. It is all very well, with your old *dhāraṇas* intact and unquestioned, to take a holiday from your responsibilities to have the feel of being released from their burden. However, it is quite another thing to resort to contemplation of mind-breath to undo all the false *dhāraṇas*, to undo one's sense of identity with the body, the senses, desires and thoughts and even with the motion of breath. If a man undertakes the meditation of the Name for the purpose of freeing himself from the very yoke of existence, then hell will lose itself upon him, volcanoes will erupt and furies cruel and destructive, to make him go mad and distraught. He will immediately seek an escape from them to live and breathe and to perceive and think, if he would not escape from death or suicide. The way of *yoga* is not easy to tread, like the sharp edge of a razor is this path, to quote the famous

Upaniṣadic saying, a living death, or dying before one's death, as the Master would often say. The sense of one's ontological loss should be strong enough in a man to make him a seeker of his lost home and strive for it. He may not have enough of disillusionment to die immediately for it as the sanctified sufferer has, that recipient of grace in the form of suffering without a hope, but he must have enough of it to know for certain that the world is a mere place of exile, that to live here is a tragedy absolute and that he must find his real home to escape from the inevitable fate ordained here for him. And it is only a sage of the highest realisation, the sage who has come to find his home, that can make him know for certain that there is really and truly the home he seeks and that there is a way to it. His own understanding cannot convince him conclusively about the truth of the goal he seeks; our probabilities can only rouse our interest in them but they cannot make us put all our being at stake for their sake, all that we are and have. Our understanding, even our experiences, can give us only probabilities but not faith in the true sense of the term. Only a seer can, he alone and his life and demeanour alone. What kind of a person that *im-person* is, what kind of death his life is and what kind of absence is his presence and what kind of impact and what influence he can have on our life can be sensed a little from my biography of the Master. It should be remembered that the way of *yoga* is not as smooth as I have put it above. Nor is it as straight as 98 may lead us to believe. The way, as I said above, is, of course, distracting and dangerous but that is not the end of the story. What is far more dangerous and distracting is the joy that the 98 speaks about. It is at this state that the seeker needs the support of his preceptor most. The bliss is truly sublime and transforming, an ecstasy of self-loss as it were, making one forget one's entire being, being placed and related. And the return from that trance of self-oblivion is truly ecstatic, transform as it does the look of the world into a world of unbearable beauty and man himself into an unbearable joy as it were. In the midst of this blessedness, a man is apt to forget that self-oblivion is not self-loss, that his joy is not bliss, that the love of it, of his joy, will take him back to his sordid and fallen state. His fall is possible, rather highly probable, because he, that man of ecstasy, is not yet dead, not yet fully dead, to avoid it. It is only the life of his true teacher that will make him understand the smallness of his joy, its meanness as it were, to make him distance himself from it for ever. His other *dhāraṇās* may end but not this *dhāraṇa* of bliss, it does not die with ease, this hardest of all illusions.

The faithful often claim, in their fervour, that the grace of the guru alone is their saviour, equating that grace with some unknown and mysterious power. The grace of the guru, however, falls on man the striver in the form of patience, patience in the midst of the great and maddening agony that his meditation will release, and in the form of disillusionment with his joy and ecstasy, in the form, that is, of patience vis-a-vis that joy and ecstasy. The last is the real, saving, grace, for to bear that ecstasy is not within the reach of mortals; they may bear the madness of hell but not the curse that their paradise is. Only God can bear and be patient with his bliss, not man the miserable being that he is. And man has to die as bliss to be the Lord, whom nothing can touch, no state of being, neither that of misery nor that of joy. What mortal is there who will sacrifice even that patience that God *for* him? Only a seer of the highest realisation can, it is he who can take him to regions beyond the reach of even our God. That is the reason that a seer of the highest order is considered greater than even God.

22. God is the son of the sacrificial man, and the true act of sacrifice that sanctifies man, makes of him the true sacrificial victim, is the yogic meditation as described above. In the death of all the adjuncts, all the states of being with which man identifies himself, in the death, that is to say, of himself lies the birth of him as God, and in the death of him as God, his Bliss, lies his liberation, his *mokṣa*.

23. That witness is innocent of himself because he is always the witness and never the witnessed, is always the knower and never the known. Who would know the knower? asks the Bṛhadāraṇyaka Upaniṣad. For what comes to be known as the self is only an *upādhi*, an adjunct, of the self, not the self itself. The self remains behind all that one knows as one's self. To be the self one has not to know it, for to know it is to phenomenalise it, make of it an object. All that we know of the self is other than the self.

24. In the Word the divide between the name and the named, between name and form is healed. That is the real, that Word, that is God and that is the *ātman*, the self, that *name proper* of each and every being, of all that is and all that is not.

25. Yoga of remembrance consists of four stages, namely, that of remembrance, that of *bhajana* – adoration –, that of *dhyāna*, contemplation, and that of *samādhi*, absorption in the real, to become one with it. For details, see 4.2

26. The spirit behind these Vedic rituals is to remind man of his mortality. Man is not, in truth, a being of the world and a being along with others, he is a being in death and along with the dead. To live as a mortal is to live a redemptive life, to live as a being related to the world and others is to live in death and for death. Unfortunately, the ritualists did not pay heed to this spirit of their rituals for the dead, they continued to perform them as mechanical ceremonies unaware of their existential implication. They forgot how mere mechanical ceremonial piety is the *āsurika* piety, piety practised by demons. The Upaniṣads would have them substitute rituals with meditation on them. But that was not to be. The priests interested in their fee would encourage people to perform them mechanically and the people continued to buy their well being in the other world through that fee. Hence the text rejects these ceremonies in toto.

27. Self-burning, burning of one's passion and desire through self-denial.

28. *Vidyā*. *Vidyā* undoes one's sense of identity with all that one knows and perceives. It says No to every state of being one identifies oneself with.

[29] The *Śatapatha Brāhmaṇa* says that demons perform sacred rites at the external altars, the gods within their mind. That is the way the Upaniṣads would look at the acts of piety – they are there to be performed in the mind, to be internalised. The text, in the same spirit, lays emphasis on internal purity. The real place of pilgrimage is the *ātman;* that is the holy shrine man must visit, the holy lake to take his final dip in. To perform acts of pilgrimage to external places is like seeking the self in the phantoms that the *buddhi* in its ignorance has set up. It is only the expression of our passion for the *other* in another form and garb, the expression of our *ajñāna*, our false and deluded ways of looking at the real.

[30] The three constituent principles of *prakṛti*, that *before* of creation, namely, *sattva*, *rajas* and *tamas*. For explanation of these terms see Index.

[31] Every being that finds himself with a name and a form, finds himself as endowed with this quality or that quality or attribute and engaged in this activity or that activity, is a being given to idol worship. Every being that has come to live in the world takes his body as his self, desires the gross things of the world and acts for their acquisition. He perceives the gross, desires the gross, strives to acquire the gross and thinks of the gross. There is no One for him to worship, only the many are. To be an inhabitant of the world of space and to act in it under the impact of the modes of *prakṛti*, namely *sattva*, *rajas* and *tamas*, is itself idol-worship. So no man is a believer here, all are non-believers, for all believe in the visible and live for it.

[32] For it is in the nature of the mind to think of the other, to desire the other and work for the other, other the gross and the material, for that is the real for it, the gross and material world. There can be no mind without that other, without the body and the world.

[33] The text equates *Māyā* with *prakṛti*. *Māyā* is often equated with names and forms and *prakṛti* with their unmanifest state. The *guṇas* of *prakṛti* are in a state of equipoise in their unmanifest state, whereas they operate in tension in their manifest form. This means that *Māyā* is the name for both the manifest and the unmanifest forms of *prakṛti*. We may recall that the text uses *māyā* and *ajñāna* too as interchangeable terms.

[34] Knowledge which has no *other* to know, is consciousness alone and absolute without its object. That is the ultimate of us mortals, the proximate of our proximates. But it is only when all has become consciousness itself that there can be consciousness without its other. To call that state self or *ātman* or consciousness is to determinate it in terms of self-negating paradoxes, paradoxes that negate all the determinates of our determinating faculty. Formulations of this kind with their own negations written into them lead us to innocence, innocence absolute, that other name for liberation, liberation from all the formulations of our intellect.

[35] That is, one's dead ancestors now living in the world of the *pitṛloka*, the world of the fathers ruled over by Death.

[36] The entire argument may be summarised as follows. A living being is

a duality with consciousness and the object of consciousness as his two constituent principles. Consciousness character subsists as inself and what it is conscious of ever changes to disown itself. The sense of entity that one has with regard to the objects of consciousness, be they gross or subtle, material or mental, is the gift of consciousness. This consciousness cannot, however, subsist in itself or by itself, it must have some object or other to get identified with and, thereby, come to know itself. A living being is thus this consciousness conscious of itself, conscious of itself as something other than consciousness. To be and to know that one *is*, is false knowledge, it is *ajñāna*, the cause of recurring deaths and births. *Recurring* deaths and births because there is no such thing as pure duration, there is only coming to be and ceasing to be. Here things, beings, moments come to be and cease to be. Every moment is a birth and a death. And it is a birth and a death because consciousness that knows it lends it an entity character. Duration without succession is inconceivable. So consciousness that knows itself has to be a mortal consciousness, consciousness that affirms itself only to deny itself. It is its passion to *be* and to know itself as the being in question that turns its being into mortality. And it is its fate to fight a losing battle against that its mortal lot. This is the unhappy condition that our existential condition is.

We cannot simply be without some bodily form and name. We cannot be mere ghosts and spirits, for there can be no being without some form or the other to identify with. This means that consciousness cannot subsist as consciousness without its *other*, without some name and form. We call our being eternal consciousness only in relation to the perishable form it has assumed. Consciousness in itself, without being conditioned by its *other*, is not consciousness at all. What it is when its *other* has been eliminated cannot be described because all that we can determinate about reality is inevitably inflicted by duality. We say that consciousness sets up its *other* to affirm itself, to know itself. But there can be no consciousness without that *other*. We say that the *jīva*, this living being, sets up a form to affirm and know himself, but there is no *jīva* without a form to set up that form and know himself as that form. The text may seem here to speak in this kind of vein in some sentences. But that is only a concession made to our understanding and its concepts. What the text actually says here is that consciousness when divested of the *other* turns into Brahman the *Absolutus* that would reject every predicate, be it in terms of its eternity or infinity or consciousness.

It is the *jīva*, the being conditioned by some name and form, that is said here to set up another form to identify himself with together with the *other* of that form, the world, to contend with. An embodiment of *ajñāna*, he continues to set up forms one after another and their respective others, the worlds. But this account only means that an individual ever and always will find himself flanked by his past and his future, will find his placed being flanked by his past placed beings and his future placed beings. Without that doer, that link between the past and the future, there can be no world and no placement. The so-called objective thinking envisages the past and the future of an objective world, existing independently of a perceiver. This is an unsustainable position. Hence the world is to be explained as a process of recurring births and recurring deaths and not as something existing independently of its perceiver. Man is a participant in the creation of the world, man the creature of the world. But why this frightening play of *Māyā* at all? This is a question that should not be asked. For questions and answers belong to the sphere of *ajñāna* itself. To ask questions and seek answers is to be a part of this unhappy condition. One must live with those questions, those questions alone; if they arise in one, one is not to seek their answers. The question will turn into the truth when man calmly submits to it, to the question that he is and his world is, to the question for which there is, there can be, no answer.

The present Instruction was given to villagers who would not come to visit the Master for fear of the ghosts and evil spirits that they believed haunted the place of his sojourn in the ruins of an old fort. But in the process the Master has given an exposition of the ontology of the individual. With no formal education in these matters, how could he speak so masterly about the Sāṅkhya and Vedāntic matters should be a matter of wonder for the reader. He may be a little sceptical about what I say about his education. He may go through my biography on his life to know the miracle that he was and his life was.

37. The reference is to the ceremony in which offerings are made to one's dead ancestors for their sustenance and well being in the other world. The *Brāhmaṇas* that constitute the ceremonial part of the Vedas give elaborate accounts of such ceremonies. To believe literally in the effectiveness of such ceremonies, as the 'pious' would do, or did until recently, is of course a belief that modern man would ignore completely, would not even think of refuting it. The text here censures such beliefs because when this section was composed, such ceremonies were quite in vogue, especially in the countryside of our land [See *To the Home that was Nowhere*]. The Upaniṣads, however, we may recall, prefer meditation on these acts to their actual performance. When meditated, this ceremony turns out to be a meditation on death, giving rise to the feeling and conviction that one's true relations are not the living but the dead, that it is their clan, the clan of the dead, that one belongs to in reality. The thought of offering food etc to the dead ancestors, meditation on this act, will establish an intimate relationship with them, resulting in the disposition of distancing from the world and its affairs. The contemplative remembrance of the dead is a redemptive remembrance, remembrance that the doctrine of *samatā* would approve and applaud.

38. The individual cannot come to be himself unless he has a body composed of the five gross elements and also the power to determinate, the power to desire and deliberate on the objects of desire, and also the I-sense. The I-sense cannot be wished away, it cannot be equated with what we may call the intellect-mind-body complex, it resists to be so equated. The ego-sense can easily look upon intellect-mind-body complex in terms of its possession, distinguishing itself from the complex. Similarly, the

intellect, the power that determinates – call it Understanding or the conceptual faculty, if you like – has to be there in order to determinate the phenomenon for the I-sense to get identified with, distinguishing it from other phenomena of the same class or of other classes. And *manas*, mind, must also be there, the faculty of desire and deliberation on the objects of desire, to make the being in question a being in the world. The concept of a disembodied spirit thus turns out to be a figment of imagination, as would the concept of the individual as equated with the body will be, or as equated with body-mind-intellect will be, for the I-sense will not be so equated. Behind all these is the *ātman*, the self, the witness for which/ whom all these components from the *buddhi* to the element of earth constitute the sphere of the witnessed. It is impossible to conceive of the I-sense without these other elements. So it cannot be their witness. Nor can be the intellect which can determinate only when there is something to determinate. Without that *other*, the intellect cannot be conceived. The *manas* is of course only an orientation towards the world, without that *other* the *manas* is simply inconceivable. As for the world, it is dependent for its being on the assemblage of the eight elements, as the assemblage of the eight elements is dependent on the world.

The text adds another element of complexity when it says that the eight elements are set up by the *jīva* himself, by that which has come to live. We know that the *jīva* is *jīva* the embodied, the embodiment being the very condition of his being. How can he, then, set up these elements before he comes into being? This question confronted us at 2.*1ff* also. The meaning is there is something like a *before* of *jīva* the manifest that sets up the seeming *jīva*-world duality. It is not in truth a duality because one pole cannot be set apart from the other pole. *Jīvā*-world duality is an illegitimate and inadmissible term, because there is no such thing as *jīva* to constitute the world and no world as such to constitute the *jīva*. There is a *before* to this appearance, this inconceivable appearance, and that *before* is also called here *jīva*. This latter *jīva* cannot be equated with the *ātman*, that self ever the same. Then who is he, if he is not the *ātman* and not the embodied *jīva*? That is the question that has puzzled all thinkers and theologians. Some eliminate the unmanifest *jīva* and make God himself the creator of the world, inviting all the problems associated with this notion. Speculation about creation springs from our passion to know reality, to enframe it within our concepts. We would reduce the real to our concepts, forgetting that no concept can exhaust the real, that it, the real, will ever and always escape its grasp. The *before* of creation is not an existent, it is only the ontological *excess* inherent in each object, the excess that would not let itself be set limits to, which our intellect is always anxious to do. We find the *jīva* a duality, we also find the world a duality. We would go behind them or beneath them to find their cause. We call that cause *prakṛti*, the unmanifest form of nature or the unmanifest *jīva*. But this too is an illegitimate talk because with the manifest *jīva*-world duality being problematic, we cannot reasonably speak of its *before*, of its unmanifest form, which will remain as problematic as was its manifest form. In our attempt to remove one veil we will be setting up another - without an end.

So, how can we say then that there is a self or the *ātman*? When the rebuffs of ill fortune strike us hard, we withdraw from our doing self into our thinking self. The thinking resorted to as one's existential prop is, however, a killing thinking, only those who are *relatively* secure in the world can enjoy it, not those whom the world has spurned and rejected. Their thinking turns diseased and freezing (no figurative term, please!). When thus the body turns scalding and the mind a torture and thinking a mere heat in the brain and in the nerves, when the entire body-mind complex is thus set aflame, then the I-sense comes to know and realise the sheer otherness, the destructive otherness, of what it has identified itself with, and would step out of it sooner than later. It is in this moment of anguish in excess that it finds itself a prisoner of life, life that is death itself. With this realisation becoming deep and stable, the I-sense becomes humble enough to distance itself from all that it knows and is. A time comes when the I-sense actually withdraws itself from its phenomena and comes to be too thin to know its place and being. With its thinning, the body-world too becomes thin to remain a place for its being. It is at that moment that the dependence of the *jīva*-world duality on the I-sense becomes evident. And when, eventually, the I-sense completely steps out of the intellect-mind-body complex, it turns or dies into the *ātman* itself and so does its *other*, the world. When the I-sense persists, the world too will persist, and when it ceases to persist, the world too will cease to persist. It is in this sense that the *jīva*, the I-sense, is the creator of the world. They rise together, the I-sense and the world, but with the I-sense having an ontological priority over the latter.

39. This sentence should not be taken at its face value. What we call noble or good deeds are not pure in the true sense of the term. Actions become pure when performed with no desire in mind. Actions thus performed make one live with and reconciled to our mortal lot. To live with our life as a motion towards death, to live our mortality, is indeed to live as liberated.

40. This belief was quite prevalent during the times of the *Brāhmaṇas*, the ritualistic portions of the Vedas. The *Brāhamaṇas* to some extent and the Upaniṣads quite explicitly tried to spiritualise this and other primitive practices. These ceremonies were, they emphasised, only to remind man of his mortal condition, to make him realise that he is not a being -with-others but a being –with- the- dead. He was to remember that his *arche* was his *telos*, that he was not destined to live with his descendents but with his *pitṛis*, his dead fathers, his true relations. But the ritualists would not live the spirit behind those rituals and would believe that their forefathers did in fact live in their world and the ceremonies they performed here in their memory would indeed appease those ancestors of theirs and enable them to find their goal. It may be noted that this view about the *spirits* of the dead living in their world does not, despite all the formulations, easily fit with the doctrine of rebirth and liberation.

Anubhava Four

SECTION I

Samatā-dhāra, Holding on to *Samatā*

(i) Samatā-dharma

Saying 1. 'Dharma' means *dhāraṇā* [< *dhṛ*, to hold, to wear, to carry]. It means to hold on to something with mind, with speech and action. To hold on to the untrue and unreal is called *adharma* and to hold on to the true and real is called *dharma*.

Saying 2. Samatā-dharma is the true *dharma, dharma* the full and perfect. When *buddhi*, the determinating faculty, remains self-same and perceives the self-same, when it desires nothing and sets up or enframes nothing, when it comes to be itself, comes to enter into the bliss that is the *ātman*, when no fear of birth remains for it and no fear of death, and when it loses itself in its real being, then and then alone does it attain to *dharma* the full and perfect. For, that is *dharma* in truth, that attaining to the state of *samatā*, and that is the end of the investigations of persons the true and great.

Many a means towards that end did they reveal unto the world, those persons great, means that constitute the very spirit of *dharma* - means like right deeds, right thinking, right belief, right effort towards the realisation of the goal of human life and right association. To cap these all, they revealed unto the world the difference between bondage and liberation. To the *samatā-dharma*, that peace eternal and indivisible, will attain the man that knows this way the truth about *dharma* and has interiorised these noble traits constitutive of it.

Saying 3. A prisoner of doership, this embodied being finds himself immersed in and identified with all sorts of states; this his passion for selfhood, for self-projection[1] never lets him find himself in his real being. This state of instability leads him to perform deeds good and evil in many ways and shapes, the passion for their results ever consuming him with anxiety and unrest. That is his soul's delusion, its dark night. Every being carries this darkness in him, this consuming anxiety and unrest. No position, no status is there to save him from this darkness and this delusion.

Saying 4. The way to *samatā* is the way that leads him from this dark delusion to bliss the transcendent - leads him straight and without much delay. That should be the endeavour great of every being, the endeavour to redeem himself through the way that leads to *samatā*, to the state ever the same. A being that follows [this] *dharma* will purify himself, purify his body, the mind and his *buddhi*, his faculty that determinates.

Saying 5. A man who purifies his body, his mind and his *buddhi*, his determinating faculty, alone knows what *dharma* in its truth is. A man who does not direct his endeavour towards this end can neither know what *dharma* in its truth is nor can he find the peace that he is truly in search of. Every great person has taught the way to bring about purification of these three constituents of one's being. But cowardly beings, with their self-interest as their sole concern, would not resort to this redemptive way of self-purification. They would divide people in the name of religion and faith, closing their own way and that of the people at large to peace the true and real. This division among religious sects, this their conflict with each other, is *ajñāna*, is ignorance, dark and dense, a block and an obstacle in the way to the peace that the state of sameness is.

Saying 6. A mortal has to take recourse to *dharma* for his own good and not to create conflicts and tensions or to earn cheap respectability. **When he has won over all his weaknesses, when, that is to say, he has merged into the bliss that the state of sameness is, then let him, that gifted being, spend his life pure and noble in the service of the people. That is the way of prophets and incarnations.** For, the faith and the way that led them, those great ones, to bliss the supreme is the faith and the way that will lead to it many another too. To abide by the instructions of a great one and to follow his lead, of him that has attained to this holy state and spends his life in service of the people, is verily the way to liberation.

Saying 7. The great ones have formulated many ways of purification of the body, the mind and the determinating faculty. The purpose of this purification is attainment of the peace that sameness is. Man is to purify his determinating faculty [of all its enframing and conceptualising functions] and attain to the infinite bliss that the Word is. Any other concept of *dharma* is a mere pretence and falsehood and evil. This mortal being is ever a prisoner of self-interest, that eternal misery of his. The *dharma* that caters to his self-interests is no *dharma* at all; it is a mere business transaction, a transaction that demands something for this body, this false appearance, in exchange for one's piety.

Saying 8. The piety that is resorted to with some self-interest in mind has only the pleasures of the body for its end, pleasures that are the source of misery ever and always, desire and fear never leaving the man addicted to those pleasures. The state of *samatā*, that peace true and real, ever remains beyond the reach of the man that is alive to the sense of pleasure and pain with regard to the body. And that sense no piety motivated by self-interest can ever undo. Therefore, his movement from one birth to another birth continues as before, of the man given to this kind of piety, his deeds determining the form of those births. Not until he comes to be endowed with the *buddhi* dedicated to the supreme reality, solely dedicated to it, will he find his eternal being.

Saying 9. The *dharma* dedicated to the supreme reality is *dharma* in its truth; it implies, this *dharma*, a firm belief in that real, in that state of *samatā*, and dedication of all one's efforts to attain to that state ever the pure. Only this disposition can give one the peace real and true. A being suffused with the spirit of this disposition has nothing to do with religious disputes and conflicts; his spiritual progress remains his only concern and effort. To stay steadfast in his true being, ever distant from all the deviations native to the embodied mode of being becomes the very mode of his life. Only he knows what *samatā-dharma* is, only a being suffused with this kind of spirit and disposition.

Saying 10. The body becomes purified through a wash, through pure intake, through acts of purity and through right and pure association. The mind gets purified through reflection on the real, through giving, through *tapas*, self-denial, through dispassion and through a sustained meditation of the Name True. The *buddhi*, determinating faculty, becomes pure through steadfast and dedicated devotion to the Lord that one's true being is. When a being's *buddhi* totally gives itself up to the *ātman*, he comes to have his mind and senses firmly under his control and, as for himself, he ever remains immersed in the pure and eternal being that he, in truth, is. To the state of peace real and true, peace that is sameness itself, *samatā* itself, does he attain then. No self-mortification, no violence done to the body will be of any avail to him unless his body, his functions of sense and actions, his mind and his *buddhi* get purified. A man who took no step to cure the disease inflicting him [disease of embodiment] and spent his life in discourses persuasive and eloquent merely wasted his life and lived to no purpose. As water cannot appease the thirst of a fish, so his gifts could not appease his thirst, of this man who would talk knowledge but would not live and practise it. A fool he remained, with all his gifts.

Saying 11. All philosophies and all investigations show forth, in the long run, how mortal life is only a search for peace. [2] A being who did not purify himself through reflection on the truth lived only as an animal and not as a human being. Every great soul had only this finding to reveal, *viz.*, that man should find the true bliss of sameness, that panacea for the malady that his life is, before its term comes to an end.

Saying 12. A man who does not care to make any progress in matters relating to the *ātman*, who resorts to all sorts of measures to serve his self-interests but never makes the Lord the anchor of his life and being - a man of this deluded thinking is nothing but a fool. No [spiritual] striving can bear its fruit if it is not resorted to with full faith in the Truth. A man who knows not in truth and strives not for the truth and who does not spare a thought for the end destined for him, a man who knows only occasional piety, piety he resorts to, to serve some end of his, is a man that knows not what piety in truth is, what *dharma* in truth is.

Saying 13. Every system of castes and stages of life[3], every religion and every sect have for their end the state of *samatā*, that ocean towards which flow these streams and rivers. That is the light supreme and the knowledge supreme that they seek and would find. But a man with a small mind does not know this truth about them and would seek to indulge in religious conflicts and disputes, ever at odds with the precepts he would profess to believe in. This folly is Satanic through and through, a folly that defames the prophets and makes a living of their sacrifice. Men of this sort are born to destroy the true *dharma*, with the very possibility of salvation denied unto them. As for those that come near them and under their influence, even the very thought of that blessed state is beyond their reach. In disputes futile they live, men of this kind, and in ignorance do they fade away. That has been their fate and that shall be their fate.

Saying 14. Every place bears the mark of the power of the Lord, same mark of that power, and so does every time. In the same way Great Ones throughout the world have shown unto the world the path that leads to that Peace, though their formulations of the means and disciplines to attain to that end may have the stamp of their individual life and experiences. Those sincere souls that adopt those means and disciplines will no doubt attain to their goal some day. But a mere chatterer will remain where he is to mislead [himself and] others. Of no use will be he to himself and of no use will he be to others.

Saying 15. Every *sat-puruṣa*, every man the real, attained to the real, waking up from his ignorance, the ontological sleep he was lost in. And the way he reached his goal blessed he taught unto others. The religious books are only records of thoughts about the ways that lead one to the final goal of life. Anyone who follows what these books contain will no doubt move towards that goal, at least to an extent. But those who merely swear in the name of their religion and would not follow its precepts will never understand their holy books nor will they know the glory of their prophets. In mischief mere is wasted their life.

Saying 16. The fount of bliss flows within every mortal. But no one can drink at that fount without purifying his mind. In no way can he attain to that bliss unless and until he orients his mind to the Lord of the all, his mind that has strayed from the Path and would deny that Truth. A tragedy is this life in the world, a tragedy great and deep. Only an enlightened being can understand the magnitude of this tragedy. A benighted soul will, however, mistake the malady for the cure to live in everlasting misery, peace the real beyond his ken and reach.

Saying 17. The way out of this misery the *sat-puruṣas*, men the real, have revealed unto the world, the way that leads one to the Lord of the all dwelling within every mortal being. Knowing that Lord, his self the true and his being the true, this pilgrim from death to death and from birth to birth will find his ordeal come to an end. To *samatā* will he be then said to adhere to, to hold on to the vision of the same. So let man ever be aware of his death, for that will put an end to his folly and ignorance, this his constant awareness of his mortal lot, and lead him to bliss the supreme.

Saying 18. One should know what *dharma* means in each and every of its aspects. The mortal being comes to be redeemed when everything turns the same for him. Let him, therefore, ever seek that vision, the vision blessed and blissful. Let him know for certain that there is no hope for him except that vision of all as one and the same. For, everything that is here is sustained by *samatā*, by ever the same; anything that loses that support ceases to be itself. This is verily the wonder that the power of the Lord is.[4] Let every being ever seek within him that truth, the truth ever the same.

Saying 19. Let no man be heedless. Let him find his life true, life that is *samatā* alone. A man who would not be heedful and wears his faith merely as a mask will not find the bliss his prophets found. For strayed has he from the path they showed, knowing not what they, those prophets of old, strove for and lived for.

Saying 20. In this very body shines the Master of the whole world. But the veil of selfhood will not let man perceive that Light. *Dharma* or faith is there to undo that concealment that his selfhood, his sense of Me, is and to lead him to that Blessed Lord of the all dwelling in him. That will be the moment when he will come to be the same to perceive the same, the moment when he will find all as one and one as all. Infinite will he turn then, his woes and sorrows left behind. This is the highest reach of the wisdom of prophets and seers the perfect, its final culmination and its ultimate end.

Saying 21. Religious disputes and quarrels will be of no avail to any man. Not until he dedicates his life to the path shown by prophets and seers will he be delivered from his unhappy condition. Man is born to find the bliss real and true, bliss that sameness is, sameness the perfect. So let him give up his follies and believe in the *ātman,* that truth itself, and give himself up to contemplation of it. Let him be ever patient, whether in weal or in woe. Let him know that they visit him only in obedience to the will of the Lord. Let this be his way, the way that will lead him straight to his redemption.

And let him meditate the Name of the Lord with his mind intent and concentrated. For, he should remember that only the Lord is real, all else is mere fear and delusion. So, let him be awake and give himself up to the Lord and His will. That is the means highest to lead him to his goal. And that is the endeavour to lead him to the vision of all as one and the same. Therefore, let his thought be ever turned towards the truth and, equipped with it, let him always stick to the path to the truth. Let him be ever earnest and serious, for his body is decaying every moment and each.

Saying 22. Let no one waste away his life in sectarian and religious conflicts. Let him move forward on the way to his *ātman,* let him, that is to say, purify his thoughts and his conduct and seek to find what his life in its truth is. Let him remember that all his energy derives from the Lord of the all and let him remember His name with concentrated attention and find within himself the Life bright and splendid and the Power that It is. Let him be ever awake to that Life within, taking his joys and sorrows as ordained by It. With this firm resolve guiding him, a man becomes capable of shedding all his illusions and delusions and comes to merge in Word the Brahman. Then is it that he comes perceive the same in full and be the same in full, with no calamity to inflict him and no ignorance to engulf him. That state is the state highest, within the reach of only those who have done their best and utmost, done their best and utmost in the true way. For, that is what all *sat-puruṣas* sought and found, giving up all their desires and cravings - sought and found that blessed state where all turned into the same. All that they accomplished and all that they had - all their qualities and all their traits that the world would accomplish and would have - emanated from only that state of bliss. Therefore, it behoves every man to give up futile disputes and seek the *samatā-dharma*, the way straight and right to the state that abides ever the same.[5]

Saying 23. The sense of Me and Mine (*mamatā*) is *ajñāna*, ignorance, itself; it is identifying oneself with what is a false appearance. *Samatā*, on the other hand, is knowledge itself; it is establishment in what one truly and really is. All kinds of beings, without an exception, stray and wander in the mazes of *mamatā*, wander in them confounded and bewildered and in fear everlasting. Not a moment of pause and rest from that fear is allowed them. With the vain hope that what they do and have done will bring them the desired result, they wander from one birth to another without an end [the looked for result never falling to their lot]. This is what this world in fact is.

Saying 24. The desire for the result of what he does ever makes this being a prisoner of attachment and aversion. This thirst is never appeased, whatever he may accomplish, whatever he may attain. Fearful and astounding is the power of this spell of *Māyā*, of its magic play. There is no way to escape from this labyrinth except the way that leads to *samatā*, to state ever the same.

Saying 25. An unrest ever deludes this mortal being, an unrest that ever deludes him to turn him into a compulsive doer of deeds good and bad. There is no relief for him from this condition of unrest and doing, no moment when he may cease to be doing [and just come to *be*, free from the fretful condition of becoming ever and always]. Only the way to *samatā*, to the state ever the same, can redeem him from this, his existential condition. The desire for the fruit of actions ever keeps this being under its spell, strong and powerful. Not until he is blessed with the vision of *samatā* can he free himself from that web, that bewildering spell that *Māyā* has cast on him. This verily is the unhappy condition of every mortal being, unhappy in the extreme.

Saying 26. The one and only purpose of righteous and holy way of life is to free this being from the manacles of action and make him rest in Brahman the Supreme, Brahman that is ever still and ever itself. A being that resorts to righteousness to serve some self-interest of his will find his efforts bear their fruit without much delay, but, then, misery alone waits for him after he has enjoyed that fruit. There is no way out of the compulsion of coming and going except action without a desire.[6]

Saying 27. To believe in something or some power other than the Lord, to seek one's being in and through it is the resolve of the dull witted. For, that is the way of desire and of self-affirmation and self-interest, the way of many means and ends and of being ever insecure and anxious. A being given to this disposition never comes to be himself, never finds the peace final and supreme. To wander from birth to birth and from death to death is to be his lot and portion.[7]

Saying 28. Let man know what the true path is and work for his salvation. Let him remember that his worldly condition is hard to transcend. Let him, therefore, purify his *buddhi* [deframe all that it has enframed] and stick with every care to the right path. For, that is how the mind will dissociate itself from all the adjuncts that it has identified his being with and will come to find the peace that is sameness itself. Free from the thought of the Me and Mine will it be, his mind.

Saying 29. Man should ever remember what it is that *karma*, action, leads one to. And let him ever keep himself away from sinful deeds. And let him follow, in association with the seers of truth, the way that leads to his truth. And let him not seek to live to serve his self-interests, let him live ever given to the will of the Lord and remember Him ever and always. And let him do whatever he can to alleviate the misery of the unhappy, the helpless and the orphans - do so with the disposition of service. And let him have full faith in the Lord and deviate not from the right path. Equipped with this disposition, this disposition that sums up all righteousness, he will extinguish all the miseries that go with his condition. He who ever lives faithful to the right and true path is the soul truly saintly and holy.

Saying 30. To think of the Lord as the support of the whole world and to know Him as bliss the eternal and perceive His light in each and every thing and being is to live truly the righteous way. And to surrender one's desire for the fruit of what one is called upon to do to His will is to be righteous. And to be of a humble disposition and to seek the good of all that live and breathe, seek it ever and always. And to let one's body exert for the good of others, one's mind think and feel for others and one's speech be of comfort unto others. And so is to give up the vanity with regard to one's body [its looks and relationships] and to respect the noble quaiities of every gifted being. And to ever strive for one's salvation and to cease to have any interest in one's body even when one is alive and to remain absorbed in the bliss that the *ātman* is. When a man comes to live this way, into Brahman the Word will he be absorbed, into that Being ever the same, that origin of the world and its blessed end.

Saying 31. To bring peace to man is the purpose of all the sacred deeds and holy life. A man who does not have faith in the Lord, does not live and breathe for Him, and who does not think of the end reserved for his life is a man given to and lives by selfishness. In no way can such a man know what the true Law is, much less can he live in accordance with it. By remaining true to the right principles [like simplicity, truthfulness and others], the *buddhi* comes to be powerful [does not seek the *other* for support and sustenance] and comes to rest in its own ontological being. It is necessary, therefore, that man should, with every effort, orient his mind towards the truth and to the way to it. For, that alone will lead him to eternal bliss and freedom from every calamity.

Saying 32. Every mortal being lives ever busy doing evil deeds. That is the law of *prakṛti,* that unmanifest cause of the manifest world. To believe in *dharma*, in the way to one's truth, one has to orient one's mind with every effort towards good deeds. This steadfast orientation alone will lead a man to the Real that he is. Those of noble and gifted dispositions, therefore, ever strive for their redemption and do not let their minds give way to evil. For that is the way to attain to one's true being and self.

Saying 33. Desire has set aflame the entire world as a mighty fire engulfs a great forest. The way out of this conflagration is the way of *dharma*, of righteousness. Therefore, let a mortal being follow the path to liberation that seers of truth have revealed unto mankind. That is the end true that a being, blessed with human birth, is to seek and attain to. So, let every being make the *ātman* alone his support, ever distancing himself from the labyrinth of *karma*, action. Let him cure his mind of that malady [of doership] and find the place truly secure. To live this way and to this purpose is to live in accordance with the Law, Law the real.

Saying 34. A being who is immersed in evil acts, who does not think of right and wrong with regard to his pleasures and acts, is a being that has strayed far away from the right path. His *buddhi* has turned dull and his life is a stain, ever anxious he lives for acquisitions and possessions. Most unhappy he lives, this being evil and sinful.

Saying 35. That man alone is great and all adorable, the knower of *dharma* and blessed with wisdom absolute, the man who has found the Lord as his only refuge in this unreal and transient world. And who from all the bodily pleasures is emancipated and has drunk deep of the Name disclosed unto him and who, with his mind given to good will, engages his body and spends his possessions in service of the world and sacrifices his comfort for the comfort of the unhappy. And who is humility itself and love itself. And who in solitude contemplates the *ātman*, the self, with no inclination left in him for all that is worldly and of the world. And who perceives the *ātman* as the support and base of the body and who leaves the fruit of his acts to the will of the Lord, that Son of man the sacrificial victim. And who has perceived the Witness within him and remains ever absorbed in It. And who has risen above all the activities of the body and its end and has come to stay still in the Word. And whose *buddhi* is no longer under the sway of dualities, those deviations from their being. He alone, a man of this mettle, is great and all adorable, a knower of *dharma* and blessed with the highest wisdom. A blessing is his life for mortals, his word the word of redemption. He is the man the world should revere and do obeisance to. He alone knows what *samatā-dharma* is, what sameness is and the way to it is. Blessed is he with the bliss of sameness, bliss that is his being and self, the bliss that those that live by the Law find and attain to. Full and whole he leaves the world [he who was born an ontological lack]. In his blessed life one finds manifest the glory of *dharma* in its form full and infinite. Think with *sat-buddhi*, with intellect pure [pure of the passion for the *other*], and orient your mind towards the truth. Therein lies your joy true and bliss true.

Saying 36. Conflicts among religions and sects flourish in and out of *ajñāna*, in and out of false knowledge. When, that is, a being identifies his being with the body, he comes to identify himself with these too, with religions and sects. There is, however, no religion as such, religion that one could hold to and identify with; only the bliss that is ever the same is *dharma* the pure, only that is what one can hold to and adhere to. All else is merely his projection, what he has set up and got ensnared in. And only *Māyā* or delusion is that - all that he has posited to project himself into. When he breaks up the ties that he has forged for himself, he comes to attain to the bliss that is the real state of his being. And that state, that Real, is called *samatā*, the state ever full and infinite, that centre of this moving world, to find which is to find oneself as bliss itself, the state that every prophet attained to in truth, and every seer [with all their seemingly different formulations of it].[8]

Saying 37. The ways and means that *sat-puruṣas*, the truth-become souls, revealed unto the people of the world for the extinction of their false identities, for their liberation from them, those very ways, and the thoughts they formulated for that purpose, came to be known as various religions. He who lives as those formulations ask him to live will find himself liberated from his ties, as did those persons the true.

Saying 38. He that has come to live is in search of freedom, but, not knowing his true being, he seeks it in what his action brings about as its result. With this ignorance of his true being, he moves on from birth to birth without an end, the bliss he is really in search of ever eluding him. *Prakṛti* is nothing else than a network ever on the move, ever in motion. To confuse his being with it is to find himself a compulsive doer, the disposition leading him to be born again and again. The knowledge of *samatā*, however, is there to bring to an end this ignorance of his, ignorance that makes him forget his true being and seek it where it is not; it is the knowledge that makes him full, makes him get absorbed in his true self and being.

Saying 39. Any man gifted [with nobility and insight] adopts the teachings of a *sat-puruṣa*, of a man that attained to his being and truth, for his own salvation and not to enter into disputes with those of other faiths. Striving every hour to attain to the Lord, as those teachings would have him strive, he will surely find, one day, the bliss he seeks, the bliss full and infinite.

Saying 40. Sure is it that a man who contemplates Person the Witness in him and ever seeks to distance himself from the mess of *karma* will find the light of Brahman and will be liberated from the adjunct of duality. He will find that light and that liberation because he will act without a desire, giving up all thoughts of self-concern, thoughts that ever darken one's soul. He will, instead, dedicate himself to the well being and happiness of others and will become one with the Name of the Lord. A man made of this mettle alone will know what *dharma*, the way true, is and he alone will be a *sat-puruṣa*, man the true and real, his word a joy and blessing for those who hear it. Imperative it is that man give up all religious disputes and dedicate himself to the way of life that would lead him to his *ātman*, his self the real. There is no *tapas* like living according to the true Law, living so with full faith, and attaining thereby the blessed state of *samatā*. Let that be one's constant effort and endeavour.

Saying 41. The founders of religions, one finds, lived the principles they taught unto the world, their lives were embodiments of freedom from desire and pride and of disinterestedness in mundane affairs and of stillness. They lived for others and for the good of others. Then, why these tensions, these conflicts, these acts of enmity among various religions and sects? The answer is straight and simple: fanatics confuse customs with religion and fall victims to intolerance and hatred on that account.

Saying 42. Rituals regarding ordinary and daily life are incidental and transient. To quarrel on their account is a sign of folly. Religion in its essence makes the mind pure, makes it have faith in the Lord and frees it from pride, arrogance and jealousy. Religion in this sense brings salvation to man, liberation from recurring births and deaths. Rituals regarding daily life are, of course, different in different religions; these are mere external symbols prescribed for identifying a man's faith, their forms dictated by the contingencies of the times [and places]. But mere adoption of those symbols will be of no use for a man if he remains ignorant of the truth his faith reveals and continues with his old wicked ways. A man of this nature cannot be called a true follower of the faith he professes, no rituals and no symbols can make of him a man righteous and set him on to the path to the truth.

Saying 43. Rituals and symbols do not turn a man into a pilgrim to the truth. He may grow hair or keep it uncut, or he may get his head shaved or may wear the holy sign on his forehead or wear other marks, or he may mortify a part of his body to make it wither, turning it into a life-long indication of his faith but of no avail will be these acts of his, of no spiritual value. A mere pretence are they, a mere notice of one's faith and religion.

Saying 44. Mere imitation of external signs and forms that marked the outward lives of the founders of religions will not bring a man the joy he seeks, the blessed joy of ever being the same. He must follow in their footsteps and give up every self-concern and act without a hope and desire. Wearing of symbols and tokens are like entering a school. One has to proceed forward to attain to his goal, as a freshly admitted child into a school has to learn a great deal before he graduates into scholarship. To remain confined to mere symbols and rituals is like a child's staying for ever at the first standard.

Saying 45. Outward symbols and signs are introduced as conditioned by the time, the place and the ways of life of the people concerned. They have been undergoing changes with the changes in time, place and cultures. They do not constitute the spirit of *dharma*, mere customs are they, mere mores. To quarrel about them is not to be human. One should learn from every religion what constitutes its right spirit; there is no sense in indulging in useless disputes and make one's mind stray from the right path.

Saying 46. Let every man of faith adopt the true principles of life that his faith has taught him and find thereby the peace eternal. That is what his faith asks him to do and the prophets and founders of that faith. If he does not purify his mind and is content to wear mere signs of his faith, a vain bragger will he remain, a mere fool ignorant of what his prophets have taught. At no time will he be welcome in the Divine Hall of the Lord.

Saying 47. There is no name intrinsic to anything in the world; its qualities and its functions determine the name it has or has been given. As the name of a thing indicates its qualities and its functions, similarly the name of the religion that one professes should make one know what it really is and reach the goal it has set for man. That would make one a true follower of his faith and would bless him with redemption., with bliss of *samatā*.

Saying 48. Every prophet's teachings have two aspects and every religion too teaches two ways to salvation. One is the way of disinterested action and the other is the way of contemplation of the Supreme and Eternal Being with faith full and complete. The aim of these two ways is the same, namely, attainment of the state where no desire obtains. Desire is the malady that inflicts all that have come to live. These two ways are there to cure the *buddhi* of this malady and wash off that stain of it to enable it to find the bliss that is ever the same.

Saying 49. Disinterested action, action without a self-interest to prompt it, is an action the results of which have been left to the will of the Lord. It implies going beyond the reach of joy and sorrow alike. And that is what the bliss of *samatā* is, the bliss of dwelling in the same and as the same. The other way is the way of knowledge, knowledge of the Lord. It implies dissociation from one's being as the doer and taking oneself as the Lord Himself, the Lord of all that is. This latter way has been termed as *vijñāna-yoga* by *sat-puruṣas*, men the real. The first way [that of *karma-yoga*], implies worship of the Lord of the all as the doer, Him alone; the other implies worship of the same Lord as the non-doer. Both these contemplative dispositions are present in every man on the path to the truth [that of dissociation from actions by attributing them to the Lord and that of dissociation from actions by attributing them to the mind-body complex and of staying as one with the witness self]. Either way can lead him out of the snares that perverted knowledge has woven for him.

Saying 50. A man who does not strive to wake up from his forgetfulness will not find the bliss he seeks whatever religion he may profess to believe in. Every religion and every path teaches man that he, a mortal living in this perishable world, seek the Being Imperishable, that bliss beyond every pain and every sorrow. To be patient and calm is his *dharma*, his sacred duty, for that is what Prophets and seers of old embodied in their lives. Let every man wake up from the sleep of ignorance and do his best to free himself from that malady called desire and offer himself to the *samatā-dharma* to attain to the blessed state of sameness, his real home. Let him ever put in his best effort for that purpose, for therein lies the joy true and eternal.

(ii) *Regarding the Path of* Samatā

Saying 1. Belief in the *ātman* and dedication to the service of the people are the primary constituents of the path of *samatā*.

Saying 2. In this path participation in *sat-saṅga* is considered indispensable to know wherein lie one's weaknesses and lapses and to get inspiration to live by other regulative principles [namely, simplicity, truthfulness, service and yogic meditation].

Saying 3. To adopt the qualities and traits of the gods and goddesses and to live in accordance with the ideals they pursued and attained to constitute the true worship of the gods and goddesses or their images. That alone is their worship true, according to the path of *samatā*.

Saying 4. In the path of *samatā,* resort to *sat-saṅga* is the primary means for self-purification and to redress the wrongs one may have done.

Saying 5. In the path of *samatā* remembrance of the Name of the Lord and contemplation of the Lord every morning and evening is an absolute must.

Saying 6. In the path of *samatā* it is absolutely imperative that one adopt, with every sincerity, the principles of simplicity, service, truthfulness, *sat-saṅga* and remembrance of one's being true and real.

Saying 7. In this path, one must study the books that speak of the *ātman*.

Saying 8. In the path of *samatā* it is considered necessary that one do one's meditation at the time fixed for that purpose. Abstinence from intoxicants too is a must for everyone that follows this path. From places of show and display[9] should he also keep himself away. These two principles must be strictly adhered to, namely, punctuality of the time with regard to meditation and keeping oneself away from intoxicants and places of show and display.

Saying 9. In the path of *samatā* participation in a true *sat-saṅga* alone is the act of pilgrimage.

Saying 10. In the path of *samatā* to believe in the Lord alone is *parama-dharma,* the highest act of faith. To believe in something else is to believe in the wrong and the evil.

Saying 11. In this path it is one's own efforts, efforts at one's best, that can bring about liberation. To believe that one can help others or to believe someone else will help one to attain to that end is a foolish thought. In other words, one must purify one's mind in accordance with the teachings of *sat-puruṣas,* men that have attained to the Real.[10]

Saying 12. In the path of *samatā, niṣkāma-karma,* disinterested action, is the primary means to liberation - that is to say, surrender of all one's acts to the Lord and acceptance with full faith whatever He ordains for one. To worship gods and goddesses and the planets with some self-interest in mind and to ask favours from them is strictly forbidden. There is no power that can prevent the *prārabdha karman,* the part of acts done in the past lives responsible for the present birth, from unfolding itself. One must endure it taking it as if ordained by the will of the Lord. There is no way other than this to turn this necessity into an opportunity for one's salvation.[11]

Saying 13. In this path, one must adore the Lord before undertaking any good deed. One must not rely on anything else.

Saying 14. In this path of *samatā,* worldly customs are to be observed in a most simple way, and only those among them that do not involve any sinful act. All other acts that create doubts in one's mind or make it polluted must be discarded.

Saying 15. One who follows this path of *samatā* must serve every deserving being, serve him as much as one can. But this must be done for one's self-purification and not for self-display.

Saying 16. Let a man that follows this path see to it that he does everything at the right time, that his endeavour is right, that his belief is right and that his company is right.

Saying 17. A man on this path must think seriously about the condition of his embodied state and adopt, with every effort, the path of *dharma* in accordance with that condition.[12]

Saying 18. Those who have chosen to follow this path should make their families too incline towards it. This is their paramount duty, especially acquainting their children with its basic teachings.[13]

Saying 19. Those who follow this path are to firmly surrender their life to the Lord's will. They should know what is action and what is non-action. *Sat-saṅga* is especially meant for knowing the difference between these two.

Saying 20. In the path of *samatā*, devotion to the Lord means contemplation of the *ātman*, of the self, and resort to acts that lead a man towards the self.

Saying 21. With regard to Hinduism and other faiths, *samatā* teaching is like unto a thread with regard to the beads of a rosary.

Saying 22. The Doctrine of Samatā permits its adherents to attend the places of worship of all religions and learn what they teach and also to invite people of all faiths to participate in its *sat-saṅgas*.

Saying 23. The customs [and insignias] attached to different religious sects are not the points to be discussed about.

Saying 24. The Doctrine of Samatā teaches that man make every sacrifice for the sake of a noble life, and a life dedicated to the Spirit within and also to the service of his land or country. He is to live this doctrine [in addition to understanding it].

Saying 25. The Samatā Doctrine instructs man to investigate in the right way the Law of Nature and make one's life accord with that Law.[14]

Saying 26. The Doctrine of Samatā teaches man that he pay every heed to the ideals that every founder of religion and every seer of truth lived for and attained to and also to live for and by those ideals.

Saying 27. If you find a man asleep to the Law Divine and immersed in many a doubt, wrong belief and practice, you are duty bound to tell him the truth but this you are to do with every care and concern for his feelings.

Saying 28. You are to leave it to his will to consider with every care what you say unto him and to take resort to the right way. It is not for you to enter into useless disputes with him. This Doctrine would not approve of the latter approach.

Saying 29. For the path of *samatā*, noble deeds performed in the spirit of disinterestedness constitute the real effort and striving. That is what seers of truth declare as the way to the truth.

Saying 30. The Doctrine of Samatā asks of man to follow the path of *dharma*, the path that leads him to his being, his *ātman*, and delivers him from the doubts that gnaw him and the wrongs that mislead him. Let every being that breathes deliberate on what it teaches and live by the principles it propounds to make his life full absolutely and in every way. This way will he find the end and goal of his pilgrimage - namely, the peace transcendental, the peace beyond the ken of man.

(iii) The Buddhi *and its Forms Consummate and Not-consummate*

(a) The Buddhi's Four Forms of Darkness

Saying 1. To deliberate on what constitutes the *jīva's* condition of bondage and that of his release, and on how to get rid of the bondage that one's identification with the activities of *prakṛti* is and on how to strive for liberation from that bondage is the purpose of a real *sat-saṅga*, of participation in a holy company.

Saying 2. Those who participate in *samatā sat-saṅga* must think of every shortcoming and weakness with regards to their daily life and their spiritual life and adopt in their life the [five] principles. Let them give up every evil deed, the deed that destroys one's sense of the spiritual truths.

Saying 3. Let every act, worldly or those regarding the life of Spirit, be performed strictly in accordance with the time and place reserved for them. Let there be a time to be awake and a time to sleep, a time to eat and drink and a time to associate with holy company, a time to give and a time to meditate and glorify the Lord.[15]

Saying 4. Let every man think how action originates and how it ends, which forms it assumes and which forms it does not assume. Until a man knows for certain what is the truth about action and its ways, he cannot make any progress towards his real goal.

Saying 5. Let a man participate in *sat-saṅga* and try to know wherein consists the true consummation of the *buddhi*, where and how it reaches the state of its perfection. For, let him understand that the entire world moves depending on the states of *buddhi*, its state higher and lower. The state of dissolution of *buddhi* is the *ātman* itself, that truth itself; when it is active, it is a mere passion for the fruit of actions. In that latter state alone it finds a world, world set up by itself. When it comes to be still in *samādhi*, the state in which the knower and the known come to be one, it turns into (*anubhava*) bliss, into that alone.

Saying 6. The *buddhi* operates in seven forms and sets up varied phenomena [those, its sustaining and negating *others*] to move from joy to pain and vice-a-versa, assuming many a form. This is all that the world is, the world so hard to transcend. But to transcend that is the only purpose of human birth, to transcend the *buddhi* and the world it sets up.

Saying 7. The *buddhi* has four stages of darkness and three of light. As long as the *buddhi* is caught up in its benighted forms, it cannot free itself from desire and the compulsion of setting up its objects [its *others*].

Saying 8. Its first benighted form consists in its equating itself solely with the body, taking it as its self and being and, under this delusion, remaining ever busy to serve that false self. In this stage of darkness all its actions are devoted towards only one end, namely, to serve the interests of the body-self. A being of this dark disposition does not believe in any teaching, despite all appearances to the contrary, nor does he believe in the existence of the Lord. Whatever he does, he does to serve his own [narcissistic] purpose. This disposition is all-polluted; it is the disposition of a being who is unfit to be a being-in-relationships, his desire, like fire, consuming all that comes its way.

Saying 9. Its second benighted form is assumed by those people who resort to magic and chants to obtain their desires or worship tombs, cremation grounds, ghosts and spirits and indulge in all sorts of evil actions for that end. People of this disposition do not hesitate to do any evil act if it serves some purpose of theirs, these beings that imagine themselves very clever and intelligent. No faith they have in the Lord, their minds polluted by false and evil beliefs. They tend to mislead others too, people of this kind, mislead them into their own dark faith. Pretence and wile are the forte of people of this disposition. Exceedingly miserable is the life they live, a torture and misery, their sinful ways ever magnifying it, that torture and misery.

Saying 10. The *buddhi's* third stage of darkness finds its expression in the life of those who resort to all kinds of rituals and penance to fulfill their desires and offer sacrifices to gods and goddesses for the same end. Their acts of charity too have the same purpose and so has their piety. To possess and to acquire is the sole aim of their life and their occupation. People so disposed have no genuine faith in the Lord nor have they any interest in matters relating to their Being nor do they ever strive to attain to that Being. They see no one else to rival them in intelligence, these self-opinionated beings. They would devise all sorts of ways to win the admiration and applause of others, but not for a moment will they think of doing them any good. This state too is a state of misery, misery acute and deep.

Saying 11. The fourth benighted condition of the *buddhi* expresses itself in the life of those who worship the planets, spiritual teachers, saints and incarnations but only to serve the interests of their false self, the self embodied. People of this kind may and do often make a display of their piety and holiness. They do resort on occasions to *tapas*, to penance, and to meditation and also do acts of charity but, again, for the sake of their worldly well being. They also visit places of pilgrimage and resort to other religious practices but, despite their apparent piety, their obsession with themselves and their self-interests does not ever leave them. Their acts of piety are often prompted by desire to be well thought of by others, this passion being a mark of their life. But there are occasions when people of this kind deliberate with a measure of seriousness on the lives and teachings of great souls. And there are also occasions when they get somewhat pensive about death too. But in spite of these redeeming factors, men of this sort never come to be rid of their obsession with themselves, that darkness ever enveloping them. As to genuine faith in the Lord, they never come to have it. Unhappiness great and deep is the mark of this form of life too.

The first two dispositions are marked by darkness dense and absolute. They constitute the very demonic form of life. Those of the two latter dispositions can find the way righteous if some great soul comes to wake them up from their sleep.

(b) The Buddhi's Three Forms of Light

Saying 12. Understanding fully the instruction about the difference between what is real and what is not real marks the *buddhi's* first form of light. And to be inclined towards the righteous acts too is a characteristic of it. A being living in this state of life lives in fear of death and ever thinks of getting himself rid of the obsession of every mortal being, the obsession for the false self and its interests. He makes a true seer of the truth his guide and mentor, and orients his efforts towards the realisation of his *ātman*; ever anxious is he to be of some service to others and is of a disposition just and fair. To be firm in his faith, to be disposed well towards others, to be honest and fair in his dealings, and to give up his sense of identity with the body and to believe in the Lord and the word of his guru, his spiritual preceptor - these are some of the traits of the man in this state of being. There remains no frivolity in him and no vulgarities. He thinks of *parama-śānti* alone, of peace the supreme and transcendental, and lives by the noble principles of simplicity, truthfulness, service, *sat-saṅga* and yogic contemplation. He would know, and know full and well, the truth about the mind, the adjunct that he has taken to be his self, and would distance himself from this his taint through the yogic meditation as taught by a truth-become soul.

When this being acquires and lives this disposition, he comes to have a foretaste, a fore-understanding, of the peace he seeks, and comes to think of the real goal and purpose of life. A being who has attained to this state of *buddhi*, endeavours, with every earnestness, to attain to that goal and to purify himself of sins, those gifts of his past lives. He alone is a true devotee, he who has given up all false beliefs and evil ways and has given himself up to contemplation of the *ātman*. Attain shall he, one day, through his endeavour true and genuine, the end supreme of life, that being noble and gifted.

Saying 13. The second state of light expresses itself in the disposition that finds the Lord alone as real and the world a mere delusion. A man gifted with this disposition has no interest left in the things of the world, his passion for them having been spent. He becomes steadfast in contemplation of the Lord, contemplation as his guru true has taught him, his weal and woe left entirely to His will. With every good will he serves every being that needs his service, serves them with all the resources at his command - material, mental and physical - and bears all the troubles that others may inflict on him, never giving them any in return. All generosity he lives and all forgiveness. Contemplates he the Name of the Lord with steadfast devotion and leaves the fruit of his bodily actions to His will. A being of this *parama-tapa[s]*, this supreme and fervent ardour, is verily a god in the shape of a man; found has he the peace transcendental within him and made it his sole refuge and anchor. He alone knows what true bliss is, he alone embodies devotion and he alone is blessed with knowledge true. He is the one who knows what the world in its truth is, and he alone has truly dedicated himself to the way that leads to liberation. Nothing desires he, nothing except the Lord, that man the blessed. Before long will he merge in the Lord as He indeed is and will attain to the goal supreme and ultimate.

Saying 14. The third state of illumined *buddhi* consists in its getting detached from all the deviants that go with the embodied state and in its coming to be established in the *ātman* as it truly is and in attaining to Word the Real within. A man who has attained to this state ever remains absorbed in the bliss that the Lord is, to be or not to be being of no concern for him, or happening or not happening. With his *buddhi* free from all enframing and determinating, he remains ever lost in the One Lord, drinking of that bliss the supreme. He alone knows what this state is, he alone who has attained to it. He has won the final victory over the world, beyond the reach of time he dwells, dwells in eternity itself. This alone is the state of peace that passes all understanding. Every act of piety, every righteous way has only this state for its end. If a man, who has had the privilege of being endowed with gifts of insight and purity, does not strive to attain to this state, vain has been his human birth for depart will he from his life unappeased and unfulfilled. It is the duty supreme of all gifted men to remain steadfastly committed to finding this state of illumination, this abode real of each and every being, attaining which he becomes Brahman itself to find himself all-bliss itself. The man who has attained to this state is verily the Lord Himself in the form of a man, he is God the Incarnate, verily God Himself is he. Knows he all the play of the world, knows it in its truth and reality, remaining all-absorbed in his true being. Bliss the supreme it is, this state.

Let this be the goal of all your endeavours and all your efforts!

(iv) *To See the Same and Be the Same*

There was never a man who could see the Same and be the Same in mere theoretical terms. These two conditions indicate how deeply one has come to be established in the *ātman*. It is only when one really and truly comes to be so established that one comes to know what that blissful state really and truly is. One could write many a book on these two states but there is neither the time for it nor is there any need for it. Only very briefly are described below these two states. Try to realise them in your life!

On the seer of the Same: To be beyond the reach of happiness and sorrow, to be free from the desire for the fruit of one's actions, to remain ever established in the *ātman*, to remain still when the organs of sense and action are active. And to perceive the same *ātman* within and without and to perceive all that happens in the world as grounded in it, in the *ātman*; to rise above the sense of me and mine with regard to the body and to remain ever given up to the *ātman*. And to remain distant from all the dualities like those of friend and foe, profit and loss, from those false appearances that the *jīva* in ignorance of his true being sets up before him. These are the characteristics of a seer of the Same. In sum, to remain self-same in activity and inactivity, happening and no happening, to remain firmly established in the *ātman*. The seer of sameness is also called *jīvana-mukta*, one who has become liberated in his life itself. A man of this attainment is a blessing for the world.

On one who lives and has become the Same : There is no taking for him and no giving, his being only the bliss that is the *ātman*, so deeply absorbed is he in it. Transcends he the body even while alive, the formed and the gross having disappeared for him. Not a trace of doership remains in him, for all oblivious he remains of his doings and what they bring about. Only Brahman he knows, only Brahman he becomes ! The great men who have attained to this state are unable to do any good to the world, for they can neither speak nor hear. Ever immersed they remain in the bliss of their *ātman*, their being.

Devotee of the Lord! Only a very brief account is given here but give your serious thought to it. It is no easy fare to become a seer of the Same, the highest reach of *yoga* is his state. And harder still is to live and be the Same. Mere talk will not lead one to become the seer of the Same or to become the Same itself. You have to live all disinterested and act all disinterested to reach this highest state of *samatā*. *Niṣkāma-karma*, action without a desire, eventually leads one to this state ultimate, this abode of both the seer of the Same and of the person who lives as one with the Same, has become one with the Same.

If a man who has not realised the self within and has not become one with it, who is a prisoner of the pleasures of sense - if a hypocrite of this kind pretends to be one with the *ātman*, to be ever lost in it, in that sameness, pretends to be so for the sake of mere these pleasures, benighted absolutely is he, a man mean of mind and intention. A man becomes first a seer of the Same, only then can he become and live one with It, transcending absolutely the state of embodiment. Therefore, resort of *niṣkāma-karma*, action without a desire, to attain to the state of *sama-darśī*, the seer of the Same! The state of *sama-vṛtti*, that of one who lives as the Same, has become the Same, will follow on its own. Not before a man has realised the *ātman* can he become a *sama-darśī* or a *sama-vṛtti*. If one thinks of himself to be one, he is a rank hypocrite and evil. For, only that man can attain to this supremely holy state who has freed himself from all the deviations associated with the body, from all its failings and aberrations and has come to rest in his own being, in his *ātman*.

Knowing that to be established in the state of *samatā* is the highest goal of his life, let a man give up his desire for the fruit of his actions, let him act with an absolutely disinterested disposition. As he progresses towards the bliss that is the *ātman*, he will find himself increasingly suffused with the vision of sameness, this vision culminating finally in his becoming one with sameness itself, that state of liberation from the body, that state of bliss the supreme. Let it be clear that perception of all as the same and to be the same are the states of the realisation of the self, of the *ātman*, the *ātman* that abides ever transcendent, beyond the body and its experiences. Few are there that can attain to the self and be the self.

In sum, one should first resort to *niṣkāma-karma*, action without a desire. to give up all the hopes that action holds out to a man. When this endeavour of his becomes firm and sustained, he will come to rest in the self, will come to attain to *samādhi*, where no desire remains and no setting up of its objects. A man who has attained to that state, the state of *samadhi*, spends his life to work for the uplift of the world, for all that he had to attain he has already attained. He alone is a *sama-darśī* (*sama-darśin)*, a seer of the Same, he alone is a *jīvana-mukta*, liberated in his life itself. When he comes to rest in the self all the more deeply, he comes to be a *sama-vṛtti*, transcending the body even when it breathes and is alive. One should, therefore, strive first to attain to the state of a *sama-darśī*, that state free from every desire and resentment and anger. For, that is the state which one has to attain to before one can attain to the state of a *sama-vṛtti*.

A man who pretends to be a *sama-vṛtti*, pretends to remain the same in his enjoyments and pleasures, is not a human being, but an animal [who cannot distinguish the right from the wrong]. *Sama-bhāva*, to be ever the same, is indeed the goal of this living being. But forgetful of this goal ever the calm, the world is lost in all kinds of conflicts and disputes. To wake up people to their goal the doctrine *samatā* has manifested again by the will of the Lord. Let your life embody this doctrine so that you may find the bliss that you truly are and be a balm for the unhappy world. *Samatā* is the goal ultimate of Hinduism. The lives of all the prophets and founders of the great religions also reveal *samatā* as their ideal. But what confusion has seized the world today! The wise and the foolish, the preceptors and the preachers are all caught up in conflicts and tensions, in disputes and quarrels, forgetting the state of *samatā*, that rest and refuge ultimate of every living being. The Lord has willed that the doctrine of *samatā* appear again before the world. Let it guide you to your self and being, dispelling all your false beliefs! May you make blessed thereby your human birth![16]

SECTION 2

Samatā-yoga-siddhi, On Attaining to *Samatā-yoga*

State 1 - Simaran, *Remembrance*

Saying 1. A man should be steadfast in remembering the Lord if he wishes to attain to the vision of *samatā*, that blessed state of being oneself without an *other*. Remembrance means silent contemplation of the Name within, with the tongue still and the lips closed. When this contemplation comes to be natural and spontaneous, one's mind no longer sets up its *others* to sustain itself and comes to live with the Name alone as its support. With every lucidity and clarity it can then discriminate between the real and the unreal.

Saying 2. When the mind comes this way to stay with the Name, it comes to be still and passive, no mental process distracting it from its still concentration. That alone is remembrance in truth, this concentration of the mind without any distraction. To attain to this disposition of concentration the man on the path should see to it that his food is pure and his dealings straight and honest and his company noble. For, only a mind suffused with purity can make the Name its support.

Saying 3. False appearances of name and form ever keep the mind distraught, letting it not a moment's respite from its obsession with things passing and transient, from one thought or another. This unrest alone is the cause of happiness and unhappiness and of birth and death. As long as one does not contemplate the Name with a true intent and does not become steadfast in that contemplation, one simply cannot free oneself from this misery and futility, this compulsive passion to set up false appearances to sustain one's false being.

Saying 4. With every faith in the Lord and devotion to Him, the mind extricates itself from names and forms, from those the false appearances and comes to repose all its trust and faith in the Name true, comes to be concentrated on it. That is the moment when the peace and calm dwelling within one will spring up to make the mind rest and repose in it. That is why, remembrance of the Name is preferred to other ways of reaching the *ātman*, for remembrance of it leaves a deep impact on the mind to make its thought-process pure without much ado and delay.

Saying 5. When a man comes to stay still with the Name and repose in it, he will have no interest in the world left in him, his devotion and allegiance being directed solely towards the Lord. Mere doings of the body then turn his actions, as mere happenings he accepts them, his desire for them having ceased and gone.

Saying 6. It is at that moment that that blessed man finds devotion, in its form true and fervent, sprout up in him to lead him to liberation, that state blessed in every truth. Only remembrance of the Name can bring about this noble disposition of exclusive concentration, no holy discourse can bring it about, no narration of sacred events, no pilgrimage, no giving and no act of sacrifice. That is why this form of yogic practice has won the homage of all the *sat-puruṣas*, of persons attained to the truth.

Saying 7. Anyone who would be blessed, would be liberated from his worldly condition, should first resort to remembrance of the Name, that means supreme, to attain to that end of his. This indeed is a privileged means to salvation, this method of exclusive concentration on the Name.

Saying 8. One should know what the right method of remembrance, of concentration on the Name, is. Some remember the Lord by adoring him in words loud and articulate, others remember Him by singing melodies in His praise. No doubt these methods have some little merit in them, for they do appease and soothe the mind for a while. But the peace the mind is really and truly in search of does not come one's way through these methods. Only remembrance of the Name, only silent and inner meditation of it, contemplation absolutely steady and exclusive, can lead one to that peace the real.

Saying 9. A man who would bring his mind to rest must, therefore, resort to the right effort and with the right method. There are quite a few gurus who would utter a *mantra* in the ears of their disciples to the great puzzlement of the latter. Many are there who initiate their disciples into five names, little knowing the significance of even one among them. This incomplete understanding [of the method of meditation] can never lead one to the bliss absolute.

Some among those who knew Real the Absolute expressed that hidden truth in many a verbal form [name] but the content of their diverse expressions was the same. The diversity lies in the way they hailed and praised the truth, not in the truth itself. For the purpose of meditation, however, only one Name should be chosen, meditation of that alone will lead one to the goal supreme, not of many names, as some teachers would have their disciples believe. It is a difficult fare to master even one Name; as for mastery over many of them, it is simply out of the question. People that try to meditate many names simply waste their time in deluded beliefs.

As for true remembrance, it consists of coalescence of breath and mind, with the inward current and the outward current of breath being of the same duration.

Saying 10. As the first step, one on the path to the truth must be steadfast in remembrance, in the meditation of mind-breath. When this meditation becomes mature and steady, he will attain to the state of *bhajana*, of joyous adoration. With that state attained, he will move on next to the state of *dhyāna*, of passive contemplation. And the last state he will attain to is that of *samādhi*, the state where the knower and the known, the contemplator and the contemplated, come to be one, the state, that is to say, of merger in the Real. A man who would resort to *dhyāna* without first becoming steadfast in remembrance will never attain to *nirvikalpa-dhyāna*, contemplation in which the contemplator knows nothing else than the object of contemplation, not even himself. Let him not mistake the lights of varied hues that he may see with his eyes closed with Brahman the Word, for they are only the [subtle] forms of the elements, not that Reality the Absolute.

Saying 11. Many are there, the pompous charlatans, who speak of many inner states described by seers true and genuine without an iota of any experience of these, without even a genuine effort to have those experiences. Their claim to be guides unto others is a mere charade and simulation. Incapable are they of finding peace for themselves or for those they pretend to guide. Anyone who would be a genuine devotee of the Lord should take refuge in a perfect sage [for initiation into meditation of the Name].

Saying 12. Those who initiate their disciples into five names, depending on the words of the *yogīs* of old, too are ignorant of the yogic way. The Word is one and one only, though its manifestations are many, depending on the extent to which the mind gets absorbed in It. This does not mean that the Name changes at every state of the Word's manifestations. In no case can meditation of many names lead the man in question to his real goal.

Saying 13. That indivisible and imperishable Word resounds in many a way but all through the same Name should be meditated on. Change of the Name on the way will cause the contemplator's decline from the state he has attained to. It is true that seers of the highest order have revealed that home ultimate and goal ultimate through many names, depending on the states and inclinations of those they addressed. But inwardly they continued to abide in one Name only. Every seeker of the truth should be aware of this truth.

Saying 14. With each state this pilgrim covers, he sees before him many a spectacle unfold themselves one after another, spectacle strange and wonderful of Power the Perfect. But it is the same Name he continues to meditate, lose himself in. A day will come when this, his constant meditation of only one Name, will lead him to his Abode the Supreme. On the other hand, the man who changes one name after another on the way will not find the rest he seeks, rest the perfect. This verily is the secret of sages and seers the perfect. Those who have been instructed into five names will not find their contemplation come to be mature and stable nor will they find the Word true and become one with It. One should never forget that it was the various stages of the manifestation of the Word that the *yogīs* of old were referring to when they spoke of the five Words; they did not mean that there were five Names to be contemplated.

Saying 15. Remembrance of the Name will lead the contemplator to **the state nameless**. That is to say, he will be absorbed in Word the indivisible, will be lost in it. Therefore, he should make it a point to believe in one Name only and steadfastly contemplate it. That is the way to his redemption. Seers have given many a name to Brahman the Transcendent, that Lord Supreme of the world. But remembrance of only one Name among them will bring about the desired result. Let the pilgrim to the truth, therefore, absorb his mind in the self-same Sacred Name, the Name with which began his yogic practice.

Saying 16. Mind is by nature unstable; when it leaves one way, it finds it difficult to adopt and abide by another. It is not easy for it to give itself up to another Name when it has been its practice to contemplate a particular Name, its attention deeply concentrated on it. Instead of reposing in the second Name, it will turn self-conscious and vain. So one should absorb one's mind in a single Name alone. For, that is the way to attain to the highest goal.

Saying 17. There are some teachers who would have their disciples start their yogic practice with *dhyāna,* with passive contemplation, itself. This is, however, not the right way to success. For, until and unless the Supreme Reality manifests itself within, how can one contemplate it? The lights one may see with one's eyes closed are only the lights of the elements. The mind cannot stay with and passively dwell on them. It is only the mind that has been purified in the fire of remembrance that can come to stay passively with the Real dwelling within every being.

Saying 18. The seers that have attained to the goal always initiate their disciples first into remembrance, into meditation, of the Name. For, remembrance alone can make the *buddhi* free of its enframings and lead it to adore the Word, to passively dwell on it and, finally, to get fully absorbed into it. Let a man who resorts to remembrance remain in silence as much as possible and, when circumstances so demand, utter only sober, serious and soothing thoughts. Speech of this kind leaves a good impression on the mind.

Saying 19. Meditation of the Name should continue in every physical state and condition. Only a man given to this kind of meditation will find Brahman the Word manifest within him. Let him, therefore, be ever persistent with his meditation of the Name, withdrawing his mind from every other thought. Only then will his mind live for and by the Name. If the mind is not held in restraint, it will give up its meditation to conjure up many a fancy to inflame all the more its passions of attachments and aversions, intensifying its agony and its unrest as never before.

Saying 20. Let every seeker of the truth give himself entirely to the meditation of the Name with all the resources of his mind and body. Let him give up his I-sense and believe that all that is there is of the Lord and, with this belief held firm in his mind, let him give himself up to the meditation of the Name with a fervent devotion. A man who does his meditation this way will soon find himself blessed, his taints and faults, taints and faults he inherited from many a life past, washed off him.

Brahman the Word will find the man given to this kind of ardent meditation of the Name.

State 2 - **Bhajana,** *Joyous Adoration of the Name*

21. When the contemplator of the Name finds the Word manifest within him and his *surati,* his consciousness devoid of all its enframing and determinating, comes to get all concentrated on it - that is the moment when he comes to attain to the state of *bhajana,* of joyous adoration. All intent, he drinks of the divine bliss, the pleasures of the world having lost every charm for him.

Saying 22. Joyous adoration of the Word, that intent and fervent concentration on it, matures with time into the state of *dhyāna,* the state in which the mind gives up all its thoughts and activities and comes to be concentrated exclusively on Brahman the Word. A myriad of sounds and melodies he hears in that state of *dhyāna,* of passive contemplation, perceiving all that is as ordained by the Lord, erasing thereby his sense of the Me and the Mine.

Saying 23. His *surati,* that innocent consciousness of his, rises up from the lower parts of the body to come to stay in the forehead at the root of the nose [at the midpoint between the two eyebrows] to experience there Word the

Brahman. Then it is that he may be said to attain to the state of real *dhyāna,* the state of passive contemplation. Distancing itself from the activities of the body, the *buddhi* becomes pure [of all determinations] and comes to be still in Word the Brahman.

Saying 24. The thought of Me and Mine with regard to the body will throw him back to his earlier, fallen condition. So the blessed man that has attained to this state devotes himself with his body, mind and possessions to the service of the world and will find a good deal of time to praise his Lord, keeping himself distant from his bodily activities.

Saying 25. Let not that man, that pilgrim to the truth, reveal what he has attained unto others, let him ever keep it to himself. And let him not show unto others his miraculous powers. For these two weaknesses are the sure hurdles in his way to Bliss. Let him ever remain steadfast in meditation of the Name and adoration of the Word to become steadfast in *dhyāna,* in passive contemplation of the Word.

Saying 26. The man who has been blessed thus should not let his mind think of and desire things of the world; let him efface himself before the will of the Lord.

Saying 27. With his meditation becoming still and steadfast, he comes to experience progressively the light of Brahman within him to remain absorbed in devotion to it, his passions for the world all extinguished. Let him of this state be ever forgiving and compassionate, let him do good unto others, be humble and free from desire and rise above the ways and dealings of the world. It is necessary that he cultivate and strengthen this kind of disposition, otherwise his mind will not stay with the divine bliss, it will slide back into the pleasures of the world. Let him be moderate in his intake, let his sleep be short and light, and let his dealings with the world be few and brief. Let his time be spent as much as possible in *bhajana,* in adoration, of the Lord.

Saying 28. Let him concentrate with deep intent and every moment on the Word within him, his passion for work left to the will of the Lord to decide and direct. This contemplation and this disposition will make him dwell *in* the Word, will lead him to the state of *dhyāna*. His adoration of the Lord will be a joyous adoration, joyous in the extreme. Let him not be carried away by it, let him absorb that joy in himself, keep it under restraint and live and move all humble in the world.

Saying 29. A man who is more dedicated to *simaran* [*smaraṇa*], meditation on the Name, and to *bhajana,* joyous adoration of the Lord, and less distracted by the pleasures of the world, will find his mind get pure of the latter. Soon will he be absorbed into Brahman, this man of pure heart and mind. For long has the passion to set up false phenomena pursued this living being, for too long this disease of his mind has inflicted him, letting him not even a moment's respite from frustrations and unrest. Therefore, there has to be no let off in his endeavours, no relaxation in his efforts to make his mind come to be still and established in the Word. For, only then will he come to be still and action-free, only then will he find that peace eternal and indivisible.

Saying 30. A man who makes his mind dwell and get concentrated on Word the Indivisible, dwell on It each and every moment, refusing to identify himself with every state of being that comes his way, shall come to rest in the state of *dhyāna,* in the state of passive contemplation in all its truth.

State 3 - **Dhyāna,** *Passive Contemplation*

Saying 31 When the mind withdraws from all that it has set up[17] and comes to stay still in Word the Brahman and when it ceases to posit the gross, material world, that is the moment when the seeker of the truth comes to attain to the state of *dhyāna,* of passive contemplation. Blessed is the man who has found this state.

Saying 32. A man who has matured into *dhyāna* comes to find Word the Brahman to stay all quiet and tranquil in that his being and truth. In myriad forms the *Nāda,* that immortal sound, resounds in him then and also flash and blaze many a lightning. Joy in excess then comes to suffuse him, his relationships with the beings of the world, relationships that condition his very being and constitute him, coming to cease. To remain still in that Pure and Holy becomes that sole objective of all his indeavours.

Saying 33. Each and every activity that his mind-body complex is called upon to perform, he attributes to the command of the Lord [and not to his will], accepting the results of those activities, those dualities, with equanimity, be those results happy or unhappy. His life turns into a mere unfolding of Nature, he himself standing apart from it without a desire and without a passion.

Saying 34. He who has come to repose in the state of *dhyāna* alone is a *yogī* (*yogin*) in truth and a *jñānī* (*jñānin*), a knower, in truth. No desire remains in his mind and no positing and setting up of the *other*, established he remains in his being real and true. Nothing he desires and would have and be, and nothing he hates and would discard and give up. Immersed he remains ever in Love, that Joy itself.

Saying 35. With his *dhyāna* getting deeper, he hears the *Nāda* sound within him ever and indivisible. All rapt and absorbed he lives in it and abides by it, the entire world turning into its emanation, of the *Nāda*, that Being Supreme. Nothing is there in the world to tempt him any more from the Name of the Lord, that life and being of his.

Saying 36. Passive contemplation of the Lord is verily a redemptive contemplation, but not without giving up desires, each and every, can a man find it. Only a man who has surrendered all his weal and woe to the will of the Lord and keeps his mind ever established in Word the Truth can attain to this state happy and blessed. In complete humility should he live, he who has established himself in *dhyāna*. A little association of his self with an act, a trite of it, shall bring about his fall from that blessed state.

Saying 37. Few are there of this state who will commit this mistake, that of identifying their self with an action. For, suffused with knowledge and realisation are they, those established in *dhyāna*, and completely surrendered to the Lord do they live in the world, with the Name only their support and prop.

Saying 38. A man of this state of yogic contemplation should not let his mind be tempted by the miraculous powers that may come his way. A servant should he live of the world, given to every humility. Let no desire ever tempt him, desire for the things of the world. And let him ever abide in faith, faith in the Lord and bear with patience whatever may befall him, happy or unhappy. Only then will he attain to knowledge the full.

Saying 39. With his mind divested of all its activities, with his consciousness become bare of all its passion for setting up its *other*, and with all the fruit of his actions surrendered unto the Lord, can a man attain to this passive contemplation of Brahman, a man of this blessed disposition.

Saying 40. When that obsessive compulsion of man comes to cease, compulsion to do and to act, when his life is spent for the well being of others, when the entire world turns into and becomes for him the Lord Himself, and when, within himself, he stays still and passive, all lost in the bliss that is Brahman - only then can he attain to Brahman, that man the patience itself, only then can he attain to *samādhi*.

State 4 - Samādhi

Saying 41. When the *buddhi*, the faculty that determinates, comes to stay still in the Word [discarding all its determinations] and ceases to posit, when its sense of the I comes to be completely extinguished and when it comes to know itself as Brahman Itself, then is it that the man of patience attains to *samādhi*, that state all effulgent.

Saying 42. A man who attains to this state of immersion in the self experiences on every side nothing but Brahman. Time ceases to move for him, his self staying apart from the body and from every action and activity. These latter he finds as belonging to the realm of *prakṛti*, that objective sphere of being [posited by the passion for being]. He indeed is the knower of Brahman, he is the teacher of the whole world. From the web of *Māyā* he has disengaged himself to stay all quiet in his being true and real, finding himself a still passivity, untouched by any action whatsoever. He knows all, he who has attained to this state, his consciousness appeased in full and to perfection.

Saying 43. The man who is established in *samādhi* never becomes active with the body, apart from its activities he stays still and stable in Brahman the Sound (*Nāda*), that still passivity. In the whole world he finds himself interfused, his love overflowing to each and every being. But in the deeps of his deep he remains apart from the world, absolutely distant from it. This is the abode highest, the home ultimate of every being, this state of enlightenment. Attaining it, that state of *samādhi*, that man of high wisdom, loses himself in the *akhaṇḍa-nāda*, in the Sound indivisible and Immortal.

Saying 44. Absorbed in Word the Brahman he remains self-same whatever he may [apparently] be doing or undergoing. Transcending the duality of happiness and sorrow, pleasure and pain he stays in bliss the highest, stays in it all unmoved. He is the sage ultimate and he alone is the blest supreme.

Saying 45. Within him and without him he finds himself one with the *Nāda*, lost in it all entranced and ecstatic. In every vein of his body, in every bone and pore of it he finds the *prabhutā* of the *Nāda*, finds its glory primal and primordial. A seer of the same [*samadarśī* or *samadarśin*} is he, this dweller of stillness, this man that has transcended all activities and actions.

Saying 46. Deep within himself he finds his self, self apart and all different from the body and its functions. Only he knows what that state is, that state blessed and blissful, only he that has thus found his being and self. For, *that* is to find and not to tell and proclaim, that state ineffable.

Saying 47. A man who has attained to the state of *samādhi* ever finds himself inactive in the midst of action, distant and apart from every state of being, ungrounded and omniscient. His beginningless passion for being (*vāsanā*) extinguished, he stays stable, indivisible and beyond the sphere of the three *guṇas,* the three constituents of *prakṛti,*[18] his body a mere shadow for him. Worthy of every tribute is such a man and by every being; a support is he unto them, and a base, this rarest among the rarest, this man established in Brahman, this man who has become Brahman.

Saying 48. Standing apart from all the ideas, thoughts, impressions and desires sendimented in him during his long pilgrimage from birth to birth, he remains unperturbed by any pleasure and pain of the body. For, the acts of the body and the hard turmoil of the three *guṇas,* the three strands of *prakṛti,* cannot force him out of the Alone into which he has merged. Nameless is that state of his and indescribable; few are there that can attain to that state supreme, that end absolute.

Saying 49. A man who remains established in the Lord each and every moment, giving up every passion for the things of the world, whose one anchor is only the *Nāda,* the sound imperishable - he alone can attain to this light supreme, this state without its *other* to negate it.

Saying 50. The pleasures of the sense and motor organs ever lead the mind astray. Therefore, the man who has decided to burn himself into his true being ever keeps it, his mind, away from the functions of his organs of cognition and action and focusses it ever on the Name of the Lord. The *vāsanas* of the body, its passions and urges, he leaves to the will of the Lord to decide about. As for himself, he remains ever awake, every minute and every hour, to Word the Brahman resounding within him. He is the man to attain to *samādhi*, the man suffused with this kind of fervent devotion.

Saying 51. The fate of those caught up in the whirl of action awaits those charlatans who have not attained to *samādhi* and yet boast of their knowledge, knowledge of the Ultimate. Proclaiming themselves as divine incarnations or world teachers, they would guide and redeem the entire world! Life after life will these impostors remain immersed in the mire of *karmas* and their results, the possibility of their deliverance remaining distant from them. One should remember that a man requires surpassingly hard effort to reach this desire-free state, this state of establishment in Brahman. He must have faith in the word of his teacher and should have no interest in and hope from the affairs of the world. And, above all, he must live in the presence of a seer of the ultimate truth. He should understand that only that man can attain to *Nāda* the Brahman and can stay still in it, the man who ever perceives his body decay and die and who, freeing himself from all the passions natural to the body, ever stays steady in contemplation of the self.

Saying 52. The first step towards this blessed state consists in giving up those actions that are ruinous, that is to say, actions sinful. The next step consists in getting oneself initiated into the Name by a perfect seer and in resorting to *niṣkāma karmas*, actions without a desire prompting them, and dedicating oneself to devotion of the Lord. In other words, he, the seeker of the truth, should give himself to meditation of the Name and to adoration of the Lord, giving up all *vāsanas*, all that lies deposited in the mind by way of the impressions of the lives past. With meditation of the Name deepening, time and action that keep one moving from death to birth and from birth to death will tend to cease. With their cessation, the person on the path will find Brahman the Word within him, this his finding leading him to get absorbed in It, in the Word. Let this be the faith, the holy faith, of everyone in search of liberation.

Saying 53. With faith absolute and with endeavour unsparing can one reclaim his lost home. Not the prattlers that claim to be liberated, quoting in profusion words of scriptures and sages of old. Foolish are they, for waste do they their time, desires for pleasures their constant misery and torture. Destroyers of *dharma* are these prattlers, many a low and wretched births will be their lot and portion.

Saying 54. Let his own redemption be man's priority. Not until all his taints and blemishes have been washed away can a man know the real in its truth and explain it aright. Those imposters who would win the allegiance and devotion of ordinary people on the strength of their false eloquence and word play and fleece the latter for their own gain will be born in infernal conditions, and so will those who follow in their foot steps.

Saying 55. Only that man of wisdom will find the state true and real, the man that has freed his mind from all its taints and faults and has subdued all desires for the things of the world. For, only he is the man to remain ever focussed on Brahman the Sound, and he is the man to live among people as if their servant. No fraud has he or any despair and regret, or, for that matter, any desire. Freed from every sectarian and ceremonial piety he lives, his life ever given over to the Lord.

Saying 56. When a man has been instructed into the secret of *yoga*, let him interiorise that instruction and meditate the Name. And let him make it sustained, this meditation on the Name, ever renewing his effort and resolve. With his mind purified this way, he will gradually move on from the state of remembrance to that of *bhajana*, adoration of the Lord, from there on to the state of *dhyāna*, passive contemplation, and, finally, to the state of *samādhi*.

Saying 57. There is no way to attain to and stay in Word the Brahman until the sense of one's being a doer of actions, that primal darkness, comes to be dispelled. Therefore, only the man that is ever focussed within himself on the Name can find his *buddhi*, his intellect, stand apart from every action. With his faith in the Indivisible and Eternal Reality his only support, he, that man the greatest, alone finds the highest *samādhi*, he alone is liberated from further deaths and births.

Saying 58. The world of experience is nothing but the turmoil of action. Only true devotion to the Lord and true knowledge of the self can cut it asunder to lead one to find the goal highest, that of immersion in Word the Indivisible. Let man, therefore, ever strive to find that, his home absolute. That verily is his highest duty, of him blessed with human birth.

Saying 59. Awful and fearsome is the mind of man. It requires long and persistent struggle to focus it on the Name and make it quiet and tranquil enough to become inwardly oriented, the world and its things tempting it no more. Its obsession with work no longer holding it under its sway, it comes to attain to bliss the highest, the bliss that is called *samādhi*, that state blessed in which all delusions come to cease. In *samādhi* one finds only the Lord, that Real Absolute, only the Lord to become one with Him, to find Him as one's self and being (*anubhava*).

Saying 60. Only the man endowed with the highest devotion can find Word the Brahman to lose himself in It. He gives up his sense of identity with the body, that false appearance, and gives himself up, each and every moment, to meditation of the Name of the Lord, seeing all that happens as ordained by Him and His will. Few are there who find their life dedicated towards this end, the end of establishment in one's being, being the full and infinite. He indeed is endowed with the highest wisdom, he who is blessed with devotion to the Lord, devotion suffused with all humility and self-submission. Attained has he bliss the absolute, his life a support for others, and the ideal he sought and attained an inspiration for them.

Saying 61. Only the *buddhi* most profound and insightful can give up its passion to stick to what it has identified itself with and its passion to project itself into the world in the shape of a doer. And [more importantly] it alone can extricate itself from its thirst for transcendence from every given state of being. Only the *buddhi* freed from these three *guṇas*, from these three strands of *prakṛti*, would free itself from every desire and would not posit its *other* to sustain itself. Only this kind of *buddhi* can find the bliss supreme, cutting asunder the false net of *karmas* that keeps it ever ensnared and entangled. Only Word the Brahman it finds then, that bliss highest and supreme, that home true and peace eternal.

Saying 62. Every gross element has its subjective counterpart in the form of a deviation to taint the *buddhi*. It is only when it dissociates itself from those deviations, those taints, that it comes to get concentrated on the Name true. When this concentration becomes firm and stable, the *buddhi* acquires the ability to understand the most profound matters, ability that makes it all patient and forbearing. Only the Word Indivisible, Word the *ātman*, it finds to be the real then, and the entire *prakṛti*, that posited *other*, posited *a priori*, it finds a mere false appearance. With this understanding becoming firm, it lets itself dissolve into Brahman the Lord Supreme. This is verily the way, this is the striving of those that find the truth to become one with it.

Saying 63. A man of firm faith in the word of *sat-puruṣas* and deeply aware of how helplessly bound and shackled he is - he alone will seek to find his true, blissful self, seek it with all the energies of his mind, speech and body [literally, action]. Freed from the web of *Māyā*, he will fully give himself up to remembrance of the Lord, to adoration of Him, to passive contemplation of Him to merge finally in Him in *samādhi*.

Saying 64. All mysterious and eerie is this struggle called the world. No one is there to escape from it except those who reflect deeply on what *sat-puruṣas* teach them and follow in their life that teaching. The passion to be a doer, the passion deeply embedded in each and every being, ever distracts the *buddhi* from its true being. Only he can repose in bliss the supreme, he who, following the instructions of the truth-become souls, has turned his back upon all the pleasures of the world and has made his *ātman*, his true self and being, his sole refuge. All the twenty-four hours of the day he keeps his mind concentrated on the Name, withdrawing it from every of its preoccupations. A man of this disposition is a man of true and highest penance; he alone will find the truth supreme, he alone will be blessed, a man of this surpassing glory.

Saying 65. Thought pure and untainted [thought on the revelatory word, not thought indulged in independently of the revelatory word] accompanied by practice in accordance with what the revelatory word teaches is verily the best means to lead one out of the mazes of the world. Let the man desirous of liberation have firm faith in the Lord, let him cleanse his mind of all tainted and false beliefs [about the nature of his self]. And let him believe that the Great Lord, the Lord that was there when this creation was not, alone is the creator and destroyer of everything. And let him take all his worldly power and glory to be His gifts, His alone. And let him remember Him with a mind stable and steadfast, his food pure and his dealings straight. And let him dissociate himself from the body, let him undo his sense of identity with it, and, giving up all thoughts of concern with this false self, bring himself to rest in the Supreme Reality that he really and truly is. This in every truth is the way of devotion, devotion true and real.

Saying 66. Knowing that to serve others is his primary duty, let man ever be of comfort to those in distress. And let him leave with all determination the care of his weal and woe unto the Lord and meditate the Name regularly morning and evening and find, with mind concentrated, within him Word the Brahman, that Real the fine and subtle. And let him stay still in that Word, that being real of the Lord, let him merge into it, withdrawing his mind from all that the nine apertures of the body provide him by way of experiences, pleasant or unpleasant. Blessed will be such a man with vision divine, suffused with which he will perceive all that is and happens within and without him as illumined by the One Lord.

Saying 67. Let his *buddhi* be steadfast in *dhyāna,* in steady and inward contemplation [of the Word] and let him give up all his *vāsanas,* all the ideas and impressions that lie imbedded in him, leaving everything to the will of the Lord. And let him be of service and be a comfort unto others but let him not harbour any desire for any result from those noble deeds of his. If ever a man comes to be blessed with the spirit of this kind of renunciation and this kind of understanding, understanding that can clearly tell apart truth and untruth - if a man ever comes to be so blessed, he will surely transcend the mazes of *Māyā* with its three strands, those of *sattva, rajas* and *tamas,* and will come to be established in his self, his being, his thirst ever quenched, for attained will he have the state that is bliss the eternal itself. That is what is called *samādhi,* this state where no desire, no trace of it, remains, no motion and no deviation. He is verily the seer of sameness, he who rests in this state, his life a blessing unto others. Every act of his is a wonder, and every word of his. The Name alone is his support, the Name alone is his family, the Name alone is his dealing. Alive is he liberated, the knower of the knowable is he. Having known the all he is lost in the Full and the Infinite, his life the peace eternal and his state the state supreme.

Saying 68. Realisation of one's *ātman* is the paramount duty of man. If he fails to direct his efforts towards that end, delusions of *Māyā* will seize him, prompting him to do sinful deeds of the worst kind. Many a birth he will have to take and many a death he will have to die to reap the wages of those his acts. So, let every being blessed with human birth do his best to attain to the State Supreme. This verily is the teaching of every seer of the truth; to adopt this, their teaching, is their worship true.

Saying 69. That man is a devotee in truth, the man who remembers every moment that to be mortal is his inevitable lot, and, ever remembering this his lot, contemplates his *ātman*, that witness within him. For each and every being he has only good will, and serves he them with no desire for a reward. As for his mind, it is ever given to meditation of the Name, each and every moment. He alone will find bliss the supreme, find it with no hurdle to stand in his way. For, only the man who effaces himself thus, who sacrifices his very being to follow the way of the *sat-puruṣas*, will find the self, that bliss transcendental.

Saying 70. A man can find that home supreme only when he gives up every desire, every trace of it, however dim and faint, and gives it up here in his life itself. So, only those who live in contemplation of their true being, their *ātman*, each and every moment of their life, can come to be established in that supreme state, only those gifted souls. Born are these high and rare souls for the good of the world, for it is they alone who can make people aware that there is a God to rule the world and that there is a way to extinguish the fires that burn unabated in every being. Their word, of these rare souls, can lead a man to his truth, to his blessed truth, if he makes of it his guide and himself its faithful follower. So, let every breathing being give up every dispute and purify himself and give every moment of his life to meditation of the Name and be unto others as a servant is unto his master. Only this disposition can lead one to the state transcendental.

Saying 71. All the *sat-puruṣas*, spiritual preceptors, *pīrs* [teachers of Islamic doctrine] and divine incarnations taught the way to salvation only when they had first attained to their real being. That the *jīva*, he that lives, comes to be deluded by *Māyā* because of his false and vicious understanding has been the essence of their teachings, of each and every one among them. And also that the way out of his misery lies in passive contemplation of his true being, devotion to it and realisation of it. So, anyone gifted with a noble disposition, who, following their instructions, endeavours to undo his false and vicious disposition will undoubtedly attain to peace the transcendent.

Saying 72. This world holds a seductive charm about it but it is, in its essence, an unhappy and tragic world where death alone rules the roost. Those born in it have only woe and anguish as their lot. With his brittle body ever in danger of death, a wise man ever strives to find his real home, the home he has lost. Even when alive he will find the bliss transcendent, in this life itself, find the real beatitude, that state imperishable and stable.

Saying 73: He who would know and be the truth that he is should ever make his mind inward oriented and meditate the Name true, opposing all desires [which would drag him outwards]. He should see to it that the food he takes is pure, that his worldly life is straight and honest, that his thoughts are untainted and that his company is good and noble. Let this be a principle of his life, let him maintain strict purity in these matters, for that will lead him to find the *ātman*, his self real and true. This has been the way of the great souls and this should be his way too.

Saying 74. He should take only the food that is pure and that too for the sake of appeasing hunger; and, on occasions, he should abstain from eating and resort to fasting. Let this be a rule with him, his holy vow. Let him be straight in his dealings in business and those relating to give and take and spend his earnings in deeds that lead him to the truth. Let him not resort to deception in this matter; let him hold in check all his sense and motor organs. And let him also see to it that these activities of give and take remain within limits. These are the rules regarding economic or commercial activities that he should make it a point to observe. And let him be pure in thought and in word; let him not be fraudulent in his dealings with others; let him ponder over the lives of great souls, ponder over them time and again, and orient his mind towards the truth, be devoted to it, and be suffused with good will towards each and every being. Let this be his vow vis-a-vis thought and reflection.

Saying 75. And let him keep company with those who have become the truth itself and obey the word of the truth, word that speaks through them. Let him give up the sinful *vāsanās*, those thoughts and desires that dwell active and inactive in him, and, with these given up, let him give himself up in devotion to the Lord, devotion free of every desire and self-interest. And let him make the Lord the sole anchor of his breath, his life, and nurture well and strong the disposition oriented towards service of all beings and take lightly the honour that the world may bestow upon him; let him not let it make him proud and arrogant. And let him take everything as the Lord's and, with this thought, give himself up with determination to the remembrance of His Name and with affection and regard to the service of those that need and deserve it. That is the way to observe, in truth, his vow about *sat-saṅga*, about holy association. He who observes these great and holy observances [about food, about business, about thinking and about holy association] alone can remember truly, adore truly and contemplate truly and attain to the state of *samādhi*. Let a man do everything to purify his life so that he may break his fetters even when alive and find that home where no fear is and no threat.

May the Lord make every seeker know where the truth abides so that he may give his thought to this revelation, revelation beyond the ken and comprehension of mankind, and strengthen his resolve to purify his life!

SECTION 3

(i) On the State of the Guru, the Preceptor

Saying 1. The word 'guru' means, 'one who dispels darkness'. In truth, only Word the Supreme Lord is the real teacher, He alone transcends all the darkness of delusion, He alone dispels it, that darkness, He the Light Eternal that shines in each and every mortal. When the *buddhi*, the faculty that determinates, experiences that Supreme Being, it leaves all darkness behind and merges into the Lord that is Light itself.

Saying 2. Teachers worldly and of the world too are there, teachers that teach the ways of the world. They are also called *gurus.* Their teaching, however, relates to the transient world and its affairs [and not to truth the absolute]. This *jīva,* this embodied being, is ever and always in need of instruction, whether about the truth absolute or about the facts and ways of the world. Without that instruction, he can neither understand the world nor can he find the truth absolute.

Saying 3. Only he can be a teacher of the truth absolute, he who has come to abide in the Eternal Lord and has gone beyond the reach of desire, that deviation and fall from one's being and truth, to remain ever absorbed in the light supreme that shines within him.

Saying 4. One that knows only the way to the Lord is not the true *guru* but only he who has been absorbed into the true being of the Lord, into the bliss that He is. One that merely knows the path does not qualify to be called a *guru,* a spiritual preceptor, but only he who has dissolved himself into the Lord that abides within him, dissolved himself with every faith, every devotion and fervour.

Saying 5. Mere imposters are those that have not attained to the truth that the Lord is and yet, vain of their learning, indulge in sins great and ruinous. Voluble teachers of this kind can neither attain to the peace true nor can they lead their followers out of sins. Wasted is their life here and waste shall it go hereafter and so w1ill be the fate of those that follow them.

Saying 6. There are preceptors who know Brahman in words only. In the body alone they find their being, there only, and make their disciples worship it. They rob their disciples of their possessions to indulge in pleasures of the world. They are not teachers but predators of righteousness. Only sins do they breed and wickedness.

Saying 7. There are teachers, mere practitioners of words, who proclaim themselves as different and detached from their deeds. They emphasise before their disciples the transcendental nature of the *ātman*, of the self, attributing all virtues and vices to the body. They claim themselves as the *ātman* itself, beyond the reach of every action. Their disciples should not, therefore, they say, pay heed to what they do and what they do not do, Brahman the transcendental as they are. The former - their disciples - are, they further say, to serve them with every faith, taking them for what they are, Brahman itself. Fraudulent teachers like these spread the cult of the worship of the *guru* for the sake of sense pleasures only, making many men and women their disciples for that purpose. Their life style of ease and extravagance leads to the destruction of the Law, their spiritual prattle and sinful life contaminating the people at large. All sorts of tensions and conflicts then come to inflict the life of the people, resulting in great misery for each and every being. That is the price that the world at large has to pay for their hypocritical rhetoric.

Saying 8. It is exceedingly hard to attain to the status of the *guru*. Rare is the soul that can attain to that status, soul that lives solely prompted by the *guru* and not by its own thoughts and inclinations (*gurumukha*). Only that person can attain to the state of the *guru*, he who has given up all the pleasures of the body and ever abides in the self, his true being. And who lives for the good of others, all his care and concern meant for them, for each and every being, and not for himself, for what he gains and what he loses, for the heat he has to bear and the cold. And who does not give thought to who is his friend and who is his foe, no fear assailing him and no delusion, his *buddhi*, his intellect, no longer determinating such dualities, for abides it ever in Brahman the Word. In sum, only he can be a *guru*, he who has dispelled his own darkness first and has attained to the Light Divine, his word alone can redeem others, and of no one else.

Saying 9. There are prattlers that make their disciples dedicate all that they are and have, their bodies, their minds and their possessions, to the *guru*; that is the solemn promise they extract from the latter. And in accord with their teachings, their disciples serve them and worship them, serve them with their bodies and worship them with their minds. For convinced are they, at the word of their masters, that their salvation lies in devotion to the *guru*, in that only. Deluded by *Māyā* themselves, their masters make these false claims for themselves, those fraudulent souls. It is necessary, therefore, that one carefully considers these matters before entering into a master-disciple relationship.

Saying 10. The true preceptors, on the contrary, instruct their disciples to spend their possessions in good deeds, giving up their sense of mine vis-a-vis those possessions, their physical resources in the service of all living beings, and their minds in meditation of the Name of the Lord shining within them. Devotion for the *guru* consists, for the true preceptors, in following the instruction true, in attaining salvation thereby. They do not ask their disciples to serve and worship them; they ask them to serve all creatures. In the service to the latter do they see their own service.

Saying 11. There are teachers, crooked and crafty, that make their disciples, men and women, worship their bodies, worship them with all the paraphernalia that go with idol worship: lights, incense, flowers and other offerings and the ceremony of taking the wash of their feet. They would have their disciples offer to them in secret whatever the latter have, leaving all the care for their redemption to their *guru*, who would never fail them and their faith. They also forbid their disciples to participate in a *sat-saṅga* other than theirs. This is a mere fraud and pretence to rob their disciples, this talk and instruction. No one was ever redeemed this way nor will ever be. For all darkness is this, this way of worship and devotion, this way of disgrace and ruin here and hereafter.

Saying 12. A genuine preceptor teaches only the worship of the Lord and service of the people in general, making his disciples understand that service of the people is service unto to the teacher himself. He would not accept any money or other things from his disciples for his bodily comforts or pleasures. On the contrary, he would himself serve his disciples, serve them with every care and love. Teachers of this mettle alone can teach what is right, they alone can redeem their disciples from the worldly mode of being. Their instruction reveals what is true renunciation and illumines the souls of their disciples with the light of the Bliss Supreme.

Saying 13. There are teachers that resort to chants and magical rites for wealth and self-honour and spread the cult of *guru*-worship for that end. Devotion to the teacher is their constant and consistent theme to intimidate their disciples into devotion unto them. Every cunning they would adopt, every craft for that purpose to ensure a luxurious living for themselves. To serve a fraudulent *guru* of this kind is to ensure a place in hell for oneself. It is naivete par excellence to believe that swindlers and pretenders of this kind can ever do any good to anyone. Rather, to follow them would mean the end of the Law, of the very way to redemption. Let no one entertain any fear about the curse that a cheat of this kind may utter; rather, he himself will invite the nemesis for his evil intention. A genuine teacher would not inflict a curse upon anyone - not even upon one who would murder him; let there be no doubt in this matter.

Saying 14. Only he can be a spiritual teacher who has gone beyond the reach of dualities, those false appearances, and has come to be established in the Lord as He truly is, losing every sense of the charm that things of the world have for the beings of the world. An authentic *guru* is one who is fervently devoted to the Lord, who steadfastly contemplates the Word true within him to lose himself into It and who knows all that happens within and without him. For the sake of others he lives, for their good, all patience is he in the midst of the worst of misfortunes, and kindness itself is he vis-a-vis every being and creature. His pleasure is the *ātman*, his support is the *ātman*; in the entire world he finds its presence, of the *ātman*, his self. No dualities can interest him, no conflicts of the opposites, dualities that every being finds set up before him. In the Self-Same he remains absorbed, in that alone, his true being. He alone is teacher the true, this knower of the truth absolute. His teaching blesses every being, saves him from the worldly condition, the teaching of the teacher all liberated from *Māyā*.

Saying 15. There are teachers, fake and false, who would impose upon their disciples the belief that all that the latter have belongs to the teachers alone, and that their deliverance consists in placing, with every faith, all that they own and possess in the service and at the disposal of their teachers. All this talk is a mere fraud. Everything [all one perceives or may possess] belongs to the sphere of *Māyā*; there it comes to be and there it ceases to be. The relationship between the teacher and the disciple has nothing to do with such appearances, with the things of the world and giving them or taking them. Let this be a clear conviction with every seeker of the truth.

Saying 16. The disciple needs the *guru* for his liberation and the *guru* needs the disciple for giving him what is his due, his deliverance from birth and death. It is their bounden duty that makes them seek each other. There is no question of obliging and being obliged in their relationship. This is the Law, the Law of the *Māyā* of the Lord.

Saying 17. The disciple is to liberate himself from the shackles of the worldly mode of life the way the teacher liberated himself. He is to follow the latter's instruction for that end. The guru should be his ideal for that purpose, the ideal kept firm in his mind.

Saying 18. And the teacher is there to instruct the disciple into a sense of care and concern for others, into dedicating his life for that end and make him have faith, firm and deep, in Real the Supreme, in goal the supreme. He is to free his disciple from the deviations that go with the embodied mode of being, from all the passions and perversions of that mode, and instruct him into a living faith in the Lord. He is to make his disciple dedicate his life and being to Him, dedicate it so firmly that *Māyā* may not charm him away from that holy path of his. That is all that *guru-śiṣya* relationship, master-disciple relationship, consists in.

Saying 19. This relationship has nothing to do with give and take of the things of the world. The *guru* must liberate himself first [from the give and take that the worldly mode of being implies and consists of]. And the first instruction he is to give to the disciple is that the latter have a disposition dedicated to the service of others, a service that expects no reward in return. He does not teach his disciples to serve him, as would do impostors and cheats. Nor would he, unlike the latter kind of teachers, teach them to worship him and his body. It is the worship of the Lord alone that he will ask them to adhere to. He will also ask his disciples to live and practise all the precepts he has taught them; he would not promise them salvation, irrespective of what they do and do not do, as would the charlatans. Mere fools are these charlatans and so are those that are taken in by their false promises, their disciples. Only darkness do they breed, teachers of this kind and those who follow them.

Saying 20. The *guru* is there to save the disciple, save him with no self-interest whatsoever, expecting no return in any form from the latter. It is the duty of the disciple to serve his teacher to the best of his capacity and strive to redeem himself, following the teacher's instructions. Only those teachers can redeem their disciples from their fallen condition, only those teachers who initiate their disciples into the path of service unto others and self-purification. The latter, namely, self-purification, they make their disciples understand, is their primary objective.. There is no place for self-interest in this relationship, only the fraudulent teachers have that objective, not the genuine ones. One should consider this point [when entering into that relationship].

Saying 21. A prospective disciple should try a *guru* as a smith would test a piece of iron. If the subject of his test happens to be a genuine *guru*, the test will strengthen his faith and if he happens to be a fake one, it will expose the latter. The test is a must before one embarks upon this relationship; one should not be duped by mere appearances.

Saying 22. A *guru's* instruction becomes fruitful when the disciple turns his back upon the false appearance that *Māyā* is to direct his endeavours towards the attainment of the Lord, that Bliss itself. Only surpassing faith and untainted devotion can make him successful in this his endeavour. A disciple who does not give himself up to the right endeavour and depends solely on his *guru* the prattler for his salvation will never attain to that goal. Nor can he truly become a devotee of the *guru*. Conviction in terms of mere words can be of no avail to him. Only his endeavour and striving can lead him to his goal. No other way is open to him.

Saying 23. The *guru* must give away all that he has for the sake of his disciple's liberation and the disciple should follow his instruction to the point of self-extinction. Only this relationship where the soul of the one thus flows to that of the other can be a redemptive relationship. Self-interest, whether on the part of the *guru* or on that of the disciple, will make this relationship fail in its purpose.

Saying 24. The teacher is to give to the disciple whatever he is eligible to receive from him; he is not to make disciples for consideration of self-gain. Lower births, very many of them, will await both a teacher and a disciple if any such consideration has polluted their relationship.

Saying 25. No incompetent person should be initiated into the spiritual path, or children or young maidens. A *guru* who does this will bring only disgrace upon himself and will bring ruin to *dharma*, the way righteous, the Law. Instruction in matters spiritual is of no avail if it is given to those devoid of true faith and understanding. A woman, desirous of initiation into the spiritual path, should receive instruction either from her husband's preceptor or from another teacher, with her husband's permission and in his, the latter's, presence. Instruction received this way will do good to both, to her and her husband alike. If her husband is dead, then she should receive instruction in the presence of a near relation of hers. To receive instruction from a teacher, without making sure for herself that he is a genuine one, to do so out of mere self-assertiveness will not bring any success to her. Rather, it will bring a bad name to her, violate as her conduct will all normal norms. As for as a young maiden is concerned, she is not to seek a *guru* nor should a *guru* accept her as his disciple. To act otherwise will violate the Law and the traditional norms of behaviour and generate evil and sin.

Saying 26. To let women worship him, the teacher, as people would worship an idol is a violation of the Law. In no circumstance he should let a woman sit alone in his presence. Nor should he give a discourse in a congregation consisting solely of women, with no man present in it. To act otherwise will bring only dishonour to a teacher and disgrace to the name 'teacher'. For breeds this kind of conduct only evil in the world. A *guru* is to instruct people according to the latter's ability. A seeker of the Real should be instructed about the Real, a seeker of well being should be instructed in good conduct. That will bring peace to both kinds of seekers, each according to his deserts.

Saying 27. It is men that a teacher should mainly instruct. Women should be instructed through them, through men. If a teacher is to instruct a woman, he should do so in the presence of her husband. He is not to instruct her directly or make a request for anything to her. To act so would be to act against the Law. It will only pollute him.

Saying 28. One is to keep at an arm's length a *guru* who is fond of sumptuous food and showy dresses, the hypocrite who waxes eloquent in speech, speech varied and diverse, but gives no evidence of practising what he so preaches. To come into contact with him is to come into contact with moral pollution and with misery.

Saying 29. A teacher that stays perfect, speaks perfect, endures perfect and sits still and firm is guru the redemptive. He should know what knowledge the perfect is, his life an embodiment, embodiment in full, of what his word proclaims, leaving no divide between what he is without and what he is within. Misfortunes are not to disturb him nor are good fortunes to elate him. For long should he be able to sit [without fatigue, boredom or unrest], not a desire dwelling in him. It is a guru of this mettle who can draw and establish the line between *dharma* and *adharma*, righteousness and unrighteousness. Only he can liberate living beings from their embodied state.

Saying 30. The *guru* that just abides, abides in and as the *ātman*, should ever instruct his disciple for the latter's redemption. He should do his best towards that end without an iota of self-interest. Let his grace flow out into the disciple out of compassion and sheer generosity of his soul. As for the disciple, he is to undo himself in obedience to the word of such a gracious teacher, as obedience itself is he to abide. Righteousness comes to prosper in the world when teacher-pupil relationship comes to be established in this way; when their respective dispositions, those of the teacher and the pupil, dispositions of this sort, come to have their impact on the people in general, their life turning into a blessing. Let the Lord make every guru aware of what the station of the guru is and make the disciple fit to receive his due! Let all devotees of the Lord understand this thought with a mind given to the truth and abide by it!

Vision of the Guru in his Truth

Behold guru the man as Word the Real,
Behold his glory in every form and shape,
His action the restraint of senses
And knowledge true his food eternal,
And grace his wear,
And desire stilled his home!

Beyond the reach of joy he shines
And beyond the shadows of pain,
The Eternal is he and Grace abounding,
Knowledge is he and contemplation is he,
All forgiving is he, all content is he,
Devotion is he and love is he,
Uniquely so and without a parallel.

Ever absorbed he lives in the truth within him,
In that light eternal, in that joy beyond joy;
Still his life and without a stir of desire.
And his word the Word of the truth,
And his act the act that sheds its Other,
And his walk the walk of humility.

In fervour for the *ātman* abides
Worship of the guru,
And in contemplation of it the wash of his feet,
And in the good of all his saving *mantra*.

Beyond the five he dwells,
And beyond the five and twenty;[19]
Seek you, noble friend, his abode, of the guru!
No more shall he die, no more shall be born,
He, the pupil, who thus knows the guru.
Liberated will be he from every evil thought,
And attain the state supremely blessed,
He who knows the glory of the guru,
Ever awake to what he says and reveals.

Eternal is the guru's abode and indestructible,
That home of Bliss Supreme,
Measure will he the worlds three,
He who knows him thus and perceives him thus.
Of Maṅgat is this the word true.

(ii) Samatāvāda: *The* Samatā *Canon*

Saying 1. Let a believer in the *Samatā* Doctrine make it his bounden duty to follow the [five] divine principles with no ill will against any religion whatsoever. Let him live as the Lord wills him to live, let him remain ever the same whatever be his existential condition. Let this be his highest religion, this way of life.

Saying 2. Whatever the faith he is born in, let him seek purification for himself and blessedness for others. That should be the main purpose of his life.

Saying 3. Let him free himself from narrow religious and sectarian customs and rituals. Let him stay away from disputes regarding these and steadfastly adhere to redemptive deeds. Let his piety be all disinterested, let him not seek any reward for it.

Saying 4. The disposition to remain ever the same in every condition is truly a redemptive disposition. The state of *samatā*, of being ever the same, is every being's being in truth, his own and real home. That alone is righteousness, that state, the objective of striving for those that strive as the guru prompts them to strive [and not their own natural or personal dispositions]. Let a believer in the Doctrine of Samatā, therefore, come out of the narcissistic sectarian concerns, steadfastly adhering to the right principles with an earnest sincerity. Let him be self-controlled, ever and always, each and every moment. For, in that lies his peace, in this endeavour and in this steadfastness.

(iii) On the Northern Course and the Southern Course

The moving world has two aspects, two facets, the two aspects expressed in varied ways. Whatever the terms in which these are expressed, they establish only one thing, namely, the dual aspect of the transient world. Consider it well.

Fire the Bright - that Brahman, the Real: From that proceeds the world of the two states. A being that dwells in his thought on the dual nature of the world can reach the truth [his own and that of the world].

Everything here has its opposite, nothing stands by itself alone. Where there is day, there is night also, where there is the bright fortnight, there is also the dark fortnight. This way the year too is taken as constituted by two opposite principles - darkness and light, six months constituted by the fortnights of darkness and six months constituted by the fortnights of brightness. In these very twelve months every being comes to be and ceases to be, some coming into being in their dark halves and others in their bright halves. Every being has to pass through these two opposites, through brightness and darkness.

The [life of the] body too has two ways open before it - the internal way and the external way. The internal way is the way up, the way northern, the way bright like the day and the bright fortnight. Anyone who dies lost within [his self], dies into the Imperishable and Eternal Being that he, in truth, is, Being ever bright like the sun. On the other hand, a man who dies as oriented outwards, as oriented towards action and the results thereof, towards that smoky darkness, darkness like that of the night [of the new moon] of the dark fortnight, dies into a state like that of the waxing and waning moon, dies into the state of recurring births and deaths. For informed by desire is this external way.

The internal way is bright as the bright fortnight of the waxing moon is, as the day is and as the sun is. And the six months that the sun moves northwards and the six months that it moves southwards also have the same [symbolic] implication, that of the internal way and the external way. These months too have the bright and the dark fortnights to constitute them, each one of them. Everyone is born either in the six bright months [consisting of twelve bright fortnights] or in the six dark months [consisting of twelve dark fortnights]. The implication is that whatever the time of the year he dies in, the determining factor is the orientation inwards or outwards, the way to the sun and the way to the moon, the way to Brahman and the way of desire to act. The two ways, the internal and the external, may be compared as follows:

THE INTERNAL WAY	THE EXTERNAL WAY
The Northern Way	The Southern Way
The sun	The moon
The bright fortnight	The dark fortnight
Six bright months of the year	Six dark months of the year
The light eternal	Smoky and ever changing

Only the internal and external ways have been described through these images or descriptions, the internal way leading to liberation and the external way leading to recurring births and deaths. As for the death of Bhīṣma [in the epic *Mahābhārata*], the poets have invoked the images of the northern way and the southern way to describe the greatness of his soul. [That does not mean that the man who dies during the six months when the sun moves northwards will die into liberation. For,] these two images are only the symbols of the internal way and the external way, the way to liberation and the way to bondage. The internal way is the way of work without desire, it is the way of becoming one with knowledge that is one's true being; it is the path of the gods. And the external way is the way of work with desire, the way of the fathers. Thus these two paths lie open before a mortal, one leading to the state of liberation, the other to that of bondage. Only those incapable of discrimination confuse these ways with objective and natural occurrences [like that of the sun moving northwards or southwards], but, in actual fact, these two movements of the sun [symbolically] relate to the inwards and outwards orientations of the embodied being. But only the *yogins* who follow the internal way to its end can know what the external way in truth is, a mere delusion. They alone can say what is liberation in truth and what is bondage.

These two orientations sum up, in fact, the entire knowledge of the world but only a *yogin* who knows what is within him can know this truth. Therefore, ever withdraw your mind within and focus your attention on the Name. Only then will the Light that is Brahman shine bright within you, setting you at rest, setting you free from the bondage of actions. That is the state of *mokṣa*, liberation, this state of freedom from the bondage of actions. However, if a being is outward oriented, he is a slave to desire, desire sedimented in him by his previous lives to compel him to be born again and again for its fulfillment. Like unto the moon he ever changes, now waxing and now waning.[20]

SECTION 4

On Life the Sanctified

To cross the ocean, vast and deep, that the world is,
man must linger on thought the pure.
Let him resort to a seer for that end,
and drink in deep what he says and proclaims.

Let him read the truth, let him hear the truth,
and let him dwell deep on it,
let this be his endeavour long and steadfast,
and find the light shine bright in him.

The ways to redemption
have all been here revealed unto him;
let him take to any with faith and devotion
and reach the end he seeks to reach.
This verily is Maṅgat's promise unto him.

Saying 1. Man is born to know what is good life and what is evil life. In this lies his superiority over other creatures. Generally, beings are interested in sanctifying their bodies and not their minds. This disposition leads them to do all kinds of evil deeds to turn their life into a mere frustration. It is incumbent on man, therefore, to know wherein lies the purity of mind and act and strive for it. For, therein lies purity the true, in purity of the mind. Without knowing what in truth the purity of mind is, in what it consists, a man will not turn in earnest and in truth to noble deeds, he will not have enough enthusiasm for them. And in the absence of those deeds, he is bound to fall into evil ways, those ways to pain and frustration absolute. So, it is necessary that man should try to know in earnest wherein lies the true purity of mind, let him put in every effort of his for that purpose; that shall open unto him the way to redemption the supreme.

Saying 2. Verily, this body is the world itself,[21] with several faculties operating in it. To live is to function in accord with these faculties. They include the five sense organs, the five motor organs, *manas*, *buddhi* and *prāṇa*, breath. *Manas* or mind is thinking or deliberation about the objects of the sense- and motor organs that it would seek. And *buddhi* or the intellect is the power to discriminate the taints of the *manas* or mind in terms of good and evil.[22] In other words, the mind operates in accordance with what the *buddhi* or the intellect determinates or understands, and the sense- and motor organs operate in accord with how the mind works and operates. The purity and the impurity of the organs, of what they sense and perform, depend on the purity and the impurity of the *buddhi*. The purity of the *buddhi* makes it do good actions through the said organs resulting in peace the true for it. Its impurity, on the contrary, leads it to do wicked actions through the organs resulting in constant discontent for it. So what form one's life takes depends on the purity [or impurity] of the *buddhi*. In fact, purity is nothing else than the purity of the *buddhi*.

Saying 3. The *buddhi* or the intellect comes to be purified when it gives itself up to true thought, to the right conduct, to the right faith and the right endeavour.[23] The truth though remains that it is only the *ātman* that is supremely pure, that dispenser of life; only that is beyond the reach of every deviation and every fret, that absolute and full bliss. That dispenser of life alone is what the seers call Lord the Supreme, Brahman, Knowledge and so on, and it is the same Spirit that shines beyond the *buddhi*, the deteminating faculty. It is only when the *buddhi* self-submits to that Spirit the Great that it comes to be purified, purified in truth. And what is called thought the pure is nothing else than the thought of and about that Spirit the Great. And the right act is the act performed with one's will submitted to It; the action done in this disposition alone is action without a taint. And true faith or belief is only faith in that very Spirit, to live as anchored to It, as grounded in It. And the right endeavour is the endeavour for attaining to It, to find that Spirit.

Saying 4. The *buddhi* comes to be truly purified and find peace the true when it comes to be one with that Being the Prior and the Supreme, that Consciousness the Pure. The *buddhi,* that faculty of knowing, remains a mere frustration, a mere non-fulfillment, as long as it remains identified with the three *guṇas,* with the three modes of being, that of remaining static *(tamas),* that of projecting oneself into the activities of the world, identifying oneself with them (*rajas*)and that of transcending all the states of being, each and every (*sattva*). The buddhi's involvement in these three modes, its confusing of its being and self with these make it find itself a doer and to be ever on the move. Its threefold desire, that informed by these three *guṇas* or modes of being, compels it to do all kinds of acts, good or bad, turning it into an eternal frustration, frustration that never allows it to ever come to be itself and be at peace with itself. This identification with these three modes, this sense of finding its being in them, is evil the absolute. Without undoing this sense of Me, the sense of Me resulting from its identification with these three modes, the *buddhi* can in no way become pure nor can become pure the actions it performs with the body [as an embodied being].[24]

Saying 5. To know the glory of the Lord that is the truth itself and to know well the taints of the body [of the embodied mode of being] is the duty paramount of man. And, equipped with this knowledge, to self-submit to that Truth is [the way to] redemption absolute. The ego of the doer, on the contrary, leads one to become a prey to all kinds of *vāsanās,* that load of the after-effects of past lives, lives without a count, and to the cruel duality that every action is. This duality makes the intellect a subject of attachments and aversions, with lasting misery for its portion. All tainted indeed is this state of being.

Saying 6. Let man dwell closely on the truth revealed unto him to understand what in truth his life is and let him direct all his endeavours towards attaining to that truth. Let him do so with all his might, for therein lies all purity and his redemption ultimate. As long as the *buddhi* is a prisoner of the I-sense [the result of its sense of identification with activity of the *prakṛti*], there can be no possibility of its freedom from the passion to act. And as long as it continues to move under the compulsive force of that passion, it will not know wherein lies its purity, will not know the state beyond the reach of every trouble or distress. Therefore, let man ever self-submit to that truth. Let him ever strive in that direction, for therein lies his liberation and his purity, in that spirit of self-submission. Let him understand that that is the high duty assigned to him, that of self-submission to the truth absolute.

Saying 7. The *buddhi,* by its very nature, remains immersed in the enjoyment of the pleasures of the body it finds itself identified with. For it is with the emergence of the body that it comes to be aware of those pleasures. It is the nature of that body that determines for it what it is to eat and drink, when to sleep and to be awake, what to give and what to receive, who is its friend and who is its foe and makes it seek other things. Getting thus aware of those pleasures, it spares no effort for their acquisition. That, in sum, is the world for it, this its life.

Saying 8. The *buddhi* can never become pure unless and until it does not cease to be tainted, does not, that is, cease to find the pleasures of the body as blessedness the supreme. With this dark disposition seizing it, it finds itself immersed in those pleasures, to be a prisoner of sex and anger, greed and infatuations, and of the I-sense, their fiery intensity, of those passions, ever scalding it and rendering it all the more tainted and contaminated. A veritable disaster, great and tragic, is this kind of life.

Saying 9. When in the grip of this false sense [of being the body-sense-mind complex], the *buddhi* makes the pleasures of the body its life's end and resorts to all kinds of cruel deeds for their acquisition. Falsehood, theft, fraud and sharp practice come natural to it to undo others, which it would do ever and always. Inflicted with this blind passion, it provokes every misery and disaster to visit it many a life, one after another. Evil all is this kind of life, all contamination is this state. To escape from this evil, it is necessary that one understand the meaning of the pilgrimage that one's life is.

Saying 10. The truth of the matter, its very essence, is this. All forgetful of the Supreme Reality that the *ātman* is, that Being, the *buddhi* comes to be inflicted with the I-sense to fall a prey to the *Māyā* of the three strands to find itself in the grip of actions of various kinds. This, its ego of agency, its sense of being the doer of actions, leads it to crave for their results. Of the nature of dualities are the results of actions, each informed by its opposite. They never let it feel secure, those dualities, those results of actions. So the process moves on endless, this tainted wheel of action set in motion by *avidyā* [that confounding of the self with the not-self is].

Saying 11. When the *buddhi* comes to realise this kind of life for what it is, life informed by darkness [of delusion], it seeks to strive for the truth and self-submit to it. The Lord alone now becomes for it the sole truth and bliss the absolute and the pleasures of the body [of body-sense-mind complex] mere fret and misery. To be that truth absolute then becomes the sole object of its endeavour. It is then, and then only, that it comes to know wherein lies its purity and how to attain to it.

Saying 12. The *buddhi* comes into being as informed by a fixation for the passions of the body, informed, that is, by the passions of sex, anger, greed, infatuation and the I-sense. Inflicted with the intensity of these passions, it turns all polluted and miserable. To understand this miserable condition of being for what it is, is the purpose of all genuine thinking, therein alone lies its true function. But all embodied beings continue to burn in the fire of these passions, these deviations and fallings from their true being, taking them, in their blindness, to be the truth of their life and being, with no way to purity and peace opening out for them. All dark and blind indeed is this mode of life, this life given over to these passions.

Saying 13. He who does not understand what this mode of life in its truth is cannot have genuine faith in the Lord, that truth absolute, that dispenser of purity absolute and peace absolute. To understand the truth of this frustrating mode of life is to understand in truth, for that understanding is the way to blessedness the supreme, to peace the absolute, the way to find that blessedness and peace in this very life, in life the mortal. Therefore, let all the resources of one's endeavour be directed towards the truth, let one be firmly committed to the truth to wash oneself of every pollution and depravity.

Saying 14. Each and every being that has come to be born in the world is ever engaged in making up the lack informing his life. But instead of making it up, he, in his ignorance, sticks to that lack, taking it as profusion. Confusing his ontological lack with desire for objects of senses, he directs all his efforts towards acquiring those objects, little realising that the pleasures of the senses cannot appease that desire, they will only intensify it. It is only at the time of death that he comes to know what those pleasures in their reality are - tragedies absolute. All tainted lives the man who does not or would not know this truth.

Saying 15. Knowing well this truth about his life and its frets and regrets, let every being give up this passion, dark and evil, with the Lord as the sole anchor of his being, the very breath of his life. Let him be truthful in speech, noble in behaviour, of disposition forgiving and compassionate; let him be ever content, his love flowing out to all beings. Blessed and holy will he live, his frets and regrets all left behind. An ideal will he be for others, the man gifted with this kind of disposition.

Saying 16. Blessed is the man, his life a fulfillment, who strives for the betterment of his life, with the Lord, that Being before every being, the sole refuge of his faith. Those who find the Lord alone as Being in truth and bliss in truth and the embodied state as a mere means for attaining that bliss, they alone will attain to purity the absolute and goal the highest.

Saying 17. Not without self-submission to the Truth within can the *buddhi* ever come to be pure. Without that anchor and refuge, it ever remains stained and polluted, given over to all kinds of perversions and deviations, misery eternal falling to its lot, and self-destruction. For, that is the end-result of the excess of indulgence in bodily pleasures. Let every being give an authentic thought to his existential condition, and know what it would lead to. Let him devote himself to the truth, devote himself with every fervour, to find the purity supreme and absolute.

Saying 18. The Lord Supreme alone is purity, purity itself, He alone is bliss the eternal. The entire domain of *prakṛti*, that seed of creation, is the domain of pollution and frustration. This truth dawns on a man when he realises in him the glory of that Lord Supreme, that Being before every being. As the light of the sun makes one know what misery is darkness and what glory is light, so to know the light that is the Being before every being is to know the darkness that *prakṛti* in truth is, that *before* of creation.[25]

Saying 19. Let man free himself from the taints intrinsic to embodied mode of being, let him do so through self-surrender to the self as it is in itself, the self that is the Great and Primordial Lord Himself. And let this spirit of self-surrender remain constant with him, for that spirit alone can free him from the great misery of the false mode of being that he has identified himself with, that source of every taint and evil. Equipped with this disposition towards truth, the *buddhi* comes to triumph over all the deviations and fallings intrinsic to embodiment to move on towards its redemption. For, the intellect endowed with this disposition of self-surrender to its ontological truth, finds itself grounded in it. With this finding does it come to know the misery that the passions of the body, those perversions, are, the realisations making it determined to free itself from their sway. This striving on its part culminates in attaining to the highest end of life, that goal all transcendental.

Saying 20. Through self-submitting in *toto* to Being, to the Lord, the *buddhi* comes to acquire the power to triumph over all the deviations of the mind and the organs of cognition and action. Only the intellect thus self-submitted to Being, to the Lord, can come to know what purity in its truth is. There is only one way to free oneself from the deviations that the mind and organs give rise to, namely, the understanding that submission to them is to fall from one's being and truth and that this fall is misery and evil the unmitigated.[26] With this realisation alone can the intellect strive for its purification, not otherwise. Self-purification will not come easy to one who does not find the passions of the body as fallings from his true being, as deviations from it.[27]

Saying 21. Evil itself is the body. That is the truth about it. But there are actions that open the way up for an embodied being, and also others that cause its downfall and bring it to woe. The *buddhi*, in its ignorance, often chooses the latter kind of actions, with the worst kind of disasters awaiting it. These include acts like these: to cause misery to others for the sake of one's own well being, to commit theft, to indulge in gambling, to resort to fraud and to falsehood, to be arrogant, greedy and wrathful without a measure, and observing no restraint while indulging in the pleasures of the flesh. Add to them the evil in the shape of serving one's own ends, without a let or a limit. In opposition to these acts are the acts that purify man of the evil [he inherits with embodiment]. They include acts like these: truthfulness, to be free from covetousness and infatuations, to be of a disposition of humility, to have every concern for the well being of others and to strive for that end, and to be content with whatever falls to one's lot in terms of worldly prosperity or otherwise.

Saying 22. Whether the *buddhi* follows the ways of gods or those of demons depends on the extent of its self-submission to Being or to conceit or arrogance. [Self-submission to Being is all blessedness and] to give oneself to conceit is to invite every disaster upon oneself. It should be man's endeavour to self-submit to Being, to what *is*, to wash himself of every stain and to live the good life. That is the way to purity in its perfection and to peace in its truth.

Saying 23. To resort to Being is to be on the way to redemption. Man must, in other words, know the body and the world as what they are, as mere transitory appearances, appearances ever changing and ever disowning themselves. And he must find the bodily pleasures too as in fact they are, as mere grounds for all misery. With this conviction grounded in him, he should fulfill his commitment to Being. That indeed is his way to purity in its perfection. Let him put a check to [the inclinations of the senses towards] the bodily comforts or pleasures, let him set a limit to them, a limit that sanctifies those comforts or pleasures[28]. And let him give up his comforts for the welfare of others. That is how he can make his mind pure of its stains.

Saying 24. With his mind open to Being, let man ever think of and strive for the well being of others and devote himself to steady contemplation of the Lord, that Being *before* beings. Let him, with this holy and redemptive disposition made steadfast in him, be of spirit disinterested and of humility and of a bent of mind devoted to the good of others. And let him be free from every passion, all his illusory hopes from those passions having been dispelled. When the *buddhi* thus comes to be firmly established this way, it finds itself steadily absorbed in Being, Being that never deviates from itself and its purity absolute.

Saying 25. Let man ever part his company with falsehood and be open to Being the truth. Let him be ever unconcerned with his self-interest and be of service unto others without a desire for a return from it. And let him ever strive to free his mind from its taints and blemishes. And let him give up all backbiting and covet not another man's possessions. And let him not desire another man's wife, let him avoid that desire as he would avoid a deadly poison. These are the means to lead him towards his goal. For, undo these means *vāsanās* (desires) of the most fierce and fearful kind, to give a rest and repose to the *buddhi*. This verily is the path redemptive, the path divine and of the gods.

Saying 26. The *buddhi* all dedicated to Being, dedicated to It in its acts and thoughts, will find all blemishes and evils fall off it on their own. Like unto light vis-a-vis darkness is this dedication vis-a-vis evil desires. Before long this conduct dedicated to Being turns into fervent devotion for that Purity to lead the *buddhi* to get established in the transcendental peace that is knowledge itself[29], lead it to that abode of the light eternal without a trace of either a fear or a deviation in it.

Saying 27. Knowing full well what the embodied mode of being is and implies, man should refrain from all the ill deeds. Let him keep himself away from the life of fashion and luxuries, from intoxicants and the company of those given to evil ways. And let him give up all activities of the mind through steady contemplation of the Lord. This, truly, is the way to make his life noble, this truly is the way to purity absolute, and this, verily, is the way of those who became one with their truth, of *sat-puruṣas*.

Saying 28. And let him give up every passion that this body, this false appearance, stirs up in him. Let him be of benefit to others and desire not anything in return for this his service unto them. And let him not be proud of anything relating to his body, let him, instead, be all humility and forgiveness and full of compassion. Let him be an embodiment of these and such like virtues. And let him not think of names and forms, those false appearances, those facets of the not-self, let him, instead, contemplate the *ātman*, the self, alone, that truth, that reality, absolute. All pure shall he turn if he lives this way, this way of dissociating himself from all the deviations that go with the embodied mode of being and self-submitting to Being in its truth. For all *vāsanās*, dense and dark, all the dark desires and passions that inalienably go with the bodily mode of being, come to be eroded as one treads this path to self-purification.

Saying 29. With obsession for the bodily pleasures is born each and every being; that, verily, is his inheritance. And under the impact of that vain obsession does he spend his entire life. An animal is he born and an animal he lives, his life fruitless, a vanity meaningless. To free himself from this obsession with pleasures should be his goal. That way alone will he live the life true and authentic, life that will bless him with the peace eternal and everlasting, life that is life the human in its true meaning and essence.

Saying 30. Unappeasable is the passion for bodily pleasures, whatever the extent of those pleasures at one's command. Rather, these increase and intensify that *vāsanā*, that passion. The body will come to fall, but there will be no softening down of the fury of that passion. This is how the wheel of *Māyā* moves, moves round and round[30]. One should understand the truth about this [purposeless] motion, dwelling deep on the thought revealed to man [not fabricated by his own thinking] and, equipped with that understanding, self-submit to Being [bare of all the concepts superimposed on to it].

Saying 31. Living under the sway of overweening passion for pleasures leads a man to ways cruel, cruel in the extreme, ways to his ruin utter and disastrous. For, in the grip of that passion, a man resorts to all kinds of evil to satisfy it, withstand its fury as he cannot. The passion, however, remains unappeased as ever, but his cruel deeds cannot but bring about their tragic results. This is how the strange wheel of life moves. Many gifted men, gifted in rich abundance, move tied to this wheel, resorting to all kinds of evil ways for the appeasement of their minds [their desires], appeasement that ever eludes them. All frustrated they depart from the world, their pilgrimage here of no purpose. Seeing the end those gifted souls met, one should understand how this wheel of the world moves and find the Being he is truly in search of.

Saying 32. Every being in the grip of bodily *vāsanas* is out to destroy others - that is what his life, in sum, is. And that is what bondage means, bondage wrought by *prakṛti*, that seed of creation. The way to undo this bondage, this darkness, lies in self-submitting to the Supreme Lord that is Being itself, in worshipping and contemplating Him, Him alone and in serving the world, His creation. And in ever remembering the moment when the body will inevitably come to fall. This is the noble way to purity, to be washed of every blemish of the *buddhi*, the way upward and to redemption.

Saying 33. A man should ever rely on his own effort to get rid of the faults and blemishes of his mind, on his right conduct. He should follow the instruction of *sat-puruṣas*, of those that have become Being itself, to turn his own true teacher. This is how the mind gets purified and oriented towards Being to be blessed with peace the absolute and purity the absolute.

Saying 34. Embodied beings wander about in the world in the grip of desires for bodily pleasures, doing good and evil deeds for their appeasement. Bodily pleasures, however, end up in sorrow for them and in their undoing. Vain goes all their efforts for those pleasures, with frustration alone falling to their lot. Knowing the darkness that this worldly pilgrimage is, one should give oneself, ever and always, to devotion true to the Lord, to that Power Primordial, that Being *before* beings, for only that can lead him, that devotion, to the state all transcendental.

Saying 35. True devotion [to truth the absolute] dawns in man when his *buddhi* knows for certain that the body with all its pleasures is nothing but suffering itself, that alone, and strives to self-submit to the *ātman* within, to his being that is also Being the Absolute and Power the Great. When this self-submission to that Lord Supreme becomes steadfast and steady, all the faults and blemishes of the *buddhi,* all its evils and deviations will come to fall off on their own, all the noble traits suffusing it spontaneously, without any external cause or compulsion. Humility will come naturally to it, and so will the disposition of love for all beings. The pleasures of the world will lose their charm for it, ever ready will it become to sacrifice them for the sake of others. As for troubles and misfortunes, it will come to bear them with every patience and fortitude. With this *tapas,* this burning ardour, informing it, the *buddhi* will come to be blessed with knowledge that is purity itself[31] and bliss the infinite[32] and eternal.

Saying 36. It is the desire for bodily pleasures that constitutes the journey called life. All their life beings remain occupied to fulfill that desire but in vain. For, life comes to an end but not the desire for those pleasures, its non-fulfillment necessitating another birth to continue the same journey all over again, the journey for the fulfillment of the same desire. All beings wander here in pursuit of fulfillment of the said desire, be they kings or the starving beggars, be they rich or poor, be they married or single, wise or foolish, humans or not-humans. But no one among them can find the end of their pilgrimage until he comes to have the knowledge of the Real. One should, therefore, know it well, the nature of this pilgrimage of life, and strive to rise above its compulsions.

Saying 37. For a bare moment stay the pleasures of the body and in a moment comes to cease the body. To seek peace the real in them is only folly par excellence. But beings live infatuated with this folly and resort to all kinds of evil deeds to sink all the more in those desires and die helplessly fettered to them. Strange indeed is this pilgrimage of life!

Saying 38. The body is ridden with lack and so are its pleasures. Man is not to nurture the illusion that these can give him the fulfillment he seeks. Let him wake up to the truth, giving up all illusions. For that, his wakening, will make him turn to his real self, to his *ātman*, that Being the Real, that cessation of all the frets and all the anguishes. One should know for certain that every pleasure is but a pain, that every act is but a bondage and a tie and that only the *ātman*, the self, that Reality Absolute, stays action-free, fret-free, all pure and all still. With this understanding and this disposition should a man direct himself to the path of gain the real, the path to peace secure and absolute.

Saying 39. In giving up all the pleasures of the body lies one's gain the true, and in directing all one's efforts towards the attainment of the great bliss that the *ātman* is. As the *buddhi* comes to be suffused with Being, its passion for the embodied mode of being comes to find its end. For, it is that Internal Peace, Peace the true and real, that frees it from all the passions relating to the body. Gifted and wise people choose this path to the self [as against the worldly people who seek their being in the body and its pleasures].

Saying 40. Those who would seek the path of transcendence from the impurities [of the bodily mode of being] and come to stay stable in their devotion to the Lord and, on the strength of that devotion, shed all the deviations of the mind, are indeed men the noble and men the true. Truly will they find themselves all uplifted and all glorious, their striving for the truth an example and paradigm for others to follow and emulate.

Saying 41. When all bodily pleasures appear to a man as what they, in truth, are, namely, as pain itself, they cease to hold any charm for him. This, his disillusion with those pleasures, sets him firmly on to the path to the truth. Only then the Lord appears as truly blessed and blissful, and the only thing to be known. That is the moment when a man comes to strive in truth for the purity of his mind. Supremely gifted then turns he to bring his pilgrimage to its true end, to his being true and blissful, realising which he crosses all the hindrances and hurdles in his way.

Saying 42. Let man ever do his utmost to make the Lord his sole refuge, let him regularly participate in *sat-saṅga*, in holy congregation, to think about how to make his mind rise above its natural inclinations. And let him be ever steadfast in service to orphans and guests. And let him, ever remembering his end, give himself up to holy[33] devotion to the Lord, devotion that can dispel all life's fevers and frets.

Saying 43. To shed the impurity that the desire for bodily pleasures is, a man should devote himself fully and without a qualification to the *ātman*, to the self that is the witness of the body and is the reality absolute and consciousness itself.[34] As one's devotion to that Real becomes deeper, one's sense of pride with regard to the body and one's infatuation for it come to cease, pride and infatuation that are the root cause of all the woes and all the evils. This, verily, is the way to peace the secure and certain.

Saying 44. The desire for the pleasures of the body, entraps its victim all the deeper to make him all the more polluted and bring him every woe. Therefore, it is imperative that man should make the truth his sole anchor and refuge, and keep his pleasures within limits, limits that save him from sin and pollution. In other words, let him take only that food that is pure, let his dealings be honest and above board, his association holy and his endeavour redemptive. This is how he can attain to his real and ultimate home, this is how he can come to be truly blessed. Creatures that are ever scalded and roasted by desires for pleasures come to be blessed only when they find the peace that their self is, for that alone, that *ātman*, is the peace supreme and the joy supreme. Let every being be firm in this belief.

Saying 45. The Lord alone is to be known and His name alone is to be remembered. The I-sense is there to be given up, that root cause of every evil. And the thing to understand is the way to one's rise, and to unravel is the secret that is death. And the thing to honour is the way of life of the truth-become souls, and the thing to accept is their instruction true and redemptive. To associate with are the guru and the truth-become souls, and to contemplate is the *ātman* in its truth and reality, the *ātman* ever attained. And the thing to strive for is one's establishment in the truth; all noble is that, that striving and endeavour. This indeed is the high duty of every being, this spirited endeavor to get rid of every impurity and pollution.

Saying 46. Only those wise beings attain to the highest goal that direct their minds counter to the deviations that they, their minds, are prone to, and embrace, in their stead, the conduct high and noble. Let that be the constant endeavour of every being, for death is there ever to pursue and overwhelm him.

Saying 47. Let one's mind be pure before the body comes to fall, let one be free of every fear before that hour. That is the way to find the highest reach of life, its very acme. The pleasures of the body are ever ridden with a lack, miseries verily and alone are they. And darkness thick and dense is the confusion of the self with the body, that window that opens out to the world, that itself is the world, each body its own world. But the body has its beginning and its end [and so has the world it reveals], too ephemeral is it to be one's being and the self and to be infatuated with. Only the *ātman*, that reality the supreme, that life of the body, is to be believed in and contemplated, contemplated with sustained intent. That alone is the way pure and the intent pure.

Saying 48. With every intention, pure and settled, should one remember and passively contemplate Him that is the life of the body, Him the Friend Supreme, Him the Protector and Companion Eternal. For, it is that remembrance and contemplation that can bring about the extinction of all the faults of the mind and bless one with peace the true, with the state all secure and fearless. To have this faith faultless, to have it ever, is indeed to be blessed, blessed supremely.

Saying 49. In mystery strange moves the wheel of the world. Here every beginning has an end, and in sorrow ends here every joy. And cease will all that has come to be and into the other will turn what is one's own. Into despair will turn here every hope, and fall will the body, that prop of every pleasure. That is the way the world moves, that is the play it plays. Let every man know it and understand it and seek and strive to attain to the state of being true and real. In that lie his virtue and his purity, in that seeking and striving.

Saying 50. In a bare moment comes to an end this life of man. Let him, therefore, ever remember and contemplate the Real as it is, remember and contemplate it with a sustained steadfastness. That is the way particular and distinct to that Real, the way of remembrance and contemplation. Remembrance of the Name leads to the cessation of the memory of names and forms, those false appearances. And to attain to the bliss of His is to cease to have every *vāsanā*, that name for every woe and suffering. And to self-submit to the Lord, that Being *before* beings, is to cease to self-submit to the body, that darkness absolute. Self-submission to the Lord makes strong the *buddhi*, enabling it to shed the I-sense, that delusion primoridal, and find the peace pure, peace not to name and not to describe.

Saying 51. The body may come to fall any moment. So no noble duty should be postponed, a man should do it here and now, freely and irrespective of his existential conditions. Let him give up his own comforts for the sake of the unhappy and the deprived, give them up with every and lasting humility. Let him perceive the world as a mere recurrence of coming and going and know only the self as a-temporal and remember it with a devotion steady, constant and exclusive. Anyone who lives with this disposition and this conviction will find all that is to be found, will find it in this very world, in this very false appearance. Supremely appeased will he be and find the state beyond the possibility of any fall or deviation.

Saying 52. To find the gain true in this one's pilgrimage alone is to live nobly, truly and in reality. Let man remember the Great Lord that makes alive this false appearance, this body, and that sustains this visible creation composed of the gross elements[35]. Let him remember that Great Lord and obey His holy commands. He who thus spends his life remembering Him and obeying Him will find his self-concerns come to cease, no longer will that fire of selfishness burn and scald him. His life will turn into a giving[36], that purity absolute.

Saying 53. A man who self-submits to the Lord with a mind pure[37] and puts all his comforts at the disposal of others, who ever contemplates the Being dwelling in his heart and lives above, and disinterested in, the affairs of this ephemeral life, and who, further, remains still and steady in honour and disgrace, in gain and loss and in prosperity and adversity - a man of this mettle alone can know what purity in its reality is. Whatever comes to him as his duty will come only to redeem him.

Saying 54. A man who takes his life as meant for the service of others, who lives ever self-submitted to the Lord and takes all his bodily activities as ordained by Him - he alone can wash himself of *vāsanā*, that pollution born out of perverted knowledge and thought. His actions will be all pure, sanctified as they will be by the spirit of self-surrender to the Lord. And he will come to find the bliss all pure, the bliss that the self is. That is how the wise should live and strive. This kind of life will bless them with liberation and will be a blessing for others, a guide to their salvation.

Saying 55. To the extent a man rises above his bound condition and dedicates himself to that end, to that very extent others too will follow his example to endeavour for their liberation. This relationship gives rise to awareness of what peace the real is, what one ought to do and what is the true Law, awareness that brings about the end of every sin and evil and makes one supremely blessed. With every endeavour should one ever seek the Eternal, that ever Full and Undeviating. Truly rewarding will turn a man's life when he gives up all deviations and fallings that go with the body and comes to be established in the Real, that bliss supreme.

Saying 56. A man who endeavours to attain to State the Real, giving up all the flaws that taint the mind and has no arrogance and no infatuation, his body, his speech and his mind ever at the service of all beings - he alone is the man who knows what is real and what is not real. He alone knows what is endeavour the true, what ought to be done, what is the right practice and what is the true, the real state of being. He alone attains to the state bereft of all thoughts, the state of purity absolute to transcend all the blots and blemishes of *Māyā* of the three strands. Rare to find is the man who chooses this way of life.

Saying 57. The way to purification of the internal organ - the mind - lies, to put the matter briefly, only in devotion to the Lord and in disinterested service of others. That is the way to one's uplift, the way holy. To self-submit to the Lord is to put an end to all one's distresses and miseries, to make the *buddhi* free[38] of all constraints and purified of every passion of the body. Purified thus, it comes to drink the bliss that the self is to be liberated from time and every activity. This verily is the state of eternal peace.

Saying 58. To discharge his duty to the truth is indeed the highest endeavour for a mortal, for it is that only that leads to the cessation of all the tainted desires and to the manifestation of peace the true and real. Let him, therefore, ever remain firm in contemplation of the Lord, leaving all his weal and woe to His will. Let him ever consider his comforts as meant to alleviate the distress of others. Let him ever be of a humble disposition, let him seek holy association for the revelation of truth and let him be ever intent on contemplation within him, for it is there, within him, that the Lord abides, that Bliss eternal and infinite.

Saying 59. When the *buddhi*, purified of all the passions of the body, passions that lead one astray from one's being - when the *buddhi*, purified this way, gives itself up to the meditation of Name the True, it comes to be purified of every *vāsanā*, that benightedness itself. That is the moment when it comes to experience, becomes one with (*anubhava*), Word the Eternal, with the *ātman* that ever abides beyond the reach of every *vāsanā*, every action and time itself. Attaining that state supreme, it never returns to the world consisting of recurring births and deaths.

Saying 60. Having self-submitted to Being, a man should meditate the Name all exclusively and be of a self-sacrificing disposition vis-a-vis others. This is how he will be liberated from the fetters that *prakṛti*, that seed of creation, has forged for him. Sustained and exclusive meditation of the Name leads to the manifestation of the Real within, the only thing one should know and adore. When the *buddhi* thus attains to this state, it comes to be blessed with all knowledge and all realisation, shedding all its passion to do and act. That is the state when it comes to be truly pure to lose itself in the bliss eternal, its being and self in truth. That is the state, the only state one should know. Blessed is the man who has given up *vāsanā*, that [primordial] blot, to repose in the self, the self that has no *other* to constitute and de-constitute it. He has come to be full and fulfilled in the ever-unfulfilled moving world (*saṃsāra*), his surpassingly pure life a lasting and redemptive ideal for others.

Saying 61. One must know what this pilgrimage of life in its untainted truth is. And having known its truth, let a man shed his I-sense, that ignorance dense and inert, that root of every folly and wickedness and their disastrous consequences. To be free of this curse, that of I-sense, is to be blessed indeed. Every being born in the world is born inflicted with this curse of I-sense. It is the kind of I-sense that causes the *buddhi* to project a body and its *other*, the world, project these in accord with that kind. This is the wonder that world the creation is.

Saying 62. To give up the I-sense, that perverted sense of 'I am the doer', is to liberate oneself. That verily is the paramount duty of man, to shed that perversion. The extent of one's freedom from the blot of I-sense depends on the extent of one's ability to self-submit to the Real and that self-submission depends on one's ability to know the real from the unreal, to discriminate between these two. This spirit of relative freedom from the I-sense and self-submission to the Real puts one on to the way of peace the secure and everlasting. It is the density of I-sense that makes the *buddhi* mistake the pleasures of the body for the bliss absolute to ever burn in and be scalded by its passions perverse and perverting. For, blinded by the I-sense and its dark shadows, it takes woe for weal to lose the way to peace true and eternal. To strive for freedom from this dark ignorance is to strive for the goal supreme.

Saying 63. An abysmal ocean of deviations and perversions is the body composed of the five elements. Attached to those deviations and perversions, the *buddhi* ever moves restless, taking them to be all-joyous. But in a moment come to an end all the pleasures of the organs of cognition and action, leaving behind desire for them all the more intensified. Indulgence in them, in those pleasures, therefore turns into a scalding misery for the *buddhi*, misery both internal and external and of very many kinds. Fear everlasting inflicts it, the pleasures of the sense giving it no satisfaction and the desire for them never getting appeased. He does well who seeks to free himself from this foolish and polluted disposition.

Saying 64. An unmitigated misery is the end of bodily pleasures, and the body itself too turns into an appalling pain in the end. In this life destined to end this way, not to draw a limit to the bodily needs and pleasures and not to give up the sense of identity with the body and not to make the supreme reality, that consciousness that dispenses life to each and every being, its support one and only, is to self-destruct oneself, is to invite death on oneslf. With every consolation denied to him dies a man who lives this way, a despairing remorse his inescapable lot. Let there be no mistake about this his fate.

Saying 65. For an insignificant moment lasts the life of an embodied being, its end inhering in it and its joys and pleasures turning into tragedies absolute in the end. That is the truth about this life, truth that every being should know and understand. And having known this truth about it, one should take to the right course to attain to the peace absolute and eternal.

Saying 66. All suffering is the body and all bliss is the *ātman*. Mortal is the body and immortal is the *ātman*. The body is all activity and, for this reason, dies each and every moment. A man must, therefore, extricate himself from this eternal recurrence and seek his being in its very truth. That, verily, is the endeavour great for him.

Saying 67. Let a man take Being alone as the very anchor, the very breath, of his life (*viśvāsa*) and orient his mind firmly towards finding It, that Being. That kind of holy faith will free him from every falling and every deviation from that Being that he in truth is. This verily is the Law. Let him, therefore, live all self-submitted to that his self the true. When the *buddhi* lives thus firmly self-submitted to the *ātman*, that Being the Supreme, it sheds its orientation outward, towards the objects of the senses, and seeks to orient itself inwards, and to stay still in that its orientation inwards. This spirit of its life leads it eventually to the Real, Real the Holy, the Unsupported [support of all that is] and the Immortal, to the Real Immortal that is the peace immortal.

Saying 68. When the *buddhi* contemplates, with an exclusive devotion, the mind-breath combination, taking the One Self in each and all as the doer and undoer[39], it comes to find its sense of being a doer, that primordial darkness, come to cease and itself stand apart from every deviation natural to the body. It finds itself, in other words, delivered from every attachment and aversion, from that its scalding torture, leaving the fruit of all its actions to the will of the Lord.

Saying 69. When the *buddhi* finds the One Self as Being itself, that Self alone, and perceives the entire visible world and also its body too as grounded on that Real the conscious, it ceases to identify the self with the body and self-submits to that Real alone. Blessed with this disposition, it puts its own bodily comforts at the service of others, and gives itself up, with all intent and devotion, to a sustained contemplation within of that Real the Supreme. It is then, and only then, that it comes to realise that Being, giving up all its *vāsanās*. Only a man given to this kind of spirited penance attains to the supremely holy state, to the peace that the extinction of his false identity is. He it is, he alone, that has brought his life-pilgrimage to its fruition true.

Saying 70. When the *buddhi* comes to know for certain that the *ātman* alone is its ground and that the *ātman* is it that illumines it, it comes to shed its sense of identity with the body, giving itself up to an exclusive contemplation of the *ātman*. Names and forms, qualities and activities, those false appearances in the shape of thoughts and counter-thoughts then no longer concern it, only Name the true claiming its exclusive devotion. That is how it attains to the bliss that the *ātman* is, that beatitude supreme and absolute.

Saying 71. When the *buddhi* comes to find Word the Imperishable, Word that is the *ātman* of each and of all, the passions of the mind can no longer lead it astray from its self nor can those of the organs of cognition and of action nor can those of the body. For all pure does it then become of these. Only the *ātman* does it contemplate then, no thoughts distracting it from that contemplation. As for the bodily activities, it performs them without a desire for anything. In that all blessed state it stays then, the state all holy and pure.

Saying 72. When the *buddhi* finds for certain that the *ātman*, that Real, is bereft of every activity and every desire, it comes to shed the *vāsanās* that go with the embodied mode of being and comes to be established in its being the true. All freed from the passion for the fruits of the bodily deeds it turns then, fruits the dualities, with their others inscribed into them. All still it rests then, all still and stable.

Saying 73. When the *buddhi* finds within *ātman* the unattached and formless, finds it so with utmost clarity, it stands apart from the entire visible creation. Attaining to that One Self, that Real Itself, it comes to be blessed with the vision of all as the same, all the taints of the body and of the mind falling off it. Fully absorbed in the Real then it abides, only in that. Bliss itself it attains to then, its being consisting only in that.

Saying 74. When the *buddhi* contemplates the self with every intent and determination, it gives up all the passion for the objects of the senses to become aware of the *ātman* within, *ātman* the Word Imperishable, Word the all glory and all power. This realisation turns the transitory world into a shadow bereft of all life. Only the One Self then appears as all illuming and as all. This verily is the essence of all knowledge, this vision.

Saying 75. When the *buddhi* finds the self within as

unattached and beyond the three *guṇas*, the three strands of *prakṛti*, it ceases to hanker after Creation constituted by those strands, setting it up no more. The bodily acts too cease to bind it; it does them as a mere instrument bereft of all desire and aversion. Beyond every *vāsanā* then it abides, all holy and pure.

Saying 76. When the *buddhi* finds the self as free of all dualities, it ceases to be affected by the dualities that all activities of the body-mind complex are and comes to be established in the Eternal, established therein steady and unchanging. Attaining that *samādhi* the eternal, it abides in that which is bliss itself, abides in the Imperishable Word, and beyond the reach of every pain and pleasure, those false appearances set up [by the 'I am the doer'-sense].

Saying 77. When the *buddhi* contemplates the Name Imperishable[40] with a steady intent, losing every interest in the pleasures of the organs of cognition and action, it turns (*anubhava*) within into a glory to which no means of knowledge can lead, where all means of knowledge turn into no means, all thoughts of it mute and inarticulate and all descriptions no descriptions.[41] All peace is that glory, no regrets ever touching it and no troubles, not an iota of them. To know this state is to attain the Real, the Real that illumines this body. Everyone should ever make that Real his refuge, make it with every endeavour holy and pure.

Saying 78. With intent devotion, intent endeavour and earnest awareness should a man resign to his Life the true and, through this spirit of resignation, get rid of and isolate himself from the taints of the body, that misery bitter and fretful. When thus the *buddhi* commits itself to the Real, it turns free and powerful enough to triumph over all the blots that constitute the body.

Saying 79. In the struggle that his life is, a man should live with a *buddhi* purified of all taints to give up all the unholy desires and ideas inherent in him. With these given up, let him resort to desire fervently holy and pure, and earnestly strive to realise and attain to Being the desire-free, to *ātman* the eternal, dispelling thereby his perverted and deluded understanding, that blinding darkness in which he wanders lost and restless. No unrest will then remain to inflict him and no fear to gnaw him, no further births and no further deaths. All will be peace, peace the absolute.

Saying 80. Let him do his best for the uplift of his life, observing the holy principles for that purpose and purifying his mind of all taints. To State the Real he shall attain, State the Imperishable, that goal absolute of every being, the object real of his desire and endeavour. All wise is the man that earnestly works for a life holy and true and to remain steadfast in it, and who knows how to bring to an end all that has brought about his fall. He alone is man the discerning, of discerning absolute, and he alone is supremely blessed, a light and guide is he and his holy endeavour for others to follow and to emulate.

Saying 81. In this pilgrimage that life the worldly is, there is only one way to get rid of all the deviations, deviations from one's being and truth: thoughtful reflection on the life of those that have attained to the truth. For, that life of theirs is life in truth and life the ideal. An inspiration is it for those in search of genuine redemption, a moving spirit to guide them in their path. Let every being remain ever steadfast in his faith in One Lord the Imperishable, Eternal and Supreme and ever dedicate this his perishable body to the duty holy and sacred.

Saying 82. When the *buddhi* takes to its duty the pure, it turns holy enough to give itself up to a steadfast devotion and contemplation of *sat*, of Being. It eats what is pure, transacts what is upright and associates with the holy to dedicate itself without a deviation to remembrance and contemplation of the Imperishable and Eternal Lord. As for the body, it seeks to direct it ever to the good of others without an expectation of a reward. This, verily, is the way to purification of the internal organ, of the mind. In a moment will fall this body, but before that moment arrives, let man utilise it with every earnestness for the highest truth - that grace abounding. With the spirit of striving for that end be blessed every being, for that goal true of their life!

This discourse is verily an intercourse with the truth, beyond the reach of human ken. Let those oriented towards their guru listen to what it proclaims, think on it and contemplate it with a sustained intent. That, verily, is their duty highest and paramount. For, that will open out their way upward. Let them know that it is their purity that will make possible purification of others, that it is with their uplift that uplift of others can come about. Let them hold on to this sacred truth firmly and with conviction!

NOTES

[1] In ordinary language *svārtha* means self-interest or selfishness. Here the text deepens the meaning of self-interest to connote the passion for self-hood, for projecting oneself, for positing oneself in and through the *other*. And since the *other*, the object of consciousness, is ever on the move, therefore, this being projected as a situated being cannot stay as himself.

[2] The text repeatedly asserts that the real search of a mortal being is search for the state of *samatā*, the state in which all distinctions give place to oneness, the state in which distinctions between the mortal and the immortal, man and God, bondage and liberation, fall and redemption cease to be. One can say that the anguish and discontent of a mortal being cannot come to an end unless and until he has attained to that state of *samatā*. In this secondary sense alone can one say that a mortal being's true desire is desire for peace the eternal, peace that falls to the lot of a man when his *other* turns into his self and his self into the *other*. If we do not remember this point, we are in the danger of confusing this 'peace' with a state of the mind, a state which we can experience and enjoy and which, for this very reason of our enjoyment of it, will disappear to make our life more miserable than before. In the Chapter on *Vāsanā* we will further dwell on this point. Scriptural writings often resort to the vocabulary of the agreeable to orient mortal beings towards the Real. But a true seeker should be able to discriminate between 'eulogistic statements' and 'statements about the truth'.

[3] The reference is to the four castes and the four stages of life. The four castes are: that of brahmins, men devoted to prayer, piety and meditative life; that of *kṣatriyas*, of heroes, that of *vaiśyas*, merchants and agriculturists, and, lastly, that of *śūdras*, the servant class. The four stages of life are: that of students, that of householders, that of forest dwellers and that of wanderers or renunciates. The *varṇas*, castes, and *āśramas*, stages of life, constitute the Aryan path.

[4] How is *samatā* the sustaining principle of the world and of each and every being and thing in it? Phenomena of the world are enframed phenomena, phenomena classified, phenomena with their limits set to them. They are interpreted phenomena, interpreted in terms of concepts and relationships and also contrasts. The world we perceive is said to be a system of such relationships and contrasts. But the things of the world and the world itself do not consist of

merely these phenomena and their relationships with each other and their contrasts to each other; there is also existence to inform them. We do not perceive concepts or classes, we perceive existents informed by concepts or classes. And the world too is not merely a system of relationships and contrasts, as it is said to be; it is also a world that is informed by existence. No doubt, we do not perceive existence as such, or, as we may put it, Being as such. But we do perceive it as the informing principle of all that is and could be. In all our thinking and knowledge, we remain concerned with what we can conceptually understand about things, we do not notice Being that is their sustaining principle. And that Being, that Existence, ever remains self-same, whatever the nature of the thing it informs. *Samatā* is this existence divested of concepts in terms of which we would understand and know it, know it as existents. What is the shape and mien of existence divorced from existents is not for our concepts to know and investigate. To know it and be it we have to be innocent, absolutely innocent of them.

There are some passive moments vouchsafed to some, when a thing before them, an ordinary thing before them, suddenly acquires a power to compel their attention, attention exclusive and one pointed, attention that sets aside the entire world to get focussed on that particular thing alone. That thing then becomes *the* thing, the only real thing, the rest of the world getting lost in a vague, undifferentiated background, absorbing the beholder too into it. At this moment, which is no moment, because it would not register its presence, the thing in question sheds its enframing concepts to exceed the limits those concepts set to it to turn into infinity, swallowing both space and time into itself. That is the moment when one comes to be the self-same, comes to be *samatvam* itself. A deep calm, an all-swallowing calm precedes the onset of the disintegration of conceptual limits, turning eventually into that state of sameness. This calm is what one turns into before one merges into sameness itself.

This sameness, this *samatā,* is what makes our interpretations turn into existents. This Being impoverished of all beings is the dispenser of being to things and the whole world. There could be no world and no things, there could be no thought and no concept, no precept and no percept, if this calm, this bliss, this sameness itself was not there to give them their being and life.

5. All the true ethical norms emanate from the Real, from the Word, from the Bliss that is ever the same, that is sameness itself. It is not for

man to formulate any ethical norm, his thinking being determined by his *vāsanā* and the passions that spring from it. But it is not on the word of revelation or of seers alone that we have to depend for understanding this truth. The nature of the three *guṇas*, the three modes of being, when attended to, will reveal how *the* ethical norm is vouched to every being. The mode of *sattva* compels every being to transcend every state of being, every knowledge and every act. This ontological negation is to be the true norm of our life. Other ethical norms are either distortions of it, perversions of it or, in some cases, partial embodiment of it, of this primordial and final ethical act. This point has often received our attention.

6. Action with desire is action that fights against mortality, action without desire is in consonance with mortality. The former results in rebirth because it would seek some resort, some anchor to escape from our common mortal condition, but action without desire will not seek any such resort. Dying itself is life for a being given to action without desire, that is his act of sacrifice, therein lies his redemption and freedom.

7. To believe in God and to self-submit to His will is to cease to seek any state of being to identify oneself with. It means to live in uncertainty, to live one's mortal lot, to acknowledge it as one's being and truth. God is present for a believer as absence in him and the world. There is no state one can find, imagine or aspire to where He will come to be a presence. To believe in Him thus means dedicating oneself to absence, to not to be. A being so dedicated accepts his mortal condition without a desire to transcend it, for no state of being can he envisage where God will come to be a presence and where he too will come to be a presence. He will thus live not as a being ever moving towards death, he will come to be a being that is already dead and ever dead. In other words, his *buddhi* will no longer set limits to things and to him, will not, that is to say, seek to *presence* them. Only existence will he come to be, existence without existents, existence not grasped and *presenced*. Thus to give oneself up to the will of the Lord is to give oneself up to one's mortal lot, to accept it, live it without a demur or a question.

8. It is the *jīva*, he that lives, that sets up the appearances of the world to identify himself with them, to assert and try to affirm his being in and through them. The *jīva* should not be confused with the embodied being, for he, the *jīva*, is the creator of those phantoms. Who is it that lives in the assemblage called the body-mind? Is he to

be equated with the latter, or has he some reality that cannot be equated with it? The *jīva's* attempts to equate his being with any of these appearances is doomed to fail, causing him insupportable pain and suffering, the pain of being a being. This, his frustration, shows that his sense of identity with these appearances is a false and deluded sense and he should get rid of it as soon as he can. When the *jīva* has freed himself from this delusion, he will find his true self to become that self.

9. That is to say, from cinema, etc.

10. This saying should not be taken at its face value. One's efforts are indispensable for one's liberation but only to the extent that they help one surrender one's will and effort to the will of the Lord. But not until the whole of one's *sādhanā*, one striving for salvation, turns out to be all-futile can one wait for what the pious call *grace*. It is the man of despair, complete despair, who is eligible for 'grace', not the one who *believes* in grace, believes in it with the easy self-complacence of the pious. And grace is nothing else than this despair, this 'loss of hope in hope itself'. Spiritual despair alone is grace, for it indicates the collapse or weakening of the doer-identity one has falsely superimposed upon the *ātman*. To strive and strive hard to the extent of realising the futility of that striving is grace, that alone. 'Grace of God' is only a palatable phrase meant for the pious to make them know that there is much more to salvation than their piety.

11. This should not be taken to mean, as some 'faithful' would tend to do, that surrender to the will of the Lord will free man from the obligation of going through what his *prārabdha karman* unfolds for him. His worship of God or gods will not save him from the inexorable unfolding of that destiny. But taking the results of his past acts as if willed by the Lord and enduring them without elation and despair will enable him to acquire the disposition of *samatvam* with regard to those results. Looking alike on his fortunes and misfortunes, his weal and woe, he will come to attain the state of *samatā* where all will become one.

12. A man must know where he stands before he embarks upon the path of *samatā*. No one, out of his vanity or pride of learning, should imagine that he can dispense with the five principles and indulge in an arm-chair kind of contemplation. He must pass through the hardship of a stern discipline before he can think of saying, '*Ahaṃ brahmāsmi*', 'I am Brahman'.

[13.] There is the danger of a pitfall in doing this duty. A man who imposes every discipline on himself, adheres to a stern mode of life, tends to become, out of the pride of his righteousness, a masochist, which expresses itself, when it comes the turn of his family, in the form of sadism. He has to rue this cruelty all his life and bear an intolerable burden of guilt. The sin of *sādhanā* is a deadly sin. It reveals in the clearest possible terms the meanness of one's piety and the inability of every virtue and piety to undo the original sin of *kartāpan*. Man must and has to believe, ultimately, in the sinfulness of every act of his and the ultimate falsehood of every teaching. He has to know, know with every pain and anguish, the untruthfulness of every scripture and every message. The *Samatāprakāśa* says that not before the man on the path has seen the end of teacher-student relationship and has forgotten the life of the Messenger and his Message will he bring his mind to come to cease:

pīr murīdī riśatā ṭūṭā hadīs nabī bisarāyī/
manuā māra cadhe gadha ūpar vijaya niśāna lakhāyī//

[14.] One is not to equate the right investigation of the Law of Nature with scientific investigation. Scientific discourse, like other human discourses, enframes the real in its concepts, superimposes them on to the real. One can find the truth of Nature not through concepts of various discourses but through freeing oneself from every concept and every framework of investigation or interpretation. Only innocence can know the real; it can know the real because it itself is the real. As long as the real is the *other*, that is to say, as long as it is *prakṛti* and its manifestations, the real will remain opaque and unknowable. It is only when it becomes the self that it comes to be, we humans in our folly will say, known.

[15.] This kind of discipline is an imperative for a beginner. It is not applicable to one who has seen through the illusions that his mind sets up for him, more importantly, the illusion about his righteousness and its efficacy. The path to the truth is not, ultimately, a path. Without a defence one has to live and without a support. Even God does not remain one's companion on this path; even He deserts one. Alone he has to move and to the Alone.

[16.] These are the contents of a letter from Śrī Gurudeva to one of his disciples.

[17.] set up as its constitutive *other*.

[18.] Three forces are there to constitue *prakṛti* in its unmanifest and manifest forms. There is the passion to remain coincided with oneself, the passion to preserve and remain what one is. This is called *tamoguṇa*. There is also another thrust operating in every being, the thrust to transcend oneself, to go beyond oneself. This is called *sattva*. And there is a struggle between these two urges, the struggle that expresses itself in action, with the world as the context and condition of that action. This last passion is called *rajas*. The man who has attained to *samādhi* has nothing to stick to, nothing to transcend, and nothing to struggle against to turn into the uncertainty between the two, the uncertainty that a doer is.

19. The five gross elements, namely, earth, water, fire, air and *ākāśa*, empty space, in which dwell all visible things. 'Twenty five' are the bodily counterparts of these five elements, each element having five of these counterparts. Thus earth has its bodily counterparts in the shape of skin, marrow, nerves, bones and hair. Water has its counterparts in the shape of blood, semen, spit, urine and perspiration. Fire has its counterparts in the shape of hunger, thirst, sleep, indolence and splendour; and air in those of running, galloping, inertness, shrinking and expanding; and *akāśa* in grief, infatuation, fear, shame and fame.

20. The Vedic concept of the northern and southern ways, referred to in the Mantra and Brāhmaṇa portions of the Vedas, acquires a deep symbolic significance in the Upaniṣads. The interested reader is especially referred to the Bṛhadāraṇyka, the Chāndoyga and the Praśna Upaniṣads. The translator has elsewhere dwelt at length on the symbolic implications of their accounts.

21. The body and the world are the constitutive others of each other.

22. This means that the choice between the good and the evil that the *buddhi* makes is not a genuine choice. The choice remains restricted to the taints of mind, between one taint and another taint, one evil and another evil. Our concepts of good and evil are informed by the evil that our concepts can never hope to comprehend or capture.

23. True thought does not mean what the *buddhi* thinks on its own but what has been revealed to it. Man is only vouchsafed the true thought, he is not privileged to find it by his powers. Similar is the case with the right conduct, the right belief or faith and the right endeavour. For these too he has to depend on what a sage reveals when lost in *samādhi*.

24. All kinds of ethical thought fail of their purpose as long as the *ātman* does not become the regulative principle of the ethical life, its

goal and end. No action is either free or good as long as it is determined by the intellect, intellect that operates in association with the mind and the sense- and motor organs. It is only when the intellect disorients itself from the mind and the organs and becomes oriented towards the self that it comes to act rightly. However, not before the intellect loses itself in the *ātman* can the ethical urge in man reach its fulfillment.

[25.] Two *befores* are there, the before of creation and the before of that before. The first *before* is called *prakṛti* and the second *before Prabhu*. The first belongs to the domain of the not-self, the second to that of self the *absolutus*, self the *absolutus* because there is no other to that self, all is that alone, that self, even what we term as the not-self, the *prakṛti*. That self is Being the Primordial and the Final and what lies between these two, creation itself. As long as a divide obtains between the *ātman*, the self, and *prakṛti*, the objective domain, evil and misery alone rule the roost. When it is said that *prakṛti* is the domain of evil and misery, all that is meant thereby is that the sense of the divide between the self and *prakṛti* is that evil and that misery. All evil is consciousness-of, consciousness conditoned by its constitutive *other*, all misery is it and all tragedy. It is only when this divide is healed that that misery comes to cease and that evil. This means that all one thinks of and is conscious of, including consciousness itself, is evil absolute - all thought, all actions, all hopes, all one's endeavours and ideals. Evil is written into consciousness-of, consciousness informed by the *other*. Man has to become all innocent in thought and desire-free in disposition to heal the divide informing him. All concepts he has to give up, his *buddhti*, the power that determinates, has to cease to operate, if he would be pure and blessed.

[26.] *duḥkha*. *duḥ* - evil, *kha*, space. *Duḥkha* thus is universal.. It is the misery of being a being, misery of being a being in and of the world. It is not mere sorrow as it is commonly taken to be.

[27.] The intellect is given to determinate phenomena, to enframe them in concepts, to delimit them as against other phenomena, visible and invisible. Self-submission to Being, bare Being or Existence, implies shedding these enframing concepts and letting Being itself stand out and suffuse the intellect with itself. As the world of multiplicity is the *other* of the active intellect, Being, bare existence, is the self of the innocent intellect, its *self*, not its *other*. For, there is no *other* for innocence. Conceptual understanding posits an embodied being as the self, with the world as the *other* of that self. It is all misery and evil, this positing and the self-world it sets up. Every event here is evil, every action, howsoever sublime it may appear to be. Every thought is an error, every knowledge ignorance and every joy a curse. In innocence alone lies one's hope, therein alone, neither in thought nor in action. Self-submission to Being, Being divested of all phenomena, means only this passive innocence, this total disinterestedness.

28. When bodily pleasures do not distract one from one's ontological commitment to Being, they do not harm one. When they distract one from the path to Being, they turn evil. This is the implication of the sanctifying and sanctified limit of those comforts.

29. Knowledge without its *others*, viz, the knower and the known. This is one of those terms that seers and scriptures often use to describe Being, terms that negate themselves in their very formulation. The faithful often confuse these terms with the truth, creating all kinds of misconceptions and disputes.

30. Creatures caught up in the web of *Māyā* move round and round the same point. Their journey has no goal and end.

31. Knowledge without its *others*, namely, the knower and the known.

32. Literally, ocean.

33. Devotion untainted by any self-interest.

34. '...the witness of the body and is the reality absolute and consciousness itself.' 'The witness of the body' and 'the reality absolute' negate each other and, through that negation, negate themselves. The witness of the body cannot be the witness of the body without isolating the body from the field of vision and, by implication, the field beyond the field of vision. Secondly, becoming its witness it cannot but be conditioned by what it perceives and does not perceive, by what it is the witness of. It cannot, in other words, isolate itself from the entire field of observed and not observed things. But what is here suggested is that this witness is the Real Absolute, that only the Real Absolute can be the witness of the body, not the witness conditioned by the body and its *other*, the known and unknown world. So consciousness in its truth and being is the Real Absolute, at once the knower and the known-unknown, the individual and the all. We understand consciousness, know it, as conditioned by what it knows and does not know; we do not know consciousness the unconditioned, consciousness that is One only

without a second. The expression '...the witness of the body and is the reality absolute and consciousness itself' unsays what it says. The real is these and yet is not these.

35. Earth, water, fire, air and space.

36. Giving is virtue, purity and divinity; acquisition is evil, impurity and demonic. Giving is life, acquisition is death. The Lord gives Himself up to creation and creation too must and has to give itself up to God, sacrifice itself into Him as He sacrificed Himself into it. This sacrificial vision of reality finds a pride of place in the Vedic Revelation. With all their concern for knowledge of the self as Brahman, the Upaniṣads revoke this vision time and again. To be the act of sacrifice itself is to be self the real and Brahman the Unconditioned. .

37. With a mind pure of all self-interests.

38. To self-assert and self-affirm is to be in chains and bondage. For, it means identification with something that is other than the self; it means to be at the mercy of that other, of its nature, its tendencies, or its passions. Not to self-assert and self-affirm is to be free of the *other*, the constraints it, the latter, imposes upon one's self. To self-submit to Being *before* beings is to self-submit to Being *before* concepts, it is to be one's self without the other. The way to freedom lies in discarding all concepts and all enframings and the sense of doership that goes with enframing. For, to be a doer means to be conditioned by the past and the future. To affirm oneself, in other words, means to invite death and mortality upon oneself and a losing fight against it.

39. The One Self in each and all is beyond the reach of every concept, including those of the doer and the undoer. The *buddhi*, the self as reflected in the determinating faculty or the intellect, falsely attributes, in its ignorance, all actions to the self, the self conditioned by it. To free itself from this, its delusion, the *buddhi* has to take the self as the doer and itself as the not-doer. This false attribution of doership to the *ātman* and of not-doership to itself frees it from the primordial malady of doership. This, in essence, is what is called *karma-yoga*. In the practice of *jñāna-yoga*, the process is reversed. Here the *buddhi* imagines itself as self the not-doer and takes every action as performed by the breath-mind-body complex, thereby distancing itself from every action. This isolation of itself from every activity also leads to the same result, namely, freedom from the malady of doership.

40. The Name Imperishable is the Name that is given to a seeker of

truth by a teacher that has become one with the Real. This Name is a name in a human language but unlike the names of a human language, this Name is not to be taken as the Name of the Real but as the Real itself. It is Name the Real and Imperishable because when contemplated as the Real, contemplated with all intent and concentration, there remains no *Othe*r to constitute it, Other in the form of a language as a whole and in the form of what that language articulates as its referent. The Name Alone becomes the All and the All the Name, there remains no other to undo it. The Name turns imperishable only when man dies into it; it is his self-sacrifice that makes it, a mere word, eternal. It is in the sacrifice of the I-sense that all glory lies, all immortality and all life and reality. And all knowledge.

41. Man cannot help trying to know the Real in his own terms, conceptual or experiential. He seeks to know it in terms of means of knowledge available to human nature, think about it in terms of his thoughts and concepts, thoughts that are linguistically articulate and communicative. And yet when he attains to it, his means of knowledge are all left behind, and his thoughts remain no thoughts, with language, their informing principle, having been left behind. The text persistently asks man to put all his efforts, all his thoughts and all his meditations in the service of one end, namely, knowledge of the self. Yet all his efforts will fail to reach it, all his knowledge and all his thoughts. In other words, that self is something to be known, not that it is knowable or can be known. We have to seek to know it, only seek to know it, so that we may cease to seek and know and to think and to act. In their cessation lies our life and being, in the cessation of all that we are and can be, of all that we can dwell in and relate to. That is the purpose of all spiritual instruction, namely, to bring about the extinction of man's passion for being, for knowledge and for transcendence, for going beyond himself and his existential condition. To know the self can only be our goal, a goal that will redeem us not through our success but through our failure, complete and absolute.

Anubhava Five

Samatā-bodha, On Realisation of Sameness

Treasure 1 - On Understanding Vāsanā[1]

Saying 1. As long as a man is not vouchsafed *nirṇaya*, truth the conclusive,[2] about this visible and transient world, there will open up no way for him to redeem himself. So, it is incumbent on man that he understand what this marvel, this play of the ever moving world is, what its truth the hidden and secret is. That, verily, is reflection the true and that, verily, is his duty the true and highest. Otherwise, he will remain, as do others, ever immersed in the business of life, happy or unhappy. Not a moment will he find without that fret and fever, the moment without an activity.

Saying 2. To reflect on this feverish unrest and to work aright for the state still and passive is endeavour the true, that only. Reflection deep and serious[3] will reveal unto man the truth about his life, if he resorts to it, to that reflection. And that truth is the truth of his thirst, thirst that is the very constitutive principle of his life, that force that ever compels him to stray and wander deluded and in error. Try as much as he may, it does not get appeased, that his thirst. In that he lives, in that lack, and in that he dies to take up another form, another body, to strive for the attainment of what he seeks, the state of being all full and perfect. This, verily, is what is called coming and going, moving on from one birth to another, to do acts good and evil, purposeful and not purposeful and reap their rewards, happy or unhappy. And this process goes on without a pause, this process of recurring births and recurring deaths, and ceases not until he has attained to bliss the full and absolute. This eternal recurrence of birth and death is all that this creation, this world on the move, truly is. Fettered by what he has set up, every being wanders about in this his life-journey, taking upon himself many an action and duty [to reap their results here and hereafter].

Saying 3. To seek the peace eternal is the object real of all his endeavours, of this mortal being. That, verily, is the true, inner urge behind all his strivings and efforts. But in the absence of reflection and contemplation, reflection true and contemplation true, his endeavours turn into naught, direct as he does them, his endeavours, towards evil purposes to end up in the vortex of fret and unrest. His end comes to him with remorse woeful and grievous about the blind folly that led him astray and to evil. But to no purpose will be that remorse, for reap one must what one has sown, good or bad. That is the way of *Māyā*, mysterious, marvelous and incomprehensible.

Saying 4. Let every being think deeply and with care about the meaning of the pilgrimage that this world is. He should try to know the cause of this his journey and the measures he should adopt to bring about the fulfillment he ever seeks, fulfillment complete and full. If he thoughtlessly goes about the business of the world in search of the fullness he seeks, vain will be his effort, for the rest he seeks, rest the full and infinite, will ever elude him. And die shall he beset with every woe grievous and overwhelming. So, let him think about life comprehensively and, equipped with right understanding, resort to right effort to reach the real goal, the goal redemptive. He will live his life in its very truth and essence, if he reflects thus and strives thus.[4]

Saying 5. Behind all the unrest that every mortal being is subject to lies *vāsanā*, that cause primordial of all that he perceives, all the spectacles strange and curious that provoke him to enjoy them or avoid them. That verily is the primal delusion, this subjection to *vāsanā*. And that alone is the world so hard to cross! Unless a mortal dedicates all his efforts towards its eradication, he will not succeed in his purpose. But a helpless prisoner of it, he does not ever pause to consider whether *vāsanā* will bring him weal or woe, and directs all his efforts towards its appeasement. For that purpose, all kinds of acts he resorts to, good or bad, and reaps their results. Thus unrest alone falls to his lot, unrest perpetual and unending but not that peace he truly is in search of. A mortal must know this malady great for what it is, must reflect upon it aright and find the cure for it. Knowledge true and real consists only in this, in this reflection and in this effort.

Saying 6. Vāsanā alone is the world, that phenomenon strange ever on the move, without a beginning and an end and without a limit set to it. The mortal being, under its impact, sets up in many and varied ways and each and every moment, the entire creation, gross and subtle[5] to identify himself with it[6], to earn for himself every weal and woe. Not a moment can he find where he may rest still and unmoving. This ever on the move condition of his is, verily, the world ever on the move, this condition alone. Not until *vāsanā,* that darkness, comes to cease, will he find and be the Being, Being the truth, consciousness and bliss, that peace eternal and absolute.

Saying 7. It is *vāsanā,* that ignorance, alone that sets up before a mortal, and throws him into, many a whirl without a way out of them. The irony, however, is that he, in his ignorance, puts in every effort to augment this darkness, seeking in it the bliss true and real. But where and how can he find that bliss, that peace absolute, in this endless but baseless fabrication, which perishes the moment it comes into being? Lost in and inflicted by this darkness, this delusion that *vāsanā* is, he will find other fabrications set up for him, other phantoms to entangle and beguile him.

This is, in every truth, the play that *Māyā* plays for every mortal being.[7]

Saying 8. This way, this mortal being perceives many a projection of *vāsanā*, projections as unstable and ephemeral as are the ripples of water, and, a victim of desire (*kāmanā*) for these, resorts to many an act to get them and thereby appease that desire.[8] But no appeasement of *vāsanā*, that blind passion for being, comes to be possible through appeasement of desires for objects set up by it. For like unto an infernal river it flows, that *vāsanā*, letting no one cross it. Compelled by it, by *vāsanā*, beings take on and shed off many bodies, bodies that are the worlds themselves, move on deluded from one birth to another birth and from one death to another death - without a let and without a pause. This verily is the wonderful *līlā*, play, of the Real, its unmotivated manifestation. To transcend it, to go beyond it, is to attain to one's abode the final and ultimate, to get established in one's being the imperishable and fearless.[9]

Saying 9. A prisoner of *vāsanā*, this mortal being does not find even a moment's respite from unrest, the dualities of weal and woe, those fruits of his actions, keeping him ever on the move. Under their impact, of these dualities, he assumes every cleverness and cunning to achieve his ends but to no purpose. For, all his moves result only in making him all the more involved in these dualities, those results of his actions, his cunning and cleverness proving to be merely his ignorance. Only misery falls to his lot, misery perpetual and unending. That verily is the way of the world, the way hard to follow and to discard, the way dark and not to see through. To transcend this way of the world is to transcend into fulfillment, full and complete. That is the truth, the truth indeed.

Saying 10. When this *jīva*, he that lives, identified himself with actions, when he fell into the grip of 'I am the doer'-sense, he found himself a prisoner of the *vāsanā* for the dualities that constitute the results of actions, dualities that are mere products of the five elements that compose the world.[10] This sense of identity with action is what a *jīva*, being that lives, in fact is. There is no why to the rise of this sense of identity with action. That is why, they term it, this false setting up of oneself as a doer, as *Māyā*. And *Māyā* alone is it. For, nothing definite can be said about it, no conclusion can be drawn about it. One can determinate only the real, not that which is not and which only appears to be. For, the moment it is sought to be investigated, it ceases to be. One may, however, say by way of conclusion, that the deluding *Māyā* is nothing else than this false setting up of oneself as a doer. When the *jīva*, this mortal being, sheds that setting up, then all delusions leave him and he comes to be the Alone, comes to be the Being that he really and ever is. This state of being, the state where he comes to be truly and really himself, is however, a matter for realisation, not something to discuss and dispute about. The first step towards its attainment is to get rid of the false notion that one has about oneself, the false notion of oneself as a doer. When one comes to shed that false understanding, that sense of me and mine, then the state of bliss that *samatā* is, is attained spontaneously and on its own, the bliss that is the Alone, beyond the reach of what one could say and utter. [11]

Saying 11. It is identification with action, it is one's sense of oneself as a doer, that gives rise to the web that *vāsanā* is. As long as this primordial delusion, this one's sense of one's being as a doer, does not get dispelled, it is not possible to get rid of *vāsanā*. And as long as *vāsanā* holds a *jīva*, a mortal being, under its grip, there is no possibility for him to escape from the misery that recurring births and recurring deaths are. Therefore, man must undo the delusion that inflicts him, the delusion of doership through thinking that is pure and unpolluted[12]. Therein lies his redemption, in this endeavour, and therein lies his duty befitting his human birth.

Saying 12. Out of identification of the self with activity and superimposition of the concept of doership on to the self arises *vāsanā* in the form of three *guṇas**, strands, those of *sattva, rajas* and *tamas* to create the world moving and unmoving. Every being that comes to live here finds himself fettered by the *vāsana* of the three *guṇas* to be compelled to do activities of all kinds to get immersed in it again and again[13], in that passion past one's understanding. Rare is the man endowed with a rare wisdom who can extricate himself free from this dense web to lose himself in the Real. It is the duty highest of every being blessed with the human birth to ever move towards that goal, that truth, that state blessed and fearless.

Saying 13. The ever moving world is nothing else than *vāsanā* consisting of the three *guṇas*. That alone is the cause of its coming to be and its ceasing to be, of this world. The net that *prakṛti* spreads out for entangling a being, all that he can perceive and conceive [and also what he cannot perceive and conceive], is nothing else than the self-projection of *vāsanā*. *This truth one comes to know only when one attains to the Real and becomes one with It*. Only by striving for and attaining to that Real Supreme, that light of consciousness[14] , can one put an end to *vāsanā* and attain to peace the eternal. That should be the considered end of a man's life. That alone is faith in its truth, this orientation of one's life towards the Real.

Saying 14. A being acts and lives as goaded by the *guṇa* operating dominantly in him. And it is the tension among the *guṇas*, their tendency to dominate each other, that spreads out the darkness that *vāsanā* is. And it is *vāsanā* that drives a mortal being towards bodily pleasures to live infatuated with them and for their sake wander in the world, deluded and bewildered. His blind passion for the body and for the visible world is nothing else than the working of *vāsanā*, of that alone. Until *vāsanā* ceases to be, the wheel of recurring births and deaths will continue to move to keep this being the mortal far away from the state of *samatā*, from that peace eternal.

Saying 15. A helpless captive of the *guṇas,* this being invents and plays many a role, strange and weird, to fulfill his heart's desire. But where to find that fulfillment in this mortal life, that wheel of recurring births and deaths set into motion by the awfully mysterious *Māyā*? Only frustration becomes his portion when he is made to depart from his body. Before that moment arrives, let him, therefore, strive for the truth, for Being to remain no more a victim of the delusion that *vāsanā* is, the delusion that has ever pursued him life after life.

Saying 16. All that this being does, good or evil, he does under the compulsive force of *vāsanā* as conditioned by the three *guṇas*. His being as a living being is nothing else than manifestation of the *guṇas*, their unfoldment. A being with the *sāttvika vāsanā, vāsanā* conditioned by the *sattva* abiding dominant in him, lives given to acts sublimely noble, his very nature unfolds itself in and through them. Truthful he lives and given unto the service of others, ever forgiving the wrongs they may have done unto him. With faith he lives, faith in the Lord, that Being *before* beings, and ever given to noble conduct, contentment, simplicity, care and regard and love for others. These and other high traits spring out of the *sattva* in him[15]. To live for others, for their joy and well being comes first in his priorities. A man endowed with this disposition and given to this kind of life and effort alone can attain to the state of being where no *vāsanā* abides, to the state of bliss that *samatā* is.

Saying 17. A being dominated by *rajas* remains ever busy in accumulating all kinds of things that give him pleasure or serve his other ends and interests. His passion for them knows no limits, the whole world would he command, if he could, to satisfy his ambitions and appease his desires. But all that he accumulates and enjoys turns into grievous woe for him when the moment of death arrives and his body comes to perish. In frustration he departs from the world, frustration overwhelming, his desires all unappeased. A man given to an overweening *rājasika* nature, nature predominantly conditioned by *rajas*, lives ever a prisoner of bodily passions and pleasures. Excessive sex, excessive wrath, excessive greed and excessive pride sum up his life and being. No moment , even a little, can he find in which he could breathe free of the selfishness darkening his soul and being. To live in pursuit of material goods becomes his way, his life solely dedicated to it. Deeply dense is this darkness, this *vāsanā* fashioned by *rajas*. Not a moment does it spare for man to breathe free of fear and apprehensions.

Saying 18. A being possessed of *vāsanā* conditioned by *tamas* lives all suffused with unrest and wickedness. No limits he sets to his passions, pleasures alone constituting the regulative principle of his life, they being the highest bliss for him. There is no aberration he will not embrace, no deviation he will not resort to. Fraud and cunning, insolence and wantonness, theft and murder, foolish and unconsidered beliefs and other great evils sum up the way of his life. Grievous and woeful shall be his end and his coming lives, very many of them, will be a retribution and a punishment for his sins.

Saying 19. The entire world moves as the three *guṇas* would have it move. When the *sattva* comes to dominate the *rajas* and the *tamas, dharma*, righteousness, comes to rise and flourish. In peace then live the *jīvas*, in calm and quiet, trying to restrain their passions for the pleasures of the flesh, to be calm of mind their goal and their way.

Saying 20. When the *rajas* assumes dominance, acquisition and accumulation of wealth becomes the guiding principle for mortal beings, with pleasures their obsession. Goods of comfort and luxuries they produce in profusion, goods passing strange and incredible. To accumulate and enjoy the pleasures of the body becomes their way of life, their days and nights spent solely for that end. The ways they invent for their physical well being mesmerize them into self-complacence to the extent of denying the existence of the Lord, the physical well being their sole concern and aim. No consideration for peace of mind survives in them, their pleasures eroding the very thought of that peace. A time, however, comes when their prosperity too ceases to be, their addictions incapacitating them to sustain it. As for their spiritual uplift, they have already denied its possibility. When this comes to pass, this state of decadence and decay, *vāsanā* suffused with *tamas* through and through comes to seize every being to bring surpassing disaster for them, and every heavy woe. This verily is the play that the *Māyā* of the Lord plays on and ever.

Saying 21. When the *vāsanā* suffused with *tamas* comes to possess beings, they come to be so deeply entrenched in narcissistic ways as to lose the very sense of what belongs to others and to them. To acquire and possess turns a blind and violent obsession with them, leading them to murder one another for that purpose, murder without a count. When this self-destructive state comes to prevail, destruction of one another becomes a daily affair with them, leaving not a way for them to live together and in peace. No word can they utter which is not fraudulent and deceitful, their souls all benighted with *vāsanā*. Then evil appears to overwhelm the world and its creatures, their *tāmasika vāsanā* leaving no opening for either prosperity or redemption. Misery alone becomes their lot and their portion.

Saying 22. This *vāsanā* of the three kinds, *vāsanā* that enwraps every being, is it that sets up before him phenomena of myriad kinds to ever goad him on into actions good and evil and reap their results, happy or unhappy. Whatever the state of being he may attain to, he finds the peace eternal ever eluding him. This verily is the way of the world, that movement from birth to death and from death to birth. No better than a mere beast is a man who does not think about the web that *vāsan*ă weaves out for him, does not know the delusion that it is, and does not pause to weigh what he does or does not do. Waste and barren will go his human, birth, for, fail will he of its purpose, viz., to make his mind stay ever still and unruffled. In births other than human this mortal being cannot find the way out of his passion for the body and the weal and woe that go with that passion. Only in human birth can he unweave the web that *vāsanā* weaves out for him. That is the role assigned to him as a being human. Let him not fail in this his highest duty, let him ever strive to redeem himself from that his given condition.

Saying 23. That man is man the noble and man the righteous, he alone, who reflects deep on *vāsanā* and the net it spreads out to catch every being in it, in this delusion all enwrapping, and who adopts the necessary measures to free himself from it, from this universal delusion. For, that is the end of every true and sacred Law, namely, liberation from *vāsanā*.

Saying 24. Every being knows well and for certain, knows as a creature of *vāsanā*, what he is to do and not to do. His *vāsanā* lets him entertain no misgivings on that account. All his life is spent in thoughts and worries about acquiring what he deems to be good for his well being. That remains the life long passion of every being, pious or not pious. Not a moment will he spare to sit quiet and still. This is how this wheel of delusion moves. Let every being consider with all seriousness what his condition in its truth is. Let him free himself from *vāsanā*, sparing no effort. That is the way to be steadfast in one's duty towards the Law.

Saying 25. All those measures that help dispel this darkness of *vāsanā* from the mind and bring about a steadfast conviction about the truth and reality of the *ātman* constitute *dharma*, the Law; and all those tainted ways of life that help intensify that darkness of *vāsanā* and prompt one to sink in sinfulness constitute *adharma*, violation of the Law. That is the truth about these two ways, that of righteousness and that of unrighteousness. To think thus and to stick and remain faithful to the way of righteousness is the way straight to peace the real and true.

Treasure 2 - On Eradicating Vāsanā

Saying 26. One must first recognise *vāsanā* for what it in its very truth is: a fearful snare and mesh. Then comes the turn of taking measures towards its eradication, measures appropriate for that purpose. That is the way proper to get to that end. One should, therefore, know what it is that binds a being and what it is that frees him. This comes to be possible, this understanding, when one lives with those that have attained to the truth and become one with it. Only their instruction can make one clearly discriminate between these two, bondage and liberation, and, enriched with that understanding, dispel this darkness that *vāsanā* is. A time will come when this restless being will find the rest he seeks, rest in its purity absolute.

Saying 27. Identification of one's self with actions and attachment to what ensues therefrom is verily the delusion that binds every being. As long as this delusion does not get dispelled, it will be hard indeed for one to find the way true to Being of all in each, to that bliss of sameness. To give up this identification of one's self with actions, to this superimposition of those on to one's self, is to give up supremely, for that giving up, pure and holy, leads this homeless being to his home true and holy.

Saying 28. Let him ever seek instruction from the seers true, for that alone will lead him towards his goal. Let this be the law primary for him, this his seeking instruction from them. With *vāsanā* for his inheritance, every being wanders about in the world as if compelled by his nature. To free himself from this helpless and compulsive wandering, from this his inherited darkness, he cannot but be obliged to resort to right measures. And those measures are precisely the ones that the seers of truth adopted to attain to their goal. It is those very measures that he must adopt and remain steadfast to. For these constitute the means to reach the goal he seeks.

Saying 29. A dreadful thing is the state of being the mind. Hard it is to subdue it, hard to the very limits of extremity. But this being that has come to live in the world *can* find the way to stillness, the way without a pitfall. And that way is the way of eradication of one's sense of identity with actions, their superimposition on to the self and of the self on to them. But the eradication of this false sense of one's being, this root of all delusion, does not come to be possible until the *buddhi*, the mind and the five organs of sense come to converge, come to be one.[16]

Saying 30. The first measure one should adopt for the said purpose is the measure in the shape of purification of one's ordinary life, life given to one's own interests, but in accordance with the teachings of the seers of truth. For, that leads to the realisation of the highest truth, this purification of one's life dedicated to one's interests. Purification of that life implies purification of the entire ambit of a man's life, of what he eats and transacts with, of the company he has and of the thoughts he thinks. Let him keep himself pure in all these aspects of life, for this kind of conduct will suffuse his *buddhi* with faith in the Real and make it strong enough to turn to It. Without this faith, strong and steadfast, no being can hope to put an end to the darkness that *vāsanā* is and dispel the fears it inflicts upon him.

Saying 31. To know the body for what it is, know it as a mere adjunct, as other than what one truly is, will itself lead one to believe in the Real. That is to say, to know the difference between the body and the spirit that dispenses life to it is discrimination real and pure. ***Buddhi, mind, the I-sense and the five gross elements constitute this instrument called the body*** with the life spirit or *ātman* illuminating it. The *buddhi* knows all the functions of this body-complex but cannot know that which dispenses life to it. Still and motionless stays the buddhi when it comes to know that living spirit, and as for *vāsanā*, it meets its end the moment that knowledge dawns upon man.[17]

Saying 32. The *buddhi* ever persists as identified with the activities of the body-mind and in enjoying or suffering the results of those activities – those results, happy or unhappy, ever keeping it on the move. This is how the body as a whole[18] functions, rendering the *buddhi* ever distressed by the desire to have or not to have. Only knowledge of the one self, that reality one and absolute, can lead one from this darkness to light, that bliss absolute.

Saying 33. Only surrender of one's life and breath to the Real and contemplation thereof can lead one out of this illusion, this confusion. That sums up the teachings of all the great seers. *Vāsanā* is nothing else than identification of the self with the body, with this assemblage of sense, mind and *buddhi*. And to abide as the self ever the same is *yoga* the highest and peace the supreme. To undo the sense of the Me with regard to that body is to undo *vāsanā*.

Saying 34. To undo one's sense of identity with the body is an exceedingly hard undertaking, for this living being, compulsively attributing actions to himself, cannot distance himself, even for a moment, from bodily[19] experiences. To break this fetter wrought by *Māyā*, fetter eerie and uncanny, is to be all-victorious. He alone is the knower of truth, of the very essence of all that is, he who has, with a noble effort, burnt up all the defects of the mind for love of the truth and has attained to the bliss that is *samatā*, that goal the purest.

Saying 35. A man who believes in and contemplates the one *ātman* and looks upon all the pleasures of the body as mere false appearances of pain and suffering, and who offers all his comforts in service of others - only a man of this faith true and given to care and concern for others can free himself from the grip of the darkness that *vāsanā* is and attain to the abode supreme.

Saying 36 To undo *vāsanā* and find the state of *samsatā*, a man is to know for certain that the body is nothing else than destruction itself and that the *ātman*, the self, alone is imperishable. He is to ever give himself steadfastly to the contemplation of the self, contemplation right and genuine. And he is to live in the world as humility itself and a devoted servant of each and every being, dedicating all his actions to the Lord and His Will, and to look alike on weal and woe. If he has truly taken to this kind of fervent devotion and contemplation and remembers the Lord's Name each and every moment, he will surely come to know what *samatā* is, this man made of the supreme mettle. And he alone will find the state where no *vāsanā* is, that state of eternal bliss.

Saying 37. A man who has resorted, with a settled constancy, to the path of disinterested action, leaving the fruit of his action to be ordained by the will of the Lord, and gives his mind exclusively to the meditation of the Name, unaffected by the dualities his actions may result in - a great man so disposed will surely come to know the state of *samatā*, that state ever the same. In the bliss of the self will he remain absorbed. With every effort he, that gifted soul, will remain steadfast in contemplation of the Sound[20] of the self to triumph over *vāsanā*. A blessing will be his life for every embodied being.

Saying 38. The living being lives ever involved in the conflict of opposites that every fruit of action is. If one thing pleases him, another distresses him, his life an unhappy tale of attachments and aversions. A mere unrest he lives, whether a man of power and influence or a man helpless and destitute. This meaningless but miserable fabrication does not allow him to know the Real that ever remains self-same in every condition.

Saying 39. To disentangle oneself from the cruel duality that the result of every action is, the duality that constitutes the sense of me and mine, there is a way straight and plain, the way of action without a desire for its fruit. Whatever this organism does or is made to do should be left to the will of the Lord, one's inner attention ever fixed on the Name vouchsafed by a seer of the truth absolute. This resolute contemplation of the Name, leaving whatever happens or does not happen to the will of the Lord, this exclusive devotion will wash the mind free of every pollution, the *buddhi* within finding the Word, that Brahman the Supreme, and becoming one with It. This is what realisation of Real the Same is, this becoming one with the Word. In other words, looking alike on every fruit of action, the *buddhi* ceases to be a doer. A moment of staying still in this passivity is enough to make it know the truth about the self, that peace absolute.

Saying 40. Self-identification with action indeed is the source of the darkness that *vāsanā* is. Without its cessation, of this superimposition of action on to the self, there can be no cessation of *vāsanā,* whatever the measures one may take towards that end. Every moment this living being imagines himself a doer and attached to action to find himself happy or unhappy. 'I am a doer' is the constant refrain of his speech, this meaningless and miserable refrain. For, that is his very being for him, this sense of 'I am the doer,' the sense that ever keeps him immersed in *vāsanā* and fear birth after birth and death after death, that wheel of recurrence ever moving on for him.

Saying 41. Only a rare man endowed with a rare power of discrimination tries to free himself from this self-identification with action, and only a rare man, dedicated to *sādhanā,* to striving for that goal, comes to attain to the state of not-doing, that blissful state ever the same. **For, a man may resort to every sacrifice and every self-denial, may resort to every yogic meditation and give away his possessions all, spend himself in the service of others and otherwise do every physical penance and at every moment but no measures he adopts will lead to cessation of his *vāsanā,* to cessation of the darkness that it is. On** the contrary, these high deeds of his will make his *buddhi* all the more proud to make it fall of its purpose true and lead it astray all the more into self-concern and self-indulgence, with unending unrest for its portion.

Saying 42. All these measures were taken to bring *vāsanā* to its extinction, but, instead of that, the density of that darkness increased manifold. Surpassingly strange indeed is this phenomenon! This living being cannot attain to the state of no-desire, that state blessed where one remains just oneself without a hankering for the other, cannot attain to that state if he is bereft of a clear sense of distinction between the real and the unreal and the grace of a true seer. No display can work here and no pretence.

Saying 43. Self-denial and learning, meditation and passive contemplation and such other measures are there to put an end to *vāsanā*. But if these means are adopted without true faith and belief in the real and without dedicating one's life to the goal of self-redemption, then of no avail will be that effort and that striving. For, instead of purifying the mind, these measures will increase one's vanity to fierce proportions to inflame one's *vāsanā* as never before.

Saying 44. Teachers of holy lore abound here in plenty and men given to charity and men of learning and knowledge, their number swelling ever. But hard it is to find, extremely hard indeed, a man whose *vāsanā* has come to be extinct. It is their sense of identity with those acts, of these men given to noble acts and to the sacrifice of their lives in great acts of piety, that does not let their *vāsanā* die down. As for the bliss of no-desire, it ever remains beyond their reach. Their resort to noble deeds of varied kinds does not mean the end of desire for their fruit in terms of happiness, it persists unabated in their hearts to lead them to further births and deaths.

Saying 45. If a man takes recourse to acts of piety and nobility for the sake of prosperity, vain will be his effort and his endeavour. For, no conviction will he have about his self the true, concerned will he remain with the interests of his self the false and imagined, making his fetters stronger than before. This *jīva*, this mortal being, has no choice but to act and do, in no way can he escape from this his predicament. The only option available to him is either to act without attributing the acts he is made to do to his self or attributing those acts to it. The first disposition is one of knowledge, the second that of ignorance. The action done with the spirit of the first disposition will not bear any fruit for him, the action done with the spirit of the second disposition will lead him to further births. In brief, the bliss of no-desire will ever elude man until he persists with his sense of identity with action, associates his self with it. The interests of his false self will ever motivate his acts of discipline, howsoever hard.

Saying 46. Only understanding, clear and solid,[21] can redeem man from his fallen condition. Therefore, one should resort to right effort with full understanding about what constitutes the way of action and what constitutes the way of no-action. That way alone can one come to be blessed. Every action leads inevitably to its result, action done with knowledge the true or action done without knowledge the true. Action done with knowledge means action done with the understanding that it is ordained by the Lord, by Him alone. Action done with this spirit will not destablise the *buddhi* from its equanimity vis-a-vis the result it bears forth, in no way will it attach itself to it, identify the self with it. But action done with the sense of I attached to it, to its doing, will destablise the *buddhi*, forcing it to take further measures to get rid of the pain that its destablisation gives rise to. This way the passion to act, that *vāsana* to act, will continue to spread out to force the concerned person move from one birth to another without an end.

Saying 47. Renunciation in truth means renunciation of the dualities that every action results in. Not until the *buddhi* comes to renounce these will it ever come to be stable, despite its apparent renunciation of everything. The passion for the duality that every act has for its result will not cease without a sustained contemplation of the Real. Loquacious beings that go eloquent about Brahman will not find the state of no-desire until their *buddhi* gets purified of I-sense through contemplation pure and genuine. Their inferences and other means of knowledge will all go waste, whatever their count.

Saying 48. Knowledge means, in its essence, attainment of the state of *samatā* and freedom from the great malady of *vāsanā*. Theoretical knowledge is of no use if one remains inflicted with the desire for the duality, the conflict of opposites, that every action results in. Mere sight of water will not quench one's thirst, only drinking of it will. Theoretical formulations about the real can come easily to man but not getting suffused with it. Only a rare being, who knows for certain what is truth and what is not truth, can purify his mind of every pollution by dedicating his life and being to the truth. He alone is the person who is blessed with knowledge the true. Rare is such a being and rare his life.

Saying 49. *Sādhanā*, striving for the goal of life, is meant for one's own liberation. Pretence of it will be useless and futile. A benighted being, bereft of every light, cannot be a light unto others. It will all be a fraud, a mere deceit. Glory lies in getting rid of the defects of the mind. This is as true in the case of a householder as in that of a renunciate, of a man given to piety or a man given to depravity, of a rich man or a poor man, a king or his subject, a teacher or a disciple. No one can reach that goal without following the path true. So, let every being adhere to the path of genuine knowledge for his uplift. That is the *dharma*, the Law, for him. Infinite bliss will he find, the being who follows this Law, will find it even before his mortal life comes to its end.

Saying 50. The wheel of *saṃsāra*, of recurring births and deaths, moves inexorably letting no one escape from it, not easily at all. It requires a very great effort on the part of a mortal to attain to the state beyond the reach of every fear. It is in the nature of this being to act and live in accordance with what he has set up. It is not easy for him to cut asunder what he has set up and take to the path that will lead him to the truth. His experience fashions his determination and his determination fashions his acts. That is the play that ever enacts itself within his mind. Therefore, it is necessary for him that he should be fully aware of what constitutes the right way for him. He should, that is to say, know for certain which effort will lead him to the very core of his being and which effort to misery and wretchedness. He should be able to decide the matter in actual and concrete situations. For this purpose, he must live among the seers of truth. For, it is from them that he can hear wherein consists the right way to the real, and, after knowing it, give himself up to reflection and contemplation of it as did those seers when they sought and strove for their salvation. Everyone should know for certain wherein consists his bondage and wherein his liberation.

Saying 51. To live as *vāsanā* would dictate one to live is to live in bondage. To live free of *vāsanā* is to be liberated. Every being wanders in the world as his *vāsanā* makes him wander. Only a rare enlightened soul attains to the state of no-desire. He is the real guide of the world, for reveals he unto the world the faith in the Supreme and the love for the Supreme. A blessing is his life for the world, such is its glory, of the life he leads. One should understand that if no cure is found for this malady called *vāsanā*, it will swell to destroy one's life. It is absolutely necessary, therefore, that one should steadfastly stick to the ways that can bring about its end. For in that alone, in its end alone, lies one's well being, well being true and genuine.

Saying 52. An instrument of actions is this body, a constant source of activities it is, activities of all kinds, making the living being blindly attached to their results, of those actions, for takes he the body as his self [and its activities as the activities of his self]. This attachment ever keeps him restless, ever on the move, with no moment falling to his lot where he could rest with and as himself. The first step, easy and straight, towards the cure of this unrest lies in giving up wicked deeds that bring about disastrous results for the embodied being, do not let him flourish and prosper. The second step consists in his dedication to noble deeds, deeds that bring about purification of the *buddhi*. One should, however, resort to these deeds as if they were the results of the Lord's will and not one's own. To live with this spirit of self-surrender is to live for one's salvation.

Saying 53. Observance of great means to redemption, means like simplicity, service, truthfulness, association with seers and meditation of the Name infuses the *buddhi* with the strength to shed all its wicked deeds. Without resorting to these means, the *buddhi* becomes a victim of all kinds of wrong traits to turn deluded and misguided. All this becomes evident when one reflects deeply[22] and in earnest. There is only one way to salvation, namely, self-submission to the Lord, accepting the weal and woe of life as ordained by His will, by that alone.

Saying 54. The body has action always associated with it but not so has the *ātman*, the self. And the *buddhi* is always busy in attributing the nature and doings of the body to itself. The death of the body leaves the *buddhi* unanchored to force it to find another body to fulfill its desire [to be]. The process continues unchecked until the *buddhi* comes to stay still in the *ātman*, the self. To believe in the *ātman* is, therefore, the very foundation of one's real and genuine well being. [23]

Saying 55. The *ātman* is the life principle that dispenses life and being to the world, pervading it in its fullness and every part of it. Even in a blade of grass it resides in its infinity as it resides in the whole world. The seers have hailed it with many a name without a count, that Real the Supreme, that one and only to be magnified, that peace eternal that abides ever the same in every condition. That is the truth, that is consciousness and that is bliss, that *ātman*, the self, that life of body each and every. Forgetful of that *ātman*, the *buddhi* with its false sense of selfhood perceives many a phenomenon, its own projections, seeking some and avoiding others. Not until it comes to know the self and be the self, this false appearance of the world, this darkness spread out by *vāsanā*, does not come to be dispelled. Therefore, one should approach a seer to find that truth, that being without a desire.

Saying 56. Within the body itself can the *buddhi* find that Real the Supreme [and not in the world]. For it has, that Real, no colour, shape and form that the *buddhi* could perceive and there is no sign that could indicate it. An enabling power is that Real, the only enabling power, power that dispenses life and being to the entire visible world and sets limits to everything in it. There is no thing that can have a form without it, or can stay as itself. In other words, the whole world composed of the gross elements has the light of that consciousness-existence as its informing and sustaining principle. The *buddhi* can find it, that Lord the Supreme, that Consciousness itself, only when it comes to be still and motionless.[24]

Saying 57. And when the *buddhi* comes to find the Real, it dissolves itself into It. This its dissolution is what is called *mokṣa*, liberation. As long as the *buddhi* does not find that Consciousness, that Word, it remains inflicted with the I-ness to immerse itself in the whirlpool of *vāsanā* and action, with everlasting fear for its portion. There is only one thing to know and adore for this being lost in this transient world, and that thing is the one *ātman*, one self, that Son of Man[25], that support the highest, attaining which the *buddhi* comes to be appeased fully and in perfection, comes to be the Alone, leaving far behind all *vāsanā*, all that blind passion [for the *other*].

Saying 58. That Real the absolute, that *ātman*, is present in all its fullness within and without the body to be a light unto it and the world. With the intellect purified [of all its determinations] should it be remembered and contemplated. That is the way to wash away all the blots and stains polluting one's being. There is no noble deed like the contemplation of the Lord, that piety surpassing all other pieties. All noble and sacred acts are there only to purify the mind, that internal organ, to enable it to self-submit to the Lord, that Bliss the absolute.

Saying 59. The *ātman* pervades the body as fat pervades milk. But only right endeavour can make one find it, find the Word, that reality the supreme. To contemplate the Lord with a steady intent, to perceive the living principle in the body as emanating from that very Real the Supreme, as grounded in It, to surrender the duality that the fruit of every action is to the will of the Lord, and to remember, as one with the breath, the Name Eternal: these, verily, are the measures that constitute the highest *yoga*, the way supreme to union with the Real. A man who ever remembers this way the Name of the Lord will find his mind all concentrated, its activities having come to an end. That will be the moment when his mind will find within the Word indivisible and imperishable, that Life itself of the whole world. Then will he be said to have attained to the state of no-*vāsanā*.

Saying 60. As long as the mind continues to conjure up names and forms, names and forms that constitute the world, it continues to wander restless in the darkness of *vāsanā*.[26] To dispel this delusion, one has the easy and straight means in the form of contemplation of Name-breath, if that contemplation is adhered to properly and in the right way[27]. Any man, noble and cultured, who turns away from names and forms, from these mere appearances, and makes Name the True the sole anchor of his life and being, and leaves all the cares of his life, pleasant or unpleasant, to the will of the Lord and concentrates all his thoughts on the Name alone - he truly is the man of knowledge true, that man given to contemplation steady and sustained. He is the man who will find the Real within him and be supremely blessed by It.

Saying 61. The *buddhi* on the move is ignorance itself and the *buddhi* still is *tapas,* the redemptive, itself. As long as it is associated with the I-sense with regard to acts, identifies itself with the latter, the *buddhi* remains on the move, lost in the darkness of *vāsanā*. When, however, it leaves all the actions of the mind-body complex to the will of the Lord, leaves them with determination, it comes to experience the Word within, that light of Brahman the Absolute, that bliss the perfect of sameness. With fervent devotion it then lets itself be merged in that Real the most High, that Abode the most High. Blessed indeed is the man who attains to this state.

Saying 62. It is, however, hard to attain to this state unless and until a being does not get disillusioned with what the body can offer him and does not find devotion, fervent and deep, for the Real welling up in his heart. Therefore, it is necessary that he should have this kind of devotion, genuine and spontaneous. For, it will enable him to triumph over all his deviations to lose himself in the joy of Real the Supreme. To be genuinely devoted to the Lord is nothing else than to self-surrender to the Lord and do without a desire whatever one is called upon to do. In other words, devotion means to live for others, shedding all selfish thoughts and giving up all one's comforts for others' good, desiring nothing in return. This is the way of pure discrimination, this way of devotion. Any being of noble intent who takes to this path with faith in the truth will attain to the bliss of the *ātman,* his passions for the bodily pleasures having lost their grip upon him.

Saying 63. It is the bodily pleasures that tempt the *buddhi* into the cycle of recurring births and deaths. They, these pleasures, indeed are the source of every misery, misery of the worst kind. There is no happiness that does not turn, in the long run, into woe. For, to entertain the idea of pleasure with regard to a thing is to pave the way for pain. As long as the thing in question gives a being pleasure, he remains obsessed with it. But with the end of that thing, his very pleasure turns into misery. This is how his deluded knowledge makes him wander about in the mazes of the world. To work without a hope alone is the way straight out of those mazes.

Saying 64. To give away one's own comforts for the comfort of others, to give them in all humility, to spend one's resources - physical, mental and material - to the maximum for that end, with the Lord alone one's stay and support, is the way open to man, that way of genuine renunciation. To tread this path of care for others is to tread towards self-purification culminating in faith, deep and steadfast, in the Real and a sense of disinterest in the things of the world. Pure devotion for the real comes to sprout in a man when he comes to have this kind of disposition. No physical pleasure or well being will carry any value for him, the will of the Lord being his only anchor. In service of others will he entirely spend himself. Living this way that blessed man will have made himself eligible enough for the bliss that the *ātman* is[28].

Saying 65. As long as a living being remains immersed in the pleasures of the body, he cannot find the joy that has no *vāsanā* for its cause, the joy that lies in being oneself alone, in being that state quiet and tranquil. For the *buddhi* tainted with impurities, true bliss lies in physical pleasures and well being alone. It is only when it gets purified with reflection [on revelation or the sayings of a seer of the truth] that it comes to know what these pleasures in their truth are, mere misery in their garb. With this realisation dawning upon it, the *buddhi* turns towards bliss the desire-free, spends itself out for that end to find the Real as its being, the Real that is all bliss in Itself, bliss the highest.

Saying 66. The pleasures of the body[29] alone are the cause of misery. If contact with a thing causes pleasure, separation from it is bound to cause pain. This process of contact and separation constitutes *karma,* action and its recurrence, with no possibility of any escape from it. In their ignorance, beings would have everlasting happiness through action, but this is simply impossible. For nothing can stay here permanent, time in which everything abides ever makes it disown itself. No contact with a thing, which has a beginning and an end, can give genuine happiness. Think of this truth, consider it with all seriousness! When the body itself is subject to decay, where is the possibility of its pleasures being real and genuine? It is delusion that makes the living being seek lasting peace in the perishable body, forgetful of bliss the absolute that the Real is. The body, however, does not stay as itself and joy the real that he seeks through it ever eludes him. With false fabrications as his being and knowledge, he leaves the world deserted by every hope and expectation. A man must, therefore, reflect on the delusion that has come to inflict him and seek to know the essential purpose of human birth. Let him, that is to say, ever seek the truth and self-submit to it; let his life and being be ever dedicated to that end.

Saying 67. It is in the nature of every living being to be ever doing something or the other, something that binds him to the world or liberates him from it. Discrimination, true and genuine, lies in doing that which liberates him from the worldly mode of being, makes him rise above it. If he is immersed in activity without discriminating [between what binds him and what liberates him], he will only tie himself to sin and defile himself. Therefore, one must resort to reflection pure and untainted to find the way to peace the true and real. Therein alone lies the dignity of life, in reflecting thus and in striving thus. One has to reap the result of what one does. That is the law. Therefore, a man should refrain from a deed that may bring disaster for him. To self-submit to the One Lord is the best way out of every malady and every suffering. Therein lies the very essence of thinking, in having this disposition of self-submission.

Saying 68. A man of discrimination who makes the One Lord, that Being *before* every being, the anchor of his being and contemplates Him with a sustained intent and does holy deeds without any self-interest will find himself liberated from action. To ever the same peace shall he attain, peace still and beyond the reach of every activity. To perceive the whole world as Lord the manifest, to find it as His light, of that Being *before* beings, to perceive one's cardinal duty in being of comfort unto others, and to be ever pure in one's intentions and in one's deeds is to be truly devoted to the Lord. To union with that Being *before* every being, to immersion in His being as it truly is will lead it, this devotion pure and holy. Therefore, fail not in your striving, in your endeavour true and holy.

Saying 69. A man who has resorted to the right endeavour for the eradication of his inclinations for sin, and who, following the teachings of those that have become one with truth, has made Being *before* every being his refuge and resort, and who does good unto all beings with a sincere heart and ever thinks of the end of his life, and who thinks of his body, his mind and his possessions as of the Lord alone, and ever lives obedient to His will and a servant unto all beings - a man given to this kind of life will find a fervent love for the Lord well up in him, love that will extinguish all his agonies and sorrows. To devotion exclusive for the Lord will he find himself given, devotion undying and imperishable.

Saying 70. When a man comes to be blessed with this kind of pure and holy disposition, he gives himself to contemplation of the *ātman* as instructed by the seers that have come to be established in the truth. Never does he let himself get slack in this his endeavour true. A time comes when his effort, sustained and holy, culminates in the realisation of the *ātman*, the *ātman* that is the source of the entire world and is the home, blessed and holy, of every being. He alone has found the life true, the man so blessed, found the life to which time holds no terror. Rare is his glory, rare is it to find in this perishable world.

Saying 71. Let man ever direct his mind to contemplation of the *ātman*, giving up his worldly possessions, giving them up in disinterested service of others. Let the One Lord be his sole refuge and resort. And seeing what the whole world is, a mere passing appearance, let him strive to establish himself in the *ātman* before his body comes to fall. This verily is the way to eradicate the darkness that *vāsanā* is and to find the unblemished bliss that the state of *samatā* is.

Treasure 3 - On the End of Vāsanā

Saying 72. The darkness that *vāsanā* is, is verily the source from where spring deviations like desire, anger, greed, delusion and the I-sense. As long as *vāsanā* does not come to cease, no one can free himself from these deviations. Therefore, to eradicate *vāsanā*, that primordial sin, is, in every truth, to redeem oneself, liberate oneself. Making the Lord one's sole refuge, doing every effort towards that end, is the way to eradicate the delusion set up by *vāsanā*, that awful delusion that sets in motion the wheel of recurring births and deaths. In eradication of *vāsanā* lies true *sādhanā*, the true striving toward the goal of life.

Saying 73. When a man comes to have steadfast faith in the Lord and surrenders all his actions to His will, surrenders them unconditionally and without a reserve, with a mind fully suffused with a fervent devotion to Him, he will find the Word within him, Word the bliss absolute and peace the all abounding. That is the moment when the *buddhi* comes to stay still and stable in the Lord, shedding all its darkness, to eventually merge itself in Him, replete with the sense of the glory of that Great Power. This state of the dissolution of the *buddhi* in the Lord alone is the state all pure of *vāsanā*, the state truly of *samatā*.

Saying 74. Hard indeed it is to eradicate one's sense of identification with *karmas*, actions. Every moment it would delude the *buddhi*. Only a man blessed and gifted can tear apart the darkness of *vāsanā*, a man given to discrimination, he who withdraws his *buddhi* [from all the web spread out by *vāsanā*] to know the Lord in His truth. With that end in view, he remembers the Name True with faith true, establishes himself in that remembering, purifying the taints native to the body, purifying them with traits like truthfulness, noble conduct, contentment and self-restraint, traits constituting the very way of his life.

Saying 75. *Vāsanā* cannot come to cease until one comes know the Lord, that Being prior to every being. As long as the *buddhi* does not find that, its home true and being true, it cannot shed the darkness that *vāsanā* is. Therefore, if there is one way to put an end to all ills, it is the Name of the One Lord; that alone can dispense eternal peace [to the restless soul]. A man who remembers the Lord as the sole doer and destroyer, remembers Him as all-powerful - he alone can redeem himself, that blessed man of steadfast disposition and devotion. Let man, therefore, make the One Lord the one and only prop of his life, know that Supreme Reality as the ground of the whole world. Placing himself in every way in that Truth (*śraddhā*), let him remember and contemplate Him. Washed away will be all his blots and taints.

Saying 76. All subject to destruction is every phenomenon of the world. To be infatuated with them is to be infatuated with misery itself, misery in the extreme. Therefore, it is necessary that man should remember only the Imperishable, contemplate it and love it and have faith in it, establish himself in it. That alone is the way to the peace true. Let that bliss the great be his sole refuge, that knowledge, that Being before every being. Let him be firm in this resolve, for that is the only great gain one can get out of this false and unreal world. He alone is a man of supreme discrimination who has made the One Lord his sole refuge and does his best to do good unto others with a disposition of a servant. He is the man who will free himself from every *vāsanā* and will attain to the state called the Real.

Saying 77. A wise man is he who has given up all the bodily pleasures and has self-submitted with every intent unto the *ātman*, who lives patient alike in weal and woe, and remains ever absorbed in the bliss of the Imperishable Word. All-wise is that man because he it is that will transcend all *vāsanā* to lose himself in bliss the supreme. He is the man who has understood in full what the world in its truth is, he is the man who has attained the goal supreme and he is the man who knows the Real in truth.

Saying 78. A man who has extinguished all his mental processes out of love for the Lord, whose life inner and outer is spent with the Name alone as its sole support, whose gains cannot tempt him and whose losses cannot distress him, and who, distanced from the body, lives within ever established in the Real - he alone is *the* man to transcend every *vāsanā*, he alone knows what knowledge the pure is.

Saying 79. A man who has found the Word within, Word the still and passive, and abides in that Word the truth, distancing himself from the conflict of opposites that every fruit of action is, he alone is the knower true, he alone is man the wise. Giving up every infatuation with doing, he reposes well in Real the Supreme. And perceiving all his activities as the works of *prakṛti,* that *before,* that seed, of Creation, and his self as unmoved by those actions, unmoved in the absolute sense of the term, he lives as one freed from *vāsanā,* from that darkness and delusion.

Saying 80. A wise man within whom has manifested Brahman, that Word indivisible and imperishable, and who has drunk deep at that fount of the immortal drink, drunk at that fount of the Real with no thought of anything else, he alone will find his *vāsanā* cease to torment him. In light all pervasive will he abide, in that bliss the absolute, finding the whole world its light and manifestation, of that Real the Supreme. In himself will he find that Real the Supreme and himself in that Real the Supreme, find himself all full and infinite. Attain will he, that is to say, the Alone, the knower of Brahman will be he, he alone, the man of this mettle. Rarely one comes across a sage of this kind.

Saying 81. He who has overcome the fierce conflict that action is and abides self-same in the ever a-doing light - he alone comes to be blessed with a disposition of generosity and an intellect unassailed by any doubts. He alone attains to freedom from *vāsanā*, that man of wisdom, and comes to be blessed with the bliss that *samatā* is. Nothing remains for him to do in the world, for free becomes he from all deviations of *prakṛti.*

Saying 82. To be convinced of the reality of the self, to self-submit to the self and to find the self and be the self are the ends true of life. A man who pursues these ends with a mind free and spontaneous is the man of right endeavour and true discrimination. For, he will tear asunder the net that *vāsanā* has woven for him and will find the bliss native to and innate in him. When he finds the flame of the self burning bright within him, he will find extinct all his blind passions for the body. Invincible will he turn, that man, his struggle against *vāsanā* turning all-triumphant. In the Real Supreme comes he to stay, stay firm and established.

Saying 83. The activities of the body ever keep restless the living being. The duality that is the fruit of every action, the duality in the shape of conflict between weal and woe, ever keeps him on the move. However, when suffused with the love for the *ātman*, for that power that keeps the body alive, he discards all his blind passion and infatuation for the body; he ceases to have any fear whatsoever, for all maladies that tormented him come to be cured then. To the very state of liberation he attains then, liberation from the worldly mode of being.

Saying 84. A man who has dissociated his mind from the passions of the organs of sense and action, passions that bring about his fall from his true being, and ever strives to stay still in the Name, and giving up all the sinful deeds of the body stays still and steady in contemplation of the *ātman* at a place of solitude - he is the man to attain to the bliss that the *ātman* is, that man given to sustained contemplation of the self. There can be no attainment of the self without an endeavour and there can be no cessation of *vāsanā* without the attainment of the self. Let there be no doubt about this matter.

Saying 85. A man who has purified the memory of his mind through the one Name of the Lord will alone find the self and be established in it, that man blessed with noble gifts.[30] To be established in the self is to be established in *samatā* itself, in Aloneness itself, the state where the visible world, that world of forms, comes to be lost in the self, giving place to Light the Formless. That, verily, is the primordial source of the whole world, that state eternal and imperishable. Those who attain to that state never regress into the darkness of *vāsanā*. Having attained to their real being, full do they become and infinite.

Saying 86. When the mind sheds its activities and processes and abides solely grounded on the Name, it turns still to get absorbed in its own true being. When this happens, one sees one indivisible and eternal reality abiding in all its fullness and infinity in each and every being and thing. This verily is the state of attainment the perfect. To realise this perfection one must devote oneself to a sustained meditation of the Name, giving up all the deviations that go with embodiment and engaging himself in the well being of others without any desire for any reward for himself.

Saying 87. A man who has ceased to identify himself with any act [of the body-mind complex], taking it as ordained by the will of the Primordial Being, that Being *before* every being, taking it so with a devotion unfailing and unwavering, and, having thus given up this ego of agency, abides all still in the Name, intermingling his mind and breath - he, indeed is *yogī* the supreme, that man endowed with this spirit and disposition. He it is that finds Word the Indivible within him to give himself up exclusively to its contemplation, contemplation appeasing all his thirst, thirst for being. From the burning flames of *vāsanā* does he resurrect. All victorious becomes that great man, victorious over all the *prakṛti*, with no fear assailing him any more. He alone knows the truth in its very essence, that man the great.

Saying 88. A man who believes, firmly and without a reservation, that whatever happens, happens by the will of the Lord, as decreed by Him and looks at the entire world as His unmotivated manifestation and, within himself, ever meditates the Name, meditates it with every faith, he alone attains to the *ātman*, to the self, that man dedicated to the truth, finding in it his life and being. He alone loses himself into the state of Nirvāṇa, that state unmoving, indestructible and without a beginning.

Saying 89. Only that person can find Word the Eternal, he who has found every pleasure a pain and has come to understand that it is the *ātman* alone that decays not, dies not and is immortal and eternal. With this insight embedded firm in him, he gives himself up to sustained contemplation of the Name, contemplation pure and uncontaminated. His mind turns still, given up to the *ātman*, self-submitted to it, its stains and blots all washed away. There is only one way to redemption, one endeavour and striving, namely, to anchor oneself to the *ātman* alone, to get established in the *ātman* ever and always, giving up all attachments to all that belongs to the sphere of the not-self, the sphere that is misery itself. Freed from every distraction and every other interest, man should ever undo that misery, that attachment with the not-self. For that is how he can find the Lord Supreme, that Bliss Supreme.

Saying 90. He alone is a man of discrimination, supremely endowed with it, whose mind is oriented towards attaining to the bliss eternal, finding his life and being in it alone, in that bliss, and who has given up all the pleasures associated with the embodied mode of being. In the Lord alone he finds the base of his life, in Him alone. Only he, a man of such disposition and determination, can find within him the Truth, Truth the Blessed. So ever do good unto others. For that is the way to purity of every kind, purity that will culminate in the disposition of self-submission to the Truth.

Saying 91. Rare is the man who has distanced himself from every pleasure, who has only ***saccidānanda***, Truth-Consciousness-Bliss, as the sole anchor of his being, its ground and base, and who is ever given to the service of all beings, his body, his mind and possessions ever at their disposal. His spirit of service brings about the end of all his maladies, of this man given to matchless *tapas*, fervent ardour. Finds he, this *tapīśvara*, this man of matchless penance, finds he within himself the Immortal and the Eternal, losing himself into that peace, peace supreme and infinite. Blessed is such a man, his bliss flowing unto many an unhappy soul, redeeming them, very many of them, before he departs from the world. He alone is born to be truly successful, a man so blessed, his life an ideal for others, truly a redemptive ideal for them.

Saying 92. Serious minded is the man who has given up the disposition of selfishness, the disposition that ever scalds and burns him, and has come to stay stable in *parmārtha*, in orientation towards Real the Supreme, taking the sufferings of all beings as his own suffering and giving away all his comforts to relieve those beings of their miseries, his own being given up to the Truth (*śraddhā*). Serious minded is he because only he can have the noble disposition that finds the *ātman* alone as the real and can live self-submitted to it, to *ātman* the Lord, that Being *before* every being. No distortions remain to pollute him, no deviations from his true being; ever self-submitted to the Lord he lives, his being abiding in the truth, in that alone. Only he lives life the pure and only he knows what life in its truth is. For, lives he as a mere pilgrim in the world, a mere traveller, ever lost in devotion to the Lord, to that Being *before* every being. He alone is the knower of truth, he who lives in the world but not as of the world, his mind untouched by it. He alone comes to extinguish *vāsanā*, the fire in which burns each and every being.

Saying 93. Doing every action, he remains untouched by every stain that goes with action, his mind ever surrendered to the Lord, given unto that Being *before* every being. It is he who knows what the disposition of *niḥ-karma* truly is, the disposition that stays inactive [in every action]. He alone has waded across the ever roaring and furious currents of *vāsanā*. With the *ātman* as its ground and being, his life finds the fulfillment it ever sought, was ever in search of, the blemishes of the body touching him not. Away from these he lives, from those blemishes, his being abiding in consciousness alone, in the light that it is. Ever abides he in and as his self, in the eternal *nāda*, that sound immortal transcending the body. He alone knows what has been his way and his end, he alone. For abides he in the state that no word can describe, and no revelation.

Saying 94. A man of knowledge, he who has withdrawn into himself all the net of illusions that desire has woven out for him and has come to stay stable in himself, will find the truth within himself, his intellect having come to rest and repose. The truth infinite will he find, with no here in it and no there. Staying above the nine gates of the body, the gates that relate one to the external world, he dwells in the great space united with Brahman the Supreme, dwells there ever stable [with no possibility of fall from that state]. Of all the creation he is the knower, of the whole world that has come to be. He is the *yogī* true, the seer of past, present and future.

Saying 95. Only the man who has triumphed over the sway of his senses and motor organs can attaint to the bliss that the state of *samatā* is, the state beyond the very reach of *vāsanā*. For, only he finds Word the Real in him and becomes one with it, his mind and speech having come to be extinct. Ever stays he in the Truth that itself is its own predicate, stays there with his intellect concentrated solely on it. The five gross elements that constitute the gross world have no impact on him, for stays he where these have no reach, stays there without a possibility of fall. For truth has he found, its very essence has he found, of the truth that it really is. His very word is redemptive, redemptive for those that pay heed to it and live and strive as that word would command them to live and strive.

Saying 96. The first step that a man that would attain to the self, would abide in that state that ever abides as itself - the first step that he should take is the one directed towards purification of his acts and deeds. He must give up all his sinful deeds and resort to acts that are noble, acts that straighten his path to the truth. The next step consists in leaving the fruit of his noble acts to the will of the Lord; it consists in resorting to the path of *niṣkāma-karma,* action done without the prompting of any desire whatsoever. Along with this disposition of disinterested action, he should remember the Lord in the right way [as instructed by a seer true and perfect], remember Him with every steadfastness. Only a man with this unwavering disposition can attain to his *ātman*, only a man blessed with such discrimination. No one can reach that goal without striving for it, striving in the right way. Therefore, having been born into this world of tensions and conflicts, it is necessary that man should ever put in every effort to triumph over these tensions and conflicts, triumph over them in truth and reality. Let him be punctual in every act he does, whether that which is worldly or that which is directed towards attaining to the Goal Supreme. Let there be no lapse in this matter.

Saying 97. It is imperative that man should observe the regulative principles in his worldly life and live in self-restraint for attaining to the true goal of life, that goal supreme and highest. He should understand that without this observance and without this self-restraint it is exceedingly difficult for him to sail across this vast ocean of the world, the ocean so hard to traverse. Let him, if he would attain to his goal, regulate his daily activities within the necessary limits, limits that would save him from straying away from the path to that goal. Let his food be pure, his dealings straight and honest and his association holy and ennobling. Let there be no negligence in these matters. For that purpose, for attaining to Being that is real and true, let him observe self-restraint, let him, that is, live with the Lord as the sole guide and guardian of his being and life. For, that is how he will wash himself of all the stains that pollute his life and being. Let him also resort to truthfulness, to noble conduct, to contentment, to service of others, to doing every good to them and [above all] ever give himself up to the contemplation of the Name, contemplation pure [contemplation as instructed by a seer]. When a being resorts to this kind of endeavour, endeavour true and noble, resorts to it without a lapse and a failing, he will, verily, become free from every *vāsanā* and, as a consequence thereof, will come to attain to the truth to become the truth. The superiority of the human birth consists only in this that man purify his mind and attain to the supreme state, sparing no right effort for that end.

Saying 98. A man noble and gifted should ever stick to his time schedule. There should be a time for worldly activities and a time for spiritual endeavour. If he observes this rule, sure it is that his maladies will all cease and he will attain to the state beyond the reach of every fear. But a man who, prompted by inordinate greed and perversities, lives ever busy in his worldly pursuits is a benighted soul, his depraved mind ever gnawing and scalding him. No way will he find any peace, no promise of it. Let this be a clear maxim for every being that restraint of mind process leads to spiritual uplift and peace the supreme and to let that restless process flow unchecked leads one to tragedy absolute. A man of folly is, therefore, he who will not put a check on the natural propensities of the mind and let himself be carried away by its polluted *vāsanās*. Deluded will he ever wander, a man of this disposition, ever impatient and restless. Noble deeds it is that compose the mind and sinful deeds it is that make it all restless. Let a mortal, therefore, be ever thoughtful, let his mind be focussed on truth, on thoughts of truth. For therein lies his redemption, therein lies human life in its truth.

Saying 99. There are men learned and loquacious doling out spiritual instructions to others; mere fools are they if their minds have not come to rest and their physical passions have not been restrained. For, to know truly is to know the truth as it is in itself and to give up *vāsanā*, *vāsanā* that dwells malignant in man [and for that matter, in every being]. It means attaining to the state of *samatā* where no *vāsanā* is and can be and to stay ever stable in it, in that state. For, as long as *vāsanā* holds its sway in and over one's mind, one's knowledge will be vain and so will be one's contemplation. All will remain ineffective, knowledge and contemplation. For to be desire-free, to be *vāsanā*-free, alone is knowledge; that alone is *yoga*, that alone is *tapas*, fervent ardour, and that alone is discrimination. A man who adopts these measures for mere show, is a man given to fraud. From light unto darkness will lead him this way of life. Vain are the instructions that he doles out to others, that hypocrite. It is incumbent on man, therefore, that he follow in practice what he has learnt so that his mind becomes pure. Therein lies the essence, the true meaningfulness, of his learning and knowledge. Only that knowledge is full, only that contemplation and that *yoga*, which spring out of one's experience within, experience so vivid and authentic as to turn into the very self and being of the person concerned. Only these can bring about extinction of the flames of *vāsanā* and only these can bless him with bliss the supreme to stay stable in it, bliss the supreme that is his own being in every truth and reality. Supremely wise is the man who has thus attained to that state, that state of the bliss purified of every *vāsanā*. He alone knows what *samatā* the truth is and only he can instruct people into their salvation.

Saying 100. Let every man resort to life the righteous, let him ever purify his mind of all its taints through that mode of life. Therein lies his faith true and genuine. There is no being that does not understand [in the depths of his mind] what he has set up for himself, good or bad. If, in spite of this his insight, he follows not the path of his redemption, then a mere animal is he and not a human being. He should understand that only that knowledge is redemptive knowledge that can bless him with peace the true, and only that contemplation. Vain will be his learning, howsoever vast and deep, and futile will be his cleverness if that peace does not fall to his lot. Rather the pride of his learning will bring about the inevitable fall. Let there be no doubt about this.[31]

Saying 101. The essence of human life lies in purification of mind, in that alone. So let every man dedicate his mortal life in the mortal world to the good and well being of others, with the Lord alone his sole refuge. For his body will fall one day and its pleasures will not stay for long, for phantoms are they all, the creations of the Lord's *Māyā*. Let man know, with mind pure, let him seek to know that Player of this play, the play His *Māyā* is. For that is the way out of the darkness of this delusion, the delusion of *vāsanā*. And that is the way to the peace he seeks. For to be free from *vāsanā* is to attain to one's Being in full, to wallow in *vāsanā* is to live as a being with a lack inscribed into his being. Therefore, to be Being in full is to find the very end of life, every step towards that is a step towards purification, towards life in its essence, towards life the genuine. Let man think over this thought, think over it pure of mind and lead his life towards its goal, that goal of redemption. For it is one's deeds that bind a being and it is they alone that set him free.

Saying 102. Let man ever know that ***Prabhu***, that Being *before* every being, is the truth itself, the real itself and the Witness of all that is. Let him, therefore, do only deeds the pure and make Him his sole refuge, Him that is ever compassionate unto those that are lowly and humble. That is the way he can shed the evil that sticks to him. With disposition noble he should live as He, that Compassionate unto the lowly, may will him to live, ever patient with what falls to his lot as the result of his deeds [of this life and of the past lives], results that have their others inscribed into them. Let him be all kindness to other beings, irrespective of what they do unto him. And let him devote himself with every intent to the Real, never allowing his worldly concerns distract him from his contemplation of the Lord, for the latter should be more dear to him than the former. When this disposition, pure and holy, comes to stay stable in a man, he will find the light of the truth shine within him, light that is all peace, all attainments, all purity, all realisation and all fullness. He who knows this holy secret is all adorable, is all wise and is Bliss itself. Attain to this supreme state should every human being, attain to this home true of his, that state of *samatā*, that not-based [base of the whole phenomenal world].

Saying 103. Redemption has to be earned, earned through hard striving. Therefore, he who is born a man should make it a point to find the way right and true so that he may find the purpose of his life, purpose full and perfect. Let him therefore be ever thoughtful, thoughtful of the truth of his being and the world's being, and let him ever seek to find and attain to that truth. And let him ever be good unto others and do the good unto them. He should know that acts prompted by selfish interests pollute the *buddhi*, that faculty of knowing, making his life a mere tormenting hankering for pleasures. Therefore, he should give up such acts and dedicate himself to doing good unto others, a dedication that will ever orient his life and deeds towards the Real, towards that alone. He should understand that as long as his deeds do not become pure [do not get oriented towards the truth of his life and being], the peace he seeks will ever evade him, peace that is beyond the reach of every fear, peace the inviolable. Without the purification of one's acts, no *yoga*, no *tapas* and no knowledge can make a man find state the desire-free, that supreme goal of life. A mere show will remain his *yoga*, his *tapas* and his knowledge, a mere pretence and mask - of the foolish man who resorts to these without first purifying his actions and deeds.

The purity of one's acts thus is the precondition for bringing about purification of the *buddhi*, purification that enables it to strive in the right way for peace the non-doing. Futile is yogic meditation and useless is all *tapas* without the purification of one's deeds and conduct. For, only holy deeds can make one self-submit to the Lord, anchor one's life and being unto Him. Faith in the Lord alone can free a being from the passion for doing and all that it implies and brings about - can make him live all self-submitted unto Him. This self-submission to the Lord gives rise in him to the one-pointed devotion unto Him, devotion that brings about the cessation of all *vāsanā*, that taint of his being. Steadfast devotion reveals the Being true within him, putting to rest the ego of agency, that *vāsanā* primordial, that root of the entire phenomenal world. With its cessation, cessation of the ego of agency, one no longer identifies oneself with any state of being; one comes to be absorbed in one's being true and ontological, being without a conflict, being that abides self-same and eternal. No longer moves then the wheel of recurring births and deaths for the *yogī* the perfect that has attained to this state. For full he becomes, all full in himself, with no desire, with no *vāsanā* [that dark passion for the *other*] ever tempting him away from his self. Supreme is that *puruṣa*, that man. Hard it is find him, to have a mere sight of him.

Treasure 4 - On Conduct the Noble

Saying 104. A seeker of salvation should make it a point to keep his conduct pure and noble, his conduct vis-a-vis his worldly life and affairs. For he should understand that without this purification of his worldly life, the Real will ever elude him, Real the desire-free. Therefore, no man should ever transgress the limit, the dividing line [between the good and the evil] in his worldly life. For observance of this rule will lead him to holy knowledge, to peace the desire-free, lead him to it without much ado.

For, the *buddhi*, under the impact of the stains inhering in the sense- and motor organs and the mind, is apt to fall a prey to the pleasures of the senses, those deviating temptations, and, as a result thereof, bring about the end of all possibilities of well being, worldly no less than spiritual. Man should, therefore, see to it that the senses and the organs of action in their varied pursuits of pleasures do not seek to dominate one over the other, that the seeking of one organ ever remains in harmony with that of the others. For, therein lies the essence of good conduct, in this equality or harmony among the organs and their respective objects. As much as the intellect comes to be so equanimous with regard to the tendencies of the senses as much will it be at peace with itself, its thoughts pure, its acts pure and its joy all-surpassing.[32] When, on the contrary, the *buddhi* comes to be blindly attached to organs, identifies itself with them, then acquisition of the objects of pleasures becomes an obsession with it - it will have them howsoever evil the means it may have to adopt for that end. Falsehood, theft, gambling, fraud, dacoity, lust and intoxicants then come to constitute its way of life, their results scalding it more than fire itself. Men of this kind of dark disposition bring about an end to even material advancements and achievements. As for spiritual attainments, there remains no possibility of these for them, not even a trace of it.

Saying 105. A prison is this body and the living being a prisoner confined in it. With unrest lives this prisoner, frustrated and in discontent, doing the functions related to the nine gates that open out to the world, doing those functions sometimes righr and sometimes wrong. And that punishment, punishment in the shape of imprisonment in the body, goes on unchecked until he brings himself to reflect on *sat-vicāra*, on the thought revealed by the Word. Birth after birth he will have to undergo and death after death. Purification of the *buddhi* comes to be possible only when it frees itself from the faults innate to these nine gates. So one should give up all those acts which makes the *buddhi* restless and deviate from itself. Therein lies the true *dharma*, the true way. Good deeds free the *buddhi* from every fear and wicked deeds make it a victim of every fear.[33]

Saying 106. Therefore, freeing himself from the impact of the organs[34], man should give up all evil deeds - for therein lies the way upward. Let him ever seek to be pure in his actions, in his thoughts and in his dealings with others. Let his food be pure and his company noble. And let him ever be truthful, of a noble disposition and ever content with what falls his way; let him be ever chaste and forgiving and doing good unto others, his life and being given over to the will of the Lord. For, that is how he can wash his mind of all its stains. Verily, these are the traits that comprise good conduct; these are the traits that lead one to the state free from every desire, every *vāsanā*. To think with *manas*, with mind, that oreintation towards the organs and their objects, is to think in terms of some way of life, good as well as bad. For, that is what its thinking means and implies. One should, therefore, purify one's *buddhi* from the evil way by freeing it from that thinking by the mind. For, therein lies the superiority of human birth over other births.[35]

Saying 107. It is his thoughts that decide whether a being is to rise up or to fall down in the scale of existence.

When noble thoughts come to stay stable in his mind, he, the being in question, comes to be a being of pure conduct, his noble deeds making him happy and full of joy. When, on the contrary, a being comes to be possessed by evil thoughts, then lost in darkness he does all kinds of wicked and violent deeds. Stained with evil then he becomes, with utter ruin for his reward and his life a hell, hell absolute. Whether one's life is dark or bright thus depends on one's thoughts, good or evil. For as are one's thoughts, so will be one's life. And so will be one's acts and the results they bring about. It is, therefore, imperative that he adopts thoughts of the right kind and not thoughts of the evil kind, if he would redeem himself from the condition he finds himself in. And it is for this reason, the reason that thoughts play a decisive role in determining one's mode of life, good mode or bad mode, that *sat-saṅga* is so important as a constituent of the way to his redemption. For, it is there, and there alone, that a gifted soul can learn thoughts that are true, thoughts that accord with and lead to the truth.

Saying 108. A man who would tread the way up should ever seek to be pure in his thoughts, thoughts that the *sat-puruṣas*, those that abide in the Real and as the Real, have given unto mankind in the form of their instructions, instructions true and about the truth. When the *buddhi* adopts the noble ways revealed in those instructions, it comes to self-submit to the Real to find itself free of all sins and all fears. Verily, it is one's devotion to the noble traits that determines the depth of one's devotion to the truth and faith in the Lord.[36] One should not forget that mere ceremonial worship of the Lord has no meaning unless and until one has purged his mind of all sinful propensities dwelling within him. To understand this truth is to understand in truth. The Lord is the Power that never deviates from Itself, is bliss the absolute itself, all pervading is He and all-supporting. As long as this embodied being does not live self-surrendered to that Power, he remains surrendered unto all kinds of sinful deeds, his life a woe and misery great and deep. Therefore, let man have faith true in the Lord and be free from the sway of sin and evil. That verily sums up what is called belief in the existence of the Lord. All peaceful is the Lord and all passive, and all restive and all active is the *jīva*, the embodied being. Devotion to the Lord is meant for the latter's freedom from the grip of doing, from the sense of his identify with the process of doing. Verily, the man who devotes himself to the will of the Lord with this disposition and for this end, is the man of faith the perfect; only he will attain to the state pure and unblemished, he who lives and acts this way for the truth.

Saying 109. The One Lord is all-powerful, ever abides He as self-same. The whole visible world is, on the contrary, ever on the move, ever deviates from itself. Therefore, this living being lives in constant fear as long as he lives oriented towards that changing world. It is only when he lives self-submitted to the Lord, self-submitted in every way, that the taints that besmear him come to be washed away, he getting absorbed in the Lord Himself, Lord the Fearless. That is the state full, the state perfect, this his absorption in the Lord. Therefore, only those acts are good acts that purify the intellect, make it oriented towards the Lord. And all evil are those acts that make the *buddhi* identify itself with this state or that state and deny the very existence of the Lord. These are the acts that lead the living being to the states of being low and degraded. Man should understand that his being as a worldly being is ever tied to doing, that he lives as conditioned by doing. Whatever he does inevitably brings about its reward in the shape of well being or ill being. Therefore, let his thoughts be pure and his actions pure, thoughts and actions oriented towards the Real and leading to the Real. For that is what conduct good and noble means.

Saying 110. With its dedication to good deeds deepening, the *buddhi* comes to be suffused with the spirit of renunciation, a continuous endeavour in that direction leading it ultimately to renunciation the absolute, renunciation implying absolute freedom from *vāsanā*. It comes to abide, that is to say, in Brahman the Desire-free. Good deeds that are done without the ego of agency and with the spirit of self-surrender to the Lord lead to the purification of the mind, purification all surpassing. A man endowed with this disposition, disposition that perceives every nobility in him as not *his* nobility but as a gift from the Lord, does not have to strive hard for the supreme state, on its own will it come unto him. One should know and understand that only that man is truly dedicated to doing good unto others who does so unselfconsciously, as if ever taking upon himself the misery of the others and giving away his own pleasures and comforts unto them were inscribed in his nature and being. And only that man is man the forgiving who ignoring all the faults of others dispenses peace unto them through his noble traits. He alone is a man of *tapas, tapas* the highest. And only that man is a man of pure conduct and a man of truth who believes in the One Lord, knows for certain that his own acts are there only to pollute and stain him and yet accepts them as if willed by the Lord. The *ātman*, the self, abiding in him he sees as abiding in all, and, enriched with this perception, he finds in the good of others his own very good.

Saying 111. Richly gifted, supremely contented and blessed with faith steadfast is the man who perceives the wheel set in motion by *karmas* as the will of the Lord, and who perceives all that is as the glory all wonderful of the Lord. And who distances himself from the body, mind and his possessions, never identifies himself with them. And who lives in the world ever to serve others with no expectation of any recompense whatsoever. And who perceives every weal and woe that visit him as mere enjoyments or sufferings of *prakṛti* and ordained by the Lord, never associating himself with them whether in terms of doing or enjoying and suffering. A man who lives this way and strives this noble way will find his pilgrimage to *nirvāṇa* a smooth and straight affair. For he alone is the man of conduct supremely pure, his life a source of peace for creatures, creatures without a count and number.[37]

Saying 112 He alone knows what *brahmacarya* is, what abstinence and chastity is, he alone who has linked his *buddhi* with the Lord as He is and has given himself to His contemplation, and has been able to cleanse his organs of cognition and action of all their stains. And who ever perceives the life and energy of his body as flowing out of the Lord, and whose food is pure and so is his thinking and his association. And whose actions bespeak of his simplicity and innocence, and, ever given to abstinence, who looks upon all women as he would look upon his mother, his very life a life of service without a vanity. He alone is wise and he alone is glorious and suffused with the splendour of the Spirit, his blessed life a blessing for the world, for from its misery will it save the world, his life pure and blessed. In the service of the Lord he spends his life and in the service of his country - that is the *dharma*, the guiding principle, of his life. Only this disposition, disposition that has only the good of others for its end and purpose, can disseminate peace in the world.

Saying 113. Anyone who is given to noble conduct in this way, and is, in addition, devoted to his teacher will find the state desire-free without much ado. For, one should understand that only that person can be wise and discriminating whose actions are rightly oriented. Pilgrimage to holy places, *yajña*, charity, *tapas* and *sat-saṅga* bear their fruit only when they turn one into a man of noble conduct. Ever given to perversions is this mind of man; he should, therefore, bring it to rest through orienting it towards the Real. Ever thoughtful should he be of what is right for him and ever wary of what is wrong. This constant vigil on his part will bring rest to his mind and strength to his *buddhi*. Let man therefore ever remember the fate that awaits the body and be aware of the restiveness that a stained and polluted mind is. And with this awareness, let him ever strive to be desire-free. Only this disposition can make him a man of noble conduct.

Every being lives identified with the body, with the mind and with his possessions. This, his identity makes of him a creature of desire endless and unappeasable, to satisfy which he resorts to all kinds of wicked and evil deeds, turning his life into misery itself. Therefore, let him do whatever he is called upon to do but without a reference to his own interests. Let him, with this spirit of disinterestedness, spend his resources - physical, mental and material - in the service of others. For, that is the way he can save himself from his miserable condition and that is what noble conduct in its very truth is.

Saying 114. As long as a being is subject to desires relating to body, mind and possessions, as long as he does not distance himself from these desires, he cannot but find himself a doer, the identity that is the root of every *vāsanā*. And as long as he finds himself a doer, he cannot come to be established in Being, Being that he really is. So, let a man of culture earn his living through upright means and spend it in the service of others without any self-interest in mind. That, verily, is the way to pave the way to his redemption. For, only he who has purified his body and mind through noble deeds and has dedicated his life to the path that leads a man to the truth, dedicated it with every determination - only he will have the humility to know for certain what his *ātman* is, what his self really and truly is.[38] And only he, the man dedicated to life the pure, will triumph over all his failings to find the eternal Word - that bliss secure and fear-free - to get absorbed in It. Hard is this path, exceedingly hard! So to life the pure should every mortal dedicate his life, dedicate it ever and always, if he would redeem himself from his misery.

Saying 115. When good conduct brings about purification of the *buddhi*, when, that is to say, it, the latter, loses all interests in the pleasures of the body, it comes to be established in contemplation of the *ātman*. Steadfast contemplation of the *ātman* puts an end to one's sense of identity with action [with the doer], that root cause of *vāsanā*. And with the end of its identity with doing having come to rest, it, the *buddhi*, attains to its native being, the blessed being ever the same and ever full. To attain to that state the non-dependent, the first step to take is that of noble deeds. For, as long as the *buddhi* identifies itself with the fret that every action is, it cannot become aware of the Real, the Real as it truly is. Therefore, one should resort to noble acts and thereafter to the path true, the internal path of *yoga*. That is the way to avoid regression into evil ways, the way of *yoga*. He who leads a life pure with steadfast faith and gives himself to the internal way of *yoga* , he is the man that will come to know the real from the unreal and, blessed with that wisdom, to know the *ātman*, the self, know it directly, unmediated by any means whatsoever, and attain to the final goal of life straight and unhindered. Anyone who has dedicated himself to this holy *sādhana*, this blessed *endeavour*, should take only pure food and with restraint and earn only a simple living and that too through straight and upright means, and should serve fellow beings with intention holy and pure. He should also fix his time for these worldly activities, should not let these activities take away the time he has fixed for his passive contemplation of *ātman*, that Truth. For, all exclusive has to be that contemplation, undistracted and undeviating. A man who observes this rule of regularity, observes it fully, be it the night or the day, is truly a man of steady and sustained contemplation; only he will qualify to attain to the *ātman* that he really is.

Saying 116. The first step one should take to attain to the goal true is to make his spiritual preceptor his sole refuge. For, only he, his teacher, can make him know the real as against the unreal and only he can reveal the secret of the contemplation of the Name to him. Blessed thus with his guru's grace, he should contemplate the Name with a steadfast devotion. He should understand that any action that distracts him from the contemplation of the Name is an evil action and he should make it a point not to do it. To do that contemplation perfectly, he should resort to solitude and sit in a posture steady and stable, should eat only pure food, eat it with restraint and at the proper time and only to satisfy his hunger. He should also make it a point to earn his living through straight and upright means and that too well within the time fixed for that purpose. And, lastly, he should seek the company of the *sat-puruṣas*, those who have attained to the truth, and follow their instructions. Anyone who, observing these rules, follows this path to the truth with fervour and devotion, the path of contemplation of the Name, is a devotee of his guru in the true sense of the term. He is the man that can follow the latter's instruction to the point of self-extinction to get merged in the Real. He alone is the hero true, he who triumphs over all his stains and faults through striving true and steadfast.

Saying 117. When the *buddhi* comes to be disengaged from actions, actions that tie it down to the embodied mode of being, it self-submits to Being as it really is. In other words, it wakes into Word the bliss supreme abiding within man. What is that blessed state is not a matter for *buddhi's* thought; for, it can abide stable in that truth only when it has distanced itself from every *vāsanā* for the embodied mode of being. And when it comes to stay stable in that Truth, like unto a dream appears then the whole world to it; only the light of consciousness does it experience then, the light permeating the entire world, each and everything in it. Only a *yogī* of the highest order attains to this state, the state of his native being to ever abide in it, with no desire stirring up in him. Absorbed he remains then in the Word within, ever drinking that drink of immortality, his desires all appeased. Every deviation intrinsic to the embodied mode of being he comes to transcend, stays he still in his being true, his self true. Anyone, any knower of the truth that attains to this state of yogic oblivion knows what life the ever lasting is, he only and no one else. Rare is this endeavour and by a rare man, a blessing is it for the world, this his holy endeavour. And blessing is he himself, the man who has striven thus and lives thus.

Saying 118. When the *buddhi* comes to be still and passive, it comes to stay stable in the self within to know the play that that Being the transcendental and adorable plays, the Being that illumines all and yet stands apart from all. Finding that Being Itself Its own measure and proof and finding no other measure to measure It up, the *buddhi* merges in It, paying It every tribute and every praise. Infinite indeed is the glory of that light supreme. To find it and know it is to get free from every *vāsanā* and every desire. Into Brahman the Truth Supreme turns everything then, Brahman the eternal and ever the same, Brahman that is peace itself. Like unto a shadow appear then the body and its activities, appear to the man blessed with that vision and wisdom. The seer of the highest order is that man, the man who has attained to this transcendental state. Dwells within all he to know all and ordain all. Only a sharer of all, only a supremely blessed man can find a seer of this order. For only his instruction, instruction true of that seer true, can make him turn a true and faithful pilgrim to the Real, with nothing to distract him from his resolve and his path.

Saying 119. Let man live in the world ever striving for his liberation, keeping a careful watch on the temptations ready to undo him, concealing the truth, the truth redemptive, from him. Let him therefore reflect, reflect with *sat-buddhi,* with the *buddhi* awake to Being within, about this world, about this play all-destructive, this play that is destruction itself. And enriched with insight into the truth about this world, let him contemplate the Real [in the form of the Name] and come to be blessed with knowledge true and with its content, content that he is ever in search of. In darkness dense are enveloped the world and its ways, mere shadows pursue every being here, ever and always. And shadows will he continue to pursue as long as he does not know the Witness of the shadows that every being pursues through his acts and endeavours, shadows ever elusive and beyond his grasp. Therefore, when blessed with human birth, let him equip himself with mind the pure to win a decisive victory in the war against the delusion laid before him. That has ever been the glory of the *sat-puruṣas*, of men the real, men that abide as one with the Real.

Saying 120. Right action and self-submission to the Lord alone will make a mortal blest and liberated. Blessed is the man, the noble man that remains steadfastly faithful to way the righteous and strives with every care for life the peaceful and desire-free, spending his resources - physical, mental and material - for the good of the people. He alone knows what life is, what its essence is, the man who lives this way and strives this way, with humility lives this way and strives this way. Only a man who has thus resorted to the way of *niṣkāma-karma*, of action without a desire, is a man truly devoted to the Lord, truly self-submitted to Him. To the bliss desire-free will he attain, that man of devotion true. All blessed is he, the man who, though born to tread the ways of the world, remains steadfast to the way of the truth. Supremely blessed is he, his glory hard to attain. But those who do not seek their being true and real, do not strive to attain to it, given to perverse and wicked acts, are out to destroy themselves, their life a tale of delusion and misery, birth after birth. Therefore, one born as a man should ever think of his truth and the world's truth, if he would be free from every fear. From *vāsanā* should he free himself, from that delusion, and from the wheel of recurring births and deaths it sets in motion for him, and establish himself in the Real as it truly is. For, that is the wisdom true and endeavour true and supreme.

Observances

Observance the First - **Sat-saṅga**

Saying 1. It is desirable that *sat-saṅga* should be resorted to daily, for it is there that one comes to acquire the ability to discriminate between the real and the unreal, the ability that enables one to free oneself from sins with a relative ease. *Sat-saṅga* should be of the right kind: only those thoughts should find expression there that could make one free from despondency and pride. The weekly *sat-saṅga* should be held at a comparatively large scale and the monthly at a still larger scale. In the annual *sat-saṅga* as many devotees should participate as possible to reflect about and resolutely adhere to the means for their spiritual uplift, means like simplicity, service of others, truthfulness, holy association and contemplation of the Real.

Observance the Second - **Abhyāsa: *Sustained Contemplation***

Saying 1. Sustained contemplation of the Name is indispensable for attaining to the blessed state of sameness. Anyone who is a *premī*, devotee, of *samatā* and has been initiated into yogic meditation should adhere to its practice daily and without fail. From the age of 15 to 30, he must devote an hour in the morning and an hour in the evening to the contemplation of the Name. Strictly regular and punctual should he be in this regard. From 30 to 40, the time for contemplation should be raised to one and a half-hour in the morning and one and a half-hour in the evening. From 40 to 60, the duration of the time should be two hours in the morning and two hours in the evening. And after 60 he should devote as much time to contemplation of the Name as possible to make his mind pure [pure of thoughts]. If a man is new to the contemplative mode of life, then he should seek progress in it steadily - in accordance with his age. One should understand that the mind never comes to be calm and stable without sustained meditation, nor can one have full faith in the Lord's power. Simplicity of food and dress and straight and upright dealings deepen one's devotion to the Name. Purity of mind is a must for one's spiritual uplift, and contemplation of the Name it is that can bring it about. So one must do it every morning and every evening without a let and omission. From every misery and every fear will this contemplation free the *buddhi*, enable as it does the *buddhi* to self-submit to the Lord.

Saying 2. One's fervour for spiritual uplift should match the passion of the men of the world for their worldly well being. For, all well being lies in it, in spiritual well being. It helps free the body from its ailments and prolong its life and makes the *buddhi* free from the shackles of mind and body and self-submit to the Lord. To this truly blessed and blissful state of being it leads the *buddhi*, the state of being where alike become well being and ill being, weal and woe. With humility should one do this meditation, without a self-interest in mind and with a disposition of good will towards all. Only this kind of meditation can lead one to the supreme goal. Taking oneself as of no account, surrendering one's life and being to the will of the Lord should one lead one's life, life of complete anonymity, uttering not a word about one's spiritual state. For, to proclaim one's inner state unto others before one has attained to the ultimate end is to tempt pride. And that shuts out every possibility of reaching the home one seeks. Let there be no mistake about this. Only he can bring his meditation to fruition, he who has left everything to the will of the Lord, he only and no one else.

Observance the Third - **Sevā**: *Service*

Saying 1. One-tenth of one's earning must be spent in the service of *dharma*. If a man finds his savings more than the requirements of his simple life, then he should spend one-fifth of his income in the service of others. He should understand that unless he sincerely dedicates himself to the service of others, service without any self-interest to serve, he cannot hope to make his life pure and noble. And with the spirit of *samatā*-teaching should he render that service unto others. He should, that is to say, serve the orphans, the guests, the helpless widows and the sick. Or others as the rules for charity would dictate. All blessed will be the man who serves others this way.

Saying 2. It is harmful to spend the said one-tenth of one's earnings on one's own self. This is the rule of conduct laid down by *sat-puruṣ*as. Rather, a man should be as generous as possible when it comes to the question of serving others. For a generous disposition of this kind will lead him to the real goal of life. A follower of the Doctrine of *Samatā* should see to it that he has a disposition suffused with the spirit of self-sacrifice. For it is a disposition of this kind that wakes up people to the true Path and brings about peace in their land.

Observance the Fourth - **Fasting**

Saying 1. A day in a week should be a day of fasting or, if this becomes too arduous, then at least a day in a month. The day of fasting should be the day devoted mostly to *sat-saṅga* and meditation of the Name. It should be a day of comprehensive self-purification.

Observance the Fifth - Tapa[s] - ***Fervent Ardour***

Saying 1. If any seeker of the truth can find some leisure from his worldly activities, he should spend some of it in *tapas*, in, that is, solitary meditation, his intake and communication reduced to the bare minimum. During that time, spiritual uplift should his sole concern, his mind fully occupied with that end. The duration of *tapas* should be regulated according to one's disposition and maturity. As a first step, one should stay in solitude for some hours, then for days and then for weeks and experience the bliss that one is, one's own self is. Of course, daily meditation of the Name morning and evening and according to the rules is itself enough to bless one with that bliss. However, if a person has the ability and the time to stay away from his worldly concerns and relationships, then let him resort to solitary meditation to stay stable in it. Solitary *tapas*, however, cannot succeed without a deep devotion to the truth. There should also be no physical ailments to distract the person engaged in *tapas* from his purpose. To very many people will this kind of *tapas* bring peace, people that live in the world and for the world, and as for the person engaged in it, it will verily bring him bliss the supreme. During the time of *tapas*, acceptance of any gift from anyone will prove harmful.

However, a man who is not fully successful in his daily meditation cannot perform this meditative *tapas*. One should understand that regular daily meditation itself is *tapas* of the highest order. That is what should be adopted and adhered to with full resolve and determination.

Saying 2. One should cultivate a disposition that can stay unconcerned with worldly affairs when one is apparently engaged in them. This disposition can be cultivated only through the daily meditative practice and through other principles meant for that purpose.[39] These constitute the real means, daily meditation and other principles, to bring into being that passively active spirit. *Dharma* or righteousness flourishes in the world only through purification of one's own life. That is the way to propagate it. Therefore, let a man who would cultivate this kind of passive disposition associate with the seers of the truth, let him serve others with every care and concern, let him remember the Lord and leave his own concern to His will. That is the way of purification, purification of his life and to stay all stable in Being ever the same. And that is the way he can uplift his country in the righteous way and make his life all successful and victorious.

Saying 3. To be ever disinterested, to be all humility, to stay above the tumult of the world and to be ever stable and to be given to the good of others is to be ever the same. Thus these traits - those of disinterestedness, humility, transcendence, stability and doing well to others - constitute what *samatā* is. These are the absolute imperatives for attaining to the state of *samatā*. Disinterestedness springs from noble thinking and self-submission to the Lord. Humility springs from perceiving the Lord as the light that reveals the whole world and from perceiving the body as a mere momentary appearance. Steadfastness in yogic meditation leads to firm conviction about the reality of the *ātman,* and this conviction about the reality of the *ātman* leads one to stay above the affairs of worldly life and to stay stable in that transcendental state. In other words, a being can and will truly come to *be* only when he perceives the body as a mere false appearance and longs for and becomes one with the *ātman*. As for the disposition that thinks well of others and does well unto others, it emerges when a man leaves all the results of his actions to the will of the Lord. To have these traits means to dispel all the darkness of the mind in every truth and reality; unto the Light do they lead the *buddhi,* unto the light of Sameness, of that bliss, to abide steady in it, in that light and in that bliss.

Saying 4. Holy association, holy and steadfast meditation, and service unto others in the right spirit verily enable one to triumph over every evil and every sin. Greatly noble are these traits, those of disinterestedness, of humility, of unconcern with the affairs of the world, stability and the will to do well unto others. When these suffuse the mind, they make it all blissful and all blessed, these great traits and dispositions. A man in whom these traits come to dwell and stay is verily a light unto the whole world.

Therefore, it is incumbent on every mortal that he regulate his life according to the true principles and give himself to contemplation of the Name. If he succeeds in doing so, he will find the bliss ever the same and will merge into it to become that bliss itself. Only then shall he [qualify to] do real service unto beings, each and every. Only then will *dharma*, righteousness the genuine, and peace the true will prevail in the world and all *jīvas*, all living beings, will live in harmony with each other.

Let all the *premīs*, all the devotees, of *Samatā*, see to it that they practise all these observances and other true principles of conduct if they would find fulfillment the absolute. May the Lord bless them with belief in the word of the teacher and orient them towards the uplift of their life and being!

NOTES

[1] As explained earlier, 'vāsanā' is derived from the root, *vas*, to dwell. A mortal being is born inheriting all kinds of desires, conscious and unconscious, ideas and dispositions. Thinking himself as constituted by them, he lives and acts as these *vāsanas* dictate him, never tasting a moment of freedom from them. These *vāsanas* he inherits, to put the matter rather simplistically, from his previous births to bring him into being and his *other*, the world. We will dwell on the implications of these points in some details while we go through this chapter.

[2] *Nirṇaya*, truth the conclusive. This can only be revealed unto man, not that he can find it by his own intellectual endeavour, conditioned as it is by the conceptual framework within which it must and has to operate. Man can only fabricate reality, he cannot find it, his intellect cannot but delimit it, enframe it within its concepts, clear or ambiguous, or multivalent. One may, however, add that even the conclusive truth revealed to him is not truth the absolute; it is conclusive only in the sense that it can lead him, through undoing his concepts, through self-negating concepts, to a state of innocence open and wide enough to let the truth find a place for itself in it.

[3] I.e. reflection on the truth the revelation, not the truth that a discourse would fabricate.

[4] Some may take this as an appeal for what is called metaphysical thinking, thinking that cannot find the answers to the questions raised here. A man in search of truth has to raise these metaphysical questions, it is absolutely necessary that he ask them and invoke them. To ask these questions is to recognise and acknowledge the mystery that life and the world are, their depth and agony, of these questions, will be a testimony of his sensitiveness and his earnestness. He will not find the answers to these questions, because those answers, if found, will be answers couched in terms and concepts, terms and concepts that would undo the mystery, would capture it in the framework of his understanding, unmindful of the depths hidden beyond its reach. The answers may modify and transform his terms and concepts, may 'enrich' them [as some would say] but they will not let the real come forth and be itself, they will again confine and enframe it. The fruit of metaphysical thinking ripens only when reflection gives place to pensiveness, to thinking that

stays still with questions without the hope of finding answers to them. To this disposition, melancholy, sad and disillusioned but calm and passive, the revelation will disclose its truth and secrets. Only before this disposition the truth about the world as the *other* of the embodied being and the truth about the recurrence of the body together with its *other*, the world, another body with another world, will shine forth and not before the restless thinker who would seek answers, answers he can know and understand, whatever their complexity. The latter will welcome every complexity but not bareness, not Being the bare, which only a passive opening out can accommodate.

5. The material world and its subjective counterpart. The subjective counterpart consists of the senses, the mind, the *buddhi,* the determinating faculty, and the I-sense. These are called the subtle constituents of a human being. Behind these subtle constituents lies breath and behind breath the unmanifest seed of creation, *prakṛti.*

6. This identification involves the element of the *Other* as its constitutive principle. Identification involves isolation from all that is other than the thing one identifies oneself with. One can identify oneself only with a finite thing and not with the entire world, which one can never know and, consequently, never be. But the paradox is that it is this finite being, this victim of *vāsanā*, that sets up the spectacle of the world, the world as the *Other*, beyond the power of his reach and understanding.

7. Notice how 6 and 7 present a paradox before us. We are told that it is a mortal being that, under the overwhelming impact of *vāsanā*, sets up the world, gross and subtle. And also that it is *vāsanā* that creates that world for that mortal being. What the text, through these paradoxical expressions, would convey is the interdependence of *vāsanā* and a mortal being. The two assume each other and constitute each other. And with these *dvandvas*, dualities, coming into being also comes into being their constitutive other, the world. This idea constitutes the basis of the teachings about rebirth. There can be no world without *vāsanā* and a being inflicted by it, they constitute the very condition of its coming into being, of this very world that seems to precede and succeed me, this world that seems more real than me, is, ontologically speaking, prior to me. This *other* has to be like that to make of me an individual, a being that identifies itself with a small part of it. This small part must have the entire world as its constitutive *other*, with all its seeming infinity and its endless duration. But this

very world, beyond the power of my knowledge and action, has me only, the me identified with this fragile and perishable body, as its constitutive principle. I create this world in order to be a being in and of it, a being helpless, fragile, and ever in search of being that he, as a situated being, will never find.

One may, however, urge with every reason that I am not an individual in and by myself. I am a being in relation to and contrast with others and that without those others I cannot be what I take myself to be, an individual. In other words, I am not a subjectivity but an intersubjectivity and the world is not the *other* of a subjectivity but of intersubjectivity and that I, others and the world rise together, constituting and constituted by each other. So, if I take myself to be a real, I have also take others and the world too as reals. There is, there can be no ontological priority of one vis-a-vis the other two. This way, the world is not set up by me, I am not its creator. I have no being apart from others and from the world to be their creator.

The doctrine of rebirth, however, takes the world to be the *other* of me. For this doctrine, the world is not the world in and by itself, it is I-world. When I affirm myself as an I, I posit something to identify myself with. It is as one with that something that I can affirm myself as *I*, know myself as such. Since that something is something in a world, so the world too comes into being the moment I affirm myself, comes into being as the *other* of what I take myself to be. I think of the world as an objective world, existing independently of me, but without me there can be no world, the world that I perceive and experience. But who is this *I*, the I identified with something, the body, for example? This I is a mere search for an identity, for that is what the present moment is, moment in search of itself. A doing moment it is, not even moment a process. The I is present in it as a doer, a doer that ever fails to find itself or himself. If the moment had been only a process, a bare temporality, there would have been no awareness of it, for there would have been no one to know and notice it. I know that moment as the doing I. And it is this doing I that divides the world into its past and its future, and it is the same doing I that divides itself from the world, that field of its doing. Others too it determinates as *others*, in relationship with and contrast to whom it can affirm and assert itself as an I. It is true that this I in relationship with and contrast to others and the world cannot precede these, but that I is the I conscious of itself, it is not the I that projects itself into an object to know itself. That latter I is alone and is ineliminable, it is the cause, the projector of the world of dualities, it itself is not a duality because it cannot be determinated as this or that.

When the doctrine of rebirth speaks of rebirth, it is the rebirth of this I the unmanifest, not of I the manifest, the I born as situated and related in a particular given set up. The latter comes to an end at the time of death but not the former. What prompted that I to project itself as a particular given object, still persists in it; it does not die with the death of the situated and related being. And what persists in it as the cause of the said projection is the passion to affirm and assert itself as I, to know itself as such. That is the primordial *vāsanā* dwelling in and with it. Under its impact the I in affirming itself affirms the Other, Other in the form of the temporal and spatial world and in that of other beings, belonging to the same specie and of other, countless, species. A whole hostile world springs into being to undo this I, the world that the I has isolated itself from, and so do other creatures, known and unknown, friendly or hostile. And time too springs into being for this doing I to bring it to decay and destruction, in fact never allowing it to be ever itself. The I projected itself in order to find itself a being, but being irrevocably deserted it. Only death remained to smash it and it to fight a useless and tragic fight against it. This process will ever continue until this passion for being oneself does not die down, this original *vāsanā*, this original sin, this source of the original fall. The I is our deadly enemy, our fatal disease and delusion. For, it is not the I but only a blind passion or *vāsanā* for being an I, the passion that brings us death instead of being, brings us death each and every moment.

The faithful believe that they really have had to pass through births and deaths infinite in number. As one cannot know the beginning and the end of the present world, this *other* of the present me, me the situated, so there is, there can be no count of the births and deaths that have preceded one's present life and no count of births and deaths to come. A grim view of life presents itself before beings, the view of a rigid determination. They believe their life is an unfoldment of the deeds that they did in the past and since that past is beginningless, there can be no end to their reward and punishment. This is a simplistic understanding of the doctrine of rebirth by people who have a simplistic understanding of their situated and related self. They think of the latter as an entity and imagine it as passing through births and deaths without a count. They must pause and think about the matter in all seriousness.

When I find my situated and related-derelated being as a result of the primordial act of self-projection, my understanding of the doctrine of rebirth will undergo a radical transformation. I will, of course, find a vast, seemingly infinite world, extending before me, a world largely unknown and, ultimately unknowable, and also each and everything in it, experienced or not experienced, and also an unknowable past preceding it and an unknowable future succeeding it. Nevertheless I, I a nonentity almost, a mere speck as it were, will find myself at the centre of all that is and could be. For, it will be in relation and opposition to me, the me that I do not and cannot find, that the entire fabric of the world, with all its causes and its possibilities, will be found to exist. There will be no past without me, no present and no future, without this uncertain and indefinable moment that I am. That means that I will find myself as prior to the body and its *other*, the world, and also as posterior to it. And yet I will not find this self at the existential level because I will remain situated and related as ever. But that does not mean that I will find myself merely a relationship and a contrast, a mere contextuality, because the I that I am will not let itself to be reduced to that, to a mere contextuality. It will show itself forth, with a steady persistence, as immersed in contextuality but not encompassed by it. In other words, my attempt at identification with the not-self will not succeed, for it will remain the not-self as ever. This would mean that I alienated myself from my self the moment I asserted, 'I am.' My past has been a story of failure and so will be my future and so will be my so-called present. Eternal loss will be the characteristic of this unidentifiable I that I would find and be.

And as there is no beginning and no end to my search for being, so there will be no beginning and no end to the world where I would seek it. Without that passion for being, there can be no world, it is rooted in that passion, that *vāsanā*. If the world was there in the past, then I and my passion too were there to project it and if it is going to be there in the future, I too will be there to project it. My past is as long as is the past of the world and so will be the case with my future. But this will be a false belief, conjured up by my passion for being, passion my understanding finds too strong to overpower. When talking of rebirth, I believe in the factual reality of the past and the future, forgetting that they are only the constitutive conditions of my projected self. So my births, past and future, are not real facts, as the past and the future of the world are not real facts, they are merely the *others* of my birth as my birth is their *other*. With the cessation of my self-projection as this or that being, my past births too will end and so will end the possibility of other births. And with the end of that self-projection will end the world too and also its past and its future, those constitutive others of it.

There can be no world, along with its past and future, without my self-projection, and there will be no self, self the projected, without its past and its future incarnations flanking it. They rise together with my projected self to lend it a semblance of reality, as the past and the future of the world are there to lend it a semblance of objectivity. So, as along as I believe in the fiction, 'I am,' I cannot escape from the burden of my past births and future births, without which there can be no past and no future of the world. But the moment I distance myself from this projection and from the not-self with which I identify myself, I will cease to be that false projected self, that other with which I identify myself, and so will cease to be my past and future and so will cease to be their *others*, the past and the future of the world. If I am deeply entrenched in my projected self, if my sense of identification with a thing, a body, is unquestioning, my past births will be as real, as inexorably real, as will be the past of the world. And as the world, that objective pole of the I-world, is rooted causally in its past, so will I be rooted in the past of the subjective pole of the I-world, namely, in my past births to give rise to the so-called future of the I-world. If the world is there, then I have also to be there to project it. There is no scope for one to escape from the other. And what kind of births will be those births, past and future, depends on the kind of my present birth. If I live completely at the mercy of my passion to *be*, then my past will determine me as inexorably as does the past of the world determine its present appearance. As a natural being I will live at the mercy of my past, or my past deeds, as the scriptures put it for the consumption of natural beings, as live /exist the other phenomena of the world. If I extricate myself from that cruel state, then my past will not determine me as a cause determines its effect. For, I will then project myself as an effect determining its cause instead of being determined by the latter.

That precisely is the dilemma of man, a determined being trying to determine his determining factors. That is his glory and his tragedy, his mean sublimity and his sublime meanness. His meanest acts speak of his attempts, desperate though, to extricate himself from the helpless, inert I that he as a projected self is, and his sublimest acts of his immersion in that killing inertness. The former is a revolt against his condition, the latter a confirmation of it. A pious and upright man is a victim of illusion if he thinks of himself pious and upright. True piety will only make him aware of his sin, making of him a conscience ever unappeased. His joy is his curse and his frustration an indication of his possibilities, the possibilities of his salvation from his fallen condition. An upright man, if he does not allow himself to be seduced by the feelings of self-esteem, is upright because he will know the frustration that he is. The brute passions of the body will not let him be what he would seek to be, hurting his sense of being good at every step, save those moments when the sense of his self-esteem has the better of him. A man thus dissatisfied with his attempts at so-called righteousness will stand apart from his actions, knowing them for what they are, mere vain attempts to invest his determined being with freedom. He will stand apart from that doing self of his to be the self, the humble self, that he is, the self anonymous that will not give itself a name and a form. With this humility and passivity characterising it, it will cease to affirm itself, to name itself, and with that will come to an end its self-projection and the chain of births and deaths it brings about and also the *other* of that chain, the objective world.

The doctrine of rebirth is true only for the self that would project itself, it is not the truth for the self that would not project itself. The doctrine of *samatā* will add deeper dimensions to this understanding of *bandhana* and *mokṣa*, bondage and liberation. For those dimensions we now return to the text.

8. *Vāsanā* dwells in man as his constitutive principle, it is a blind passion for being as against *kāmanā*, desire related to an object. *Kāmanā* is a derivative form of *vāsanā*. Having identified with the given projected object, *vāsanā* turns into the ontological and existential needs of that projected object, the creator turning into a slave and creature. Desire, that expression and emblem of the lack of being that characterises the projected object, is a tragic frustration because it will fail in the purpose of *vāsanā's* passion for being.

9. Mortals are born to go beyond *vāsanā* and the worlds it sets up. In that lies their salvation and liberation, in crossing beyond that realm of fear and death. But what is a curse and fall for mortals is a happy play for the Real, this Its sacrifice into the agony of mortal life. Mortals are to sacrifice themselves into the Real, the Real that ever sacrifices

itself into the mortal, is the act of sacrifice itself. Its self-sacrifice is its *līlā*, its play transcendental. He who would live, the *jīva*, has to live as he who would die, who would sacrifice himself into the act of sacrifice. In that alone lies his bliss, in not being himself as the bliss of his Lord lies in not being Himself. Only that man is truly free who looks alike on liberation and bondage, on knowledge and ignorance, on mortality and immortality. Not he who draws lines of distinctions between these.

10. The inert earth is present in man in the form of hunger, that expression of greed and acquisitiveness. . The moving water is present in man as desire, more especially, as sex-desire. The flaming fire has for its subjective counterpart in the form of the passion of wrath and anger, the air in the passion for relationship and space for the passion of self-assertion.

11. Notice once again the ambiguity about *jīva*, the living or mortal being. It is he that identifies himself with actions to turn into *jīva*, the mortal being that he is. The ambiguity puts into question the reality of both the *jīva* and the sense of doership. That precisely what a duality is, one pole of it asserting itself at the cost of the other but in doing so affirming the other pole, thereby negating itself. Dualities are not realities, as many a thinker would have us believe. The Vedas explain the truth about dualities through the image of the *saṃvatsara*, the year. The year is constituted by two principles, each the food of the other, the principles of *agni* and *soma*. When summer starts in, the principle of *agni*, fire, is on the rise and *soma*, the principle of cold, is on the decline and when winter arrives the process gets reversed. What was food at the setting in of summer turns into the eater of food at the commencement of winter. By 'eating' *soma, agni* turns into *soma*.and by eating *agni, soma* turns into *agni*. That is what dualities are, the enactment of constantly becoming the other. When some thinkers assert the reality of dualities themselves, they forget about the conflict inherent in them, conflict that does not let remain themselves the opposites constituting them. So, when these cannot be identified, these conflicting elements, the dualities too cannot be identified. The Sanskṣrit term for duality, *dvandva*, conflict of opposites, highlights this point which the term duality does not. We must remember that all dualities that we know of are dualities in time and as such only seek to be but never come to be. So, dualities come to be considered realities when they are thought apart from their existential contexts, when they are looked at as bare concepts.

Abstraction from their existential contexts is the cause of much philosophical confusion about them.

The other point that this paragraph highlights is that relating to the concept of *Māyā*. We cannot identify the cause of the rise of *jīva* or the sense of one's identity with action because the *buddhi* cannot determinate it as such and such. The *buddhi* can determinate only what is real and not what is a mere appearance. 'One can determinate,' the text says, 'only the real, not what is not and only appears to be.' And the unreal appearance is that which cannot withstand investigation, 'for the moment it is sought to be investigated, it ceases to be.' This means that it is the *buddhi* that can decide about the truth or otherwise of things. In other words, what it can clearly identify is real, what it cannot identify is unreal. All that we perceive and conceive, however, fails the test. One simply cannot say of anything here that it is *this*. For, every *this* has the not-this to set limits to it, thereby negating it and itself. I and my world and what is beyond the world are *Māyā* because nothing in them and about them can bear investigation, can be determinated truly. This unintelligibility of all that is turns it into *Māyā*. This fact adds a further complexity to our rather hasty conclusion above, namely, that what the *buddhi* can clearly identify is real and what it cannot so identify is unreal. The fact in question implies that when the *buddhi* fails to find anything to coincide with its concepts, it too ceases to be. For, the *buddhi* is the faculty of determinating and when there remains nothing to determinate, the process of determinating too ceases to be. In other words, its criteria of truth can apply only to the things that fail to measure up to them; it can only decide what is unreal and not what is real because the real would not appear before it. The *buddhi* too is a *dvandva*, it too is a duality, in negating its *other*, its objects, it negates itself too.

[12] Only that thinking can be pure and unpolluted which is not prompted by desire for what we ordinary call knowledge and power. The thinking that we ordinarily do is prompted by our desire to measure things in accordance with our concepts, concepts that are rooted in the 'I AM' in us. Thinking done by this 'I AM' is necessarily narcissistic, it is not loyal to Being in itself but to Being conditioned by the 'I AM' and its concepts. True thinking is thinking that is passively open to what is and lets itself be suffused by it without an attempt to determinate and enframe it. Before this passively awake disposition dawns in us, we must deliberate on revelation and the

words of those that have attained to the truth. Only those disillusioned by their knowledge and power will dwell on the words of revelation or those of seers, not those who are centred on their ego. Disinterested opening out to the words of revelation and of seers will enable one to open out genuinely to what is and self-submit to it.

· *Guṇas*, we may recall, are the strands that compose the rope that binds a being to the worldly mode of being in the form of recurring births and deaths. *Tamas* is the strand that would bind him to inertia. *Rajas* is the strand that binds a being to activities and to the world where they come to be possible. *Sattva* is the strand that makes him transcend every state of being. A being and his *other*, the visible world, are embodiments of the tension among these three forces.

13. to get born and die again and again.

14. 'Light of consciousness.' I am conscious when I am identified with the *buddhi*. The term '*buddhi*', as explained earlie, is not exhausted by the term 'intellect'. That is only one aspect of the *buddhi*, the aspect that determinates, places an end and limit to, what it perceives, conceives and understands. In this its aspect, the *buddhi* functions as the conceptual faculty. There is, however, another dimension of the *buddhi*, the dimension of passivity, in which the *buddhi* does not determinate so much as it perceives, perceives passively and lets the phenomena it, as the conceptual faculty, determinated reveal themselves on their own. A still another dimension of the *buddhi* is the state of consciousness where it does not merely let the phenomena reveal themselves, it lets them possess it, suffuse it. In this thoroughly open disposition, the *buddhi* exceeds itself to find the phenomena exceeding their limits, it turning into, so to say, infinity along with the phenomena. It is then that it turns into the Real, that light of consciousness.

When consciousness determinated its objects, it also determinated itself, determinated itself as consciousness-of as opposed to the objects it determinated. But the *buddhi* cannot, on its own, assume the form of consciousness. Concepts are not consciousness, concepts of whatever kind — defining and definite, complex or simple, ambiguous or multivalent. It is only when the *buddhi* distances itself from concepts that it turns into consciousness, almost a passive awareness. But this awareness too is awareness-of, awareness of thoughts, images, concepts or feelings. It is these latter that lend it the characteristic of consciousness. In those moments of passivity, the *buddhi* experiences itself as subsisting unchanged in the midst of the succession of thoughts. Many equate this seemingly unchanging consciousness with the *ātman*. But consciousness as experience of something other than itself has to be temporal too; it cannot be totally a-temporal and still be consciousness, as it cannot be temporal and still be consciousness. Consciousness is an ontological outrage for conceptual understanding, resisting as it does both the concepts, that of temporality and that of a-temporality and also, by implication, of their reconciliation. Consciousness thus refuses to be encompassed by any concept whatsoever, consciousness the passive. With this realisation, the *buddhi* sheds its conceptual character to find itself exceeding itself, that is to say, to find itself ceasing to be. It is that excess in it, the excess it finds itself getting transformed into, that is the light of consciousness, the light that informs consciousness, makes it what it is. It is the informing principle of *buddhi* the conceptual faculty, *buddhi* the passivity and *buddhi* the self-exceeding principle. That is the light that makes *buddhi* the unconscious turn, seemingly, into consciousness. Consciousness is called the *ātman* because it is the expression of the Real, not that it is the Real. Consciousness has to die as consciousness to turn into the Real that one is. Thus the *buddhi* itself is bereft of light, it is the *ātman* that turns it into consciousness. The phrase 'light of consciousness' implies all these matters.

15. *Sattva*-guṇa is, we said, the transcendental principle operating in every being, in a few dominantly, in most as dominated by *rajas* and *tamas*. The dispositions and acts mentioned here help one to transcend his worldly mode of being, the mode of being that seeks itself in being situated and related.

16. Their coming to be one, of the *buddhi*, the mind and the senses, implies becoming one of their constitutive others too. The senses have their *other* in the material world, the mind has its *other* in the world in the form of its own projection and the *buddhi* has its objective counterpart in the *avyakta*, the unmanifest. *Avyakta*, the unmanifest, is always prone to become manifest, the emanation turning into the frozen, inert and oppressive world. It is only when they, namely, the unmanifest, the manifest and the material *other* come to be one for a being, when he remains self-same in all these conditions of quietness, of joy and of misery, finding no difference among them, that he comes to be free of *vāsanā*, not before. Cp. Kaṭha Upaniṣad 1.3.13:

yacched vāṅ mānasī prājñas tad yacched jñāna ātmani,

jñānam ātmani mahati niyacchet tad yachec chāntātmani.

Let the man of discrimination merge his speech in the mind and the mind in the knowing self and the knowing self in the great self and the great self in the tranquil self, the quiet. .

17. Cp. Ibid. 2.3.10:

yadā pañcāvatiṣṭhante jñānāni manasā saha,

buddhiś ca na viceṣṭati tam āhuḥ paramāṃ gatim.

When come to rest all the five cognitions along with the mind and the *buddhi* too stays still and passive, that is the state they call the highest.

18. That is to say, the embodied being, *vide* 31.

19. We should keep in mind that the body connotes the organism consisting of the body, the senses, the mind and the intellect. We should also add breath to the list.

20. i.e., the *Nāda*.

21. Understanding that attribution of action to the self is a false attribution.

22. on revelation and the words of seers.

23. The body is a curious complex of the inert and the moving, the inert providing the moving with a sense of being, the moving making the inert as if instinct with life. The inert, however, is not the being that the moving life seeks, it is only an illusion of being. And the moving too is not the life that the body would be endowed with, it too is only a false appearance of life, only a make believe. To be is the overriding passion of this organism, of this body-mind complex. But the being of the body lies in the inert, to that it would return, ever and always. The element of life in the organism would however seek being the pure, not being that the body provides, being in the shape of the inorganic matter. So the so-called living being is a duality, a conflict of these two opposing principles. Seeking life the eternal it moves inexorably to the inert and to death. .

Yet the inert cannot be there in the absence of ever moving consciousness and this consciousness cannot be there unless there is a self to experience it, experience consciousness as consciousness. This self is however conditioned by the *buddhi*, *buddhi* that determinates everything, enframes it in concepts. To enframe itself, it has to enframe a body and to enframe a body means enframing it as against the context of a world. So awareness of the self as the stable principle of the moving consciousness leads the *buddhi* back to the body and the world, leads to them the moment it seeks to determinate it. The only way it can find the life it seeks, life the eternal, is not to determinate the witness of consciousness but to self-submit to it, giving up its function of determinating. When it does so, the body will melt into that witness and so would the world and so would the *buddhi* itself. That is the Life it seeks, the life it calls eternal. But where will survive the *buddhi* to call it eternal? Eternity and temporality too are dualities fashioned by the *buddhi*, dualities that the *ātman* disdains serenely, as Rilke would say.

24. All that a being is and his world is, is haunted by absence. Every living being finds himself endowed with consciousness but he cannot find consciousness as such. And everything in the world is suffused with existence or with being but that being ever remains unidentified. There is nothing in the world that can be, and yet it is very much there for us to find it an existent, as endowed with being. There is nothing in me that can be and be conscious and yet it is and is conscious. So what is That which dispenses being and consciousness to the world remains a mystery, a mystery that haunts every sensitive and thinking mind, a mystery that would not let such a mind rest in and for itself. We call it Being and Consciousness because it dispenses being and consciousness to us, not that it itself is being and consciousness, this mystery unknown and unkowable. The *buddhi* cannot know it because it, as the determinating principle, cannot determinate it, set limits to it, but it can find that Being of being if it ceases to determinate, if it, that is to say, ceases to be itself. In no way the *buddhi* can find it except by ceasing to be *buddhi*. That is what is implied by **'Within the body itself can the *buddhi* find that Real the Supreme [and not in the world]**.' The world and the determinating principle that the *buddhi* is go together. Seeking being in enframing and in the enframed will be of no avail, only by ceasing to be itself can the *buddhi* find its life and being.

25. the son born out of the sacrifice of man. When man dies only then does that Lord come into being.

26. The rich ambiguity implicit in the sentence should be kept in mind. Mind is constituted by name and form, as name and form are constituted by mind. Some would contend that mind is nothing else than name or names. But that will mean ignoring the other

dimensions of the mind, dimensions like its tendency to remain coincided with its given state of being, its tendency to project itself into the world in the form of actions and its urge towards transcendence. To confine the mind within mere names is to unduly emphaise its *tāmasika* nature and ignore its *rājasika* and *sāttvika* aspsects.

27. I.e. as instructed by a seer of the highest truth.

28. True bliss is the bliss that does not depend on the *other*. To be oneself, absolutely and without a qualification, is to be in bliss true and genuine. Now, unless and until all that is the *other* turns into the self, one cannot find, rather, *be* that bliss.

29. We should not forget that 'body' here means the whole organism, it means body, the senses, the mind and the intellect. The pleasures of the senses and the joy that springs from satisfaction of varied desires, from realisation of one's ambition and from understanding and knowledge — all end up in our misery in the long run. At the basis of all these desires lies the desire to *be*, to be in and through the body, that primary cause of our ontological pain.

30. False memory is the memory of the *other*, of the world. True memory is the memory of one's loss, one's ontological loss. The Primordial Being has deserted the being but has left behind the traces of its absence in the form of its Name. We can regain our loss only through remembering that Name, contemplating it to the extent of becoming one with it. The Name of the Primordial is itself the Primordial, becoming one with it is to become the Primordial. Our purification, our redemption, lies in becoming one with the Name.

31. How is it that every being is born blessed with wisdom true, with no exception, whatever his ways and mode of life? The three Vedas, we are told, were revealed as soon as the world sprang into being. That is why they call these Vedas eternal. When creation lies concealed in the *avyakta*, in the Unmanifest, they too lie there unmanifest, when the *avyakta* turns into *vyakta*, into the Manifest, the Vedas too turn manifest. The three Vedas, as explained earlier, represent what later came to be called the three *guṇas*, the *guṇas* termed *sattva*, *rajas* and *tamas*. Every being that comes to be born into the transient world is born endowed and suffused with these three *guṇas*. The man who is given to *tamas* and would do everything to preserve himself knows, in his heart of hearts, that his ways are wrong, for there is no mortal who is not aware that all such

endeavours would come to naught. And the man given over to *rajas* also knows that all his ambitions and activities will turn, in the long run, futile. And the man given to *sattva*, the transcendental thrust, too knows that unless and until he comes to be extinct, his search for the beyond will not rest. So death in a way is the fourth Veda, the teacher supreme of our truth. For any one who has the patience to reflect can know, and know fully well, all that the Vedas reveal; for, born is he as a knower of the Vedas. His learning and other forms of kowledge will only conceal this primoridal knowledge which, if realised and followed, will lead him to his lost home. That is why in times ancient wisdom was sought not in civilisation but in the forest, where man lived as himself alone with no myths clouding his mind, whether those myths are those of superstition or of what the self-complacent term Enlightenment.

32. The senses are as much narcissistic as is man himself. They would dominate each other, would enjoy themselves at the cost of each other. When a man while seeing with the eye does not neglect the ear, has his mind open to the latter, the eye will become blind and the ear deaf – blind and deaf suffused with the tranquillity of the mind. And if while seeing and hearing thus, the mind does not cease to inhale and exhale with the sense of smell, it will step out of thoughts to mingle with the incoming and outgoing breath. And if it remains heedful to the sense of touch, while breathing in tranquillity, tranquillity blind and deaf, it will find the body suffused with a still calm, a soothing and peaceful sensation spreading out to every pore of the body and every sense of it. When this stillness comes to suffuse the mind to bring it into a still repose, even the tongue will not fail to feel satisfied, it will taste as it were that peace, that coming to rest of all activities, that quiet stillness.

The senses, however, cannot sing this song in unison, this 'song of the five friends', without a preparation. A man must ever remain open to all that the eye can reveal, from the distinct objects it can perceive to the excess in them, excess that no measure can measure. He must, in other words, be open to all the possibilities of that revelation. He must also let the ear realise all its possibilities, allow it to hear not only all kinds of sounds but also silence and the depth of that silence. As for touch, he is not to limit it to sexual pleasure but should feel the *touch* of touch in every limb of the body, every part of it, every pore of it; he should let the sensation of *touch* touch him. For, he should know that the body itself is the sensation of touch and that the possibilities of touch can be realised when he stays and lingers at every touch that body gives him, in each of its parts, in each of his pore. As for the sense of taste, it will be appeased only when it tastes itself, tastes that touch of itself. If a man tries this way to let the senses sing in unison, does not let one sense dominate his mind at the cost of the satisfaction of other senses, he will be acting in the right way. He will be a man living in a world happy and enchanted, his mind at rest, his senses all appeased. This his heedfulness towards all the senses will truly make him a man of right conduct, a man truly righteous and noble.

Men of thought have given their thoughts to ethical matters for centuries, but have often remained dissatisfied with their own findings and formulations. But what they sought to know lay on the surface itself. We blame the senses for leading us astray, forgetting that their seeking is not a false seeking but a true seeking. That seeking becomes perverse because we do not pay heed to the seeking of each one of them; we would appease one and starve others, with the result that all our so-called satisfactions turn into frustrations. The hedonists should be true hedonists, all comprehensive hedonists. .

33. Good conduct lies in harmonising the functions of the sense and motor organs, but purification of the *buddhi* lies in one's stepping out of the organs to look at them as different from oneself, from one's being or, to put it in the Vedāntic terminology, to look at them as belonging to the sphere of the not-self, of the *anātman*.

34. Organs cognitive and motor and also the inner organ, the organ of thinking.

35. The term 'mind' is a comprehensive term. *Manas* is often translated as mind, as has been done in this passage. But strictly speaking, *manas* comprises thinking of objects of the sense in terms of desire and action vis-a-vis those objects. Thinking by the *manas* thus has no role to play in determinating the objects concerned, in setting limits to them vis-a-vis each other. That is the function of the *buddhi*, not of the *manas*. The *buddhi* becomes pure when it frees itself from the thinking of the *manas*, stands apart from it. When it does so, it will find itself a being in relation to the objects it determinates as existents. The *manas* does its thinking as a prisoner of objects, the *buddhi* merely posits those objects. The desire that prompts it do so is the desire for being and the objects it posits are there to create the illusion that it indeed is an existent, which it is not. When this

realisation dawns on it, the *buddhi* self-submits to the *ātman* to become one with it. True purity lies in this its merger in the *ātman*.

36. The truth and the way to the truth come as a revelation to man, they cannot be formulated in any human discourse. And the true principles of good actions too are a gift of revelation, of that alone. What is called the truth is the same what the faithful call God. The God of our discourse is, of course, no God, as the Good of our discourse is no Good. One should, however, understand that even the truth and the God of revelation are not ultimate truths, for formulated in terms of concepts, human concepts, they come to us with their negation inscribed in them. The only difference between revelatory truth and the truth of discourse is that the former negates itself not in terms of concepts, as the latter does; it, the truth of reveltion, comes to be negated only when man comes to be united with it, is merged in it. Then neither revelation remains nor does the God or the truth of revelation nor does the seeker of revelation. Human formulations are the products of the *buddhi* and that too when it is in the grip of the propensities of the *manas* and the organs of sense and cognition. They are the products of *avidyā* and relate to and abide in *avidyā*, in that alone. For a detailed description and analysis of revelation and its difference from human discourse, the reader may consult the chapter, 'The Starry Pastures' in the author's biography of Śrī Gurudeva and also preface to The Word Speaks to the Faustian Man, Volume 3.

37. Notice the paradox that runs through the entire fabric of this text. It has been a consistent theme of this text that we creatures are all fallen in the world as a result of our identification with the processes and doings of *prakṛti* and that this state of being is our curse and tragedy, curse and tragedy absolute and unmitigated. And yet the way out of this curse and tragedy is not the way of fighting against it but of accepting it as the glory wonderful of the Lord, as the expression of His Being and Will. In other words, man has to look alike on liberation and bondage, on Māyā and Brahman. That is the way to step out of his being the embodied, out of the body, the mind and the world. And, paradoxically enough, that is the way to flow out to others in love, love true and genuine. And that is the way to abide unaffected by the sorrows and pleasures of life.

The spirit behind these paradoxes should be clearly grasped and understood. For, a mortal that has come to realise that all his strategies against his mortal lot are vain and foolish cannot but find his salvation in Brahman, Brahman that is at once the ground of his being and the goal of his being. For him, truth abides not in what he perceives and experiences, not in what he finds himself to be and his world to be but in that source, in that support and in that end of his life and the world's life. He would attain to that end where there is no fret and no fever, no restive desires and no frustrating ends, no birth and no death, where all is peace, peace the absolute and eternal. Which, in other words, is the being, being the absolute that he ever aspires to be, this mortal that would be immortal. A projection of his own aspiration is that reality, which he terms as reality the absolute. But he does not know the way to the realisation of that his end absolute, the end where his primoridal desire for being will get finally appeased.

He cannot find the way to that goal because his intelligence is outward oriented, oriented towards the phenomenal world, world transient and devoid of being. He longs for a guide, guide that can lead him away from the hell that he is and the world is. And the guide comes in response to his fervent longing and prayers to show him the 'path' to that source and end of his life. And he will follow that path with sincerity, if his disillusion with the world is complete and unqualified. But when he has done all that it is possible for him to do, has striven to the utmost reach of his strength and energy, he finds that his endeavours have gone awry and wasteful, that the goal remains as distant as ever, despite his sincerity and his guide's assurances. It is at that time that the truth dawns upon him that the distinction that he drew between his present state of being and the state of being that he would attain to is a false distinction. For, if the Brahman of his imagination and aspiration had been the sole and single reality, there would have been no creation and no world, no striving and no end, no truth and no falsehood. But these *are* there, these distinctions and the tragedy that goes with them. There is the world before him with its doom written into it and there is he with his undoing inscribed in him. And there is also eternity that he ever seeks but eternity whose truth is dependent on the falsity of the world, for it is in relation to the falsehood of the world that Brahman can be posited as real. And it is on the degradation of the actual that the glory of the ideal is dependent. He cannot possibly deny anything or affirm anything, neither the reality nor the unreality of the world, nor the reality or the unreality of Brahman, neither falsehood nor truth, neither the pain nor the bliss and neither knowledge nor ignorance. He has to accept all, without a question, without a protest.

This is how he will come to find the world as the glory of the Lord, each the affirmation and the negation of other. .And it is this disposition, this disposition of acceptance of all that is without a judgement that would make him step out of the mind, the body and its *other*, the world. He will become a passive witness of the whole world, subjective no less than the objective, to melt ultimately into the eternity that he sought. Through the passive acceptance of the world and his bondage he will find Brahman and his liberation but only to undo himself and with that to undo that embodiment of his ideal too, that Brahman and that bliss. What is the real in itself man cannot know and he cannot find, because the moment he finds Brahman, his own ideal, *his* own ideal, he will not remain to find that ideal nor the ideal will remain to attain to. ***This way man is to strive, strive with pain and agony, for the goal of his life, the goal eternal and immortal. That is the beginning, the beginning he is not to deny or can deny. He has also to find the guide to lead him to that goal of his. And he has also to find that the path revealed to him will not lead him to that goal because the goal is not*** **the** ***goal but only*** **his** ***goal, of him the mortal. Next comes his acceptance of the given reality and also the ideal he seeks. And with that comes about the weakening of his selfhood, of his identification with the body, the mind and the intellect and also*** **prāṇa*****, breath. And then follows his attaining to his ideal and the cessation of him and that ideal. The ultimate truth, the ultimate mystery, is not for man to visualise, to strive for and attain to. He has to accept and submit to every state of being in this his pilgrimage, pilgrimage to he knows not what. That uncertainty will be his salvation, his blessing and his*** **mukti*****, his liberation.***

[38.] Many a theoretical Vedātins would know the self only through study of scriptures and through reasoning. But the self will ever elude them if they do not distance themselves from the passions of their sense and motor organs, from their thinking and deliberations and from their *buddhi*, the faculty that determinates and *places* phenomena. And this never comes to be possible unless and until they are free from desire, from self-interest and from the passion to be and to do. Unless the man in them dies, their self will not reveal itself. The path to self-realisation is the path of self-extinction, self-extinction of their false self, the self that identifies itself with the *other*, and this way murders itself. Thinking, however, profound, will always conceal self the real, for it will always superimpose its concepts on to it.

If a man knows for certain that the body is nothing else than destruction itself and the *ātman*, the self, alone is imperishable and ever gives himself and steadfastly to the contemplation of the self, contemplation right and genuine; and, if he lives in the world as humility itself and a devoted servant unto each and every being, and, looking alike on weal and woe he dedicates all his actions to the Lord and His will - if he indeed takes to this kind of fervent devotion and contemplation and remembers the Lord's Name each and every moment, he will surely know what *samatā* is, this man made of the supreme mettle. And he alone will find the state where no *vāsanā* is, that state of eternal bliss.

39. Other principles like those of simplicity, truthfulness, service and holy association.

Anubhava Six

(i) *On Understanding* Samatā

Saying 1. The Real reveals itself, discloses itself unto a *sat-puruṣa*. And the *sat-puruṣa* proclaims that revelation unto the world. And that is the truth final for a seeker of the Real, the Real as proclaimed by a *sat-puruṣa*. And it is that latter truth, truth final and conclusive, that a seeker has to understand. For not until he understands the meaning of that articulated truth can his mind find the peace it seeks. [1] The superiority of the human birth consists only in this that man can know the Real to become one with It to purge his mind of all the disastrous appearances it has set up before itself. That is how he can find the peace absolute even while alive and know, in truth, wherein consists the superiority of the human birth over other births.

Saying 2. The *sat-puruṣas* have articulated that truth in many ways, depending on their respective experiences. The meaning of what they say and proclaim is, however, the same; the differences one perceives in their teachings are differences, more or less, in terms of concepts and ideas, not in what those concepts and ideas are about. However, not until one resorts to a sustained contemplation of the Real can one believe in It fully, can one have full conviction about It. So, one should, first, understand that Real [Real as articulated by a *sat-puruṣa*] and then contemplate it to attain to the state of *samatā* to become one with it.[2]

Saying 3. Flawless contemplation within leads to knowledge true of life in all its aspects. Therefore, one should remember the Real Supreme and Eternal in the right way to attain to the final goal of life and peace the absolute.

Those who would resort to mere thoughts and learning bereft of contemplation are cowardly souls; forever will they live in fear, their efforts gone vain and fruitless.

Saying 4. The truth-become souls found the Real when they turned still and passive within; and they revealed what they found unto the world at large in the forms of thoughts. The purpose behind their formulations was that people should resort to the right ways to attain to the same state of passive stillness and let the Real reveal itself to them so that they find the rest they seek and the bliss and the enlightenment they are in search of, enlightenment full and all-comprehensive about the truth of the world! Mere listening to those formulations cannot bring anyone what he longs for, namely, peace the absolute and enlightenment the all-comprehensive. A seeker of truth must resort to the right way; in that lies his duty the paramount.

Saying 5. Every being is born conditioned by *prakṛti*, by that Other, by that seed of creation. From his very birth he is aware of all the deviations that go with embodiment, are implied by it, in whichever country he may have been born, in whichever faith, in a town or a jungle. His life in the world is determined by his understanding of what his body or the mode of his embodiment desires and projects or sets up. This is how *Māyā* plays its mysterious play.

Saying 6. Karma is a duality, a conflict of opposites. That is the snare it spreads out for every mortal being, the snare of dualities like well being and ill being, gain and loss, happiness and unhappiness, friend and foe, life and death, Me and the Other, receiving and giving, honour and disgrace, attainment and non-attainment. Other dualities too *karma* spreads out, dualities like grief, obsessions, desire, anger, shame, fear, hunger, thirst and heat and cold and very many others. Every being is aware of these dualities in accordance with his power of understanding and deliberates about what they will bring him, happiness or unhappiness, and acts, with every cunning and cleverness, as prompted by his calculations. This is all what life in the world is, this search for freedom in bondage, for peace the fear-free in actions prompted by this condition of helplessness. Not until he finds the Real can he find the rest he seeks. Vain will turn his efforts, with discontent as his eternal lot. This delusion alone is *Māyā*, this seeking misplaced and this endeavour misdirected.

Saying 7. All beings live bonded to *prakṛti,* live helplessly tied to doing, identified with it. And identified with their mode of being, mode of being that is not their own real being, they mistake satisfaction of the desires native to that mode of being for real peace and seek that satisfaction and strive hard for it. But this their seeking of peace the true in the satisfaction of desires goes vain and waste, for satisfaction of desires gives rise to further desires, desires without a count. In this vain endeavour goes waste their life, in seeking the satisfaction of desires, with peace the real, that ontological need of theirs, ever and always eluding them. This verily is their life, their life in the world, the world hard to traverse and cross. All their life they spent in pursuit of peace the real, did all kinds of efforts for that purpose but to reap despair only for their reward. Every human being is aware of what is going to be his portion in the end, but how to redeem himself from this his condition and in what way he does not know, never comes to know. Unhappy and miserable he departs from the world, having wasted his life in appeasing desires false and unreal. Curious and strange is this spectacle that *Māyā* sets up before beings. In misery alone do they stray and wander, stray and wander in search of peace life after life, birth after birth. This is all that the spectacle of the world in its truth is.

Saying 8. From birth to death and from death to birth move beings tied to their desires, desires very many and countless, and the objects of those desires, objects set up by those desires themselves. In the pleasures of the organs of cognition and action would they seek happiness true and real, wasting away all their life in this false pursuit of peace the eternal in those pleasures. But momentary are those pleasures, their enjoyment intensifying their infatuating passion for them, with misery for their portion in their life and in their death. Let every human being be aware of this truth. With all his efforts, with life long efforts ranging from birth to death, only frustration falls to man's lot; bereft of hope is he born and bereft of hope will he die, whatever be his life, whether that of an emperor or that of a beggar. Their beginning is the same and their end is the same. Blessed indeed is the man and blessed his life, the man who lives aware of this truth.

Saying 9. Let man be aware of the appalling snares that *Māyā* weaves for him; let him endeavour for his liberation from those snares, endeavour in the right direction. That is the real duty laid down for those blessed with the human birth. Beings, each and every, live prisoners of the sense of the ego of agency, of Me and Mine, and perceive a world set up by their mind and their desire[3] to experience pleasure and pain in it, their identification with doing never dying and so not their desire. Their bodies change ever and always, inflicting every pain on them, their thirst for being never coming to be appeased. Not a moment comes in their life when they can feel secure and at peace with themselves. That is the truth of their life, the truth that every human being should know well and perceive.

Saying 10. In the journey of life beings wander compelled by their desires, good or bad, good desires making them happy and the evil ones making them miserable. As prisoners of desire do they wander here in many ways and in many forms [birth after birth], unaware of the peace eternal and unchanging dwelling within them, peace that is the reality supreme, the reality ever the same.

Saying 11. And as long as desire to do and to act persists in a being, there is no escape for him from dualities like happiness and unhappiness. And desire to do and to act will not cease until the ego of agency, his sense of his identity as a doer, does not come to cease. Thus this, his sense of his identity as a doer, is the root cause of every misery and unrest. And the appearance of the world, appearance in the form recurring births and deaths, too, is, in its essence and original form, nothing else than this his identification with doing, this identification of the self with it[4]. As a prisoner of this illusion, this attribution of the concept of the doer on to the self, makes of him a being infatuated and obsessed with action and its result, giving rise to further actions and their results. Thus ever remains he discontented and frustrated, doing all kinds of actions and reaping their results, actions and results ever perpetuating themselves.

Saying 12. This sense of his being a doer is inborn in every being; that is what constitutes his being for him to make him live and act under its prompting, of this primordial *Māyā*, of this false appearance of himself. As long as this confusion persists, this false attribution of the concept of the doer on to his self, his world too will persist, his passion for doing ever projecting it before him, rendering him ineligible for the eternal peace that liberation is, that light and enlightenment.

Saying 13. Redemptive is the path that leads to the cessation of this being's false attribution of the concept of the doer on to his self and being, of this darkness and ignorance primordial, making him, as a consequence thereof, know and be the Real, Real the still and ever the same, Real the Bliss unchanging and undying.

Saying 14. And a curse for this being is the other path, the path that augments this false attribution, attribution of the concept of the doer on to his being and self, the fulfillment he seeks and ever strives for never coming his way. The fulfillment he seeks, that peace the full and infinite, he can find only when this false attribution comes to an end, not when he sticks to it. That verily is the last word of those who have attained to the Real to become one with It.

Saying 15. That false attribution of the concept of the doer on to his being and self, that I-sense, lies at the root of the unrest that inflicts this embodied being. For as long as this false attribution persists, the passion to do and act will not leave him, and as long as this passion to do and act persists in him, this being will ever remain insecure and a victim of discontent. That verily is the truth about his life, the truth that he must know and realise. Therein alone lies wisdom and knowledge true, in this realisation.

Saying 16. Since this mortal being is born with this false attribution inscribed into his being, it is extremely difficult for him to free himself from this primordial ignorance. He has to die, in every truth, before his actual death, die into a new life, life the passive, life that is the light of consciousness, life that is peace itself, peace the inviolable. That is what this being is ever in search of, of that Full and Infinite.

Saying 17. This false attribution of the doer on to one's being verily constitutes *Māyā* of the three modes of *sattva, rajas* and *tamas*. This embodied being will not come to rest until he crosses this threefold *Māyā,* until he ceases to seek to coincide with himself, ceases to change one sate of being into another and until he ceases with the cessation of the transcendental thrust in him. No pleasure can appease his thirst for true being, not even the transcendental joys of the transcendental beings, of gods, joys lasting for years in their millions. Hope will ever elude him; in his death he will not find it as in life he did not. This, in its very truth, is his journey, of this mortal being, this confounding journey of ever lasting non-fulfillment. Let man be aware of this way of the world to find the way of deliverance from it.

Saying 18. Māyā is nothing else than this false sense of oneself, this confusion of one's being with being the doer. And that verily is time, time the death, this false sense of one's being as a doer. Only the not-doing light of consciousness[5] is the Real, that only. As long as the *buddhi* does not free itself from this darkness, from this false sense of its being, of being as the doer, and does not find and be the Passivity that it truly is, unrest and frustration will remain its everlasting lot. Let man, therefore, ever try to extricate himself from the sense of Me and Mine, let him do so through the right way and means. That is how he can liberate himself from the recurring process of births and deaths. That verily is the endeavour true and the finding true in the eyes of seers true, this striving for liberation and attaining to it.

Saying 19. Every human being seeks to be blessed but that never comes to be possible unless and until he ceases to be a doer, unless he ceases to be that false identity of his. Without the extinction of that false self, there will be no peace for him, peace beyond every possibility of disruption. That is the truth which every being should know, know for certain. So he must have, as the first step, firm faith in the truth of Power the Not-doing and, as the second step, he must surrender himself to that still 'passivity' to put an end to all his deviations and failings. That will lead him, this his endeavour, to the realisation of Real the Supreme, of Word the Imperishable, that Life in its truth and reality. This verily is *upāsanā*, worship, the genuine, this faith and passive surrender to the Passive.

Saying 20. To be self-affirmative and self-assertive is ingrained into the very being of every creature, it verily is his being and nature, this selfhood, and is, for this very reason, hard to eradicate. To affirm oneself as a doer, to have this ego of agency, is to give rise to *vāsanā*, and *vāsanā* in turn gives rise to actions. In the grip of their bondage lives every mortal being, lives their helpless prisoner, knowing no way out of this his helpless condition. Not for a moment can he think of what peace in its truth is, nor can he believe in [the very possibility of finding] it. Ever devoted to serve his interests, he lives a life ever benighted, no ray of light guiding him out of its darkness. Let man, therefore, surrender his life and being to the Real, surrender it with a firm and steadfast intention, if he would escape from this awful labyrinth. Let the results of all that he does be left to the will of the Lord, left without a let, his mind firmly intent upon the holy contemplation of the Name. That is the way to eradicate *vāsanā*, this contemplation with every self-interests surrendered to the Lord, this devotion the true and genuine. This path of disinterested action [and contemplation] will bring to an end all *vāsanā* to lead one to the realisation of the Eternal and Indivisible dwelling within him, the Eternal and Indivisible that is peace the immovable.

Saying 21. Obsessed with this false sense of identity, the identity of the doer, a mortal being resorts to actions ever thinking of the results they may bring him, no action of his being ever free from this stain [of motivation and calculation]. With desire he ever burns and with aversion, this being the doer. To give up this false self, the self as a doer, to give up this false sense of Me, there is the smooth way of self-submission to the Lord Ever-the-Same, preceded by renunciation of the fruit of all one's deeds to His will, and letting no feeling of joy and sorrow touch one. When a mortal comes to live thus and be thus, he will find within him Real the Supreme, that peace ever secure and eternal.

Saying 22. To know within oneself the Eternal Real, that still passivity, is to undo the darkness that positing of the self as a doer is. To bring about that state of peace absolute one must resort to sustained meditation of that Real, remember It and contemplate It. The world that one perceives and finds oneself entangled in is, in its depths, projected by the *vāsanā* for action alone. The *buddhi* can find the final rest only when it comes to know the *ātman*, self the real, self that is stillness itself, extricating itself from the web that action has spread out for it. It is only when the *buddhi* knows that *ātman* and becomes one with it that one's activities and actions will find their fruition true and absolute. To know that life in its truth is to be blessed in every truth.

Saying 23. Every living being is born a slave of action, is born as conditioned by action, which condition only knowledge of Power the Still can put an end to. And that Power the Still only the *ātman* is, that Real the Absolute, that Word the Imperishable. That *ātman,* that Word the Imperishable, shines in its fullness within and without but cannot be known unless one's mind has been purged of all its impurities, when, that is, it has ceased to identify itself with doing and the doer. With every effort, therefore, should one purify the mind, with every right effort, and resort to devotion the true to undo that false sense of one's being, and find the Truth Absolute, that rest absolute and eternal. This verily is the way to be blessed and liberated.

Saying 24. This ever moving world is nothing but [the constitutive *other* of] the self conditioned by doing, the self that posits itself as the doer. But this doer-world duality is rooted, originally and ultimately, in the light of consciousness[6], in that Stillness. And it is knowledge of that Stillness and abiding as one with it that can bring about cessation of the recurring process of births, and deaths, of, that is, the innate passion for doing. To know that Stillness, that light of consciousness, is, therefore, to attain to the highest goal of life, is to find the peace supreme.

Saying 25. The world, gross and subtle, springs from *kartāpan,* from positing the self as the doer and is also sustained by it, by this wrong conception of the self. And *Māyā* too is this false positing, *Māyā* of the Lord. It ceases to be, this *Māyā,* this false identity, when the Lord is realised within, when all that is is found to be that *ātman,* that Real the Highest. Of peace the still is this state, the only state one should know and be.

Saying 26. These two powers the truth-become souls have revealed unto the world, in varied ways and forms. One is the power that dispenses life and being to all, the power that is ever the same and is bliss the eternal itself. And the other power is the one that projects itself as the doer, posits itself as such, the power that is *Māyā* itself and is conditioned by origin and end. Inflicted with this false conception of the self as the doer, the *buddhi* remains ever unhappy, thinking compulsively of the origin and the end of things. When, however, it comes to be aware of the Stillness within, it finds all that is as that very Stillness and lets itself be absorbed in It. That verily is liberation and peace the still and unmoving.

Saying 27. When the self is posited as the doer, the origin and the end of the world too get posited. In self the still there is, however, no *saṃsāra*, no world of recurring births and deaths. To know that self, that Real the Alone, is, therefore, to find peace the transcendental and attain to the goal supreme of life. For the eradication of this delusion, of the self as the doer, is meant the contemplation of the living self, to remember and contemplate it through its Name. That verily is the way to redemption and blessedness.

Saying 28. From *kartāpan*, from that confounding of the self with the false appearance of the doer, springs the instrument of action, the body-mind-sense complex. And from attachment to the fruit of deeds spring the great maladies like those of desire, wrath, greed, infatuation and the I-sense, those passions of unrest endless, passions that keep every mortal ever unhappy and frustrated. So the only way to salvation from this all-unhappy condition is to know the self and be the self, that One and Supreme Reality, that Power the still and placid. This verily is the essence of the teachings of seers of the truth, teachings that everyone should learn and live by. The glory of human birth lies only in this, in knowing the self and in being the self, self that is the Real itself.

Saying 29. Sat-puruṣas, the truth-become souls, have formulated these two states, those of bondage and liberation, in varied ways, but the content of their teaching in its essence and purity is the same. It is the bounden duty of every man to reflect on the teachings of those seers of truth and orient his life towards that truth, ever move towards it. Let him know the truth underlying the varied formulations of these two conditions, know it in experiential terms, and self-submit to the *ātman*, that single and sole reality, and attain to the highest goal of man's life.

On the Conditions two of Life

Peace the secure	**Unrest**
1. The Power called *samatā*.	The Power called *mamatā*, Me and Mine
2. The Power that is the *ātman*	Power the *anātman*, the not-self
3. Power the *niṣkarma*, not-active.	The Power called *karma*, action
4. Power the Compassionate and Timeless.	Power the Time
5. Power that is Brahman	Power that is *Māyā*
6. The light of the truth	The Power of *moha*, of delusion
7. *Gurumukhatā*, orientation towards the Guru	*Manamukhatā*, orientation towards the mind
8. *Ānanda*, Bliss	*Dvandva*, duality
9. *Nirvāṇa*, Liberation	Rebirth
10. *Sūnyatā*, Void or Emptiness	Time and *Kalpanā*, setting up
11. The Power that is the Lord	The Power that is *Prakṛti*
12. *Guṇātīta*, beyond the three modes	*Māyā* of the three modes
13. Consciousness, the light	Inert the dark
14. Power the Divine	Power the Demonic
15. Power the unattached	Power of Me the fallen
16. State the Enlightened	State the regretting

17. Knowledge	Delusion
18. The State one's own	Journey without an end
19. Light	Darkness of *vāsanā*
20. To find all as one's self	Disposition the deluded
21. To have no disposition	To be possessed of disposition[s]
22. The Alone	The Deluded
23. To be ever the same	To be conditioned by origin and end
24. The Indivisible and Nameless	The false and with name
25. The Formless and A-dual	The Formed and Dual
26. *Nāda*, the Sound	*Bindu*, the Dot
27. The Undecaying, Ineffable, Fearless	Ever-dying and Painful
28. All-knowing and All-powerful	Little knowing and attached
29. Beginningless and Unborn	Conditioned by beginning and end
30. Infinite and the Ground	Ever Grounded on the other
31. One and Only	Momentary and multiple
32. Unthinkable and Indestructible	Ever restless and destructible
33. *Qādir*, the Powerful	*Qudarat*, the Power
34. Light the pure, Desire-free and A-dual	Desire endless and the Imagined
35. Being	Not-Being
36. Light and Bliss the Absolute	Pleasure the painful
37. Wisdom	Folly
38. *Anubhava*, Knowledge-Being	The Visible

39. Name the True	Appearance the False
40. To be established in Yoga	To be immersed in enjoyment
41. The Lotus Feet, the Sound of the self.	Mind, speech and appearances false and painful
42. Non-violence	Violence
43. Power the Passive	Power the active
44. Non-attachment	Attachment
45. The Unembodied	The Embodied
46. Realisation of the Real	Knowledge of the Unreal

Other expressions too, very many of them, have been used to describe these two states. But the gist of all such expressions is that projection of the self as the doer is the root cause of all delusion and the misery that it lets loose and that one should step out of this falsehood to know the Real that one truly is, the Real to be adored with all the epithets noble and sublime. For, that is all peace and all bliss and all fullfilment. [7]

Saying 30. To know that Real is to know all else, to attain to it is to be supremely fulfilled— to attain to that Imperishable Word Fearless abiding within all to illuminate all. To remember that and to contemplate that with a one-pointed mind is to find the bliss full and absolute. That verily is the way to the highest treasure.

Saying 31. To withdraw the mind from everything that is the not-self and to self-surrender to the *ātman*, to the self, is to bring peace unto it, unto the mind. Therefore, giving up all doubts and false beliefs, one should believe only in the Power of life abiding within one and contemplate it with sustained intent to attain to the goal and state the highest. For that purpose, it is necessary that one should associate with the seers of the truth. For, it is in their company that a man can come to have belief and faith in the *ātman*, faith and belief that will enable him to stand apart from the world and its endless appearances, and, with that disposition gifted, attain to the Real abiding within him. With that will come to cease all his fears, with abiding as one with the Real within him.

Saying 32. As long as confusion of the self with the doer persists in a man, as long as he imagines himself a doer, he should believe the *ātman* itself as the doer and the undoer and as the Lord of the whole world. That belief will undo that his false attribution to the self. With this belief and this disposition he should ever remember and contemplate the Name True with an exclusive intent, contemplate it silent and within. That will lead him to the realisation of the Word, his *ātman* true and being true. This verily is devotion pure and *upāsanā* pure, passive contemplation pure, *upāsanā* in the shape of viewing every occurrence and non-occurrence as willed by the Lord, taking himself as of little account. This disposition is the way to eradicate the attribution of the false identity of the doer to him and to attain to the realisation of the passively still *ātman* within. Therein lies his highest duty, of the man who lives oriented towards his guru, in purifying his mind through this disposition of devotion pure and love pure. For that is how he can attain to Being the real, of his and of the whole world.

Saying 33. This devotion pure brings to rest every passion for doing. With that coming to rest, there comes to manifest within man the Word Imperishable, that still passivity, bringing to an end all that the *buddhi* has set up, all the false appearances. That is the moment when it merges into the Real, finding itself different from the whole of *prakṛti*, that *before* of creation, that seed of creation. That verily is the attainment surpassing every other attainment, and that verily is the source of the whole world, that state of being. The blessed man that has attained to that state is verily the man adorable, worthy of every worship and tribute. He only knows the truth about the world, the truth hidden from everyone else. And he alone abides in the state that abides ever the same.

Saying 34. To liberate oneself from that false identity, identity of the doer, one must believe that the Lord alone is the doer and the undoer, and believing thus, one should steadfastly meditate that *Sacidānanda*, that truth, consciousness and bliss, meditate Him in the shape of His Name. This kind of devotion to the Lord brings to cessation all the *vāsanā* ingrained in man and culminates in the realisation of the Full, making the *buddhi* stay still and calm. Freed, that is to say, from the passion of doing, it merges into Light the Pure, that Ever the Same, that Passivity Still.

Saying 35. Knowing that stillness, that ever the same consciousness, that light, a *jñānin*, a man of wisdom, ever abides in the bliss that state is, the state ever the same. But an *ajñānin*, a man inflicted with ignorance, falsely imagines himself a doer to wander purposeless and ever in the false appearances that his *vāsanā* weaves for him. Ever attached to pleasures, pleasures of the body, he finds unrest alone as his portion, unrest in the shape of pleasure and pain, weal and woe. A man should, therefore, give a serious thought to the two states of being mentioned above and try his best to give up the false notion that he is a doer, and release himself from the thick and dense web it spreads out for him, this false notion about his self, this his sense of Me and Mine. And having given up this false notion, let him devote himself to the remembrance of the Name and contemplation of the Word, remembrance and contemplation that will lead him to peace the highest, peace beyond every reckoning. Every man, wise and accomplished, should have firm faith in the reality of the *ātman*, of the self, to dispel the darkness that the *anātman*, the not-self, is, darkness bereft of every life and being.

Saying 36. The sum and substance of all this is that one should believe and know that the *ātman* alone is real, that it alone is the light that illumines the whole world and that it alone is its sustainer, that of the world, and that it alone, that reality the supreme, is the life and being of all that is. And equipped with this belief and knowledge, one should remember the Name and contemplate the *ātman* steadfastly and with faith the true. If a man believes this way and contemplates this way, he will, through this *yoga*, attain to the goal highest, the goal ever the same, for that is the way one can eradicate the false notion that one is a doer. Let every man reflect on this redemptive thought, let him interiorise it, make it a living thought, and resort to the true path and attain all that is to be attained, namely, the bliss that *samatā* is.

Saying 37. Within every living being, every mortal, abides that bliss the eternal, shines that light the eternal, but the darkness that the false appearance of the Me and the Mine is, does not let one know it, that Real the Absolute. Therefore, one should adhere to the right and true path to eradicate the false identity one has identified oneself with, the false identity in the shape of the doer, and adopt the disposition of devotion, devotion pure of all taints. That is how one can attain to all that is to be attained to, that is the way one can find the peace one seeks. Only that endeavour is holy and pure in the eyes of seers, of those that have become one with the Real, the endeavour that eradicates all the pain and anguish of life, eradicates it through self-surrender to the Real. That is what every mortal who has come to be born in this transient world should make the concern of his life.

Saying 38. Devotion the pure means worship within of the One Name, meditation of it ever and always, leaving one's acts and deeds to the will of the Lord. It means self-surrender to the Lord, having ceased to determinate and to desire. That is the true devotion, the devotion that enables the *buddhi* to free itself from the desire to act and to stay still and stable, its intention all focussed within. No action can then bind it, for all-concentrated it remains on the Word, that Real the Imperishable. That is the state of redemption the highest, the state of *samatā*, that bliss ever the same.

Saying 39. When the *buddhi* breaks itself free from the ties of action, action that holds in its grip every embodied being, and leaves every consideration of its well being or ill being to the will of the Lord to become all-focussed on the One Name - when the *buddhi* gets oriented this way, it comes to know the Truth within to become one with that Truth, leaving far behind all its *vāsanā*, that source of every pain and misery. Supremely blissful is that state, that state of *samatā*, one's own true and native being.

Saying 40. The desire for bodily pleasures ever keeps the *buddhi* restless, forcing it into action again and again, birth after birth. Therefore, one should keep in balance all the pleasures of the body, letting not one dominate the other, and live solely as the Lord wills one to live. With this disposition of self-restraint and self-surrender should one give oneself to a sustained meditation of the true Name. That is the way man can redeem himself from his condition of perpetual unrest. Let him cease to determinate, let him free himself from this futile and disastrous function. Let only the Name occupy him, ever and always, whether he is active or at rest, his weal and woe left to the will of the Lord. That is how his *buddhi* will shed the identity of the doer, that darkness primordial, and come to know and be *ātman* the still and passive and be ever blessed in itself. Knowing the light that is consciousness and becoming that light, it will become still and stable, no happiness touching it and no unhappiness. No desire will stir up in it then and no action, passively still it will remain, lost in bliss the supreme that *ātman* the Word is. That verily is the state of wakefulness true and real, the state in which the *buddhi*, washed clean of the desire to act and of all that desire fashions and projects, merges in the Imperishable Stillness, that Reality the transcendent to become one with That. He alone can know what this state is, only he who has known it and become one with it. Blessed is that man and blessed is his glory, his very word a word of redemption.

Saying 41. Self-surrender to the Lord means dissociation from the pleasures of the organs of cognition and action, that only. When the *buddhi* makes the One Name its sole refuge, it sheds all its failings and deviations and remains ever absorbed in the *ātman*, that purity itself. That is what has been called the state still, the state action-free, the state in which the *buddhi* no longer identifies itself with the bodily actions, staying stable in Word the non-active. That is what absorption in *yoga* too is, this, its staying still and passive in and with the Word. To stay apart from the pleasures associated with functions of sense-cognition and conation, giving oneself solely to the meditation of the Name, is the way to eradicate one's identification with the body. That verily is renunciation the true, the renunciation that leads to the realisation of the self within, that light eternal and peace the highest.

Saying 42. The pleasures of the organs of sense and activity are merely another name for misery and suffering. The world itself is nothing else than these pleasures, it is these that constitute the motivating force behind the recurring process of birth and death. It is these pleasures that keep one away from the bliss that one's own *ātman*, one's own self, is. One cannot however get rid of those pleasures unless one ceases to identify oneself as a doer. No renunciation can help one eradicate the passion for them, not even the life of a forest dweller. For that passion stays obstinate in man unless its root, identification of the self with doing, is uprooted.

Saying 43. As long as a being imagines himself a doer, he will remain an enjoyer/sufferer too. And as long as he is an enjoyer/sufferer, he will be inflicted with the feelings or the sensations of pleasure and pain. And as long as these sensations of pleasure and pain are there, there will be desire, worry, fear, infatuation and other deviations to seize and hold him under their grip. This is all that *Māyā* is and what it projects.

Saying 44. To free oneself from this grip of the passions of the organs is a task hard and difficult, which only a man with a true heroic mettle can accomplish. To accomplish this rare feat, one should, as a first step towards that end, keep in restraint his desires for pleasures, bring them into harmony with each other. This he can do if he earns a simple living, and that too through honest and upright means, with his *buddhi* ever concentrated on the meditation of the Name. He must have every faith in and devotion for the Lord and his guru, his mind disinterested in each and every pleasure of the sense- and motor organs, pleasures that last not beyond a moment. Equipped with the strength of devotion true, he should give up every desire, his life surrendered fully and absolutely to the will of the Lord. That is how the *buddhi* comes to shed its determinating nature and gives itself up to the contemplation of the Name, its hunger all appeased. This is what *bhakti*, devotion, in its truth is.

Saying 45. One comes to truly extricate oneself from the grip of the pleasures of the organs, when one comes to be concentrated on Word the Imperishable, with nothing to distract one from that concentration. And that verily is what brings full satisfaction to this mortal being, that devotion true and exclusive to the Word. To make the Lord one's sole refuge, to do so with faith true and genuine and never to deviate from one's true being and self is the paramount duty of every mortal, duty that he must perform. For, it is only when its passion for the pleasures of the sense- and motor organs dies down that the *buddhi* truly comes to meditate the Name and attain to the Word, that Bliss the Eternal and Desire-free, that Peace Eternal and Indestructible. It is then, and only then, that it, the *buddhi*, comes to be free from the ties of action. Remembrance of the Name it is that brings about the end of one's false identity, identity of the doer, and leads the *buddhi* to merge itself in the *ātman*, that light the still and passive. He who has attained to this state, has truly attained to that which is beyond the reach of the sense- and motor organs, beyond the ambit of the phenomenal world, beyond the sphere of the three *guṇas*, beyond time and beyond the reach of every measure, every means of cognition. To self the true and real has he attained, to self the holy and pure, self that never deviates from itself. To bliss the full and the highest has he attained, to the state beyond the reach of every regret and affliction, himself turning into peace itself. He has known what is worthy of being known, the state of sameness, the state of *nirvāṇa*, the state where there is no going and no coming, no birth, no death and no rebirth. Only the man that has liberated himself from the pleasures of *prakṛti*, that primal Other, and has come to stay with and as his own being, his own true self, he alone is the man adorable. Rare is a man of this mettle, his life all glory, to which every being should pay every tribute. His long pilgrimage has found its end, pilgrimage without a beginning, his desires all appeased, his peace eternal, and his very being [a] being-without-a-desire. Redemptive is the very sight of such a soul, and redemptive is the word he speaks.

Let every *premī*, every devotee, reflect on 'On Understanding *Samatā*,' on this holy text; let him do so with the mind of a true seeker of the truth. And let his false identity, identity as a doer, come to be extinct, that source and root of every pain and misery, giving place to the all-blessed devotion to the Real. Let him this way find within him Word the Imperishable, Word ever the Same. That is the duty of every human being, his duty the highest and noblest. May the Lord bless every being with effort the true to attain to goal the true, to the Truth itself!

(ii) *Hidden Instruction of the Preceptor True*

Instruction 1. Seek the life true, giving up every pleasure of the mind. For that will lead you to peace the full and infinite.

Pleasures of the mind are misery itself, to be immersed in them is to miss the end of life, to remain unaware and ignorant of that end. Seek to know what life in its truth is; that indeed is true seeking and true investigation, that investigation of the source and secret of life. But unattained it remains, that life the true, until one ceases to identify oneself with the mind, with the body, with the organs of sense and activity and with breath. Life the Power that dispenses life and being to beings, is all full in itself, is verily bliss itself. Only fervent devotion to that Real, Real the Supreme, can enable one triumph over all the deviations that go with the mind. To live all dedicated to that Real is to work for one's true end and goal, end and goal of the being called man.

Instruction 2. The mind, the body, the organs of sense and activity and breath ever deviate from themselves, but with their deviation, that Life, that dispenser of life, never deviates from itself. Ever the same it remains, in all the three dimensions of time. Fear and delusion will ever pursue the *buddhi* as long as it remains tied to and oriented towards the mind, the body, the sense and motor organs and breath. When it becomes aware of that Life within, it dissociates itself from the mind, the body, the organs and breath, losing every interest in them and the world they experience or deal with. That is its moment the blessed, the moment when it comes to finally rest and stay still. That verily is the goal of life, that blessed state of becoming stillness itself, peace itself.

Instruction 3. Ever active remain these - the mind, the body, the organs and breath, never do they come to stay and be still. Associating itself with these and their activities, the *buddhi* reaps the results of their activities to turn happy or unhappy, its happiness and unhappiness ever keeping it on the move, without a let or a respite. Let man, therefore, steadfastly remain faithful to Word the Real, let him make that *ātman*, self, his sole refuge and anchor. For that is how he can withdraw from his mind, his body, his organs and from the breath he breathes, that is how he will stand apart from them to know and be Word the still and imperishable and find the peace he is truly in search of. Therein lies his endeavour the true to attain to his goal the supreme.

Instruction 4. To move with the organs, those of sense and activity, means to identify oneself with the body. To move with the mind means to identify oneself with those organs. And in the motion of breath lies the motion of the mind too. As long as the *buddhi* does not perceive the motion of breath, perceive it every moment, staying still and passive, it cannot undo its identification with breath. It behoves, therefore, every seeker of the truth that he give himself to meditation of the Name, the Name vouchsafed to him by a preceptor true, make it his sole refuge and support. For, that will lead him to triumph over this instrument of *Māyā*, this complex of body, organs, mind and breath. Therein lie the highest *yoga*, the highest devotion and the highest *tapas*, in this self-submission to the Name.

Instruction 5. When the *buddhi*, whether active or withdrawn, self-submits to the Name vouchsafed to it, when it gets so suffused with devotion to It that not a moment passes without its remembrance of the Name, it will find the Word Imperishable to become one with It, with Word the bliss supreme, that life and light of the world. Blessed with knowledge, knowledge that is not an acquisition but its very being and self, it transcends all the deviations that *prakṛti* is subject to. No sense of Me and Mine then remains to inflict it, the sense that conceals its own truth and being from it. It merely stays with the Word to finally merge in It. Here all its unrest comes to cease, its passion for self-affirmation having come to rest. Let this thought become the guiding principle of your life and being to lead you onwards. Let it lead you to your being the true and real, being without a relationship and without a desire, being that is the Real itself, that is Word the Imperishable, your very own self! Abiding in That alone will you abide ever the same.

Saying 1. Every mortal being, in the depths of his being, seeks peace the holy, peace that he cannot find unless and until his needs and desires, each and every one of them, do not come to be extinct. And desires will come to be extinct, when he ceases to identify himself with the body and makes the Lord alone his sole refuge, leaving his very life and being to His will. And identification with the body comes to an end when he makes simplicity, truthfulness, service of fellow beings, self-submission to the seers and to the word of revelation and yogic meditation and such other observances the guiding and regulating principles of his life. He is to balance his desires one with the other, keep a harmony among them through self-restraint, giving up every unnecessary need. This mode of life will lead him to leave his life to the will and care of the Lord, bringing to an end his identification with the body and the disposition of selfishness that identification gives birth to. That is the way he can find his salvation.

(a) *On Self-submission unto the Body*

Saying 2. a) To live ever immersed in the pleasures of the body.

b) To live self-submitted to one's family, to be ever active for the sake of its interests.

c) To live self-submitted to one's sect, one's religion and one's society - to remain active to make them flourish and progress.

d) To live self-submitted to one's country - to sacrifice oneself for its reformation.

However, if a man is inflicted with thoughts of selfishness, he will do no good to himself or his family, his sect or religion or his country. To bring that about, he has to first surrender himself, his very life and being, to the Lord, for only that can bring about the purity of his mind, that spirit of self-surrender, only that can make possible every triumph and bring about every kind of peace and harmony [personal, familial, religious and national and inter-national].

(b) *On the Spirit of Self-submission unto the Lord*

Saying 3. Giving up all one's interests, to live as the Lord wills one to live and think well of others and do well unto them as much as one can - this way of life sums up the spirit of self-surrender unto the Lord, this disposition. The body comes to be sanctified by this spirit of self-surrender, and so do one's family and clan, and so do flourish one's society and one's country. Only by living according to the Divine Law can a richly gifted person reform himself and his family, his society and his country. Giving up all thoughts of self-interest, he is to do well unto others, to all living beings, as much he can, do so as duty-bound and with utmost humility, without a reference to himself. That is the way to peace, peace within and peace without. Without this spirit of self-surrender to the Lord, no being can bring about any genuine change for the better in any sphere whatsoever. For, his mental stains will not let him follow the right path with a firm resolve - will not let him do genuine good unto others, not steadfastly. The spirit of self-surrender unto the Lord alone is the centre of every progress, the source perennial of every kind of peace, personal or social. The very acme of joy is He, the Lord, the Truth itself is He, the very Spirit that dwells in every mortal body, dispensing it life and being. A living being must turn within to pray unto Him, to that Being *before* every being, to contemplate Him and live as He ordains him to live. Only then will he find the true purpose of his life, the purpose that will put an end to all his unrest and seeking. And only then will come to an end his dark ignorance, his identification with the body, his self-submission to it and the selfishness that goes with that self-submission. To be brief, only the spirit of self-submission to the Lord can undo his passion for the false appearance that the world is - as much the extent of that self-submission so much the extinction of that passion. The process, this process of progression, ultimately culminates in his merger in the Lord, in *nirvāṇa*, in peace the eternal, peace that is Sameness itself.

(iii) *On Reforming Oneself and Society*

Saying 1. To adhere to the five regulative principles, those of simplicity, service, truthfulness, *sat-saṅga* and yogic meditation - to adhere to them firmly and resolutely is to ensure every progress and every well being: personal, social and spiritual.

Saying 2. Let every member of the *saṅgat*, of the assembly of those that strive alike for the end alike, whose effort is for the truth and whose goal is the truth, make it a point to do every act of service, whether high or low. For that is the way to live in harmony and for uplift [true and genuine].

Saying 3. To be well intentioned towards such co-pilgrims and towards mankind at large, one's very being flowing towards them with feeling and delight, is the way to the uplift - one's own and of others. Let it be remembered that service unto others is just another name of *Samatā*.

Saying 4. To reduce his needs, reduce them in abundance, and spend his resources - physical, mental and of possessions - spend them without a self-interest, is an imperative duty for every *premī*, every devotee of *Samatā*. Therein lies every progress and every kind of uplift and every kind of peace, in the observance of that duty.

Saying 5. Those members of the *saṅgat* that dedicate themselves unto service of every kind, dedicate themselves to every possible extent, will find their glory spread out in the whole world, howsoever small their number may be.

Saying 6. An example should be a man to his family, to the members of the social group he belongs to - an inspiration for noble conduct and upright life. Great good will come out of it, and peace and harmony. Every person that lives surrendered to a seer of the truth and his word should see to it that he be an example of this kind.

Saying 7. Myriad kinds of people live in the world, some gifted with high intelligence, others with low intelligence. But if and when an occasion demands, they all stick to the right path, making every sacrifice for that purpose, and, despite their sacrifice, take no credit for it but take it as mere their duty, then these persons by setting their example will turn a blessing for the people of the world. For, reveal will they, these devotees of the truth, the true *dharma*, the true Law, unto the world.

Saying 8. If a *premī*, a devotee, of the *saṅgat*, lives true to the five regulative principles of *Samatavāda*, then it is the bounden duty of his brethren to give him every encouragement. And if there is a member of the *saṅgat* who deviates from his principles, then with utmost consideration and care should he be brought back to those principles. For, only love can purify a misled *buddhi*. To hate him and slight him will be a harmful approach. When that fallen being comes to realise his mistake, he will receive every censure by the *saṅgat* with utmost regard for it. An example will he become for the *saṅgat*, that repentant soul. Love alone is the cure for all faults, that alone can lead the *saṅgat* to prosper and flourish.

Saying 9. If the *premīs* of the *saṅgat* diligently observe the regulative principles, the very embodiments of love will they turn into to breathe life and soul to their caste and country. Let there be no doubt about this.

Saying 10. Let every *premī* of the *saṅgat* avoid debates and disputes. Let his life itself be the means of communication to others. That is the way to do good unto others and to spread among them the right ways of life and conduct. Those who confine themselves to mere talk and theories never reach their goal. That is the truth that every *premī* should know.

Saying 11. Let every *premī* regularly participate in *sat-saṅga* and learn the true instruction there. Let him reflect on that instruction and, then, live and regulate his life according to that instruction. Only that *saṅgat* can flourish and prosper that knows and lives by this truth; only that *saṅgat* can become all-powerful and show the way of peace to the world.

Saying 12. Only one's noble conduct can reform others. Therefore, only that *saṅgat* can and will flourish that does good unto others, does so in real, practical spirit.

Saying 13. Let there be no hurry in reforming the wrong customs and practices prevalent in one's caste and country. The process should be slow, more through example than through precepts. That is the way to make all beings follow the right path and adopt the right conduct, follow these willingly without a fret and without a resistance.

Saying 14. Let there be no doctrinaire disputes with other *saṅgats*, whatever their faith and principles. Only their inner troubles should be understood and recognised, recognised and understood with every good will. If you adopt this approach of understanding and good will towards them, they will spontaneously adopt your principles and your mode of life.

Saying 15. The *saṅgat* should be fully open minded towards what seers and prophets have taught unto the world, taking every inspiration from the life they led and the sacrifices they made. If a *saṅgat* is equipped with this disposition, it will find its message spread out in the whole world. For, all living beings are, in their heart of hearts, inflicted with the same frustration and the same suffering, and the cure for that existential malady of theirs is also almost the same - the cure in the form of life dedicated to the Spirit within. A careful thought will make this point clear and lucid. But only the example your actual life presents before others, the kind of life you actually lead, can wake others into the life dedicated to the Spirit, and not mere your words and precepts.

Saying 16. Every being perceives the world and lives in it as determined by what he finds himself to be. The world is as his being is. Therefore, one must redeem one's own life before one can think of redeeming others. This verily is the Law, Law the Divine.

Saying 17. A being that offers his joys and pleasures unto others, is verily an ideal for the *saṅgat* and for the country. If every *premī* of the *saṅgat* imbibes this spirit of self-sacrifice, then blessed will turn other beings and blessed will be their lives.

Saying 18. Every living being lives obsessed with himself. That is the truth about him. Motivated compulsively by this his nature, he ever increases his wants and desires, posing a threat to others around him, thereby causing great distress to himself no less than to other beings. When a sub-society or a land comes to be possessed by this obsession for selfhood, it is bound to lose its power and glory to meet one day its doom. For, this obsession is all evil and all discord. To save oneself from this obsession for self-concern is to be human, human in truth.

Saying 19. A mortal that purifies his life and conduct, knowing for certain that the world he would possess and relate to is a mere passing show, he alone can be a teacher true for his *saṅgat* and for his land. When alive, he dispenses peace unto others, and when dead he becomes an inspiration for the people, an ideal to emulate and follow.

Saying 20. A man who keeps his needs in restraint and in balance, who, in other words, has made simplicity a regulative principle of his life, and who, shedding all cunning and fraud, ever strives to be truthful, is verily the man of noble conduct, his life noble and oriented upwards. Spacious enough is his heart to accommodate ideals that all seers and prophets cherished and lived for, a true participant in *sat-saṅga* is he, the man of this generous and open disposition. Lives he in service of others, spending his resources - physical, mental and material - for the welfare of others. And finding in the Lord alone the soul and anchor of his being, he ever stays stable in meditation of the Name, the Name that a seer of the highest order has initiated him into. Only a man of this noble mettle can reform his life in truth, a life that will be an inspiration and example to emulate for his *saṅgat* and for his land and country.

Engaged in purifying itself this way, the *saṅgat* [dedicated to *Samatāvāda*, to the Doctrine of *Samatā*] too should offer itself to the uplift of other people. A blessing in all times is this *sādhanā*, this endeavour, and the very essence of human life. For, all that is, is the *ātman*, the self, itself and all living beings ever wander in search of *śānti*, of peace that passeth understanding. Therefore, it is necessary that the *saṅgat* should understand what *samatā* in its essence and spirit is, and surrender itself to the Lord and give itself to the service of others. That is the way to make one's country and social life move forward in the true sense of the term. And that is the way to be blessed in mind, to be suffused with peace the transcendental. When a man's life comes to be so pure and so full of care and concern for others, disinterested will become his *buddhi* vis-a-vis the affairs of the world. On the Name will it become focussed, on that alone, this all exclusive contemplation culminating in its absorption in the *ātman*, that supremely blessed state, its being and home ultimate.

Saying 21. The sum and substance of all that has been said is that it is the extent of a being's belief in the reality of the *ātman* that determines the extent of his capacity to give up and renounce. And it is his renunciation that can lead him upwards, only that. Therefore, let a being understand what the path of Samatā in its essence and truth is, and give up his sense of identity with the body so that he may come to find the *ātman* alone as his life and being. Let him know and understand that his worldly life is of little account. And with this thought staying firm with him, let him do whatever he is called upon to do without a self-concern and a self-interest. That is how he can sanctify his pilgrimage, a pilgrimage that will be a blessing alike for him and for others. This verily has been the way of those that lived for the truth and became the truth, the way that has been a light and inspiration for all mortals.

Saying 22. To be excessively concerned with one's own interests is to invite ruin upon oneself. It is, therefore, imperative for man that his concern for his own interests should not transgress the norms of righteousness and also that he should strive to attain to the Real, his goal ultimate. Only that *saṅgat* can truly flourish that lives committed to these two, to the purity of worldly life and to striving for the supreme end. For, that is what life the divine really is.

Saying 23. A true *saṅgat* would uplift itself through noble thoughts, would ever strive for that end, with good will for all its guiding principle. Not even the wheel of time can undo such a *saṅgat*, the wheel that lets nothing to stay and persist. With patience it would endure every hostility and every adversity. A *saṅgat* so nobly oriented and so meekly disposed will, one day, shine bright in the world, to be a light and a guide for the whole world. That verily is the Law, the Law ordained by the Lord.

Saying 24. Those who, endowed with cultured minds, seek to take up with every pure intent great undertakings in their life will find the ways to their goals spontaneously open out before them. For, it is only good will and service of others that constitute the real basis for every great undertaking. But only that man can do good unto others who has first done good unto himself, done it through giving up his self-concerns and self-interests. Only through this way can one redeem oneself. A man or a *saṅgat* that seeks to find the highest reaches of his or its possibilities should, therefore, adhere firmly to this way, for it is through seeking the good of others that one can find one's own good. That is the way to *parama-śānti*, to peace the transcendental.

Saying 25. There is no greater blessing than that the mind should come to rest. That is what every being, in the deepest of his deeps, is ever in search of. But that does not fall to one's lot unless one gives up his own comforts for the sake of others, keeping for himself only as many as do not come into conflict with each other, one comfort or pleasure with other comforts and pleasures. Therefore, those souls that lived for the truth and as the truth found the essence of life in giving their own comforts to others and taking their miseries upon themselves and in remaining steadfast to the contemplation of the *ātman*, that bliss the highest. Rare is a man of this noble disposition, a revelation verily of the Path is he, and a guide and light for his land and country. Let every man endowed with noble culture adopt this way, adopt it with a firm conviction. As for the devotees of *Samatā*, they should ever live by this thought, purifying themselves thereby. Let them ever remain faithful to this path, taking it as their duty the most imperative. That is the way to every attainment and every achievement, the goal of peace the absolute, peace that has no other to constitute it. And that is the way to lead others too from their darkness to light. In that lies the glory of the human birth, in following this path to deliverance. May the Lord bless people with a disposition ever open to Truth the Ultimate![8]

(iv) *On Power: the Conditioned and the Unconditioned*

Saying 1. Power is, in the ultimate analysis, of two kinds: Power as conditioned by the Other, and Power the Alone, Power without an Other.

Saying 2. The doer, doing, the result of doing, the world, that is, of the five elements, constituted by them, is Power conditioned by the Other, the Power called *Māyā*. And Power the Alone and Absolute is the *ātman*. Beyond the reach of every change of the other Power called *Māyā*, this Power subsists ever the same, this Real the Highest and Imperishable. Without a support it subsists, all different and all transcendent.

Saying 3. Without becoming aware of these two Powers, aware with every lucidity, the *buddhi* cannot find peace the absolute and fear-free [peace without an other to negate it], cannot win triumph the irreversible. One should therefore do one's best to understand what the Power without an Other is and what the Power constituted by its Other is.

Saying 4. Without knowing and becoming one with Power the Alone and Unconditioned, one cannot possibly determinate and establish what the Power along with and conditioned by its Other really is. Therefore, to know the Power without an Other, to cognise it as what it truly is, is to be redeemed from one's being the conditioned.

Saying 5. From Power along with its Other, Power the Conditioned, from, that is to say, changes in the five elements that constitute the visible world, spring the hugely degrading passions of sensuality, wrath, greed, infatuation and self-hood. These passions, these products of the elements, the *buddhi* attributes to itself to live ever insecure and in fear and find the body it has identified itself with fall in no time. Thus in despair it departs from this transient world. That is the kind of life it, the Power conditioned by the other, unfolds before it, life dark and beastly.

Saying 6. When, on the contrary, the *buddhi* comes to know Power the Alone and Unconditioned, that *ātman* the sole and single reality, it comes to be free from desire, turns truthful and humble to stay unconcerned and stable in the midst of what happens or does not happen, its life dedicated to the welfare of others. These are the redeeming traits it comes to acquire then, traits that enable it to become one with that Power the Alone. In this very life, it finds itself blessed with peace, peace the still and transcendent, to be a guide to mortals to their salvation. *Sat-puruṣas,* men the true, are they that have become blessed thus and live blessed thus.

Saying 7. All forms of progress, whether that relating to a body (individual) or to a social group or to one's land

and country, belong to the sphere of Power the Conditioned, conditioned by its other. But no real and genuine progress in these spheres is possible without faith in the Lord, faith unfailing and absolute. Only allegiance and fealty to that Real the Supreme, that *ātman*, is *the* way open for human beings, the way to their prosperity no less than to their liberation.

Saying 8. It is only through self-submitting to Power the Alone that the *buddhi* can subdue Power the Conditioned. It is only that kind of *buddhi* that can reveal unto the world the regulative principles of life, principles suitable and in accord with the given conditions and circumstances. Only that *buddhi*, *buddhi*-in-peace, can emanate peace unto others. That has been the way of seers and the enlightened.

Saying 9. The conflicts inflicting the conditioned mode of being cannot be composed and reconciled without resorting to Power the Alone, resorting to it as one's being and self. For, that Power, Power the Unconditioned, is unto Power the Conditioned as a root is unto a tree. The *buddhi* can make a proper use of *prakṛti*, the forces of matter, only when it finds its being in the *ātman*, not when it is pitted against them [as it does when it seeks in the body the support for its being] to invite their hostility upon itself. But that is how *Māyā* operates - in terms of dualities and opposites.

Saying 10. A social group or a country where people live self-submitted to the *ātman*, live disinterested, humble and truthful and given to good will for, and to the spirit of service unto, others - only that social group or land can reveal to other social groups or lands how to make the right use of Power the Conditioned. This is as true in their case as it is in the case of an individual vis-a-vis other individuals. And it is such individuals and such groups and lands that can inspire in others a living faith in Power the Unconditioned, Power that is, in every truth, one's very life and being. On the contrary, those individuals or social groups or countries that are given to wicked ways, to fraud, arrogance and self-seeking, and nurture hatred and jealousy towards others live bereft of every belief in the truth and bring only ruin upon themselves. People of such lands lose every capacity to live together as a social group and live under subjugation of those nations or groups that live and conduct themselves in the right way, way oriented towards the truth. That is how operates the Law in the social context.

Saying 11. Therefore, it is incumbent on any individual or society desirous of self-development to adhere to the true principles of life - principles that help one self-submit to the *ātman*. Then and only then can Power the Conditioned be directed towards accord, harmony and patience - the traits that ensure all harmony and achievement - to make life free of anxiety and fears.

Saying 12. When a man comes to live with Power the Alone and Unconditioned as his sole refuge and support, he comes to be free from all the good and the evil that Power the Conditioned is inflicted with, with all his passions spent out and extinct. To *Samatā* the Bliss he attains to then, that man the great, to *nirvāṇa*, to liberation from the ever-recurring process of births and deaths.

Saying 13. To believe in *ātman*, *ātman* that is all power and all life, to find it as one's very being and support is to attain all that is to be attained, to acquire all the power that is there, to be all pure and to be all successful. With that as his refuge and anchor, let man shed all his tainted *vāsanas*, let him reflect on the truth revealed unto him and augment thereby his devotion for the Lord, his sole resort and support. Let him live for the true principles, let him spend himself in their observance, his concerns for himself given up. Let him live for the Lord and for others, with every pure intent, without a self-interest. That is the way, *the* way to his redemption, to his liberation.

Saying 14. With the deepening of the *buddhi's* self-submission to the *ātman*, its freedom from the sway of Power the Conditioned too deepens, from, that is to say, the dualities that the results of actions are, results with their negation inscribed into them. With that freedom attained, it comes to be full in itself, giving up all its desires even before the death of the body. Into the all blissful *ātman* it merges then, attaining the state highest and supreme.

Saying 15. If the *buddhi* orients itself towards the opposite direction and, obsessed with Power the Conditioned, does every action motivated by desire for the the results it can bring about, then all the dark *vāsanās* come to possess it to undo it and others. This is how live those persons whose souls have ceased to be living souls, have turned all dull and inert. To live a life of restraint, keeping in harmony all one's needs and desires, is to be human. Man must think and act and desire as self-submitted to the *ātman*; let him not think, act and desire in a way that leads him away from the *ātman*. For, that is the only way he can live blessed here and attain to the Truth hereafter. Let all devotees give their thought to what has been said here about Power the Conditioned and the Unconditioned and strive for the true goal of their life. May the Lord bless them with genuine faith and belief!

(v) Samatā: *the Highest Self-Sovereignty*

Saying 1. Peace the full is *Samatā,* and knowledge the full, state the perfect and seeking the perfect. And striving the perfect it is and purity the perfect and experience the full of life the human. And bliss too is it, bliss the highest and transcendental.

Saying 2. Knowing That and becoming That, one finds one's needs become all fulfilled. Nothing more remains for one to desire, nothing more to know. For to know that Life the Pure and free from every desire, to know that One that is the all, to know that Word the still and without a beginning is indeed to know all and live the very essence of life. To be absolutely free it is - to know the Word and be the Word -, to be the absolute Sovereign unto oneself. For no desire can bind one there, for beyond the reach of desire it is, that Bliss itself.

Saying 3. Let this be a conviction with every human being that it is one's own purity that can make others pure, that it is one's own self-sacrifice that can [prompt others to strive for their] deliverance. For, only through giving up one's own comforts can one give comforts to others and that it is only a liberated soul that can inspire others to liberate themselves - to make every sacrifice for that end. And that it is only what one knows and has become one with that can inspire faith in others to work for their self-purification. The entire *prakṛti*, the entire sphere of the not-self, moves alike in all its spheres: the passions of the organs of sense and action and the desires of the mind burn alike each and every being here, forcing him to act for their fulfillment. But instead of fulfilling them, his efforts intensify them all the more, making him miserable all the more, his obsession with the Me and the Mine never letting him know what bliss the state of *samatā* is. Frustration and despair alone fall to his lot when he departs from the world. All folly is this mode of life, all-dry and bereft of spirit.

Saying 4. Human birth is a cherished birth, for in this birth it is possible to dispel the darkness that the sense of Me and Mine is. Here, in this birth, a being can attain to the state of absolute sovereignty that the state of *samatā*, sameness, is and make his life truly blessed and be an example and ideal for others to follow and emulate.

Saying 5. Without being fully faithful to the principles he cherishes, faithful in his life and being, a man can redeem neither himself nor others. It behoves him, therefore, that he first reform his own life; that is the way to bless himself and others. Every being knows the evils that reside in his mind, but feels helpless to get rid of them. That is the universally valid truth. So, if there is a man who has been successful in understanding and eradicating his own faults, he will have the ability to be a guide to all others, he alone can redeem them and save them.

Saying 6. As long as the *buddhi* cannot bring the organs of sense and activity and the mind under its full control, it cannot find the bliss that is ever the same. Restraint of the organs of sense and activity and of the mind alone, thus, constitutes true freedom and peace the transcendental. To live given to them, to the organs and the mind, is verily misery the absolute. From bondage to bondage moves that man, he who lives subject to them.

Saying 7. As long as the *buddhi* is associated with the I-sense, it remains a slave to all kinds of *vāsanā*, the changes of mind and the organs ever keeping it on the move. No effort on its part can bring it peace, peace with no *other* to undo it, its life remaining a life of misery, misery the absolute.

Saying 8. There is only one way to save oneself from this appalling misery, that of dissociating the *buddhi* from the deviations of the organs and the mind through right effort and with a right disposition. Only then can the *buddhi* find the bliss that is ever the same, with no duality to inflict it, bliss that is stillness itself, that is Word the Imperishable Itself. For, knowing it, the *buddhi* will turn into it, into that very bliss. Then and only then can one become a true sovereign unto himself.

Saying 9. It is only when one's *buddhi* becomes free from the taint of selfhood that one comes to be absolutely pure. Only the *endeavour* directed towards that end can bring one *śānti*, the peace that passeth understanding. Therefore, let man purify himself through contemplation of the Name vouchsafed unto him by a seer abiding in the Truth and as the Truth.

Saying 10. Let the organs sense and act in harmony, let them not come into conflict with each other. For therein lies conduct the pure and holy. And let man abide in the Truth, staying ever still and stable in obedience to the will of the Lord, his mind at rest, its passions fell all extinct.

Saying 11. In one word, to contemplate the Name revealed unto a being, contemplate it with faith the steadfast and the full in the *ātman,* the Real, giving up the results of all his actions to the will of that Inbeing is the way to dispel the darkness that identification with action is, that primal seed of the moving world, of recurring births and deaths. Ever aware that the world he perceives is a passing appearance, let him make the *avināśī puruṣ*a, Man the Imperishable, his sole and final refuge, his body, mind and possessions ever in the service of others with no expectation of a return. Let him be ever humble, his mind purged of every desire, solely given to devotion to the *ātman.* Into *Samatā* will he merge, a man of this disposition and endeavour, into that state all enlightened and all still. Return will he to his home, his own native home. Apart from *prakṛti* will he stay, from the snare of the five elements it has woven for him, abiding with Real the Supreme, abiding as that Real the Supreme, all fulfilled and appeased.

Saying 12. When the *buddhi* becomes purified of the ego of agency, it abides unattached to the activities of the mind and the organs, cognitive and motor. No thoughts arise in it then and no counter thoughts, ever awake it stays then in and by itself. When one's *buddhi* comes to be purified thus, one lives the life true and highest. Only the man who has attained to this state knows what self-sovereignty in its very truth is. He has cut asunder all the ties that *Māyā* forged for him, has dispelled all the darkness that the state of bondage was and has come to attain a state which no fear will ever visit. Holy will be his endeavour, truly a dispenser of life unto others.

Saying 13. Let a being get rid of all the defects that stain his mind. Only then can he attain to the self-sovereignty that the state of *samatā* alone is. Let him ever do good unto others, with a disposition devoid of pride, that enemy the worst, his life ever given to the care of the Lord. Let him ever stay still and alike whether in prosperity or in adversity. Let him deliver himself from the grip of desire, that misery the absolute, taking his refuge in devotion to the Lord, devotion that blesses a man with every perfection and every peace. And let him find and realise *ātman* the true, that support of all abiding ever the same.

Saying 14. Truly noble is the man who has adhered to this holiest of all the holy endeavours, holy will be his conduct and holy his state of being, holy will be his knowledge and his abiding as that knowledge, and all holy will be the fervour of his devotion. Countless mortals will he save thereby, by these traits of his. He alone is the Person, Person the true and real, a knower is he of all that is to be known. His word will be redemptive and redemptive will be his proximity. Let there be no doubt about this.

Saying 15. Every being should know wherein lies the true progress of life so that he may, with that knowledge, strive for the state of being true and real, freeing himself from the dark delusion that his unappeasable desire is. Let him thus make blessed his little and mean life. Let him ever abide in conduct the pure. And let every being be disposed well towards his fellow beings, a relationship of love binding them together. Therein lies the glory of the human birth, that alone is humanity the true and genuine.

(vi) *The Message of Word the Truth*

Samatā alone is Life the Eternal, Peace the Eternal and Self-sovereignty the Eternal

Saying 1. A prince one may be or a beggar, a man of wealth may he be or a man of penury, a land may be ruled by the system of monarchy or the system of democracy, but the sense of Me and Mine will not cease to reign supreme in life, personal and social. Accordingly, seeking the good for oneself and the ill for others becomes the ruling passion of life, negating the very possibility of concordance and content. Every being thus lives in discontent and dies in discontent, every hope deserting him at his last hour. Making every effort, his life remains a frustration, fulfillment, fulfillment the true, ever evading him.

Saying 2. Investigation of matter, of the gross elements, howsoever deep or thorough, cannot appease this being's thirst and seeking. Only investigation of the Spirit can, of the Power that dispenses life to all beings, the Spirit that is *samatā* itself.

Saying 3. No social group or nation can sustain its progressive thrust by increasing its wants and desires, giving them a full vent; it can be sustained only if it is accompanied by investigation of the life spirit within. Unbridled increase of wants and desires often leads to ruin and destruction. That is what one should ever keep in mind.

Saying 4. The desire of every being, desire real and ontological, is verily the state of *samatā*, it is the desire to stay self-same ever and always. But swayed by his passions, he turns all narcissistic in his life, whether as an individual or a member of a social group or a citizen of a country, provoking destruction alike for his soul and for others. In unrest he lives and in unrest he dies, unrest without a measure, the full appeasement of his real thirst never falling to his lot. His entire endeavour, endeavour prompted by self-love, does not let this pilgrim find his real goal and end. Therefore, let every being try to understand what the goal of his life truly is and ever strive for that goal, the goal called *samatā*, striving that will bring peace to the individual and true well being, material or otherwise, to his social group and his country.

Saying 5. Only highly upright conduct and intensely concentrated *buddhi* can find and realise in full the state of *samatā*. One should, therefore, bring his desires to extinction, desires that ever burn and scald him. And realising in full how the world is a mere passing appearance, let him be devoted to the seeking of the Truth. That is the way his desire will come to cease and the darkness of his ignorance will get dispelled to let the knowledge ever the same shine forth within him, that light of the *ātman*, his ontological being.

Saying 6. When the *buddhi* finds passivity in activity, the unrelated in the related, all knowledge in the little knowledge, the formless in the formed, eternity in temporality, the unimagined in the imagined, safety in fear, one in many, the compassionate in the selfish, sameness in dualities, the desireless in desire and life in the inert body, then and only then can it find peace the full and invulnerable, find itself all blessed, shedding the taint of self-hood. Attaining to that state of *yoga*, state that is life the true itself, life that every being seeks and desires, life that is generosity itself and all knowledge itself and yet is all transcendent, it, the *buddhi*, comes to merge in Self-same the all blessed. That is what every body should seek and investigate, every being that has come to sojourn in this passing world. Only then will he know how supremely blessed is this human birth.

Saying 7. Two states open out before the *buddhi* in the pilgrimage of its life, that of *samatā*, sameness, and that of *mamatā*, mine-ness. Identification with the body intensifies the sense of Me and Mine, whereas self-submission to the *ātman* brightens one's awareness of the reality of *samatā*, of sameness. *Mamatā*, the sense of Me and Mine, alone is ignorance and that alone is time the killer. When its obsessive passion for the body turns blind and infatuated, the *buddhi* too turns inert with the body, the dark mode *tamas* overwhelming it. Wicked it turns then to do wicked deeds, wicked in the extreme, to reap misery itself, misery in the extreme, as the reward of those deeds. This is the fate awaiting all beings that wander aimless in the labyrinth fashioned by *prakṛti*, that primal seed of creation.

Saying 8. When identification with the body gets blind and intense, then all beings fall under the spell of excessive *vāsanā* to turn destructive of one another, causing devastating upheavals and disruptions. Human birth is verily an opportunity for understanding these hidden truths about life, understanding that can lead, if accompanied by the right endeavour, a man to liberation from this, his miserable condition.

Saying 9. To identify itself with the body is natural to the *buddhi*, with the result that it gets obsessed with the pleasures of the body to do all kinds of evil acts for enjoying those pleasures, acts that bring only woe to it as well as to others. Ever tragic is this kind of life, inflicted with ignorance. A man who has understood this truth would ever self-submit to the Truth, this self-submission of his leading him to find the all-peace that *samatā* is.

Saying 10. All embodied beings wander in this transient world with the taints of their minds determining what good they do or what evil.[9] When the *buddhi* lives self-submitted to the Truth, it adopts the way of all-peace, the way of self-sacrifice and dispassion, fully awake to its affinity and equality with others. And to love it gives itself up and to service, to truthfulness and noble conduct, remaining all content with itself. With traits these enriched and with others, traits divine and transcendent, it ever works for its liberation, its striving and finding leading it to *samatā* the true self-sovereignty, to liberation, that is. A man who has found this way open out before him and follows it the way described, will verily transcend the domain of *Māyā* of the three *guṇas*, of the three strands, to attain to the peace that *nirvāṇa* is, that extinction of his false self is.

Saying 11. Those who follow the path contrary to the path of self-submission to the Truth, given up wholly to the body, mistaking it for their self, follow the path to darkness dense and absolute. Wholly given up to the passions of the body and its pleasures, they would resort to untruthfulness and to theft, to deceit and fraud, to jealousy and hatred, to greed unchecked and infatuation, to sensuality unrestrained and wrath, and to egoism overweening and in excess. These their dark dispositions disrupt every peace and concord, their own no less than that of others. Miserable do they live, scalded alike by the passions of the body and those of the mind. As demons do they live, their life nothing else than death itself, for that is what their demonic traits are, destructive alike of themselves and of others.

Saying 12. Bound thus by the dread *prakṛti*, beings, each and every, move helpless towards their doom and misery. To stem this compulsive drive, there is only one way: self-surrender to the Real that one truly is. Knowing well this plight that life in its truth is, let every being shed the physical and mental taints and evils that go with embodiment and self-submit to the Real, his life dedicated to the good and service of others. That is the way to self-sovereignty the real and supreme, self-sovereignty that only the state of *samatā*, that peace inviolate, is. Only one right has been vouchsafed to man: that he seek his salvation through truth, renunciation and service. That alone is the way to all-peace, to liberation, to self-sovereignty the invulnerable. Only that man is hero the invincible who has given up the sense of Me and Mine, that ignorance and bondage, and with the Truth alone his sole refuge, lives and acts freely, without the compulsion of any desire. Only a man of such a heroic mettle can be all victorious, the hero who remains self-same in the midst of all the tumults of mortal life. Greatly wise is that man, the only one who knows what self-sovereignty in its very truth is.

Saying 13. All well being follows, spontaneously and on its own, the man that lives holy and in service pure, his life all directed towards Spirit the ever Self-same. His very conduct and the spirit of his service ensure that well being, well being material, social or national, of that noble and great man, that hero victorious alike over himself and over the world at large. With hope he departs from this world, hope all full and rich, abiding in and as bliss ever the same. That verily is the way high of those that would find the truth and become the truth. Every *premī*, every being devoted to the path of *samatā*, should ever seek his home the true, doing, this way, good unto him and others, doing it without a consideration of self-interest. That verily is the highest duty of man. May the Lord bless every being with true enlightenment, with life everlasting and with peace and harmony!

(vii) *On Self-protection*

Saying 1. With every means and measure this being would protect his body from dangers within and without. All steps he would take for that end, all resources pile up, his days and nights spent in that hard and fierce struggle. This entire struggle for self-preservation has, of course, only one goal, the goal of peace the real and genuine. But that never falls to his lot, that peace the real, for lives he in everlasting fear, with no respite for even a moment. That is the truth about life in the world and its struggles. No protective measures can ultimately save this body, protective measures within and without, for perishable it is and bound to fall in the end. Protection within means protection through the intake of all kinds of invigorating things. And protection without means protection from every contingency or happening that may pose a threat to its safety. In that self-protection beings spend the entire span of their life, but to no purpose. That is the truth about mortal life and that is the truth about its compulsions.

Saying 2. Finding this struggle vain and futile, the seers of the truth that became the truth disclosed unto mortals the way they had discovered to the Fearless, disclosed it unto them immersed as were those miserable beings in unrest never ending and in fear never ending. The way out of man's predicament lay, for those seers, not so much in the protection of the body as in the protection of the mind and the *buddhi*, the intellect. Whatever protection the body needs, protection within and without, is taken care of by the very nature of a living being, spontaneously he gives that protection and unselfconsciously. Whatever is legitimately needed by it in terms of food, water and clothing and heat or cold a being will naturally provide it, without a conscious formulation of those needs. But despite that legitimate care , the body will fall one day - for that is what the life of a mortal is, that is the truth about it.

Saying 3. Protection of the mind and the *buddhi* means protection of the *buddhi* from the flaming fire of *vāsanā* by every possible means. That has been the finding of *sat-puruṣas,* of seers of the truth. So, with this holy purpose in mind, they ever keep their *buddhi* all-focussed on *ātman* the Truth, focussed with every steadfastness. When the *buddhi* comes to stay stable with the *ātman,* that Word the Imperishable, that Light the Supreme, its passion for self-protection, inner and outer, comes to an end, leaving it all free and liberated. For, the *ātman* alone is life, that alone is desire-free, is eternal and all-full and bliss itself. Abiding all still in that *ātman,* the *buddhi* lives in the body free from every compulsion, lets the body function as it would function on its own, it itself looking alike on weal and woe, for ever absorbed it remains in that Imperishable Real. That is the real and true state of protection, where no fear abides. Shedding all its greed, its infatuation and the I-sense that accompany its passion for the protection of the body, the *buddhi* ever stays still with the *nāda,* that sound immortal. That, its state, is the state of *nirvāṇa* itself, of liberation from the dread terrors that time and action are.

Saying 4. Contrary and opposite to this way is the way of the disposition that believes merely in self-assertion, making it the basis and ground of its being, instead of self the real and true. Asserting its being and self in and through the body, this disposition takes every measure, internal or external, to preserve the body. Many a comfort and pleasure it would gather for its well being and many an external means it would adopt for its security, so that all-secure and strong, it may subdue or eliminate every rival and competitor to shine all bright and glorious. But despite all these measures, the body will not stay forever, it will fall in the end, rendering all one's power and strength of no avail and leaving only remorse and despair as one's portion. Every seeker of truth should reflect on this truth about his worldly pilgrimage, that is his real and sacred duty.

Saying 5. Over-protection of the body leads to its early end. This is equally true of communal, social and political life. Excessive and unjust power, military and economic, acquired through greed and arrogance, cannot but spell an early ruin for a society or country so disposed. Only that progress, material, social or national, can be sustainable that is in harmony with the true endeavour, endeavour directed towards the attainment of the Truth, not detrimental to that attainment. A blessing indeed will be that progress for mankind, progress in harmony with the spiritual endeavour. Though, in the end, this progress too will meet its decadence, for that is the Law of the *Māyā* of the Lord. Only the *ātman*, the self of each and all, stays as itself, only that real. This is the truth, this alone.

Saying 6. Equipped with this understanding, a true seeker of the truth should seek to stay still in the *ātman* alone, *ātman* the truth, letting his personal life and his relationships with others unfold themselves on their own. That alone is the way to security the true and to peace the absolute. For, a being can become fearless, truly fearless, only when no desire remains to assail and disrupt him from his still absorption in self the real. But effort in the right direction, effort great and sustained, is required to attain to this state, the state that is the state supreme, that is *nirvāṇa* itself, liberation itself.

Saying 7. Peace within and harmony without depends on giving up *vāsanā*, the depth of the former determining the extent of the latter, of that giving up. Unbridled *vāsanā* is indeed the cause of every fear and every ruin, for the very acme of sin it is. Its cessation is *śānti* itself, peace the transcendent itself and the end of every fear. For, the supreme righteousness is it, this cessation of *vāsanā*. And on self-surrender to the *ātman* depends its cessation, the stronger the self-surrender, the weaker the *vāsanā* and deeper one's fulfillment. So let man believe in the Supreme Lord, have every faith in that Person the Supreme, the Person that is the self of all and each. Let Him be his sole love, the very goal of his life, his efforts all directed towards that goal. For that faith, that love and that dedication alone will bring every *vāsana* to its extinction to lead him to the state unvisited by any fear whatsoever. Only that man can call himself a believer who believes this way, lives this way and strives this way.

Saying 8. Opposed to this way of life is the life of those who, owing to their infatuations and pride, give themselves up wholly to the pleasures of the body, doing actions wicked and evil in the extreme, their fierce passions consuming them every moment. In no way can such beings find peace the true, their very life mere hell itself, hell in its deepest deeps.

Saying 9. There is no misery like the misery that unbridled *vāsanā* inflicts on a being. And there is no peace like the peace of freedom from *vāsanā*, peace the real is that and righteousness itself is that, that freedom. And from *vāsanā* the *ātman* alone is free, while the whole world is merely its projection. Those who come to reflect on this truth of life should do their best to free themselves from *vāsanā* and self-submit to the *ātman*, if they truly wish to protect their life. For that alone is the way to redemption the true.

Saying 10. When the *buddhi* truly makes the *ātman* its sole and only refuge, it loses all interest in the imagined world of mind and organs, those of cognition and action. For all that the mind and the organs find set up before them appears a mere passing show to it, only the self, their witness, abiding imperishable and fearless. To the latter then it becomes wholly and exclusively devoted, eventually losing itself in it. This verily is all knowledge and all devotion, knowledge and devotion possible solely in human birth. Let every seeker of truth, therefore, seek the company of the seers of the truth to make steadfast his self-submission to the *ātman*, giving up his sense of identification with the body. This devotion, holy and fervent, will free the *buddhi* from the yoke of *vāsanā*, that dark ignorance, and make it lose itself into the *ātman*, the light that illumines consciousness. This alone is the way to real self-protection, to bliss the absolute, the way to liberation from recurring births and deaths, setting at final rest all passions and all desires. And this is *sādhanā* the holy, striving the holy, that every human being should consider as his real and prime duty. Otherwise, birth after birth, human or others, they will find themselves burning in the fierce flames of *vāsanā*. For, only the human birth can bring liberation to them, provided they resort to the right path. In that possibility alone lies its superiority over other births.

Saying 11. The first step to this real and genuine protection consists in giving up *vāsanā* of the darkest kind. That comes to be possible when one resorts to *sat-saṅga*, to holy association, and serious and steadfast reflection on what is right and wrong. With that *vāsanā* given up, one comes to live a life as it should be lived, life in accord with what one has learnt about good life from that holy association. Good life led this way makes the *buddhi* strong enough to submit itself to the *ātman* as against its self-submission to the body, its passion to identify itself with the body. As its *vāsanā* comes to be pure so do its acts come to be pure, their purity culminating in its contentment with itself. Understanding this truth, a seeker of the Real must try, ever and always, to break himself free from the grip of *vāsanā*, giving himself to sustained contemplation of the self, contemplation holy and pure, contemplation as revealed unto him by a seer of the highest order. That is the way that can lead him to the highest state of being, the state free of every *vāsanā*, state that is the peace of *nirvāṇa* itself. That verily is the ideal that those who have become one with the truth, are that very truth, have set for mortals to live for.

Saying 12. Let every being of noble traits realise within him, realise in full, what has been said here. That is how he will find for himself protection the perfect and safety the perfect, a safety which even death cannot undo, for even in that hour his peace will not be disrupted, peace the eternal. Inevitable is the fall of the body and inevitable is the tragedy of a mortal's life, tragedy that mortality itself is, unless he finds peace the real and genuine. Therefore, let him ever purify himself through reflection the true, through belief the true and through contemplation the true. That verily, that alone, is his bounden duty, holy and high. The Lord bless every being with disposition the redemptive!

(viii) *On Nonviolence: the Still Passivity*[10]

***Saying* 1.** Every being, in the pilgrimage that his life is, is ever busy, mentally or physically, prompted as he ever is by one desire or other residing in his mind. But despite all the pleasures he may have enjoyed in his life, he departs from the world all discontent and disconsolate. This is all that his life is, a mere regret and unrest. Only the effort true can save him from this his fate, and sustained contemplation. These alone can lead him to the state free from every activity, to the state where no violence is and no cruelty.

Saying 2. The body, that form visible, along with the organs of cognition and activity, is the location in and through which the *buddhi* enjoys the fruits of actions, enjoys them visibly and invisibly, obsessed with and attached to them. Involved ever and always in accepting and rejecting, it turns a victim of desire and aversion, those dualities that the fruits of actions give rise to, never letting it rest and pause. This is the wheel that *Māyā* sets in motion, wheel all mysterious and awful, to which is bound every being to move helpless with it, with no hope of release in sight.

Saying 3. To activities and actions is ever oriented this visible form of the body, activities and actions without a count and number. And actions ever change, every moment do they change to give rise to the dualities that their results are, dualities ever in conflict with themselves. This verily is creation and dissolution, creation and dissolution in a fine and subtle form. All benighted and infatuated, the *buddhi* gets attached to those dualities, those results of actions. Finding life in one pole constituting a given duality and death in the other pole, it ever seeks the former and avoids the latter. This is all that struggle for life or existence is, the struggle in which every being finds himself helplessly involved. But no struggle can succeed here, for die he must sooner or later. This is how moves the wheel of time the destroyer.

Saying 4. To liberate oneself from the dualities that action gives rise to in the form of its results, to be free from this awful recurrence, is to be still and passive, is to be truly nonviolent and free from every regret. Only supreme disillusion with the world and dedication to and giving oneself up to the Truth can bring about this state. Only that man is *puruṣa*, person, the true who would ever live surrendered to the truth to undo the pain and misery inflicting his inner being.

Saying 5. The body is body-in-action, ever changing and deviating from itself. That is why it is called unreal, a false appearance, a delusion. As opposed to this is the *ātman*, that light the true, that Word the still and without a beginning and indivisible. That alone is the Truth and support of the whole world, that *ātman*, to self-submit to which is to live supremely the human life, for, redemption itself, liberation itself is this spirit of self-submission.

Saying 6. True *satyāgraha* means self-submission to the Supreme Reality. It means dissociating, each and every moment, the *buddhi* from the dualities that results of actions are, actions done by the psycho-physical system. It means putting one's comforts at the disposal of others without an expectation of a return. This kind of *satyāgraha*, *satyāgraha* the supreme, frees the *buddhi* from the violence that the results of actions are, results the dualities, to make it stay all still and not-doing, stay, that is, in bliss the non-violent, in *nirvāṇa* itself, that home of it true and ultimate.

Saying 7. As long as the *buddhi* is affected by misery that results of actions, results the dualities, are, it ever remains unstable, happy with the results favouring it and unhappy with those not favouring it. And as long as this condition prevails, it cannot find its *ātman*, cannot become that, its true being, the being where no conflict is and no violence and no fear. Immersed in dualities, in conflicts of opposites, it ever remains busy adopting one course of action as opposed to the others, all outlets from this misery, misery the absolute, having been closed unto it.

Saying 8. Knowing this unhappy truth about his life, let a man live ever self-submitted to the Truth. A being is born bound by *karma*, by action, action that does not let him experience even a trite of peace. Whatever peace that results of actions promise, those dualities, are mere false appearances set up by delusion, appearances that tempt this being from darkness to darkness, his *vāsanā* getting stronger along with that his misery.

Saying 9. The passion for the results of actions, for the dualities that they are, intensifies *vāsanā* to make a being all destructive, of himself no less than of others, his actions all wicked and his life a restless misery, life the demonic and of dark ignorance.

Saying 10. To liberate oneself from the passion for the results of actions and the conflicts that they embody is to be a hero, hero the great and supreme. But self-submitted to the body, that locus of actions without a count, the *buddhi* cannot extricate itself from that passion, that root of all violence. Only its self-submission unto the *ātman*, unto self the not-doing, the non-violent, the unmoving and imperishable, only its self-submission to that *ātman* can purify it of that malady.

Saying 11. The *buddhi* can turn non-violent, non-violent truly and genuinely, only when it self-submits to the *ātman*, giving up its sense of identity with the body, with its passion for its pleasures all spent and over. In Word the *ātman* it comes to stay then, stay still and stable, its bodily comforts given up for the welfare of others. Only then does it give up its violent nature, only then. To peace the pure that his *ātman* is, his true and real self is, it then attains, to that blessedness, blessedness the absolute.

Saying 12. Only by resolutely self-submitting to the *ātman*, by resorting to this kind of *satyāgraha*, can the *buddhi* save itself from the dread tragedy that its identification with the body is. For all conflict is this state of being, the state of being that its identification with the body involves. With that resolute self-submission unto the *ātman*, its self, it comes to find that Word the Imperishable, that holy and still Passivity, as the informing spirit of each and every being. And only then does it come to give up its violence, only then does it come to stay still in that Word the not-doing, that Love that is the all, its frets and troubles over, its desires lost and extinct, its ver being merged in That.

Saying 13. Its self-submission to the body, self-submission blind and deep, makes the *buddhi* all restless, its *vāsanā* fierce and aflame. With this unrest and this *vāsanā* for their motivating forces, the organs, cognitive and motor, operate only to give rise to unrest both for oneself and for others. Whatever the *buddhi* then perceives or cognises and whatever it does turn only into instruments of violence for it, violence the full, fear ever pursuing it. That is the beastly life that it then comes to live.

Saying 14. To have the sense of identification with the body, to have the sense of Me and Mine with regard to it, alone gives rise to the passions of sex, wrath, greed, infatuation and egoism. To satisfy these passions, the *buddhi* ever indulges itself in the pleasures of the sense- and motor organs to bring unrest for itself and for others. Therein lies the whole tragedy of life, tragedy fierce, oppressive and dreadful - in equating the body with one's self and being, in identifying oneself with it.

Saying 15. When the *buddhi* ceases to identify itself with the body to give itself up, resolutely and firmly, to the Real, self-surrender unto it, and contemplates the Name, letting no exterior thought to distract it from its contemplation - when the *buddhi* lives thus and contemplates thus, it breaks itself free from the grip of *vāsanā*, that darkness dense and deep. With this its freedom from *vāsanā*, its passions for the pleasures of the sense and motor organs, pleasures with their *others* ingrained in them, become dead and extinct. And with the *ātman*, that stillness itself, its sole abode then, it turns a protector of itself and of others, protector in every truth. Any man who has attained to this state is a man of absolute non-violence. With no regret or distress to trouble him, he takes away the troubles of all other beings, takes these away as their true self and being, of those unhappy souls. He alone is the guide of the world, its preceptor and teacher, that man of peace the infinite, that man blessed with the vision of the Real as it is in itself.

Saying 16. Identification of the self with the body gives rise to a disposition of violence and prompts the organs of actions to do acts disastrous and painful. The threefold misery that inflicts every being, namely, the misery that the psycho-physical system gives rise to, the misery that the external world causes and the misery that the Will Divine showers upon man, is in fact only a product of equating one's self with the body. It sets a mortal ever on the move without a pause and without a rest, this knowledge false and deluded, this ignorance that equates the self with the body. One should live in the company of seers to put an end to this delusion and surrender oneself to the Truth that one truly is. Therein lies man's first duty, for therein alone lies one's safety true and real. Anyone who strives for this end is truly a gifted soul, a soul that lives in absolute peace with others, doing no violence to any being whatsoever.

Saying 17. This kind of *satyāgraha,* this self-submission to the one *ātman,* is the way to eradicate one's obsession with the interests of the body-self. So, one must adhere to this self-submission and concentrate one's mind and intellect on the Truth within, losing all interests in the pleasures of the senses. This verily is *tapas,* is self-denial the holy, *tapas* the supreme, and dedication to *ahiṃsā,* to non-injury. And that verily is self-protection pure and holy.

Saying 18. The bodily desires alone are the causes of *hiṃsā,* of violence. Destruction absolute are they, those desires. Therefore, it is necessary that man should purify himself of these passions and make the Truth abiding within him his sole refuge, giving all his thought to contemplation of that Truth. Therein lies the way to absolute purity that Word the Imperishable is, Word the still and passive, Word the peaceful and non-violent absolute.

Saying 19. Giving himself up to the Truth within, a man should free his mind from its distresses, spending his body, mind and intellect in the contemplation of that Truth. That is the way of *yoga, yoga* the redemptive. If a man resorts to this way, resorts to it without a deviation, there will remain no bodily passions to sway his *buddhi* from its contemplation of Word the Truth. To his very home will this way lead him, home all safe and protective.

Saying 20. The body is all activity, activity become visible, visible with a form. To free itself from it, from this bondage, the *buddhi* has to abide all stable in Word the Indivisible, the Word that is all still and transcendently passive. Only then can it find the bliss free of every desire and beyond the reach of every tumult and every distress. That alone is pure of every violence, that bliss and that peace. Redemption itself turns the man that has to this state attained. Verily has he found the bliss that is native unto him, found it having given up all his attachments.

Saying 21. When the *buddhi* distances itself from the actions of the body to abide still and stable in Word the *ātman*, when its actions, those of the body, no longer concern it nor do the dualities those actions give rise to - when the *buddhi* comes to stay stable in this way, it rises above all its *vāsanās*, its absorption in Word the Redemption becoming deeper and irrevocable. When a being attains to this state, the state devoid of all thought and dualities, he comes to be non-violent in the full sense of the term, for transcending all his desires he reposes in the Eternal itself. One may remember that only desire gives rise to *hiṃsā*, violence, only desire, compelling the *buddhi* to ever remain engaged in the acts of welcoming one state of affairs and rejecting others. When, however, the *buddhi* comes to be purified of all desires, then the acts of the body-self can no longer bind it, its stay in the Imperishable Word, that Real the Absolute, becoming firm and unwavering. All different it then finds itself from the body, that *buddhi* the pure. Of *ahiṃsā*, of non-violence, is verily the incarnation a person that abides, abides ever and always, in this state. For, dwells he ever in the bliss that his very own being is, his very *ātman* is, *ātman* that transcends every desire, every thought, every conflict, every projection and every relationship and is the light that illumines all that is. Ever blessed he lives, this soul blessed, beyond the reach of the tumults and discords of temporal life. Pure is he, purity itself is he, that being the blessed. To attain to this blessed state there is only one way open to man, the way of firm self-submission to the Truth abiding within him, the way, that is, of contemplation of the Name with a disposition that has distanced itself from all the pleasures of the body. That verily is endeavour the successful, that verily is the way to salvation.

Saying 22. Every man is duty bound to turn himself into a true guardian of life, of the life that redeems all lives. This he can do only when he realises the truth about this pilgrimage of life, pilgrimage all transient, pilgrimage that in a moment comes to an end. Let him, that is to say, do good unto others but without a thought of self-concern and self-interest. Therein alone abides genuine *ahiṃsā*, non-violence, in this disposition. And so does *dharma*, the Law, and so does *nīti*, ethics, social and political. Only that kind of disposition can lead a man to the state beyond every act, beyond every violence and beyond every unrest. Let every being ever strive for realisation of the truth, his and of the world!

(ix) *A Return to Holy Association*

Saying 1. Deliberation on Devotion to the Lord: At a *sat-saṅga*, the concept of devotion, devotion to the Lord, should receive the first consideration. One should know what Truth in itself is and should seek to abide in That, in Truth.

Saying 2. Deliberation on Simplicity: Emphasis should be laid on the principle of simplicity, on simple food and simple dress, on giving up wasteful expenditure.

Saying 3. Deliberation on the true spirit of Service: service unto humanity and protection of other beings. It must be emphasised that these two are obligatory acts.

Saying 4. Deliberation on the regulative principles of life as formulated by the truth-become souls: on moulding one's life in accordance with the ideals they set before humanity.

Saying 5. Deliberation on actions purifying and truth-oriented: deliberation on actions in accordance with the Law and in discordant with the Law, on how to adopt the former and avoid the latter.

Saying 6. Deliberation on out-spreading the Law: Emphasis is to be laid on the truth that only the purity of one's life and conduct can benefit others and not one's words.

Saying 7. Deliberation on cultivation of a disposition straight and unbiased: Emphasis on moulding one's life in accordance with the true regulative principles and refraining completely from vain disputes and theories irrelevant to existential conditions.

Saying 8. Deliberation on the teachings of prophets and seers of each and every faith: The purpose should be to know what kind of ideals they pursued and lived for, leaving aside all fanaticism and useless disputes.

Saying 9. Deliberation on how to regulate one's life in accordance with one's age and condition. It should be emphasised that to purify one's mind, one has to meditate the Name with strict punctuality, with no let and omission.

Saying 10. Deliberation on how to get rid of the evil customs prevailing in one's family or social group: It should be brought home to the participants in a *sat-saṅga* that the customs of this kind are useless and harmful and should be given up.

Saying 11. Deliberation on the life and conduct of traditional family preceptors or those of the social group one is attached to: It should be made clear to every body that a preceptor of an evil conduct can do no good to any one and should, for this reason, be given up. Only a seer who has become one with the Truth can lead one to purity, lead one through his own purity. Accordingly, only his company should be sought, and his proximity.

Saying 12. Deliberation on how to purify one's mind and thoughts. Only the life dedicated to the Law can bring about this purification. Everything should be dedicated to that life, one's body, mind and material possessions.

Saying 13. Deliberation on how to make one seek holy association: This comes to be possible when one is made to realise that holy association is redemptive association, participation in which can genuinely re-form one's life.

Saying 14. Deliberation on how to look alike on all living beings and how to work for their good.

(x) *Regulative Principles*

Saying 1. To take pure and simple food, abstaining from all intoxicants, meat and everything injurious to health.

Saying 2. To wear simple and plain dress, avoiding clothes with a look expensive and showy.

Saying 3. To participate *in sat-saṅga,* in holy association, in order to do what seers and prophets command one to do, taking their commands as absolute imperatives.

Saying 4. To cultivate the disposition oriented towards doing good unto others. This implies compassion for all beings and firm adherence to noble conduct.

Saying 5. The daily observance - to contemplate every morning and evening and with every devotion the Name of the Lord as revealed by a preceptor true.

Saying 6. Whatever one does should be done with punctuality and with a free spirit.

Saying 7. One should refrain from seeing imitative shows [like cinema, etc]; they extinguish the light of the soul within man.[11]

Saying 8. One should be a seeker of the Real, giving up all one's failings and orienting one's life and being towards it, towards the Real.

Saying 9. To be well disposed towards every being, to wish for his well being, spiritual and otherwise, desiring nothing in return.[12]

Saying 10. Let one's entire thinking, one's entire power, one's entire learning and one's whole effort be directed towards purification of one's life, purification the perfect. And let one attain to the state fearless, to be all-blissful with one's own being before the last hour arrives. Then alone will have one led the life truly successful.

Saying 11. Let a man ever resort to holy association to know wherein lies his good and how to attain to it. Let him know that therein alone abides the superiority of human life, in that knowledge redemptive and in that endeavour redemptive. Having come to this transient and perishable world, let him be ever devoted to the Real, if he would be liberated from himself. And let him not resort to acts that bring unrest unto him, let him only take to the way ever peaceful, with his mind solely oriented towards his teacher. Knowing the inevitable end destined for this momentary appearance, this body, let him strive for the truth and devote himself to the truth, if he would not depart in unrest and frustration from this world. Let this momentary life truly prosper, setting at rest the eternal unrest that inflicts the mind. Let him dwell in Word the Imperishable, that abode fearless of peace, that Lord the Supreme and Brahman the Transcendent.

Saying 12. And let him distance himself from every sinful *vāsanā*, self-submitting himself unto the Real. For, only the pure of mind can find the Light, not those of mind the polluted. Supremely accomplished is he, supremely rich is he and supremely pious and heroic is he, the man who has purified himself of all the taints of the mind and lives ever self-submitted to the Truth abiding within him. He lives as a light and inspiration unto others to die into *nirvāṇa*, that peace transcendent, dies triumphant over the false appearance that the all-triumphant world is. Rare is his life and rare his striving, a life and a striving that every being should emulate, for therein lies the true purposefulness of human life, its superiority over other forms of life. May the Lord enrich every being with the spirit of self-submission to the Truth!

(xi) *The Seeker of the Truth and His Holy Resolve*

Saying 1. He who would know the truth will shun the pleasures of the organs cognitive and motor as he would shun poison itself. For the sustenance of his life will be his intake and that too of the simplest kind. And with the *ātman*, the self, alone as his sole refuge, he will give himself up to sustained meditation of the Name. To the *ātman* will he attain, to his self the true, that blessed seeker of this kind and mettle.

Saying 2. When he is called upon to act, he will do so with the results of his acts surrendered unto the Lord, his contemplation of the Name bringing unto their end his desires all and his imaginings all. Not a moment will that spirit of self-surrender he let pass, such will be his devotion unto the Lord, devotion the transcendental. Find shall that devotee supreme his self the true, find shall he *nāda* the imperishable - find shall he that Sound to turn into It.

Saying 3. He who has distanced himself from all his failings, failings of his mind, body and organs, cognitive and motor, his mind all concentrated on the Name, he alone will find the self within him, find the *yoga* supremely redemptive.

Saying 4. He who would find the *ātman* to become the *ātman*, his passion for the pleasures of the mind, body and the organs all spent - he alone is the man of discrimination, he alone can tell the truth from the untruth. Of the Lord is he the devotee true and of the seers the servant true, his inner being given up to the Name and his outer being given up to the Lord, his actions as if willed by Him, actions resorted to for self-sustenance or for the good of others. All humility he lives and all humility he acts. But whether outwardly active or at rest, his inner being ever remains anchored to the Lord, his sole support and refuge. Light the Supreme will he find, this person of true discrimination, bliss will he find, bliss that is native to his being, not dependent on the *other*. Find will he that bliss to become that bliss to repose for ever in peace that passeth all understanding, peace the supreme and transcendental. No pleasure will then remain to tempt him and no pain to distress him, that rare man of rare spirit and life.

Saying 5. The being that has found the self within him and become the self will transcend all the threefold woes, woes inflicted upon him by his psycho-physical system, by the material world around him and by the forces unknown and mysterious, beyond the reach of his senses, thought and intellect. Alone will he abide in the Alone, Alone the still and passive, in Whom no desire dwells and no conflict - each moment of his life an abiding steadfast in That. From his great woe will he be released, from *Prakṛti,* that Seed the Unmanifest. His knowledge alone will be knowledge of the Real, that culimination of *yoga* the highest and his being itself the bliss everlasting. And all success will be his endeavour, his glory all singular.

Saying 6. A seeker of the truth will make the Name his sole support, on the Real alone will he concentrate his mind, withdrawing it from his organs of action and cognition. To his self will he attain, to the self free from all desires, that seeker given to contemplation steady and unrelenting.

Saying 7. No longer finding his self and being in the body, to the Word, that Real the Imperishable, self-submitted , staying far away from the dualities that every act of his results in, that seeker true sits near the truth, ever absorbed in it. Delighting in the self, in the self alone and not in the *other,* rejoicing in that beatitude, he loses himself into that ecstasy his own and native.

Saying 8. Perceiving vividly the body perish every moment, he loses all interest in the pleasures of the organs to abide in the self, separating the real from the unreal. Free from the bondage of the three *guṇas,* the three strands of *prakṛti,* that seed primordial of the manifest world, he stays as their witness, supremely blessed in himself.

Saying 9. The pleasures of the organs alone constitute that bondage. A man of *tapas* is he, of *tapas* the highest, he who dissociates himself from all those passions and pleasures, steadying his mind in the contemplation of the Name his teacher has revealed unto him. From his own acts he stays apart, passive and still, their results, of those actions, left to the will of the Real, to that Witness of all that is. Staying alike in weal and woe, that seeker will attain to the *ātman,* to his being the real and true.

Saying 10. A seeker of the truth perceives the bodily form as the form ever doing, as ever in motion towards an end, and all subject to destruction. And the *ātman*, his real and true being, alone he knows as staying ever still and unrelated, knows it as such and abides in it as such. He alone is the seeker attained to the state of *yoga*, the seeker of this sight and this knowledge, with his *buddhi* all motionless and at rest. For, knows he the enlightened state of *anubhava*, of knowledge that is being itself. Verily, the home true of every being is that, that state of the *buddhi*.

Saying 11. Whatever is done and accomplished for the sake of the bodily interests is like unto an all consuming fire in his eyes, in the eyes of a true seeker. Ever awake he remains of Real the Supreme, the affairs of the transient world touching him no more, and the pleasures of the organs. For, staying ever awake to his imperishable self, that Real the absolute, he attains to *nirvāṇa*, that *yoga* the highest, his striving become all redemptive.

Saying 12. Indulgence in the pleasures of the senses sets aflame all the more the desire for those pleasures, turning one's lives to come into lives of pain the surpassing. That is the truth that every seeker should know, the truth about the end of self-indulgence. For, only that knowledge will prompt him to escape from those burning flames, those passions false and desires. That realisation alone will make him seek refuge in a teacher, that realisation of the inevitable results of self-indulgence, to know in earnest the reality supreme and highest. With his passion for the world all extinct and his devotion to the truth all fervent, he will make, that seeker true, his mind rest all still on the Name his teacher has revealed, letting no other thought to distract him from his concentration. With his self-absorption in the Name deepening, he will find Word the True manifest within him, that bliss the eternal, to become, eventually, one with It, his desires all extinguished, and he himself turned into peace itself, into peace transcendent. That verily is the goal final, this one's transformation into peace the transcendental. For, broken will have that seeker all his fetters, realised will he have his being true and immortal, his fears all dispersed. Life the Eternal will he have found within him, Life that is Word the Indivisible, and known will he have all that is to be known, such his resolve the true, and such his glory the rare.

Saying 13. The *buddhi* ever remains in the grip of the three *guṇas*, the three strands, and as such ever remains deluded by false names and forms, qualities and activities, unable to be certain and sure of anything whatsoever, not even for a moment. A seeker who has come to perceive this unrest that his mind is will come to understand, if he has found the preceptor true, understand for certain, what his being in its truth is, shedding his sense of identity with the three strands of *prakṛti*. In and as his own native being will he dwell then, being the imperishable and eternal.[13]

Saying 14. Great effort is needed to dispel the darkness of this perverted understanding. There has to be steady and genuine discrimination, there has to be steady and genuine dispassion and there has to be steady and genuine meditation. Indispensable are these to make a being's *buddhi* distance itself from the not-self that his body is, to bring about the cessation of its sense of identity with the body, its projection of the self on to it, and find and be the Real that it truly is. Only then will it shed all its *vāsanā*-s to stay all stable in That, in that Goal the Final and Ultimate.

Saying 15. Genuine discrimination implies perception of the entire *prakṛti*, that realm of the not-self, as perishable and of the nature of suffering and, equipped with this understanding, self-submission of oneself unto the Imperishable, distancing oneself, ever and always, from the passion for phenomena, for those *others*. It means, that discrimination the genuine, constant striving to know and be the Real. Only this kind of fervent devotion can truly strengthen one's power of discrimination, only this can redeem a man from his unhappy condition.

Saying 16. Genuine dispassion implies authentic and lived perception of pain and misery in all the pleasures of *prakṛti*, it implies living their perishable nature. Truly redemptive is this anguished perception of one's mortality in one's pleasures. For, it makes a man distance himself from all the bodily pleasures and experience the divine flash in him and stay steadfast in that light and revelation. There alone does he find the peace authentic and the life authentic.

Saying 17. And genuine meditation means exclusive contemplation of the Imperishable Word by the mind, with a spirit of self-surrender to the Truth and to bring to cessation all the thoughts and images, those false appearances, that the mind sets up. It means, in other words, living with the Name alone for one's support, staying all stable and alike in weal or woe. Only the man who acts this way can attain to his being the true, can know and be his real *ātman*, his self. Ever blessed he becomes, enriched with his knowledge, knowledge the living to attain to the very highest reach of *yoga*.

Saying 18. Only the preceptor true, the preceptor who has known the Real and has become the Real, can instill in one the spirit of genuine discrimination, of genuine dispassion and of genuine meditation. To live in his company, of that seer of the *ātman*, and to serve him is verily the supreme support of a seeker of the truth, that alone is his teacher the supreme, his refuge the supreme and his life the supreme. All blessed is the man that has been portioned out this holy association and this holy service. For, only that seeker of the truth will escape from the delusions that this dread mystery, this Māyā, has woven for him, only that seeker who has undone his selfhood through the *yoga* revealed unto him by his teacher true and has thereby become ripe enough to receive his grace. Then and then only will he find the being that he truly is to become a teacher unto himself and a guide unto all living beings, a guide to their redemption.

Saying 19. Only the knower given to the spirit of authentic discrimination, authentic dispassion and authentic meditation will dispel the darkness that duality of action is, duality to which he ever finds himself tied.

Only he can stay stable in his self the true, only in that self. He alone knows himself and knows the all and he alone can be the teacher true.

Saying 20. As long as the *buddhi* superimposes the self on to the body and the body on to the self, as long as it confuses that self the real with the body, it will continue to be scalded and consumed by desire, by wrath, by greed and by infatuations and the passion to *be*, to be the I and the Me. It resorts to many a way and many an act to assuage these passions but all vain prove its efforts, for the body, the very means of those efforts, is itself the seat of those very passions and deviations, passions and deviations the *buddhi* would bring to rest. To think of it, of the body, as *being* is to be ever frustrated, for delusion all it is, all ignorance, this confusion of the self the true with the body.

Saying 21. A seeker will attain to the Imperishable Word, that Being the true, if he brings to an end his sense of identification with the body through the way his teacher has taught him and nurtures with care the spirit of authentic discrimination, dispassion and contemplation. That is the way to bring to extinction the fierce flames of desire burning in him and attain to Word the Imperishable. To its very end the final brings he his embodied journey, journey that is time the death itself, mortality itself, to find the self, that refuge true of his and the being true of his, that peace the eternal. Not many can live his life and find his purpose.

Saying 22. Let there be no let in one's effort to undo this confusion of the self with the body; therein lies devotion the true and dispassion the true. Any seeker of the truth that finds himself thus devoted is a hero, his triumphs all pure and all authentic.

Saying 23. To distance oneself from the body is verily the attainment supreme and the peace supreme. All wise is the man and all compassionate, the man that stays firm away from the body to repose for ever in self the eternal and immortal, in that being his own and eternal.

Saying 24. The body is, verily, actions the embodied, actions without a count and an end, and the *budhhi,* that faculty of knowing, experiences those actions in terms of pleasure and pain, experiences them each and every moment to remain ever displaced from itself. The seeker of the truth that knows in full what an unrest his life-condition is will distance himself from it to self-submit to the *ātman* within him, that witness real of all that is, will distance himself as his teacher has instructed him to do. His fervent devotion to that *ātman*, that witness of all, will undo all the taints of his mind, the Name alone the focus of his mind and being. With no organs will he identify himself, with no activities of theirs, the Name being his sole concern and attention. He alone will be the master of *tapas*, of fervent ardour, he alone will find the Real and become the Real, will become that Peace the all. Noble has been his seeking, a light of himself is he unto himself, his knowledge all blessed, his knowledge of the Real. Only seeking the steadfast, seeking the pure and authentic can bring about the peace without a support, support of the *other*, peace that is the all. And only that seeker is seeker the noble, he who stays still in contemplation of the Name, giving up every interest in the pleasures of the body. A day will surely dawn upon him when his human birth will bear its real fruit for him, success the supreme smiling upon him, his goal attained, the supreme goal of man's life. In this world where every being wanders deluded and confused, few can be true seekers of the truth, and fewer still will be those who strive for the truth, follow the path to it as shown by their teachers true. To beings without a count their doings will bring peace, their word a revelation, revelation of the Truth and the Law, a blessing will be these to all, their doings and their word. One comes across them, these swans[14] devoted to their teachers, only when destiny smiles all benign on one, when one's portion of Grace turns full and overflowing. Let every being be the seeker true and seek the peace true, for that is how this frail and fragile life, life that perishes the moment it comes into being, will bear its true and redemptive fruit!

Let a man be the seeker true
And reflect on the Revelation true,
And in himself find the being his own,
His delusions dispelled, his deeds dispersed.

In himself will he find the Word,
Word the true and indivisible,
Word the *Nirvāṇa*,
Knowledge at once and Being.

Let him die into the word of his teacher,
To die into it to live again,
And find the knowledge,
Knowledge in its truth.
And let him earn Name the One,
All unconscious of the Me and Mine,
And bring to an end the fevers three
And find the home secure and safe.
Let him remember the truth,
Let him realise the truth,
Let him live for truth.
Forget shall he that false projection,
Projection they call the body.
Into the *ātman* shall he awake,
Into that self the very true.

He who drinks in the joy of the self,
Joy of the Word eternal and true,
Will attain to *nirvāṇa*, his goal and end,
He, the seeker true.

Seek, gentle soul, the way to deliverance,
Seek it with mind intent on the Name,

Human birth the rare is yours,
Make a use true of it
And earn *dharma*, the Good -
That profit rare and rich.
That Lord of the yonder world
Is your very life and being,
Ever find him there, within your mind!
That indeed is the act sublime,
Heed you the word of Maṅgat true!
Worship that Real within
And find the State Supreme.

Here ends the *Samatāvilāsa*, the Word Realised.
Prevail the Will of the Formless!
Brahma Satyaṃ Sarvādhāra!

NOTES

[1] Only he who has become one with the Real can communicate what the Real is, only he can 'interpret' it, can clothe it in communicative terms. Not others. The sentence in the original is too condensed for a rendering immediately comprehensible. So, an explanatory rendering of it has been given here.

[2] There is a gap between the Real as Revelation of Itself and the articulation of the Real by truth-become souls. There is, further, a difference in the respective depth of the latter's experiences of the Real, experiences in the sense of their merger in the Real. So no articulation of the Real, even the interpretation given by a seer of the Real, can ever embody the Real. There will always be a schism, a divide between the Real and the word, between the Real and the idea. The Real will vouchsafe only its intimations, but will not be comprehended by a concept or word. Its articulation by a seer intimates its reality to a man precisely because it emphasises the absence of the Real in his discourse. Other discourses are false precisely because they would 'capture' the Real in words and concepts. The speech that disowns itself as untruthful is, in truth, speech the truthful and the speech that would cling to itself, would nurture the passion to be truthful, is speech the untruthful. So one should believe in the 'untruthful' interpretation of a seer, believe in it as truth itself, to attain to the Real and self-extinct in it. Only then will he become the Real through this self-sacrificial disposition, not otherwise.

[3] Projected by mind and desire as their constitutive *other*.

[4] The projection of oneself as a doer and the projection of the world as the field of doing, rise together. Constitutive *others* are they, each of the other.

[5] 'The light of consciousness,' means, the reader may recall, the self that illumines consciousness, that manifests itself as consciousness, but is not to be confused with consciousness, as it should not be confused with the doer in us.

[6] *Vide* note 5.

[7] Human thinking cannot escape dualities and opposites. Its fallen state is conditioned by its redemptive state and the redemptive state is conditioned by the fallen state. There is no Brahman of our thinking without *Māyā* as there is no *Māyā* without Brahman. Man must die into Brahman, his ultimate goal and seeking. That is the truth *for* him. When he has died into Brahman, then distinctions between fall

and redemption, bondage and liberation, *Māyā* and Brahman will cease to be. For the benefit of our understanding that state [?] is termed as One only without a second. For the benefit of our understanding only!

8. Reformation of society is possible through self-reformation. But self-reformation cannot come about easily. Man is a being that is constituted by others and it is as that being, being *along* with others, that he has to begin the process of self-reformation. Not, however, as a member of the society as a whole, but as a member of a sub-society, a sub-society oriented towards the Truth Ultimate. This sub-society too cannot come into being unless there is a guide to lead it towards that goal. A *saṅgat* without a preceptor is impossible. People come together and strive together, strive for the same goal only under the care of a true teacher and guide. It is his life and renunciation that can inspire others to emulate his ways. Thinkers seek to find their ways to goodness and to salvation through their thoughts and concepts, but these are too frail and self-negating to guide one to that goal. Only that thinker can follow the guide true to the goal true, only that thinker who has found all knowledge, actual and possible, as ignorance. And also those who have striven for the goal but have found themselves all weak and sinful. Disillusioned alike with their virtues and with their strivings, they surrender themselves to the teacher and wait for his command, for that only. Those that have found their worldly achievements vain, their pleasures woes and their successes failures alone can be the faithful followers of the true teachers. Thus the humble alone can constitute a true *saṅgat*, humble in their thought, humble in their efforts and humble in their success and achievements. For, only they can follow a seer of the truth, not those who are proud of their achievements: economic, political, ethical or spiritual. Only such members of a sub-group oriented towards the Truth and not towards the world can, under the guidance of their seer-teacher, reach the goal of life, their individual lives augmenting the resolve of one another. A solitary thinker cannot make his concepts his guides, nor can a man of morality his moral principles, for all our thoughts and moral principles are rooted in our self-love, revolve around that Narcissus within us. The Truth ever and always gives its call, call in the form of the transcendental thrust in us, but our projects and pursuits do not let us pay heed to it. It is only when the Truth appears before us in the form a seer to proclaim Its call that we come to be aware of It and pay heed to It.

Otherwise, we ever remain deaf and blind, striving for we know not what. But when those that obey their guide and teacher come to live in our midst, their life and demeanor cannot but make us aware that there is such a thing as the call of the Truth and the need to obey it. Thus only a *saṅgat* true of a guru true can make society in general aware of the transcendental thrust in us and follow it to save itself from the disastrous effects of its exclusive interests in its projects and pursuits.

9. Even what are called good actions are not free from the stain of evil. For, mind is evil in the end, the difference between good and evil actions being only a difference of degree. All actions are tainted by the primordial evil of self-hood.

10. *Satyāgraha* (literally, favouring the truth or real as against the untruth or unreal) peaceful civil obedience, and *ahiṃsā*, non-violence, were the two great weapons that Mahātmā Gāndhī employed against the British in his long but successful struggle for independence of India. In this section deeper dimensions of these two concepts are explained, dimensions that can bring about [relatively] stable peace to society in general and absolute peace to the individual. My biography of Gurudeva explains these points in details.

11. Art critics may protest against this assertion. They may invoke the dramatic masterpieces, tragic and of other genres, to say that artistic imitation is not merely an imitation, it is an imitation of human life enriched by deeper dimensions, dimensions unknown to ordinary men and women. One cannot say that a Sophocles or a Shakespeare merely reproduces some slice of life but does not add any meaning to it. This is, of course, a comment too obvious to emphasise, even to mention, as every sensitive reader would agree. The point is well taken but only in relation with and contrast to ordinary or the so-called realistic sensibility, more accurately speaking, lack of sensibility. But what about the man who, perceiving the meaninglessness of our ambitions and achievements, the demonic fury of our blind and sordid passions and the sadism and masochism involved in our relationships will care for the findings of these artists.? His agony will be too deep to be redeemed by the aesthetic distance these works will create in him. For, even the contemplator of our sordid life, the passive witness of it, passive in the artistic sense, will not escape his searching and penetrating gaze. This passive witness of the tumult of our passions, this creative soul, that man of complete disillusion will find too deeply narcissistic

to tempt him into aesthetic pleasure. For, in the midst of our mortal life, this aesthetically distant self would stay calm and quiet with its disinterested pleasure. This disinterested pleasure is the experience of an inauthentic self, for it would forget the truth of our mortality. It is sinful because it does not care to come to terms with death, that ultimate truth about our life. And the life that does not find its meaning in death is a life vain and meaningless. It is bound to end up in frustration, frustration without a qualification.

So all art, in the final analysis, is an imitation of life projected by a sensibility distanced from the humdrum of our daily concerns but unaware and insensitive to the dance that death plays in each and every moment of our life. You 'create' a reality that is only a contemplative imitation of life. And this imitation kills the voice of the Law within us, the Law that sternly reminds us, each and every moment, what we truly are : mere mortals that are born every moment to die that very moment, are mere passions for being, but passions completely unfulfilled and frustrated and frustrating. The tragic masterpieces are strangely but in every truth not tragic enough; they are mere imitations of our true tragedy, an escape from it through a false contemplation of it.

[12.] People endowed with this kind of disposition should refrain from expecting any spiritual reward for them. That is the temptation that they should resist.

[13.] The *buddhi*, the determining faculty, functions as conditioned by the three strands of *prakṛti*, namely, *tamas*, *rajas* and *sattva*. The *tamas* would prompt it to determinate a thing as a presence, the *rajas* would impel it to make of it an equipment to transform other things, and the *sattva* would reveal the thing in question as ever transcending itself. The *buddhi* thus ever finds a phenomenon as negating itself, as never being itself, the forces of *rajas* anxious to change it and the forces of *sattva* ever finding it exceed itself, exceed itself with absolutely no limits. So a thing as a presence is ever a presence changing itself and a presence ever changing itself is ever a presence transcending itself. The three *guṇas* ever remain in conflict with each other, *rajas* and *sattva* never letting *tamas* to rule the roost, *tamas* and *sattva* never letting *rajas* to have its sway over them, and *tamas* and *rajas* never letting *sattva* to dominate them. Everything here is ever negating itself, is, as a matter of fact, self-negation itself. There is nothing that can be determinated here, our *buddhi* functions as mere frustration itself.

There are however moments when the *buddhi* turns passive, passively alert to this destructive dance of the three *guṇas*, when it perceives them unconcerned and unaffected by their tumult. It is at that time that it comes to be that calm witness, still, passive, and unchanging, of the restless, active and ever changing drama played before it, played within man and without him. When its calm deepens, it no longer identifies itself with the play of the three *guṇas* but stays still and quiet whatever may happen or not happen. That becomes a being's life then, not the dance that death enacts before him. With his calm deepening further, he ultimately ceases to be even the witness, and turns into innocence absolute, into an ecstasy of not knowing. Then alone he attains to liberation from birth and death and the tragedy that they are.

[14] Swans are said to separate milk from water. The seers too are swans because they can separate truth from falsehood, reality from delusion.

Appendix

Supplement 1

(i) Samatā - *Its Vision of Life*

On Life the Successful

Saying 1. Every embodied being is busy here, in this transient world, to attain to success in his life. His days are spent for that end and so are his nights. But only remorse and repentance falls to his lot in the end, success ever eluding him. That is how *Māyā* operates and how it binds.

Saying 2. Embodied in the body constituted by the five elements, he would seek success the true in his percepts and acts, those functions of his organs of cognition and those of action. He would, that is to say, seek eternal peace through their pleasures, pleasures the momentary that cannot but culminate in pain and anguish great and deep. Wisdom, lies, lucid and pure, in understanding this truth.

Saying 3. Suicidal is the disposition that would not hold in restraint its passion for the perceived and the wrought upon, would not discard that passion in accord with the regulative principles of life, principles pure and noble. Unless a man understands this truth, unless he interiorises it, he will not come to be a seeker true of the truth.

Saying 4. True success in life depends on one's freedom from the passion to sense and to act. Salvation will not come to bless a man until he does not shed his desire and aversion vis-a-vis what he perceives and acts upon, pleasant and unpleasant. The world, the world so hard to transcend, is nothing else than this passion to sense and to act.[1]

Saying 5. A captive is this being of that passion, the passion to sense and to act, that verily is his life and the source of every desire, high and low. No way he finds out of the grip of these desires, his life a misery, misery the absolute, and he himself all helpless.

Saying 6. Diagnosis of a malady can make possible the cure. And the malady that inflicts every embodied being is the passion for the objects of senses and their manipulation. Success will smile upon a man, success the supreme, when he finds the peace true and genuine. But that will come to be possible only when he knows for certain where lies his bondage and where his emancipation.

Saying 7. To understand this existential condition and to redeem oneself from it is to live the ideal human life. All the principles and all the measures which can free a man from the grip of this passion to sense and to act are the principles true and the measures true, for freeing him from this his passion they lead him to submit himself to the Real, the True. That is the way true, the way that takes a man away from this his false orientation towards the senses and the organs of action and what they perceive and deal with to lead him to his establishment in the *ātman*, that truth the imperishable. And that is the search that man should engage in, search pure and holy. This is the truth that every human should know and live.

Saying 8. It is thus gratification of this passion, the passion to sense and to act, that leads this being from one bondage to another, those results of his good and bad deeds. In fear he ever lives and in unrest terminal. That comes to be his lot, of this being fated to move from acts to results and from results to further acts, the process never ending. Man is born to escape from this condition, unhappy and tragic. That is the duty assigned to him, his paramount duty.

Saying 9. Identification with the body and the passion to sense and to act go together. That is the delusion inflicting this being, this his projection of the self on to the body. To undo this delusion is to know the truth, the aim of all true *jijñāsā*, of all true investigation.

Saying 10. And identification with the body does not cease, unless one does not believe in, does not find himself tied to, the *ātman*, that witness of all that is. And the passion to do and to sense will not die until one does not cease to project himself on to the body, does not cease to identify his self with it. Therefore, only belief in and self-submission to the Lord the Supreme, to that Light the dispenser of all life, to that Truth the absolute and transcendent is the way to one's salvation, to one's liberation from the embodied mode of being. That is the truth one should realise.

Saying 11. The extent and depth of one's belief in and self-submission to that Truth, that Real, will determine the extent and depth of one's release from that passion to sense and to do. That will lead him to become pure in thought and in action, to the way of renunciation for the well being of others, to the way, that is, of *sat-dharma*, of righteousness the true and genuine.

Saying 12. When the passion to sense and to act gives place to the passion for the bliss unborn and imperishable, there arises in one dedication to the Real, to the True, dedication that breaks the fetters of this being, now turned into a seeker true of the truth. Giving up all his cognitions and doings he orients himself to the contemplation of the *ātman*, of that alone. That is worship and that is devotion, worship and devotion in their very truth.

Saying 13. Dedication to the Real, to the True leads to cessation of the passion to do and to sense, the *buddhi* giving itself up to the contemplation of the Name, abiding with it still and passive. That is the moment to know wherein lies true success, in, that is, still passivity beyond the reach of all *vāsanā*. To stay passive this way is to be a master of *yoga*, of its very acme and highest reaches.

Saying 14. The body is all active, is activity itself, and the *ātman* is all passive, is passivity itself. As long as this being, his *buddhi*, remains self-submitted to the body, the passion to sense and to act will not leave it nor will leave it weal and woe and the unrest that goes with them. Tied to activity will he live, live to die and die to live, without a pause and without an end.

Saying 15. Belief in the *ātman* is belief in the Real. Devotion to the *ātman* is devotion to the Real. To stay in the *ātman* is to stay in the Real. This belief, this devotion and this stay lead to freedom from action and to peace the passive and to bliss the eternal, to success the supreme, that is. Nothing more remains then to know, nothing more to achieve or attain to. For to the peace of *nirvāṇa* one attains then, to the Real that it is to turn into bliss itself.

Saying 16. Only belief and faith in the Real and devotion to the Real can lead one out of the mire of failings that this pilgrimage of life here is. And that is what one should have, that faith and that devotion, with every effort directed towards that end. Giving up all sense of Me and Mine, one should live surrendered to that Real, leaving all one's deeds and their results to the will of the Lord. That is the way your teacher has shown you, the way to redemption the supreme.

Saying 17. Only surrender to the Real can release one from the grip of the passion for the unreal and its charms. Only that can purify one's conduct and action to be a blessing for oneself and for others. Let the Real alone be your support if you will be free from all your taints and all your faults. In that lies all redemption, in this spirit of surrender, redemption yours and of others, in that lies your success the true and pure. Let that be your way, that spirit of self-surrender to the Real, to save you from all your deviations, deviations from your Being, from those your burning tortures. Peace then will come unto you, peace the true and transcendental.

(ii) *Life and the Essence of Life*

Saying 1. Know for certain that the world is changing and the body is changing.

Saying 2. Know that to live pure and doing the pure is your obligation, you who are born a man.

Saying 3. You are not to have any ill will for any man, for all will pass away. Love alone is to be the principle of your life; that is what will make you noble, and your life.

Saying 4. Restraint of the organs of sense and action and steadfast conviction about the reality of the *ātman* alone can redeem one from this dreadful darkness of ignorance, only that can make one stay in the truth and as the truth. [2]

Saying 5. Liberation from living is the goal of living. And that comes to be possible only when you have given up all the *vāsanā* abiding deep in you. Therefore, let your mind be given up to the Truth, and so be your speech and so be your acts.[3] With these so given up, let your life be a life of service unto others, but service without a self-reference. To live this way is to live life the pure and in its truth.

Saying 6. To live dedicated to your resolve, resolve the pure, will lead you to attain to all that you would attain to; to the Real will it lead you, to Being all blessed, to the Bliss unsullied by any regret [unlike the pleasures of the world].

Saying 7. Like unto a storm of dust is this transient world, storm blind and blinding. Only dust can it give and promise, only unrest and doubts. Self-submission unto the Lord alone is the way out of this storm fierce and strong, only that can lead you to rest and to calm. That has been the way of the wise, their way to salvation.

Saying 8. Let you be good unto others, let your life be dedicated to their well being, as much as it can. Let this dedication be true and sincere. In this perishable world, that is the way to peace the real, this holy endeavour; that is the glory true of your life and of every other human being.

Saying 9 Let your mind find peace the true and so do your functions of perception and action. Let you act and endeavour for that end and that purpose. Let these find the bliss pure of every *vāsanā*, bliss unconditioned by any orientation towards their objects. That is the search noblest and that is the seeking noblest, search and seeking for this peace and for this bliss.[4]

Saying 10. True success lies in knowing for certain that the world is a mere passing appearance, and in doing what one is enjoined to do, and in purifying the mind of every desire, in, that is, establishing oneself in the Real to abide and stay all stable in it.

This is the conclusive formulation about life in this moving world. Every gifted soul should adopt this disposition and seek and attain to well being true and redemptive.

(iii) Life, a Pilgrimage

Saying 1. In ignorance of Being the Imperishable lives this being, his *buddhi* entrenched in the decaying body of the five elements, to sense and act its overweening infatuation and the unrest of pain and pleasure its eternal portion. Misery itself is its condition, of the *buddhi* immersed in the body.

Saying 2. The experiences of the body, its perceptions and actions, are the props of the *buddhi*; in these it sees the life and the death of the body, in these perceptions and activities. Not for a moment can it distance itself from these, from these, for it, its very life and being. Its passion for them does not die with the death of a being, it sets up other bodies to satisfy that passion, one after another and without a count and an end. This is all that life is, that this world is, the way it moves, this mystery and this wonder.

Saying 3. Man is born to know the truth about this pilgrimage of life, know for what it is, a mere working of the passions of the body, and what the objects of those passions are, mere passing appearances. With this realisation of the truth of his life, he must distance himself from his infatuation for the embodied mode of being and know the life principle in him, to believe in it and contemplate it without a let and distraction. That is his privilege, of the being that has been vouchsafed the human birth.

Saying 4. With thus given up to the Real, the *buddhi* comes to be disinterested in the pleasures of the body, restrains its passion for them to stay stable in the contemplation of Name the true. This is what renunciation is and devotion is, this life directed towards this end.

Saying 5. When the *buddhi* thus orients itself towards the Real with every conviction and belief, when it considers the body not as a means to pleasures but as a means to attain to the Real, it comes to stay free from every sin and pollution to give itself up to the contemplation of the self, contemplation all focussed and undistracted. That is how one is to do sustained contemplation of the self.

Saying 6. When the *buddhi* ceases to think about weal and woe to stay stable in the contemplation of the Name, it comes to find the Imperishable Word within, Word the *ātman*, finds it straight, unmediated by any means of knowledge. No longer attaching itself to doing and the results of doing, it comes to pay heed to Word the still, Word that is liberation itself. Then it is that it truly comes to attain to *yoga*.

Saying 7. Identification with the body, to be suffused with the sense of that identification, leads to the birth of the *vāsanā* for the pleasures of the body. That *vāsanā* results in actions evil and dreadful. And those actions result in woes surpassing and in fear. But when this sense of identification with the body comes to be extinct, and the *buddhi* self-submits to the Real, to That alone, it, the *buddhi*, comes to be purified of all the *vāsanā* for the pleasures of the body to stay all concentrated and stable in the Imperishable Word within, in that Still Passivity. To *nirvāṇa* it attains then, to peace ever the same. To understand this is to understand the truth about life.

Saying 8. Belief in the *sat*, in the truth, and contemplation of the *sat* is verily the cure for all the aberrations inflicting the *buddhi*, that is the way to attain to peace the absolute, peace that nothing can undo. Therefore, let a man be a protector of himself and with a holy and firm resolve seek the truth. That verily is the way to his salvation. Let every noble being resort to the right means to earn his salvation. That is what his life is meant for, namely, to strive in the right way for his redemption. May the Lord bless every one with noble thought and understanding!

On Reforming Life

Saying 1. All his life, from birth to death, every living being wanders in the world a victim of attachment to the body, a prisoner of that passion. The bodily activities with dualities of pleasure and pain for their results ever keep him engaged in avoiding pain and in seeking peace the real through satisfaction of many a desire. But not even a moment's peace falls to his lot, for the dualities that satisfaction of desires result in are of the nature of polarities, with their poles ever in conflict with each other, conflict that never lets any mortal being even an iota of true rest. This is what mortal life is, that web of *Māyā* past understanding.

Saying 2. One must understand this secret about life, understand it in every truth, to find the way for progress in life, progress holy and sanctifying, and adhere to that way with every sincerity. Therefore, every gifted soul should try to understand the truth about this unhappy pilgrimage of life so that he may follow steadfastly that blessed way to peace the true and eternal. That is the way one can make one's life truly and supremely fruitful.

Saying 3. The bodily actions change each and every moment and so does the body. The pleasures the body cannot, therefore, give one the peace one seeks, peace the true and real. On the contrary, a being who lives blindly attached to those pleasures will find them turn into pain the all despairing when death comes to visit him. This is the truth that every being should know and realise, for in knowing it, in knowing this truth, lies all wisdom and true discrimination. For, when this understanding dawns in a man, he purifies himself of all the impurities of the mind, the fervour of his seeking for the truth become strong and steadfast.

Saying 4. To hope for peace in the ever changing body and its acts is an act of unmitigated folly. Only unrest can one get from them, only pain without a measure, from the body and the acts of the body.

Saying 5. Knowing well what this bodily pilgrimage in its truth is, a man should focus his thought, thought purified of all taints, on the power that brings the body into being, projects it and makes it visible. That is the power that seers of the truth call *ātman*, the self, bliss the true, the Immortal and the Eternal, and the Lord and the Giver of life. Countless are the names they have given it, that power. Let your thought be all concentrated on it. Only then will you become a believer in the truth, a man of faith in it.

Saying 6. The essence of the matter is that the body is a great bondage and so are its actions and the results of those actions in the forms of pleasure or pain. These inflame a being's thirst, the body and its actions and their results, to scald and torture him, peace the true ever remaining beyond his reach. To avert this misery the absolute there is only one way open to man: that he have full faith in the Lord, leaving each and every moment the results of his actions to His will. This verily is *bhakti*, is devotion, this disposition of self-surrender to the will of the Lord, this way of life that can liberate man from the misery of his condition, condition that is merely a conflict of opposites.

Saying 7. The *ātman*, the self, alone is peace the true, peace that passes all understanding. And that peace a man can attain to only through self-submission to the Lord, leaving each and every action to His will and giving his mind each and every moment to the contemplation of His Name. There has also to be a disposition that remains self-same in all the joys and pleasures of embodied life. When this kind of true faith comes to stay in a man, he cannot but know directly and immediately the *ātman* that he is, that peace the true and real.

Saying 8. The gifted man who has been blessed with this holy and steadfast disposition of self-surrender unto the truth, will find direct and straight the *ātman*, find that Word the Brahman without the mediation of any means of knowledge to attain to the state still and non-active, that peace the indivisible. That verily is the state of supreme satisfaction, that state the still and non-active, and that very peace is peace the supreme. For having attained to that state, the *buddhi* becomes purified of all deviations and perversions of the embodied mode of being to stay stable in Word the Imperishable. The very acme of *tapas* is this stability and of meditation the highest reach.

Saying 9. To live and act with the spirit of self-surrender to the Lord and without a self-interest is to live the very essence of life and its activities. For that is the way to the peace of *nirvāṇa*. That has been the inner life and effort of every *sat-puruṣa*, of every truth-become soul.

Saying 10. To live with faith the true and to contemplate the right way, to shed all useless and disastrous desires and to remember and contemplate the Imperishable Truth within and to act ever watchful of the limits one is not to transgress, to act, that is, nobly without self-interest is the way to reform one's life in the absolute sense of the term. For, that is the way to one's redemption. All devotees of the Lord should give every thought to this formulation so that true success may come their way.

(iv) *Life the Holy and Redemptive*

Saying 1. Fearful are these times when the entire world is permeated by unrest and unrest alone. Symptoms of evil appear day after day to undo one another. The cause behind all this mischief is the intensity of *vāsanā*, that result of excessive addiction to pleasures. This excessive addiction to pleasure is the result of impoverishment of the ability to discriminate between the real and the unreal and between good and evil. And the result of this impoverishment is that for most people today life of pleasure has become *the* life, to *that* alone are directed all their efforts and endeavoours, the life of fulfillment well beyond their reach. That is how the *Māyā* of the Lord operates, letting no one escape from the whirl it has set in motion. Strange and marvelous are indeed its ways, of the *Māyā* of the Lord!

There is only one way of escape from this scalding and fearful whirl of *Māyā*, the way of self-surrender unto the Truth, self-surrender firm and unflinching. With this spirit of self-surrender should also go a life free from excessive *vāsanā*, a life straight and natural, a life dedicated to simplicity, truthfulness, service and other redemptive principles with full understanding that genuine truthfulness and renunciation alone constitute the binding duty of man. For, dedication to these is the way to transcendental peace and authentic love for all creatures. That has been the way of gifted persons, the way that made them live in peace and be an example unto others to redeem their lives. And this is the way that every gentle soul should lead his life, this way of redemption from the dark and blinding *vāsanā* and the chaos and confusion that it has made of their lives. And following their example, people in general too will come to have a disposition of disinterestedness and live in peace and harmony with each other. Therein consists true self-sovereignty and spirit of non-injury, in life inclined towards disinterestedness. Every man should live this kind of life, life truly non-violent, truly pure and redemptive.

(v) *Establishment in Life the True*

Saying 1. Beings merely breathe in the world, they do not truly live. For, helpless they live in the grip of their *vāsanā*, their life a mere unfoldment of it, of their *vāsanā*, a mere projection of it, with ephemeral pleasures and everlasting woe for their lot and portion. That is the way *Māyā* moves, this calamity that life the temporal is.

Saying 2. In no way the misery born out of this passion for embodied mode of being would abate nor would abate, becasue of the very misery, that passion with the result that only remorse accompanies a being at the hour of death, that gift of frustration from a life led in this world, world with lack and want for its being. Understanding well the truth about this their pilgrimage, men of sight and insight withdrew themselves from it to live self-submitted to the Real. They did whatever they were called upon to do but with no personal end in view, for they took it as the command of their Lord, their sole refuge and support. They lived a life holy and dedicated to the truth but without self-glory, for all humility they lived. With their faith in the Lord firm and strong, they contemplated the Name with a mind concentrated and undistracted. They were the persons who were true *tapasvīs*, true burners of their *vāsanā*, and they were the persons who were truly devoted to the truth, devoted to the extent of becoming one with it. And they were the persons that attained to the state supreme, their thirst appeased all and for ever. Their life attained its purpose, attained it fully, fulfillment itself it became, that rarest of the rare lives.

Saying 3. Every man of culture should, therefore, know towards what end his life is moving and, gifted with that understanding, he should try to establish himself in the Real the Imperishable, the Real that no duality can reach, no conflict of opposites. With his mind turned inward, let him ever remember the Supreme Person dwelling within him. For it is this holy remembrance, remembrance become ripe and mature, that can lead him to the bliss unblemished by any desire, to come to rest in the Imperishable Word, freed from all *vāsanā* for action. To the peace that is *nirvāṇa* will he attain, the man given this way to remembrance of the Word. This verily is life the redemptive, life oriented towards the true preceptor, life that leads one to rest in the Real and become the Real. All the devotees of *samatā* should strive to live for the truth, devoted to it and dedicated to it, to live that life bright and splendid.

(vi) *The Final Word on Life*

To have a true understanding of the truth is the purpose of human life and not for following the beaten track. The time was when brahmins lived in glory as high as the sky itself. But now you find that glory all lost and gone. And the reason for their decline lies in their forgetfulness of spiritual progress, their vocation true and indeed of mankind in general. Many a superstition and false practice have seized the brahmins of today resulting in the decline of their social prestige and of their intellectual power. Give your serious thought to their condition and the cause that brought about that condition and try to direct your life towards the truth so that the failings that have come to inflict you may come to an end.

The questions that should engage your mind in the first instance are the following:

1. What is the cause of birth? What is the cause of one's embodiment?
2. What is the relationship between life and the body?
3. What comes to be the fate of this living being when his body comes to perish?
4. What is the way to get liberated from the body?
5. What is the difference between the body and the world?
6. What is the real being of the body and of the living being?
7. Does man come to be blessed with a mere sight of, by merely coming into contact with a seer of the

truth or by following his instructions?

8. What is it that brings about salvation to a man? His acts in the form of hearing of the truth from the lips of a seer, his reflection on what he has thus heard and his meditation of that truth? Or, the doings of another person of which one has no immediate and direct experience?
9. Whose is the way and the end (*gati*)? Of the body or the living being?
10. What is the right way to one's redemption or liberation?
11. What is the difference between *dharma*, the way to salvation, and mere customs and mores? How can one bring about reformation of the latter?
12. What is the instruction of the truth-become souls, their instruction in its truth? How can one attain to their state of being? What are the principles that one must follow for that purpose? And what is the meaning of worship of those souls?

Now, consider the answers to these questions given below, and measure with care your ways and attitudes and compare them with the duties laid down for you. Let your *buddhi* be all absorbed in thought. Only then will you find the truth.

1. Desire is the cause of the *jīva's* embodiment. Desire and embodiment rise together. Projecting his being into the body, taking it as his very being, he goes on to strive for the fulfillment of his desire. Desire alone is *Māyā*, that alone is the primal delusion.
2. Take the relationship between the living being and the body as you would take the relationship between the owner of a house and the house. Like unto that owner the living being dwells in the body. Consult Chapter 8 of the *Bhagavadgītā* in this regard. There you will find the Lord of sacrifice, that dispenser of

life, described as the Lord of the entire cosmotheandric *prakṛti,* of the entire cosmotheandric world. Give a serious thought to that exposition.

3. With the fall of the body, the living being takes on another body, takes it on as determined by his desire and the very moment his body comes to die. This is what Śrī Kṛṣṇa taught Arjuna. The *jīva,* he says, takes on a new body as a man puts on new clothes discarding the old and worn out ones. Not for a moment can he abide without a body.
4. Disinterested action, action done without a desire, leads to liberation. That is the essence of the teaching of the *Bhagavadgītā* and that is the final conclusion of all the seers and prophets. Acts done with desire make one immersed in the pleasures of the body and acts done without desire free one from the passion for them. Lives of truth-become souls embody this very truth.
5 There is no [ontological] distinction between the body and the world. It is only when one takes on a body that one perceives the goings on of the world. When the body comes to fall, the world one perceives too disappears. The body and the world have the same form. Where the body is there the world too is. The world, in truth, has no being of its own independent of the body. As one's body is so is one's world. And when one comes to have control over the body, one will come to have control over the world too. Let there be no doubt about this matter.
6. The body is nothing but a totality of acts and the *jīva*, the living being, is the experiencer of those acts; that is the essence of his being, of the living being. As long as he takes himself to be the doer of acts, he continues to have his identity in the shape of a living being to experience weal and woe. When he ceases to identify himself with actions, when he ceases to

be a doer, his identity as a living being gets dissolved into the Same, into the Power that is Brahman. He melts into the latter as ice melts into water to turn into water itself.

7. One can attain to salvation only by following the teachings of the truth-become souls. Mere contact with them, mere perception of them will not be of any avail. Duryodhana came into contact with Śrī Kṛṣṇa but that contact did not bring him salvation. Nor did the sight of Rāma brought salvation to Kaikeyī, his stepmother. Examples countless could be quoted in this connection. If a mere sight of a *satpuruṣa* could bring one salvation, Arjuna would not have been seized by cowardice as he was when the great war of Bhārata was about to commence. And there would have been no need for Śrī Kṛṣṇa to instruct him. Therefore, try to live by instruction the true given to you. That is the true worship of a *satpuruṣa*, of a truth-become soul, and that is the way to one's salvation. Consider it well, this thought.

8. Only a living being's own deeds can redeem him from his fallen condition. No one else can free him from this Law the Divine. Those who would not be heedful about their deeds and would depend on sons and priests for their deliverance are fools plain and absolute. They should understand that a man's own doings will liberate him and his own doings will bind him. That is the law of *karma*. If others could free a being from his bondage, where would be the need for holy acts and where could be the need for instruction about *karma-yoga* that Śrī Kṛṣṇa gave to Arjuna? The law of *karma* is inexorable, one cannot but reap the reward of one's deeds, happy or unhappy. That is the final finding of all the seers of the truth. And that is what the doctrine of rebirth means and formulates. So resort to noble deeds to find the truth, the noble deeds that all the prophets

have formulated for mankind.

9. *Gati*, end or goal, means salvation. Cremation is the end of the body, or burial or immersion in flowing waters. The Hindus prefer cremation to other forms of its disposal. As for the *gati* of the *jīva*, the salvation of the living being, it depends upon his deeds alone. No other factor can be of any avail.
10. One must resort to *sat-karmas*, actions that lead to one's being and truth, if one is to be liberated. What one eats, what one wears, what one thinks, what one associates with and what one strives for - all these should have the stamp of holiness. For, it is these that will lead one to find one's true being, to find which is to find one's redemption.
11. *Dharma* or the Law of life and death is inexorable and universal. No country is free from the rule of that Law, and no religion. Every living and sensate being is born as embodied, every being is swayed by the desires for pleasure and every being is, ultimately, destined to find liberation from this his existential condition. That is the Law as against customs that change with the times and assume different forms in different social and cultural contexts, forms in the shape of principles of conduct, conventions etc. But not the Law, for eternal it is and unchanging.
12. Devotion to the Lord is meant for liberating the living being from the bondage of recurring births and deaths, and from woes that go with this worldly condition. It is there to deliver a man from the disease of desire to lead him to the joy true and real, joy the eternal, joy that is the bliss innate and native to one's own being. Any devotion resorted to for worldly gains will not yield that joy and bliss, joy and bliss the real. Let this truth be understood clearly and thoroughly. Those who do not believe in God too have their share of happiness and unhappiness as

the believers have. For the sake of one's salvation alone one is to believe in the Lord, not for the sake of worldly prosperity.

13. One is to adopt instruction of the seers of the truth for one's spiritual uplift, one is to adopt it for shedding one's sinful and evil ways and to resort to noble deeds, to remain dedicated to those deeds. To accept their instruction as the truth is to worship them, worship them in the true sense of the term. For that is how they came to be the seers of the truth - through resorting to noble deeds. Disinterested they lived and acted, all humility were they and dwelt above the tumult of the world. To be still and steadfast was their life and dedicated to doing good to others. These constituted their life, these traits and these ways. And these constitute their instruction, these ways. To follow this their instruction is to worship them.[5]

(vii) *Instruction the True*

Saying 1. Let a man reflect on the way the world moves, reflect in the right way. And understanding what the way of the world in its truth is, let him keep himself on to the path of peace the holy, keep to it with a resolve firm and steadfast. Therein lies a mortal's duty high and noble, and therein lies the way he can illumine his life, illumine it with the light of the truth. And therein lies his true profit, in finding that peace the holy and that light the enlightening. May self-submission unto the truth be your way and life! May the Lord bless you with this blessing! Let you be a follower true of the doctrine of *samatā*, let you be a guide unto yourself on this your path and then be a guide unto others, then only. That is your duty, duty the highest. May the Lord give you the power to perform this duty, may He give you the power to remain steadfast in this your effort true!

Saying 2. To live self-submitted to the unreal and not to the real is to give oneself up completely to a life given to the pleasures of the body. It is to live as a consumer through and through, a state of being that lets *vāsanā* spread its net widely, *vāsanā* that would not be appeased by any pleasure, would not let one's mind rest and repose. That is the way of the world today, the way that lets no body be at peace with himself, be he a ruler or the ruled. The truth is that the way the cult of greed is spreading, it has set almost every man against every other man, to be an obstruction unto the latter, to be a hindrance in his way. In these cruel times, it is the bounden duty of every man of culture to orient his mind towards a steadfast spirit of self-submission unto the truth. Let him keep under restraint greed, greed that is progressively on the increase these days, and direct his life towards a spirit of restraint of desires and harmony among them. Let his mind be directed towards the good of others, and so be his speech and his actions. Let this be his constant endeavour and effort. Only then will his mind be suffused with the thought of the truth to lead him to peace of mind that every being, in the deepest of the deeps within him, is really in search of. And only then will he have done what he was born to do.

Saying 3. Only fear can lead man to the disposition of self-submission to the Truth, be it the fear of the Lord or the fear of death. This fear is an imperative for man to lead him to think of uplifting his life, to put it on a higher course. And this kind of thinking it is that gives rise to the spirit of devotion to the Lord, culminating in love the pure and holy. To remain steadfastly dedicated to this way is to be on the way to the peace of the mind. That should be one's belief and conviction.

A man of a disposition contrary to this, he who is proud and arrogant and has no fear of any perversities and perversions, is a man given to wicked ways and acts mean and degrading. In wretchedness he lives, a torture unto himself, his scalding suffering knowing no end and limit. That is how you are to think, that should be your understanding. Let fear of the Lord lead you to noble ways, to dedication to *dharma*, for that is the way to peace the true, this dedication. May the Lord bless you with right understanding!

(viii) *On the Teacher-Disciple Relationship*

Hard to tread is the way of *dharma*, difficult to find and hard to cover! Let no one choose this way to truth, for death will be his companion sole and alone.

The guru thou hast found lives on love; drinks in he that springing out, but you would not know this his life, and would beguile him with mere food and drink!

You would not pay the price, you would not measure his measure. And yet would you be a sharer of his share. Waste will you away your labour hard, seeking the thing where it is not.

Your head is the price the guru demands. Less than that will not satisfy him! For all grim is this relation. Not without life dedicated all unto him will you find the truth concealed. The give and take will be settled thus.

You cared not for him when he was there alive before you! But now that he has gone, you would relate with him and be with him. Of no avail is this, your belated relationship. Now, the game is lost, only remorse is yours and anguish ever lasting.

With thought and insight are you to forge this relationship between this pole and that other. Only then will end this give and take, only then will your life be blessed.

Play the game of life with your head at stake! All will be over in the end, nothing will remain, no bonds and no ties, only isolation will remain and desolation. Serve you, therefore, your Master and worship the Name he gave unto you! That will break the ties that bind you to the world, all your fetters and your shackles.

With the teacher your sole guide and guardian, let this

relationship endure up to the end. Your fame will spread holy and blessed to give you the peace holy and blessed.

(ix) *On Husband-Wife Relationship*

On Wife the Chaste

A woman dedicated to her lord will find her heart at rest, its desires all appeased, a woman blessed with understanding all true.

Let her husband be her God, let her worship him as God, obeying every command of his, but command only the just. Let this be her way, with the Truth her sole support.

And like unto a slave should she serve her husband's family, modest and upright her way, all noble her speech, and pure.

And let her home be the focus of her *dharma* and of her dedication full and entire, her delight the noble association and the good of others her heart's intent.

And let *dharma* the true be her life, of the woman given thus unto the truth! Blessed will she live, the mother of children divine and transcendent.

Let her be truthful, let her be good unto others, her life simplicity itself. Let her live ever obedient to her lord, obedient in body and in mind. Wife the chaste shall she be, her life here like that of gods, all praise and all glory. Mother of the whole world would be she. With that name, Mangat, will the world hail her!

On the Dharma of Man

Noble in conduct, in mind all humble, devoted ever to his teacher, the Lord alone his life and being, his life given unto deeds the noble. Let a man lead this way the householder's life, the way all holy and pure, his mind intent on his teacher's word, word holy and redemptive.

Like unto his limb should he treat his wife and serve her as the Law would command. And like unto a mother should he look at another man's wife. And let his company be all pure. Let this be his way, let this be his life.

And let his food be pure and his thoughts be pure and his dealings all truthful. To his parents should he ever be obedient, his mind devoted unto their service.

And let his life be a comfort unto others, a blessing to all that live and breathe. Unto simplicity be devoted his life, and unto the Lord should be devoted his love, perceiving all as ordained by Him. That should be his resolve the firm.

Devoted unto *dharma* should he make his own, his own life ever in tune with the truth. For the orphans and the unhappy let be his care. To the essence of life thus may he find his way.

This way of the householder is hard to tread, this his way dedicated unto *dharma*. But blessed will be the man that would stick to it. In the world like unto a god shall he live. This verily is the word of Maṅgat.

(x) *On Ghosts and Spirits Again*

Saying 1. There are three kinds of diseases:

1) Diseases caused by mental delusions;

2) Diseases relating to the body, those caused by unbalance of the elements, what are ordinarily termed as diseases proper.

3) Diseases caused by external factors like accidents etc. in the shape of injuries, wounds etc.

Excessive grief, excessive fear and excessive joy throw the mind out of balance and into a state of swoon in which the patient narrates many an incident. A being inflicted with this kind of disease or disorder of the mind is often termed as a being possessed. But the truth is that this disorder is a manifestation of excessive sinfulness, it is one's sinful deeds that conjure up such fearful phantasmagoria.

Excessive grief, excessive fear, excessive anger and excessive joy give rise to such disorders. The remedy for this disorder lies in removing the cause that has brought about the state in question. Some resort to charms and rituals to drive away the spirit that they think has possessed the patient in order to free him from his fears etc. and have the balance of his mind restored to him. But methods like these are the products of deluded beliefs and speak of sinful dispositions of their practitioners. The real treatment of disorders of this kind lies in goods deeds and meditation of the Name. To resort to charms etc. is to make the *buddhi* all the more weak and vulnerable to all kinds of delusions, which, devoid of all faith in the Lord, tends to entangle itself all the more in these maladies of the mind. Lest these maladies should overpower the mind, these measures should never be allowed to become an option for one.

Seers of the truth have prescribed only one remedy for mental disorders, namely, good conduct. One is not to give ear to those who proclaim the efficacy of charms etc., for the products of deluded beliefs are they. That will keep your mind sound and healthy, your good conduct. For, diseases of this kind are the creations of a deluded mind that conjures up illusory appearances of ghosts, spirits etc before it. For, no reality have these ghosts and spirits. Belief in their existence will make the matters worse for one inflicted with troubles of this kind. Therefore, let your faith in the Lord be ever steadfast and your deeds ever noble and virtuous. Whenever such troubles come to possess some men of faith, they invoke the Name revealed unto them by a seer of the truth and also recite the *mantras* meant for charming away 'ghosts' etc and also resort to some ritualistic worship.[6] This way they free the mind from its fears. That the Name given by a seer of the truth has this power, that of restoring the mind back to its normallty, should be a conviction with you.

Know for certain that it is only sinful ways that make the *buddhi* vulnerable to these troubles which people name differently [according to their belief and understanding]. There is, however, one way to cure all kinds of diseases, mental or physical, the way, that is, of faith in the Lord and of noble conduct. Let your mind be ever self-submitted to *dharma*, to the Law, to the way righteous. No fear will ever seize your mind then, and no malady your *buddhi* . Let this be your faith and belief. There are, in truth, no ghosts and no spirits; these are mere false projections of a diseased mind, a state that sometimes overpowers some beings. The physical troubles that these maladies bring about are to be treated with contemplation of the Name given to one by a seer of the truth and through association with him, association that is his worship itself. The issue you have raised is, however, not a very important one. People understand these maladies in different ways but the truth is that they are mere manifestations of the fear of the mind. Those who live according to the law of *dharma* and give no room to such superstitions will never fall victims to such dangerous maladies.

(xi) *The Nine-fold Devotion*

What have been described as the nine kinds of *bhakti*, devotion, reflect the ways the mind, when directed inwards, worships the *ātman* within man, worships that shining one in accordance with the kinds of disposition it has come to be or has. But foolish people confuse these inner states of the mind and the ways it opens itself out to the self within with mere outward forms of behaviour they sometimes manifest themselves in. Without deep reflection on the truth mental aberrations would not end, nor will the mind turn desire-free. External postures will serve no purpose. Only inner devotion can bring peace to gifted men, devotion pure and noble, only that can free their minds from fear. The nine-fold devotion is to be performed within the mind, that indeed will be the right worship, not external aping of it. The latter cannot give the peace pure and real. The truth about the nine-fold devotion may be understood in the following way.

Saying 1. Śravaṇa, hearing: Knowing the body and the world for what they are, mere perishable phenomena and the *ātman* to be all-pervading and imperishable, one should hear the glory of the *ātman* at a *sat-saṅga* and strive to hear the Word within. This latter kind of hearing will purify the mind of all its faults and failings and enable it to find the rest it seeks.

Saying 2. Kīrtana, joyous celebration: When the *buddhi* hears Word the true with its attention directed inwards, it finds the world to be of little account and that Real the Full to be all glory. Its love for that all-fearless Bliss then overflows to suffuse its mind, its speech and acts. That is how it, that Bliss, becomes manifest. The lives of *sat-puruṣ*as often embody that glory, are manifestations of it. It manifests itself through their minds in the shape of their humility and distance from the affairs of the world, through their speech in the form of its praise, and in their acts in the form of the good they do unto others. Their staying apart from these manifestations, their distancing from them embodies it all the more effectively. This what *kīrtana* in its truth is, *kīrtana* that one can know from the way a knower of the truth lives, speaks and acts and the way he keeps distant from it, from that *kīrtana*. Many are there who would ape the seers of the truth, who would sing and dance as if seized by the glory of the Lord, but all this exercise ends up in a mere passing amusement with no substance in it. There have been many great souls that have sung the glory of the Lord through their songs and melodies, but that became possible only because they had experienced the divine melody, the indivisible Word within them to strike them with wonder and amazement. This their sense of wonder overflowed into their songs and words to manifest that their state of ecstasy. That ecstatic joy only they knew, those great souls. Ignorant of that inner secret, men of the world only ape their behaviour, of those great souls. This way, they waste away their life, knowing not what that ecstatic song of praise in its truth is, the song that he who has once heard will not have any interest left in him for anything else. Only the man who has heard that praise sung within him can know what *kīrtana* in its truth is. All else is a pretence and mere amusement.

Imitation cannot please the Lord, nor can it give peace unto the soul. Only those who have attained to their goal, have perfected themselves know what it is to sing into love and self-forgetting ecstasy, not those who merely ape them unaware of the celebration of the Word within. These latter kind of people, often given to dissimulation and fraud, mislead and cheat the people, resulting in loss of the latter's faith and devotion. The false *kīrtana* they do is very much in vogue today, but has this celebration ever undone the delusion that people nurture about their being and led anyone among them to be suffused with devotion for the Lord? Fraud can breed only fraud. For, only the experience of the Word within can burst into true celebration, celebration that will make you flow into the Word to become one with It. And that will be the time when you will forget the whole world. This forgetting of the world is peace the fearless, that alone. Only those who live fully obedient to the word of the guru can know this secret and attain to the true spirit of *kīrtana* and devotion. Think about this matter with care and concentration.

Saying 3. Simaran, Remembrance or meditation: Meditation of the eternal *ātman*, one's being in its truth, with the mind all turned within and suffused with a sense of its glory, of that *ātman*, is *simaran*, remembrance or meditation. The point has already been explained in details. Remembrance means remembrance exceeding into identity with what is remembered or meditated. To remember the Lord this way leads to the end of all sins and evils. Few are there, few blessed saints who can remember the Lord this way, can devote themselves to Him this way. Only they know what remembrance is, only they can attain to it.

Saying 4. Pādasevana, adoration of the feet: To perceive all beings as the Lord and to adore them and please them is adoration of the feet of the Lord. A man who gives joy to people with this spirit of desire-free love truly adores the feet of the Lord. Perceiving the self-same and indivisible presence in all beings, he serves them with all his resources - physical, mental and material. That seer of the Same adores the feet of the Lord this way to become, turn into the Lord Himself.

Saying 5. Arcana, to glow with adoration: He who with all humility forgives all and is compassionate to all and soothes them with comfort burns the true and holy incense. He alone glows with adoration for the Lord, he alone knows what this play, this manifestation of the Lord is, and he alone is the devotee supreme and noblest. Ever steadfast he remains absorbed in the *ātman* within him, the world and its temptations, that net of *Māyā,* having no power over him. Only a man who is humility itself and has gone beyond the reach of each and every desire can glow with adoration this way.

Saying 6. Vandana, Homage: A man that finds the whole world as a mere transient and perishable appearance and only the Real as imperishable and pays all humility every homage to every being[7] as its manifestation, manifestation of that Real, is a man given to *vandana* true and genuine. Only a yogī of the highest order can pay this kind of homage to the Lord, only he can have this spirit of devotion. A man who has attained to this kind of holy humility alone can transcend *Māyā* of the three strands, only he can become one with the *ātman,* with the self.

Saying 7. Dāsyabhāva, to have the disposition of a servant: A man who contemplates the Lord with every humility, contemplates Him this way ever and always, knowing him to be the doer and undoer of all that is, is the man to find and attain to the indivisible Word. From being the servant of the Lord, from being His slave, he turns into the Lord of the all.

Saying 8. Sakhābhāva, Friendly disposition: To know the ever present, ever found, *ātman* as the witness of the body, to know that self as one's supreme friend, one's all time protector is to worship the Lord with a disposition of a friend.

Saying 9. Ātmanivedana, self-communication: To experience all that is within and without as the *ātman,* as that alone, to lose the false sense of the Me and the Other is the state where the self speaks to the self. A man who has attained to this state knows only the self, the self alone.

These are the parts or constituents of devotion. Anyone who worships the Lord within him will find himself attain to all these dispositions to eventually merge in the *ātman.* Think about this issue with a pure mind. To reduce these dispositions to mere external gestures or ceremonies will not lead to Nārāyaṇa, that Lord the fear-free. Only the light of devotion within can. Every person who knows the self will find all these dispositions of devotion within him, these dispositions that purify the mind of all its false and evil thoughts. Only the man who self-submits to the Lord with his attention all turned within can know the true secret of devotion. All else is mere show and darkness. Think about this matter with a mind pure [of all its natural inclinations]. To do all actions without a self-interest and with a spirit of self-submission to the *ātman* and contemplate the Name each and every moment, leaving all considerations of weal and woe to the care of the Lord is devotion the true. For this disposition, when turned firm, leads to the end of one's sense of identity with the body, to that state the imperishable. He who seeks will find. Mere words will not be of any use. May the Lord bless you with life the true!

(xii) *On Action and the Spirit of Self-surrender*

Saying 1. Taking itself as a doer, the *buddhi* takes the activities of the body as its own activities and binds itself with the results of those activities or actions in terms of the pleasure and pain those results may bring it. This state of its being is a state of ignorance and regrets, this state in which the *buddhi* ever finds itself in the unrest that its consideration of pleasure and pain vis-a-vis the results of those actions generates in it.

Saying 2. Many desires, desires without a count, then take hold of it, the dualities that the results of its actions are keeping it, the *buddhi,* ever in their grip. Caught up thus in the dire vortex of pleasure and pain it finds unrest alone as its eternal portion. That is the truth about the worldly state of being, this state of dense ignorance and woe the existential and absolute. To bring to its end this ignorance, there is the way of *karma-yoga,* the way of doing one's acts with the spirit of self-surrender, the way straight to the supreme state, the state in which one comes to be truly one's self. In other words, when the *buddhi* tries to give up its sense of identification with actions, tries to give up this primal cause of all unrest, with full determination, a realisation will come to dawn upon it that the *ātman* alone is the doer of every action. And when this realisation comes to mature fully, it will find itself free from the anguish and regret of the duality that every result of every action is. Its polluted *vāsanās* will then come to an end giving place to faith in the truth, to service of others and to devotion to the truth and, eventually, in contemplation of the true Name.

Saying 3. And when the *buddhi* gives itself up to the contemplation of the Name, contemplation all stable and continuous, and surrenders the fruit of every action to the will of the Lord, it, the *buddhi,* so disposed, comes to be concentrated and pure. It then acts only as an instrument of the Lord, its *upāsanā*, its meditation, getting deep and fervent, leading to the realisation within of Word the Indivisible, of that Real the Imperishable. Peace the transcendental then descends upon it, peace the all fulfilling. For, it will dissolve itself then in the *ātman*, becoming one with that indivisible self, self without a regret in it, without a desire in it and without an activity in it, the self that is *nirvāṇa* itself. No action and no activity can bind it then, for all distant it will stay from the body, will stay all still and ever the same. The wheel of births and deaths will cease to move for it, it will stay in itself as fullness and perfection itself, its state of being beyond the reach of the tongue to say and of the pen to write about. Blessed is the man who finds this all holy state, suffused with a calm that nothing can disrupt. Find does he his being the true, his finding ever lasting. A teacher rare is he, a teacher unto the world, this blessed man, with a blessed life that dispenses blessedness unto all. This is the secret thought about the secret truth. Meditate on it repeatedly and cultivate within you the disposition of self-submission, cultivate it to perfection. For, that is the way to desirelessness and sinlessness and to realisation of the truth. May the Lord bless you with the spirit of self-submission to the truth and the power to ever abide in it!

(xiii) *On World Peace*

Saying 1. Without investigating the truth of life, it is exceedingly difficult for a man to act rightly. And without the right kind of effort, no one can find the peace the transcendental that every being is ever in search of. The primacy of human life lies in precisely this that man can know what his life is, life that is the world itself, and orient himself towards the uplift of that life and find its end, the end in the shape of peace the perfect.

Saying 2. All beings live in search of peace the real, be they human, animal or inert. All their strivings and their efforts are directed towards that end. But all that they may accomplish and achieve turns out to be inflicted with a lack, a want, an incompleteness. That is what serious reflection would make plain and clear. As a matter of fact, their endeavours intensify their unrest, intensify it manifold. That is the way the wheel of this all unhappy world moves, the wheel marvelous and past all understanding. Therefore, only that investigation is the true and genuine investigation that leads one to peace the supreme, to satisfaction the supreme and fearlessness the supreme. Otherwise, all effort will go waste, all effort that every being makes day in and day out. Let there be no doubt in this matter.

Saying 3. Truth the conclusive about life is this and this only: The *buddhi* inflicted with the In-sense, with that pollution, takes on itself a body, body that is the world itself, to get oblivious of the truth of the Real, to get oblivious of the truth of the dispenser of life. And with this oblivion overpowering it, it busies itself in making the untrue true, in transforming the unreal into the real and in seeking peace the real in that unreal. For that purpose it roams about in the visible world, roams about in the world all forgetful of the dispenser of life. A prisoner of the I-sense it lives there, of that pollution, ever denying to itself the truth of the change informing the body and its pleasures. This insensitiveness to the transience of the body and its pleasures makes it all dull and stupid, the bodily pleasures becoming its life and being, the source as it were of the peace it ever seeks, peace that is its ontological need. The very state of ignorance is this state of being, the state of denial of the truth, the state of naturalism and of consumerism.

Saying 4. This its identification with the body leads the *buddhi* to acquisition of all kinds of the means of pleasure. That becomes the purpose of all its endeavours; not for a moment does that passion leave it alone. Since indulgence in those pleasures does not quench its thirst, does not give it peace the true, it directs itself all the more towards acquisition of pleasures to the extent of acquiring even a vast empire for itself. But nothing will appease its thirst, nothing will give the peace it truly seeks, peace the true and genuine. That is how the wheel of life moves, this wheel all marvelous and mysterious.

And in pursuit of those pleasures, the *buddhi* would resort to all kinds of evil deeds, deeds like those of theft, murder, gambling, drinking, promiscuity and fraud and deceit to create all kinds of troubles for itself, turning its life in the world into a life in hell itself. Evil acts like these intensify its I-sense to the extent of inertness as it were, inertness that proves suicidal for it. In misery great then it leaves the body. That is the end result of life dedicated to consumerist ways.

Saying 5. For the sake of peace it took upon itself a body and for its sake did it go through all the struggles but the end result turned out to be all wrong and adverse! That is the truth about this kind of life, the truth that every man of culture should know and understand.

Saying 6. Immersion in the pleasures of the body it is that prompts the *buddhi* to investigate the external and gross elements, to find that investigation the only genuine investigation. This investigation of the gross elements leads to the discovery and invention of many a wonder, wonders that make it ever restless and blind to its own truth and being. These wonders, those results of investigation of the elements, lead to tragic and disastrous results. To seek peace the true in them is a sure sign of stupidity. One should understand this truth about this commitment to the I-sense. Dedication to this false I-sense may end up in mastery over the sun, the moon, air, water and other forces of nature but it cannot put to rest the unrest that troubles every mortal being. For, every investigation of external elements, investigation that has the passion for the pleasures of the organs of sense and action for its cause, and the discoveries and inventions that this investigation leads to for the supposed happiness of mankind, are, as a matter of truth, the source of every unrest, unrest in the extreme, and every fear. That is the truth about this investigation, truth that every thinking being should understand. And this precisely is the effect that scientific investigation of these days is producing on everybody's mind. Instead of finding ways to sustain life, people are inventing ways to destroy it. One should be aware of what this external investigation leads to, this excessive commitment to the gross, material world. It can lead, this worship of matter, only to killing tensions, degraded ways, fraud and deception and self-destruction. Instead of investigation of matter, it is the life force within that should be investigated. For, only that investigation can lead one to the way to peace the supreme, that goal true of life, only that can make human life truly successful.

Saying 7. Dedication to matter, to, that is to say, the pleasures of the functions of sense-cognition and action cannot but have complete disaster for its result. When mankind in general totally give themselves up to a consumer culture, with no thought of its implications, their *vāsanā* swells to lead them to all kinds of evil and mischief. People in the grip of this kind of *vāsanā* ever think of finding ways to destroy others, inviting retribution on themselve. That is the result of their excessively evil and wicked ways.

Saying 8. Tainted by the I-sense the *buddhi* finds itself completely identified with the body of the five elements to seek final satisfaction in the modifications of those elements, in their subjective counterparts, namely, sexuality, wrath, greed, stupidity and egoity. Its increasing immersion in these passions pollutes it further to lead it to all kinds of troubles and miseries for it. Not a moment can it find to breathe freely and without fear. That in sum is the worldly mode of life and being. Worship of matter, dedication to it, inflames these passions to an excessive extent, leaving no scope for any possibility of self-restraint. Human beings then turn worse than beasts, inviting complete destruction upon themselves. For worship of matter leads to increase of desires, resulting in exploitation of others for one's own pleasures and well being, provoking consequences that cannot but create every unrest for beings, unrest in the extreme. This is the life style of demons, the very embodiment of complete self-destruction.

Saying 9. Knowing what this consumer culture is, knowing well this naturalistic disposition and this life that is oblivious of the real, knowing what consequences can this disposition and also the false investigation they have committed themselves to can bring about, the people [of this age] should dedicate themselves to the investigation of the spirit within. Only that can lead to peace inner and outer. Those given to worship of matter and to life given consumeristic ways cannot but find themselves ever in the grip of desire, that cause of every unrest and trouble. Those who live victims of this unrest of the mind cannot bring about peace in the world, their prattle cannot conceal the game of deceit that they play with themselves no less than with others. When they are themselves unaware what peace in its truth is, in what way can they show others the path to it? So to find peace within his own self, peace without a fret and fear, should be the first priority for every man. Only then can he show the way to others, through his life no less than through his instructions.

Saying 10. No one can free himself from the grip of the five passions, those forms of every unrest and every disquiet, unless and until he becomes free from his orientation towards the material world. As a matter of fact, if he persists in that orientation, his unbridled passions will only destroy him and others. This is the way of *asuras*, of demons, the way that lets no good name to survive, and no progress.

Saying 11. When the *buddhi* realises the disastrous results of this worship of matter, this dedication to materialism, when, that is, it realises with every conviction the transient nature of the body and the bodily pleasures, then it seeks to free itself from this its passion and dedication. He who understands this transient nature of *prakṛti* alone is man the awake. When the *buddhi* thus comes to realise in concrete and immediate terms the transient nature of the body, it seeks to distance itself from the bodily faults and failings. In that consists the real investigation of the truth.

Saying 12. With the softening down of its sense of identity with the body, the *buddhi* finds itself shedding the taint of I-ness, suffused as it is then with the ability to discriminate between the real and the unreal. That is the moment when it truly becomes engaged in seeking the real, that dispenser of life to this perishable body. With its conviction about the truth of that dispenser of life becoming deep and firm, it transcends its orientation towards matter and its pleasures. That truly is the manifestation of peace the supreme, this its transcendence from matter and its pleasures.

Saying 13. When its contemplation of that dispenser of life within becomes sustained and firm, when it, the *buddhi*, seeks to know that dispenser to the extent of becoming one with it, its passion to sense and to act loses all charm for it. With the extinction of that passion its desires cool down to make it feel blessed in and with itself. Eventually this its blessedness turns into fervent love and devotion to lead it to stay still in and with the real, resulting in complete extinction of the sense of Me and Mine in it. That is the moment when it comes to realise in truth the *ātman*, that power of life, that peace the transcendental. Here, in this state, one comes to be completely enlightened, completely wise and completely satisfied. Here one comes to be replete with hope, hope the full and satisfaction the full, hope and satisfaction that every being is really and truly in search of.

A brief description of the implications of investigation of matter and of investigation of the dispenser of life is given here. It is necessary that men of thought and culture should know the implications of these two kinds of investigation so that their life may get oriented towards investigation of the life-spirit within. For, in that orientation lies purification of mind of all its faults and taints, and in that lies the way to redemption, redemption of each and all. Worship of matter, when augmented into a commitment, can only bring unrest to mankind, for it inflames the passions to do and to act, passions that can bring only unrest and tension to all. Investigation of the life spirit, on the contrary, brings about a disposition of true renunciation and that of true good will for others and to be of service unto others. To purification from all the faults and taints it leads, this investigation of the life spirit. Therefore, the way to one's well being and to well being of all lies only in self-submission to that truth, in turning the flow of life towards it.

Saying 14. Lack of peace characterises the life of mankind in general no less than the life of an individual. Therefore, dedication to the truth, that primary rule of life, alone can lead mankind to peace that they seek, only that can make the individual peaceful, a family peaceful, a society peaceful and life the political peaceful. Therefore, it is imperative for mankind that they become aware of the hold of the worship of matter over them and orient their life towards the truth. For that alone will enable them to cultivate a disposition towards renunciation and to keep their increasing wants and desires in check and within limits. It is this increase of wants and desires that has brought about all kinds of tensions and decadence in the world; that in truth is the cause of the unrest that has engulfed the entire world today.

Saying 15. If, on the contrary, they persist in this their worship of matter, then their wants and desires will continue to increase to create an atmosphere of enmity and tensions and conflicts among them and all kinds of troubles that go with these. Therefore, faith in this life of affliction, this life that never truly comes to be life, must give way to faith in the life spirit, in that truth and reality, to self-submission to it. And wants and desires too must be brought down to the minimum. For, that is the way to well being and purity the true and supreme. This thought is a difficult thought to understand; its depth and profundity require very many books for exposition. Here only a brief exposition of it is being attempted for men of thought and culture so that they may try to put a check to the passions of matter-worship, self-worship and pleasure-worship, passions that have engulfed the world today. Only their own purity and dedication to the truth, of these gifted souls, can hope to do so, not mere theoretical expositions. For, if this swelling deluge is not brought under control, it will lead to complete disaster and destruction, and the show and splendour of this material culture and civilisation will be lost in darkness absolute. For, that is what wor5ship of matter often leads to. Therefore, all gifted souls of these times should try to do right and true investigation of life so that they may attain to a life dedicated to true renunciation and acts of good will towards others. That is the way to attain to the state of imperishable peace, peace where no *vāsanā* is and no fear, the state every being is ever in search of.

Saying 16. One can come to have peace only if one dedicates himself fully to the right conduct, brings under control, that is, the passion of sensuality, anger, greed, infatuation and the I-sense, passions that deviate one from one's true being. This is equally true of others too, they too can attain to peace only through their noble conduct. This is the only way to peace and tranquillity, this way of dedication to the right conduct. If, discarding this way, mankind adopt way the devious, the way given to passions, they will only bring unrest to their lives, degrading themselves to the state of being worse than that of animals. To only undo one and another will they live.

Saying 17. Only self-submission to the Real can make one righteous, self-submission firm and strong. Therefore, only that ruler can generate noble dispositions among his people, the ruler that is the defender of the noble way of life and who himself embodies every aspect of righteousness. For, his spirit of renunciation will inspire his people with the said noble disposition, noble disposition that will lead to the manifestation of peace the perfect in their lives. For, everybody will becomes a well-wisher of everybody else. When people live this way, their life becomes truly life the divine.

Saying 18. There are some that believe that service done unto others is the thing and not one's private life and conduct; if the former is done well, then nothing else matters. People of such persuasions are ignorant of the way Nature operates. For, they should understand that in human relationships the first thing that affects one another is their conduct. A man of noble conduct can easily find a way into the hearts of the people, whereas one of evil conduct and cunning can never win their confidence in spite of the service he does to others, and to whatever extent. As a matter of fact, the service that the latter may render to others provokes their hostility towards him. One must understand this truth about life, understand it well.

Saying 19. A man desirous of uplifting his life in the true sense of the term should first self-submit to the Real and purify his conduct to the utmost extent possible. Only then can he redeem himself and others, only he, the best among men. That verily is the way of *sat-puruṣas*, the truth-become souls. Only one's own self-sacrifice and dedication to the truth can inspire the spirit of renunciation among others, only these can give rise to noble dispositions among others, noble dispositions that embody the very spirit of true peace. Therefore, every man should try to purify his mind in the true spirit, for that is the way to the supreme well being and to be all victorious, and that is the way to peace. Every man of thought should read this write up with care and orient his life towards what it says. Only then will he find wherein consists the true uplift of his life.

Saying 20. Not many will be there to give their careful thought to the deep ideas expressed here. But those who will try to do so will find these ideas truly reflecting their inmost state of being. A warning has been given here against the expanding materialistic mode of life and thought, a mode of life that must be brought under check to put an end to the awful moral degradation of these days and to give rise to a way of life dedicated to nobility and to truth. For, only then can humanity live in concordance and every individual in holy peace to make his pilgrimage of life find its true end and purpose. And then only will this age turn into an age of gods!

(xiv) *On an Ideal State* - Rāmarājya

Saying 1. An ideal state flourishes where people keep their needs within limits, where people refrain from life given to fashion and exhibition and indulgence.

Saying 2. Where people live with faith in the *ātman*, where false beliefs have no place.

Saying 3. Where there is harmony between public servants and the people.

Saying 4. Where public servants are impartial, are not greedy and are given to righteousness.

Saying 5. Where students live simple and celibate and dedicated to the righteous way of life.

Saying 6. Where women enjoy limited freedom but are well instructed in spiritual matters.

Saying 7. Where all intoxicants and impure foods are banned.

Saying 8. Where time limit is set to all activities concerning one's livelihood and business. People should see to it that they keep such concerns and activities within limits.

Saying 9. Where boys and girls study in separate schools; for, education and good conduct should go together.

Saying 10. Where very student can receive the kind of education he/she is fit for.

Saying 11. Where the financial resources of the government have education as their first priority.

Saying 12. Where every being has the liberty to uplift his life in the right way and receives every aid and help for that purpose.

Saying 13. Where the true principles of life, like those of simplicity, truthfulness, service unto others, equality, harmony and the like are widely disseminated among the people at large - these high traits.

Saying 14. Where the public servants are fully devoted to their duty, duty high and noble.

Saying 15. Where the public servants and the public in general have firm faith in the reality of the Spirit and are fully given to noble conduct and to devotion to the Lord and to their land, treating all beings as equals. If they are blessed with these traits, the public and the public servants, they will truly form an ideal state.

NOTES

[1] That is to say, the world is nothing else than the constitutive *other* of the passion to sense and to act.

[2] One cannot know for certain what the *ātman* is. The *ātman* is, as the Upaniṣads would say, the knower but never the known. Though the *ātman* cannot be known as we know an object, know it in terms of concepts, know it in terms of something predicated of it, we cannot doubt its existence in the sense that as the witness of our knowledge and ignorance and their objects, it is ever and always there. Even the man who denies the existence of the *ātman* affirms it. As for as our perception of things is concerned, we do not perceive only the things or objects in question but also their existence, though it, existence as such, remains inarticulate and unnoticed. We come to be suffused with existence or Being only when we have de-predicated every concept of it, when we have turned into innocence and passivity. The *ātman* will reject even the concept of is or is not, for, 'The *ātman is*' too will turn the *ātman* into the not-*ātman*, into an object of consciousness. The *ātman* may condescend to tolerate its description, 'The *ātman* is innocence, innocence absolute' but only condescend to tolerate it but not to accept it as adequate. Knolwedge of the *ātman* means only *neti, neti,* Not this, Not this. Yet one can, as the Kaṭha Upaniṣad would say, be the self as it is in its truth only by worshipping it as 'It *is*.' When a man gives himself up to the *ātman* as *is*, the *ātman* in its truth will turn benign unto him to reveal itself:

> *astīty evopalabdhavyas tattvabhāvena cobhayoḥ* /
> *astīty evopalabdhasya tattvabhāvaḥ prasīdati.* (2.3.13)

[3] The mind, *manas,* means thinking about the objects of the senses and about the projects to be carried out by the organs of activity; it means thinking about them in terms of pleasure and pain, gain and loss and also in terms of volition. When the mind gets disoriented towards the world revealed unto the organs of sense and action, it comes to be oriented towards the *ātman*, self-submits to it. Speech determinates phenomena, sets limits to them, makes them known as against the background of the unknown, selects them as against what it ignores and rejects. Speech does this function not, of course, independently but as an instrument of the *buddhi*, that faculty proper of determinating. When the *manas* or mind ceases to be interested in the so-called objective world, speech-*buddhi* too gets disinterested in

determinating phenomena. This its passivity with regard to determinating is its self-submission to the *ātman*.

I act as a being-in-the world, placing myself as the point of connection between the past of the world and its future. I am the uncertainty that the present moment is, that link between the past and the future. I am that linking and connecting act. My action is the action of a placed being, a being driven by the past but desperately seeking to free itself from its burden in order to escape into the future. But conditioned thus by the past and the future, I cannot escape from either the burden of the past or from the compulsion imposed on me to escape into the future. I am act the conditioned but the act that would be free. When, however, I cease to be a doer and my act turns into a mere event, then my act will be an act without my ingression into it, for I will only be a witness of that act, or, to be more accurate, that event. That will be the moment when that act of mine will be the act of self-surrender.

4. The senses come to be blessed when they give up their passions for the objects, when they stay in and for themselves. The mind becomes blessed when it ceases to be an orientation towards the senses and their objects and ceases to deliberate about objects in terms of pleasure and pain and about what to do with those objects in order to get pleasure or to avoid pain.

5. Man would reconcile the two polarities, would make them one, the two polarities in the shape of One and Many, the idea and the image, substance and qualities, existence and the existent, Me and the mind-body complex and so son. For him to exist is to exist conditioned by name, form, qualities and activities and functions. In the absence of these latter there can be no being. That is the belief of common sense and the considered view of most of the philosophers and thinkers. But the two polarities would not get reconciled, would not be encompassed one by the other. Man always finds himself divided against himself, his self and his existential condition would not get reconciled, with all his struggles and all his efforts. His entire life is spent in this vain toil but his isolation from his so-called being would not end, the *other* would persist to constitute him and undo him. Wisdom lies in accepting the inevitable schism, the inevitable divide and the tragedy of every attempt to make it whole. That is why the text here insists that he that lives in the body is not to be equated with the body, as ,common sense would do, as most philosophers or scientists would like to do. One must own up to this

division and strive to attain to Being the Unconditioned, that Other of our existential condition. It should be understood that Being the Unconditioned is *our* truth, only of us mortals; it is not the truth absolute. For, when one has transcended the conditioned mode of being, Being the Unconditioned too will not remain to beckon him towards itself. It is as the *telos* of the conditioned being that Being the Unconditioned is there, not in its own right. Being the Unconditioned thus is conditioned by being the conditioned. But being the conditioned has to accept it as its goal, for that is written into its being, its fealty to that Other Being. That is the truth for it, truth the absolute, but truth the absolute for a being that is destitute of that Being, a being that can conceive that Being only in its own existential terms and thereby obliquely condition it and falsify it.

6. A patient is not likely to understand that there are no ghosts and spirits to possess him. He is too deeply seized by his visions to be open to such a suggestion. Therefore, the *mantras* are recited for driving away the ghosts to win the confidence of the patient. Meditation of the Name and recitation of the *mantras* and the worship of the guru rid the mind of its malady. With that gone, its projections in the forms of ghosts, spirits etc too will disappear.

7. Literally, takes the dust of their feet as inaccessibly blessed.

Appendix (Continued)

Supplement 2

On the Path of *Samatā*-knowledge

(i) *On the Path of Yoga*

(a) The Consumerist Way of Life

Saying 1. Every embodied being born into the visible world ever strives for his own satisfaction. This is equally true of man as it is true of other beings. If one reflects deeply, one may come to understand what seers have proclaimed as their decisive truth about this one's condition. In the absence of such reflection, every being strives for that satisfaction under the blind impetus of his natural inclinations and propensities, devising many a way and project for that purpose. That in sum is the life he is made to live in this dreadful world, the centre of peace and the cause of his unrest equally evading his understanding. Ignorance is the mark of this state, and is inertness.

Saying 2. To probe into the nature and essence of this life committed to ignorance is to be human in the true sense of the term. For, to understand this one's condition is to know the way of one's salvation; it is to set oneself on to the way of the truth, the way that leads one to peace the real and true. In this lies the superiority of man over other creatures, in this understanding and this dedication. If a man has failed to grasp the essence of the decisive truth propounded by seers, if he has reposed all his hope in the life dedicated to blindness and ignorance, if he would seek all his well being in that kind of life only, vain has been his human birth, his life worse than that of beasts. For, in this pilgrimage of life, it is imperative that man should understand the truth about life's purpose and orient his life towards that end. Therein lies the gory of human birth and therein lies the way to one's salvation.

Saying 3. Every living being, of whatever species, seeks, all his life, pleasures of the body in the hope of finding them all fulfilling. Whether or not those pleasures give him the fulfillment he seeks in them, his seeking continues unabated in the depths of his heart. That verily is the way of the world, this seeking of fulfillment where no fulfillment is.

Saying 4. Embodying himself in the body composed of the five elements, every living being finds himself a slave of the five passions[1] and the pleasures of the five organs of cognition and of the five organs of action. In those pleasures he would seek peace the eternal, his entire life devoted to that end. But the ephemeral pleasures cannot give him what he seeks in them; instead of the peace he seeks in them he finds only unrest in those pleasures. This is how the unhappy world moves, this ephemeral world.

Saying 5. Embodying himself in the body composed of the five elements, the body that is the transitory world itself, every living being ever strives to find happiness the secure and invulnerable. But the body comes to naught in a moment, its pleasures unappeasing and his life a despair without a let and a pause. To make his pleasures all fulfilling a king would establish a kingdom, a man of wealth would amass wealth and a man of family worries about his family welfare. The motive behind all these activities and accomplishments is one only, namely, that he should find the rest true and real. But all these pleasures cannot bring about the fulfillment that he seeks; rather they make him all the more restless and frustrated than ever before. This is the way *Māyā* functions, the way past one's understanding. Human life is meant for understanding this truth about life

- that first step towards the ontological peace that every being is in search of.

Saying 6. The body is verily the world; to be embodied is to be a being of the world and in the world, it is to be compulsively oriented towards the pleasures of the body [and thus towards the world]. Acquisition of the said pleasures, however, intensifies one's sense of frustration all the more. That is the portion of every embodied being, be he an emperor or a pauper; born is he, each and every being, with everlasting unrest and frustration for his lot. That is the truth blind and dark about his life, truth that every human should understand so that he may find rest the true and real. Blessed is indeed the man that understands thus and strives thus.

Saying 7. All mysterious moves the wheel of *Māyā* but its truth lies disclosed before the seers, truth that may be formulated in the following terms. The living being, that is to say, the *buddhi*, superimposing on to itself the I-sense or 'I am the doer'-sense, projects before itself threefold desire, desire to remain coincided with itself, desire to act and project and desire to transcend. With this threefold desire prompting it, the *buddhi* takes upon itself the gross body composed of the five elements, the body that is Creation itself, is the duality called the result of actions. With thus superimposing the body on to itself, the *buddhi* becomes oblivious to the eternity that the imperishable *ātman* is and seeks peace the true in the body, that visible form ever transient and changing, to find itself ever insecure and stricken with fear. That is all that life is, that this transient world is. This verily is the state of being given to ignorance, to naturalism and to nihilism.

Saying 8. With the I-sense superimposed on it, the *buddhi* ever remains infatuated with the body, that Creation itself, causing eternal unrest unto itself. That is to say, it finds itself ever scalded by desire in the form of five perversions that its association with the body of the five elements gives rise to. Every moment it seeks satisfaction in these five perversions, namely, sensuality, anger, greed, infatuation and the I-sense. For that satisfaction it wanders in the visible world but all in vain, for these passions never come to be appeased. As for attaining to peace the eternal and fear-free, it never comes to fall to its lot. To know this truth about life is to know in truth.

Saying 9. Embodied in the body composed of the five elements, the *buddhi* comes to be a prisoner of the five passions to satisfy which it ever remains compulsively attached to the bodily activities. These perversions, these passions, never let it free itself from their sway, making it impossible for it to find the peace it seeks, peace the true and real. That is its tragedy, tragedy absolute. When greed comes to overcome it, it busies itself in earning wealth and possessions, throwing to the winds every consideration of the good and the evil. Discontent without a measure prompts it to act this way. When infatuation or attachment comes to possess it, its sense of me and mine vis-a-vis itself and its family becomes so strong as to prompt it to undo and destroy others to serve its purpose. When sensuality comes to overpower it, it gives itself up to excessive self-indulgence to invite ruin upon itself, its life and conduct a degradation and depravity. With anger becoming an obsession with it, it is seized with the suicidal passion of undoing others. The obsession with itself, with its ego-sense, makes it arrogant beyond every measure, jealousy becoming its life and being. Of untold regret and discontent is this its life, life that is all ruinous and destructive.

Saying 10. In the flames of these five passions, passions that deviate one from one's self, burn all embodied beings, each and every. And all the misery of the world is nothing else than the manifestation of these very deviations, of these very aberrations. For, to be identified with the I-sense means for the *buddhi* to be identified with the body of the five elements and identification with the five elements means identification with desire in the form of these five deviating passions, passions that torment the *buddhi* ever and always. Unable to get rid of the I-sense it wanders all helpless in the world, a slave to these deviations. This is all that the world is, a mere motion of misery and in misery from birth to death and from death to birth, misery all appalling and fearsome. The ever-moving wheel of *prakṛti* has these very passions for its driving force.

Saying 11. These five aberrations and the pleasures and strivings they give rise to verily constitute the truth of life for the *buddhi* that has, under the impact of ignorance, come to be oblivious of the unchanging self, self that never deviates from itself. For, forgetful of its own being, its own *ātman*, it comes to identify itself with the body of the five elements and with the inert dullness of these five aberrations, these fallings from one's being. Seeking fulfillment in and through these ever deviating passions, fulfillment complete and perfect, it projects itself, through the body, into a pilgrim in a moving world, its pilgrimage ever extending and expanding. For these ever deviating passions never come to be satisfied and appeased, indulgence in them ever inflames and intensifies them. To hope for true satisfaction or peace in and through them is the root of all hedonistic beliefs; it is folly exceeding every limit. .

Saying 12. The *buddhi's* identification with the I-sense gives rise to desire in the form of these five deviations, identification that compells the *buddhi* to seek satisfaction, satisfaction real and true, through these very deviations of it. Like unto a patient seeking the cure of the disease inflicting him through things he has been asked to strictly abstain from, the *buddhi* seeks the cure of the malady inflicting it through indulgence in these deviations that cannot but inflame it all the more. With care should one ponder over the disease that inflicts every being from within. For, not without this careful pondering can one find the cure for it.

Saying 13. All living beings endowed with forms consisting of the five elements ever deviate from themselves, striving for the appeasement of these passions. Ever in the grip of action, they move towards death, the real peace they are truly in search of ever eluding them. For never can come to be fulfilled these ever changing passions. Like a deer in a desert seeking to slake its thirst through the waters of a mirage is this being seeking fulfillment through these passions. That is all that his life in the world is. The cause of these passions is desire and the cause of desire is the I-sense. As long as that sense inflicts this being, he cannot get rid of these five passions, passions that are his tragedy absolute.

Saying 14. The obsession for the gratification of these deviations, this bondage, is indeed a great misery, obsession that ever keeps the *buddhi* on the move and in delusion, never letting it be free from its gnawing fears and sense of insecurity. To keep these blinding drives in check and in proportion is therefore the very essence of good conduct and noble life. All the measures that can make the *buddhi* triumph over these deviating passions - measures like knowledge, holy association or influence - are the redeeming measures, for they make the *buddhi* strong enough to know the truth that never deviates from itself and come to be blessed with peace the transcendental.

Saying 15. There is no misery like slavery of these blind drives and no bondage like their bondage. Ever restless remains the embodied being that lives ensnared by them. For, born under the grip of these deviations, he does not need to be instructed into them. Seeking their gratification is a compulsion with him, no cunning and cleverness will he spare for that end. This is how *Māyā* ensnares every being. Mysterious are her ways, beyond every human reckoning. To indulge in these passions is indeed a calamity, calamity that every human being should free himself from. That is how his life can have meaning and purpose. For, the truth imperishable will he find if he can so free himself.

Saying 16. For all living beings, whatever their kind, life consists of nothing else than gratification of these deviations. With full determination and passion do they indulge in them, such is the sway of ignorance over them. It is hard for them to extricate themselves from this bondage, this great calamity and disaster. Of supremely heroic mould is made the man that can earn this freedom, for hard is the way to this state supreme. Only a man blessed with true and pure power of discrimination— discrimination of the real from the unreal— whose passion for the worldly mode of being has been spent up and who finds himself all oriented towards the truth, oriented towards it exclusively and with purity, can realise the truth that his imperishable *ātman* is. Only he will find the state that knows no change and no misery; only he will be absorbed into it, lose himself into it, into that blessed state which is peace itself, peace that passes all reckoning.

Saying 17. As long as the *buddhi* does not realise how every bodily pleasure is a pain and distress, it remains dull and inert and totally incapable of extricating itself from the sway of the perversions that these pleasures are. To free oneself from this demonic disposition, one must resort to discrimination, discrimination true and pure, discrimination that enables one to know how every mode and activity of *prakṛti,* whether subjective or objective, is an affliction and misery. For, only this realisation can prompt one to take appropriate measures for the all-blessed liberation from the bondage of *prakṛti*, subjective and objective.

(b) Discrimination the Pure and Holy

Saying 18. The *buddhi* superimposes the I-sense on to itself to find itself a prisoner of the *vāsana* of the three modes, that motivating force behind all its activities, cognitive or motor, motivating force that ever keeps it on the move. All pain is this state of its being, this state of its attribution of all these activities on to the self, attribution that makes it a prisoner of the threefold desire, *sāttavika, tāmasika* and *rājasika*. This threefold desire impels it to project itself into activities without a count and indulge in all kinds of pleasures, pleasures relating to functions of sense and activity. Add to this the misery that the desire for the fruit of its action is, fruit that ever and always partakes of the nature of duality, giving rise to all kinds of feelings of aversion and attraction in it, in the *buddhi*, and the misery that these dispositions lead to. Not a moment of rest can it find in this its misery, not a glimpse of the peace that it is truly in search of. To know this its unhappy predicament is what is termed discrimination in its truth.

Saying 19. Projecting oneself as the doer gives rise to the *vāsanā* for doing and the passion for doing, one's indulgence in it, gives rise to the duality that the result of every action is, duality that expresses itself in the form of acceptance and rejection, seeking and aversion. Bondage to this duality is the end result of that projection of oneself as the doer. For the sake of *sat-śānti*, peace in its truth, the *buddhi* takes upon itself the identity of the doer only to find itself a prisoner of the conflict of opposites that the experience of the result of every activity leads to. This conflict of opposites leads the *buddhi* to take upon itself other acts, gross and subtle, acts of innumerable kinds, finding no reprieve or let-up from this its confounding and fearful predicament, not even for a moment. This verily is its state of bondage, this its pain and its tragedy, pain and tragedy without a measure and absolute.

Saying 20. Projection of oneself as the doer leads to the projection of the world; that projection of oneself verily is cause the primordial, the very root of this world-tree. *Vāsanā* is it that makes this world the tree grow and expand. And the dualities of the result of action are its branches and its tender shoots, dualities that go on unabated to project the world. Thus from attribution of the identity of the doer on to oneself springs *vāsanā* and from *vāsanā* springs the duality that the result of every action is. Thus continues without a pause this unrest of the *buddhi*, unrest great and forbidding. To know this truth about one's pilgrimage of life, this truth unhappy and all distressful, alone is wisdom the true and absolute.

Saying 21. This projection of itself as the doer on the part of the *buddhi*, this its bondage, and this its seeking of peace the real in the result that its activities lead it to, result that partakes of the nature of a duality, culminate in the unending process of rebirth. But the peace it seeks does not fall to its lot, its frustration getting compounded birth after birth. This is how the cycle of rebirth moves, this process of death after birth and birth after death. False is the notion of one's identity as that of a doer, a delusion it is and a mere imagining. And the fruit of action, that duality, is ever on the move, is ever changing. From where can one find the peace one seeks in this wheel ever on the move, this wheel that this false world-projection is? Only from woe to woe can one move here.

Saying 22. The duality that the fruit of every action is, is necessarily subject to change and deviation, to ward off which the *buddhi* adopts many measures, one after another and without an end. In other words, the fruit of action, that happiness-unhappiness duality ever the move, the *buddhi* would convert into only one pole of this duality, namely, happiness, and would negate its other constitutive pole, that of unhappiness. But the conflict of opposites that every fruit of action is will not let happiness stay, the other opposite cannot but replace it, the opposite in the form of unhappiness. Consequently all the efforts of the *buddhi* go waste and fruitless. Ultimately, in misery alone it takes on itself another body to continue its futile search for another form of happiness. But how can any perishable happiness give it the rest it seeks? This is the truth everyone should know and understand; therein lies every wisdom and every insight.

Saying 23. To seek and find happiness alone in the pleasure-misery duality that every fruit of action is, is an act of utter stupidity, for pleasure cannot but give place to pain, that is the end reserved for it. But life after life, the *buddhi* busies itself through all kinds of means to negate misery, that other constitutive pole of every fruit of action, to find its striving doomed to fail, for misery cannot but be its portion in the end, despite all the pleasures it may have accumulated for itself. That is how the wheel of *saṃsāra* moves, that ever-moving wheel of recurring births and deaths.

Saying 24. Gone densely inert by the superimposition of the notion of the doer on to itself, the *buddhi* seeks in the duality that the result of action is peace the true and real, duality that is a mere modification of the five gross elements. Many an action it undertakes, many an activity for that purpose of rest and peace, undertakes these each and every moment. But ridden with conflicts as every duality is, it can hold no promise of that peace. That is why the *buddhi* ever remains in search of other and new kinds of pleasures, the fear of impending misery ever gnawing it. From the five elements arise the body, that appearance, with its five organs of cognition and five organs of action with their respective functions. These functions culminate in the duality called the fruit of actions, with one pole of that fruit favourable for the doer and the other unfavourable. The favourable pole arouses the *buddhi's* attachment for it and the unfavourable arouses its aversion to it. Ever caught up it remains in this conflict of opposites that the world is, impatience ever inflicting it, without a moment's pause. That is the truth about the worldly mode of being, that process of moving from birth to death and from death to birth, that ever recurring process of misery itself.

Saying 25. This seeking of peace the true in the pleasures of the organs of sense and activity, in the pleasures that inevitably have their *others*, others in conflict with them, as their constitutive principles, cannot but find its seeking a pain and misery, pain and misery great and surpassing. That comes to be its portion as a result of the inertness it superimposes upon itself in the form of doership. For the sake of appeasement of its *vāsanā*, its desire and passion, the *buddhi* seeks the pleasures of the organs of cognition and action, but instead of appeasement only frustration falls to its lot. Every new measure it adopts, every action it undertakes for that purpose, only adds up to its misery and woe. Fearful and appalling indeed is this recurring process of birth and death that the world is.

Saying 26. Projection of one's identity as the doer gives rise to *vāsanā* and *vāsanā* gives rise to attachment to the duality, the conflict of opposites, that the result of action is. This attachment gives rise to all kinds of actions, one after another, intensifying all the more the *vāsanā* that prompted those actions. That is the reason no embodied being ever comes to have patience, not even for a moment. His torments continue to augment themselves, his desire fiercely scalding him. To know this truth about the worldly mode of being is to know in truth.

Saying 27. To be a slave of *vāsanā* is misery the utmost and to be free from it is bliss the supreme. All beings resort to activities of one kind after another for the fulfillment of their *vāsanā*, forging all kinds of bonds for themselves. But nowhere can they find their desire come to be fulfilled. This is the net of delusion that *Māyā* has laid out, delusion past every understanding. To hope for fulfillment of desire in the dualities that the results of actions are is an act of folly, folly without a parallel. For, the change that the tension between the opposites constitutive of that duality generates intensifies desire all the more instead of fulfilling it. Attachment to the result of action can bring no hope to man; a sign sure is it of ignorance and stupidity great and dense.

Saying 28. Desire arises from projection of one's identity as the identity of the doer, and desire spreads out from the enjoyment of the duality that the fruit of every action is. There can be no scope for any optimism in this fearful web, only folly can entertain any hope from this condition. But the unhappy truth is that very many gifted souls wander deluded in this ever moving wheel of the moving world, wander from birth to birth, but no hope, hope in full, ever comes to smile upon them. For as long as the intellect imagines itself as the doer, is caught up in that delusion, there can be no deliverance from the desire for the results of the actions that it undertakes. And as long as the desire for that result subsists in it, new desires will continue to well up in it to set up worlds after worlds and pain after pain. For, that is how the wheel of *prakṛti* moves.

Saying 29. The way the wheel of life moves confounds every power of understanding. But with a disposition pure can its truth be grasped, which every being should grasp to take himself on to the path of complete fulfillment, which alone is his desire in every truth. For, to be a creature of desire is tragedy the absolute and to be free from desire is to be supremely blessed. But not without discarding the identity of the doer, that source of desire, can a being bring to an end his attachment to the fruit of action, that duality, that expression of the expansion of desire.

Saying 30. For, the *buddhi* bereft of every understanding comes to be have cunning alone for its disposition, a disposition for which enjoyment of the fruit of action, of that duality, alone becomes *the* thing; in that alone it reposes all its hope and expectation. This false belief on its part leads it to acquire as many pleasures of the sense- and motor organs as it can. These days one finds many scientists and materialists embodying this kind of attitude and belief. But one should understand that indulgence in sense pleasures only intensifies *vāsanā*, that misery without a parallel. To understand how great is the misery of life, life that is the world itself, is to take the first step towards one's redemption. That is the truth one should keep in mind.

Saying 31. Blindly obsessed with the I-sense, the *buddhi* ceases to understand the truth about its inner misery; with the pleasures of the sense- and motor organs its sole care and concern, it ever remains restless and impatient. In the world of time [that inevitable *other* of this its disposition] and its motion it vainly seeks peace the true to find eternal unrest for its portion. To live awake to the unmitigated tragedy that this life is, is to live truly life the human.

Saying 32. Not without eradication of the density that false attribution of the identity of the doer on to it is, can the eternal unrest of the intellect come to cease. For, that false attribution inevitably results in the enjoyment of the fruit of action, enjoyment that has misery itself as its constitutive *other*. In this world ever on the move, the superimposition of the false identity of the doer on to the self swells the passion for doing and this passion swells the misery that conflict of opposites that it results in is. To get rid of this misery, the *buddhi* resorts to many a way and means, taking on itself many a body of many a kind. But the false attribution of the identity of the doer on to itself, this pollution, does not let it find the state free from this false attribution, the state of the *ātman* all blessed and truly peaceful, ever still and ever free from desire.

Saying 33. Attribution of the identity of the doer on to itself, the *vāsanā* for doing and the duality that the result of every doing is verily constitute the discontent that inflicts every being, discontent the absolute. As long as this primordial delusion, this darkness, does not cease to have its hold on a living being, there can be no realisation for him of the *ātman*, that peace the real and supreme.

Saying 34. The essence of all understanding and wisdom lies in realising that there can be no escape from the misery of the passion for doing and for the duality that the result of doing is, unless and until the *buddhi* sheds the false identity of the doer, that primordial ignorance that makes it attached to the inert, confound its being with it. For, that false identity alone is the cause of desire and the world, that is to say, of the recurring cycle of births and deaths. Therefore, there is only one way to liberate oneself from this world so hard to cross, namely, freedom from this false sense of its being and identity, this false I-sense, that source of every pain and every misery. For, that is the way to get absorbed in the *ātman*, *ātman* the ever non-doing, that truth the eternal and imperishable, that stillness absolute, that redemption itself.

Saying 35. Under the impact of the blind delusion about its true being , the *buddhi* wanders from birth to birth, seeking peace the true in the bodily pleasures, seeking eternal (*sat*) peace in the perishable body. For that purpose, it seeks to acquire as many bodily pleasures as it can. But pleasures do not last beyond a moment and the body too does not last for ever, rendering all its efforts futile, only discontent falling to its lot, discontent without a pause. But its false sense of its identity does not let it pause to think and understand about this its predicament, the nature of that its false being compelling it to preserve for ever its body and its pleasures, a feat impossible to realise. In vain is spent its entire life, in the pursuit of this vain illusion, its body coming to die but not its frustrated desire.

(c) Dispassion the Pure

Saying 36. Projecting a false identity for itself, the *buddhi* in its obsession for that identity does not ever care to understand what its embodied condition implies nor can it realise the end of that its journey. Ever busy it remains with preserving for ever its body and the pleasures of the body, such is the depth of its self-complacency and its delusion, a delusion that can have nothing but despair for its end. That it should find being in the perishable and seek pleasure in pain is a marvel that only *Māyā* can project, that mystery unfathomable. All embodied beings, of each and every kind, wander helpless in this maze of delusion, except for a rare soul endowed with the power of discrimination of the highest order. Only he knows that the entire play of *prakṛti* is doomed to destruction, it is he only that, with this realisation prompting him, seeks the true state of being, seeks it with every firmness and determination.

Saying 37. Human birth is blessed because in this birth a man can understand with lucidity the meaning and purpose of his mortal life. All that shines bright and splendid in the world and all the efforts one puts in, in pursuit of these phenomena are dependent on the body, have their being anchored to it. One should know what these phenomena and their pursuits are in their truth and essence. To follow the beaten track without this understanding will render one's life futile and meaningless, with despair alone as one's lot in the end. That verily is the portion of every being when their bodies come to fall.

Saying 38. Inflicted with the I-sense, the *buddhi* takes on itself the body, body that is the whole world itself. This its false sense of its identity makes it seek peace the true in the pleasures of the body, devoting all its life to their pursuit and enjoyment. But the body is mortal and perishable are all its pleasures. Instead of the real peace the *buddhi* seeks, it finds in them only disaster the great and absolute. That is all that its pilgrimage in this darkness can give it, that disaster great and absolute. With careful thought should one try to know the truth about this life. There is nothing else that becomes a human being so much as such an understanding; there is nothing else more rewarding for him.

Saying 39. This its taking on itself the body, the body that is the world itself, and this its seeking happiness, secure and lasting, in the pleasures of the body is an obsession with the *buddhi*, obsession born out of its ignorance of the truth about its real being. All its life is wasted in this false and deluded and deluding obsession. It cannot realise that anything that has a beginning and an end and appears only to perish, perish in a moment, cannot give it the peace it seeks in it, peace the true and genuine. This foolish belief must be given up, for it renders one's life meaningless and purposeless.

Saying 40. Only pain, pain the utmost, is the result of this, of the *buddhi's* identification with the perishable body, and of its obsession for the pleasures of the body, and not peace the real it seeks in these. That is the truth that every human being should know about his life; blessed will be his human birth if he comes to know it, this truth. He should know that his body will not last for long, nor will its pleasures give him the content he seeks in them, for all pleasures inevitably end up in pain. That is the law of *prakṛti*, of that *before* of creation.

Saying 41. With the body of the five elements for its being, the *buddhi* finds itself burning with the five passions, those deviations and perversions great and grim, seeking every means to gratify those passions, hoping to find peace in that gratification, in that fierce and burning flame. For, with every gratification of these passions, the flame of desire burns all the more fiercely to scald the *buddhi*. That verily is the fate of all embodied beings, to burn forever in the fire of these blind passions. One must wake up to this truth of life to devote oneself to find the peace that never deviates from itself, peace the real and eternal.

Saying 42. Verily, the body is the world itself. To be embodied means to spread out, to expand, the five passions [those subjective counterparts of the five elements], the five deviations, to find these deviations one's very life and being. For, all one does and performs in life is nothing but the expression of these five perversions, of these five passions. Let there be no misgiving about it. In all embodied beings operate these pervert drives, but in an individual one among them often operates as the dominating factor to determine the entire course of his life. Some are born as particular victims of *moha*, blind attachment, for example; others as those of anger, still others as those of greed; others as victims of sexual passion and some of pride and egotism. It is the dominating passion that determines what kind of life the man in question will live, how he will fashion it and towards what end and purpose. That is how the course of their life is determined, life of all embodied beings.

Saying 43. Prakṛti is bereft of consciousness and the *buddhi* immersed in *prakṛti*, identified with it, partakes of its nature, of *prakṛti*, mistaking the gratification of the five passions for the peace it is truly in search of. But gratification of these blind passions intensifies its desire all the more, making it more miserable and frustrated than before. This verily is the state that the disposition dedicated to dead matter, to denial of the Spirit and to consumer life finds itself in. These are all the discontent and misery of life, these passions; and to be and remain their prisoner is all ignorance. And all the pleasure of life, that mean and insignificant pleasure, is also the product of these deviating passions, pleasures that have absolute tragedy for their inevitable end. And all the turmoil and disquiet of the world too spring from these. Let every being be wide awake to this truth.

Saying 44. The extent of the *buddhi's* immersion in the dullness of I-ness determines the extent of its immersion in these passions. And the extent and depth of this immersion in them determines the extent of the all tragic world it comes to create as a result of that its immersion. All agony it undergoes in this world, all the pain and torture before it leaves the world. All beings ever burn in the fire of these deviating passions, all beings whether a prince or a beggar, a wise man or a foolish man, a householder or a renunciate - all beings burn in them in accordance with the kind of bodies they have. Strange indeed are the ways of the world, strange indeed is the play it plays!

Saying 45. Unless and until the *buddhi* comes to understand the nature of this dark life, this life inflicted with every deviation, understand it through discrimination pure and redemptive, it cannot find a way out of the scalding tortures that these passions are. It is these passions that make all embodied beings deadly enemies of one another, out to destroy one another. And it is these passions that are at the back of all the changes in and of the world. For, the *buddhi* under their sway loses every power of thinking and every patience, using these very passions as the motivating force for all its perverse and adverse actions, actions that bring about total disaster and destruction for it.

Saying 46. All embodied beings, each and every, have an innate understanding of the ways these deviating passions operate. A savage understands them and so does a citizen of a rich and cultured city. Even birds and animals and inert beings live subject to these urges and spend their lives under their sway. Natural and inborn is the experience of these urges. To experience them is to experience *prakṛti* itself, for *prakṛti* is nothing else than these urges.

Saying 47. Man's superiority over creatures of other species lies precisely in his ability to free himself from the hold of these innate urges. All knowledge is meant for attaining to this freedom, for that alone, and so is holy association and the vision of the Lord, for lead these means a man from the state of despair to the blessed state of hope the absolute. In that lies the sole significance of human birth, its very essence, in this endeavour high and holy. For, only in human birth can one bring to their extinction these passions. If a being who has been blessed with human birth does not resort to discrimination the pure for the extinction of these passions, then waste has gone his birth, his life being worse than even that of an animal. For instead of redeeming himself, he has directed all his efforts towards his own destruction.

Saying 48. There is no misfortune except these five deviations, no ignorance and no darkness. To triumph over these is to triumph indeed; that is the glory of the human species, viẓ, to triumph over them through right thinking, thinking about truth and untruth. The instruction of *sat-puruṣas* is meant for their eradication, the *dharma* in its truth is directed towards that end, and the justice true of the ruler too has the same end and purpose. Through right thinking are they to be subdued, through the rule of the law and through the power of *tapas*, of self-denial. For, that is how the people in general can come to live according to the Law to direct their peaceful lives towards the state that ever remains itself, the state pure of all deviations.

Saying 49. All misery are they, these deviating passions. A man truly comes to be himself, comes to have the true human identity, when he keeps these passions within limits. All ethical conduct consists in this and all human mores - in containing these passions within limits. When these drives come to dominate human beings, they turn nihilists, deniers of the truth, to invite every doom upon themselves. Let there be no doubt about this consequence of this state of affairs.

Saying 50. All violence are they, these passions, and all disquiet and discontent. A man can do good unto himself and unto others only to the extent he can purify himself of these passions, purify himself through dedication to the right kind of reflection. Therefore, let every human being give himself up to right reflection, for only that can purify him of these passions to make his life truly blessed. For when these blind passions come to dominate human beings, then theft, fraud, deception, murders, falsehood and corrupt conduct become the order of the day to culminate in total discontent and destruction.

Saying 51. To give himself up to the right kind of reflection is the primary duty of man, that verily is knowledge the noble and wisdom the true. For, only right kind of reflection can cool down the disquiet of the *buddhi*. And only that can generate in it love for the truth, devotion to it, devotion that will bring to rest all these passions to lead it, the *buddhi*, to the realisation of *ātman* the unchanging and imperishable, to that blessedness itself. To move from the state of self-deviation to the state undeviating alone is to progress in truth. That alone is effort the true and redemption the true. Not to rise above these pollutions of the mind is to waste the gift of the human birth; it is to take oneself on to the path of degradation, to the path that leads to a state of being worse than the human. It is imperative that every man should know this truth about his life, truth hidden from him.

Saying 52. To subdue these internal enemies through pure understanding and knowledge is to make the only noble endeavour, for these alone are one's primal misfortune and misery, their very root and source. Swayed by them, the *buddhi* forgets the *ātman*, that eternal stillness, to move on from one misery to another that these passions give rise to, with fear alone for its companion. To move from this ever changing and ever perishing life to life the eternal and unchanging alone is to live all victorious and all peaceful.

Saying 53. It is only when the *buddhi* comes to know through pure discrimination what these blind passions lead one to, to misery the unmitigated, that it tries to dissociate itself from them and seeks to know the truth that the *ātman* is, *ātman* the unchanging and all-blessed, beyond the reach of every pain and affliction. To investigate the five elements is to augment these five passions, to investigate the *ātman* is to free oneself from their sway. The extent of the *buddhi's* self-submission to the truth that the *ātman* is determines the extent of its freedom from the sway of these deviations. Therefore, investigation of the truth is the paramount duty of man, his all noble endeavour. And the real is that which illumines this unreal and lifeless and ever-moving world. Knowing it, one comes to know all and attain to all to bring to cessation all *vāsanā*, that source of these deviations, one's *buddhi* becoming all peaceful and all blessed, no fear besetting it. This seeking is seeking the true and this way of life is the true way of life, for leads it to life the eternal beyond the reach of any fall or deviation.

Saying 54. When the *buddhi* perceives with utmost clarity the momentary nature of every bodily pleasure and the very embodied mode of being, then and only then does it seek to free itself from the grip of the bodily deviations and passions. And it is then only that it finds within itself a gleam of true love and devotion for the *ātman*, that [never witnessed] witness. With its devotion for the *ātman* deepening, it finds within itself the state all restful and desire-free. To strive for acquisition of bodily pleasures and, hoping for peace the true in their enjoyment, to pursue them day in and day out with exclusive determination - that verily is the way these primal deviations express themselves in a being's life. Add to this also the discontent that ever accompanies him whether he is in possession of those pleasures or is deprived of them. This state of being, all dull and inert, is the gift ultimate of these deviations.

Saying 55. When the *buddhi* sheds the I-sense, that pollution it has projected itself into, it comes to experience in its very truth the way the wheel of *prakṛti* moves. Every moment it finds all that is formed, including its own body, originating and ceasing, with a beginning to it and an end, and inflicted with every pain and misery. Ever restlessly active it finds this entire motion of *prakṛti* then, ever changing and all dreadful, with nothing in it giving it, the *buddhi*, a promise of any rest or peace, for every thing there it finds ridden with conflict with other thing/s, conflict deadly and destructive, and in this process disowning itself, that thing in question. The *buddhi* perceives all this in its very truth and being when it comes to have this disposition, this pure disposition of *vairāgya*, of dispassion.

Saying 56. When the *buddhi* comes to be enriched with this kind of pure *vairāgya*, pure dispassion, it distances itself from all these deviations, deviations that go with embodiment, to become suffused with devotion for the True and Imperishable, the True and Imperishable that abides transcending each and every misery. Then it is that it ceases to anchor itself to the body, finding it all restless and inflicted with every misery and seeks to anchor itself to the witness of the body, to that its self. To be disposed thus is to truly believe in and affirm the truth.

Saying 57. When the *buddhi* finds the entire world process as a process of self-disownment and inflicted with every woe, it ceases to have any interest in bodily pleasures and seeks to free itself from their sway. It is then only that the genuine desire for the transcendental happiness comes to spring up in it, for that joy ever lasting and eternal. For, it perceives, when in this disposition, all the perishable joys and pleasures as ending up in disaster in its very extreme. With discrimination pure and dispassion pure it comes to be blessed then, discrimination and dispassion that enable it to perceive with clarity the truth about the world-process, the way it really operates. It is only when this clear eyed vision dawns upon it that the *buddhi* genuinely seeks to purify itself of all the *vāsanās*, of all those false appearances. Blessed indeed is this state of being, blessedness itself is it, this state.

Saying 58. Destitute of this kind of dispassion and devotion, this kind of blessed dispassion and devotion, the *buddhi* cannot find the truth it seeks, that peace the blessed and transcendental. Therefore, it is the bounden duty of man to know what the world process, that moving wheel of recurring births and death, in its very truth is. For, only then can he distance himself from the life he finds himself leading, life that finds its being in bodily pleasures alone, and from the way he has given himself up to them because of this his false vision and understanding. And only then can he give himself up to Being, to anchor himself to It. He should understand that this alone is the all-redemptive way, this kind of effort and striving.

Saying 59. The first step [towards one's salvation] consists in understanding truly the truth about life, to know it without any illusion. Then comes the turn of right striving, striving directed towards freedom from the misery that every being finds himself caught up in. That is how a man can attain to all surpassing purity, to the highest kind of renunciation and to patience the supreme, attain to these through this kind of blessed endeavour. And only then can he redeem the entire world. For, abiding in the real, he purifies all beings of their faults and blemishes to bless them with peace the blessed. That verily is the power of one's abiding in the real.

Saying 60. A deviation from its being, a falling from it and all pain and ignorance is the entire ambit of *prakṛti* and the web it has spread out. As opposed to it is *ātman* the true Being, *ātman* the all blessed, all knowledge and peace the eternal. Knowing this truth the final, one should distance oneself from all the transformations of *prakṛti* and give oneself up to the Truth, self-submit to it. For, as long as the *buddhi* surrenders itself to the perishable body, is identified with it, there is no escape for it from the passions of the body, not even for a moment. Hard to break is the web that *prakṛti* has spread out to entangle beings in it.

Saying 61. To know the *prākṛtika*, natural, condition for what it is, namely, all painful and perishable, one should seek to know the truth as it is in itself, seek to know it with firm determination. There is no effort, no endeavour like the effort and endeavour to have devotion, devotion fervent and pure, for that which has dispensed being to the unreal body and which by its very presence illumines this world, this death itself, and which pervades all beings, each and every. Only this devotion, pure and fervent, for that Real can free one from all mental deviations and perversions.

Saying 62. There is no beginning to that Truth and no end, no time obtains in that and no action and no *vāsanā*. Ever selfsame that abides, with itself as its support. All knowledge and all bliss is that and ever full and infinite. That is what one is to self-submit to, that truth that is one's being. Therein alone lies one's redemption, redemption the supreme.

Saying 63. To seek to know that which purifies the mind of all its taints, which reveals unto mortals peace the invulnerable and which itself is eternal and imperishable - to seek to know that with determination is the way to one's redemption. A man should know what his condition is. Tainted is he born with the taints of *prakṛti* to live a life all restless and discontented. Many ways he adopts and many means to escape from this his condition but only despair falls to his lot in the end. Ever desiring to live, he is doomed to meet death in the end, fear and a sense of insecurity haunting him all his life. With every pleasure of life at his command, he still lives in fear of impending pain. And ever seeking liberation, ever striving for it, **he finds nothing but perpetual bondage for his portion.** This in truth is his existential condition, this life that is death itself. Knowing it as what it is, a man should do everything to self-submit to the Real, to make that his sole refuge and anchor. For, that is the way to put an end to all the taints inflicting him and to get established in the *ātman*, that joy eternal and impregnable, that one's haven, that abode supreme of peace the eternal.

Saying 64. To know one's in-being is verily to put an end to all desires, each and every, and to all the agony of time and action. To find it is to find the supreme fulfillment, is to know and be the state where no dualities obtain, no conflicts of opposites. That very in-being is one's *ātman*, that consciousness abiding ever the same. That is what one should seek to know with every determination, that *ātman*, that one's inmost being. This seeking, this striving, this knowledge and this fervent devotion - this way of life alone can free one from the hold of all the falsehood that every *vāsana* is. A man, who has thus come to be established in the truth, has come to stay still in and as that truth is verily a man adored by the whole world, he is it that can bless others with life the blessed and redemptive.

Saying 65. To know that supreme reality is to know the all, to know all the mystery that creation, sustention and dissolution of the whole transient world is. That is all that one should seek to know, that eternity itself. That verily is the beginning of all, that which itself is without a beginning. And when all kinds of knowing turns into *anubhava*, when, that is to say, knowledge turns into what it knows, then only that beginningless beginning of the world, that real the supreme, reveals itself as knowledge itself, as consciousness itself. To know that consciousness, to know that light the supreme, that *ātman* itself, to get truly established in it is to be redeemed supremely. And that is all that one should strive for in every way and every truth.

Saying 66. All calamities and misfortunes that *ātman* takes away from mortals, ever protector is it, ever attained and nearest of all, that dispenser of life eternal, that light the true, that *ātman*. To make it one's refuge is *the* endeavour, the supreme endeavour. And to be devoted to that ever living *puruṣa*, to be devoted to him in every earnest, is to dispel the darkness that duality is and to stand apart from it, from that deadly conflict of opposites. Towards that end should be directed all one's endeavour to attain to the state free of all desire, to attain to it even when one is alive in the world.

Saying 67. All darkness is the life dedicated to pleasures. And discontent ever lasting is the ever moving wheel of action. There is no way out of this darkness and this unrest except the way of remembrance and contemplation of one's ontological being, one's *ātman*. With earnestness should, therefore, one resort to that *yoga* the genuine. It will release you, that yogic contemplation, from the agony of the false pleasures that you seek, from that scalding fire, and bless you with peace the genuine, that life in its very truth.

Saying 68. To believe in the unreal, to anchor one's life and being to the body and the pleasures of the body in the hope of getting peace the true from them is the false disposition that every being in his heart is obsessed with. From this false belief and disposition, one should awake to the real, surrendering his life and being unto it, unto the eternal *ātman*. That is the endeavour one must undertake, for only the *buddhi* thus self-submitted to the truth can purify itself of all the mental modifications inflicting it, all those failings and perversions, and can come to be blessed with joy the everlasting and eternal. Only this kind of endeavour can free the *buddhi* from its passion for pleasures, only that can make it stay still and stable. Therefore, freeing oneself from all these fetters one should follow the path to the truth, follow it with steps firm and steadfast.

Saying 69. Firm faith in the truth leads to eradication of one's attachment to the untruth, one's immersion in it. With that attachment gone, one comes to stay stable in the truth. That is the way blessed to Blessedness, this way of staying stable in the real, having distanced oneself from the unreal. In the company of seers and sages, it is possible to orient one's life towards the real and to have true faith in that real and to be fervently devoted to it. Therefore, one must seek their company for this purpose, company of seers the perfect, those who have made their life blessed and, bidding goodbye to all desires, have come to be all appeased and fulfilled.

Saying 70. When a man comes to know for certain that one *ātman* alone is the support of the body and the moving spirit behind all the activities and motions of the whole world, he comes to shed the tainted disposition that finds that world dead and inert. With that vision dawning upon him, he gives up all *vāsanā*, that false base and ground of his being, and comes to be convinced that the *ātman* alone is the sole ground of his life and being. All redemptive is this lucid faith of that man, this his finding his being as grounded in the *ātman*, in that alone. One must cultivate this holy faith and belief, with discrimination pure and lucid should one seek it.

Saying 71. The *buddhi* comes to be truly discriminating only when it finds the whole world of forms as dead and lifeless and only the *ātman*, that consciousness itself, as the support of all that is. And it is then only that it comes to give up every desire and every false notion to give itself up to contemplation of the self, self the redemptive and the ground of the whole world, to stay still in it. With its self-submission unto the self deepening, it gives up all the passion for action, for that duality, to dive deep into the bliss the *ātman*, *ātman* that abides within [all beings].

Saying 72. To know the *ātman* as the light that illumines the world and, endowed with this knowledge, to perceive all the activities of the body as grounded in it, in that self, and to give oneself up with every love, love the pure, to remembrance of the *ātman* and to stay still in that contemplation is, truly speaking, belief the pure and faith the pure. This kind of faith eradicates all the after-effects left by what one did and experienced life after life during one's long journey in the world, after-effects all false and unreal. With these becoming eradicated, the *buddhi* self-submits to the *ātman*, all its efforts directed towards one goal only, namely liberation.

Saying 73. To make pleasure the sole aim of one's life, to live by the principle that pleasures alone are the things that matter, is to live a life inert and dull. One must awake from this torpor and shed all the passions that make one deviate from one's being, for these passions, these bodily passions, have only misery in store for man. Only when he gets purified of all these passions can a man redeem himself. Let his food be pure, his dealings honest, his conduct noble and his association holy. To abstain from meat and intoxicants means purity of food. To remain content with what one earns through honest means is purity in one's dealings. To orient one's speech and actions towards the real is purity of conduct. To ever associate with people of noble conduct and with those who live ever open to the real is purity of association. When purity of this kind comes to be attained to stay stable, then the *buddhi* wakes up to the forbidding intensity of its attachments, intensity beyond every measure, and turns into a pilgrim to the truth, to its redemption. This is the first step to take for moving forward in this pilgrimage, the step consisting of these kinds of purity.

Saying 74. When a man's daily life turns all noble, when, that is to say, he lives by the noble principles of simplicity, truthfulness, holy association and yogic meditation, and becomes pure of mind (*buddhi*), giving up all its devious ways, then true faith comes to dawn in man, and authentic devotion and authentic contemplation of the *ātman* - faith, devotion and contemplation that will lead him to his salvation.

Saying 75. With the *buddhi* all purified should a man take to the path of noble conduct so that all his polluted *vāsanās* may come to cease. Let him, in other words, give up the disposition to steal and to gamble. Let him refrain from all fraud, jealousy, hatred, and from the tendency to do evil unto others. Let him be truthful, upright and of high moral conduct, be content, compassionate and forgiving and acquire other noble traits. When he comes to be blessed with these celestial dispositions, let him devote himself fully to the contemplation of the self. Soon will such a man attain to the highest goal of life, the man who resorts to contemplation of the self with a mind so blessed with purity.

Saying 76. A man on the path to the real should make it a point to be punctual in his life and do every kind work, work noble and redemptive, accordingly. He must, in other words, set apart the time from his worldly activities to devote it to the attainment of the supreme goal of life. And he should stick to this rule firmly and without a relaxation and should devote most of his time to yogic contemplation, to service of others, to *sat-saṅga* and other means that can lead him to that goal. Only this way can he get rid of his mental blemishes - get rid of them soon, to give himself up entirely to the truth and stay stable in that disposition of self-surrender unto it.

(d) Contemplation the Pure

Saying 77. Only when the inevitable result of all bodily pleasures dawns on the *buddhi*, the result in the shape of woe, woe the absolute, does it try with every determination to self-submit unto the real. That real, real that is one's own being and self, fully pervades the body as does fat milk and fragrance a flower. But that real, that truth the supremely blessed and redemptive, can be realised within only when the *buddhi* devotes itself to contemplation of it with exclusive determination, when it contemplates it with every effort and devotion sincere and authentic and with method the right and true.

Saying 78. In the shaped body dwells the unshaped *ātman*. In the dual dwells that a-dual, in the active and desiring that inactive and not-desiring. In the body with a beginning and an end shines that self without a beginning and an end, in the miserable the not-miserable, in the one with little knowledge the one with infinite knowledge, and in the composite, composed of infinite number of atoms, that non-composite. Untainted by the taints of the body, pervades it that self, that infinite, that bliss the eternal, that consciousness itself.

Saying 79. No means of knowledge is there to reveal it, no example and illustration, no number of them. To seek that unapproached, that unknown self the Word, to remember it, to contemplate it and to realise it, that *ātman*, is the path of *yoga*. With every steadfast effort should one stick to that path, for that is the way of release from the taints of *prakṛti*, the way all-victorious and all-conquering.

Saying 80. Bound to the body, the body that is the world itself, the *buddhi* moves from one activity to another each and every moment, inviting everlasting misery upon itself because of this its obsession. To escape from this forbidding and tragic condition there is only one way, namely, investigation of *ātman*, to be all committed to that investigation. To investigate that self, self the supremely real and fear-free, it is necessary that one should have the guidance of a true preceptor, one who has come to be established in that Real the Supreme. For the great souls so established live a life totally unconditioned by the compulsive laws of *prakṛti*. Their freedom from every desire, their humility all comprehensive, their transcendence from every situation, their repose and stability and their disposition to do good unto others - in brief, their purity and their inner stay, stay undeviating and all stable, in that which is consciousness itself, lend every authenticity to their word. Even a man burdened with low understanding can easily attain to the truth when such souls, souls that have become one with the real, instruct him into the truth. For their instruction alone is instruction the true.

Saying 81. Only he can be one's true guide on the path to the truth ultimate, only the sage that has found the *ātman* within him and has transcended all the blemishes of the body. For, only he is the one to stay untouched by the functions of the organs of cognition and action, functions ever in conflict, one against the other. His instruction, instruction the true, and his proximity, of a sage of such high self-denial, alone can bless one with success on that path. The *buddhi* inflicted with I-sense will ever find itself caught up in the impurities that go with embodiment, will ever think of those impurities, those drives responsible for its fall. Not a moment of rest can it find from those drives and the activities they lead it to. Only the sage who has ceased to identify his self with this dark mode of life, who has awakened to contemplation of *ātman* the ever still and has come to be the seer of the Real - only that man the true can show the yogic path, path the pure, to a seeker of the truth, only he and no one else.

Saying 82. His word speaks the truth supreme and his action reveals the goal supreme. In the *ātman* alone he stays, in that Word the Imperishable beyond the reach of *prakṛti* the gross. Stays he there all passive and still, that blessed seer of the peace beyond the pale of *vāsanā*, no deviating drives of the body ever binding him. That is the kind of seer a seeker of true devotion and *yoga* should approach; he, that sage, alone is his refuge for that end.

Saying 83. It is only when the *buddhi* comes to be completely pure and seeks to extricate itself from the misery that all the modifications of the mind are that its association with a seer of the highest truth can appease its thirst. This comes to happen because the seer in question has purged himself of all the pollution called the I-sense and has come to drink at the fount of the *ātman*, that purity absolute, to bring to extinction all his desires and all his acts. To contemplate with a sustained intent all that he utters will put the seeker concerned on to the path to the truth.

Saying 84. Identifying itself with the body, body that is the world itself, the *buddhi* finds itself in the grip of many a thought and disposition of the mind, the misery of name, form, qualities [or the three modes of *prakṛti*, namely, *sattva*, *rajas* and *tamas*] and action - the misery of those false appearances having it, the *buddhi*, in its grip. Not without giving itself up to contemplation of the *ātman*, that Real, can it escape from the misery of the false appearances of names and forms - those subtle roots of the phenomenal world, those evils that ever set in motion the wheel of birth and death to tie every being to it. Of *Māyā* of the three modes are these the expansion - these false appearances of names and forms [and qualities and actions].

Saying 85. When the *buddhi* identifies itself with the process of thinking, it is called *mana[s]*, the mind. To think about the pleasant and the unpleasant activities of the senses in terms of liking and disliking, in terms of seeking and aversion, to think about them this way ever and always and each and every moment is the nature of the mind; that is what mind in fact is. Thinking this way about sense activities of all kinds, kinds without a limit, the mind ever identifies with name, form, qualities and action - those constituents of the transient world, world gross and subtle. And as long as the *buddhi* remains a prisoner of this senseless and disastrous thinking, it remains a prisoner of the mind to do, ever and always, deeds evil and unlawful.

Saying 86. Speech, that delusion, ever operates in the shape of name, form, qualities and action - in terms of these false appearances. And as long as the *buddhi* does not free itself from this misery of speech and mind, it cannot know the *ātman*, that liberation itself from recurring births and deaths. To escape from these false appearances of name and form [and qualities and actions] that the *buddhi* finds set up before it, there is only one way, namely, firm dedication to the contemplation of the *ātman*, that Real. For, contemplation of the Real brings to an end all thinking about those false appearances of name and form, thinking that turns the *buddhi* inert and bereft of life. And with the eradication of these false appearances, the *buddhi* comes to realise Word the Imperishable to turn all blessed.

Saying 87. Firmly associated with name, form, quality and action, firmly identified with these miseries, the *buddhi* imagines itself a doer and an enjoyer/sufferer to find itself ever engaged in the conflict of opposites that every action [and its result] is. That is its disposition, disposition of ignorance, in this its condition. When, however, it gives itself up to contemplation of Name the True, throwing the burden of all acts and their consequences on to the Lord, on to that Consciousness, that Doer the Supreme and the Undoer, it would no longer set up any name and form before it. On itself then it becomes all concentrated, on itself alone. Only the Truth it finds then and the Truth it becomes, attaining to blessedness the supreme and absolute.

Saying 88. When thus with the right method the *buddhi* contemplates the coming in and going out of breath, its inhaling and exhaling, along with the Name, it finds itself becoming one with the Truth all pure and calm, all the false appearances it has set up before it melting away. To that state it then attains to, the state that never disowns itself, never deviates from itself, where, distancing itself from all the functions of the organs of sense and action, the *buddhi* gives itself up to the One Name, makes it its sole refuge and anchor.

Saying 89. The projection of name and form is the primordial source from which springs this whole world, this whole complex of dualities, of opposites at once constituting and negating each other. This false appearance has come to stay firm in the *buddhi* [this duality in the form of name and form]. And it can come to an end, this false delusion, only through contemplation of Name the true, when it is resorted to in the right way and with pure devotion. With the weakening of its orientation towards those false appearances of name and form, the *buddhi* finds itself getting all the more concentrated on contemplation of the Name. With that concentration deepening, it finds the world set up before it come to melt away, the vision of its being and self dawning on it, the vision that absorbs the *buddhi* in itself, makes it one with itself. That is how the *buddhi* becomes an adept in the way of *yoga* the pure and holy.

Saying 90. Contemplation of the self, sustained and unfailing, will redeem a man [from his fallen condition] if he resorts to it with every modification of the mind subdued, subdued with discrimination pure, discrimination that can tell the real from the unreal. He has to resort to this contemplation with the disposition of pure *vairāgya,* of pure disinterest and dispassion. Therefore, it is important that he should give himself to the contemplation of the Name to his utmost capacity, for it is this contemplation alone that can bring to an end that false appearance of names and forms, that primal cause of all the self-deviations this mortal being is subject to.

Saying 91. Knowing all his bodily strength and pleasures as grounded in the *ātman,* as derived from it and sustained by it, one should contemplate the self with devotion fervent and exclusive. That is how a man can redeem himself, with this disposition and this conviction. For, the *buddhi* cannot disown its sense of identity with the body unless and until it believes for certain that there is the Real that lights up this body, makes it come to be and known.

Saying 92. For, it is only when the *buddhi* knows the *ātman* to be the source-life, to be the life of all that lives, that it comes to shed the body-ego and gives itself entirely to the contemplation of Name the Holy to find and become the self all pure and holy. This contemplation it resorts to thinking of the *ātman*, that Lord the Supreme, alone as the doer and undoer of all that is done and undone. Only then does it find the bliss bereft of all thought, bliss beyond the reach of mind.

Saying 93. With every effort, with every devotion and with every wisdom should one purify oneself of all the stains of the mind to remain ever immersed in the contemplation of the Name. For, the *buddhi's* self-submission to the Name means cessation of its self-submission to the body - its freedom from that original fall from its real and true being and its awakening unto it, unto the latter.

Saying 94. Only the Name vouchsafed by a *sidhha-puruṣa,* the man who has attained the highest goal of life, Name the Seed[2], Name that can be contemplated along with the full currents of incoming and outgoing breath, of exhaling and exhaling, is Name the True. With the guru one's sole refuge, that Name is to be meditated each and every moment, all the mental processes merging into it to repose all still in it, in that their ground and being. That is what meditation of the Name or *yoga* in its truth is.

Saying 95. A man initiated into yogic meditation by a saint who has yet to dispel the darkness of his mind cannot hope to succeed in reaching the goal he seeks. For, without the grace of guru the perfect, it is exceedingly difficult for anyone to come to be established in the truth. Fraudulent teachers can initiate people only into worldly affairs and not into the path of redemption, as is evident from the effect their instructions have produced these days. Instruction given by an imperfect saint cannot do any good to anyone nor can one have full faith in his instruction. Every aspirant to truth should clearly keep this thing in mind.

Saying 96. A disciple will sacrifice himself only if his guru has sacrificed himself, he will be pure only if his guru is pure. And it is the guru's dispassion vis-a-vis the world and his devotion to the truth and his sustained contemplation of it that can inspire his disciple to embrace every noble quality to undo all his faults and blemishes. But if the guru himself is all depraved and his knowledge a mere talk, then the disciple too will end up like him. For, it is only the guru established in the truth that can help a disciple shed all his blemishes and all his stains.

Saying 97. When a perfect seer instructs a man, his noble qualities will spontaneously inspire that disciple of his into contemplation of the Name, into that devotion the pure, his *buddhi* becoming strong enough to shed all its blemishes and evils and get established in the state beyond every impurity. He will follow with every determination in the footsteps of his guru to attain to that supreme state where no desire obtains.

Saying 98. When a man is instructed into yogic meditation by a soul that has transcended every attachment, his *buddhi* will ever strive to make the Name its sole refuge. This way through its self-submission to the Name, it will attain, without much ado, to the holy state of *yoga,* that state all blessed. Therefore, it is necessary that one should seek, with every effort and determination, the company of a seer the true to make his yogic meditation firm and stable, meditation that will purify his mind into joy, joy free from every fear.

Saying 99. One's meditation of the Name becomes stable when one's intake is pure and light, one's dealings are upright and within limits and one's company is only that of seers and one's study only of their lives. Giving up all other supports and anchors, the *buddhi* then makes only the Name its sole support and anchor. Then it is said to have attained to the state of devotion holy and pure.

Saying 100. The *buddhi* self-submits to the meditation of the Name only when the seeker in question reduces his worldly engagements to the [indispensable] minimum and devotes most of his time to the meditation of the Name. That is the way the *buddhi* comes to be disengaged from the deviations and perversions that inhere in the embodied mode of being to find the Truth manifest within the body. That verily is *tapas*, ardent fervour, at its best and highest.

Saying 101. When the *buddhi*, immersed exclusively in fervent and devout contemplation of the Name with every breath it inhales and exhales, surrenders all the fruits of its actions, those dualities, to the will of the Lord, it comes to be delivered from the taints that its actions are, gets dissociated from them. The mind then comes to be purified of all actions, those taints inflicting the *buddhi*, to lead it, the *buddhi*, to the state transcending all desire, to *ātman* the Word abiding within it. With its passion for the duality that fruit of action is, with that passion cooling down, it comes to be all patient, its polluted identity as the doer, that primordial delusion, dying down.

Saying 102. To surrender all the dualities that results of action are to the will of the Lord through giving oneself up to the contemplation of the Name and to look at one's actions too as willed by Him is devotion in the true sense of the term. This self-surrender, this holy self-surrender, alone makes the *buddhi* transcend all its impurities to find itself all blessed. To be immersed in that conflict of opposites that every fruit of action is, is to intensify the very *vāsanā* that led one to the act in question. And the intensification of the said *vāsanā* intensifies all the more one's passion to posit one's self as the doer. One is, in other words, compelled to act further for the appeasement of the desire for pleasures. That is the hard battle that life is, battle [one bound to this condition] cannot but lose.

Saying 103. With their minds all concentrated on the Name, and with their worries about what their acts will result in, in what kinds of dualities - all surrendered to the will of the Lord, *yogins* would do noble acts but as mere instruments of the Lord. Distanced thus from every action, that fetter, they come to attain to the state free from all activity, the all still state that is the Real itself.

Saying 104. Men given to the supreme fervent ardour do every act that they are called upon to do, all the acts of their body, without associating their being with any of those acts. Neither with their doing do they identify themselves nor with enjoying their results. For them the Lord alone is their doer and He too is their enjoyer. As to themselves, they are mere instruments of the Lord for that doing and that enjoyment. Endowed thus with this spirit of self-surrender they find themselves ever absorbed in the contemplation of the Name, absorbed in it all still and concentrated, contemplation that culminates in their realisation of the *ātman*, of their ontological self.

Saying 105. Only those men can attain to the highest goal, attain to it without a hurdle, only those men, endowed supremely with the power of discrimination, that ever remain immersed in the contemplation of the Name, remain so immersed each and every moment. For, this their uninterrupted meditation of the Name-mind-breath trio and their fervent devotion to the Real will lead to the eradication of all their mental faults. Beings ever think about false appearances. Only meditation of the Name, meditation firm and uninterrupted, can put an end to that false and deluded thinking to lead the *buddhi* to get concentrated on the Real and stay all stable in It.

Saying 106. For those ever open to the truth, ever ready to reach out to it, the Name alone is their support, the Name alone is their food and the Name alone is the object to deal with, the object supreme and highest. It is men of such dedication to the truth that find all that deviates them from their true being, all the passions and desires, fall off them to leave them all pure and untainted. And it is they only, men so dedicated, that will come to be established in the *ātman*, that peace the true, peace that ever dwells within each and every being. But it is only when the *buddhi* ever remains immersed in the Name, without a pause and interruption, not even for a moment, that it finds all its desires and all the false appearances it has set up melt away leaving no trace of theirs in it. Then it is that it, the *buddhi*, comes to be awake to the Imperishable Word within, Word the Real and all glorious.

Saying 107. When contemplation of the Name brings to an end the appalling world in the shape of one's identity as the doer and the dualities that one's actions result in, only then will one come to be aware of the Imperishable Word, that Stillness itself where no desire stirs up and no regret. Therefore, one should resort to contemplation of the Name with every effort, stick to it firmly, so that all the after-effects of one's past deeds and lives come to an end and one comes to realise the Word, that Purity Absolute, that State Supreme bereft of every despair [that destination ultimate of all embodied beings].

Saying 108. Only those *yogīs* can attain to their *ātman*, their self, the supreme *yogīs* that give up the false identity of the doer and the passion for doing through self-surrender to the Lord, with the Name alone their support and resort. To contemplate the Name along with incoming and outgoing currents of breath, to contemplate ever the Name-breath this way is remembrance of the highest kind. And, along with this contemplation, giving up one's identity as the doer through surrendering all thoughts of the results of one's actions is devotion of the highest kind. This is the kind of *upāsanā*, of meditation, that makes the *buddhi* pure, pure superbly, when it is resorted to without a distraction and without an interruption. And it is then that the *buddhi* comes to realise the Imperishable Word, that Self, that Alone.

Saying 109. To be free from all *vāsanās*, from those delusions, and to remain all passive when the body is active, to stay all unattached from those its activities, is *yoga* in its very truth. And that comes to be accomplished, this kind of *yoga*, only when one makes the Name one's sole and only resort. With all its passion for the bodily actions spent, the *buddhi* then comes to be all concentrated to find within itself the Imperishable and Eternal Word, with all its fears and their possibilities faded out.

Saying 110. As long as the ego of the doer and the passion for doing persist in mind, one should meditate the Name with the faith and belief that the Lord alone is the doer and the undoer, that He alone is the dispenser of all well being and is the support and protector of all beings. With this kind of devotion alone, devotion all fervent and pure, can the *buddhi* shed its dull disposition bereft of all spirit, disposition born out of its allegiance to untruth. And with this kind of devotion alone can it self-surrender to the Truth and find within itself the Purity Transcendent to become one with It.

Saying 111. When the Name turns for the *buddhi* what water is for a fish, then alone does it come to be free from the tyranny of the bodily pleasures, only then does it attain to the self, self transcending every passion for those pleasures. With its obsession for the embodied mode of being become extinct through its meditation of the Name, meditation firm and deep, it withdraws itself from the nine openings, openings unto the world, to turn inward oriented. This inward orientation of it leads it to find itself as one with the Indivisible and Imperishable Word beyond the reach of every deviation and every woe. All blessed turns the *buddhi* then, the functions of the nine openings unable to make it deviate from its identity with the Imperishable Word.

Saying 112. Passions burn all fierce in man. Only contemplation of the Name, contemplation pure and undistracted, can make them extinct. Therefore, it is imperative that all one's effort should be directed to that contemplation. For, that alone is *tapa[s]*, fervent ardour, that alone is *bhakti*, fervent devotion, and that alone is *yoga*, that meditation of the Name. Even the dull witted can attain to the highest goal of life if they resort to the Name with every faith and discrimination, give themselves up to its meditation.

Saying 113. Contemplation of the Name, if resorted to with the right disposition and with the right method, will lead to *parama-tapa[s]* the highest kind of self-denial, to *parama-japa*, the highest kind of recitation, to *parama-tyāga*, the highest kind of renunciation and to *parama-sthiti*, to the state supreme. To contemplate the Name in the right way means to contemplate it mingled with the equalised incoming and outgoing currents of breath [the incoming current reaching downs to the navel and the outgoing current rising from the navel to mingle into the atmosphere again to resume from there the same process]. When the Name is contemplated this way, it comes to stay stable in the mind, to put an end to all desires related to name and form, those false appearances, and culminate in the realisation of Word the Imperishable. Therefore to stay stable in and as the Name is to redeem oneself from one's fallen condition. That should be man's paramount duty, namely, contemplation of the Name.

Saying 114. Only men of discrimination of the highest order can attain to *ātman*, to the state beyond the reach of every fear. With all determination do they devote themselves to the Name, make it their sole resort, giving up all their passion for the results of whatever they are called upon to do. Only good will do they have for others, these men of true discrimination. For, not without true discrimination and true devotion can one sustain this meditation, sustain it without an interruption. Few among the innumerable pilgrims to the truth can reach their ultimate goal, for few can separate the truth from the untruth and devote themselves exclusively to the truth.

Saying 115. Not without giving up all passions for the bodily pleasures can a man find his self. Nor without a firm faith in the word of his teacher can he reach that goal, and without being ever alert with regard to his meditation, without devoting each and every moment of his life to it. Only to him, to the man blessed with this kind of fervent devotion, will be vouched the vision of the *ātman*, the vision which no speech can express and no pen can describe.

Saying 116. Sustained and undistracted meditation of the Name leads to the cessation of all mental processes - those dualities - culminating in the state of *dhyāna*, that passive contemplation that frees the *buddhi* from each and every duality, those opposites that at once constitute and negate each other. When this comes to happen, one experiences within oneself Word the true, that light of the self. At first, the Word manifests itself in the region of the navel, afterwards that indivisible current rises up to the midpoint between the eyebrows. When it comes to stay stable there, the *buddhi* sheds all its bodily desires, getting all concentrated on the *ātman*. With the deepening of this state of *dhyāna*, this passive contemplation, the Word rises up to the crown of the head, the crown all empty and silent, to resound there as *Nāda*, as Sound the eternal and indivisible. That is the moment when the *buddhi* sheds the shadows that delusion cast upon it to rest all quiet in its own true being, leaving behind all the taints that constitute the body. No hunger survives then, no thirst and no sleep and no misery of the dualities of attractions and aversions, those opposites that at once sustain and negate each other. No more does it, the *buddhi*, enjoy or suffer with the organs of perception then or with those of action, for all passive it stays in the midst of their activities, happy or unhappy. To the very highest reaches of *yoga* then the *buddhi* comes to have attained.

Saying 117. Formidable indeed is the power of the perversions inflicting the mind, seldom do they fail to pervert the *buddhi* too, with all its efforts and struggles to the contrary. Only a supremely wise man can succeed in this path of redemption, in this path of *yoga*. For, the confusion of the *ātman* with the false identity of the doer, the confusion that does not allow the *buddhi* to know and be the self that it truly is, does not get dispelled without an exceedingly hard effort and struggle.

Saying 118. But sustained meditation of the Name, carried on with firm determination, and surrender of the fruit of all one's actions to the will of the Lord can lead one smoothly to that goal, the goal of the eradication of one's false identity as the doer. The latter disposition of self-surrender to the will of the Lord is also called *bhakti-yoga*, the path of devotion, and *karma-yoga*, the path of [disinterested] actions. Not without this spirit of self-surrender can one succeed in meditation of the Name, cannot sustain it to perfection. For, the conflict of the opposites that constitute one's life does not allow one to rest all passive and innocent even for a moment. And to think of knowing the *ātman* and to be the *ātman* without that rest and passivity is the dream of only the naive and foolish.

Saying 119. For, the world is nothing else than the *buddhi* on the move, and knowledge of the self, one's true being, is nothing else than the *buddhi* the still and at rest. As for the *buddhi*, it cannot be still and at rest, cannot free itself from the compulsion of being ever active and on the move, as long as it does not cease to project itself as the doer. Its actions will continue to result in conflicts of opposites, setting aflame its *vāsanā* all fierce and awful to compel it to act further without a let or a pause. Therefore, the only way, way the redemptive, open to man is the way of self-surrender, the way he should stick to with every effort and determination. Let him shed his false identity as the doer, let him know and believe that it is the Lord alone, that Witness, that does all and undoes all. Let him stand apart from the misery of dualities, let him never engage himself in those ambiguities with their polar opposites ever in conflict with and destructive of each other.

Saying 120. Non-doer is the *ātman*, non-activity itself is it, and inflicted with the identity of the doer is the *buddhi* and with the passion for doing. It, the *buddhi*, cannot, therefore, know the *ātman* unless and until it is purged of its sense of its identity as the doer, that darkness primordial. All forms of *yoga* - that of *bhakti*, devotion, that of *karma*, action, and that of *jñāna*, knowledge - have only one aim, namely, eradication of the false identity of the doer which the *buddhi* has superimposed on to itself and, with that eradication, to know and be the *ātman*, that self beyond every misery, that light the supreme.

Saying 121. It is the malady of that false identity with which the *buddhi* has confounded its being, its self, that compels it to get immersed in what its actions result in, viz., the dualities with their constituents out to undo each other. This, its immersion leads it to fall a prey to *vāsanās* without a count and actions without a number, *vāsanās* and actions that ever keep it on the move. Not even a moment can it find to be at rest with itself, to be free from passion or desire. To be in this condition is to live addicted to delusion and falsehood and to nihilism [or atheism].

Saying 122. To extricate oneself from this web of delusion, from this self the doer, from this delusion past every understanding, there is only one way, namely, self-submission to the *ātman* that abides as the *sākṣī [sākṣin]*, as the witness, of all that is, and, with this spirit of self-submission, to know and be the *ātman*, that all peace and all quiet. Self-submission to the body must give place to self-submission to the *ātman*, for only through this self-submission can one know that self the real and be that self the real. Therefore, one must have all faith in the *ātman* and all devotion for it, devotion true and genuine. That is the only way to free oneself from the shackles of bodily pleasures and to give oneself up to that real, to make it one's sole refuge and resort. That will wash one of all one's taints and evils, that spirit of self-surrender firm and constant.

Saying 123. To strive to know that self, to ever strive to know that Real the absolute, is to be blessed truly and supremely. Beyond the sphere of every activity abides the self, inflicted by no desire whatsoever, staying all still in itself and never deviating from itself. Acts it not, enjoys it not and suffers it not; all indivisible it stays, all undifferentiated, all-knowing and eternal, no taints of *prakṛti* touching it. To remember that eternal presence (*avigata*), to contemplate it, is, for the *buddhi*, to break all the ties that bind it with the evils of *prakṛti*, to be free from them. This verily is the way thrown open to man, the way to his liberation.

Saying 124. Man is not to prefer the way of *kartāpan*, that false identity superimposed on to his self, to the way of self-submission to the self, that reality absolute. For, in that lies his degradation, degradation below that of animals, in that false sense of his identity. In dualities, those results of his actions, will he find himself immersed, that doer, dualities ridden by self-conflicts, to make him all dull and asleep to his true self, a victim of *vāsanā*, all fierce and destructive of him no less than of others. For, that is where these two lead one to, his false sense of his self as the doer and his passion for the dualities his actions result in. All evil and demonic his life turns then. For, this ignorance, this confusion of one's self with the doer, leaves one ever frustrated, one's passion for the fruit of actions never coming to be appeased. Rather, gratification of that passion makes one all the more obsessed with the pleasures one has enjoyed, those fruits of his actions, obssesed to the extent that he would not hesitate even to do deeds of utmost cruelty in order to satisfy that passion. Death alone he provokes then, his own no less than that of others.

Saying 125. It is the privilege of man that he can, he has the ability and the capacity, to dissociate himself from the awful misery that the net of *prakṛti* is. It is his privilege alone to attain to that peace the transcendent, peace that every being is ever in search of. The unhappy fact however is that instead of dissociating themselves from the net of *prakṛti*, beings get immersed in it to seek that peace eternal, falling asleep [to its true abode, namely, their own self, their own *ātman*]. Of ignorance, ignorance dark and deep, is this their state of being.

Saying 126. The Vedas call upon man to free himself from this delusion, this his superimposition of the concept of the doer on to his self and to know the a-doing real that he truly is, the imperishable real, that peace the eternal. And so do call upon him all other scriptures and those that have attained to the final goal of life. With every effort he should seek to know that self, with every power of discrimination, with every devotion and love - should know the self seeking his redemption, redemption the pure and real. Let him have every faith in that spirit, that dispenser of life in all its forms, let him contemplate it with every firmness. Only then will he find it, will have an all lucid vision of it, of that his own native home and place.

Saying 127. The *buddhi* is to look at all the passions of the body as what they really are, as mere perversions of its true being; it must have a lucid understanding of what these passions can bring it - mere discontent and unrest in their very excess. Only when it comes to have this understanding and this vision will it self-submit to the Real, only then. With this its disposition of self-submission deepening, it finds itself shedding its identity as the doer, that pollution inflicting it. At last a time will come when, with its fervour of devotion swelling, it will come to know and be the Real that it truly is, its fears all gone and dispelled.

Saying 128. There is no way to self-purification, self-purification the absolute, except this disposition of self-surrender to the Universal Witness abiding within each and every being. To resort to it is to shed all polluted *vāsanās* and all sinful deeds; the deeper this spirit of self-surrender the greater its freedom from that *vāsanā* and those deeds. Freedom from polluted *vāsanā* leads to freedom from sinful deeds, and freedom from sinful deeds leads to the empowerment of the *buddhi*, to its becoming strong enough to strive for the spirit of self-submission to the Real, for that spirit only. True devotion to the Lord lies in this very disposition, in this very spirit of self-surrender.

Saying 129. To no avail has lived the man that has not purified himself of the stains of mind and who has not surrendered his being to the Real with every sincerity. His piety will be a mere display and show, an expression of a mean mentality. An impostor will he live to bring ruin and destruction to his soul.

Saying 130. Every embodied being would redeem himself, that is his search and endeavour right from his birth. But through pleasures of the body would he seek that end, such is the density of his ignorance, of his deluded understanding. With every cunning would he acquire those pleasures, make every effort for that purpose. But *prakṛti* [that site of his endeavours] is ever subject to change and inflicted with every misery. To seek the redemptive peace in it, redemptive peace that every being is in search of, is a mere folly, folly in its extreme. There is a lack inscribed into the body and into the pleasures it can give and promise. They cannot give this being what he seeks in them. Only Real the Full can make whole that lack, only its search can fill him with hope, hope all full and perfect. And that Real the Full only the *ātman* is, the light that illumines this inert world, this death [*kāla*] of every being.

Saying 131. To seek that infinite and imperishable Real is verily to be redeemed. One should, therefore, surrender oneself to the one *ātman* with every effort to extricate oneself from the grip of *vāsanās*, those all unreal and all painful appearances. It is not for bodily pleasures to appease *vāsanās*, only knowledge of the *ātman* can accomplish that end. That is the truth one should never forget.

Saying 132. The whole ambit of *prakṛti* is the play of *vāsanā*, that is what sets it up, that play. And *vāsanā* it is that brings about every change in every thing, compelling every being to be ever active to fulfill it, fulfill *vāsanā* itself, this their very misery, but fulfill it through things that themselves are ridden with *vāsanā*. So, instead of fulfilling it, beings set it aflame all the more to find discontent alone as their eternal lot. That verily is the truth about the worldly condition that those lost in that condition obstinately refuse, in their ignorance, to take notice of. However, those who come to have insight into this their truth should never fail to seek to know the *ātman*, that truth the infinite, truth that transcends every desire and every taint.

Saying 133. To bring about fulfillment of *vāsanā*, to be free from the misery of doing and from ever recurring births and deaths, to bring that ever moving wheel to the final rest, one should seek, firmly and with determination, to know and be the *ātman*, *ātman* that ever abides self-same and imperishable. For, that is the way to be supremely blessed, the way to liberation final and absolute.

Saying 134. Let one have firm belief in that Real the absolute, and having that belief bring all blessings to oneself and to others. That is, in ever truth, the way of the gods. One must rely on his own efforts, efforts right and noble, to break one's ties, to dispel one's delusion and one's discontent and unrest. Only that can bring about supreme beatitude, one's own right effort. Eternal misery pursues those who, instead of depending on their own effort, seek to depend on their imagined gods, for ever tied will they remain to this ever moving and cruel wheel of *prakṛti*.

Saying 135. Let a mortal be wide awake to this his deluded condition, where the wheel of birth and death ever moves on for him, let him be ever awake to it to find the way to redeem himself from it, for death approaches him inevitably and inexorably. Wise is the man who reflects deeply on this his mortal condition and who has lived through the misery of bodily pleasures, has felt it, that pain, felt it deep in him. Only he will tread the path of truth, that man of wisdom, and attain to the goal supreme of life.

Saying 136. With discrimination pure can the *buddhi* attain to and sustain the meditative disposition, meditative disposition true and pure, and through association with seers of the highest truth. When it comes to be so enriched, all the effects and traces that its past lives have inscribed into it come to be extinct without much of a trouble, leading it to repose and rest in its own true being.

Saying 137. When its dissociation from all the deviations of *prakṛ*ti and its adherence to meditation of the Name become firm and stable, the *buddhi* finds knowledge of self the non-doing dawning within it, knowledge that culminates in its becoming one with that self. Peace the transcendental does it find then, its passion for bodily actions and activities all dead. This is its natural state, its state innate, of the *buddhi*. A man who has attained to this state knows in full the world, knows its way and its goal, his life an inspiration for others, an example to emulate.

Saying 138. When the *buddhi* stands apart from the body to find the self within it, then all the actions and activities of the body, those taints and evils, fall off it, for the self at no time either acts or suffers. But it can know the self, self different from the body, only when no passions of the body, passions that deviate the *buddhi* from its true being, can ever tempt it away from its disposition of self-surrender to the *ātman*. Without this distancing from the body and the taints of *prakṛti* and self-submission to the *ātman*, no one can ever hope to find his being and self, howsoever learned he may be. His condition, of that mere prattler, will be like that of a man who would slake his thirst from the waters sketched on a map.

Saying 139. With every effort should one try to break one's fetters, those deadly fetters of delusion, effort sincere and pure. And with every effort and determination too should one try to know, know for certain, that there is such a thing as one's *ātman*, one's true being and self. For only this certainty about the truth of the self, about its reality, can free one from every false belief and from every attachment. A being who does not have this kind of belief in the *ātman* and seeks peace the true in the sphere of the not-self will find in his last hour every hope desert him and every way closed for him, with woe, woe all overwhelming, for his sole companion to the life to come.

Saying 140. The world is ever on the move and so is the body, body of each and every being. Ever aware of this change, this eternal process of self-disowning, one must seek to know and find the *ātman*, that self the eternal, that self without a beginning. Here in this world the wisest man is all-unwise, the richest man is a discontent, and one of long life would still hope to live more. This is how moves the wheel of *prakṛti*, with its all ensnaring illusions. A mortal must free himself from this delusion and seek to know *that*, that being and truth, to know which is to know the all and to find which is to find the all with all one's hopes fulfilled. Only the *ātman*, that Real itself, can hold out this promise and redeem this promise. He alone is the cleverest among the cleverest, he who has come to this understanding and this conviction.

Saying 141. Only through self-submission to the *ātman*, to that Real the absolute can a mortal redeem himself from the misery that his life is, from every pain inflicting him. For, to be convinced of the truth of the self means eradication of one's orientation towards the *other*, towards the not-self. And contemplation of the self leads to the end of every deliberation about the not-self. And to know and be the *ātman* means the end of the world, of that recurring process of birth and death, that recurring delusion of the *buddhi*.

Saying 142. When the *buddhi* comes to be concentrated on itself to know and be the Real that the *ātman* is, it attains to peace the alone, peace beyond one's ken and expression. The forbidding desire for the body, for that would itself - desire that keeps every being on the move and compels him to do acts of all kinds and without a count then comes to cease, leaving the *buddhi* all still, its *vāsanā* and its passion to act finally set at rest.

Saying 143. With its self-submission to the *ātman* getting deeper, the *buddhi* finds this entire *prakṛti*, *prakṛti* bereft of life, as rooted in the *ātman*, in that Living Spirit, finds its being in that Being, and its life in that Life. With this vision dawning upon it, the *buddhi* comes to turn into mere 'contemplation-of-the-self,' that only, its all-surging love undoing the doer in it, that false projection of itself. In the *ātman* alone then it comes to stay and established, in that still no-activity alone.[3]

Saying 144. When the *buddhi* gives itself, with every devotion and love, to the contemplation of the self, its desires, each and every, will fall off it and also all that it has set up before it. Stays it then all still in the body of the nine gates, the Word Eternal resounding there, that Real the Absolute, to appease all the thirst that has ever tormented it, life after life and death after death. Nothing remains inaccessible then for the man who has attained to this state, nothing beyond his reach, of the man so blest.

Saying 145. When its love for the *ātman* comes to suffuse the *buddhi*, suffuse it irreversibly, it withdraws itself from every relationship, its attachment for its near and dear ones coming to an end. For all appear to it ephemeral then, all bodily forms, only the formless, the *ātman*, stays imperishable for it. Finding no purpose in the love of mere passing shadows, a man of this vision loses himself in the love of the Imperishable, of that alone, his joy all pure and blessed.

Saying 146. Self-submission, self-submission firm and irreversible, brings to an end all one's passion for pleasure and aversion for pain, only contemplation of the self, contemplation all passive, coming to be the exclusive concern of the *buddhi* then. Blessed becomes it then with the bliss of the *ātman*, the bliss that is the *āman* itself, finding that self, that bliss, at once pervade the body and transcend it. Seeing this wonder, this marvel, the *buddhi* attains to the state of the supreme *śūnya*, that absolute Nothing, becomes and turns into that *śūnya*, that peace the Eternal.

Saying 147. When the *buddhi* gives itself up to a sustained contemplation of the [Name of the] *ātman*, gives itself up exclusively and without a distraction, it finds within itself the *ātman,* that sole and single reality. With *that* it becomes one, with the *ātman* that abides timeless in time, desire-free in desire, formless in the formed, conflict-free in conflicts, action-free in action, a-dual in the dual and as Brahman in *Māyā.* With that glory manifest within it, the *buddhi* turns all sovereign, all free, the bodily acts no longer grieving it, abide as it does unattached to them. To *nirvāṇa* does it attain then, to that all blessed state.

Saying 148. With the *ātman* becoming manifest[4] within it, the *buddhi* no longer identifies itself with the bodily acts. Unaffected by them it abides then, free from every desire and from the conflict of opposites. Unrelated it turns then and unattached, distanced from every *vāsanā* of the body, that all-entangling web. All glory to the man who attains to this state, this supremely blessed state!

Saying 149. The wheel of *Māyā* ever moves all mysterious, that recurring and never ending process of births and deaths. Only that man can find rest from that process, only he can find peace the eternal, he who comes to be established in the *ātman*, that reality the supreme, comes to be established in it before his body comes to fall, the bodily passions, those deviations, no longer touching him.

Saying 150. But he who is drunk with arrogance, lives a life given all to luxury and pleasures, will not find redemption but only fall for his lot. And so will he who, instead of resorting to contemplation of the *ātman,* resorts to all kinds of deities and worships them for his bodily pleasures. And so will he who resorts to all kinds of evil means for those worldly ends.

Saying 151. A man of learning who, in his pride, has studied all kinds of holy books but has not cared to purify himself of his faults is like a man who, with a light in his hand, jumps into a well. Wasted has he his life to no purpose.

Saying 152. A man who has not purified himself of the pollution of the I-sense or has not surrendered himself unto the *ātman* with every faith is verily a being given to all evil, whatever be the extent of his learning or his formal piety. For, the taints of the mind cannot be washed away without that spirit of self-surrender to the truth. Fraud, lies and pretence do not let anyone get established in the Real, great obstacles are they in the way to it, to the Real.

Saying 153. A man who resorts to the right path with a mind free from every desire and interest and ever strives to wash his mind of every fault and evil, will automatically attain to devotion pure and holy, devotion that will lead him to redemption absolute, to liberation itself. For, pure disposition it is that leads to pure endeavour, and pure endeavour it is that leads to perfection the pure. Therefore, one should resort to faith the full, to the spirit of self-surrender the absolute, for that is the ferry to take one beyond this ocean of the world, ocean so hard to cross, take one there in this very life, before one's body comes to fall.

Saying 154. Self-surrender unto the Real undoes the disposition given to untruth, disposition from where proceed all darkness and all evil. And to love, love the pure, gives rise this spirit of self-surrender unto the Real, to the holy love that leads to the knowledge of the Real, knowledge that is the same thing as becoming one with the Real. Therefore, with every determination and conviction and with every love should a man on the path seek to self-submit to the Real to wash himself of all the taints of the embodied mode of being. And he should also see to it that his mind is given to service of others, service rendered with every resource at his command - mental, verbal and physical - and with a spirit of generosity. For, to place one's pleasures at the service of others means to be awake to the bliss residing in the self, bliss the blessed and eternal.

Saying 155. A man on the path to the truth should ever think of his life as meant for the good of others, should think so with his mind all submitted to the Real and, suffused with this latter spirit, should serve others with every care and concern. This is the endeavour, endeavour the real and true, that will purify him, that man on the path, of the taint of I-ness, his *buddhi* attaining to the state free of that taint and to enlightenment all holy and unblemished. In the Real itself then it comes to stay still. To attain to that stillness is verily to attain to the highest reach of *yoga*.

Saying 156. To rise above the fall from one's true being, the fall in the shape of I-thought, a man must understand how one comes to project himself into this vast sphere of false appearances and false pleasures, taking them to be the only things that matter and are real. That is the first step he should take for that purpose, the step consisting in understanding the dread mystery of the vast expansion of that projection and those pleasures. When he comes to be blessed with this kind of discrimination, discrimination clear and lucid, he should cultivate the conviction that there is such a thing as the Life Spirit and that It is the Real itself, freeing himself from the faults and taints of his mind. He should resort, to bring about that self-purification, to simplicity, to service, to truthfulness, to *sat-saṅga* and yogic meditation, resort to them with undeviating resoluteness. Only when the *buddhi* thus comes to stay firm in this way of righteous conduct that it can bring to extinction the fierce flames of passions in the shape of sensuality, anger, infatuating attachment, greed and I-sense, getting suffused thereby with divine dispositions.

Saying 157. When the *buddhi* abides desire-free, all humility and risen above each and every existential condition to stay all stable, and gives itself up to the good of others, it, the *buddhi*, then comes to be suffused with the spirit of self-surrender to the *ātman*, self-surrender complete and absolute. That is the moment when its sense of identity with the body, that source primal of all the evils and fallings inflicting the *buddhi*, comes to be eroded. And that is the moment when devotion untainted and holy wells up in it to make it all pure, the evil in the shape of thoughts no longer polluting it. And that is the moment when it comes to stay all still in the *ātman* and attains to the goal ultimate and final of life.

Saying 158. To wash oneself of all the deviations that inhere in the embodied mode of being, of all its evils and fallings, one must stay firm in belief in the *ātman*. And to be free from all the fears and woes that inflict embodied beings, each and every, one must contemplate the *ātman*. And to be blessed, supremely blessed, one must realise the *ātman* and be the *ātman*, one's being true and real.

Saying 159. A dreadful struggle is life-in-the-world. A being who finds himself so situated, situated in the context of a world, should do what he is called upon to do by his existential situation, but do it in a meticulously upright way. For, that alone is the way to purify his mind of all its taints, that upright mode of life, and, with his mind so purified, to live all self-submitted unto Real the Supreme that his very *ātman* is. That is how a mortal is to lead his mortal life, lead it to its end. If he succeeds in doing so, all blessed will he live even here, in this very world, no fear casting its shadow upon him. All will turn into his *ātman* for him, into his very being and self. In himself will he find all fulfillment, in his own very self, desiring nothing else, needing nothing else.

Saying 160. There is nothing greater and nobler for a mortal being, a being who has come to reside in this perishable body, than to redeem himself from this his condition. That verily is what every being should work for, for therein lies his salvation, in this holy endeavour. The Path of Yoga formulated in this chapter should be carefully considered and with a mind pure and unstained so that one may give oneself wholly to it. All hidden is this Path, unknown to the human mind, but with utmost lucidity has it been revealed here so that even a low witted man may know and understand his worldly pilgrimage in its very truth and strive for his redemption, redemption all holy and pure. In the state beyond the reach of every fear, will he dwell, he that resorts to this Path of *Yoga*. May every gifted being be suffused with love for the Real and find the *ātman*, that Real itself! May he thus become all hopeful and find the state all blessed! May all noble souls find the inspiration to strive pure and for the end pure!

(ii) Final Word On the Way to the Truth

Saying 1. **To be firm in reflection on the Truth:** Firm reflection on the Truth brings an end to excessive passions of the body, passions that make a being fall from himself, from his true self. A fervour for noble conduct, fervour deep and intense, will spring up in him and the disposition of self-submission to the Real. A being in this condition finds himself ardently longing for [the grace of] a true and perfect preceptor.

Saying 2. **To be firm in one's self-submission unto the Real:** Self-submission to the Real brings about cessation of all the tainting *vāsanās* to give rise to the disposition of forgiveness, compassion, patience and devotion for the Truth, the disposition that results in sustained contemplation of the Real, to, that is to say, exclusive remembrance of the Name of the Lord.

Saying 3. **To stay firm in sustained contemplation of the Real:** When contemplation of the Real becomes sustained and firm, there survives no desire, desire good as well as bad, to disrupt the stillness of the *buddhi*. All disinterested it stays then, undistracted by any pleasure whatsoever, its uninterrupted meditation eventually culminating in its becoming aware of the Imperishable Word abiding within it.

Saying 4. **To remain ever awake to the Real:** When a being abides ever awake to the Real, then all his actions turn disinterested, no desire of his ever prompting them.

To the will of the Lord will he surrender all his actions, giving himself to pure and fervent devotion to Him, his consciousness all and ever absorbed in the Imperishable Word, that *ātman* of his, his being true and real. The very acme of devotion is this state, putting to rest all one's attachment for the gross world. The devotee of this mettle simply comes to stay still with the Being abiding within him.

Saying 5. **To stay still in the Real:** When a being thus comes to stay still in the Real, there remains no darkness of delusion to darken him, no thought of the I, that is. His consciousness, his consciousness-with-its-other, melts into the Imperishable Word, that *ātman* of his, that Consciousness the bare, Consciousness without its *other*, to turn into that itself. To *nirvāṇa* it attains then, to the peace that it is. This comes to be possible when the intellect, hailing the glory of the *Nāda,* of that Immortal Sound, contemplates that Sound the uninterrupted each and every moment with utmost spontaneity, contemplates it in its varied forms and facets. There will be moments when it will find that Sound beyond the reach of any dualities, dualities with their negation written into them. And there will be moments when that Sound will appear beyond the sphere of any *guṇa* of *prakṛti,* with nothing to stay with, nothing to strive for and nothing to transcend. A-dual that Sound will appear to it, in which no desire can stir up and no action can originate, where the very self, self the false, one has projected oneself into, self the *other*, comes to be extinct. This coming to rest of the process of birth and death will the *buddhi* find in It, and also the all silent ***śunyā,*** that void and sillness absolute, in It, in that Sound. And at the same time, this very Word the Silent will appear all-knowing to it and Light the self-same. Contemplating the *Nāda* this way, the *buddhi* will lose itself into that its own being, its own self, the conflicts of opposites, the dualities that the mind, the body and the organs are no longer touching it. Transcending these all, it will stay, no thought stirring up in it, no fear to disturb it. All still it will stay in that state supreme and all peaceful, in that final coming to rest of the ever moving wheel of recurring births and deaths. With every effort should a man try to attain to that supreme state, with every right and genuine effort, and with every disposition genuinely oriented towards that end, and with firm and sustained contemplation. To attain to that state is his duty the paramount; that is the goal he should ever strive for.

Saying 6. Let every gifted being treading this path to the truth, and anxious to stay firm on it, see to it that he adheres to all these states. Let him move on, with steadfast intent, from the state of reflection to that of self-submission to the Real, from that to contemplation of the Real and to awakening unto It and to coming to be established in It. Only then will he be cured of the dread malady inflicting him, malady in the shape of *vāsanā*. And only then will he find the Bliss Eternal, will come to be established in that Real the Supreme. There has to be constant effort to attain to that goal, and unfailing perseverance. For, hard is the path, exceedingly hard, which only he can tread who lives for the truth, for that alone, and who believes in every word of his *guru*, his preceptor true.

(iii) On Well-being the Highest

Saying 1. Taking on him the body, body that is the world itself, every being strives to bring about his well being, using all the resources at his command. That is all that his life is, a seeking for his well being. But only calamity he meets in the end, with the peace he seeks, peace the real, beyond his reach. This is how the wheel of the world moves, the world in the shape of recurring births and deaths, the wheel all mysterious and awful. Not without reflection on the truth and resorting to sustained meditation can one find that peace, peace without a fear.

Saying 2. Embodied in the body of the five elements, the *buddhi* finds itself a slave of the pleasures of the five cognitive organs and the five motor organs, its desire for their acquisition compelling it to do all kinds of actions, good and bad. The pleasures it seeks are, however, all ephemeral, not beyond a moment do they last, their enjoyment making the *buddhi* all the more miserable, its fears and unrest ever accompanying it. Charmed by those pleasures, mistaking them all blissful and [as if] not of this world but of the other, the *buddhi* makes every effort to have them at its call but only to find them all inadequate, its discontent and misery persisting as before. That is the truth about this dreadful world, that other name for every woe and every pain.

Saying 3. The *buddhi* thus seeks eternal joy in ephemeral pleasures of the organs, pleasures that are pain itself. Its indulgence in them, in those pleasures, pleasures it is addicted to, cannot undo its unrest and fear, those its constant companions. And when death comes to visit it, it departs from the body with calamity great and formidable for its companion, its *vāsanā* dragging it into another body and from that into other bodies without a count to repeat the same tragic story, its passion for the bodily pleasures causing it weal or woe. This is how it wanders in the world, that ever moving cycle of recurring births and deaths, wanders all deluded and in illusion.

Saying 4. Only unfailing self-submission to and sustained contemplation of the *ātman*, of that witness, can release a being from his passion for the pleasures of the organs, from that his worst misery. These two constitute what is called the true path or path to the truth, namely, the disposition of self-submission to the *ātman* and sustained contemplation of it. The *ātman* alone is purity itself and bliss itself, purity the supreme and bliss the supreme. The *ātman* alone is eternal and all pervasive and all inclusive. The *ātman* alone is peace the full and peace the eternal. In the realistion of the *ātman* alone lies one's well being, one's highest well being and nowhere else. To self-submit to the *ātman* with this knowledge and this belief, self- submit to it in every way, is the way sure to eradication of one's passion for the pleasures of the organs, is the way sure to one's liberation from them. A man who believes thus and lives thus is truly a man of faith in the Lord, he who perceives the end of the entire world and its phenomena in woe and misery, woe and misery absolute, and, with this conviction, directs all his efforts towards finding the Real. Therein consists true faith in the Lord, in this belief and in this disposition.

Saying 6. The pleasures of the body, transitory in nature as they are, augment one's discontent and *vāsanā*, that agony the most tragic. Knowing this truth about this pilgrimage of life, one should make the *ātman* alone, that Real the Supreme, that Life in truth, the anchor of one's being and life and contemplate it ever and always. That verily is the way to redeem oneself from this mortal condition.

Saying 7. As long as the *buddhi* fails to realise how every pleasure ends up in pain, has that alone as its inevitable end, and does not understand that it is the *ātman* alone, that Real the supreme, that matters and nothing else, it, the *buddhi*, will continue to remain inflicted with the false selfhood it has projected itself into, selfhood which makes it deny the reality of the true self that it is, that reality absolute. Seized by *vāsanā* great and intense, seized by that pain and anguish itself, it will give itself up to all kinds of polluted and polluting pleasures of the organs, scalded by all kinds of passions, passions that bring about its further fall. Such is the life it will have to live, life all fear and pain itself. For, its passions for the pleasures of the organs will ever compel it to do all kinds of wicked deeds, deeds that prove suicidal for it in the end. All darkness is this kind of life, every misery it is and every anguish.

Saying 8. The passion for the pleasures of the organs generates all unrest and all discontent for this being, undoing his faith in the truth of the *ātman* and his devotion to it. No being can stay firm in that devotion if this *vāsanā* for the pleasures of the organs persists in him. That is the truth he should know and understand. But such is the hold of ignorance on it, on the *buddhi*, that all forgetful of the *ātman*, its being the real, it would find all happiness in those pleasures only, inviting every woe for itself and every wretchedness. That is all that the way of the world is, the way so hard to transcend and to go beyond.

Saying 9. Knowing what this pilgrimage of life in its truth is, life so hard to transcend, one should ever set a limit to the enjoyment of the pleasures of the organs, limit the purifying, having full faith in the Real. That is the effort real and true, effort towards one's real well being, and that is the path of those who live ever oriented towards their gurus [and not towards their minds].

Saying 10. With mind pure of every taint should a man seek to know the truth about his mortal life, and live with the Imperishable alone as his sole refuge. Therein lies his effort true, in surrender of all his efforts to the One Imperishable. That is the effort to free him from the fearful bondage of action to bless him with the peace beyond the reach of every fear.

Saying 11. Pleasures of the organs will ever augment his discontents and fears, of the man that indulges in them, for inflame these his *vāsanā* as never before. With wisdom is blessed the man, wisdom out of the ordinary, the man who has come to perceive this truth. Delinking himself from his Being the true and real, man comes to mistake only the pleasures of the organs for happiness pure and perfect and gives free vent to his indulgence in them. That is his real confusion, this his mistaken notion, notion to torture him ever and always.

Saying 12. Death itself is the *vāsanā* for the pleasures of the organs, *vāsanā* that would set no limits to itself. From moment to moment it deludes the *buddhi* to compel it, ever and always, to do all kinds of evil acts. Worse than a beast is the man that has failed to understand this truth about his life.

Saying 13. Under the impact of the *vāsanā* for the pleasures of the organs, the *buddhi* would acquire all kinds of such pleasures in the hope of finding the rest it is in search of, little realising that every perishable thing is unrest itself and that to acquire it is to add to one's frustration and discontent. All folly is its hope of finding its rest in those pleasures and all wisdom is to perceive the restiveness that they are.

Saying 14. The spirit of self-submission to the Real originates in man when he perceives death in the body and its pleasures, and every misery in them. It is then alone that he strives to purify himself of the taints of the mind and to live self-surrendered to the Indivisible and the Imperishable. That is the kind of *buddhi* he then comes to be blessed with, *buddhi* the *niścayātamikā, buddhi* suffused with conviction.[5]

Saying 15. When the body and the pleasures related to it appear all destructive, appear so to *buddhi* the *niścayātamikā,* it sheds all its desires directed towards the world, desires that pollute and stain it, and stays still in the disposition of devotion to the Truth, finding in It the very breath of its being and life. A *jijñāsu* true and genuine is indeed such a man, a man of this disposition.

Saying 16. In the state of ignorance, the state of oblivion of one's true being, the *buddhi* lives exclusively given to setting up the body and its pleasures, for the passion for those pleasures would not leave it alone even for a moment. However, when it finds the body and its pleasures only momentary appearances, it seeks to give itself up to the Truth, give itself up ever and always. The pleasures of the body no longer tempting it, it seeks to stay still in that eternal joy, the *ātman* within it. This is what sustained meditation in its truth is.

Saying 17. The dreadful *vāsanā* that ever holds the *buddhi* in its grip comes to be dispelled when it, the *buddhi,* leaves the results of its actions, results ever divided against themselves, to the will of the Lord, of that Real . With its desire for the result of action all extinct, the *buddhi* turns into a mere instrument of actions, give itself as it does to that which is Eternity itself. When the *buddhi* comes to stay thus, it is said to have attained to true devotion of the Lord.

Saying 18. To project oneself as the doer, to get associated with actions and the dualities that those actions result in and, as a consequence of this projection and this association, to be ever on the move in enjoyment of the pleasures of the body - this, verily, is the benighted state of the *buddhi*, its state of ignorance. The only way to dispel this darkness of delusion is the way of self-submission to the Truth, self-submission firm and stable. That is to say, one must perceive all one's acts as grounded in the Truth, shedding his false identity of the doer. This disposition alone is the disposition of *styāgraha*, the disposition that *favours* the truth, truth alone.

Saying 19. With the deepening of its dissociation from the false self of the doer it has projected itself into, the *buddhi* resigns all its acts to the will of the Lord. With this resignation comes about the weakening of its *vāsanā* to culminate ultimately in its total cessation. In that it stays all still then, in that cessation of *vāsanā*, in that bliss native to its self, to that alone. To *yoga* does it attain to then, when it stays all still in its own being, in its own self, with not a trace of desire for the *other*.

Saying 20. Ceasing to set up names and forms, those false appearances, the *buddhi* resigns itself to the meditation of Name the Imperishable, knowing for certain that the Imperishable alone is the doer and the undoer. With this remembrance of the Truth getting all stable, it comes to find the world in the shape of names and forms it has set up melt away to give place to Word the Imperishable within it. Supremely blissful is this its realisation of the Word within, Word which no *vāsnā* can touch, and no action.[6]

Saying 21. When the *buddhi* comes to realise the Real as its *ātman*, its self, it comes to be disengaged from all the bodily acts to stay all still in the *ātman*, in that freedom from all acts. To Blessedness the Supreme it attains to then, blessedness which no *vāsanā* can disrupt and no activity, those miseries of a mortal. To peace the transcendental attains the *buddhi* then, peace the full and infinite.

Saying 22. The *buddhi*, to put the matter in brief, is destined to remain ever on the move, given as it is to the enjoyment of the results of actions, those consequences of the [primal] act of positing the I as the doer, the I conditioned by the three modes of *prakṛti*, modes that make it cling to itself, to transcend that clinging and its propensity to act in a world context. This conflict among these modes is all that its life is, the pain of it and the misery of it. There is no other way for it to escape from this its predicament than to live all resigned to the *ātman* and to constant contemplation of it. When a gifted man comes to live thus resigned to the Real, convinced of the inevitable misery of his condition, when he perceives all his physical resources and his weal and woe as ordained by the Imperishable that the Indivisible Word is, when he perceives these as grounded in That alone, he gives himself up entirely to exclusive contemplation of the self within him. This fervent devotion of his frees him from all the dualities, dualities always divided against themselves, his *buddhi* finding its rest in the Real, the rest it was ever in search of, for supremely blessed is that rest, that peace.

Saying 23. Knowing the truth about the pilgrimage of his life, let every man live ever self-surrendered unto the Truth. Therein alone resides the dignity of human life. Let him keep his bodily pleasures within legitimate limits, let him adhere to a life of simplicity, of truthfulness, of service of the others around him and given to holy association and to yogic contemplation. For that is how he can cleanse his mind of its taints and attain to the state supreme of eternal peace.

Saying 24. All mental aberrations, each and every, come to an end when man makes the One Real his sole refuge.

With this conviction, the conviction that that Real alone is his sole refuge and shelter, he should seek to wake himself up to the Imperishable Word within him, for only that *ātman* is pure of every *vāsanā* and every activity, and is eternity itself. As for the body, it ever dies, is death itself; action itself it is and misery itself. With this conviction in mind, one must shed one's sense of identity with the body to live given up entirely to that Real within, for that is the pathway to go beyond the reach of every woe.

Saying 25. With devotion to the Truth should a man purify himself, should triumph over sensuality, wrath, greed, his infatuations and his passion to assert and affirm himself as an I or a Me. For, embodiments of *vāsanā* are all these passions, and there is no purity and no greatness like freedom from their grip. Steadfast should he, therefore, be in his meditation of the Name and leave all the results of his actions to the will of the Lord. For, that is the way to get rid of the passions for the pleasures of the organs and, thereby, to bring to an end all one's faults and to stay as one's self, as one's ā*tman*, that purity all transcendent and supreme.

Saying 26. In owning up to one's true being lies purity the supreme and freedom from all the aberrations of the mind and the organs. Therein lies the way to be awake and alert and to stay still with no *other* to disrupt one from one's true being. For, the *buddhi* then comes to be dissolved in the supreme reality the *ātman* to redeem, truly redeem, this being from his fallen condition.

Saying 27. There is no wisdom like distancing oneself from the pleasures of the organs. And there is no understanding like owning up to one's real being after careful reflection on the instructions of the seers of truth, on what they have proclaimed as the truth. For, it is this understanding born out of reflection on the teachings of the seers that purifies the *buddhi* and dispels all one's deluded notions and false understanding. In Consciousness the Alone [without a constitutive *other*] the *buddhi* then comes to stay all still, in that peace the transcendent and a-doing.

Saying 28. There is no wealth like self-surrender to the *ātman*, that spirit of life, that Imperishable itself. There is no investigation like that self-surrender; there is no knowing and no endeavour, no resort and no sublimity like that disposition, and no wisdom. For, therein lies the way to freedom from all the faults and taints of the mind, freedom that redeems this being from this his fallen condition. Blessed is the man who resorts to this redemptive path, the gifted man that sticks to it with a determination untainted[7]. An ideal verily is his life for others to emulate and to follow.

Saying 29. When a man's mind remains firmly intent on contemplation of the Name within and his body ever engaged in the service of others, he himself staying apart from those acts of the body and their results, then pure shall he become from all the faults of his mind, the man that does not attribute those acts and their results to his self. This truly is the right endeavour, this contemplation within and disinterested service without, endeavour that every gifted man should make it his paramount duty to resort to. This body is ever moving towards death. To attain to the Supreme State, to attain to that Goal the True is to make the best use of this perishable body, the best profit one can make out of it.

Saying 30. To ever strive to attain to one's real state of being, to strive so in truth and earnest, is to live life the most noble. One should ever take care to take the purest possible kind of food, to be upright to the utmost in one's worldly dealings and to adopt the simplest possible mode of life, giving up all display and self-indulgence, and should have an earnest longing to attain to the Truth. For, that is the way to bring about the cessation of the delusion of *vāsanā*; and that is the way to attain to one's real state of being, attain to it without much of a delay. One should adopt this way of life to free oneself from all the faults of the mind and be one's own saviour. All heroic will be one's life then, heroic without a parallel!

Saying 31. With the purest *buddhi* should one try to know the truth about the world that one's life is and with steadfast intent resign one's life and being to the One Real, with one's mind ever given to Its remembrance. For, that is one's life, that Real, life that illumines this body and is bliss itself. With a firm resolve should a man resign all his acts to that Great Lord and ever strengthen the disposition of service unto others, service through his mind, speech and actions. And as for his death, let him never sleep over it. With this understanding and this remembrance, with this spirit of self-surrender to the Lord and this spirit of service towards those around him and with this his watch over his mortality, let him make strenuous efforts to realise the Imperishable, the Imperishable without an *other* to confront it. Let him realise That with a spirit free of any compulsion [of desire or passion]. For one's own home is that, that Imperishable without an *other*.

Saying 32. If a man has come to have ardent devotion for the Lord and spends his physical resources in service of others without any self-interest, he has truly lived a life of real and genuine profit, for only this kind of endeavour can lead him to get established in the State Supreme. One should, therefore, reflect on the life of the seers of the truth to make oneself firmly established on the pathway to the truth. For, that is how one can come to know oneself truly and come to be supremely blessed.

Saying 33. The whole world moves inflicted by a thirst [for being]. To bring it to genuine rest, that thirst, is the true goal of life. But oblivious of the Imperishable Real [one's Being in truth], the *buddhi* seeks that supreme and imperishable blessedness in the ever decaying body. That is its ignorance, ignorance that holds it in a firm grip. One must, therefore, wake up from this life, life that is all ignorance, giving up his sense of identity with the body and, with faith true and genuine, make the One Imperishable his sole resort, his body given to contemplation of the Name, contemplation that will lead him to the state supreme and fearless.

Saying 34. A truly gifted and wise person is he who ever lives all self-submitted to that Being, to that only. Perceiving the whole world as the manifestation of the glory of that his being, that his eternal self and reality the supreme, he serves all beings to his utmost capacity without seeking any return from this his act. His mind, however, remains ever immersed in the contemplation of the Word, in that he spends his inner life, in that contemplation. To goal the highest attains such a being, his very life a source of redemption for the whole world, for only he knows wherein consists its redemption; only his life can be an example for others to emulate. Rare is a man of this kind and rare indeed is his life!

Saying 35. Deeply immersed is the *buddhi* in the false identity of the doer. To live with this confusion about one's self is to live and find oneself a mere natural being living as Nature would determine him to live. It is there, this confusion, to deny all reality, to equate it with the false *I* one has projected oneself into, and to be a nihilist, or to mistake delusion for reality. And it is this very confusion about one's self that gives rise to *vāsanā* of the three modes and, under the impact of that *vāsanā,* to all kinds of actions and the dualities they result in, dualities ridden with self-conflicts. That is the world this projection of the self as the doer sets up to delude the *buddhi* with, the world composed of subtle and gross elements. And here, in this very world, the *buddhi* would seek peace the fearless [all secure] and would ever strive for it, for that peace the fearless! But not without disowning that its false identity, that of the doer, can it free itself from the unrest that every act of it is and every result of that act is, result that is nothing else but a conflict of opposites. That is its woe, this its mess and predicament, woe the most grievous.

Saying 36. The *ātman,* that Real, dispenses being to each and every brittle body, dispenses that to it dwelling within it. That *ātman* should one take as the doer of all and the undoer of all, for that is the way to dispel the darkness that projection of one's self as a doer is. That verily is the disposition that believes in the real, in the truth, in God and in knowledge, this disposition of taking [the not-doing] *ātman* as the doer.[8]

Saying 37. The disposition that projects all its doings onto the self, self that is the Real itself, and does so with a holy resolve, will give itself up, that disposition, to the remembrance of the Name with every devotion. That is the way the *buddhi* will extricate itself from its passion for the results of its actions, results ever in conflict with themselves, ever negating themselves. When this passion dies down in it, there will swell in it true love for the Real, love that will purify it of all the aberrations innate to the body. This disposition of the *buddhi* is sometimes termed the disposition of self-surrender, sometimes *karmayoga*, the Yoga of Action and sometimes *bhaktiyoga*, the Yoga of Devotion.

Saying 38. The projection of one's self as the doer alone is the root of the *vāsanā* for action. And the way to undo this false projection is the way of self-surrender unto the Real and the projection of all one's doing onto that very self, self the real. When the *buddhi* comes to be firmly established in this disposition of self-surrender it comes to be purified of all the *vāsanā* for pleasures to stay apart from the dualities that the results of actions are. Liberated then it becomes even before the death of the body.

Saying 39. To undo this darkness, this projection of one's self as the doer, is the way of those that live oriented towards their gurus as against their own inclinations. And it comes to cease, this darkness, when the *buddhi* knows for certain that only the Lord is the doer and He alone is the undoer, thus bringing unto rest all its *vāsanās*. When this happens, when the *buddhi* comes to be all pure of *vāsanā*, it comes to know the Real dwelling within it, Real the formless, the unborn, the a-doing, the desire-free, the conflict-free, the indivisible, the all-knowing and the all transcendent, comes to know that eternal and imperishable Word. No passion for the body survives in the *buddhi* then, the passion for projecting itself as the body. All passive then it stays with itself, all stillness. To the highest state of being it attains to then, all appeased and all peaceful. All knowledge it turns into then, and all-experience. Knowing that light, that ight the supreme, it merges into it to become it, become that light. To the peace of *nirvāṇa* it is said to have attained to then. Knowing the kind of life that can lead one to this supreme enlightenment, one should ever strive to attain to it, to that truth, shedding all the taints of the mind. That is the way one can stick firmly to the path of the truth. Every noble person, desirous of salvation, should ever live self-submitted to the truth, do so with every resolve and effort. For that is how he will make his life truly fruitful, his human life, for attain will he peace the secure. May the Lord bless every being with true understanding!

(iv) Meditation and Good Conduct

There is a conduct that leads one to the truth and there is a conduct that leads one to the untruth. The former is good conduct and the latter is evil or false conduct. The Lord alone is the truth, Lord the Life and dispenser of life. Therefore, without a true belief in that truth, in that real, all that one thinks or does is evil itself, is the very root of it. Without self-submission to the Lord and without contemplation of the Name, it is exceedingly hard for a being to be of noble conduct, for that alone is good conduct, namely, the disposition of self-surrender unto the Lord. For, as long as the *buddhi* remains self-surrendered unto the body, it cannot be good in its conduct, not in reality. The *buddhi* projects the world as conditioned by its disposition, by what it believes in, believes in with every conviction. So devoid of the disposition of self-submission unto the Lord and contemplation of Him, it finds itself disposed towards the unreal to project all kinds of deviations for itself, deviations subtle, not overtly manifest. There come to be, however, moments when those failings and perversions, hidden within it, come to be manifest in their gross forms too, in the form, that it to say, of its actions. Therefore, no one can truly be of noble conduct without self-submitting to the truth and meditating the Name.

Those who talk of noble conduct independent of self-submission to the Lord are ignorant of the truth about noble conduct. For, not until the *vāsanā* relating to the five aberrations die down in man can he ever lead a truly ethical life. And not until he comes to live by his faith, faith full and complete, in the Lord and gives himself up to contemplation of His Name will that *vāsanā* cease to be, despite all his efforts. Only in the cessation of the *vāsanā* relating to these aberrations consists the essence of all ethical conduct. Theories of ethical conduct put forward these days are not, really and truly, theories of ethical conduct but theories of ethical misconduct. When subjected to tests, all the tall claims about the ethical life of the proponents of those theories prove hollow. A man caught up in the whirlpool of *prakṛti* can hope to stick to his principles if and only if his faith in the truth is firm and his meditation of the truth is stable. For, to live by the truth, to live for the truth comes to be possible for a man only when he knows the Lord alone as the Real and the whole net of *prakṛti* as unreal. Only then the aberrations native to his mind will come to cease and only then will his *buddhi* come to be pure to act all pure.

Therefore, ever remember the Lord, remember Him with ardour and fervour. For He alone is Power the Pure, He alone is support the ultimate, and He alone is patience the absolute. All else is fall and distortion, the whole ambit of the Gross, of the Formed. Without resorting to that Real, the *buddhi* ever remains discontented, impatient and given to change and aberrations. A brief account of ethical conduct is given here, reflect well on it and stick firmly to the true regulative principles. A hard test is this world; no one can pass this test without resigning himself to the Truth, no one can redeem himself from it without that resignation. *Sat-saṅga* is indispensable to attain to this disposition. Participate in it and make others too participate in it. For, who knows when a man may come to have the right kind of understanding? This is also a kind of service - this, your appeal to others to participate in *sat-saṅga*. May the Lord bless all with the true understanding!

(v) Fervent Devotion to the Lord

Confusing his being with many a false appearance, this mortal being lives in the world ever unhappy and miserable. Not a moment does he find in which he could feel himself truly happy. No meditation can give him the content he seeks, no *yajña*, sacrifice, no charity or, for that matter, any other means unless and until he finds true and authentic love for the Lord rise up in him. For that love, love true and authentic, alone is devotion, that alone is *yoga*, that alone is wisdom and that alone is the Lord's Power. They resort to *tapa[s]*, to self denial, for the sake of this pure love, and resort to meditation too for its sake. For, this love alone can bring to naught one's confusion about one's being and self, that ignorance primal, and make manifest within one the *Nāda*, that Lord the Omnipotent, that bliss the supreme and eternal. That verily is the goal that every being blessed with human birth should seek.

Many are the adjuncts this mind would superimpose on to itself, subjecting itself to many a malady that go with that act of superimposition. This error, this malady, does not let it believe in the Lord or have love for Him truly and genuinely. One may study as much as one can, study books of all kinds and without a count and still may remain all dry, no fount of true love springing up in him. One may go on pilgrimage to many a holy water or resort to fasting and other measures of self-purification and still find his soul too dry and inert to flow out with love pure of all taints. For, projection of the self into the body ever misleads this living being into desire, into that ever burning passion. It is only when he finds himself in the presence of a holy seer and receives his instruction that his *buddhi* comes to be pure and suffused with humility. Only when a man comes to be so blessed with a pure and humble spirit that love for the Lord surges up in him accompanied by an intense longing for a vision of Him. This love and this longing purge him of each and every sin of his. Only then his efforts turn authentic and bear their fruit in the shape of his merger into the Lord. It is only then and then alone that one comes to know what love in its very truth is and what life the bliss is. Guru the true is he, prophet the true, the Incarnation of the Lord and the Messenger of the Lord - he that has attained to that Love and that Life. When a man is lost in that Love for the Lord, only then does he come to attain to the state of *samatā*, then only. In the midst of dualities of *Māyā* he stays self-same, in happiness and in misery, in gain and in loss, in pleasure and in pain, in heat and in cold, or in the midst of friends or foes. All free he lives, lost in the sea of eternal love, lives so here itself, in this very body.

A man so blessed, blessed with this disposition, will find the whole world suffused with Presence the Transcendent, his own being all ecstatic with that vision. From the malady of deeds, from the malady of recurring births and deaths, he becomes free to lose himself in that Being the True. To attain to this state is vouchsafed the human birth to a being, for that is the purpose supreme of that birth. Let every *premī* dispense with every dispute, let him give up every fraud and hypocrisy and ever devote his life to find love the true. For, that will save him from the passion of positing the perishable, from the malady of recurring births and deaths, and make him one with the Lord, with that Bliss Itself.

(vi) Samatā-vijñāna

On Realisation of the Truth propounded by The Doctrine of the Same

Saying 1. Projecting itself as the I conditioned by the three *guṇas,* as I the doer, the *buddhi* becomes a prisoner of the *vāsanā* for all kinds of actions and all kinds of the results those actions end up in. Thus it would appropriate that *other* as its own, turning that into the 'Mine' and the 'Me'. This way it would appropriate the gross body and also the subtle body - the mind - as its being to live ever in fear and ever on the move, the body-mind it appropriates this way constituting the world itself, the world as its *other.* Thus does it come to live in real unrest and in misery all surpassing.

Saying 2. With intent all inclusive would the *buddhi* ever project itself as the doer to fall a prey to all kinds of *vāsanas* and all kinds of actions and the self-negating dualities those actions result in. Conditioned thus it seeks in the body - that world itself - peace the secure, entangling itself in many a desire, to satisfy which it takes recourse to many a striving in the visible world. That is what the worldly mode of being is, this striving for the satisfaction of desires it finds itself entangled in, desires it can never escape from.

Saying 3. The *buddhi's* projection of itself as the doer is verily projection of itself as the world itself, the world conditioned by the three *guṇas.* Ever remembering that false identity of it and the *other* of that identity, the world, it spreads for itself a net of *vāsanā* to find itself ever tossed by sensuality, wrath, greed, attachment and the I-sense and other primary passions, passions that make it remain ever obsessed with the pleasures of the organs, cognitive and motor. Ignorance itself is this state, untruth itself is it, delusion is it and attachment all-obsessive is it. The whole immovable world, the whole material world, is merely the expansion of this *kartāpan,* this projection of one's being as the doer, *kartāpan* that is *Māyā* itself, *Māyā* of the three *guṇas*, *Māyā* with its three modes of being.

Saying 4. Obsessed with that false identity of it, the identity of the doer, the *buddhi* ever remains a victim of unrest. For, the dualities its acts give rise to, dualities in the shape of their results, never let it find a pause from its struggles. For, ever blind it remains to the truth of those results, those dualities with their constitutive poles ever in conflict with each other, seeing neither the change inherent in them nor the all surpassing pain and woe that change implies - such is the intensity of its passions for them, for those results. As for taking up measures to free itself from those passions, there can be no question. All inert is this condition, all folly.

Saying 5. For, the *buddhi* in this condition confounds its being with the passion for doing, the intensity of that passion being what it is. With this confusion about its identity reigning supreme in it, the *buddhi* ever remains busy with accepting and rejecting, accepting one pole of the duality that the result of an act of it is, and rejecting the other pole constituting it. From birth to birth, births of many a kind, it reaps this reward of its acts, reward in conflict with itself. That is what its coming and going means, its ever recurring births and its ever recurring deaths.

Saying 6. Doing means the interaction of the three *guṇas*, interaction among the given state of affairs, the state of affairs to be forged and the state of no affairs, the state transcendent. It means to be a prey to *vāsanās*, good and bad, *vāsanās* resulting in acts, good and bad, and the experience of pain and pleasure those acts give rise to. Ever a victim of this delusion, the *buddhi* finds itself now at a higher state of being and now at a lower. This is how the wheel of the world moves, of this *līlā*, this unmotivated manifestation [of the Lord], manifestation ever on the move.

Saying 7. As long as the *buddhi* does not come to know for certain that every action of it inevitably results in dualities, dualities that are nothing but misery itself, it cannot get rid of the false identity of the doer it has projected itself into. Constituted by the three *guṇas*, the three modes, that identity is nothing else than a delusion in the shape of *vāsanā* and its wide spread net, to disentangle itself from which is impossible for it without an insight into its tragic implications. And as long as that *vāsanā* inflicts the *buddhi* it cannot liberate itself from the ever moving wheel of recurring births and deaths. This is the way *Māyā* operates and expands itself, the way all astonishing and confounding.

Saying 8. This is all that the worldly mode of being is, the mode of being ever on the move, this immersion in the false identity of the doer and in the dualities that one's acts result in. To believe in the truth, to have firm faith in the truth, is difficult to have in this condition. Therefore, in name only people in general have faith in the truth or the Lord. Their living belief is centred on the fruit of their acts and deeds, on those dualities ever divided against themselves, compelling them to resort to evil deeds, deeds that prove suicidal for them.

Saying 9. Self-projection as the doer indeed is the world in its causal state or the body in its causal state. And the dualities, the conflicts of the opposites, that the results of actions are, are, in truth, body the effect, the body composed of the gross elements, and world the visible.[9] The world will not reveal its secret to the *buddhi* that does not know this truth, the truth that one can realise only by becoming it. Nor can it cease to be attached to it, to the world, cease to be infatuated with it.

Saying 10. Only when the *buddhi* comes to know for certain that the duality that every action results in is nothing but pain itself and grief itself, and seeks to get disinterested in it - only when the *buddhi* comes to know and strive thus can it be called *buddhi* the seeker, not otherwise.

Saying 11. There is no escape for the *buddhi* from this net of stupidity as long as it does not realise the surpassing enormity of the misery that every result of action is, result the duality. Therefore, it is the bounden duty of man to understand this truth about his life's pilgrimage, and equipped with this understanding, set himself on to the path that will lead him unto his being the true and real.

Saying 12. For, only when the *buddhi* comes to realise this truth, the truth that the duality that the result of every action is, is nothing but tragedy absolute, only when the *buddhi* comes to know this for certain that it comes to be suffused with dispassion the pure and genuine. And only then does it seek to undo its *vāsanās* for pleasures. That is the way to peace the true, and that is the way to the real, this its effort to undo those *vāsanās*.

Saying 13. Realisation of this truth about the results of actions, results ever in conflict with themselves, realisation of the misery that they are, leads the *buddhi* to a disposition of withdrawal from the false identity of the doer it has projected itself into. With its faith in the Real becoming firm, it seeks to restrain the intensity that false identity operates with. With faith, with love and the spirit of service unto others, with humility and renunciation true and genuine, it seeks to find Word the Not-doing and Imperishable, seeks It with every determination. What they call *bhakti*, devotion, or *gurumkha-niścaya*, the final choice of the one oriented towards his guru, are nothing but this disposition of the *buddhi*, the disposition that makes it seek the Word.

Saying 14. The buddhi's sense of its identity with doing, identity with the three *guṇas* inflicting it, cannot die, until one's passion for the duality in the shape of the result of one's action does not cease to be. Nor can it, without the cessation of that passion, attain to the peace that the not-doing state of *samatā* is, that peace ever the same. To know this truth is to know in truth.

Saying 15. Only firm faith and belief in the Real or the Lord can free a man from the grip of the passion for the duality in question, the duality that every result of every action is. Only that faith and belief can lead to salvation, only that. He is to resort to the Real, self-surrender to the Real, to undo his doer-identity and he is to surrender the results of his actions to the will of the Lord [to undo his passion for the results of actions]. This is all that is there to renunciation the true, devotion the true and action the disinterested, this disposition of self-surrender to the Real and to the will of the Lord.

Saying 16. Knowing that the Imperishable Real is Power the a-doing, the *buddhi* nevertheless believes, believes with every faith, that that Real the a-doing alone is the doer. It believes so because that is the way it can cease to project itself as the doer. And to that Power the Great it surrenders the results of all its actions too, not letting itself get involved in the dualities that those results enact and are. Having thus freed itself from the burden of doing and the results of doing, the *buddhi* gives itself wholly to the meditation of Name the Imperishable, its *vāsanās* and projections of false identities and their *others* ceasing to pollute it and to distract it from its concentration on the Name. To the state of purity the supreme does it then attain, the *buddhi* endowed with this disposition.

Saying 17. To believe that the [a-doing] Lord alone is the doer, to believe in Him this way with a firm and decisive intent, leaving the results of one's actions and their inherent negations to His will and to contemplate, each and every moment, the One Imperishable Name, to do so without a let or a hindrance, is the way to be still. And to be still means to know and realise the Imperishable Word, Word the a-doing, to find peace the highest. This is all that is there to true devotion, devotion the supreme.

Saying 18. All that has been said comes to this: peace the highest, peace that passes human understanding, is nothing else than freedom from the false identity of the doer that this being finds himself projected into. And that too is enlightenment the highest, this freedom from that false identity. But this freedom demands that he shed his passion for the results of actions and remain distant from the conflicts that they embody. For, without shedding this passion and without this distancing there is no way to eradicate that false notion about one's self.

Saying 19. And it is only by shedding that false identity that this being finds himself identified with and the passion for the results of actions that involve him in every conflict that he can come to know the state of *samatā*, that Real the a-doing and imperishable. Therefore, only that man can find that state of not-doing, that goal the highest, only the gifted man that strives for that end with a true and sincere disposition.

Saying 20. Identification with doing is a compulsive obsession with the *buddhi*, not for a moment can it forget that false identity it has posited for itself. That is the primordial ignorance inflicting it. But when it gives itself up with a firm resolve to contemplation of the Imperishable Name, that gift of the preceptor true, gives itself up to that contemplation for eradicating this false identity it has projected itself into, it finds its desires losing their hold upon it, disclosing thereby the Imperishable Word before it. To that Real, to that Word the Imperishable, the *buddhi* then ever remains awake. That is the glory of remembrance of the Name, this awakening unto the Real.

Saying 21. Only knowledge, knowledge the unmediated, of Power the not-doing can undo the ignorance that this attribution of the false identity of the doer on to one's self is. That alone is the highest goal and the highest state, that knowledge pure. And only giving oneself up to contemplation of the Imperishable Name can lead to the knowledge of that Power, Power the not-doing. For, sustained contemplation of the Name alone is true *sādhanā*, true striving for the true goal; to contemplate it, that Name the True, is to undo the unreal names and forms that [the act of self-projection as the doer, that ignorance primordial] has set up, and to divest the *buddhi* of all thoughts, each and every. Stays it, the *buddhi*, then still and unmoving in the Imperishable Itself.

Saying 22. As one progresses in meditation of the Name, one finds one's association with the false identity of the doer slackening its hold. And as that hold slackens, so does slacken the hold of *vāsanās* on the man on the Path. With the hold of *vāsanās* slackening, he, the man on the Path, finds himself getting absorbed in *Samatā*, that Imperishable Itself to stay still in It. That is what the state of *dhyāna* is, the state of passive contemplation.

Saying 23. When the *buddhi* comes to stay still and passive in the Imperishable Word, Word the Witness, dissociating itself from the false identity of the doer, it comes to become one [*anubhava*] with the Word, its contemplation of it becoming all deep and firm. Then it is that it ceases to find itself projected as the doer, the dualities its actions give rise to touching it not. '*Samādhi*' is the name given to this its state, or that of *yogārūdha-avasthā*, 'the state of mounting on *yoga*', the state of staying all still in the Indivisible and Imperishable Real. To peace of *nirvāṇa* the *buddhi* attains then, turning the Same Itself.

Saying 24. Bringing to cessation its false identity as the doer, that root of the world, the *buddhi* comes to be still in the Still, its bondage at an end, and its fears. Only Real the Imperishable then it finds as the cause of all that is to find itself all blessed and all bliss. To Brahman it attains then, becoming one with It. Supremely wise is the man who has attained to this state, shedding his false identity as the doer and staying away from the results of actions, from those conflicts. The knower of Brahman is he, the knower of the Real and all enlightened, the man who has attained to this state. All blessed is he to make blessed all that is.

Saying 25. In brief, only dissociation from that false identity of the doer, the identity the *buddhi* has posited for itself, can bring to extinction its passion for doing, passion to act, that cause of recurring births and recurring deaths.

That is the conclusive, the final truth [about the mortal condition].

Saying 26. There is no endeavour like the endeavour that seeks to undo that false identity of the doer. And only self-submission to the Truth and remembrance of the True Name, self-submission and remembrance firm and stable, can bring that about, bring about the cessation of that false identity. *Yoga* is only this much, this endeavour true and genuine.

Saying 27. He alone is a renunciate, he who has given up the passion for the results of his acts, who stays away from the conflicts that they are. And only he can become desire-free or *vāsanā*-free, he who has ceased to identify his self with the false identity of the doer. Therefore only the supremely devoted souls, those who renounce all the results of their acts to the will of the Lord and remember Name the true with exclusive devotion, can attain to the highest state, state all still and of peace ever the same.

Saying 28. As long as the *buddhi* associates its being with the false identity of the doer it has posited for itself, its salvation lies in attributing all doing to the not-doing Power, to the *ātman*, and in remembering it as such, contemplating it as such, as the doer, giving up all the results of its acts to the will of that Power. All blessed will prove this its resolve.

Saying 29. When that association comes to an end, when the *buddhi* ceases to posit itself as the doer, it comes to be absorbed in that Not-doer, absorbed irrevocably. No passion for the fruit of action can then tempt it, disengaged it remains from that fierce duality out to undo itself. All turns into the self for it then, [all the dualities], to knowledge of the Same it attains then, to true knowledge of that state.

Saying 30. As long as the *buddhi* finds itself projected into the identity of the doer, there is no escape for it from the results of actions, results with their destructive *others* inherent in them. Mere talk of one's being Brahman is of no avail as long as that projection persists in one and the passion for those results of actions. Talk of this kind is the result of folly in the extreme; it destroys one's belief in the Truth and the possibility of attaining to it. Mere theoretical formulations will redeem neither those that formulate them nor those who pay heed to those formulations.

Saying 31. Mere reflection on *jñāna*, on knowledge [of Brahman], will not save a man unless and until he adopts the right means for the eradication of the ignorance of doership. To dispel this darkness, darkness all polluting, alone is to attain to knowledge, knowledge the pure.

Saying 32. Faith in the Real, faith all firm and resolute, constitutes the first step towards salvation, for it is that alone that can put to an end to sinful desires and prompt one to do acts good and noble.

Saying 33. Dedicating himself to good and noble acts one should dedicate to the spirit of self-surrender to the Real, spirit firm and immovable, and to the disposition that leaves the result of every action to the will of the Lord. This dedication and this disposition constitute the path straight to the end of desires, those obstacles in the way of one's salvation, and to disillusionment vis-a-vis the temptations of the world. That moment of disenchantment is the moment when true devotion for the Lord comes to sprout in one's soul.

Saying 34. With freedom from the *vāsanas* that obstruct one's way to salvation come the ability to realise the Real and the strength to put in every effort for that end. With that ability and that strength the *buddhi* ultimately succeeds in breaking all its bonds and all its fetters.

Saying 35. With the spirit of self-submission to the Real, spirit firm and unmoving, comes to an end engagement in the fierce conflicts that every act one does inevitably throws one into. And with that self-submission and that disengagement comes concentration on the Real, on the *ātman*, on that ever the Same, concentration suffused with love the supreme and faith the supreme. To *yoga* the pure and holy does the *buddhi* attain to then.

Saying 36. When the *buddhi* finds the bliss that is of the self and is the self, its *vāsanā*, its passion for the *other*, ceases to be. In the state supreme then it dwells, dwells all still and unmoving, dwells all bliss and blessed. That is when it comes to know the Same, when it comes to be so still and blessed.

Saying 37. Having come to be born in this world, the world of death, a man should self-submit to the Real, self-submit to It fully and firmly. Therein lies the way to his true progress, to his real uplift; therein lies the glory of his human life. Let him shed the false identity he finds himself projected into, identity of the doer, to know the Real and Imperishable, to know and find that abode the supreme, the abode that is peace itself, peace the transcendental.

Saying 38. Awful is this positing of the doer as one's being and self, the positing that every being finds himself immersed in. With every effort and every cunning beings augment this darkness, with utmost misery as their sole inheritance for their next life.

Saying 39. Let every man then know the truth about his body and his world, the body with a beginning and an end and the world with a beginning and an end. Let him self-submit to the Real and to meditation of the Name. Let him do so with every resolve and determination, for therein lies his salvation, salvation true and genuine.

Saying 40. Let him do his utmost to eradicate the false identity of the doer he finds himself projected into, let him ever contemplate the Real, that alone, giving up all his passions for the results of his actions. Therein lies his true heroism, heroism that will liberate him from all the pollution of the mind and reveal unto him Word the Indivisible, that Bliss, that Same. Let every noble being know his journey through the world for what it is, let his mind be all concentrated on the Truth. Let him redeem himself in every truth, attain to the goal ultimate, to the ideal of all the seers and prophets, to the goal of redemption. Let all those who have dedicated their lives to their preceptor orient their life towards realisation of the Truth. Let that be their resolve firm and undeviating!

(vii) *On Contemplation of the* Ātman

Saying 1. Polluted with the I-sense, the *buddhi* ever thinks of names, forms, qualities and actions, thinks of those appearances false, appearances that are the *others,* not its self. Similar is the case with other things it may think about. That is all that the world is, this state of dullness, of ignorance. For, thinking of these *others,* thinking of what belongs to the sphere of the not-self, gives rise to all kinds of desires for pleasures, to the *buddhi's* immersion in those pleasures, compelling it to ever strive for what it likes and to avoid what it dislikes, this discontent summing up its life and being. This is all that the world is and promises - this life of woe the highest.

Saying 2. Only contemplation of the self, self that abides within every being to light up all that is there, only contemplation of that self can liberate this being from the darkness that his life is. Only that should be remembered, only that is to be contemplated, that self that is light the pure, light of consciousness. For, the dispenser of life and being is that, abides it ever without a beginning to it and without an end, transcending the body composed of the five elements and the mind and the *buddhi*. Only that all transcendental self is to be remembered, only that and nothing else.

Saying 3. With discrimination all pure, with all strength of the body, with every faith true and genuine, should a being devote himself to contemplation of the self, of that Word the Imperishable, contemplation all sustained. That alone can lead one to purity the supreme and to peace the transcendental.

Saying 4. A mere instrument is this body, inflicted with activities, with *vāsanās*, with a beginning and an end. All conflict it is, a negation of itself, a veritable sea of eternal woe and fear. Taking it for its being, and all immersed in it, the *buddhi* would seek its satisfaction through all kinds of acts and pleasures, seek it through this body that itself is a misery! Vain turns out this its seeking and vain turn out all its acts. Only aversion and temptation can this body promise, aversion for what is unpleasant for it and temptation for what it considers pleasant. Thus only discontent comes to be its portion and misery all scalding. Knowing what bodily pleasures lead one into, one should resolutely self-submit to the Real, do so ever and with every sincere intent. For, therein lies one's uplift, uplift the supreme, and peace the supreme, in that endeavour towards self-submission to the Real.

Saying 5. Ever stays still the *ātman*, ever not-active, ever liberated from desire and from misery. Ever attained it is and ever full, and abides it ever indivisible and as redemption itself. To that should a mortal self-submit, to that Real, to that Knowledge. For, washed of every sin he will be, of every stain of it. That is the duty laid upon him, duty the supreme and highest.

Saying 6. Let that power, that *ātman*, be the doer for him and the undoer for him. Let him meditate it thus and contemplate it thus - as the creator and destroyer of his body. Let his weal be left to the will of that *ātman*, that Lord the Supreme, and also his woe. Let there be no attachment in him and no aversion. Only the self should remain his focus, only that. That verily should be the mode of his life as long as the sense of doership persists in him and the passion for doing and for the results of his actions. That should be his first *sādhanā*, his first endeavour for his goal. Whether he reaps adversity as the result of his deeds or prosperity should not be his concern, let that be the concern of his *ātman*, of that alone. Only contemplation of the Real should be his concern, that alone; in that should he be absorbed - ever and always, each and every moment. That alone should be his *tapa[s]* the supreme.

Saying 7. This verily is the way the *buddhi* can liberate itself from its obsession for the duality called the result of an action. And this verily is the way it can come to be still in the *ātman*, in that alone, and come to know the bliss that it is, bliss transcending all action and all desire. All miseries that go with the embodied mode of being come to cease then, and the *buddhi* attains to peace beyond every reckoning. All blessed is this state that the *buddhi* attains to then, all bliss and purity.

Saying 8. When the *buddhi* stays still in the midst of what it finds and what it loses, nothing in the sphere of the not-self attracting it or repelling it, it comes to stay all still in the *ātman*, in that real and that truth. Distant will it stay then from all the desires that stir up in a man's mind, desires for the pleasures of the organs, cognitive and motor. In the Imperishable Word the *ātman* it will remain absorbed then, its passion for positing itself as the doer all spent out, and also its passion for action and the result thereof. In the self alone the *buddhi* will stay then, stay in that ever and always, in the self a-doing, a-desiring and a-miserable, the self that every man must attain to, for that alone is his duty, his duty the noblest and supreme.

Saying 9. When the sense of I-ness comes to overwhelm a man, evil comes to seize all his desires, evil in the extreme, compelling him, those evil desires, to do acts wicked in the extreme. He alone is the man of faith, he alone is the true believer, who can give up the evil in the shape of those desires and actions and lives self-submitted unto the *ātman*, to that self of his, self the true and real.

Saying 10. The disposition of self-surrender unto the *ātman* gives rise to *vāsanā* the pure [*vāsanā* disoriented from the *other* and oriented towards the self], *vāsanā* that would lead a man of this disposition to discharge his duty - duty pure and noble. That alone is conduct the pure, conduct prompted by *vāsana* the pure, *vāsanā* that self-submission to the *ātman* gives rise to. Every man should understand that he comes to be man the true, comes to be a man in the true sense of the term, only when he so self-submits to the *ātman*, finding all his bodily functions a misery, cease as they do the moment they come to rise. He should, therefore, try to purify his passions - his greed, his attachments and infatuations, his wrath, his sexual desire and his self-assertion as an *I*. Never should he let them turn excessive. To try to liberate himself from these passions should be his endeavour, for that is the goal of a life dedicated to the truth. Only this holy resolve and this holy practice can make one's contemplation of the self endure firm and stay firm.

Saying 11. When *vāsanā* in its purest form comes to inform the *buddhi*, making the latter one with itself, when the *buddhi* turns into that *vāsanā* the pure itself, then will it get liberated from the self-concerns and self-interests that inflict the embodied state of being. In the Supreme Reality then will it come to dwell, never deviating from that state. In the pure waters of the Real then it becomes immersed, the acts of the body and their results, in the shape of weal or woe, left entirely to the care of the *ātman*, to its powers. Whatever happens or not happens it sees as dependent on the *ātman*, on that alone. **When this vision dawns upon it, even the pure *vāsanā*, *vāsanā* that leads it away from the not-self to the self, comes to be extinct for it. Only *vāsanā* the momentary then survives for it [with no thought of the before and the after]. This state of being is what they term the state of disinterested action, action without desire.**

Saying 12. This state of disinterested action, action that arises to leave no trace behind, purifies the *buddhi* of all the stains that go with embodiment. Only *nāda*, that immortal sound, absorbs it, absorbs it into itself. No desire survives in it then. To state the ineffable it attains then, to the very acme of *ātma-cintana*, to the highest reach of contemplation, contemplation of the self. No thinking of the not-self then survives in it, not a trace of it. For, contemplating the *ātman*, it verily becomes the *ātman*. To state the Fear-free does it attain then.

Saying 13. In giving up evil desires and evil deeds lies the genuine progress of life, its uplift and advancement. And in adopting the conduct noble, conduct dedicated towards the attainment of the Real. The man who has given up all selfish desires and has made the Truth alone his resort and has only good will towards others, and with that good will does good to others without any self-interest, that man alone is the best among men, a god among humans is he. For, only this disposition and this endeavour can make his contemplation of the self fully steady, the self that is peace the supreme itself.

Saying 14. The superiority of man over other creatures lies only in this that he should purify himself of all the mental aberrations inflicting him and should have a disposition ever open to the truth. Let contemplation of the self be his daily endeavour, let that be his daily duty, his prime duty. Let him thus wake himself up from the darkness he is lost in, the darkness of delusion, and orient his life towards attaining to the state desire-free, that all blessed state.

Saying 15. Only in contemplation of the *ātman*, of the self, lies the supreme uplift, the supreme progress for man. Therein alone lies inquiry and investigation the supreme and understanding and enlightenment, understanding and enlightenment the supreme. The origin primordial does it lead to and to supreme realisation and fearlessness. Heroism the highest lies in it, in contemplation of the self, and purity and realisation the absolute. Through that alone can a man attain all these, through contemplation of the self. To attain to the self in straight and living terms, he is to eradicate all his mental aberrations. And for that purpose, he must orient himself inwards and contemplate the self in the right way, the way shown by a seer. Let him know that this alone is the highest achievement possible for man, this staying still as the self. Rare is the man and rare is his life, of the man who has striven for that end and attained to that end.

Let every *premī*, devotee, pay heed to what has been said here and strive properly to stay firm in contemplation of the self. Only this *sādhanā*, this endeavour, can give them peace in this degenerate age. To be heedless towards contemplation of the Name is to invite ruin for oneself. So, let them follow the path to the truth with every intent and effort to make themselves fit recipients of the grace of their preceptor to find themselves redeemed and all blessed. It is absolutely imperative that they orient themselves towards this end, those who have faith in their teacher. May every *premī* find himself so oriented! May the Lord bless them with true understanding!

(viii) Contemplative Dispositions

(a) On Yoga of Action or of Devotion

Doer art Thou and Undoer! Thy Will Prevail! Protector art Thou and Supporter! Gracious to the lowly art Thou and ever the Forgiver! Let thy Will be done! Of the fallen art Thou the Redeemer and the Eternal Ground of all, Constant Companion and Imperishable! The Beginningless Beginning of all art Thou and Father the Primordial, and of the perishable world the Lord! And of the senses the Light and Sustainer and of blessings art Thou the Giver, Thou without an End and Thou without a Limit! None can traverse Thee, Thou Gracious, Thou Doer, Thou Doer, Thou Doer! Thy Will Prevail, Thy Grace abound! All art Thou! All art Thou! All art Thou! Beginning Thou art and the middle art Thou and the end! Truth art Thou, the Unknown art Thou and the Known, Lord art Thou and the Inner Controller, Blessedness art Thou and Life art Thou! The Ordainer art Thou and the Dweller within and without and of the lowly art Thou the Master! Knowledge the general art Thou and knowledge the particular! Beyond the reach of the mind art Thou and the Lord born out of the self-sacrifice of man!

These are some of the countless dispositions with which the meditation of the Name is to be held firm and stable. Contemplation of the Name with such a disposition has been termed as *samarpaṇa-buddhi*, disposition of self-surrender, as *karma-yoga*, yoga of action, as *bhakti-yoga*, yoga of devotion, *anāsaktti-yoga*, yoga of dispassion or non-attachment, or the *saguṇa-yoga*, yoga the conditioned or relating to the Conditioned Brahman. Resolute adherence to it, to this kind of *yoga*, culminates in the cessation of the I-sense, that pollution, and of *vāsanās*, each and every. With its sense of the Me and the Mine gone, the *buddhi* transcends all mental faults, staying still and unconcerned with them. In the Word alone then it reposes, reposes all passive, in Word the Indivisible and Imperishable. To state the supreme then it attains and to goal the supreme. As long as one is not aware of the truth, as long as one is lost in ignorance, this is the way one is to adhere to, this way of *karma-yoga* or *bhakti-yoga*, for disposition of this kind easily puts an end to the evils of the mind, leading one to the knowledge of the *ātman*, to its realisation.

(b) On Jñāna-yoga, Yoga of Knowledge

***Ātman** the disembodied am I, the **ātman** beyond the reach of every action and perception, that **ātman** the eternal, that **ātman** the non-doer, that **ātman** the consciousness pure, that **ātman** the indivisible. No one is there to cut me, the **ātman** that I am! Ever-undifferentiated do I endure, I the **ātman** distanced from all that is! **Ātman** the ever a-dual am I, **ātman** the ever unborn, **ātman** the desire-free, **ātman** the all, and **ātman** the ever liberated, **ātman** the Brahman! **Śūnya** am I, the Eternal Void, beyond the reach of **guṇas** and of activities, each and every! No conflict is there in me the **ātman**, the ātman ever the same and timeless! **Ātman** the truth, consciousness and bliss am I, **ātman** the unattached, **ātman** the formless and **ātman** the bliss absolute, that beginning of all. And **ātman** the non-situated am I, **ātman** the homeless, that support of all that is! I am **ātman**, that my own native being, that life of all that is and the witness of all that is!*

To merge in the Real with dispositions like these is the way of *jñāna-yoga*, yoga of knowledge, of *Sāṃkhya-yoga*, *Nirguṇa-vṛtti-yoga*, yoga oriented towards the Unconditoned, the Real uncondtioned by the *guṇas*. When the *buddhi* meditates the Name with this kind of disposition, meditates it without a let and without a distraction, internal or external, its identification with the body comes to an end, its contemplation becoming all concentrated. That is the moment when it comes to stay stable in Word the Imperishable, that consciousness itself. To the state of *samādhi* it attains then, to the state where it turns into consciousness itself. Transcends it, the *buddhi*, then the entire sphere of the formed, and the very reach of its frets and miseries, attaining to goal the highest. However, long pratice of *karma yoga* too will lead a man to this state of *jñāna yoga*, lead as it does a man to the vision of the self. Blessed with that vision, he will find this knowledge and realisation of the Unconditoned automatically revealed before him.

It may, however, be remembered that every man who has realised the truth finds these two dispositions, that of *karma-yoga* and that of *jñāna-yoga*, possessing him, possessing him in abundance. For, both these dispositions can lead one to the *ātman*, that real the eternal and imperishable and to make him stay stable in that. To think of these dispositions as different or opposed to each other is the way of the unwise, of those wedded to blind beliefs and to mere theoretical formulations. For, every man who has attained to the supreme goal finds these two dispositions operate in him, for alike are they, these two dispositions, in eradicating the faults that inflict a being under the grip of *prakṛti*. That is the truth final in the eyes of the seers. Depending on one's abilities, either of these ways may be adopted for the eradication of the delusion that inflicts every embodied being. Either of the two can free the *buddhi* from the pollution of I-ness, either can lead it to find and get merged in Word the indivisible and eternal, lead it to that state transcendent and fearless. In the Path of *Samatā*, both these ways or dispositions are considered redemptive, for both help one reach the same state, the state ineffable and inexpressible. This is the truth that every *sādhaka*, every striver for the goal of life, should know for certain.

(ix) On Attaining to the Ātman, *to One's Being the True*

A man on the path has to pass through six stages of his pilgrimage unto the *ātman*. The first stage is the state of dispassion vis-a-vis the world. The second is that of longing to know the self; the third is that of contemplation of the self; the fourth that of finding the self; the fifth that of staying in the self and the last that of getting merged in the self.

In the first five stages, the pilgrim must keep his experiences to himself, letting no one know about them.

There are many a pitfall on the way, pitfall he should be wary of. For, the passion of the organs may stir up to lead him astray from the state of dispassion he finds himself in. And the desire for fame and glory may undo his longing for knowing the self. And impure food, unethical dealings and evil thoughts or lack of self-restraint in these matters may distract him from his meditative life. He should understand that without full faith and continuous practice he cannot but fail to bring his meditation to its fruition. And there is also the danger of fall from the state where he finds his self manifest before him. And the danger lies in his pride, pride in his meditative mode of life, in his *tapa[s]*, self-denial, and in his renunciation. And, lastly, in his pride of learning, which may tempt him into false verbosity to win the applause of the people.

There is a possibility of fall even for one who has come to stay in the *ātman*. He may be tempted into displaying his supernatural powers and may give boons to some and inflict curses on others. He may become vain of those powers, drunk in the homage he receives from the people at large!

The sixth stage, that of merger in the *ātman*, is, of course, state the perfect. For beyond the reach of the three *guṇas* the *buddhi* stays then, all still and stable, to merge in Brahman, that Real the absolute.

NOTES

[1] Those of sensuality, anger, greed, infatuation and self-hood or egotism.

[2] Name the Seed, that is to say, the Name vouchsafed by a seer of the truth to a man. Only that Name can sprout into realisation of the highest truth, the Name that is Grace itself.

[3] The phrase 'in that still no-activity' is meant to deny every activity in the *ātman*; it should not be taken to mean that it is inactive, for no concept can comprehend the *ātman*. One can only speak of it as what it is not, not as what it is. One cannot even say about it that it *is* or that it is not.

[4] The *ātman* is said to be the unknown knower. How can it become manifest before the knowing faculty called the *buddhi*, then? The *ātman* manifests itself before the *buddhi* in the form of consciousness, in the form of the dark nothingness called the *kuṇḍalinī* or in the form of *nāda*, the sound eternal. As consciousness it manifests itself as the *knower* of breath, of *buddhi*, of the *manas*, or mind, and of the sense- and motor organs, of the body and the *other* of the body, namely, the world. One knows it as the knower but cannot determinate it, cannot phenomenalise it. With one's contemplation getting deeper, one finds that even consciousness is only a reflection of the *ātman*, consciousness as the *buddhi*, it itself stands all transcendent, wholly unknown. When the self manifests itself as the void, one does find, in moods deep and profound, oneself as different from it and also from the body-sense-mind complex, that *other* of the said void. The self remains all transcendent and unknown, the seer of the void, even the seer of its seeing. When the self manifests itself as the *nāda*, the humming sound, it swallows the whole phenomenal world, subjective and objective. Not before dying into bare consciousness, into the darkness of the *kuṇḍalinī* or the all-swallowing *nāda* can one die into the Real, if the Real *can* be called the Real. One can find the *ātman* only as the all-negating consciousness, all-negating *kuṇḍalinī* or the all-swallowing *nāda*, there being no *ātman* as such and in itself. The *ātman* the real will reject the nomencalture of *ātman* and that of *Brahman* no less than that of consciousness the bare, of *kuṇḍalinī* and of *nāda*. The unknown *ātman* is not, truly speaking, the *ātman*.

[5] It is in the nature of the intellect to be ever in doubt; it is its doubt that prompts it to seek further knowledge, knowledge without an end. It is only when the *buddhi* ceases to enframe things in concepts

and perceive the things so *enframed* in the context of and against the background of a world that it can shed its doubt. As innocence alone, innocence the absolute, can it attain to knowledge the certain, not when it thinks and classifies, relates and contrasts.

[6] The Name a seer initiates a man into is only a word or a phrase in a particular language, with a clear meaning to convey or no meaning. How can it be called Word the Imperishable, then? The word or the phrase in question has to be meditated dissociated from the context of the language it belongs to and from the meaning it may have. Only the word is to be meditated, meditated unrelated to all relationships, syntactical or referential. When the contemplation turns deep and concentrated, deep and concentrated to the extent of the contemplator becoming one with it, then the word will exceed itself into infinity and so will the man contemplating it. It is the death of man into it that makes the word resurrect as the Imperishable.

[7] Every resolve or determination springs from the ego, from the false self of the doer. How can this be untainted, then, the determination that decides the course of action one is to take? Can there be a choice or determination without the doer-self? The spirit of self-surrender, that way to liberation, comes to stay firm in a man who has realised, with every clarity, the disastrous consequences of his actions and their results. It is not *his* determination that makes him stand apart from all his acts and stay obedient to the will of the Lord; it is the depth of his suffering and disillusion that decides the issue. It is he who comes to be determined into the disposition of self-surrender. The attribution of that determination to the man concerned is only a concession to those who live as victims of the false self of the doer. For them the passion for doing and the spirit of self-surrender appear as a matter of choice. A long and hard journey awaits them to know the meaning of the firm spirit of self-surrender.

[8] Notice, again, the paradox. The not-doing *ātman* is to be meditated as the doer, whereas the false doing self is to be taken as the non-doer. As long as one's sense of identity with the body waxes strong, one is to project one's actions back into the *ātman*, thereby undoing one's false identity. It is only when this false self gets negated that one will become aware of the passive depths in one. Not before.

[9] The causal body is projection of the self as the doer and its cosmic counterpart is *avyakta*, the Unmanifest. The body in the shape of the result of action is body the effect and so is its cosmic counterpart, the visible world.

The Great Chant

aum brahma satyaṃ niraṅkār ajanmā
advait purakhā sarab vyāpak kalyāṇ mūrat
parmeśvarāya namastam.

Brahman is truth the absolute
and the ground of all that is.
Samatā is the Power Absolute

Index and Glossary

[Wherever a page number is followed by ff, the entry may be looked for either on the page mentioned or on the next page/pages. It is possible that in some cases the entry may be available on the following page alone. **The Index also includes Glossary of Sanskrit and Hindi words. Where the meaning of the word in question is not given, the reader may take it that the meaning is complex. In that case, he should look into the pages mentioned first.**]

M

N

SATPURUṢA

MAHĀRĀJŚRĪ MAṄGATRĀMJĪ

(1903-54)

His life was a miracle, his face a mystery, an enigma, a thing to see and not to tell. One could not call it a face human, for it was a revelation, revelation of something that would shatter all our concepts and precepts, a face that spoke not of a man, alive or dead, but of something that was beyond life and death, beyond all that man can think of or imagine. For, even the face of a corpse has some human resemblance but that awesome enigma was not human, absolutely not. The reader will find some information about his life in the Preface. For the details one may turn to the biography of the master (vide TO THE HOME THAT WAS NOWHERE *An Encounter with the life and teachings of Maṅgatrāmjī*, Somraj Gupta, MLBD, Delhi)of the man (?) whose nights were spent in the open and in dangerous jungles, who never slept after the age of 25, whose daily intake was a bowl of tea or, when his health was perilously ruined, that of milk. In the solitudes of the jungles flowed from the lips *bānī* (*vāṇī*), speech the revelatory, flowed spontaneously and without a thought, without his awareness of what he uttered or did not utter. And yet this rock like man was all compassion, all human, sensitive in the extreme to the misery of beings, beings disinherited from themselves.

सत्पुरुष श्री मंगतराम जी महाराज

(For an introductory overview see p. 582)